THE

FINAL

PROPHECY OF JESUS

an
Introduction
Analysis and Commentary
on the Book of Revelation

by
Oral Edmond Collins

Wipf and Stock Publishers
Eugene, Oregon

THE FINAL PROPHECY OF JESUS
An Introduction, Analysis, and Commentary on the Book of Revelation

Copyright © 2007 Oral Collins. All rights reserved. Except for brief quotations in critical publications or reviews, no part of this book may be reproduced in any manner without prior written permission from the publisher. Write: Permissions, Wipf and Stock Publishers, 199 W. 8th Ave., Eugene, OR 97401.

ISBN 13: 978-1-55635-260-7

www.wipfandstock.com

Manufactured in the U.S.A.

Scripture taken from the HOLY BIBLE, NEW INTERNATIONAL VERSION®. NIV®. Copyright © 1973, 1978, 1984 by International Bible Society. Used by permission of Zondervan.

The "NIV" and "New International Version" trademarks are registered in the United States Patent and Trademark Office by International Bible Society.

The cover illustration, "Earthquake and Eclipse,"
may be found in a work by
F. E. Tower, *The Wonders of Foretold History*,
published in Hartford, Connecticut by the American Publishing Company
in 1890; unnumbered page 112

To my wife, Joyce
my children
my grandchildren
my
great-grandchildren

and to
my students
and
former students

CONTENTS

Foreward	xi
Preface	xiii
Abbreviations	xv
Glossary	xix
Bibliography of works cited	xxiii

CHAPTER ONE. INTRODUCTION TO THE BOOK OF REVELATION 1

The Special Place of the Book of Revelation	1
Purpose	2
Historical Origin	3
Authorship	3
Occasion and date	6
Approaches to Interpretation	7
Understanding Apocalyptic Writing	15
Apocalyptic and the Book of Daniel	19
Structure and Theme	35
Literary Outline	42

CHAPTER TWO. CHRIST SPEAKS TO THE CHURCH   **47**

Introduction		47
1:1-3	The Apocalyptic Prologue	47
1:4-8	The Epistolary Prologue	50
1:9-20	Apocalyptic Introduction	56
2:1-3:22	The letters to the churches	63

v

Contents

CHAPTER THREE. A DRAMA IN HEAVEN 99

Introduction 99

4:1-6a	The Revelation of Almighty God	99
4:6b-11	The Worship of Almighty God................	104
5:1-5	Christ Has Triumphed	108
5:6-10	The Worship of the Lamb	111
5:11-14	The Great Anthem of Praise	115

**CHAPTER FOUR. THE OPENING OF
THE SEALED SCROLL** **119**

Introduction 119

6:1-8	The Four Horsemen	121
6:9-11	The Souls of the Martyrs	142
6:12-17	The Great Earthquake	147
7:1-8	The Sealing of the True Israel	159
7:9-17	The Great Multitude in White	168

**CHAPTER FIVE. THE SOUNDING OF
THE SEVEN TRUMPETS** **175**

Introduction 175

8:1-5	Seven Trumpets and the Prayers of the Saints ...	176
8:6-12	The First Four Trumpets	180
8:13	The Three Woes	193
9:1-12	The Fifth Trumpet	196
9:13-21	The Sixth Trumpet	205

Contents

CHAPTER SIX. THE LITTLE BOOK, THE TEMPLE, AND THE TWO WITNESSES **223**

Introduction 223

10:1-11	The Angel and the Little Scroll	227
11:1-6	The Two Witnesses	237
11:7-10	The Death of the Witnesses	253
11:11-13	The Resurrection of the Witnesses	260
11:14	The Passing of the Second Woe	265
11:15-18	The Seventh Trumpet Sounded	266
11:19	The Temple and the Ark of the Covenant	267

CHAPTER SEVEN. THE DRAGON AND THE TWO BEASTS **271**

Introduction 271

12:1-6	The Woman and the Dragon	272
12:7-17	The Woman and the Dragon (cont'd)	282
13:1-4	The Beast from the Sea	293
13:5-10	The Beast from the Sea (cont'd)	297
13:11-18	The Beast from the Earth	315

CHAPTER EIGHT. THE LAMB AND THE 144,000, THE FLYING ANGELS, AND THE TWO HARVESTS . **327**

Introduction 327

14:1-5	The Lamb and the 144,000	328
14:6-13	The Three Flying Angels	332
14:14-20	The Harvest of the Earth	341
14:1-20	The Harvest of the Earth—Fulfillment	346

Contents

**CHAPTER NINE. THE POURING OUT
OF THE SEVEN BOWLS OF WRATH** **349**

Introduction 349

15:1-4	Seven Angels with Seven Last Plagues	350
15:5-8	Seven Last Plagues (cont'd)	353
16:1-9	The First Four Bowls of God's Wrath	355
16:10-16	The Fifth & Sixth Bowls of Wrath	361
15:1-16:16	The First Six Bowls—Fulfillment	365
16:17-21	The Seventh Bowl of God's Wrath	377
16:17-21	The Seventh Bowl—Fulfillment	380

**CHAPTER TEN. THE FALL OF THE HARLOT
BABYLON** **383**

Introduction 383

17:1-6a	The Woman on the Beast	384
17:6b-14	The Woman on the Beast (cont'd)	391
17:15-18	The Woman on the Beast (cont'd)	396
17:1-18	The Woman on the Beast—Fulfillment	399
18:1-24	The Fall of Babylon—Introduction	401
18:1-3	The Fall of Babylon	401
18:4-8	The Fall of Babylon (cont'd)	404
18:9-17a	The Fall of Babylon (cont'd)	406
18:17b-24	The Fall of Babylon (cont'd)	408
18:1-24	The Fall of Babylon—Fulfillment	411

Contents

CHAPTER ELEVEN. THE GREAT DAY OF THE LORD   **415**

Introduction 415

19:1-5	The Hallelujah Chorus	416
19:6-10	The Hallelujah Chorus (cont'd)	419
19:11-16	The White Horse Rider	421
19:17-21	The White Horse Rider (cont'd)	426
19:1-21	The Great Day of the Lord—Fulfillment	428

Excursus on the Restoration of Israel 429

CHAPTER TWELVE. THE MILLENNIAL REIGN AND THE GREAT WHITE THRONE JUDGMENT **433**

Introduction 433

20:1-6	The Millennial Reign	435
20:7-10	Satan's Destruction	442
20:11-15	The Second Resurrection and Judgment	448

CHAPTER THIRTEEN. THE NEW HEAVENS AND THE NEW EARTH **455**

Introduction 455

1:1-4	The New Home of the Bride	456
21:5-8	The Inheritance Covenant Affirmed	459
21:9-21	The New Jerusalem, the Bride	460
21:22-27	The Lamb, the Light of the City	463
22:1-5	The River, the Life of the City	465
22:6-22	The Sure Return of Jesus....................	466

Contents

APPENDIXES

Appendix 1. Observations Regarding the Hermeneutics and
    the Book of Revelation 471
Appendix 2. Observations on the History of Apocalyptic
    Interpretation 477
Appendix 3. Parallel or Continuous Structure in the
    Apocalypse? 485
Appendix 4. The Historical Antichrist 499

INDEXES

Index of Texts 513
Index of Subjects 533
Index of Modern Authors 569

Foreword

The interpretation of the book of Revelation, the last volume of the New Testament canon, has challenged many biblical students from the patristic period of the church until the present day. For most writers it has fallen into three schools of thought: the preterist, the historicist and the futurist. The preterist school explains the vision-prophecies as applying, largely if not fully, to events of John's own day. The historicist school finds their fulfillment throughout the history of the church, either in one continuing historical sequence or in visions of several parallel series of historical events, each vision-prophecy culminating in the second coming of Christ and His establishment of the universal and everlasting kingdom of God. The futurist school understands much of Revelation's prophecies to find their fulfillment in today's or shortly forthcoming events that will also issue in Christ's coming and in His earthly millennial kingdom.

Dr. Collins' work offers an important contribution in that, almost alone among contemporary commentaries, it generally follows and updates the continuous-historicist interpretation of John's volume. The historicist school became prominent during the Protestant Reformation, especially in the Reformed churches' separation from and doctrinal conflict with the Roman Catholic church. In this context the historicist hermeneutic identified the enemies of God's people and purpose in the Roman church and Papacy. This school was dominant among post-Reformation Protestant writers until the nineteenth century.

The present commentary continues that approach. There are several qualifiers, however, that I believe Dr. Collins would not wholly disagree with. First, the historicist school critiques the errors

Foreword

of the Roman Catholic organizational and doctrinal system and does not identify the judgments of Revelation with individual Roman Catholics or individual popes who faithfully believe and follow Christ.

Second, the Reformation is now 500 years in the past and most evangelical Protestants today recognize that the organizational church as such, whatever the denomination, is subject to the danger of unfaithfulness or apostasy. As Jesus' parable of the weeds among the wheat (Matt 13:24-30) illustrates, the church as 'organization' is a mixed bag, made up of both elect believers and unregenerate professing believers. Even apostolic churches reflected this mixture as the New Testament letters show.[1]

One of the significant achievements of this commentary is to bring to the attention of modern scholarship an approach to the book of Revelation that still has insights to offer and contributions to make in the ongoing discussion of 'Jesus' final prophecy.'

                        E. Earle Ellis, Ph.D
                        Research Professor of Theology Emeritus
                        Scholar in Residence
                        Southwestern Baptist Theological
                              Seminary
                        Fort Worth, Texas

---

[1] Cf. e.g. 1 Cor 11:19; 2 Cor 12:20f.; 13:5; Gal 1:6-9; 4:11; Rev 3:1-3, 15f.

Preface

The historicist approach to interpretation of the Book of Revelation lies at the foundation of our Protestant heritage. It was the understanding of Reformation scholars, prevailing as the exclusive or majority view among Protestants from pre-Reformation times through the nineteenth century. Nevertheless, the historicist school has produced no major scholarly commentary since that of E. P. Cachemaille (1st ed., c. 1911). Most of the old historicist works are now out of print. Most scholars when writing on Revelation tend to interact with their contemporaries and to neglect those older works. Though this traditionally Protestant school is still recognized as one of the four major approaches to the interpretation of Revelation, its critics usually reject it on the basis of assessments which this writer views as reflecting inadequate understanding. (For further discussion of this current situation, see Appendixes 1 and 3). This writer does not naively expect that his work will turn the tide in the direction of historicism, but this work may provide a contemporary model and reference point for students and teachers who wish to assess the historical school.

This work contains several types of material. The first chapter is introductory and foundational to the whole. The rest is commentary with several levels of treatment. In Chapters 2-13, the sections of the commentary labeled Introduction deal with general matters such as the bearing of context and literary structure on the passage at hand. The Exposition is a general approach to interpretation, primarily for explanation, practical instruction, and inspiration. The Notes are for more serious study of particulars, including those on which many interpreters disagree. On the prophetic part of the book (chapters 6:1-22:5) there is for each passage a section called Fulfillment. The author has adopted as a principle govern-

Preface

ing interpretation the fact that the meaning of the passage must in so far as possible be determined before the question of fulfillment can be properly addressed. The footnotes are for documentation, as well as for more polemical treatment. The Appendices are essays on several of the major issues.

Certain conventions are followed throughout: The text of Revelation is usually cited in bold face type. We have used the NIV because it is perhaps the most common version among evangelical readers. In the Notes, excerpts from the preceding Scripture passage cited for comment appear in bold face rather than with quotation marks. We have included transliteration of Greek and Hebrew in the Exposition sections to facilitate reading by those not acquainted with the biblical languages.

The Index of Subjects is highly detailed with the hope that among other functions it may prove useful for topical analysis in preaching.

This work has consumed a substantial amount of the author's time over a period of fifteen years. I am particularly grateful to my wife, Joyce, who has exercised unusual patience during my absence and also has read much of the manuscript. Several other readers have read the manuscript at various times during its development. For their editorial advice and their numerous corrections I am especially grateful to the following individuals: the Rev. Clayton Blackstone, the Rev. Dr. David A. Dean, Dr. E. Earle Ellis, Dr. Daniel Estes, the Rev. Louis Going, the late Dr. Clyde Hewitt, the Rev. Robert Miller, the Rev. Mary Roller, and the Rev. Gary Stevens.

      Oral E. Collins, Ph.D
      Professor of Bible
      The Berkshire Institute for Christian Studies
      May, 2007

ABBREVIATIONS

1QpHab	Dead Sea Scrolls, *Pesher (Commentary) on Habakkuk*
2 *Apoc. Bar.*	Greek *Apocalypse of Baruch*
a priori	reasoning from cause to effect, or from what may be an unsubstantiated presupposition to a conclusion
AB	Anchor Bible (series)
ABD	Anchor Bible Dictionary
Apc.	Apocalypse
ASV	American Standard Version
Antiq. Rom.	Halicarnassus. *Antiquities Romanae*
Apoc. El.	*Apocalypse of Elijah*
Apoc. Mos.	*Apocalypse of Moses*
Ar. *Ranae*	Aristophanes. *Ranae*
b. *Soṭa*	Babylonian Talmud *Soṭa*
BAGD	Baur-Arndt-Gingrich-Danker. *A Greek-English Lexicon to the New Testament*
BDB	Brown-Driver-Briggs. *A Hebrew and English Lexicon of the Old Testament*
BDF	Blass-Debrunner-Funk. *Greek Grammar of the New Testament*
bk.	book
ca.	circa
CBC	Century Bible Commentary series
cent., cents.	century, centuries
ch., chs.	chapter, chapters
Cic. *Ep. ad Fam.*	Cicero. *Epistulai ad Familiares*
Cic. *De Off.*	Cicero. *De Officiis*
cf.	confer
COT	Commentary on the Old Testament
cp.	compare
Deut	The Book of Deuteronomy
Did.	*Didaché*
D. S.	*Diodorus Siculus*
1 Enoch	*The Apocalypse of Enoch=Ethiopic Enoch*
ed.	edited
En.	1 Enoch (Ethiopic Enoch)
enl.	enlarged
Ep., Eps.	*Epistle, Epistles*
Es.	2 Esdras (= 4 Ezra)

Abbreviations

Esdr.	Esdras, 2 Esdras (= 4 Ezra)
2 Esdr.	2 Esdras (= 4 Ezra)
ESV	English Standard Version
ET	*Expository Times*
et al.	et alii (Lat., "and others")
Eus. *Hist.*	Eusebius. *Ecclesiastical History*
Exod	The Book of Exodus
Gen	The Book of Genesis
Gosp. Pet.	*Gospel of Peter*
Gk.	Greek
Greg. *Ep.*	Gregory. *Epistle*
Hdt.	Herodotus. *Historicus*
Heb	Epistle to the Hebrews
Heb.	Hebrew
Hippol. *Philos.*	Hippolytus. *Philosaphumena* ("A Refutation of All Heresies")
Hirt. *Bell. Alex.*	Aulus Hirtius. *Bellum Alexandrinus*
Hom. *Il.*	Homer. *Iliad*
IBD	*Illustrated Bible Dictionary*
Ibid.	Ibidem
ICC	International critical commentary
IDB	*Interpreter's Dictionary of the Bible*
Ign. *Ep. Magn.*	Ignatius. *Epistle to the Magnesians*
Ign. *Smyrn.*	Ignatius. *Epistle to the Smyrnaeans*
Illus.	Illustration, illustrative
Iren. *Adv. Haer.*	Irenaeus. *Adversus Haereses* (Against Heresies)
Isa	Book of Isaiah
j. Qidd.	*Jerusalem Talmud Qiddušin*
j. Tg.	*Jerusalem Targum*
JBL	*Journal of Biblical Literature*
JETS	*Journal of the Evangelical Theological Society*
Jos. *Ant.*	Josephus. *Antiquities of the Jews*
Jos. and Asen.	*Joseph and Aseneth*
JPSV	Jewish Publication Society version
Jub	Jubilees
Kgs	Book of Kings
KJV	King James Version
Lact. *Instit.*	Lactantius. *Institiones Divinae*
Lat.	Latin
Lev	The Book of Leviticus
Lib	Library
Liv. *Hist.*	Titus Livius Patavinus (Livy). *Historiae ab Urbe Condita* (History of the Founding of the City)
LSJ	Liddell-Scott-Jones *Greek-English Lexicon*
Luc.	Lucianus Sophista (Lucian)
LXX	Septuagint version of the Old Testament
m. Pes	*Midrash Pesaḥim*

Abbreviations

Mart. Pol.	*Martyrdom of Polycarp*
Mic	The Book of Micah
ms., mss.	manuscript, manuscripts
Midr. Rab.	*Midrash Rabbah*
MT	Massoretic text of the Old Testament
n., nn.	note, notes (endnotes or footnotes)
NAB	*New American Bible* (Roman Catholic)
NASB	*New American Standard Bible*
NASV	New American Standard version
NCB	*New Century Bible*
NCV	New Century version
n.d.	no date
NEB	*New English Bible*
NICOT	New International Commentary on the Old Testament
NIV	New International version
NKJV	New King James version
NRSV	New Revised Standard version
Num	The Book of Numbers
Ov. Metam.	Ovid. *Metamorphoses*
Ov. Fasti	Ovid. *Fasti*
p., pp.	page, pages
Ph. Vita Mos.	Philo. *De Vita Mosis*
Phoc.	*Phocica*
Pi. Pyth. Od.	Pindar. *Pythian Odes*
Plb. Hist.	Polybius. *Historicus*
Pliny *HN*	Pliny. *Historia Naturalis*
Plu. Pyrrh.	Plutarch. *Life of Pyrrhus*
prep.	preposition
Pss Sol	*Psalms of Solomon*
REB	*Revised English Bible*
refs.	references
repr.	reprint
Rev	Book of Revelation
rev.	revised (by)
RSV	Revised Standard version
Rule Comm.	*Rule of the Community* = Manual of Discipline
RV	Revised version
Scapul.	Tertullian *To Scapula Tertullus*
Sib. Or.	*Sibylene Oracles*
Sir	Sirach=Ben Sira=Ecclesiasticus
Sq.	Sequence (page or pages following)
St. Byz.	*Stephanus Byzantius*
Str.	Strabo. *Geographus*
T. Ab.	*Testament of Abraham*
T. Dan	*Testament of Dan*
T. Levi	*Testament of Levi*
T. Mos.	*Testament of Moses*=Assumption of Moses

Abbreviations

Tacitus *Ann.*	Tacitus. *Annals*
TCNT	*Tyndale Commentary on the New Testament*
TEV	*Today's English version*
Tg.	*Targum*
Th. *Hist.*	Thucydides. *Historicus*
TLZ	*Theologische Literaturzeitung*
Trans.	*Translation, Translator*
Treb. Pol.	*Trebellius Pollius*
Tob	*Tobit*
TWOT	*Theological Wordbook of the Old Testament*
v., vv.	verse, verses
Verr.	Cicero, *In Verrem*
Vg.	*Vulgate version*
Vit. Claud.	*Vita Claudius* (Life of Claudius)
viz.	namely (from Latin *videlicet*)
Zech	Book of Zechariah

GLOSSARY

2 Esdras. The apocryphal book also called 4th Ezra.

allegorize. To create an allegory by imposing an unnatural and secondary meaning on a text, thereby violating the hermeneutical rule that the normal sense of the language should determine its meaning.

allusive reference. An unexplicit reference to another text indicated by parallel language which reminds the informed reader of the text which is the object of the allusion.

anarthrous. An adjective describing the use of a word without the article.

anthropomorphism, anthropomorphic. A figure of speech ascribing human form or language to a deity or any non-human being or thing. Adjective, anthropomorphic.

Antichrist, antichrist. From the Greek, ἀντι, *anti* plus χριστος,, *kristos*. The preposition, ἀντι, means "opposite," "in place of," "instead of"; Χριστος means "Anointed One," "Messiah," "Christ." Thus, the "Antichrist" refers to that Little Horn power which usurps the place of the Messiah, Jesus Christ. The lower case "antichrist" is one who has that spirit or those characteristics, though not the specific Antichrist of prophecy.

antitype. See type.

Apocalypse, apocalypse. When capitalized, the Book of Revelation. Adj. **Apocalyptic, apocalyptic.** When in lower case, "apocalypse" and "apocalyptic" refer to the genre, the kind of literature which has some of the distinguishing characteristics of the Book of Revelation.

Ben Sira. The Hebraic title of the Apocryphal book dated in the second century B.C., called in the Septuagintal tradition **Sirach** and in the Latin Vulgate tradition **Ecclesiasticus.**

bishop. The church office of overseer, from the Greek *épiscopos*, "presbyter." The bishop ordinarily is in charge of the churches in a particular territory.

canon. 1. From a word meaning "rule," that collection of books which are incorporated into the Bible and believed to be the inspired Word of God. 2. A clergyman living within the precincts of a clergy house or a cathedral.

cathedral. A church containing the official chair of a bishop.

Church, church. When capitalized, the word refers to the true Church made up of believers whose names are written in the Book of Life. In the lower case, the word refers to the visible church as it exists anywhere in the world, in a particular area, or in a local congregation. The "church" (lower case) may be nominal (in name only) or it may be a true visible church, i.e., a church which faithfully proclaims and maintains the sacraments and the true Gospel. The distinction is contextually indicated.
circa, ca. About, from Latin, *circa, circum.*
codicil. A supplement to a document; commonly, a supplement to a will.
consul. One of two chief magistrates who ruled conjointly in ancient Rome.
en passim. Here and there throughout
epexegetic. A textual construction which adds or implies further explanation, as "the earth" meaning "the earth and its inhabitants"
et alii, et al. A Latin term meaning "and others"; abbreviated et al.
excursus. An appendix or digression that contains an exposition of some topic, usually of a supplementary nature.
genre. Kind, as referring to a particular type of literature, such as poetry, narrative, wisdom literature, legal literature, etc.
hyperbole. A deliberate exaggeration for effect and not intended to be taken literally.
metaphor. A figure of speech based on a direct comparison without such words as "like" or "as," for example, Jesus' description of Herod Antipas as crafty by comparing him to a fox when he said, "Go tell that fox . . . " (Luke 13:32).
metropolitan. An archbishop who has authority over a number of bishops.
N.T. New Testament
O.T. Old Testament
prebendary. A clergyman who receives a stipend from a cathedral or church.
prelate. A high ranking clergyman such as a bishop or archbishop.
proconsul. A Roman official who exorcized consular authority over a province or an army.
prolepsis. In prophecy, a figure whereby a future event is presented as if present. Adj. **proleptic**
Providence, providence In biblical theology, providence is that sovereign action of God whereby he upholds his creatures by guiding and governing all events, circumstances, including the free acts of angels and men, thereby directing everything to achieve his

appointed goals. When referring to God as subject, the word is capitalized.

pseudepigraphon, pseudepigrapha) A book regarding which the authorship is falsely attributed, in the case of non-biblical apocalyptic works, to some illustrious biblical person. Plural, pseudepigrapha

sic.   This adverb, meaning "so," "thus," when inserted in brackets within a quotation indicates that it is quoted accurately though it may appear to be incorrect..

true visible church. See **Church, church** above.

type. A person, thing, or event in history which is viewed from the standpoint of Divine providence as anticipating a subsequent person, thing, or event of greater significance. In Scripture a type is sometimes considered as a prophecy. The greater person, thing, or event is called the "antitype."

BIBLIOGRAPHY OF WORKS CITED

Adams, Jay E. *The Time Is At Hand: Prophecy and the Book of Revelation.* Phillipsburg: Presbyterian & Reformed, 1966.
Aharoni, Yohanan. *The Land of the Bible: An Historical Geography.* Philadelphia: Westminster, 1962.
Allen, Leslie C. *The Books of Joel, Obadiah, Jonah, and Micah.* The New International Commentary on the New Testament. Grand Rapids: Eerdmans, 1996.
Allix, Peter. *Some Remarks upon the Ecclesiastical History of the Ancient Churches of Piedmont.* New ed., 1821. *Remarks upon the Ecclesiastical History of the Ancient Churches of the Albigenses.* New ed., 1821. Repr., Gallatin, Tenn.: Church History Research & Archives, 1989. 2 vols. in one.
Arndt, William F. *The Gospel Acco rding to St. Luke.* St. Louis: Concordia, 1956.
Arnot, A. B. *Last Words to a Lost World.* New York: Carlton, 1975.
Ash, McKinley. *Anti-Christ Past, Present and Future.* Robbinsdale, Minn.: Osterhus, 1967.
Atkinson, Basil F. C. *The Book of Genesis.* The Pocket commentary of the Bible; Chicago: Moody, 1957.
___. *The War with Satan: an Explanation of the Book of Revelation.* London: Protestant Truth Society, 1940.
Aune, David E. *Revelation.* Word biblical commentary. Nashville: Thomas Nelson, 1997-1998.
Barclay, William. *The Gospel of Luke.* Edinburgh: Saint Andrew Press, 1953.
___. *The Revelation of John: Translated with an Introduction and Interpretation.* 2nd ed. Philadelphia: Westminster, 1960. 2 vols.
Barnes, Albert. *Notes on the New Testament: Revelation.* 1852. Enlarged type ed., Grand Rapids: Baker, 1949.
Barton, Harold E. *It's Here: the Time of the End.* New York: Exposition , 1963.
Bauer, W., W. F. Arndt, and F. Wilbur Gingrich. *A Greek-English Lexicon of the New Testament and Other Early Christian Literature.* 2nd ed. Chicago: University of Chicago Press, 1979.
Beale, G. K. *The Book of Revelation.* Grand Rapids: Eerdmans, 1999.
Beasley-Murray, G. R. *The Book of Revelation.* New century Bible. Revised ed. Grand Rapids: Eerdmans, 1978.
Beckwith, Isbon T. *The Apocalypse of John: Studies in Introduction with a Critical and Exegetical Commentary.* 1919. Repr., Grand Rapids: Baker, 1967.

Bibliography

Biblical Archaeology Review 2, no. 20 (Mar/Apr 1994). "Queries & Comments." 20, 73-81.

Birks, T. R. *First Elements of Sacred Prophecy*. London: W. E. Painter, 1843.

___. *Outlines of Unfulfilled Prophecy*. London: Seeleys, 1854.

Blass, F., A. Debrunner, and Robert Funk. *A Greek Grammar of the New Testament and Other Early Christian Literature*. Chicago: University of Chicago Press, 1961.

Bloomfield, S. T. *Ή ΚΑΙΝΗ ΔΙΑΘΗΚΗ, The Greek Testament with English Notes, Critical, Philological, and Exegetical*. Boston: Perkins and Marvin, 1837.

Boak, A. E. R. *A History of Rome to 565 A. D.* 4th ed. New York: Macmillan, 1955.

Boring, M. Eugene. *Revelation*. Louisville: John Knox, 1989.

Boutflower, Charles. *In and Around the Book of Daniel*. 1923. Repr., Grand Rapids: Zondervan Publishing House, 1963.

Bower, Archibald. *History of the Popes, from the foundation of the See of Rome to A.D. 1758*. Philadelphia: Griffith & Simon, 1844. 3 vols.

Bowman, John Wick. *The First Christian Drama: the Book of Revelation*. Philadelphia: Westminster, 1955.

Bright, John. *A History of Israel*. 2nd ed. Philadelphia: Westminster, 1974.

Brightman, Thomas. *The Revelation of Saint John . . . Together with a Most Comfortable Exposition of the Last and Most Difficult Part of the Prophecy of Daniel. . . .* Amsterdam: Thomas Stafford, 1644.

Brown, Francis, S. R. Driver, and Charles A. Briggs. *A Hebrew and English Lexicon of the Old Testament.* Corrected ed. Oxford: Clarendon, 1962.

Brown, John. *Harmony of Scripture Prophecies and History of Their Fulfillment*. Glasgow: John Bryce, 1784.

Bruce, F. F. *1 & 2 Thessalonians* . Word Biblical Commentary. Waco, Texas: Word, 1982.

___. "The Revelation of St. John." In *A New Testament Commentary*. London: Pickering & Inglis, 1969.

Burns, Thomas S. *Barbarians Within the Gates of Rome: a Study of Roman Military Policy and the Barbarians, ca. 375-425 A. D.* Bloomington, Ind.: Indiana University Press, 1994.

Burr, G.I. "The Carlovingian Revolution, and Frankish Intervention in Italy." Pages 589-591 in vol. 2 of The *Cambridge Medieval History*. Edited by J. B. Bury. New York: Macmillan, 1926.

Burton, Ernest DeWitt. *A Critical and Exegetical Commentary on the Epistle to the Galatians*. Edinburgh: T. & T. Clark, 1921.

Cachemaille, E. P. *XXVI Present Day Papers on Prophecy*. London: Seeley, Service, 1911. Later reprinted as *The Visions of Daniel and the Revelation Explained*.

Bibliography

Caird, G. B. *A Commentary on the Revelation of St. John the Divine.* Harper's New Testament commentaries. New York: Harper & Row, 1966.

Caringola, Robert. *The Present Reign of Jesus Christ: a Historical Interpretation of the Book of Revelation.* Springfield, Missouri: Abundant Life Ministries Reformed Press, 1995.

Carroll, B. H. *The Book of Revelation.* New ed. Nashville, Broadman, 1947.

Carson, R. A. G., "From Tiber's Seven Hills to World Dominion." Pages 223-40 in *The Birth of Western Civilization: Greece and Rome.* Edited by Michael Grant. New York: McGraw-Hill, 1964.

Charles, R. H. *Apocrypha and Pseudepigrapha of the Old Testament.* Oxford: Clarendon Press, 1913.

___. *A Critical and Exegetical Commentary on the Revelation of St. John: With Introduction, Notes, and Indices Also the Greek Text and English Translation.* International Critical Commentary. Edinburgh: T. & T. Clark, 1920. 2 vols.

Charlesworth, James H., ed. *The Old Testament Pseudepigrapha.* Garden City, N. Y.: Doubleday, 1983-1985. 2 vols.

Chilton, David. *The Days of Vengeance: an Exposition of the Book of Revelation.* Fort Worth: Dominion, 1987.

Clarke, Adam. "The Revelation of St. John the Divine." Pages 958-1068 in *The New Testament . . . the text, . . . a commentary and critical Notes.* New York: Carlton & Porter, n.d.

Close, Albert. *Antichrist and His Ten Kingdoms.* London: The Protestant Truth Society, pref. 1917.

Collins, Oral. "Two difficult readings in Daniel 9:24." *Henceforth* 1 (1972): 42-47. Cited 8 July 2006. On line: as "Exploring the Prophecies of Moses and Daniel as Corroborating Authority for the 'Great Tribulation' of Matthew 24," http://www.histori cism.com.

___. "Prostitution in the Ancient Near East." In *The Stem ZNH and Prostitution in the Hebrew Bible*, 26-60. Ph. D. dissertation, Brandeis University. Ann Arbor, Mich.: University Microfilms, 1977.

___. "Good Question." *Henceforth.* . . . 7 (1979): 103-107.

___. "Continuous or Parallel? The Question of Chronology in the Book of Revelation: An Evaluation." Pages 165-180 in *Our Destiny We Know: Essays in Honor of Edwin K. Gedney.* Edited by Freeman Barton. Charlotte, N. Car.: Venture Books, 1996.

Cooke, Ronald N., *Antichrist Exposed : the Reformed and Puritan View of the Antichrist.* 2 vols. Max Meadows, Va.: Truth International Miistries, 2006.

Cox, William E. *Biblical Studies in Final Things.* Philadelphia: Presbyterian & Reformed, 1967.

Bibliography

Cumming, John. *Lectures on the Book of Daniel*. Philadelphia: Lindsay & Blakiston, 1855.

___. *Apocalyptic Sketches: Lectures on the Book of Revelation*. First Series. Philadelphia: Lindsay & Blakiston, 1856.

Cuninghame, William. *A Dissertation on the Seals and Trumpets of the Apocalypse*. London: Cadell, Hatchard, & Nisbet, 1843.

Daubuz, Charles. *Perpetual Commentary on the Revelation of St. John*. London: Benj. Tooke, 1720.

DeWette, W. M. L. *Kurze Erklärung der Offenbarung Johannis*. Leipzig: Weidman, 1848.

Dollinger, J. H. Ignaz von. *The Pope and the Council*. London, 1869.

Durham, James. *A Complete Commentary on the Book of Revelation, Delivered in Several Lectures*. 2 vols. Falkirk, Scotland: Robert Penny, 1799.

Edersheim, Alfred. *Sketches of Jewish Social Life*. London: Religious Tract Society, n.d.

Edwards, Jonathan. *History of the Work of Redemption*. Boston: Draper and Folsom, 1782.

___. "Notes on the Apocalypse." Pages 97-305 in *Apocalyptic Writings*. Vol. 5 of *The works of Jonathan Edwards*. Edited by John E. Smith from unpublished mss. New Haven: Yale University Press, 1977.

Eerdman, Charles. *The Revelation of St. John*. Philadelphia: Westminster, 1966.

Eichhorn, I. G. *Commentarius in Apocalypsin Joannis*. Göttingen: Dieterich, 1791.

Ehrlich, Carl S. "Cherethites." Pages 898-899 in vol. 1 of *The Anchor Bible Dictionary*. Edited by David Noel Friedman. 6 vols. New York: Doubleday, 1992.

Elliott, E. B. *Horae Apocalypticae*. 5th ed. 4 vols. London: Seeley, Jackson, and Halliday, 1862.

Ellis, E. Earle, Paul's Use of the Old Testament. Grand Rapids: Eerdmans, 1957.

___. *The Gospel of Luke*. London: T. Nelson & Sons, 1966. Repr., Eugene, Oreg.: Wipf & Stock, 2003.

___. The Making of the New Testament Documents. Leiden: Brill, 2001.

Eusebius. *The Ecclesiastical History of Eusebius Pamphilus . . . and an Historical View of the Council of Nice by Isaac Boyle.* Translated by Isaac Boyle, 1856. Popular ed. reprt. Grand Rapids: Baker, 1962.

Ewald, G. Heinrich A. *Commentarius in Apocalypsin Johannis*. Lipsiae: Hahn, 1828.

Faber, G. S. *Dissertation on the Prophecies*. 4th ed., rev. and corr. 2 vols. 1805. London: Rivington, 1810.

Bibliography

Fairbairn, Patrick. *Ezekiel and the Book of His Prophecy: an Exposition.* 4th ed. Edinburgh: T. & T. Clark, 1876.

Farrar, F. W. *The Early Days of Christianity.* New York: Cassell, Petter, Galpin, 1882.

___. *The Gospel According to St. Luke, with maps, notes and introduction.* The Cambridge Bible for Schools and Colleges. Cambridge: University Press, 1916.

Ferrero, Guglielmo. *The Ruin of the Ancient Civilization and the Triumph of Christianity.* New York: Putnam's Sons, 1921.

Fisher, George P. *History of the Christian Church.* New York: Scribner's Sons, 1916.

Ford, Desmond. *Daniel.* Nashville: Southern Publishing Association, 1978.

Ford, J. M. *Revelation.* Anchor Bible. Garden City, N.Y.: Doubleday, 1975.

Foxe, John. *Book of Martyrs.* Edited by W. Grinton Berry. First published as *The Acts and Monuments*, 1563. Grand Rapids: Baker, 1992.

French, S. H. *The Unsealed Book.* London: Prophetic Light Publications, 1968.

Frend, W. H. C. *Martyrdom and Persecution in the Early Church.* Garden City, N.Y.: Doubleday, 1967.

Frere, J. H. *A Combined View of the Prophecies.* 1814. Corrected ed. London: Hatchard, Seeley, Nisbet, & Panton, 1826.

Froom, Leroy Edwin. *The Prophetic Faith of Our Fathers, the Historical Development of Prophetic Interpretation.* 4 vols. Washington, D.C.: Review and Herald, 1950-1954.

Fudge, Edward William. *The Fire that Consumes.* Houston, Texas: Providential, 1982.

Gebhardt, Hermann. *The Doctrine of the Apocalypse, and Its Relation to the Doctrine of the Gospel and Epistles of John.* Translated from the German by John Jefferson. Clark's Foreign Theological Library. New Series, vol. 58. Edinburgh: Clark, 1878.

Gentry, K. L. *Before Jerusalem Fell: Dating the Book of Revelation.* Tyler: Institute for Christian Economics, 1989.

John H. Gerstner. *The Rational Biblical Theology of Jonathan Edwards.* 3 vols. Powhatan, Va.: Berea Publications, 1991.

Gesenius' Hebrew Grammar. Edited and Enlarged by the Late E. Kautzsch. Revised in Accordance with the Twenty-eighth German Ed. of 1909 by A. E. Cowley. 2nd ed. Oxford: Clarendon, 1910.

Gibbon, Edward. *The History of the Decline and Fall of the Roman Empire.* With notes by H. H. Milman. New ed. New York: Harper & Brothers, n.d.

Gibson, Scott M. *Adoniram Judson Gordon, D.D. (1836-1895), Pastor, Premillennialist, Moderate Calvinist, and Missionary Statesman* (Ph.D thesis,

Bibliography

    University of Oxford; Oxford: Regent's Park College, Hilary Term, 1997).
Gill, John. *The Exposition of the New Testament*. Philadelphia: Woodward, 1811. 3 vols.
Godet, F. *A Commentary on the Gospel of St. Luke*. Trans. from 2nd French ed. by E. W. Shalders and M. D. Cusin. Preface and notes to the American ed. by John Hall. The Bible Students Library. New York: Funk & Wagnalls, 1887.
Goodwin, Thomas. "An Exposition of the Book of Revelation." Pages 1-226 in *The Works of Thomas Goodwin*, vol. 3. 1639. Repr., Edinburgh: James Nichol, 1861.
Grant, Robert M. *Augustus to Constantine: the rise and triumph of Christianity in the Roman World*. New York: Harper & Row, 1970.
Gregg, Steve, ed. *Revelation: Four Views, a Parallel Commentary*. Nashville: Thomas Nelson, 1997.
Grotius, Hugo. *Commentatio ad Loca Quaedam N. Testamenti Quae de Antichristo Agunt* [*Commentary on Certain N. Testament Texts which Deal with Antichrist*]. Amsterdam: 1640.
Guinness, H. Grattan. *The Approaching End of the Age*. 1878. 8th ed. New York: A. C. Armstrong and Son, 1884.
___. *Light for the Last Days: A Study Historic and Prophetic*. 2nd ed. London: Hodder & Stoughton, 1888.
___. *The Divine Programme of the World's History*. London: Hodder & Stoughton, 1889.
___. *Romanism and the Reformation from the Standpoint of Prophecy*. Boston: Arnold Publishing Association, 1893.
___. *History Unveiling Prophecy: or Time As an Interpreter*. New York: Revell, 1905.
Guthrie, Donald. *New Testament Introduction*. Vol. 2. *Hebrews to Revelation*. Chicago: InterVarsity, 1962.
___. *New Testament Introduction*. Vol. 1. *The Gospels and Acts*. Chicago: InterVarsity, 1965.
Gwatkin, H. M. "Constantine and His City." Pages 4-5 in vol. 1 of *The Cambridge Medieval History*. Edited by J. B. Bury. New York: Macmillan, 1924.
Hammer, Richard. *The Vatican Connection*. New York: Rineholt & Winston, 1982.
Harrison, R. K. "Cherubim." Page 264 in *The Illustrated Bible Dictionary*. Edited by J. D. Douglas. Vol. 1. Leicester, Eng.: InterVarsity Press, 1980.
Hartman, L. F., and A. A. Di Lella. *The Book of Daniel*. Anchor Bible Commentary. Garden City, N.Y.: Doubleday, 1978.

Bibliography

Hendriksen, William. *More Than Conquerors: An Interpretation of the Book of Revelation.* Grand Rapids: Baker, 1952.

Hengstenberg, E. W. *The Revelation of St. John.* 1851. Repr., Cherry Hill, N.J.: Mack Publishing Co., 1972.

Hewitt, C. H. *The Seer of Babylon.* Boston: Advent Christian Publication Society, 1948.

Hislop, Alexander. *The Two Babylons: or Papal Worship Proved to Be the Worship of Nimrod and His Wife.* 3rd ed. Edinburgh: Wood, 1862.

Hitti, Philip K. *History of the Arabs.* London: Macmillan, 1953.

Hoeksema, Herman. *Behold He Cometh: An Exposition of the Book of Revelation.* Grand Rapids: Reformed Free Publishing Association, 1969.

Holtzmann, H. J., *Briefe und Offenbarung des Johannes.* Freiburg: Mohr 1893.

Hourani, Albert. *A History of the Arab People.* Cambridge, Mass.: Harvard University Press, 1991.

Hughes, Philip. *A Popular History of the Catholic Church.* Garden City: Doubleday, 1947.

Hughes, Philip Edgecombe. *The Book of Revelation: a Commentary.* Grand Rapids: Eerdmans Company, 1990.

Hutchinson, Wm., *The Apocalypse Opened.* Glasgow: Wm. Collins, 1857.

Iranaeus, *Adversus Haereses*, 5.30.3.

James, William. *The Naval History of Great Britain.* London: Richard Bentley, 1837.

Jewett, Paul. *Infant Baptism and the Covenant of Grace.* Grand Rapids: Eerdmans, 1978.

Johnson, B. W. "Revelation." In *The Peoples New Testament*: the Common and Revised Versions, with References and Colored Maps, with Explanatory Notes. 405-505. ca. 1900. Repr., 2 vols. in one. Nashville: Gospel Advocate, 1982.

Johnson, Paul. *The Intellectuals.* New York: Harper & Row, 1988.

Jones, William. *History of the Christian Church.* 1826. 3rd Am. from the 4th London ed. Louisville: Ephraim A. Smith, 1831. Repr. Gallatin, Tenn.: Church History Research & Archives, 1883; Conrad, Mont.: Triangle, 1993.

Jonge, Marinus de. "Messiah." Pages 777-788 in vol. 4 in *The Anchor Bible Dictionary*. Edited by David Noel Freedman. 6 vols. New York: Doubleday, 1992.

Jurieu, Pierre. *The Accomplishment of the Scripture Prophecies, or the Approaching Deliverance of the Church.* French ed., 1686. Eng. translation, London: 1687.

Katz, Solomon, *The decline of Rome* (Ithaca, New York: Cornell University Press, 1955.

Bibliography

Kee, H. C. "Testaments of the Twelve Patriarchs." Pages 775-828 in vol. 1 in *The Old Testament Pseudepigrapha*. Edited by James H. Charlesworth. Garden City, N. Y.: Doubleday, 1983.

Keil, C. F. *Daniel*. Commentary on the Old Testament. vol. 9. 1884. Repr., Peabody, Mass.: Hendrickson, 1989.

Kiddle, Martin. *The Revelation of St. John*. London: Hodder & Stoughton, 1940.

Kistemaker, Simon. *Exposition of the Book of Revelation*. New Testament Commentary. Grand Rapids: Baker, 2001.

Kromminga, D. H. *The Millennium in the Church: Studies in the History of Christian Chiliasm*. Grand Rapids: Eerdmans, 1945.

____. *The Millennium: Its Nature, Function, and Relation to the Consummation of the World*. Grand Rapids: Eerdmans, 1948.

Lacocque, A. *The Book of Daniel*. London, SPCK, 1979.

Ladd, George Eldon. *The Blessed Hope*. Grand Rapids: Eerdmans, 1956.

____. *A Commentary on the Revelation of John*. Grand Rapids: Eerdmans, 1972.

LaTourette, Kenneth Scott. *A History of the Expansion of Christianity*. New York: Harper Brothers, 1937.

____. *A History of Christianity*. New York: Harper Brothers, 1953.

Lee, Francis Nigel. *John's Revelation Unveiled*. Brisbane, Australia: Queensland Presbyterian Theological College, 2000.

Leith, John H., ed. *Creeds of the Churches: A Reader in Christian Doctrine from the Bible to the Present*. 3d ed. Atlanta: John Knox, 1982.

Lenski, R. C. H. *The Interpretation of St. John's Revelation*. Columbus, Ohio: Wartburg, 1943.

Liddell, Henry George, and Robert Scott. *A Greek-English Lexicon*. New Edition Revised and Augmented throughout by Henry Stuart Jones. 9th ed. Oxford: Clarendon Press, 1940.

Llorente, Juan Antonio. *A Critical History of the Spanish Inquisition*. 1823. Repr., John Lilburne Company, 1967.

Loades, D. M. *The Oxford Martyrs*. New York: Stein & Day, 1970.

Lo Bello, Nino. *The Vatican Empire*. New York: Trident Press, 1968.

Longdon, R. P. "Nerva and Trajan." Pages 198-199 in vol. 11 of *The Cambridge Ancient History*. Edited by C. W. Previté-orton & Z. N. Brooke. Cambridge: University Press, 1936.

Llorente, Juan Antonio, *A Critical History of the Spanish Inquisition* (English ed., 1823; repr. John Lilburne Company, 1967).

Lowth, Robert. *Isaiah: a new translation . . . with a summary view and explanation of the same*. London: C. Paramore, 1791.

Lucas, Ernest C. *Daniel*. Apollos Old Testament Commentary, vol. 20. Downers Grove: InterVarsity, 2002.

Bibliography

McDougall, Douglas. *The Rapture of the Saints*. Blackwood, N.J.: O.F.P.M., 1970.

M'Leod, Alexander. *Lectures upon the Principal Prophecies of the Revelation*. New York: Whiting & Watson, 1814.

Macpherson, Dave. *The Incredible Cover-up: the True Story of the Pre-trib Rapture*. Plainfield, New Jersey: Logos International, 1975.

Manhattan, Avro. *The Vatican Billions*. London: Paravision Books, 1972.

Mansfield, Peter. *A History of the Middle East*. New York: Viking, 1991.

Manson, William. *Gospel of Luke*. London: Hodder & Stoughton, 1930.

Mansfield, Peter. A History of the Middle East. New York: Viking, 1991.

Marshall, I. Howard. *Gospel of Luke*. New International Greek Testament. Grand Rapids: Eerdmans, 1978.

Martin, Malachi. *The Decline and Fall of the Roman Church*. New York: G. P. Putnam's Sons, 1981.

_____. *The Keys of This Blood: the Struggle for World Dominion Between Pope John Paul II, Mikhail Gorbachev, and the Capitalist West*. New York: Simon & Shuster, 1990.

Mede, Joseph. *A Key to the Apocalypse, a translation of Clavis Apocalyptica*. Translated by R. Bransby Cooper. 1st Latin ed., 1627. London, J. G. & F. Rivington, 1833.

Meyers, Carol. "Jerusalem Temple." Pages 364-365 in vol. 6 in *Anchor Bible Dictionary*. Edited by David Noel Freedman. New York: Abingdon Press, 1992.

Mickelsen, A. Berkeley. *Daniel and Revelation*. Nashville: T. Nelson, 1984.

_____. *Interpreting the Bible*. Grand Rapids: Eerdmans, 1963.

Milligan, William. *The Book of Revelation*. New York: Armstrong, 1901.

Milner, Joseph. *History of the Church of Christ*. 2nd ed. Cambridge, Eng.: J. Burges, 1800. 2 vols.

Moore, George F. *Judaism*. Cambridge, Mass.: Harvard University Press, 1966.

Moreland, Samuel. *The History of the Evangelical Churches of the Valleys of the Piedmont.* London: Adoniram Byfield, 1658. 2 vols. in 1. Repr. by Baptist Standard., n.d.

Morris, Leon. *Revelation*. Revised ed. Grand Rapids: Eerdmans, 1987.

Mosheim, John. Lawrence von. *Institutes of Ecclesiastical History, Ancient and000000000 Modern.* London: William Tegg, 1859.

Mounce, Robert H. *The Book of Revelation*. Grand Rapids: Eerdmans, 1977.

Mowinckel, Sigmund. *He That Cometh*. New York: Abingdon Press, 1954.

Moyer, Elgin S. *Who Was Who in Church History*. New Canaan, Conn.: Keats, n.d.

Napier, B. D. "Lamb." Pages 58-59 in vol. 3 in *The Interpreter's Dictionary of the Bible*. Edited by George A. Buttrick. New York: Abingdon, 1962.

Bibliography

Newark, Tim. *The Barbarians: Warriors & Wars of the Dark Ages*. Poole, U.K.: Blandford, 1985.

Newport, John P. *The Lion and the Lamb*. Nashville: Broadman Press, 1986.

Newton, Isaac. *Observations Upon the Prophecies of Daniel, and the Apocalypse of St. John* (London: J. Darby and T. Browne, 1733

Newton, Thomas. *Dissertations on the Prophecies*. 1754. Repr., London: Crissy & Markley, 1850.

Nichol, Francis D., ed. *The Seventh-day Adventist Bible Commentary*. Washington, D.C.: Review and Herald, 1957.

Osborne, Grant R. *Revelation*. Baker Exegetical Commentary on the New Testament. Edited by Moisés Silva. Grand Rapids: Baker, 2002.

Payne, J. Barton, *Encyclopedia of Biblical Prophecy, the Complete Guide to Scriptural Predictions and Their Fulfillment*. New York: Harper & Row, 1973.

Pelikan, Jaroslav. *The Excellent Empire*. San Francisco: Harper & Row, 1987.

Ploetz, Carl. *Ploetz' Epitome of History*. 7th ed., tr. & enlarged by W. H. Tillinghast and H. E. Barnes, eds. New York: Blue Ribbon Books, 1925.

Pond, Enoch. *The Seals Opened; or, The Apocalypse Explained*. Portland: Hoyt, Fogg, & Breed, 1871.

Priest, Josiah, *View of the Expected Christian Millennium*. Albany: 1827.

Pusey, E. B. *Daniel the Prophet: Nine Lectures Delivered in the Divinity School of the University of Oxford, with Copious Notes*. 3rd ed. London and New York: Rivingtons; Pott, Young, 1876.

Pyles, F. A. "The Missionary Eschatology of A.B. Simpson." Pages 29-47 in *Birth of a Vision*. Edited by D. F. Hartzfeld and C. Nienkirchen. His Dominion, Supplement No. 1. Cited May 2, 2006. Online: http://online.aucnuc.ca/alli-ancestudies/ahtreadings/ahtr_s141.html; http://www.historicism. com/misc/absimpson.htm.

Ramsay, William M. *The Letters to the Seven Churches of Asia*. New York: A. C. Armstrong, 1909.

Ribera, Francisco. *In Sacrum Beati Ioannis Apostoli, & Evangelistiae Apocalypsin Commentari*j. Lugduni: Ex Officina Iuntarum, 1593.

Richardson, Donald W. *The Revelation of Jesus Christ: An Interpretation*. Richmond: John Knox, 1964.

Rissi, Matthias. *Time and History: a Study on the Revelation*. Translated by G. Windsor. Richmond, Va.: John Knox Press, 1966.

Rist, Martin. "Antichrist." Pages 140-143 in vol. 1 of *The Interpreter's Dictionary of the Bible*. Edited by George A. Buttrick. New York: Abingdon, 1982.

Robertson, A. T. *A Grammar of the Greek New Testament in the Light of Historical Research*. Nashville: Broadman, 1934.

Bibliography

Rollin, Charles. *Ancient History*. From the latest London ed., rev. and corr. 4 vols. New York: Leavitt & Allen, n.d.

Rowley, H. H. *The Relevance of the Apocalyptic: A Study of Jewish and Christian Apocalypses from Daniel to the Revelation*. 2nd ed.. London: Lutterworth Press, 1947.

Russell, D. S. *The Method and Message of Jewish Apocalyptic, 200 B.C.--A.D. 100*. The Old Testament Library. Philadelphia: Westminster Press, 1964.

Schaff, Philip. *History of the Christian Church*. 8 vols. Grand Rapids: Eerdmans, 1950.

Schoedel, William R. *Ignatius of Antioch: A Commentary on the Letters of Ignatius of Antioch*. Hermeneia. Philadelphia: Fortress, 1985.

Scott, Thomas. "Revelation of John the Divine." In *The Holy Bible . . . with Explanatory Notes*. Vol. 1 (unpaged). 5th London ed. Boston: Sam. T. Armstrong, 1831.

Scott, Walter. *Exposition of the Revelation of Jesus Christ*. 4th ed. Westwood, N.J.: Revell, n.d.

Seiss, Joseph A. *The Apocalypse*. 9th ed. New York: Charles C. Cook, 1906.

Simpson, David. *A Key to the Prophecies: Or, a Concise View of the Predictions Contained in the Old and New Testaments, Which Have Been Fulfilling, or Are Yet to Be Fulfilled in the Latter Ages of the World*. London: Booksellers, 1847.

Smiles, Samuel.. *The Huguenots in France*. New York: Harper, 1874.

Smith, Ethan. *A Dissertation on the Prophecies Relative to Antichrist and the Last Times*. Charlestown, Mass.: Charles T. Armstrong, 1811.

Smith, H. P. *A Critical and Exegetical Commentary on the Books of Samuel*. Edinburgh: T. & T. Clark, 1912.

Smith, Sidney. "The Foundation of the Assyrian Empire." Pages 1-31 vol. 3 in *The Cambridge Ancient History*. Edited by J. B. Bury, S. A. Cook, & F. E. Adcook. New York: Macmillan, 1925.

Smith, Wilbur M. *A Preliminary Bibliography for the Study of Prophecy*. Boston: W. A. Wilde, 1952.

Spurgeon, Charles Haddon. *Commenting and Commentaries*. New York: Sheldon, 1876.

Steele, David. *Notes on the Apocalypse . . ..* Philadelphia: Young & Ferguson, 1870.

_____. *The Two Witnesses*. 1859. Reprint, Edmonton, Alberta: Still Waters Revival Books, n.d.

Stuart, Moses. *A Commentary on the Apocalypse*. 2 vols. Andover: Allen, Morrill and Wardwell, 1845.

Summers, Ray. *Worthy Is the Lamb*. Nashville: Broadman Press, 1951.

Bibliography

Swete, Henry Barclay. *The Apocalypse of St. John: The Greek Text with Introduction, Notes, and Indices*. 3rd ed. Grand Rapids: Eerdmans, pref. 1908.

Tasker, R. V. G. "The Apostle John."Pages 794-795 in vol. 2 in *The Illustrated Bible Dictionary*. Chicago: InterVarsity, 1980.

Taylor, Daniel T. "The Great Tribulation." Pages 53-74 in *The Great Consummation*. Boston: Advent Christian Publication Society, 1891.

___. *The Reign of Christ on Earth: or the Voice of the Church in All Ages*. Boston: H. L. Hastings, 1893.

Tenney, Merrill C. *Interpreting Revelation*. Grand Rapids: Eerdmans, 1957.

Thompson, J. A. "Marriage." Pages 955-957 vol. 2 in *The Illustrated Bible Dictionary*. Wheaton, Ill. Tyndale House Publishers, 1980.

Trapp, John. "Revelation of St. John the Divine," Pages 740-787 in his *Commentary on the New Testament*. Evansville, Ind.: Sovereign Grace Book Club, 1958.

Tregelles, S. P. *Remarks on the Prophetic Visions of Daniel*. London: Bagsters, 1852.

Turberville, A. S. *Mediaeval Heresy & the Inquisition*. Hamden: Archon, 1964.

Turner, C. H. "The Organization of the Church." Pages 143-182 in vol. 1 of *The Cambridge Medieval History*. Edited by J. B. Bury. New York: Macmillan Company, 1924.

Victorinus, "Commentary on the Apocalypse of the Blessed John," *Anti-Nicene Fathers*, vol. 7. Grand Rapids: Eerdmans,1989.

Walvoord, John F. *The Revelation of : A Commentary*. Chicago: Moody, 1966.

Warns, Johannes. *Baptism*. Minneapolis, Min.: Klock & Klock, 1980.

Welcome, I. C., and Clarkson Goud. *The Plan of Redemption by our Lord* . Boston: Advent Christian Publication Society, pref. 1867.

Wells, H. G. *The Outline of History*. Garden City, N.Y.: Garden City Publishing, 1921.

Wilson, Clifford A. *Rocks, Relics and Biblical Reliability*. Grand Rapids: Zondervan, 1977.

Wylie, J. A. *History of Protestantism*. 3 vols. in 2. Kilkeel, N. Ireland: Mourne Missionary Trust, 1990.

Young, Edward J. *The Book of Isaiah*. Grand Rapids: Eerdmans, 1965. 2 vols.

Zimmermann, Frank. *The Book of Tobit: an English Translation with Introduction and Commentary* New York: Harper & Brothers, 1958.

Chapter One

INTRODUCTION TO THE BOOK OF REVELATION

The Special Place of the Book of Revelation

The Bible gives the Book of Revelation a high place in its library collection. The reader neglects it at his or her loss. The book begins with the pronouncement of a special blessing for those who publicly read it and also for those who hear it and who take it to heart (1:3). Indeed, John testifies here that the Revelation is "the word of God and the testimony of Jesus Christ " (1:2). For centuries, the covenant people waited for their Messiah. They believed that when he came he would deliver them and lead them into all truth. Here, the glorified Jesus, the Sovereign One, appears with his final message—his letters to the churches (1:12-16) and the unsealed prophecies of this book (5:7-9). The promise of blessing to the one who "takes it to heart" implies its great practical value.

Unlike any other Bible book, Revelation contains Jesus' explicit warning—a curse against anyone who might presume to add or take away anything from the words of His prophecy: "God will take away from him his share in the tree of life and in the holy city, which are described in this book" (22:19).

In spite of this, Revelation is one of the most neglected and misused books of the Bible. It abounds with extraordinary and strange symbols. To make understanding more difficult, several modern approaches to its interpretation give rise to radically different and conflicting explanations. In the earliest days of the church, apocalyptic writings were commonplace and the symbols for the most part were understood. Now, many do not know their meaning. It is the task of the reader (and especially of those who presume to write commentaries!) to return to those early ways of understanding and to put them into a present-day life situation.

From our perspective, at a time when the world tends to despair of the future and even to turn to pagan religions and to the occult, the believer should cherish the last prophecy of Jesus. The times demand that we give the Book of Revelation a high place in our personal lives and in the life of the church.

Purpose

Why did our resurrected Lord choose to give his people His final testimony in this book and put it at the place of emphasis at the conclusion of the Bible? We find the answer in part in the very first sentence: "The revelation of Jesus Christ, which God gave him *to show his servants what must soon take place"* (emphasis mine). Those who de-emphasize or deny the predictive element in the book must turn away from Jesus' words. "To show what must soon take place" is to disclose future events.

The introductory chapter of the Revelation addresses the sovereignty of the resurrected Christ. He is in spite of appearances "the ruler of the kings of the earth" (1:5). When the people of God suffer persecution and when earthly rulers prevail with their ungodly designs, we are to know that "he has made us to be a kingdom (1:6), the eternal kingdom of God, and that "he is coming with clouds." All the ungodly "peoples of the earth will mourn because of him" (1:7). Those who have suffered, even died, for their testimony will be vindicated. "Blessed are those who wash their robes, that they may have the right to the tree of life . . ." (22:14).

The believer needs understanding and lively hope. He needs to be on the alert to practice personal obedience, and to witness to the truth and power of the Gospel. To this end the Book of Revelation takes its place in the written Word of God as the testimony of Jesus, His final message to His people.

Historical Origin

1. Authorship

The author identifies himself simply as Christ's "servant, John" (1:1, 9). The unanimous tradition of the church fathers of the second century is that this was the apostle, the "beloved disciple."

According to the extrabiblical history, John left Judea at the time of the Jewish-Roman war (A.D. 66-70) and began an extended ministry in the Roman province of Asia, what is now western Turkey in Asia Minor. He resided in Ephesus and superintended the Asian churches. John was the youngest of the twelve. In the final decade of the first century he was held in high esteem as the only survivor of the twelve apostles.

During our Lord's ministry, John was one of the favored three, numbered with his brother James and Peter. Jesus, on at least three occasions, gave special privileges to these men (Mark 5:37, 9:2, 14:32 ; see also Gal 2:9). Tradition records that John lived at Ephesus to extreme old age and that he was regarded with great respect. One interesting tradition says that in his final years he was carried to the meetings of the church and that on such occasions he often kept repeating, "Little children, love one another."[1]

During the first century, Domitian was second to Nero as a persecutor of Christians, but he was the first to punish Christians for their refusal to worship the emperor. As he did with John, he liked to banish the accused. Philip Schaff states that he was

> as cruel and bloodthirsty as Nero, and surpassed him in hypocrisy and blasphemous self-deification. He began his letters 'Our Lord and God commands,' and required his subjects to address him so. He ordered gold and silver statues of himself to be placed in the holiest place of the temples. . . . Many Christians suffered martyrdom under his reign, on the charge of atheism—among them his own cousin, Flavius Clemens, of consular dignity . . . and his wife Domitilla, who was banished to the island of Pandateria, near Naples.[2]

The island of Patmos, located about sixty miles southwest of Ephesus in the Aegean Sea, is rocky and barren. One can still go to a

---

[1] R. V. G. Tasker, "The Apostle John," *IBD*, 2:795; Iranaeus, *Adv. Haer.*, 5:30.3.
[2] *History of the Christian Church* (Grand Rapids: Eerdmans, 1950), 1.427-428.

grotto on a southern hillside where local tradition identifies the site of John's vision. We may estimate that the Apostle was about ninety years old at the time, but in spite of the hardships, tradition says that he returned to Ephesus to die a natural death. Imagine what would have been had John retired from public life at age sixty-five.

Domitian's persecution occurred toward the end of his reign, probably in the year A.D. 96. We may date the composition and publication of the Book of Revelation at that time.

Excursus on Non-Apostolic Authorship

There is no reason to reject the unanimous tradition of the ancient fathers. They testify that the Book of Revelation was written by the Apostle John in the fifteenth year of the Emperor Domitian, A.D. 96, when he was exiled to the island of Patmos. The tradition is attested by Papias (ca. A.D. 100), Justin Martyr (in his *Dialogue with Trypho the Jew* 81.15; ca. A.D. 135), Iranaeus (ca. A.D. 185), and Clement of Alexandria (ca. A.D. 195). Iranaeus, who was born about A.D. 120, stated that Papias was a disciple of the Apostle John (see Schaff, 2:697-698).

The common argument that the Fathers were all dependent on a common ignorant source overlooks the fact that the churches in the ancient Roman world were connected by tradesmen and other travelers, as witnessed by the canonical epistles. Many ancient libraries were then intact. The arrest and imprisonment of the aged and only surviving Apostle would not have escaped the notice of most of the churches. The frequent mention of Papias in a chain of evidence is best accounted for by the fact that these men were well-known accredited authorities, surely not the only available evidence.

After Constantine's legalization of Christianity as the primary state religion in the fourth century, the premillennial doctrine common in the first three centuries, including the identification of Antichrist with the government of the Roman Empire, came into disfavor. The tradition of the Apostolic authorship of Revelation was rejected by Eusebius and others who now saw the Emperor, not as antichrist, but as the primary benefactor of the church. Eusebius disposed of the millennial teaching of Revelation 20 by arguing for non-Apostolic authorship. He appealed to a quotation of Papias which, he alleged, proved that there were two Johns in Ephesus, John the Apostle and John the Elder. Though Papias had attributed the Revelation to John the Apostle, Eusebius avoided the Apostolic authority of the Revelation by assigning it to "John the Elder." Here is what Papias said:

τοὺς τῶν πρεσβυτέρων ἀνέκρινον λόγους· τί Ἀνδρέας ἢ τί Πέτρος εἶπεν . . . ἢ τί Ἰωάννης ἢ Ματθαῖος ἤ τις ἕτερος τῶν τοῦ χυρίου μαθητῶν· ἅ τε Ἀριστίων καὶ ὁ πρεσβύτερος Ἰωάννης οἱ τοῦ κυρίου μαθηταὶ λέουσιν.

I inquired regarding the words of *the elders,* what Andrew or what Peter *said,* . . . or what Philip, or Thomas, or James, or John, or Matthew, or any other of the Lord's disciples *said,* also what the Lord's disciples Aristion and the Elder John *are saying.*[3]

A careful reading of the above indicates that Eusebius' two Johns are an unnecessary inference. More likely, Papias describes the apostles both as elders and as the Lord's disciples. From Papias' second-century point of view, the term, "elder," is probably used as an appropriate ecclesiastical title of respect due the Apostles. On the other hand, the term "disciple" as used here denoted one who, though not necessarily an apostle, had been a follower of Jesus during his earthly ministry. Papias referred to John as "the elder" to distinguish him from Aristion and to show respect for his apostleship. The reason Papias repeated John's name is found in the tenses of the emphasized verbs. John is included among the list of apostles from whom sayings have been preserved through oral transmission in the church. He also is distinguished from them because he is still living and giving personal testimony. If there were two Johns in Ephesus who were both candidates for the authorship of Revelation, Papias' statement provides no proof.

Another difficulty in affirming the tradition of apostolic authorship is the difference in style between Revelation and the other books traditionally attributed to the Apostle John. This argument is reported by Eusebius and is attributed by him to Dionysius, Bishop of Alexandria (ca. A.D. 250). As Eusebius, Dionysius was motivated by his distaste for the millennial teaching of Revelation. Though he wished to retain the book as an inspired work which, according to the fashion of the Alexandrian School, might be interpreted allegorically, he did not wish to honor it with apostolic authorship (Eusebius [bk. 7:25], 297-301).

The differences in the Greek vocabulary and style between the other books attributed to the Apostle John and the Revelation are substantial. The language of the earlier works generally conforms to the normal patterns whereas the grammar of the Apocalypse is highly irregular. However, Robert Mounce and others have pointed out that there are also significant similarities between Revelation and the other Johannine books. [4]There are characteristic words and expressions which are used in a distinctively Johannine sense (29, 30). Moreover, Donald Guthrie shows that the language of Revelation has more affinity with that of the other Johannine books than with any other of the New Testament.[5] For such reasons, scholars who reject the apostolic authorship often suggest that the author was a disciple of the apostle or a member of "a Johannine school."

While one need not insist that the John who wrote the Revelation was the Apostle, one can find other reasons for the language difference. R. H. Charles in his exhaustive review of the problem concluded that "a good number" of the irregularities

---

[3]Eusebius, *Eccl. Hist.* bk. 3.39; Gk. text from H. B. Swete, *The Apocalypse of St. John: the Greek Text with Introduction Notes and Indices* (2nd ed., 1908; Repr., Grand Rapids: Eerdmans, n.d.), clxxvi. Trans. and emphasis mine.

[4]Robert H. Mounce, *The Book of Revelation* (revised ed.; NICNT; Grand Rapids: Eerdmans, 1977).

[5]Guthrie, Donald, New Testament Introduction (4th ed., rev.; Downers Grove, Ill.: InterVarsity, 1990), 940.

of language may be explained as reproductions of Hebrew idioms.[6] Moreover, it is probable that John's earlier works were written by a secretary who edited his Greek. We know that this was the case with the Apostle Paul, who on one occasion called attention to an exceptional instance when he was writing with his own hand (Gal 6:11). One should expect also that John's writing would have been affected by the manner in which the revelation was received. He was told to write what he had seen (1:19) and the revelation came in highly dramatic, pictorial form. Moreover, he may not have had time or materials to make a "corrected" revision.

It is difficult to account for the unique character and place of the book and the respect it received in the earliest centuries of the church apart from the authority of apostolic authorship. Several scholars have pointed out that to achieve recognition other apocalyptic books of the day without exception were attributed pseudepigraphically to some more ancient and more illustrious person. Would the Revelation have been given the authority of Scripture by the Christian world at large had it not been written by the Apostle John but by some other John unknown beyond the environs of Ephesus? (Guthrie, 933-936)

Some scholars who have been looking for evidence of nonapostolic authorship of the Book of Revelation have appealed to Eusebius. All things considered, the witness of the Apostolic Church is a better foundation on which to build. The author of the Revelation identifies himself simply as "John." The most eminent John, the Apostle, to whom tradition assigns a long residence in Ephesus, is the most likely candidate. If absolute certainty is wanting, nevertheless the author most probably was the Apostle John.

2. Occasion and Date.

The tradition of the Apostolic and Early Church supports the writing of the Revelation in A.D. 96, during the reign of the Roman Emperor Domitian. Although some scholars have argued that the book was written as reflecting the Neronian persecution, the great majority have agreed in associating the book with the persecutions of Domitian.[7]

The letters to the churches contain mention of persecution shortly before and at the time of writing. The Ephesians "have endured hardships for my name" (2:3). Antipas, a "faithful witness" in Pergamum was "put

---

[6]R. H. Charles, *A Critical and Exegetical Commentary on the Revelation of St. John* (ICC; Edinburgh: T. & T. Clark, 1920), 1.clii.

[7]E. Earle Ellis in *The Making of the New Testament Documents* (Leiden: Brill, 1999), 210-216, argues with a number of British scholars for an earlier date, ca. 65-70. Though this writer finds this less than convincing, most of my interpretation which follows will not be affected by an earlier date. One need not assume on account of the extensive concern with persecution and martyrdom in the Book of Revelation that when it was written there was general or severe persecution in progress in the Empire such as exited under Nero. There is sufficient justification for anxiety on the part of the first-century reader as derived from the prediction of the war of the Little Horn antichrist in Daniel 7.

to death" (2:13). To these we may add the statement of the author, himself, "Your brother and companion in the suffering and kingdom and patient endurance that are ours in Jesus . . . " (1:9).

The Book of Revelation was given to the church to encourage Christians as they give witness to the Gospel and to give hope in the face of persecution. Christ's victory over the persecuting Antichrist power and the certainty of the deliverance of the people of God is a central theme in the book. This emphasis is appropriate to the assumption that the tradition regarding its origin is correct. In the face of the historical evidence, we assume that the book was written about the year A.D. 96, toward the end of Domitian's reign, the time systematic persecutions by Rome began. This note of assurance to the persevering believer is appropriately voiced in the letter to the church at Philadelphia:

> You have kept my word and have not denied my name. . . . I will keep you from the hour of trial that is going to come upon the whole world to test those who live on the earth. I am coming soon. Hold on to what you have, so that no one will take your crown. (3:8, 10, 11)

Approaches to Interpretation

Through nineteen centuries several schools of interpretation of the Book of Revelation developed and become established in Christendom. Here we offer a brief resumé summarizing the different approaches. Many of the questions introduced by the discussion below are treated more fully in Appendix 1, to which the reader is referred for a more complete analysis and evaluation.

During the first fifteen centuries readers commonly assumed that the book was a prophecy regarding events in the future of the church, events which began to occur soon after the time of its composition (see 1:1, 19, 4:1) and that these events extended through the period of the church age to their consummation in the second coming of Christ and the establishment of His eternal kingdom (chs. 19-22). This approach is now known as historicist interpretation and is commonly called the historicist school (see no. 3 below).

1. The Rise and Characteristics of the Preterist and the Futurist Schools

During the years when the Roman Catholic Papacy was coming to power in the church there grew up among dissenters a persistent doctrine that the Roman Papal power was the Antichrist predicted in the prophecies of Daniel, Revelation, and other Scriptures.[8] Because this understanding of the Antichrist played a fundamental role in the Reformation of the sixteenth century, Jesuit scholars as part of the Counter-Reformation movement developed and published two alternative ways of reading those prophecies.[9]

One of those commentaries written by the Jesuit priest Alcasar took the position that the prophecies had been already fulfilled in divine judgments against the Jews and the old Roman Empire. This approach to interpretation developed into the school called "Preterism" (Latin, *praeteritus*, "gone by"). According to this school, the Antichrist was one of the emperors of the pagan Roman Empire.[10]

Another Jesuit priest, Ribera, published a Counter-Reformation commentary in which he advocated that all of the prophecies in Revelation after the seal judgments in 6:1-8:5 relate to the last few years at the end of time when a future antichrist will come and wage war against the saints (8:6-18:24). This view with some subsequent modifications came to be known as the futurist school. Ribera did not, however, hold to the church-age-parenthesis theory popular among futurists today. Instead he took the seal judgments as spanning the church age.[11]

Neither the preterist nor the futurist view allowed for the then- common Protestant historicist interpretation that the Antichrist was the contemporary Roman Catholic Papacy.[12] For obvious reason, the preterist and futurist views became popular in Roman Catholic circles and still remain so.

Following negative-critical theories that arose in the eighteenth century with naturalistic tendencies that were skeptical of the possibility of predictive prophecies, many scholars of that mind set, both Catholic and Protestant, adopted the preterist school. From this standpoint, they

---

[8]For a thorough review of pre-Reformation interpretation of the Apocalypse from the Apostolic Fathers to the Reformation, see H. Grattan Guinness, "Interpretation and Use of These Prophecies [Daniel and Revelation] in Pre-Reformation Times," in *Romanism and the Reformation* (Boston: Arnold Publishing Association, 1893), 179-222. For an in-depth exposition of that history, see E. B. Elliott, *Horae Apocalypticae* (5th ed.; London: Seeley, Jackson, and Halliday, 1862), 4. 275-436.

[9]H. B. Swete, *The Apocalypse of St. John* (Grand Rapids: Eerdmans, pref. 1906), 331-333; Elliott 4.480-481.

[10]Swete, 331-332; Elliott 4.484.

[11]Swete, 332-333; Elliott 4.481-483.

[12]On Luther, see Le Roy Edwin Froom, *The Prophetic Faith of Our Fathers*. (Washington, D.C.: Review and Herald, 1950), 2.254-256, 261 and sources indicated there. On Calvin, see Froom 2.436-439; on Knox, Froom 2.450-455.

viewed prophecy, in so far as it has been proven to be accurate and beyond human capacity to forecast, as history written after the fact.[13] Unfulfilled predictions, such as the second coming of Christ, they usually viewed either as metaphor for temporal events or as pious human opinion and myth.

On the other hand, in part resulting from the Anglo-Catholic Oxford Movement of the eighteen-thirties, Ribera's futurist approach was taken up by elements within the Anglican and Presbyterian churches of England and Scotland, and about the same time, by the Brethren movement in England. This may be seen as a part of the accommodation to Rome which characterized the Romanist Oxford Movement. The futurist interpretation has an advantage in its putting the prophecies of Revelation into the unknown future rather than in the history of the church. It has in the late nineteenth and twentieth centuries been popularized in the United States by the Moody Bible Institute, the Scofield Bible, and by the many Bible colleges and other institutions which have grown out of those spheres of influence. In the opinion of this author, the futurist interpretation of Revelation exhibits an excessive literalism inappropriate to the nature of apocalyptic literature. Today, nevertheless, the teaching of the futurist school is considered orthodox, biblical doctrine by several evangelical denominations. The futurist commentaries of Walter Scott and John F. Walvoord are for many standard works within this school.[14]

Futurist interpretation characteristically assumes a church-age parenthesis between the sixty-ninth and the seventieth week of the Seventy Weeks prophecy of Daniel 9 and interprets chapters 4-22 of Revelation as pertaining to events after the rapture and during the 70th week of Daniel nine.

---

[13]The first Protestant preterists were Hugo Grotius, a Dutch scholar, and Henry Hammond. the first English preterist. In 1640, Grotius wrote against the Protestant doctrine that identified Antichrist with the Papacy, following the Jesuit Alcasar in his interpretation of Revelation. He opposed the Reformation and favored closer ties with Rome. Hammond wrote *A Paraphrase and Annotations upon All the Books of the New Testament*, which was published in 1653. On the book of Revelation he closely followed Grotius. These preterists interpreted the Antichrist and the war against the church in terms of pagan Rome. They followed the Catholic view that the millennium began with Constantine and even understood the New Jerusalem as Constantinople! (Froom 1:524, 525; chart on 528-529)

[14]Walter Scott, *Exposition of the Revelation of Jesus Christ* (4th ed.; Westwood, N. J.: F. H. Revell, n.d.); John F. Walvoord, *The Revelation of Jesus Christ.* (Chicago: Moody, 1966).

2. Current Trends.

Some scholars with a futurist orientation have recently abandoned certain key elements of their approach. They reject what they perceive in the school as excessive literalism while introducing a preteristic tendency which sees in Revelation more of the ancient Roman background and less prediction. Nevertheless, they still expect a future Antichrist and a future tribulation. Examples of this "neofuturism" may be found in the commentaries of the late George Eldon Ladd (1972) and Robert H. Mounce (1977). Although this is sometimes referred to as historical interpretation, it should not be confused with the approach of the traditional historicist school.

Within the preterist school, mediating scholars have tended to develop the approach by minimizing the predictive element while maintaining a reverent, theistic approach to the book. Examples of these may be found in the well known, standard commentaries of Henry Barclay Swete (3rd ed., 1908) and Isbon T. Beckwith (1919), or in the more recent popular writing of William Barclay (1976). Such works, however, clearly affirm or presuppose errancy in biblical prediction. Beckwith, for example, states:

> The recognition of . . . fallibility in certain details of prophecy . . . furnishes an important factor in the interpretation of the Revelation. . . . But their failure cannot give difficulty in the study of the Revelation, as a book of prophecy. . . . . They enshrine great truths regarding the kingdom of God; but the form in which the Apocalyptist saw the truth realized . . . is derived from events and ideas belonging to an age now past. That form is transitory, the truth is eternal.[15]

One should discern in such statements that the standard of truth is not the Scriptures but the mind of readers, including those truths enshrined in creeds of the church. It may be sufficient for the present to remind the reader of the Lord's statement to Moses on the subject, "If what a prophet proclaims in the name of the LORD does not take place or come true, that is a message the LORD has not spoken" (Deut 18:22).

---

[15]Isben T. Beckwith, *The Apocalypse of John* (1919; Repr., Grand Rapids: Baker, 1967), 300-301.

3. The Historicist School.

In this commentary the writer affirms the propriety of the traditional Protestant approach to the interpretation of the Book of Revelation called the historicist school. This approach sees the Revelation as a forecast of the progress and destiny of the church in its conflict with Rome and the Roman Antichrist power forecast in Daniel seven.[16] Its prophecies pertain to events from the time of the New Testament church to the end-time consummation. The approach is historical, not from the standpoint of the New Testament author, but from the standpoint of the modern reader for whom much of the prophecy has already been fulfilled. It focuses on the course of church history depicting the victory of Christ over the Antichrist, the redemption of His bride, the Church, the ultimate destruction of evil, and the establishment of Christ's everlasting rule at His second coming.

The historicist school assumes that the Revelation addresses the primary concern of the persecuted church at the end of the first century—the destiny of the church under the terrible Roman Beast of Daniel 7, and especially the predicted rise of the Little Horn antichrist power forecast in Dan 7:8, 11, 20-21, 24-26.[17]

The historicist approach to the Revelation was followed not only by nearly all Protestant interpreters during and for several centuries after the Reformation, but also by pre-Reformation dissidents from Romanism, until Jesuit scholars in the late sixteenth and seventeen centuries gave rise to futurist and preterist views. It was systematically developed by post-Reformation Protestants, both premillennial and postmillennial, and came to be called "the Protestant view."[18] Futurism and preterism largely

---

[16]This should not be caricatured, as is commonly done by opponents of this school, as a comprehensive prophetic history of the church, which obviously it is not.

[17]Opponents frequently allege erroneously that historical interpretation renders the book irrelevant to the churches to which it was addressed.

[18]The writings of the earlier pre-Reformation dissidents from Rome have by and large been destroyed by their Papal enemies. The following sources will be useful in documenting their witness: Peter Allix, *Some remarks upon the ecclesiastical history of the ancient churches of Piedmont*; *Some remarks upon the ecclesiastical history of the ancient churches of the Albigenses* (1690, 1692; repr. in 1 v. by Gallatin, Tenn.: Church History Research & Archives, 1989); Elliott, 4.381-436; Guinness, "Interpretation . . . in pre-Reformation times," *Romanism*, 178-222; H. Grattan Guinness, *History unveiling prophecy* (New York: Revell, 1905), 63-78; Wylie, J. A., *The History of Protestantism* (1878; repr. , 2 vv.; Down, N. Ireland: Mourne Missionary Trust, 1985), 1.18-56.

Leading post-Reformation works include Joseph Mede (*The Key to the Apocalypse*: *Discovered and Demonstrated from the Internal and Inserted Characters of the Visions* (1627; trans. from Latin by R. B. Cooper; London: Rivington, 1833);

replaced the historical interpretation in the later nineteenth and twentieth centuries, preterism in the mainline denominations and among many Reformed scholars and futurism, indigenous in most of the Bible institute movement and in most Protestant-evangelical churches. In the early Bible institute movement, however, there were notable exceptions. For example, A. J. Gordon, founder of Gordon College, and A. B. Simpson, founder of the Christian and Missionary Alliance and Nyack College, were historicists, as were the founders of Berkshire Christian College (then The Bos-

---

Thomas Goodwin, "An Exposition of the Book of Revelation," *The Works of Thomas Goodwin* (1639; repr., Edinburgh: J. Nichol, 1861), 3.1-226; Ch. Daubuz, *Perpetual Commentary on the Apocalypse* (London: Benj. Tooke, 1720); Isaac Newton, *Observations Upon the Prophecies of Daniel, and the Apocalypse of St. John* (London: J. Darby and T. Browne, 1733); Jonathan Edwards, "Notes on the Apocalypse," in *Apocalyptic Writings* (ed. Stephen J. Stein from unpublished mss; vol. 5 of *The works of Jonathan Edwards*; New Haven: Yale University Press, 1977), pp. 97-305; Thomas Newton, *Dissertations on the Prophecies* (1754; repr., London: Crissy & Markley, 1850); John Brown, *Harmony of Scripture Prophecies and History of Their Fulfilment* (Glasgow: John Bryce, 1784); James Durham, *A Complete Commentary on the Book of Revelation, Delivered in Several Lectures* (Falkirk, Scotland: Robert Penny, 1799); G. S. Faber, *Dissertation on the Prophecies*, 4th ed. (London: F. C. and J. Rivington, 1810), Alexander M'Leod, *Lectures upon the Principal Prophecies of the Revelation* (New York: Whiting and Watson, 1814); Adam Clarke, "Revelation of St. John the Divine," *The New Testament* (New York: Carlton & Porter, n.d.) 2.993-996; Thomas Scott, "Revelation of John the Divine," *The Holy Bible . . . with Explanatory Notes* (5th London ed.; Boston: Sam. T. Armstrong, 1831); S. T. Bloomfield, Ἡ ΚΑΙΝΗ ΔΙΘΗΚΗ, *The Greek Testament with English Notes, Critical, Philological, and Exegetical . . . .* (Boston: Perkins & Marvin, 1837), Elliott (1862); David Simpson (*A Key to the Prophecies* (London: Wm. Walker, 1847); Moses Stuart, Commentary on the Apocalypse (2 vols. Andover: Allen, Morrill and Wardwell, 1845), Barnes, *Notes on . . . Revelation* (1852; repr., enlarged type ed., Grand Rapids: Baker, 1949); T. R. Birks, *First Elements of Sacred Prophecy* (London: W. E. Painter, 1854); Wm. Hutcheson, *The Apocalypse Opened* (Glasgow: Wm. Collins, 1857); David Steele, *Notes on the Apocalypse: with an Appendix* (Philadelphia: Young & Ferguson, 1870); James Stacy, *Handbook of Prophecy: Containing a brief Outline of the Prophecies of Daniel and John, Together with a Critical Essay on the Second Advent* (Richmond: Presbyterian Committ of Publication, ca 1900); B. W. Johnson, "Revelation," *The Peoples New Testament* (1st ed. ca. 1900; Nashville: Gospel Advocate, 1982); E. P. Cachemaille, *XXVI Present Day Papers on Prophecy* (London: Seeley, Service, 1911); Basil F. C. Atkinson, *The War with Satan: an Explanation of the Book of Revelation* (London: Protestant Truth Society, 1940); Harold Barton, *It's Here: the Time of the End* (New York: Exposition Press, 1963).

ton Bible School).[19] For our defense of the historical school, see, in addition to the commentary which follows, Appendixes 1-4.

Major expository works bearing on the Book of Revelation in the nineteenth and twentieth centuries written from the standpoint of the historicist school are those of T. R. Birks (1843, 1854),[20] E. B. Elliott (1844, 5th ed., 1862),[21] Albert Barnes (1852, currently published by Baker),[22] David Steele, Sr. (1870),[23] H. Grattan Guinness (1879- 1905),[24] E. P. Cachemaille (1911, 2nd ed. 1931?),[25] and Francis Nigel Lee (2000).[26] Of these, Elliott's work, *Horae Apocalypticae,* is clearly the most outstanding. Charles Haddon Spurgeon cited it as "the standard work" on the Revelation.[27] Though a futurist, the late bibliographer, Wilbur Smith, commented regarding *Horae Apocalypticae* and its author that "this vast work is in some ways the most learned of all English works on the

---

[19]Scott M. Gibson, *Adoniram Judson Gordon, D.D. (1836-1895), Pastor, Premillennialist, Moderate Calvinist, and Missionary Statesman* (Ph.D thesis, University of Oxford; Oxford: Regent's Park College, Hilary Term, 1997), 132ff.; F. A. Pyles "The Missionary Eschatology of A.B. Simpson," *Birth of a Vision,* ed. by D. F. Hartzfeld and C. Nienkirchen (His Dominion, Supplement No. 1), 29-47. Cited May 2, 2006. Online: http://online.auc-nuc.ca/alliancestudies/ahtreadings/ahtr_s141.html; http:// www.historicism.com/misc/absimpson.htm. Founders of the Boston Bible School included A. E. Hatch, *A Handbook of Prophecy* (Mendota, Ill.: Western Advent Christian Publication Association, 1913) and F. L. Piper, *The Return of Christ* (New York: Fleming H. Revell, 1922). See especially, Piper, pp. 41-42.

[20]T. R. Birks, *First Elements of Sacred Prophecy* (London: W. E. Painter, 1843) and *Outlines of Unfulfilled Prophecy* (London: Seeleys, 1854).

[21]E. B. Elliott, *Horae Apocalypticae* (5th ed; 4 vols.; London: Seeley, Jackson, and Halliday, 1862).

[22]Albert Barnes, *Notes on the New Testament: Revelation* (1849; enlarged type ed.; Grand Rapids: Baker, 1949).

[23]David Steele, Sr., *Notes on the Apocalypse . . .* (Philadelphia: Young & Ferguson, 1870).

[24]H. Grattan Guinness wrote several major works including the following: *The Divine Programme of the World's History* (London: Hodder & Stoughton, 1889); *History Unveiling Prophecy, or Time As an Interpreter* (New York: Fleming H. Revell Company, 1905); *Light for the Last Days*: *A Study Historic and Prophetic,* by Mr. and Mrs. H. Grattan Guinness (2nd ed.; London: Hodder and Stoughton, 1888).

[25]Cachemaille, E. P., *XXVI Present Day Papers on Prophecy: an Explanation of the Visions of Daniel and of the Revelation, on the Continuous-Historical System* (London: Seeley, Service, 1911); reprinted as *The Visions of Daniel and the Revelation Explained* (New ed.; London: Seeley, Service, n.d.).

[26]John's Revelation Unvieled (Brisbane, Australia: Queensland Presbyterian Theological College, 2000).

[27]C. H. Spurgeon, *Commenting and Commentaries* (New York: Sheldon, 1876), 280.

Apocalypse to appear in the 19th century. His knowledge of history is astonishing. He knew everything that had been written on the Book of Revelation up to his time." "His 400-page [sic] history of the interpretation of the Book of Revelation is the most exhaustive of our language."[28]

4. The Spiritual Interpretation or the Philosophy of History School.

A fourth school of interpretation has been given various labels such as the spiritual school, the idealist school, or the philosophy of history school.[29] The approach may vary somewhat depending on the author, but proponents generally expound the Book of Revelation not as prediction of specific events but rather as teaching principles regarding good and evil applicable in every age. During the 20th and 21st centuries there has been considerable blending of the various schools. This is true of futurism with preterism, as mentioned above, but even more, of both futurism and preterism with the spiritual school. Historicist commentaries, on the other hand, have sometimes erred, while concentrating on questions of prediction and fulfillment, by neglecting to expound the spiritual values of the prophecy. In this work, we have attempted to take a more balanced approach.

A major characteristic of the philosophy of history school is their reduction of the specific historical Antichrist as fulfillment of the Little Horn of Dan 7:8 and the Man of Lawlessness of 2 Thess 2:3, 4 to an antichristian principle that may be reiterated in many temporal events in the course of history. This issue has great practical consequence, as it confronts the traditional Protestant-historicist understanding that helped to fuel the Reformation—that the Antichrist is the present Roman Papal church and the sacramental system of the Roman church. Protestants should not be embarrassed to affirm what the Reformers accepted as fundamental and wrote into the great Reformation creeds: "the Pope of Rome . . . is that Antichrist, that man of sin and son of perdition, that exalteth himself in the Church against Christ, and all that is called God." (West-

---

[28]*A Preliminary Bibliography for the Study of Biblical Prophecy* (Boston: Wilde, 1952), 28. Elliott's history runs to 288 pages of volume 4.

[29]Perhaps the most popular representative of this school is Wm. Hendrickson with his work, *More than conquerors*. A more recent work, very valuable in many respects, is the commentary by G. K. Beale. Both writers adopt as an interpretive principle the transtemporal nature of prediction in the Book of Revelation, thereby avoiding the necessity of correlating predictions with specific historical fulfillments. (Hendrickson, 54-56 *en passim*; Beale, 48-49.)

minster Confession, 25.6)³⁰Nevertheless, the equation is not to be made simplistically. For example, we do not assume that those who worship in the Roman church cannot experience salvation by faith alone but only that prophecy teaches that the doctrines and practices of that church, especially as they require for their members their sacramental system, are antichristian.

Understanding Apocalyptic Writing

The term "apocalyptic" originated from the Greek language form of the title of the Book of Revelation, Ἀποκάλυψις, *Apokálupsis*, translated, "Apocalypse." The word means, "revelation." "Apocalyptic" has come to be used to describe several hundred books written from the second or late third century B.C. through at least the first century A.D. because they are in their literary style much like the Apocalypse, the Book of Revelation. Scholars have difficulty, however, knowing how much like the Apocalypse a particular writing must be in order to be called "apocalyptic." Among the Old Testament writings, the best claimant to the title is the book of Daniel with its several apocalyptic visions.

Apocalyptic writings share in common several distinctive features which must be understood for their proper interpretation.

1. Symbolic Language

The most conspicuous of these is the abundant use of symbolic expression. Apocalyptists were also caught up with the sequence of events leading up to the coming of the Messiah and the end-time establishment of the Messianic kingdom. Among the visions of Daniel we find, for example, the vision of the Great Image (ch. 2), where the head is the kingdom of Babylon in the reign of Nebuchadnezzar and the various sections of the torso illustrate three more kingdoms: Medo-Persia, Greece, and Rome. These four kingdoms are represented as extending to the end of

---

[30] John H. Leith, ed., *Creeds of the Churches* (3rd ed.; Atlanta: John Knox, 1982), 222. As a reflex of contemporary trends in the interpretation of the Book of Revelation, the First General Assembly of the Presbyterian Church in America, in December 1973, when adopting the historic Reformation Confession, deleted the reference to the Pope as the antichrist (XXV,6). Cited May 2, 2006. *The Westminster Confession of Faith* (3rd ed. with corrections; Lawrenceville, Ga.: Committee for Christian Education & Publications, n.d.). Cited 3 May 2006. On line: http://www.pcanet.org/general/cof_preface.htm.

time, when a fifth, the kingdom of God, will strike the image at the feet and introduce God's eternal, universal rule. Characteristically, the apocalyptist shows how God will vanquish the dominant evil ruling power and emancipate his people for divine rule.

The symbols of apocalyptic are drawn in part from the book of Daniel, but beyond that, from the larger reservoir of symbolic language found in the Old Testament and, occasionally, elsewhere in the ancient world. Celestial and terrestrial symbolism is common in the prophets. It is used there to symbolize the demise of the authority of earthly monarchs under the judgment of God. It is important when trying to understand a particular passage of Revelation to go back to the Old Testament use of the symbol and examine that passage for its general sense. Then the text of Revelation must be carefully studied to see how the symbol is adapted in the new context to fit into the meaning of that passage. Ordinarily there will be some general correspondence in meaning but the usage in Revelation will be molded by the new context to provide a specific sense somewhat different from that found in the older text.

In the common culture of the ancient Near East, celestial bodies, characteristically the sun, moon, and stars, were seen as representing deities, which in turn were represented by rulers on earth. The darkening of the sun, the moon turning blood-red, or the falling of the stars were seen as symbols of the fall of the earthly rulers they represented. The prophets, in turn, borrowed that dramatic language when predicting divine judgments against sinful nations. We will show how all such language in the Revelation is found in the Old Testament and it is there we should learn its meaning.

The seven-headed serpent of Revelation 12 is illustrated in Babylonian, Egyptian, and Canaanite sources, some dating from the second millennium B.C. Of course, the identification of the serpent with Satan is found in the Genesis account of Eden (Gen 3:1-15).

Much of the symbolism of Revelation is drawn from the covenant institutions of Israel appropriately to convey a message to the people of God in the future ages of the church. In this category is the tabernacle-temple with its furniture, vessels, and offerings, as well as the numbering and identification of the tribes that in the Sinai wilderness camped around its courts. The Revelation reflects the first-century concept of the unity of Covenant Israel with Gentile believers grafted in, as taught by the Apostle Paul in Romans eleven.

To take such symbols literally rather than as figures would clearly be out of place in an apocalyptic work.

Why were symbols used by the apocalyptists or why should God use this means to present His message? Apocalyptic characteristically predicted the downfall of established governments. Were this done in plain language, Christians affirming these texts could have been charged with subversion of the ruling authorities. Also, Scripture characteristically veils such prophecies. This ambiguity is enhanced by the symbols. We assume that the divine Author designed this to prevent His people from knowing the future too accurately, while at the same time insuring an attitude of watchfulness in preparation for the great end-time events. (We will comment further on this in Append. 1.)

2. The Revelation as Drama

The Book of Revelation not only communicates through symbols but is presented as a drama which plays itself out before the eyes of the beholder. Scholars have seen in the interplay of action and interlude a similarity to the Greek theater.[31] This was constructed with two levels: the main stage for the dramatic action by which the plot was unfolded and often a higher level where the chorus supplemented the action with explanatory messages.

In Revelation we witness action and interlude—for example, the opening of the first six seals, then an interlude with the sealing of the 144,000 and the white-robed chorus, then the sounding of the first six trumpets (6:1-9:21). As with ancient drama, messengers often appear to facilitate the action or to orient the audience. Interludes supplement blocks of text which predict future events to provide orientation for better understanding the predictions, or to encourage the recipient of the prophecy in the face of coming judgments.

3. "Literal" Interpretation

Those who do not accept the supernatural origin of the Bible may equate literal interpretation with a naive acceptance of the normal sense of its language as true and authoritative. The position is sometimes caricatured to include ignorance of cultural conditioning and figurative language. Of course, those who target literalism in this manner ordinarily do not themselves accept the authority of the text.

---

[31]See, e.g., John Wick Bowman, *The First Christian Drama: the Book of Revelation* (Philadelphia: Westminster, 1955).

The belief that the Book of Revelation should be understood literally is complicated by the fact that in interpretation the word "literal" may have one of three meanings.

The most common meaning of "literal interpretation" is the idea that the text should be understood in its normal or ordinary sense. Accordingly, a literal understanding includes figures of speech and any other language phenomena that would normally be found in the particular kind of literature as they were known and recognized when they were written. As it is an apocalyptic writing, one should expect the Revelation to abound in figurative language, yet the book to be taken literally—that is, according to the norms by which at the time of writing that kind of language was understood. This is the method which must be pursued when seeking an authoritative message from any part of the Bible.

A less common use of "literal" is that the language in question does not include figures of speech. It would be inappropriate to argue that the Book of Revelation or any other apocalyptic book is literal in that way. There will be occasion, however, to consider whether particular elements within the book are literal or figurative. In such cases one must determine from the context which is most appropriate—which results in the most natural and suitable sense.

A third use of the word "literal" in interpretation is its use as a label for hyperliteralizing. This may involve interpreting the text as literal when it should be seen as figurative or, conversely and strange though it may seem, interpreting the text in a highly detailed, figurative manner. The latter method gives contrived meaning to details of the text, such as the number of letters in a word, irregularities of spelling, or redundancies such as repeated words. Those who have practiced such methods, because of their attention to details, have sometimes been labeled as literalists.

The first definition, which defines "literal" in terms of the literal principle of reading the language of Scripture in its natural or normal sense is one of the most important foundations of responsible interpretation. Scripture as the Word of God must be taken contextually the way it reads. We therefore aspire in this work to avoid all imaginative and creative intrusions on the part of the reader. Also essential as a principle of interpretation is the recognition that this meaning of the prophecy must be determined in so far as possible before consideration is given as to how it may or may not have been fulfilled.

In beginning our interpretive quest, it is fundamental to recognize that the Book of Daniel is the prototype for all subsequent apocalyptic prophecy. The visions in Daniel, some of which are accompanied by the interpretations of the Divine author, provide the best analogy for understanding the vision of Revelation. This fact, though commonly recognized in some of its aspects, is to a large degree passed over by many contemporary scholars, who address the Revelation as if it were written in a new and different genre. The importance of Daniel for understanding the symbolism and symbolic structure of Revelation is such that we must now examine the relationship of the two books more closely.

Apocalyptic and the Book of Daniel

Of the several occurrences of apocalyptic writing in the Old Testament, none has more bearing on our understanding of the Book of Revelation and perhaps on apocalyptic literature in general than the book of Daniel.

1. The Place of Daniel in the Apocalyptic Literature.

The book of Daniel is generally recognized, even by those who treat it as pseudepigraphic and date it in the second century, B.C., as the first of the apocalyptic books.[32] The historical setting of Daniel is the sixth century, B.C. But during the critical period of Jewish conflict with the Syrians in the second century Daniel was the prototype for the development of what is now known as Jewish apocalypticism and the apocalyptic literature. Of the hundreds of extrabiblical apocalyptic writings produced between 200 B.C. and A.D. 100 by this movement, all, unlike the book of Daniel, were pseudepigraphic and none were received as canonical. Although writings in the apocalyptic style were commonplace during this period, only the book of Daniel stood as pre-Christian Scripture, a worthy prototype for our understanding of the Book of Revelation.

Two points logically follow from this literary history: First, the entire body of apocalyptic literature, sixth century B.C. to first century A.D., including Daniel, provided the literary-historical context to guide the first-century reader or hearer in his understanding of the Book of Revelation. Although the pseudepigraphic writings never achieved the status of Holy Scripture, we know from the distribution and quantity of

---

[32]See H. H. Rowley, *The Relevance of Apocalyptic* (Rev. ed.; London: Lutterworth, 1963), 33; D. S. Russell, *The Method and Message of Jewish Apocalyptic* (Philadelphia: Westminster, 1964), 16.

the manuscripts that many were highly respected and used within the Early Church. This will have insured that at least the leaders of the Asian churches would have known the interpretive principles inherent in the nature of apocalyptic prophecy. Second, the book of Daniel as canonical Scripture would have provided the primary authoritative guide for understanding the apocalyptic style and thematic content of Revelation. This is especially enhanced by the fact that the visions of Daniel, with the exception of the last, are accompanied by inspired interpretations.

Several interpretive principles issue from this relationship of the Book of Revelation to the book of Daniel, some of them shared more or less in common also with the noncanonical apocalyptic books:

1. The dream-vision apocalyptic style of Daniel's prophecies is the medium for presenting prediction of events future from the standpoint of the author's time. We will see that this is borne out also by the claims of the Book of Revelation, contrary to some popular interpretations not entirely limited to the preterist school.

2. The interpretations given with the visions in Daniel indicate that the prophecies predict specific mundane events, sometimes in considerable detail, not in a broad, sweeping approach nor simply as a philosophy of history to be understood only in terms of principles applied in a general way to the course of the future.

3. Future events are predicted in Daniel in a sequential manner, beginning at a fixed point in history and leading up to some culminating event, usually the first or second advents of Christ. We should not therefore expect the reader to be prepared for unannounced, repetitious patterns of parallel symbols such as are often imposed on the Book of Revelation by those who hold that the seven churches are seven periods of church history or that the seals, trumpet, and bowl judgments should be construed as representing three parallel series of events (see Append. 3).

We will illustrate and address further the implications of these principles of interpretation later in this work. There is more to be learned regarding Daniel's prophecies and their implications for our understanding of the Revelation.

2. The Content of Daniel's Visions

The book of Daniel contains six apocalyptic style prophecies:

1. The vision of Nebuchadnezzar's image. 2:1-49

2. The vision of Nebuchadnezzar's tree. 4:1-37
3. The vision of the four beasts. 7:1-28
4. The vision of the ram and the goat. 8:1-27
5. The vision of the seventy weeks. 9:1-27
6. The vision of the end of days. 10:1-12:13

Each of these visions was received—the first two by Nebuchadnezzar, the last four by Daniel—on a particular occasion and independently of the others. Each of the visions except the last is accompanied by a divinely authored interpretation. Of the last it is said that "the words are closed up and sealed until the time of the end" (12:9, cp. 12:4). By way of contrast, the Book of Revelation consists of one vision received by John on one occasion. For this reason, when comparing visions from the standpoint of determining structure, one should not compare the several visions of Daniel with the several dramatic scenes in the one vision of the Revelation. One should rather compare vision with vision.

The visions of Daniel share a common purpose. They are intended to show the providential design of God in history, especially the fact that the Gentile pagan world powers which ruled over the people of God in Daniel's day will some day be put down, and that the kingdom of God will be established so that His will will be done on earth as it is in heaven.

a. The Vision of the Four Beasts (Daniel 7)

Of the several visions of Daniel, the one which appears to have most captured the imagination of God's people in the intertestamental period and in New Testament times was the chapter 7 vision of the Beasts from the Sea. Two themes from this vision became popular in Jewish apocalyptic speculation on the last days. The first was the Antichrist theme as expressed in the terrible Fourth Beast with its great power to destroy and its blasphemous Little Horn (vv. 8, 21).[33] The second was the appearance of the wonderful Son of Man-Messiah on the clouds of heaven to receive the kingdom for the "saints of the Most High" (7:13, 27).

At least from the first century until the rise of modern critical theories, Jewish and Christian interpreters recognized that Daniel's ter-

---

[33] I use the term, Antichrist, in the traditional manner to refer to that power symbolized by the Little Horn of Daniel 7, the Desolating Power of Daniel 9, Paul's Man of Lawlessness of 2 Thess 2:3, and John's Beast from the Sea of Rev 13:1-10. The term appears in the Scriptures only in the Epistles of John. For my exposition of these and other texts on the subject, see Append. 4.

rible nondescript beast which "devoured and broke in pieces and stamped the residue with its feet" was Rome. This was apparent both from the description and from her position in the rise and fall of nations, as charted in this vision and in the image vision of chapter two. (The modern critical reconstruction, because it dates the authorship of Daniel in the Maccabean period and rejects a-priori predictive prophecy, must necessarily identify the fourth beast with Greece.)

There are several parallels between the vision of Daniel 7 and the events as forecast in the book of Revelation:

Daniel 7	*Revelation*
Ten-horned beast (8)	Ten-horned beast 13:1-10)
Boastful little horn (8, 11)	Mouth to utter proud words and blasphemies (13:5)
Waging war against the saints (21)	Given power to make war against the saints (13:7)
Saints will be handed over to him for a time, times and half a time (25)[34]	Given to exercise his authority. for forty-two months (13:5)
Judgment established (9, 10) Beast destroyed (11)	Judgment established (20:4, 11) Beast destroyed (19:20)
Other beasts were stripped of authority but allowed to live for a period of time (12)	Satan bound for 1000 years, Then released for a short time (20:2, 7)
One like a son of man receives the kingdom for the saints of the Most High (13, 27)	The saints reign with Christ (20:4) New heavens & new earth (21:1-22:6)

The above parallels are sufficiently obvious to show a close tie between Daniel 7 and the Book of Revelation. There are common themes and a common chronology of last day events. Because the book of Revelation deals with the Daniel themes expansively, one may say that Revelation supplements Daniel and provides an explanatory commentary.

Moreover, because Revelation focuses on the fourth beast, it picks up the progress of the four world Gentile powers at the point con-

---

[34]"Time" in this expression means "year"; "times" is from the Hebrew dual, meaning "two years"; so the expression means "three and one-half years" and equals "forty-two months."

temporary with the author and the first century reader—that is, with Rome, that terrible beast out of which the persecuting little horn would arise.

This is entirely what one should expect from the perspective of the late first century when Domitian was enforcing Roman law by requiring Christians to worship the emperor. Would Domitian be the Little Horn antichrist? How long would the mysterious "time, times and half a time" prevail? The book of Revelation was given from a very practical standpoint to address such questions.

Is it not unreasonable to think, as the futurist interpreters generally do, that the divine answer is a revelation that addresses only the last seven years before the Judgment, a judgment which at the time, though unknown to the reader, was more than two millennia removed from the people to whom the predicted events were addressed? How much more plausible to assume that the prophecy speaks to the time of the immediate future and leads to the consummation in the manner well known from Daniel seven, as well as from other apocalypses known to them.

b. The Vision of the Seventy Weeks of Daniel 9

The Seventy Weeks prophecy of Daniel 9 pertains primarily to the coming of the Messiah and the bearing of that great event on the destiny of Jerusalem and the Jewish people. When the book of Revelation was written, the first advent addressed in the Seventy Weeks prophecy was history. However, because the Daniel prophecy does bear on the doctrines of Antichrist and tribulation, it is highly relevant for our study of Revelation.

(1) Daniel's Introductory Prayer of Dan 9:4-19

To understand this vision we must look carefully at the introductory passage, Daniel's prayer (9:4-19). This is dated in the first year of Darius the Mede, probably sometime in the year 538 B.C.

Daniel had reflected on Jeremiah's prophecy forecasting seventy years for the Babylonian captivity (Jer 25:11, 29:10). The first date for the beginning of this period was 605 B.C., the year Nebuchadnezzar subjugated Jerusalem and took hostages, including Daniel, himself. No doubt, the aged prophet, probably now eighty-five to ninety years old, yearned for fulfillment during his lifetime, hoping he might personally witness the event.[35]

It is important to recognize that Daniel not only looked to Jeremiah's prophecy, but also to the covenant promises of Moses as fundamental for understanding the desolations and forthcoming restoration of Israel. He looked not to Israel's repentance nor to any righteousness of the nation but to the Lord's merciful intent to glorify his holy name through his covenant people. We quote his prayer in part below:

> 9:4. "O Lord, the great and awesome God, who keeps his covenant of love with all who love him and obey his commands . . . . [7]Lord, you are righteous, but this day we are covered with shame . . . [8b]because we have sinned against you. . . . [11b]Therefore the curses and sworn judgments written in the Law of Moses, the servant of God, have been poured out on us . . . .[16a]O Lord, in keeping with all your righteous acts, turn away your anger and your wrath from Jerusalem, your city, your holy hill. [18b]. . . We do not make requests of you because we are righteous, but because of your great mercy. [19]O Lord, listen! O Lord, forgive! O Lord, hear and act! For your sake, O my God, do not delay, because your city and your people bear your Name."

Daniel hoped that the impending restoration would be the beginning of the new covenant era promised by Jeremiah when all Israel would know the Lord and the Righteous Branch would rule on David's throne (Jer 31:34, 33:15). But what of the Seer's earlier visions forecasting two additional Gentile governments to rule God's people? Would Gentile domination be extended still further into the future? God's answer to Daniel is the prophecy of the Seventy Weeks (Dan 9:24-27):

> [24]"Seventy 'sevens' are decreed for your people and for your holy city to shut up the transgressions, to seal the sins, to atone for iniquity, to bring in everlasting righteousness, to seal up vision and prophecy, and to anoint the Most Holy [One]. [25]So know and understand that the issuing of a decree to restore and rebuild Jerusalem until the Anointed Prince there will be seven 'sevens' and sixty-two 'sevens.' Again it will be rebuilt with plaza and a moat, but in times of trouble. [26]Then after the sixty-two 'sevens' the Anointed One will be cut off and will have nothing. Then the people of the Prince who is coming will destroy the city and the sanctuary. Its end will come like a flood. Even until the end there will be war. Desolations are determined. [27]He will confirm a covenant with the many for one 'seven,' but he will put a stop to

---

[35]If Daniel were between 15 and 20 years old when carried to Babylon by Nebuchadnezzar in 605 B.C., when he was near the end of the predicted 70 years, he would have been about 85-90 years old.

sacrifice and grain offering. Then upon the wing of abominations will come one who makes desolate until the decreed annihilation is poured out on him. [trans. mine][36]

For every year of Jeremiah's seventy year prophecy there would yet be a week of years before Messiah would come. Even then, more desolations were in store.

(2) The Structure and Meaning of the 70 Weeks of Daniel 9

In Dan 9:24, the content of the Seventy Weeks period is defined, especially as it relates to the covenant theme of Daniel's prayer. The language is juridical. It speaks of the Lord's judgments and mercies, the punishment of the nation and the redemptive work of the coming Messiah. Contrary to many of the futurist school, there is no prediction of the Antichrist within the scope of the seventy weeks.[37]

The purpose of the Seventy Weeks is stated in the several elements of Dan 9:24, as follows:

1. **To shut up the transgression.** The concept derives from the idea of holding the record of the accused for court action. The seventy weeks will bring the covenant nation to account. The idea is illustrated by Hos 13:12, "The guilt of Ephraim is stored up, his sins are kept on record." (cp. Deut 32:34; Job 21:19; 1 Thess 2:16; 2 Pet 2:9)

---

[36] I have adopted the *kĕthib* readings in 9:24 as more consistent with the juridical genre of the text. I am indebted to C. F. Keil for his defense of the *kĕthib* here and also for my translation of the difficult expressions in v. 27; C. F. Keil, *Daniel* (Repr., Peabody, Mass.: Hendrickson, 1989), 341. The *kĕthib* readings are those of the written text, while the LXX and modern versions adopt the *qerê* readings, those that the Massoretes put in the margins. The Massores preferred the marginal readings for public reading, I suspect because they better accommodated their understanding of the prophecy.

[37] The exposition of this vision is difficult and has a complicated history. It will not be possible within the scope of this work to fully exegete the prophecy. However, our interpretation follows the main lines of the traditional, Messianic view, which is given below. The reader will find thorough treatment in many older commentaries, including those of T. R. Birks, *First Elements* (1843), 169-181; John Cummings, *Lectures on the Book of Daniel* (Philadelphia: Lindsay and Blakiston, 1855), 327-422; Ch. Boutflower, *In and Around the Book of Daniel* (repr. Grand Rapids: Zondervan, 1963), 168-211; and E. B. Pusey, *Daniel the Prophet.* (3rd ed.; New York: Pott, Young, 1876), 164-233. More recent works following the traditional school include E. P. Cachemaille, *XXVI Present Day Papers, 1911*), 71-90; C. H. Hewitt, *The Seer of Babylon* (Boston: Advent Christian Publication Society, 1948), 251-273; and Desmond Ford, *Daniel* (Nashville: Southern Publishing Association, 1978), 221-238.

2. **To seal the sins.** As with "transgressions," the record of sins is in view here. Sealing probably has to do with rendering of an official verdict. That is, God during this period will have determined the verdict. The destruction of the nation which followed resulted from the national rejection of the Messiah.

3. **To atone for iniquity.** Grace enters at this point when the promise of Messianic atonement is made. Note that Daniel's introductory prayer is largely a confession of sin and a plea for God's mercy.

4. **To bring in everlasting righteousness.** This is a promise of Christ's righteousness imputed to the believer through the atonement which was to be accomplished in the midst of the seventieth week at Calvary.

5. **To seal vision and prophecy.** The first advent of Jesus served to seal the prophetic message of the Scriptures with His Messianic authority.

6. **To anoint the Most Holy [One].** Jesus was anointed by the Holy Spirit at His baptism in preparation for His redemptive work.

Daniel 9:25-27 is explanatory, giving the division of the seventy week period into three parts—seven, sixty-two, and one, the final week. Notice that there is nothing assigned to the sixty-two weeks. Their function is to indicate the span between the seven and the seventieth. It should be apparent from this as well as from the nature of a time prophecy that the seventieth week is connected to the sixty-two and not separated by an unmentioned and undefined period of time, as some of the futurist school hold.[38]

---

[38]The fallacy of a parenthesis in a time prophecy may be illustrated by algebraic formulas: $7 + 62 + 1 = 70$ whereas $7 + 62 + X + 1$ does not $= 70$, but $70 + X$, an indeterminate period contrary to the explicit statement of the text, "Seventy weeks are determined . . . ." The idea that Daniel's prophecies pertain only to Jews and not to the church and that therefore the church age is a parenthesis in the prophecies of the book is a dispensationalist conjecture wholly arbitrary from the standpoint of prophecy and contrary to the true unity of the old and new covenants, as illustrated by Paul's teaching that the Gentiles are grafted into the olive tree, Israel, so that they become a true and living part of the tree (Rom 11:17-24). One need not, however, go to the other extreme of spiritualizing those Old Testament prophecies which explicitly predict the return of the dispersed Jews to the land, the restoration of the nation, and the Messianic renewal of that nation within the land. When New Testament authors quoted these prophecies indicating elements of spiritual fulfillment in the first advent of Christ or in the birth of the New Testament Church, they made no pretense of treating them exhaustively nor of implying that nothing more remained to be fulfilled.

Dan 9:25-27 answer three questions: First, when will the Messiah come? (25a) Second, when will Jerusalem be rebuilt? (25b) Third, what will happen after the Messiah comes, after the sixty-ninth week? (26, 27)

First, when will the Messiah of Dan 9:25a come? We are told that the Messiah will come at the end of the sixty-ninth week. This corresponds to Jesus' baptism and the beginning of his ministry, probably A.D. 26. The chronological period is equal to sixty-nine "weeks" (7 + 62) or 483 "days," when each "day" means one year. In other words, "day" and "week" are used as apocalyptic symbols for "year" and "seven years," respectively. The 483 years are counted from the decree of Artaxerxes in 458 B.C., the time of Ezra's mission to Jerusalem.[39] (When

---

[39] The decree of Artaxerxes pertaining to Ezra's mission is the best option for the beginning of the seventy weeks for several reasons: 1. It results in an appropriately accurate fulfillment of the prophecy. With Nehemiah's date, 445 B.C., the span must be calculated in "lunar years," a less suitable solution. 2. There is no *decree* (Aram. שִׂים טְעֵם, *sîm t$^{e\bar{e}s}$*) of Artaxerxes for Nehemiah's mission. The decree of Cyrus is unsatisfactory from the standpoint of fulfillment. Moreover, Cyrus' decree provided for the return and rebuilding of the temple, but makes no provision for the city or its walls (Ezra 1:2-4, 6:3-12). We are left with the decree which established the mission of Ezra (see Ezra 7:13, 21).

One may object that there is no mention in the decree of rebuilding the walls of the city. However, several facts apply: *First*, the decree makes ample allowance for this work: "Do whatever seems best . . . in accordance with the will of your God" (Ezr 7:18, see also 20, 23). The amount of money given to Ezra, ostensibly to purchase animals for sacrifice, teach the law, and conduct certain reforms, was by modern reckoning well in excess of $50,000,000, with more if needed. *Second*, Artaxerxes was motivated by the need to avert "wrath against the realm of the king" (23). The context suggests that this is the wrath of Ezra's God, "the God of heaven." It is highly probable, however, that Artaxerxes was motived also by the need to maintain a strong military presence in Judea. The province, Beyond-the-river, of which Judea was a part, was the key linking Persia with Egypt. Egypt had rebelled and withdrawn from Persian rule the previous year, 459 B.C. Judea's neighbors, who had opposed the building of the temple and who later gave Nehemiah much trouble, were pro-Egyptian. Later, the Persian satrap of Beyond-the-river, Megabyzus, was himself unstable, unsuccessfully rebelling against the Persian throne, while the Jews remained loyal. Artaxerxes probably saw the Jews and Jerusalem as a stronghold having potential for stabilizing the province in preparation for the recovery of Eygpt. Egypt was in fact again subdued in 454 B.C. *Third*, there is evidence that the construction of the walls did begin before Nehemiah. Ezra 4:6 implies that for a brief time the walls were under construction at the beginning of Xerxes reign (485 B.C.) and again in the reign of Artaxerxes (4:7-23), on which occasions construction prematurely ceased. If the second occasion was prior to Ezra's mission, Artaxerxes may have been persuaded by Ezra to reverse his decision to halt the work on the ground that the complaint of Jerusalem's neighbors was badly motivated and not in the king's best interest.

adding years B.C. to years A.D. one must add 1 year, as 2 years are numbered 1 [B.C. 1 & A.D. 1]: 486+26+1=483.)

The reference to the Messiah as "Prince," one who leads or rules by virtue of his preeminent authority (Heb., נָגִיד, *nagid*) is found also in Acts 5:31 and Heb 12:2 (Gk. ἀρχηγός, *archēgos*). "In the NT this term is reserved for Christ" (*IDB*, 3:891).

Second, when will the rebuilding of Jerusalem described in Dan 9:25b occur? The seven weeks of building Jerusalem (25b) correspond to the rebuilding which was to occur under the leadership of Ezra and Nehemiah, 458-409 B.C. In the light of this prophecy, 409 is a probable date for the end of Nehemiah's second mission (Neh 13:6, 7). It is possible, however, that the rebuilding ended at that time for some other reason.

Third, what will happen after the Messiah comes, after the sixty-ninth week of 9:26, 27? "After the sixty-two weeks," two events are predicted, the cutting off of the Messiah (26a), which we infer from verse 27 was to occur in the seventieth week, and the destruction of Jerusalem and the temple (26b).

Why does the prophecy not next address the seventieth week, rather than the less definite "after . . . "? Why does the prophecy not address the two events discreetly in chronological order instead of with the repetitious pattern of verses 26 and 27? Perhaps because it designs in verse 26 to show the intimate connection between the "cutting off" of the Messiah and the further desolations which are to fall upon Jerusalem.

The rejection by the covenant nation of her Messiah and the desolations upon Jerusalem and the nation which were to result are at the very heart of the prophecy. They answer to Daniel's remorse over the Holy City's desolate state. This association is introduced in verse 26 and then both subjects are further addressed in verse 27.

Moreover, it would then also have been in the king's interest not to publicize his reversal by making explicit reference to the walls in the decree. If this was in fact the case, we must also assume from Nehemiah's report (Neh 2:17) that Ezra's rebuilding was halted, probably due to some military activity in the province at that time (see Neh 1:3). The revolt of Megabyzus occurred between the missions of Ezra and Nehemiah (448 B.C.; see Herodotus 7.89, 8.67; J. Bright, *A History of Israel* (Philadelphia: Westminster, 1952), 376-378; Y. Aharoni, *The Land of the Bible* (Philadelphia: Westminster, 1979), 412-413.

(3) The Identity of the "Coming Anointed Ruler" of Dan 9:26b-27

At this point, it is necessary to explain in a clear and careful way one of the controversial aspects of this prophecy—the several references to "the Anointed Ruler," and especially to identify "the Coming Ruler" of verse 26b. I will set out the appropriate scriptural statements for comparison:

9:25: "From the issuing of a decree . . . to **[the] Anointed Prince** [Heb: מָשִׁיחַ נָגִיד, *māshîaḥ nāgîd*] there will be seven 'sevens' and sixty-two 'sevens.'"

9:26a: "After the sixty-two 'sevens,' **[the] Anointed One** [Heb: מָשִׁיחַ, *māshîaḥ*] will be cut off . . . "

9:26b: "The people of **the Coming Ruler** [Heb: נָגִיד הַבָּא, *nāgîd habbā*] will destroy the city and the sanctuary."

9:27: "He will confirm a covenant with the many for one 'seven' . . ."

There are several "standard interpretations" of the emphasized words. Many of the futurist school have taken Dan 9:25 and 26a to refer to the Messiah while interpreting 9:26b and 27 as referring to the Antichrist. Some in the historical school take 9:25 and 26a as referring to the Messiah and 26b as referring to the Roman general, Titus, who in A.D. 70 conducted the siege against Jerusalem. They then take 9:27 as again referring to the Messiah in spite of the fact that the immediate antecedent of the pronoun "He" is "the Coming Ruler" of 26b (in their view, the Roman general, Titus).

In my translation I have capitalized the several references to "the Anointed Ruler" because the plain sense of the language requires that they all refer to the same person—the coming Messiah. His anointing is promised in 9:24 as one of the accomplishments of the seventy 'sevens.'[40] This interpretation results from a straightforward and natural reading of the text.

9:24 promises to bring about during the seventy 'sevens' period the Messianic work of redemption. Implied here is what we now know as the

---

[40]"To anoint the Most Holy [One] (Heb: לִמְשֹׁחַ קֹדֶשׁ קָדָשִׁים, *limshuaḥ kōdesh kodāshîm*)" refers to the coming Messiah. E. B. Pusey states: "The remaining clause, *and to anoint an All-holy*, must be spiritual, since all else [in v. 24] is spiritual. It cannot be spoken of the natural 'holy of holies,' which, in contrast to *the holy place*, is always '*the* holy of holies' never 'holy of holies'" (*Daniel*, 181; see also Boutflower, *Daniel*, 183-184. The allusion is best understood not in terms of the physical act but of the Holy Spirit's anointing.

first advent of the Messiah, Jesus Christ. His anointing is stated as the official and public confirmation of his ministry. Verse 25 predicts the time when this Coming Ruler will appear, at the end of the sixty-two 'sevens' period. Verse 26a predicts the violent death of the Anointed One. Twenty-six b refers to the people of *the* Coming Ruler (note the italicized article). Should not the previous reference in 26a to the Messiah as a coming ruler clearly identify *this* ruler as the Messiah? That is the natural way to read the text. Moreover, the necessary reference to the Messiah in the pronoun, "He," which immediately follows in verse 27 should seal this understanding as altogether obvious and correct.

The problem with this interpretation for many has been a reluctance to deal with the implications of verse 26. How can it be said that it would be the people of the coming Messiah who would "destroy the city and the sanctuary"? Yet the responsibility of the Jewish nation for the Divine judgment which destroyed Jerusalem and the temple is affirmed both by the Jewish historian, Josephus, and by Jesus Christ, Himself (Matt 23:37, 38).

Moreover, this understanding of Providence agrees with one of the major themes of this chapter, as indicated by Daniel's prayer of confession of the sins of his people and the resulting wrath of God, "O Lord, . . . turn away your anger and your wrath from Jerusalem, your city, your holy hill" (9:16). Daniel sees this wrath as consequent upon the sins of his people (vv. 11-16).

I conclude that the Coming Ruler is, indeed, the Messiah, and that this is the only meaning which avoids doing violence to the text.[41]

---

[41]See Jos. *War* 6.3.3-9. The Roman general, Titus, is reported to have said at the end of the battle, "We have certainly had God for our assistant in this war, and it was no other than God who ejected the Jews out of their fortifications; for what could the hands of men, or any machines, do towards overthrowing these towers!" (Josephus*War* 6.9.1 [Whiston]). Wm. Whiston added this note in his translation of Josephus: "The Romans were not only willing, but very desirous, to grant those Jews in Jerusalem both their lives and their liberties, and to save both their city and their temple. But the zealots, the robbers, and the seditious would hearken to no terms of submission" (*JosephusWar* 6.3.3 n.). The defenders not only carried out much of the destruction of the city, but destroyed the temple with fire. It is clear from Josephus' report that he regarded the whole destruction as a fulfillment of prophecies found in the Hebrew Scriptures. So also did Jesus, as stated in Luke 21:20, 22, "When you see Jerusalem surrounded by armies, you will know that its desolation is near. For this is the time of punishment in fulfillment of all that has been written." The belief that the sins of the Jews were responsible for Jerusalem's destruction is also affirmed in the *Apocalypse of Baruch* (*2 Apoc. Bar.* 1.4, 5, 78.5; 79.2-4); James H. Charlesworth, *Old Testament Pseudepigrapha* (Garden City, N. Y.: Doubleday, 1983), 1.621, 648.

(4) The Seventieth 'Seven' of Dan 9:27

Here, the vision returns to the seventieth week to indicate two more facts: First, the Messiah will confirm a covenant with "the many" for one "week," and second, "in the middle of the week, he will put an end to sacrifice and offering." Clearly, both of these pertain to the atonement as accomplished by Jesus at Calvary.

(a) The Messiah will confirm a covenant with many for one 'seven.' 9:27a

Following the year-day chronology mentioned above, the seventieth week starts with the beginning of Jesus' ministry in A.D. 26 and ends seven years later with the killing of Stephen and the persecution that drove the witnessing community of Jewish believers out of Judea into territories with predominantly non-Jewish populations. "All except the apostles were scattered" (Acts 8:1). During the first half of the week, our Lord confirmed the covenant with the many through His earthly ministry. During the latter half, from Passover of A.D. 30 to A.D. 33, the witness of Jesus to the covenant nation of Israel was continued through the Holy Spirit-anointed believing community (Acts, chs. 1-7). During this time the ancient covenant of the Lord with Israel was confirmed with the righteous remnant, "the many," and rejected by most of the leaders of the nation.[42]

(b) In the midst of the 'seven,' the Messiah will put an end to sacrifice and offering. 9:27b

Our Lord's crucifixion occurred in the midst of the prophetic week, Passover of A.D. 30, fulfilling and rendering obsolete and ineffectual the Mosaic ceremonies.

---

[42]"The many" may be a term for the elect remnant (see Dan 12:2). It was used in that way by the sect of the Dead Sea Scrolls. See, e.g., a few of many instances, 1QS (the *Rule Comm.*) 6.8-13 (four occurrences).

(5) The Determined Desolations of Dan 9:26b, 27b

Israel's national rejection of her Messiah determined the course of prophetic events. The transgression of Israel is thus sealed for the calamitous judgments of God against the nation. The statement of Daniel 9:24, "To shut up the transgression, to seal the sins," echoes the words of Moses: "Is not this [rebellious conduct of Israel] **laid up in store** with me, **sealed up** in my treasuries? Vengeance is mine, and recompense . . . for the day of their calamity is at hand, and their doom comes swiftly" (Deut 32:34, 35, ESV).[43] Similarly, Daniel says of Jerusalem, "Its end will come with a flood" (9:26).

Jesus also interprets the "desolations" of Daniel's seventieth week in terms of Moses' prophecies. Israel will be dispersed and her inheritance land will be desolated during the latter days of Gentile times (see Lev 26:33-39; Deut 28:64-68; 30:22-29; 32:15-43). Jesus alludes to this time as the "days of vengeance" (Luke 21:22, ESV), an expression which reflects the ancient Septuagint (Greek) version of Deut 32:34, 35. It reads as follows:

> In the **day of vengeance**
> I shall make recompense,
> for the day of their destruction is near (trans. mine).[44]

Explaining Daniel from this perspective, Jesus warns the faithful,

> "Let those who are in Judea flee . . . for these are [the] **days of vengeance**, in order that all things which are written may be fulfilled" (Luke 21:21, 22, **NASB**; compare Lev 26:14-33)

(a) The Desolation of Jerusalem of 9:26b

Our prophecy states that "the people of the Prince who is coming will destroy the city and the sanctuary." Moses had graphically described the destruction of all the cities and especially the horrible conditions of siege (Lev 26:27-30; Deut 28:52-57).

---

[43]My translation of Dan 9:24 reflects the Hebrew text whereas the common translations follow the marginal readings. See note 11, above.

[44]In the expression, "day of vengeance," "day" means "time"; so "days of vengeance" is a correct explanatory translation of the singular form. For a fuller discussion of this text, see Oral Collins, "Two difficult readings in Daniel 9:24," *Henceforth* 1 (Fall, 1972).42-47 (also available at http://www.historicism.com).

Jesus understood both Daniel and Moses from this perspective. As he looked at the city, he said, "As for what you see here, the time will come when not one stone will be left on another; every one of them will be thrown down" (Luke 21:6). A little later, he warned the faithful (Luke 21:20-22),

> "When you see Jerusalem being surrounded by armies, you will know that her desolation is near. Then let those who are in Judea flee to the mountains, and let those who are in the city get out and let those in the country not enter the city."

Again, when Jesus pronounced woes upon Jerusalem (Matt 23:32, 35, 36, 38),

> "Fill up, then, the measure of the sin of your forefathers! . . . And so upon you will come all the righteous blood that has been shed on earth . . . I tell you the truth, all this will come upon this generation. . . . Look, your house is left to you desolate."

(b) Desolations after Jerusalem's Destruction, 9:26c

The desolations of Jerusalem were only the tragic beginning of the tribulation which was to come upon her people. As the vision says, "War will continue until the end, and desolations have been decreed" (26c). E. B. Pusey remarks on this text that this can hardly refer to the end of the Jewish-Roman war, as that war "was the beginning, not the end, of the desolations." He points out further that the Hebrew expressions קֵץ, *qêtz*, "end" and עַד קֵץ, *ad qêtz*, "unto the end," "are terms used by Daniel to point out the close of a period appointed by God" (Pusey, 186)." The determined desolations are those predicted by Moses and alluded to earlier by Daniel in his prayer (9:11-14). Following this line of reasoning then, the time of tribulation extends on into the period we have come to call the church age, extending to the time of the end.

(c) The One who Makes Desolate of 9:27b

We are told that there will come "on the wing of abominations shall come one who makes desolate" (ESV) The "wing of" (Hebrew, כְּנַף, *kĕnaph*) is in this context rather obscure.[45] Perhaps one may understand

---

[45]Commentators usually interpret כְּנַף literally, as does the latest ed. of the NIV, as referring to some extremity of the temple. As subsequent to the predicted destruction of the temple, fulfilled in A.D. 70, this hardly seems appropriate.

the term in this context metaphorically, as indicating a connected occurrence subsequent to the preceding. "Abominations" probably has reference to the sacrilegious practices of the pagan Roman power, especially within the precincts of the holy city, the sacred temple, and the covenant people.[46] From the standpoint of the biblical and historical background of the text, there should be little doubt but that "the one who makes desolate" is the Roman power of the fourth beast of Daniel seven, including the Little Horn of that beast which was later to wage war with the saints. "The decreed end" of that power is predicted in Daniel 7:26, "His power will be taken away and completely destroyed forever."

In concluding our consideration of the Seventy Weeks prophecy, let us return to Jesus' commentary on Daniel in Luke 21. Immediately after his statement regarding the Roman destruction of Jerusalem quoted above, he says, "They will fall by the sword and will be taken as prisoners to all the nations. Jerusalem will be trampled on by the Gentiles until the times of the Gentiles are fulfilled" (Luke 21:24). Contemporary expositors usually interpret these times as either (1) the times of the Gospel witness to Gentiles through the church (with appeal to Rom 11:25), or (2) the times following the Roman destruction of Jerusalem in which Jerusalem is under Gentile control. Of these two, surely the latter is more suitable to the context of Daniel. However, as we have noted, Jesus is expounding Daniel's prophecies. It is more likely, then, that he referred to those times when Jerusalem and the Covenant people are under the sovereignty of Gentile (heathen) powers, as forecast by the visions of the Image, the Four Beasts, and the Seventy Weeks.[47]

---

[46] See William E. Cox, *Biblical Studies in Final Things* (Philadelphia: Presbyterian & Reformed, 1967), 25-29, for his excellent study on "the abomination of desolation."

[47] Scholars who see this as the time of Jerusalem's subjugation to heathen power, such as Wm. Manson *Gospel of Luke* (London: Hodder & Stoughton, 1930), 234; I. Howard Marshall, *Gospel of Luke* (Grand Rapids: Eerdmans, 1978), 773-774; E. Earle Ellis, *The Gospel of Luke* (London: T. Nelson, 1966; repr., Eugene, Oreg.: Wipf & Stock, 2003), 245; et al., are surely more on track than those who find in it the time of Gentile opportunity for the Gospel (F. Godet, *A Commentary on the Gospel of St. Luke* (New York: Funk & Wagnalls, 1887), 450; F. W. Farrar, *The Gospel According to St. Luke,* (Cambridge: University Press, 1916), 318; J. Barton Payne, *Encyclopedia of Biblical Propecy* (New York: Harper & Row, 1973), 100, 514-515; et al.), the latter quite out of the context of Daniel 9. Current scholars tend not to give sufficient attention to the developing structure of prophetic prediction in the Bible, in which the covenant preachments of Moses are foundational. Marshall rightly calls attention to evidence that the parameters of Jerusalem's future judgment were "a set theme in prophecy." There is indication of "a fixed period of rule" and a set limit (773). Daniel's visions must be

Accordingly, they began with Nebuchadnezzar's subjugation of Jerusalem in 605 B.C. and extend through the end of the rule of the fourth beast of Daniel seven. This interpretation provides a natural harmony with our understanding that the great tribulation period extends into the period we have come to call the church age.

We are now better prepared to see how Christians facing persecution at the end of the first century and hearing the book of Revelation read would bring its text to bear on their understanding. They knew that ongoing desolations were predicted for the Covenant people at the hand of the fourth beast power and they knew that power to be Rome. How would the church, believing Israel, fare with its great influx of Gentiles, vis-a-vis the war to be conducted against the saints of the Most High by the blasphemous Little Horn power? What must be suffered by the people of God before the Lord Jesus Christ would return to establish his everlasting kingdom? The Lord Jesus, himself, gave the answer in his final prophecy recorded by John on Patmos.

We are now ready to look at the Revelation, itself, to see how its message is organized and developed.

Structure and Theme

Ancient books seldom display their outlines to their readers. One of the first tasks in any effort to understand their meaning is to discover and outline in so far as possible the thought patterns and literary structure of the work. My students who over the years have been asked to read and identify evidences of structure within the book of Revelation have been quick to point out the seven churches, the seven seals, the seven trumpets, and the seven bowls. Beyond the obvious, the task is both intriguing and complicated. We will proceed to identify and discuss certain structural elements within the book and then present a literary outline.

---

understood in the light of Moses' promise of covenant blessings and curses and their further elaboration by subsequent prophets. The language and themes are often stereotyped and indicate a common understanding of the force of prediction. Given our Lord's agreement with Daniel's vision of four heathen nations which would each exercise a time of subjugation of the covenant people (Daniel 7), what could "the appointed times [Gk. καιροί, *kairoi*] of the Gentiles" mean but those predicted times? See H. G. Guinness, *Light for the Last Days* (London: Hodder & Stoughton, 1888), 20-22.

1. Introduction and Conclusion (chs. 1; 22:6-21)

The introduction to the entire book is chapter one. Here we find some of the usual conventions, such as author and title, formal greetings, and the circumstance which gave rise to the book. The conclusion of the book is found in 22:6-21.

2. The Vision as a Whole (chs. 2:1-22:5)

The latter part of the introduction includes the beginning of John's vision (1:10-20) and perhaps should be included here. However, the GO message of the book begins with chapter two, so we address the matter of structure at this point.

From the standpoint of the author's experience, the book of Revelation is not a series of independent visions, but it is one connected whole. The reader should expect that the predictive revelations will unfold as one drama, rather than as several visions which might be interpreted independently of one another. The reader should expect that the Revelation will provide whatever information is needed to determine the structure and the chronological relationships that may be implied in the several scenes of the drama. (For the implications of this relative to elaborate parallel or synchronous approaches, see Append. 2.)

The one vision is clearly divided into two parts, [1] "what is now and [2] what will take place later" (1:19). It should be apparent to the undesigning reader that "what is now" is the letters to the existing seven churches of Asia (chs. 2 and 3), and "what will take place later" begins with 4:1 and comprises the rest of the prophecy through 22:5. This is indicated where the Lord said to John, "Come up here, and I will show you what must take place *after this*" (4:1, emphasis mine). We will observe this designated pattern carefully in our exposition which follows.

One need not assume that the vision is interrupted by the letters, for the apocalyptic figure of the Lord is their author and this is explicit in their content. The words, "At once I was in the Spirit" (4:2) are not intended to indicate that the vision had ceased while John was recording the letters and at this point again resumes, but that the heightened state required for the author's extraordinary involvement in the progress of the revelation resumes.[48]

a. The Letters to the Seven Churches (chs. 2 and 3)

We will address some of the unique literary features of the letters in our commentary on the text. Here, we will deal only with those aspects which determine our general approach to their understanding and how they relate to the rest of the vision.

It is important to know that the churches addressed were real churches which existed in the Roman province of Asia, the larger parish where the Apostle John ministered in his later years. Many expositors have pointed out that the churches are addressed in the order they would have been encountered by the person traveling on the Roman road to deliver the letters. The letters resemble other New Testament epistles and, except for the descriptive allusions to the Divine Messenger of chapter one, do not contain anything that should be interpreted in a mystical or symbolic fashion.

Many expositors, both of the futurist and historical schools, have wanted to view the letters as prophecies of seven church ages. However fanciful, this has the advantage of providing one of seven perceived parallel prophecies which some look for in the book. However, there is nothing in the letters to inform the reader that they are prophecies, while it is clear, on the other hand, that they are addressed to real churches about problems which existed in their parishes.

To take them as prophecies one must assume that each letter has two divergent meanings, the plain sense and also a mystical sense pertaining to the future. Most expositors recognize that such allegorizing does not fall within the boundaries of legitimate interpretation.[49] Because we

---

[48] Although we have included the letters as within the body of the prophecy rather than in the introduction, it is possible to treat them as part of the introduction, especially in view of 1:1, "I will show you what must soon take place." This seems to indicate that the main message of the book is the prediction which begins in 4:1.

[49] The idea that the letters to the seven churches are prophecies of seven periods of church history is akin to medieval allegorizing. There is nothing in the text to sustain it. The following observations are appropriate: 1. The letters precede the "things which are shortly to occur," i. e., the prophecies of the book (4:1); they are not written in the symbolic style of the apocalyptic prediction which constitutes the bulk of the book; they are interpreted in the book as messages to seven literal churches known to have existed in the first century. Almost all scholars of the three major schools of more recent times have either implicitly or explicitly rejected the prophetic view of the letters including

reject allegorizing, we assume that the letters are to be understood only according to the plain sense and nothing more.

All the letters will, nevertheless, convey relevant messages to the churches of any age. They should be expounded as we do other New Testament epistles, recognizing both their original historical orientation and those principles relevant for general application.

b. Action and interlude

We mentioned earlier that the Revelation has some of the characteristics of a dramatic theater production. It is as if there are two focal points for the viewer. One of these is on the main stage where the action unfolds. Here, in dramatic symbol the predicted events of the prophecy are presented in sequential and chronological order. The other focal point is the upper stage where in the Greek theater the choir may have been sometimes stationed. Here, as it were, the Revelation introduces scenes of heaven where the Almighty sits enthroned, or elements of the heavenly tabernacle are revealed, or the heavenly choirs chant or sing hymns of praise and thanksgiving. As in the theater, the heavenly scenes serve to orient the observer so that he understands better some aspect of the action on the main stage.

In some instances the interludes are digressions which provide more detailed information regarding a subject already treated in the preceding prophecy. Such is the case with the description of the harlot and the beast in chapter 17, adding new dimensions to chapter 13:1-10, and also the fall of Babylon of chapter 18, expanding on the prophecy of the seventh bowl in 16:17-21.

The discerning reader can identify the interludes in distinction from the action. They are:

---

the following: Elliott, *1.75-82*; Simpson (see below), Barnes, 59-60; Cachemaille, 145-146; Eerdman, *Revelation of St. John* (Philadelphia: Westminster, 1966), 42; Hoeksema, *Behold, He Cometh* (Grand Rapids: Kregel, 1969), 48; Hendriksen, *More Than Conquerors* (6th ed.; Grand Rapids: Baker, 1952), 22; Tenney, *Interpreting Revelation* (2nd ed.; TNTC; Grand Rapids: Eerdmans, 1987), 50-55; Morris, *Revelation* (Revised ed.; TNTC; Grand Rapids: Eerdmans, 1987), 57-58; Ladd, *Commentary on the Revelation of John* (Grand Rapids: Eerdmans, 1972), 12; Newport, *The Lion and the Lamb* (Nashville: Broadman, 1986), 141-142; Mounce, *The Book of Revelation* (Revised ed.; Grand Rapids: Eerdmans, 1998), 64-65; Beale (1999), 48. Many more could be added. Without malice may I quote David Simpson, "Such conduct is making the Scripture a mere nose of wax, and doing infinite prejudice to the cause of genuine truth," *Key to the Prophecies* (London: Booksellers, 1847), 309.

1. The Almighty, the seven-sealed scroll, and the Lamb. Chs. 4, 5
2. The pretribulation sealing of the 144,000. 7:1-8
3. The posttribulation celebration of the white-robed multitude. 7:9-17
4. The seven angels with seven trumpets and the incense angel. 8:2-5
5. The angel and the little book. 10:1-11
6. The temple, the two witnesses, and the war with the beast. 11:1-13
7. A proleptic celebration in heaven. 11:15b-18
8. The heavenly sanctuary opened. 11:19
9. The Lamb and the 144,000 redeemed singers. 14:1-5
10. Harpers sing the song of Moses and the Lamb. 15:2-4
11. The presentation of the angels of the seven last plagues. 15:5-16:1
12. Excursus on the harlot Babylon and the beast. ch. 17
13. Excursus on the fall of Babylon. ch. 18
14. The victory songs of the heavenly multitude. 19:1-10

One must not assume that the interludes continue the chronological sequence of the drama that precedes them. Most are proleptic, that is they look ahead to the consummation when the saints are caught up to be with the Lord and rejoice in the experience of the final victory. It is important also to realize that these scenes, like the other apocalyptic descriptions, are emblematic and should not be pressed into too literal actualization.

c. The Seven-sealed scroll (5:1-22:5)

We encounter the next major structural element in the Revelation in the seven-sealed scroll. This scroll, containing the entire predictive part of the book, is appropriately introduced in the opening scene of the second part, "the things which must occur after this" (4:1, trans. mine).

Normally scrolls were sealed one or more times on the outside, but in some cases where multiple copies of a legal document were made, there was an additional sealed inside copy which was protected from the wear and tear of repeated reading. In the case of the scroll of Rev 4:5, apparently there were seven seals in the first section of the scroll which had to be opened before the rest of the book, the major part, could be read. As each seal is broken, another part of the introductory action is disclosed.

One should expect from the prominent place of the three series of major symbols—seals, trumpets, and bowls—that these function to indicate the flow and relationship of the major prophetic events. Each series must have its own conceptual unity so as to account for the particular symbols and their differentiation. One can notice certain patterns of style which persist, most evidently within the first two series, especially a 4-2-1 pattern, in which the first four events predicted in the series are introduced very briefly, the next two with greater fullness, and the last given only to introduce the next series of seven. The three series—the seals, the trumpets, and the bowls—determine the main sequence of events and o their chronological order within the book.

At the end of the first two series, the seventh seal and the seventh trumpet, there is no substantive prediction, but each serves to introduce the next series of prophecies. The opening of the seventh seal introduces the seven trumpets, the blowing of the seventh trumpet introduces the pouring out of the seven bowls. The pouring out of the seventh bowl, the fall of Babylon, however, is the climatic judgment which leads to the culminating events which occupy concluding chapters of the vision.

This manner of understanding the structural relation of the seal, trumpet, and bowl prophecies is called "continuous-historicist" interpretation. An alternate approach, not unique to the historicist school, is called parallel or synchronous interpretation (see Append. 3). Such innovation has contributed to widely disparate interpretations.

d. The Little Scroll (Chs. 10-14)

Another symbolic device which determines the way in which the book should be understood is the Little Scroll. In chapter 10, after the blowing of the sixth trumpet, an angel appears holding a little scroll. The presentation of this scroll suggests that the prophecies that immediately follow should be understood as the message of the scroll.

The passage is analogous to Ezek 2:9-3:9, where the LORD handed a scroll to Ezekiel and told him that "on both sides of it were written words of lament and mourning and woe." As many commentators have indicated, the scroll contained the Word of God which Ezekiel was to preach, but not just any Word of God. The description clearly indicates that it contained the specific message assigned to Ezekiel, a message of judgment against the covenant nation. The specific form in which we know this message is given to Ezekiel as well as to the modern reader in the chapters which follow, Ezekiel 4-25.

So in the Revelation, the presentation of the Little Scroll by a messenger of the Lord presupposes, not the Word of God in general, but a specific message, the content of which is found in the context of the chapters which follow Revelation 10, chapters 11-14.

Why is this scroll described as "little"? The probable answer suggests itself from a comparison with the seven-sealed scroll. We should therefore expect that its message will be found, not in all the remaining chapters of the book as some have suggested, but in a shorter passage.

The place that suggests itself for the end of the Little Scroll message is the end of chapter 14, where the vintage harvest is described, a scene which scholars generally agree pertains to the final judgment. With this, the prophecy resumes what was interrupted at the end of chapter nine by introducing the third in the series of seal, trumpet, and bowl judgments with scenes introductory to the pouring out of the seven bowls.

How does the Little Scroll message relate to the message of the larger scroll? If, as we have concluded, the larger scroll embraces the "things to occur" in the times future to John (4:1), then it follows that the little scroll message must be a part of that scroll. This also is implied by the way it is introduced as an element within the dramatic scene portrayed in chapter 10. The implied disjuncture of the Little Scroll from the larger scroll message is due to the fact that it breaks with the chronological sequence of the seals, trumpets, and bowls.[50]

Chapter 11 is an introduction which serves to introduce the Little Scroll message of chapters 12-14. The first part of the introduction consists of an explanation given by the angelic messenger addressing key elements relating to the scroll message (1-13). The second part, a brief statement that "the second woe is past" (v. 14), provides a chronological indicator for the end of the sixth trumpet prophecy of 9:13-21. The third part is a proleptic scene celebrating the victory over Antichrist yet future

---

[50]I reject E. B. Elliott's suggestion that chs. 12-14 constitute the message written on the back of the scroll (Rev 5:1). Though plausible, it is unsupported by any indication in the text (1.105, 118 [chart]). Writing on the back of a scroll is usually understood to mean that the message is unusually long or consequential (cf. Ezek 2:9; Zech 5:1-4). The assignment of a portion of the text following chapter ten to the Little Scroll is supported by Charles, 1.258, 260; Donald W. Richardson, *The Revelation of Jesus Christ* (Altheia ed.; Richmond: J. Knox, 1964), 74; F. F. Bruce, "The Revelation of St. John," in *A New Testament Commentary* (London: Pickering & Inglis, 1969), 649 (cited in Mounce, 209); and others. Beckwith's contention that Ezekiel's scroll is not intended to symbolize the message which is given to Ezekiel to deliver to Israel and is therefore not recorded in writing in the chapters which follow is arbitrary and an unnatural way to understand the text (578-588). The opposite conclusion is to be preferred, as supported by the above-named scholars. See further remarks in the commentary to follow. The particular portion to be assigned to the Little Scroll must be decided by the internal evidence of the text, which in an apocalyptic book need not be explicitly stated.

(11:15-18). A fourth part (11:19) reveals briefly the Divine perspective on the Little Scroll message.

The prophecies of the Little Scroll message in chapters 12-13 are central to the message of the whole book, as they enlarge upon 11:7, the rise of the Antichrist power and his war against the people of God. Chapter 14 provides a suitable conclusion to that message and extends the chronology of the Little Scroll to the end of the age.

The Little Scroll message gives perspective to the concluding part of the book, which in the pouring out of the bowls and the explanatory passages that follow forecasts divine judgments against Antichrist and then introduces the events of the Day of the Lord.

e. The three woes. 8:14

Another structural element that is woven into the Revelation is the Three Woes introduced in Rev 8:14 and mentioned ominously in 9:12 and 11:14 as each of the first two woes passes. The third woe is of course the seventh trumpet. The passing of the third woe remains unmentioned as it consists of the final judgments against Antichrist, the pouring out of the seven bowls, culminating in the fall of Babylon (16:17-18:24). At this point, suspense is ended, and the saints make ready for the marriage supper of the Lamb (19:1-10).

The eagle cry of the Three Woes and their sequential enumeration heighten the emphasis of the Revelation on the victory of Christ over Antichrist and on the righteous judgments of a sovereign God.

We have examined several significant structural elements within the book of Revelation. These illustrate what is almost universally agreed upon by current scholars—that the Revelation is a unified literary work of complex and wonderful design. Many lesser illustrations of this remain to be considered within our exposition and commentary which follows.

Like the Little Scroll, its message is both sweet and bitter. The glorified Christ and the blessings of his future reign is the believer's encouragement and hope, even amid suffering in this evil world. The certainty of the sinner's judgment, both in this life and in the life to come brings anguish even to the people of God and urgency to the task of both bearing and receiving the good news.

Literary Outline[51]

The Final Testimony of Jesus

Introduction. Chapter One

    A. Apocalyptic prologue. 1-3
    B. Epistolary prologue. 4-8
    C. Apocalyptic introduction. 9-20

PART ONE. "WHAT IS NOW": CHRIST'S MESSAGE TO THE CHURCHES. 2:1-3:22

    I. To the Church at Ephesus. 2:1-7
    II. To the Church at Smyrna. 2:8-11
    III. To the Church at Pergamum. 2:12-17
    IV. To the Church at Thyatira. 2:18-29
    V. To the Church at Sardis. 3:1-6
    VI. To the Church at Philadelphia. 3:7-13
    VII. To the Church at Laodocea. 3:14-22

PART TWO. "WHAT WILL SOON BEGIN TO TAKE PLACE": THE FUTURE VICTORY OF CHRIST AND HIS CHURCH OVER ANTICHRIST AND THE WORLD. 4:1-22:5

    I. Interlude: a Dramatic Scene in Heaven. chs. 4, 5

        A. The Revelation of God. 4:1-6a
        B. The Worship of God. 4:6b-11
        B. The Lamb and the Seven-sealed Scroll. ch. 5:1-14

            1. Christ has Triumphed. 1-5
            2. The Worship of the Lamb. 6-10
            3. The Great Anthem of Praise. 11-14

    II. The Opening of the Seven-sealed Scroll. 6:1-8:5

        A. The First Four Seals Opened—the Four Horsemen. 6:2-8

---

[51]For an outline of the commentary, see the Contents section above, pp. i-v.

B. The Fifth Seal Opened—the Souls of the Martyrs. 6:9-11
   C. The Sixth Seal Opened—the Great Earthquake. 6:12-17
   D. Interlude: the Sealing of the True Israel. 7:1-8
   E. Interlude: the Great Multitude in White. 7:9-17
   F. The Seventh Seal Opened—Silence in Heaven. 8:1

III. The Sounding of the Seven Trumpets. 8:1-11:19

   A. Interlude: the Incense Altar and the Prayers of the Saints. 8:1-5
   B. The sounding of the first four trumpets—portents in sky and land. 8:7-12
   C. The sounding of the fifth trumpet (the first woe)—the locust plague. 9:1-12
   D. The sounding of the sixth trumpet—(the second woe) the hordes of horsemen. 9:13-21
   E. Interlude. chs. 10, 11

      1. The mighty angel and the little book. ch. 10
      2. The temple, the two witnesses, and the war with the beast. 11:1-13

   F. Interlude (indicating chronologically the passing of the second woe and the sounding of the seventh trumpet. 11:15b-19

      1. The passing of the second woe (the plague of the sixth trumpet). 11:14
      2. The sounding of the seventh trumpet (the third woe). 11:15a
      3. Proleptic celebration in heaven. 11:15b-18
      4. The heavenly sanctuary opened with portents in sky and land. 11:19

IV. The Message of the Little Scroll. 12:1-14:20

   A. The war in heaven—the woman, the man-child, and the dragon. 12:1-17
   B. The beast from the sea. 13:1-10
   C. The beast from the earth (the false prophet). 13:11-18
   D. Interlude. The heavenly chorus of the redeemed 144,000 14:1-5
   E. The three flying messenger angels. 14:6-13
   F. The Son of Man and the wheat harvest. 14:14-16
   G. The vintage harvest. 14:17-20

V. The Pouring Out of the Seven Bowls of Wrath. 15:1-16:21

   A. The sign of the seven angels with the seven last plagues. 15:1
   B. Interlude. Proleptic view of heaven: the chorus of the redeemed, the song of Moses and the Lamb. 15:2-4
   C. Interlude. The presentation of the seven bowls of wrath 15:5-16:1
   D. The pouring out of the first four bowls—portents on sea and land. 16:2-9
   E. The pouring out of the fifth bowl—the throne of the beast 16:10-11
   F. The pouring out of the sixth bowl—the drying up of the Euphrates. 16:12-16
   G. The pouring out of the seventh bowl—the fall of Antichrist. 16:17-20
   H. Excurses. chs. 17, 18

      1. The harlot Babylon and the beast. ch. 17
      2. Lament over the fall of Babylon. ch. 18

VI. The Day of the Lord. 19:1-20:15

   A. Interlude. Proleptic view of the heavenly chorus. 19:1-10
   B. The Rider on the white horse and the call to judgment. 19:11-18
   C. The destruction of the beast and the false prophet. 19:19-21
   D. The binding of the dragon, the first resurrection, and the millennial reign. 20:1-6
   E. The release and destruction of the dragon in the battle of Gog and Magog. 20:7-10
   F. The second resurrection and the great white throne judgment. 20:11-15

VII. The New Heavens, the New Earth, and the Holy City. 21:1-22:5

Conclusion. Final blessing, warning, and a great invitation. 22:6-21

Chapter Two

CHRIST SPEAKS TO THE CHURCH

Rev 1:1-3:22

Introduction

The introduction to the book consists of three parts: (1) the Apocalyptic Prologue (1:1-3), (2) the Epistolary Prologue (1:4-8), and (3) the Apocalyptic Introduction (1:9-20). The book of Revelation is at once an apocalypse and an epistle. The apocalyptic style and structure predominate (see pp. 10-13), but the epistolary feature introduced here insured that the letters to the churches (chs. 2 and 3) were delivered to their particular historical destinations, while at the same time in principle they served all the churches.

Prologue

1:1. **The revelation of Jesus Christ, which God gave him to show his servants what must soon take place. He made it known by sending his angel to show his servant John,[2] who testifies to everything he saw—that is, the word of God and the testimony of Jesus Christ. ³Blessed is the one who reads the words of this prophecy, and blessed are those who hear it and take to heart what is written in it, because the time is near.**

| 1:1-3 | The Apocalyptic Prologue | Exposition |

This concise statement identifies the title, the divine author, the principal purpose, the human author, and a special blessing for reading and for responding to the message of the book.

How blessed we are to have before us the Word of God, "the testimony of Jesus" regarding the future of His church, the revelation of "what must soon take place." Toward the end of the first century, at a time when Christians endangered their lives if they witnessed to the Gospel, Jesus presented Himself to the church as the one who had been the faithful witness, the one who loves us and who had freed us from our sins by His death on the cross.

Having received God's grace, we also may know His peace, that enjoyment of wholeness and well-being that comes from a right relationship with the triune and sovereign God—with the eternal Father, with Jesus Christ, His Son, and with His Holy Spirit.

This revelation reminds us that we are not to cling to this world, but to be bold in our witness. As firstborn from death, Christ will overrule the kings of this world and bring us into His everlasting kingdom. He "has made us to be a kingdom and priests to serve His God and Father" (v. 6). As sons of God, we are people of destiny, destined to live forever for the glory of God.

| 1:1-3 | The Apocalyptic Prologue | Notes |

1. This book containing **the revelation** is sometimes called by its Greek title, Apocalypse (Απ οκάλυψις, *Apocálupsis*). As in this case, ancient books were often titled from the first word or phrase at the beginning of the work. Scholars commonly note that "The Revelation" probably was not written as a title statement, as the article "the" does not appear in the

Greek text.[1] The word has its ordinary generic meaning, "a disclosure." This meaning is qualified by the name of the person responsible, "a revelation **of Jesus Christ**." The divine author presented himself to John with great authority in the vision which follows (12-16). The One who appears in the first statement is the central figure in the Revelation and He will dominate the book. The phrase "revelation of Jesus Christ," does not mean "revelation *about* Christ" (objective genitive), but "revelation *by* Christ" (subjective genitive). It is comparable to "the testimony [τὴν μαρτυρίον, *tēn marturíon*] of Jesus Christ" (vv. 3, 9), a phrase which is further explained in 22:16, 20: "I, Jesus, have sent my angel to give you this testimony for the churches . . . He who testifies to these things says, 'Yes, I am coming soon.'" Similarly, in 1:5, Jesus is **the faithful witness** [ὁ μάρτυς,, *ho mártus*]. He is the author of the Revelation, which is itself the testimony. **His [Christ's] servants** is an appropriate designation for the people of God (Rom 12:1, 2). **What must soon take place** is a translation of the Greek, ἃ δεῖ γενέσθι ἐν τάχει, *hà dêi genésthai 'en táchei*, "what must begin to occur soon" (ingressive aorist of γενέσθαι, *genésthai*; cp. 1:9).[2] **His servant John** probably refers to the apostle (see pp. 2-6). **2. The word of God and the testimony of Jesus Christ** (cf. v. 9) is to be received both as Scripture and as the authoritative testimony of the Messiah. The Apostle believed that Providence had arranged his exile to facilitate the revelation (see v. 9). **3.** Revelation is the only book in the Bible which contains the promise of special blessing to the reader and to the hearer. In the context of the first century, **he who reads** refers to the public reader who reads aloud for the benefit of others. The Greek translated **take to heart** literally reads, "who hear and who keep." This reminds us that the Revelation is not intended to satisfy curiosity about the future, but to give information for practical application to daily life.

---

[1] But see A. T. Robertson, *A Manual Grammar of the Greek New Testament* regarding titles of books in Koiné Greek: "These may be without the article, being already specific enough . . . ' Ἀποκάλυπσις τοῦ 'Ιησοῦ Χριστοῦ (Rev. 1:1)." (Nashville: Broadman Press, 1934) 793e.

[2] The implications of the clause ἃ δεῖ γενέσθαι ἐν τάχει are much discussed. The ingressive aorist commends itself in view of the prima-facie evidence of the book that the elaborate symbolic forecast could hardly suggest to the turn of the first century reader an immediate consummation. Moreover, several allusions to the Daniel prophecies (2:28-29, 45) in v. 1 also argue for this; see G. K. Beale, *The Book of Revelation* (Grand Rapids: Eerdmans, 1999): "The focus of 'quickness' and 'nearness' (τάχει) in vv. 1-3 is primarily on inauguration of prophetic fulfillment and not on nearness of consummated fulfillment . . . ." (182). Cf. further, Beale, 153.

The time is near because the Lord's return is imminent. Whether by the return of our Lord or by death, in our next conscious moment we may be in his presence.

Greetings and Doxology

1:4. **John,**

To the seven churches in the province of Asia:

Grace and peace to you from him who is, and who was, and who is to come, and from the seven spirits before his throne, ⁵and from Jesus Christ, who is the faithful witness, the firstborn from the dead, and the ruler of the kings of the earth.

To him who loves us and has freed us from our sins by his blood, ⁶and has made us to be a kingdom and priests to serve his God and Father—to him be glory and power forever and ever! Amen.

⁷Look, he is coming with the clouds,
and every eye will see him,
even those who pierced him;
and all the peoples of the earth will
mourn because of him.
So shall it be! Amen.

⁸"I am Alpha and the Omega," says the Lord God, "who is, and who was, and who is to come, the Almighty."

1:4-8   The Epistolary Prologue   Exposition

Together with the conventional naming of the human author and addressees, these verses present a statement of the theme of the Revelation: the glorious destiny of the covenant people insured by a sovereign God (v. 8) and a sovereign, victorious Savior who will come with the clouds of heaven to establish His everlasting kingdom (v. 7).

The Apostle greets the churches with a reminder both of the grace of God as indicated by the Gospel and the well-being is ("peace") which accrues to the believer who appropriates that grace. These blessings are insured by the triune God, the God of history, the God of our present circumstance, and the God of all times future.

This great God loves his church. Having saved us, He has made us "a kingdom of priests." He has not assigned the responsibilities of priesthood to a special clergy class but has given to every believer the high privilege and the responsibility of serving the almighty Sovereign by bearing witness to His love and grace in the Gospel. Thus, the believer's destiny is the glory of God, to be fully realized when the Son of Man appears in the clouds to establish on earth His everlasting kingdom.

The Lord God, the Almighty, is both the beginning, the Creator of all things, and the end, the One who will consummate history in the earthly reign of Jesus, when "every eye will see him"!

1:4-8   The Epistolary Prologue   Notes

4a. John, most probably, the Apostle (see above ch. 1, Authorship). **The Seven churches** of chapters 2 and 3 are known from history and archaeology to have been located in the order named along a circuit route on the Roman highway. No doubt they were selected by the divine author for their significance and influence. But they also are representative of many other churches in the Asian province and elsewhere, both at that time and in later centuries. The Roman **province of Asia** occupied approximately the western third of Asia Minor, a part of modern Turkey. The offshore islands, including Patmos, now belong to Greece. The epistolary reference to the province indicates clearly that, like the New Testament epistles, the Revelation is to be understood from the standpoint of the historical destination to which it was originally delivered.

4b. Grace to you and peace is the early Christian greeting familiar from the Pauline epistles. Adapting the common Greek and Hebrew conventions, the expression teaches fundamental doctrine while emphasizing the common standing of Gentile and Jew in the gospel. **Grace** (Gk, χάρις, *cháris*), "gift, unearned favor," turns heavenward the Greek greeting, "Be joyful" (χαίρε, *chaíre*). **Peace**, meaning "well-being," is the traditional

Hebrew greeting, שָׁלוֹם, *shălôm*. The formula, **who is, and who was, and who is to come**, is echoed in 1:8 and 4:8, in part also in 11:17 and 16:5. The expression is known from Jewish literature as an expansion of the divine name, Yahweh.[3] **Is to come**, in distinction from the Jewish form of the formula, "He who will be," emphasizes the second coming of Christ.[4] The statement exalts the eternally existent God who is sovereign over the affairs of men, the God of prophecy. The unusual expression, **the seven spirits before his throne**, probably reflects the sevenfold symbols used later in the book to represent the Holy Spirit. In 3:1, Christ in figure holds the seven spirits with the seven stars which represent the messengers of the churches. In 4:5, God has seven spirits represented with the figure of "seven lamps blazing." In 5:6, Christ has "seven eyes, which are the seven spirits of God." The figures expound upon Zech 4:10, "These seven [lamps] are the eyes of the LORD, which range throughout the earth."[5] The "seven spirits" are the Holy Spirit, who is at once the Spirit of God and the Spirit of Christ." The unusual language of 1:4 is in harmony with the figures occurring later in the book. **5a.** Jesus Christ is **the faithful *witness*** (Gk: μάρτυς, *mártus*).[6] Traditional Jewish wisdom knew that when Messiah "comes, he will explain everything to us" (John 4:25; Deut 18:18, 19). Even a Samaritan woman knew that the true Messiah is the faithful witness whose words carry authority and exact judgment. Jesus is the **first-born from the dead** (cp. Col 1:18). Even if witness results in martyrdom, there is promise of resurrection (see 7:9-17; 14:1-5; 20:4). Our hope is not in this life but in the life to come. Jesus was not the first to be raised from the dead (witness, for example, the resurrection of Lazarus (John 11:43ff), but the first to come forth in the glorified state. The high dignity of royal primogeniture is implied here (Psa 89:27). He is also the *first-born* of many (see 1 Cor 15:19-28).[7] As witness, Jesus is the

---

[3] J. M. Ford. *Revelation*. (Anchor Bible; Garden City, NY: Doubleday, 1975), 377.

[4] R. H. Charles, *A Critical and Exegetical Commentary on the Revelation of St. John* (ICC; Edinburgh: T. & T. Clark, 1920), 1.10f.

[5] Beckwith, Isbon T. *The Apocalypse of John* (Macmillan, 1919; Limited eds. library; Baker, 1967), 424-427.

[6] Our word, "martyr," derives from this Greek word for "witness"—the result of a later emphasis, the witness-martyr theme (see the lampstand symbolism of chs. 2 and 3; also 6:9, 7:3, 11:3, 7, 14:6, 20:4).

[7] "First born" (Gk. πρoτoτoκoς, *prōtotokos*) is used figuratively here. When used in the literal sense the word describes the first-born child who has the primary right of inheritance. But the term as it functions here implies others whose inheritance is insured by Jesus (2 Cor 4:14, 1 Thess 4:14).

true *prophet*; as the dying, resurrected savior, he is the true *priest*. As **the ruler of the kings of the earth**, he is the true *king*. The idea is from the Davidic-Messianic Psalm 89, verse 27: "I will appoint him my firstborn, the most exalted of the kings of the earth." This theme is worked out in the prophecies of the Revelation that follow.

5b. Here begins a benediction, a prayer of praise: **To him who loves us and has freed us from our sins by his blood**. Christ's righteous obedience to the law is seen in his constant love (note the Gk. present tense; Gal 5:14). His love expressed itself supremely in his historic death, "He has freed us from our sins" (note past tense). When facing hardship or persecution, "the love of God, in spite of all evil experiences, is assured by an event in history—the death of Jesus Christ" (Ladd, 27). "God demonstrates his own love for us in this: While we were yet sinners, Christ died for us" (Rom 5:8). **By his blood** (̓εν τῷ αἵματι αὐτοῦ, *'en tô haímati 'autoũ*) reflects a Hebrew idiom implying the payment of a ransom price, our Lord's death at Calvary (Charles, 1.16). **6.** According to its primary usage in Old and New Testaments he **has made us to be a kingdom and priests** does not refer to the *place* but to the *power* of rule. The people of God, by virtue of their inheritance in Israel are a kingdom of priests (Exod 19:6). The point of this text must be found in the context of the Revelation, where in 5:10 it says, "You have made them to be a kingdom and priests . . . and they will reign on the earth." This refers to the future when the saints will rule together with Christ. So Jesus promised his apostles, "You . . . will also sit on twelve thrones judging the twelve tribes of Israel" (Matt 19:28, Luke 22:30). Paul remarked to the Corinthians, "Do you not know that the saints will judge the world?" (1 Cor 6:2) Rev 20:4 says of the martyrs and those who had not worshiped the beast that "they came to life and reigned with Christ a thousand years." As one might expect, the doctrine of the saints participating in future judgment is taught in Dan 7:27, "The sovereignty, power and greatness of the kingdoms under the whole heaven will be handed over to the saints, the people of the Most High."⁸ The saints will be **priests to serve**. This does not refer to the performance of priestly liturgy but "as priests of God, we are to be God-centered in our living, and our chief purpose in life is *to serve and glorify God* our Father" (Newport, 131; see 1 Pet 2:4, 5, 9, 10; Rom 12:1, 2). Ladd points out that this verse "unites the church and Old Testament Israel in a bond of continuity. The church is the new and true Israel, inheriting the spiritual privileges of the Old Testament people of God" (Isa 61:6; Ladd, 27). Thus the Old and the New Covenant people of God are one in Jesus Christ, their common Savior. The doxology looks to the future age as the time when God's glory will be more fully realized and witnessed in his created world. **To him be glory and power**. "Power," from the Greek, κρατος, *kratos*, denotes sovereignty power of the throne.

7. Look, he is coming with the clouds. The language alludes to the Son of Man text of Dan 7:13, and to the second coming of Christ. John points the reader to the culminating event toward which the predic-tions which follow lead and from which they derive much of their ultimate meaning. **Every eye will see him**. The point is that all will see him and recognize him as the coming Messiah. It does not promise that all will see him at the same time. Jesus adopted his favorite Messianic title from this Daniel text. He alluded to this and to the Zechariah text of verse 7b in Matt 24:30 (see also Rev 14:14; Matt 26:64; Mark 13:26, 14:62; Luke 21:27). The allusion to Dan 7:13 carries with it the context of that Daniel passage, the great judgment scene, victory over Antichrist, and the giving over of the kingdom to the saints of the Most High. Among those who will see him are **those who pierced him**. This alludes to Zech 12:10, a prediction that the Jewish people, who were instruments of Christ's crucifixion, will some day mourn when the Lord pours out upon them "a spirit of grace and supplication."⁹ **All the peoples of the earth will mourn because of him**. Again, this alludes to Zech 12:10 and therefore

---

⁸The participation of the saints in the rule over the nations is assigned in Rev 20:4-6 to the millennial age, where the doctrine has peculiar relevance. For the Revelation's teaching on the millennium, see our exposition and notes on ch. 20.

⁹The Zechariah text need not be understood as referring to the second coming of Christ, a common interpretation. This does violence to the order of Zechariah 11-14, which otherwise appears to be in chronological order. "They will look on me, the one whom they have pierced" (12:10), in context, can be understood metaphorically of mental vision or insight.

Chapter Two   *The epistolary prologue, 1:4-8*   55

should be understood in a manner compatible with the Old Testament context. The translation should read, "All the tribes of the land [πᾶσι αἱ ψυλαὶ τῆς γῆς, *pâsai hai phulaì tês gês*] will mourn for him." Zech 12:10f. reads, "They will mourn for him as one mourns for an only child, and grieve bitterly for him as one grieves for a firstborn son . . . . The land will mourn, each clan by itself [φυλὰς φυλάς, φυλὴ καθ' ἑαυτὴν *phulàs phulás, phulḕ kath' heautḕ'n*] . . . ." The context in Zechariah is a forecast of the national repentance of Israel and her consequent mourning over her complicity in the crucifixion of her Messiah (cf. Zechariah 13). There is no compelling reason to give it a different meaning here. The Revelation passage is a testimony to Zechariah's promise of the repentance and conversion of the nation of Israel in the time of the end.[10]

8. I am the Alpha and the Omega. Commentators are divided as to whether these words are those of Christ or of God the Father. Those

---

[10]One should understand Rev 3:7 with its allusion to the Zechariah text in a way that agrees with Zechariah. Thomas Brightman in seventeenth century English states, "This is the wailing of repentance, not of desperation, as is cleare out of Zachary, whence these words are taken . . . . They . . . shall with abundance of teares bewaile the lewdnesse of their fore-fathers in putting Christ to death. This is certaine, that *this booke of the Revelation* staieth his discourse in the conversion of these Jews . . . . And because the glory of Christ shall be then very great, as being a most lively remembrance of that which shall shine out in the last Judgment, the setting forth of this is fetched in to adorne that [i.e., the last judgment] . . . ."; *The Revelation of Saint John* (Amsterdam: T. Stafford, 1644), 6.

Consider the following: (1) Ordinarily, the New Testament quotations should be understood as reflecting their Old Testament meaning. The few apparent exceptions to this principle can be understood either as *midrash pesher* (see E. Earle Ellis, *Paul's Use of the Old Testament* [Grand Rapids: Eerdmans, 1957], 139-147); or as typological interpretation. (2) Whereas "every eye will see him" is universal, "even those who pierced him" most naturally takes its meaning from the Zechariah passage and has a delimiting relationship to the preceding stich of the parallelism, referring as in Zechariah to the nation of Israel. (3) Our interpretation respects the ordinary meaning of *'ep' autòn*, "for him," not "because of him." Quoting Beckwith, "After verbs of emotion *epí* with the acc. regularly denotes the object toward which the feeling is directed, cf. Mt. 15^{32}, Lu. 23^{28} . . . " (432). It is therefore implied that the mourning is occasioned by a penitent spirit rather than fear of judgment. (4) In the first century when there were still nuclei of Hebrew Christians in the churches, an allusion to a repentant Israel witnessing the return of Christ was consoling and entirely natural. (5) The parallel passage, Matt 24:10, should be understood in the same manner. John 19:37 simply alludes to the occasion of the spear thrust as contributing the imagery of Zech 12:10. One need not see it as referring to the soldiers looking on Jesus. Hippolytus states regarding Rev 1:7, θεάσνται ὁ τῶν Ἑβραίων δῆμος καὶ κόψονται, "the Hebrew people shall see and weep" (my transation of the Gk. as quoted in Henry B. Swete, *The Apocalypse of St. John: The Greek Text with Introduction, Notes, and Indices* (3d ed.; Grand Rapids: Eerdmans, pref. 1908), p. 10.

who hear Christ speaking appeal to the context (Ellis, Walvoord[11]), whereas those who interpret the speaker as God the Father appeal to the text, **says the Lord God** (Gk: λέγει κύριος ὁ θεός, *légei kúrios hò theós*).[12] Though the words are more often applied to the Father, what is affirmed here is also attributed to Christ in other places (see 1:5; 5:12, 13; 22:13). This affirmation of the sovereignty of God is appropriate at this place of transition. It reinforces the theme of the Revelation before launching into the specific vision which follows. The ideas are reiterated over and over in the passages which follow. **Alpha and Omega**, the first and last letters of the Greek alphabet, are explained in 22:12: "the First and the Last, the Beginning and the End." The formula reflects Isaiah 48:12, "I am the first and I am the last [also Isa 41:4, 44:6]. My own hand laid the foundations of the earth, and my right hand spread out the heavens; when I summon them they all stand up together." The formula implies the eternity of the omnipotent Creator rather than merely finite extension in time. **The Almighty** means All-ruler (Swete 11).

One Like a Son of Man

1:9. I, John, your brother and companion in the suffering and kingdom and patient endurance that are ours in Jesus, was on the island of Patmos because of the word of God and the testimony of Jesus. [10]On the Lord's Day I was in the Spirit, and I heard behind me a loud voice like a trumpet, [11]which said: "Write on a scroll what you see and send it to the seven churches: to Ephesus, Smyrna, Pergamum, Thyatira, Sardis, Philadelphia and Laodicea."

---

[11]Walvoord, John F. *The Revelation of Jesus Christ* (Chicago: Moody Press, 1966).

[12]Swete cites the following Fathers who support the Christological interpretation: Hippolytus, Clement of Alexandria, Origen, and Andreas (p. 11). In addition to Ellis and Walvoord, mentioned above, Reformation and modern commentators of this persuasion include Brightman; John Trapp, "Revelation of St. John the Divine," *Commentary on the New Testament* (Evansville, Indiana: Sovereign Grace Book Club, 1958); John Gill, *The Exposition of the New Testament* (Philadelphia: W. W. Woodward, 1811; S. T. Bloomfield, *Ἡ ΚΑΙΝΗ ΔΙΑΘΗΚΗ, The Greek Testament with English Notes, Critical, Philological, and Exegetical* (Boston: Perkins and Marvin, 1837); and J. M. Ford. Included among those who affirm the alternate view are Hengstenberg, *The Revelation of St. John* (Cherry Hill, NJ: Mack Publishing Co., 1972); Barnes; Swete; Beckwith; Charles; Ladd; Mounce; and Mickelson, *Daniel and Revelation* (Nashville: T. Nelson, 1984).

¹²I turned around to see the voice that was speaking to me. And when I turned I saw seven golden lampstands, ¹³and among the lampstands was someone "like a son of man," dressed in a robe reaching down to his feet and with a golden sash around his chest. ¹⁴His head and his hair were white like wool, as white as snow, and his eyes were like blazing fire. ¹⁵His feet were like bronze glowing in a furnace, and his voice was like the sound of rushing waters. ¹⁶In his right hand he held seven stars, and out of his mouth came a sharp double-edged sword. His face was like the sun shining in all its brilliance.

¹⁷When I saw him, I fell at his feet as though dead. Then he placed his right hand on me and said: "Do not be afraid. I am the First and the Last ¹⁸I am the Living One; I was dead, and behold I am alive for ever and ever! And I hold the keys of death and Hades.

¹⁹ "Write, therefore, what you have seen, what is now and what will take place later. ²⁰The mystery of the seven stars that you saw in my right hand and of the seven golden lampstands is this: The seven stars are the angels of the seven churches, and the seven lampstands are the seven churches.

1:9-20   The Apocalyptic Introduction   Exposition

The description of Jesus Christ found in verses 13-16 corresponds in many details with descriptions of God found in the book of Daniel. He appears here with snow white hair speaking of the wisdom and majesty of eternity past, with a burning look that pierces into one's inner being, with the purity of molten bronze, and with a voice that resounds like great rushing waters. He speaks with such clarity as to define the very Word of God. His face displays the Shekinah Glory like the most brilliant sun. Yet, he appeared before John as "one like a son of man." We know from the Greek that the language is not drawn from the Gospels, but from Dan 7:13, such a figure appears "coming with the clouds of heaven" to receive for the saints of the Most High a kingdom, the glorious future kingdom of God. We know from similar forms in the Semitic languages of the ancient Near East that "a son of man" is simply one who is truly human (cp. Ezek 2:1). The contrast between such a one and the person whom the Apostle saw in his Patmos vision is dramatic. We are reminded of the teaching of the Apostle Paul in Phil 2:5-7 regarding Christ,

> Who, being in very nature God,
> > did not consider equality with God
> > > something to be grasped,
>
> but made himself nothing,
> > taking the very nature of a servant,
> > being made in human likeness.

But here we have the reversal of the incarnation—Jesus in his post-resurrection glorified state. As the author of the testimony (v. 2), Jesus exercises his prophetic role. As the one who walks among the lampstands serving the churches, Jesus exercises his high priestly role. As the "ruler of the kings of the earth," Jesus exercises his kingly role. Jesus combines the Messianic types of prophet, priest, and king in his one person. Nowhere is this better displayed for us in Scripture than in the book of Revelation.

Our great Savior and Lord walking in the Revelation among specific, historical churches reminds us that the true church is not an abstraction but exists in local congregations wherever a body of believers functions organically with Christ as its head (1 Cor 12:12-26). He serves all of His churches as the Old Covenant high priest served the lamps in the tabernacle, helping to insure that they burn brightly by supplying the oil and trimming the wicks. The believer serves Christ as an organic part of a local body of believers. We should be conscious of Christ's presence in all the proper functions of the local church. This passage showing Jesus as high priest tending the lamps of his sanctuary, reminds us that His church is the true antitypical temple. As the Apostle Paul says, "Don't you know that you yourselves are God's temple (Gk. ναός, *naós*, "sanctuary") and that God's Spirit lives in you?" (1 Cor 3:16)

The imagery also implies that the Asian churches, composed mostly of Gentiles, were nevertheless numbered among the covenant people. So we shall observe as we progress through the Revelation that Israelite imagery abounds, not because it is a message about Jews, but because all the people of God inherit the promises by virtue of their inclusion in the body of God's covenant people, Israel. We should, nevertheless, remember and appreciate the words of Paul, "You [Gentiles] do not support the root [ethnic Israel], but the root supports you" (Rom 11:18).

Above all else, this passage presents our resurrected, glorified Savior. As we proceed to read the letters and consider the prophecies of the Revelation, His radiant and awesome presence stands before us. We do well to emulate the ancient people of God who, like John, fell prostrate in abject humility of spirit before Him.

We give ear to the Testimony of Jesus and the Word of God, not to impose fanciful interpretation nor to buttress human philosophy or doctrine, but from ground level to hear our Master speak. John wrote only what he heard. We learn only what we read. We must let the text speak. We must read and obey.

1:9-20   **The Apocalyptic Introduction**   **Notes**

9. The Apostle describes himself as **your brother and companion in the suffering and kingdom and patient endurance**: The Revelation views tribulation as present in his own day (see above, pp. 30-34). Not only did the Apostle suffer the common deprivations of prisoners, but as Victorinus reports he was consigned in his old age to slave labor in the mines, a fate which is hardly comparable to any contemporary practice.[13] Suffering is for the Christian more easy to bear with the knowledge of God's sovereignty and the assured hope of the coming **kingdom**. With hope, we receive grace for **patient endurance.** All three are experienced **in Jesus**, an expression comparable to the Pauline "in Christ." **Because of the word of God and the testimony of Jesus** alludes to verse two above. John viewed his exile as providentially arranged to receive and to record the Revelation. **10.** The Lord's Day refers to Sunday, not the eschato-

---

[13]"Commentary on the Apocalypse of the Blessed John," *Anti-Nicene Fathers* 7 (Grand Rapids: Eerdmans, 1989), 353. Such prisoners were often permanently shackled with heavy chain and consigned to hard labor until death mercifully delivered them. The accession of the Emperor Nerva within the year A.D. 96 may have saved the Apostle from such a fate. Tradition indicates that he was released to return to Ephesus.

logical Day of the Lord, as some of the futurist school hold. The Day of the Lord is consistently represented differently in the original languages of the Bible. The Greek would have ἡ ἡμέρα κυρίου, *hē hēméra kuríou* from the Hebrew יְהוָה הַיּוֹם, *hāyyōm yhwh*, whereas "the Lord's Day," here in the Greek is τῇ κυριακῇ ἡμέρᾳ, *tē kuriakȇ hēmérą*. Though not appearing elsewhere in the New Testament, "the Lord's Day" is found in contemporaneous writings referring to Sunday.[14] The phrase, **I was in the Spirit** (Greek,ἐγενόμην ἐν πνεύματι, *ėgenómēn ėn pneúmati*) indicates that John was in a Spirit-controlled state. **11.** The Apostle was told to **write on a scroll**. The several occasions when John is instructed to write or not to write indicates that the writing was to be done concurrently as the vision progressed. For **the seven churches**, see the notes on verse four.

12. At this point, we first encounter the dramatic symbolism of the Apostle's vision. The figure with the setting which follows clearly indicates that John is privileged to look into the sanctuary where Jesus Christ ministers within the new temple of the Christian church. The Old Covenant imagery is present, accommodated to the dimensions of the New. The High Priest is present in form and garb which clearly identifies both the earthly and the Divine dimensions of His person, character, and function. The symbolism of the **seven golden lampstands** derives from the original seven-branched menora of the tabernacle (Exod 25:31-40). The most holy vessels of the sanctuary were made of or overlaid with pure gold. In the Exodus typology, the seven lamps symbolize the covenant community of Israel, the people of God, who are to light the world. Here, we are told that "the seven lampstands are the seven churches" (v. 20). The context assumes that the lampstands held burning lamps. **13.** Christ is seen walking **among the lampstands**. He walks among the churches tending the "lamps" of his sanctuary. The lamps of the tabernacle were lit from evening till morning and tended continually (Lev 24:3, 4). The generic meaning of the title **son of man** is "human being," but Jesus used the term with reference to Dan 7:13 as a Messianic title. **Like** is often used in

---

[14] New Testament references to the eschatological Day of the Lord with ἡ ἡμέρα κυρίου are: 1 Thess 2:2; 1 Cor 1:8; 5:5; 2 Cor 1:14. In addition to Revelation 1:10, τη κυριακῇ ἡμέρᾳ occurs in Ign. *Ep. Magn.* 9:1 (written before A.D. 107), *Did.* 14:1 (very early 2nd century), and *Gos. Pet.* 9:35 & 12:50 (early 2nd century). For more full discussion, see Oral Collins, "Good Question," *Henceforth* 7 (Spring, 1979) 103-107; for a defense of the Day of the Lord interpretation, see Walvoord, p. 42.

apocalyptic description to indicate the element of analogy present in figurative language. The miracle of the incarnation is that the Son of God became man (Phil 2:7, 8). He appeared **dressed in a robe reaching down his feet**. The dress is that of high office, in the context of the lampstands, clearly suggesting that of the high priest (see Jos. *Ant.* 3.7.2). **The golden sash** suggests sovereignty (cp. 15:6; Dan 10:5). **14. His head and his hair were white like wool, as white as snow.** This is characteristic of God as "the Ancient of Days" (Dan 7:9; 1 Enoch 46:1). Ancient expositors took this to mean the eternal preexistence of the Son (Swete, 16). Keil on Dan 7:9 suggests that God is so described "because age inspires veneration and conveys an impression of majesty" (230). **His eyes were like blazing fire** (cp. Dan 10:6). This was a common ancient metaphor for the penetrating look which derives from superior intelligence and wisdom (Swete 16f). **15. His feet were like bronze glowing in a furnace** (cp. Ezek 1:4, 27; 8:2; Dan 10:6). The exact meaning of **bronze** (Gk., χαλκολιβάνῳ, *chalkolibánō*) is unknown, but it is believed to have been an especially fine alloy of gold or brass. The figure denotes great strength and stability. Perhaps the shining product of the smelting process also denotes purity. **His voice was like the sound of rushing waters**. The figure conveys loudness, indicating the authority with which He speaks (Ezek 43:2; Rev 14:2; 19:6; cp. Dan 10:6; Rev 19:1; cf. Rev. 17:1, 15). **16. In his right hand he held seven stars**. The **right hand** is the hand of authority and strength. Christ is head over the churches. "The **seven stars** are **the angels** of the seven churches" (v. 20). The Greek word ἄγγελοι *ángeloi* ("angels") means "messengers." Swete suggests that the stars may represent messengers sent to Patmos from the seven Asiatic churches to bring back the book of Revelation (p. 21; cp. 2 Cor 8:23, ἀπόστολοι ἐκκλησιῶν *apóstoloi ecclēsiôn*). Alternatively, some have suggested that the messengers are the guardian angels of the churches (cf. 1 Cor 11:10). Others see them as the pastors or presiding elders. The status given as held in Christ's right hand tends to support one of these last two views. They must be closely identified with the seven individual churches, themselves as sharing in their responsibilities and potential(cf. 3:1b).[15] The designation of the messengers as **stars** should not be overlooked. Elliott points out that heavenly bodies in the Revelation, as otherwise in scrip-

---

[15]For an extensive review of the question see Alford, *The Greek Testament* (Boston: Lee and Shepard, 1886), 4.560-561.

tural symbolism, are symbols for authority figures.[16] The stars as messengers appear to represent the churches and their authority to communicate the gospel of God in the world. **Out of his mouth came a sharp double-edged sword** (also 19:15, 21; cp. Isa 49:2; Heb 4:12): The double-edged broadsword used by the Roman military is a symbol here for the judicial authority of the Word of God invested in Jesus Christ, the Messianic judge. **His face was like the sun shining in all its brilliance** (Matt 17:2; cp. Exod 34:29, 30; Judg 5:31; Matt 13:43). The description appropriately ends with this attribution of the glory of God (cp. 2 Cor 4:5; 6; 3:18).

17. When I saw him, I fell at his feet as though dead (cf. Josh 5:14; Ezek 1:28; Dan 8:17; 10:15; Matt 17:6; Acts 26:14; cp. Isa 6:5). The appropriate response to the presence of the incarnate Word of God is abject humility and consequent obedience. **I am the First and the Last**. See notes on verse 8; cf. 1:17; 2:8; and 22:13. Without question, He affirms in this statement his Deity, attributing to himself the attribute of God. **18. I am the Living One; I was dead and behold I am alive for ever and ever!** This may be translated more literally, "I am living unto the ages of the ages" (Gk. ζῶν, ἐιμι εἰς τοὺς αἰῶνας τῶν αἰώνων, *zōn 'eimi eis toùs aiōnas tôn aiōnōn*; cf. 4:9, 10; 10:6; 15:7). The resurrection of Christ is the primary and central evidence of the genuineness of our Christian faith and hope (Rom 1:4; 1 Cor 15). **I hold the keys of death and Hades**. The **Keys** in this context indicate authority and control over eternal destiny. **Death and Hades** are synonyms here, referring to the first death and intermediate state (cf. 6:8; Psa 16:10; 18:4, 5; Prov 5:5). Death is an enemy ultimately through Christ to be destroyed (1 Cor 5:54-56; Rev 20:13, 14).

19. What you have seen, what is now, and what will take place later: Some (e. g., Elliott, Charles, Swete, Walwoord) take the division here as threefold—past (1:12-18), present (chs. 2, 3), and future (4:1-22:6). Others (Mounce 62, citing W. C. van Unnik and Moffatt) understand "what you have seen" as proleptic (meaning "what you will have seen") embracing the entire vision, while "what is" and "what will take place later" divides the vision into two parts: 1:11-3:22 and 4:1 to the end of the vision. The difference is not crucial, however, as **what you have seen** in the three-fold division is introductory to a chronological division

---

[16]Elliott, E. B. *Horae Apocalypticae*, 5th ed. (London: Seeley, Jackson, and Halliday, 1862), 1.74.

of the prophecy. What is crucial to a proper understanding of the chronology and the resulting prophetic referents is the clearly drawn distinction between "what is now" and "what will take place later" (NIV). If we accept the divine interpreter as authoritative, we must then recognize that chapters 2 and 3 pertain to **what is now**, and that chs 4:1ff refer to predicted future events from the standpoint of the time the Revelation was given (A.D. 96). At this point, 4:1 is decisive, "Come up here, and I will show you what must take place *after this*" (emphasis mine). This should have the effect of ruling out a prophetic view of the seven churches as representing seven church ages. They clearly fall into the place of "what is." **What will take place later** (Gk. ἃ μέλλει γενέσθαι μετὰ ταῦτα, *hà méllei genésthai metà taûta*) is better translated, "What is about to start to occur after this" (μέλλει, *méllei* with the ingressive aor. infin. of γίνομαι, *ginomai*).[17] **20. Mystery** refers to the hidden meaning of the symbols. On the **seven stars . . . in my right hand**, see the notes on verse 16 above. For the **seven golden lampstands**, see on the note on verse 12 above.

2:1-3:22   The Letters to the Churches   Introduction

Chapters two and three in the structure of the book constitute "what is now" (1:19), that part of the message that speaks to contemporary matters. Our Lord addresses each of seven selected churches (see above on 1:4). With some variation the letters may be outlined according to the following pattern:

1. Introductory formula ("To the angel of the church in . . . ")
2. A sign of authority (drawn from 1:12—18)

---

[17] The aorist infinitive with μέλλει views the action holistically as being "on the point of" or "about to" occur; W. Bauer, F. W. Gingrich, and F. Danker, *A Greek English Lexicon of the New Testament and Other Early Christian Literature* (2nd ed.; Chicago: University Press, 1979), 501-502; F. Blass and A. DeBrunner, *A Greek Grammar of the New Testament and Other Early Christian Literature* (Chicago: University Press, 1961), 174. The holistic force of the aorist infinitive with μέλλει is illustrated also by our author in 3:2, ἃ ἔμελλον ἀποθανεῖν, "I am about to spit you out of my mouth" (NIV). In all of these texts the action appears to be not only future but impending. The ingressive aorist of 1:19 would seem to be required by the extensive nature of the events forecast.

3. Words of commendation (except for Sardis and Laodicia)
4. Words of criticism (except for Smyrna and Philadelphia)
5. Exhortation and warning
6. A promise (sometimes after the closing formula)
7. Closing formula ("He who has an ear, let him hear . . . ")

Because these are known historical churches, we must assume that the messages reflect actual conditions which existed in each church. The messages may be applied principially to the present day in the same 1manner as those of the other New Testament epistles.

To the Church in Ephesus

2:1. **"To the angel of the church in Ephesus write:**

These are the words of him who holds the seven stars in his right hand and walks among the seven golden lampstands: ²I know your deeds, your hard work and your perseverance. I know that you cannot tolerate wicked men, that you have tested those who claim to be apostles but are not, and have found them false. ³You have persevered and have endured hardships for my name, and have not grown weary.

⁴Yet I hold this against you: You have forsaken your first love. ⁵Remember the height from which you have fallen! Repent and do the things you did at first. If you do not repent, I will come to you and remove your lampstand from its place. ⁶But you have this in your favor: You hate the practices of the Nicolaitans, which I also hate. ⁷He who has an ear, let him hear what the Spirit says to the churches.

To him who overcomes, I will give the right to eat from the tree of life, which is in the paradise of God.

2:1-7   **To the Church at Ephesus**   **Exposition**

Christ holds the seven stars in his right hand. The reader is reminded of that which was stated in verse sixteen. Christ holds strongly his churches. He had said to Peter, "I will build my church, and the gates of Hades will not overcome it" (Matt 16:18). As we picture him walking among the lampstands, we know that he is with and among his people caring for them.

Christ models true love in his instruction. He commends where there is merit and he admonishes where his people fall short. Love without discipline is shallow and ineffective. The Ephesian Christians were in several respects outstanding. No doubt, this was in part because Ephesus was the mother church for the Roman province of Asia. On account of her strategic location she had been called to lead. The Apostle Paul and later the Apostle John had spent years in Ephesian residence ministering throughout the Asian churches. Ephesus had enjoyed high privilege and great responsibility. Her leaders had worked hard to preserve the true Gospel in the face of strong opposition (see Paul's earlier warning to the Ephesian elders, Acts 20:28-31).

The Apostolic leaders had exercised great vigilance against the Nicolaitan heresy. They had possessed a holy hatred for the perversions of that sect. Today, when orthodoxy is often treated as a fault, we do well to observe that the Lord Jesus commended the Ephesian church for it. He praised that church particularly for their intolerance of wickedness and false teaching. The text strongly implies that the church had taken disciplinary action against those who wrongly claimed to be apostles. It "had found them false" (see Matt 18:17-18).

However, to be orthodox is not enough. We are not told what the Ephesians had neglected—we know only that it was their first love. But a stagnant orthodoxy is potentially fatal. The church will die if they do not repent of it and do their first works. There must be both orthodoxy and orthopraxy—sound doctrine must be wedded to sound practice.

2:1-7   **To the Church at Ephesus**   **Notes**

1. For **the angel of the church**, see the notes on 1:20. **Ephesus** was a leading city and western seaport of the Roman province of

Asia (see 1:4). It was also the ancient world Mecca for the worship of the love goddess, Artemis. Her temple was one of the seven wonders of the ancient world (Acts 19:23-20:1). The city, with a population of about 250,000, was one of the major ports of entrance for the province of Asia. The church, established by Paul with Priscilla and Aquila on his second missionary journey (Acts 18:19-21), was later, on the third journey, to enjoy the Apostle's residence for some three and one-half years (19:1-20), when "all the Jews and Greeks who lived in the province of Asia heard the word of the Lord" (19:10). Ephesus became the mother church, not only of the other six named here, but also of such as Hieropolis and Colossae. Tradition tells us that the Apostle John made his residence in Asia, probably shortly after the martyrdom of Paul (A.D. 68) to the time of Trajan, a period of possibly thirty years.[18]

For the **seven stars in his right hand**, see the note on verse 16. For **him who . . . walks among the seven golden lampstands**, see on vv. 12, 13. **2. I know your deeds**—the One who walks among his people to care for them knows them. **Perseverance** is not patience (KJV) in the passive sense, but active steadfastness. The verb, **tested**, which occurs here in the past tense (Gk. aorist indicative), points to some particular time or times when false apostles were brought to trial in the church. The **false apostles** probably were not Judaizers as in Corinth and elsewhere, who in an earlier period promoted legalism (2 Cor 11:12-15), but Nicolaitans, a sect which practiced libertinism (see vv. 6, 15). For an ecclesiastical trial of similarly wicked heretics, see 1 Cor 5:1-13. Traveling prophets who are not well known should be required to carry valid credentials (2 Cor 3:1), especially before their true character is fully demonstrated (Matt 5:17; Acts 20:29; 1 Cor 14:29). **3.** For persecutions in the Asian province at the time of writing, see the notes on 2:8, 10, 13.

---

[18]See Schaff, 1.424-426. Schaff reasons that John moved to Ephesus to continue the work of the deceased Apostle Paul in this critical area endangered by various heresies.

4. You have forsaken your first love. We are not clearly informed about what had been forsaken. Two interpretations are possible: (1) The Ephesians had lost their first enthusiasm, either in general, or for a particular work in which they first excelled. Or (2), they had fallen away from their earlier practice of brotherly love within the fellowship. The practice of orthodoxy is often accompanied by the internal strife of excessive judgmentalism. This seems to be the more probable situation in Ephesus. 5. To **remember** is the first step on the road to repentance (Barclay). **I will . . . remove your lampstand**: The lamp that flickers and eventually goes out may well be suffering this judgment. 6. The heresy of **the Nicolaitans** had spread through many of the Asian churches (2:15, 20-23; attested also by the Fathers of the Early Church, Irenaeas 1.26.3; 3.11.1 and Hippolytus *Philos.* 7.36). In Rev 2:14 and 15, it is identified with the teaching of Balaam, which is associated with food sacrificed to idols and sexual immorality. Such immorality was commonplace in contemporary Greek religion and culture. Nicolaitanism was a compromising and false Christianity. If tolerated, it had the potential to destroy the church.

7. He who has an ear, let him hear (cp. Matt 13:13-30). In this expression, there may be a bona fide instance of double entendre. Brightman comments, "He teacheth that all men of what kinde soever they are, ought to bend their mindes in hearkening to these admonitions of the Spirit. . . . And yet all men will not hearken and take warning, but *they onely whose eares the holy Ghost openeth"* (18). In the expression, **what the Spirit says**, Jesus identifies himself as in John 14:16-18, with the Holy Spirit. The plural, **churches**, indicates that the epistle is intended not only for Ephesus, but as it may apply, for all the churches. **To eat from the tree of life** is, to live forever (Gen 2:9, 3:22; cp. Ezek 47:12; Rev. 22:2). **The paradise of God** reflects the fact that the garden of Eden is a type of the new restored creation, the world to come, where the people of God will live in fellowship with Him (Isa 51:3; Luke 23:43; Rev 22:2).[19]

To the Church at Smyrna

2:8. "To the angel of the church in Smyrna write:

These are the words of him who is the First and the Last, who died and came to life again. [9]I know your afflictions and your poverty—yet you are rich! I know the slander of those who say they are Jews and are not, but are a synagogue of Satan. [10]Do not be afraid of what you are about to suffer. I tell you, the devil will put some of you in prison to test you, and you will suffer persecution for ten days. Be faithful, even to the point of death, and I will give you the crown of life.

[11] He who has an ear, let him hear what the Spirit says to the churches. He who overcomes will not be hurt at all by the second death."

---

[19]Paradise in the Jewish literature of the Talmud and of pre-Christian times commonly refers to the future life, *after the resurrection* (*1 Enoch* 24.4-25.6; 4; Ezra 7.36, 8.52; *T. Levi* 15:10-11; *m. Pes* 30.191b; *Apoc. Mos.* [*Life of Adam and Eve*] 13:2-5; 40:1-41:3; *b. Soṭa* 22a; *j. Qidd.* 1.10.61d). In the *Apoc. Mos.* 40:1-41:3, the body of Adam is buried by archangels in "paradise on the earth" after his death and the ascent of his spirit into the third heaven (37.4-6). "And God called and said, 'Adam, Adam.' And the body answered from the earth and said: 'Here am I, Lord.' And God saith to him: 'I told thee (that) earth thou art and to earth shalt thou return. Again I promise to thee the Resurrection; I will raise thee up in the Resurrection with every man, who is of thy seed'" (41.1). "And thereafter Michael spake to Seth and saith: 'Lay out in this wise every man that dieth till the day of the Resurrection. . . . Mourn not beyond six days, but on the seventh day, rest and rejoice on it, because on that very day, God rejoiceth (yea) and we angels (too) with the righteous soul, who hath passed away from the earth'" (43.2, 3). Luke 23:43 may also be understood of life after the resurrection simply by correcting the traditional punctuation, "I say to you today, you will be with me in Paradise" (tr. mine). This punctuation is indicated in Codex Vaticanus by a ὑποστιγμή (mark equivalent to an English comma; Robertson, 242) after σήμερον. The correction is supported by the Scriptural idiom found frequently on the lips of the first lawgiver and Messianic type, Moses: "I command you today" (19:9; 27:4; 30:2, 16), "I declare to you this day" (30:18; many other occurrences). Association with the tree of life clearly places this reference (Rev 2:7) in the age to come (Rev 22:2).

2:8-11   **To the Church at Smyrna**   **Exposition**

Smyrna appears to have been the poorest of the seven churches. Jesus said, "I know your poverty." The worth of a church is not to be measured by the extent or the splendor of its properties, nor by the size of its income or its annual budget, nor by the amount of its investments, for in spite of that church's poverty Smyrna was rich in its inheritance of the Gospel and of the promises of God.

Faithful in their witness, believers in Smyrna were greatly persecuted, falsely accused, and put in jail—even put to death. Christ reminds them of the great resurrection hope of the church by addressing them as "the one who died and came to life again"! He is "the First and the Last." He has authority and he is victor from beginning to end. It is our standing in him that gives assurance, both for this life and the life to come.

Unlike all the others, Christ's letter to the Christians in Smyrna finds no fault. We cannot assume from this that the church was without sin. Perhaps our Lord's compassion for this faithful, impoverished, and suffering congregation restrained him from any censure.

In our materialistic culture we are prone to derive our values from the things that are important only to this life and to neglect the life to come. While this world is of short duration and at best uncertain circumstance, for the faithful the world to come will be unending and glorious. Those who seek fulfillment in this world will in that day inherit suffering and everlasting destruction. Thus, Jesus ends this letter with the words, "He who overcomes will not be hurt at all by the second death."

| 2:8-11 | The Letter to Smyrna | Notes |

8a. On angel see the note on 1:20. **The church in Smyrna** for more than half a century was led by the distinguished bishop, Polycarp, born about A.D. 69, a disciple of the Apostle John, burned at the stake in Smyrna in A.D. 155 (Eus. *Hist* 4.15). He was remembered by his disciple, Irenaeus, as the "blessed and apostolic presbyter," who was particularly esteemed for his faithfulness in holding to and defending the Apostolic tradition and the Holy Scriptures against Gnosticism and other heresies. The works of the Apostolic Fathers include a letter of Polycarp to the Philippian church written about A.D. 115.[20] *The Martyrdom of Polycarp* gives an eyewitness account of his testimony and circumstance at the time of his death. Iranaeus thought Polycarp was the most outstanding Christian of his age. The church must have benefited greatly from his leadership. A letter of Ignatius of Antioch to the Smyrnaeans preserved from that period (A.D. 100-118) provides a historical commentary on the prophecy of Smyrna's suffering: "I glorify Jesus Christ, the God who made you so wise; for I perceived that you are settled in immovable faith, having been nailed, as it were, on the cross of the Lord Jesus Christ both in flesh and spirit . . . " (Ign. *Smyrn.* 1.1).[21] **Smyrna** is modern Izmir, Turkey, a large seaport and commercial center on the west coast of Asia Minor about forty miles north of Ephesus. It competed with Ephesus and Pergamum to be "first city" of the province of Asia. It was noted for its beauty, its loyalty to Rome, and its center for worship of the Emperor. Smyrna hosted a large colony of Jews, many of whom were hostile to Christianity.

8b. The words of him who is the First and the Last is an allusion to 1:18. These words give comfort and hope to those who face persecution and martyrdom. They imply Christ's agency in creation and in re-creation through the resurrection of the dead (see on 1:18). Christ is described as the one **who died and came to life again.** He was raised the "first fruits of those who have fallen asleep" (1 Cor 15:20). **9.** Christ said, **I know**

---

[20]The epistle relates to the death of Ignatius of Antioch which is reported by one source to have occurred in the ninth year of the Emperor Trajan, A.D. 107-108, but other circumstances suggest a somewhat later date (see *Schaff* 2.655-656.)

[21]Tr. of Wm. R. Schoedel in his *Ignatius of Antioch* (Hermeneia; Philadelphia: Fortress Press, 1985) 220.

your afflictions: Roman persecution no doubt was incited by the opposition of influential Jewish leaders. Here, the word **poverty** (Gk.πτωχεία, *ptōcheía*) means "extreme poverty," lit., "beggarliness" (BAGD 728a); "a laughingstock" (Brightman 20b). The reason is not given, but it is probable that the Christians were victims of pogroms by which their properties were destroyed or stolen (Charles 1.56; cp. Heb 10:34). The fact that many were slaves was a general condition in the first century church and would not account for the condition in Smyrna. The middle and upper classes were also commonly represented and in the New Testament church there would have been sharing of goods to meet such extreme needs. Yet the Smyrneans were **rich** spiritually (cp. Rev 3:18; Matt 6:20; 2 Cor 6:10). "They were rich with the riches of Christ, with the blessings of the covenant, with the graces of the Spirit, and in good works; they were kings and priests unto God, had a . . . right to the kingdom of glory hereafter . . . ." (Gill 3.707). **Slander** (Gk. βλασφημία *blasphēmía*) is used here of humans rather than of the Deity. Probably there were false charges exposing the Christians to the penalty of Roman law. Some of the common accusations were: (1) cannibalism, for eating "the body and blood" of Jesus in the ordinance of communion; (2) sex orgies, inferred from their reported attendance to "love feasts"; (3) destroying family and home, because conversions did sometimes cause such division; (4) atheism, for rejecting images and the established Roman religions, especially emperor worship; (5) insurrection, for refusing to say, "Caesar is Lord"; and (6) incendiarism, for predicting the destruction of the world by fire (Barclay 1. 98). **Those who say they are Jews** refers to nominal Jews—those who had rejected the true Judaism in rejecting Jesus as Messiah and were in conflict with Christians, especially with Jewish converts to Christianity. They say they are Jews **and are not.** Christ's testimony affirms the teaching of Paul: "A man is not a Jew if he is only one outwardly, nor is circumcision merely outward and physical. No, a man is a Jew if he is one inwardly; and circumcision is circumcision of the heart, by the Spirit . . . " (Rom 2:28, 29; cf. Rev 7:1-8). They were instead **a synagogue of Satan,** in distinction from the Jew's claim to be the true synagogue (assembly) of the LORD (cf. 3:9, Num 16:3, 20:4;*Pss. of Sol.* 17:18). Jesus earlier said essentially the same thing, "You belong to your father, the devil" (John 8:44). Those who reject the Messiah, Jesus, are allied with the alternative kingdom of Satan, who is the prince of this world (John 12:31; 16:11). In Paul's experience, such Jewish leaders militantly pursued him from one community to the next and had effective tactics for inciting the opposition of civil authorities against Christian missionaries (see Acts 13:50; 14:2-5, 14:19; 17:5-9). Probably similar attitudes and tactics prevailed in Smyrna. We read in *The Martyrdom of Polycarp* that "the multitude of heathen and Jews living in Smyrna cried out with uncontrollable wrath."[22] Then, in spite of the Sabbath, they helped to gather wood to burn Polycarp alive (13:1; Mounce, 75). **10. The prison** in the first century was ordinarily used only for temporary confinement pending sentence. Some punishment followed, often immediate execution or deportation to work in the mines, where the most tortuous conditions and slow death prevailed. Prisons were void of creature comforts except what might be provided by loved ones or friends. For some such conditions were to come, Christ promises the Smyrneans, **to test you.** For the Christian, suffering for Christ is one of the marks of genuineness (Luke 9:23; Acts 9:16; Phil 1:29; Heb 12:7-11; Rev 3:19). **You will suffer persecution for ten days.**[23] In this context of a literal epistle, the preferred interpretation is ten literal days, or understanding "ten" as a round number, a period of approximately that length.[24]

Be faithful even to the point of death: The principle is illustrated by the Smyrnaean bishop, Polycarp, the eleventh martyr of that church, who facing the flames affirmed, "Eighty and six years have I served Him, . . . and He has done me no wrong. How can I blaspheme my King who saved me? (quoted from Barclay 1.93). **I will give you a crown of life.** The "crown" (Gk. *stéphanos*) is that worn by the victor in war or athletic

---

[22]*Mart. Pol.* 12.2, as quoted with emphasis added by Mounce, p. 75.

[23]"Ten days" has been given several different interpretations: (1) ten literal days (Atkinson, Henry), (2) a figure for ten years (Clarke, Hill), (3) ten definite periods of persecution in church history (Spurgeon), (4) an indefinite period of time, (5) a long time, though definitely limited (Summers, Mounce), or (6) a short time of fixed duration (Beckwith, Brightman, Charles, Ladd, Swete).

[24]This expression will be natural if we assume that the prophecy is addressed uniquely to the Smyrna church of that generation. If taken in a more inclusive sense it will be much too brief to include the known persecutions of the succeeding centuries. The figurative interpretations must be considered, but apart from the year-day principle implicit in certain Old Testament prophecies and in the apocalyptic predictions of Revelation (see below on Rev 11:1-6), the chronological delimiter with the figurative "day" is, I believe, unprecedented, and therefore doubtful. Apart from its occurrence in apocalyptic symbolism, the prophetic use of the year-day principle is accompanied by contextual explanation. The references often cited in the commentaries for the use of "ten days" as a "short but definite period of time" must be taken rather literally either of ten actual days or as a round number of approximately that length.

competition. Here, it is a figure meaning "reward." Victory over suffering and death is a dominant theme in the book of Revelation, Christ's final testimony to his church. His redeemed church is seen repeatedly in the age-to-come celebrating this victory! (6:9-17; 14:1-5; 15:1-4; 19:1-8; cp. Isa 28:5; 2 Tim 4:8; James 1:12) **11.** For **He who hath an ear** and what follows, see the notes on 2:7. The **second death** is the destruction of Gehenna. The expression is defined in the only other occurrences in the New Testament, Rev. 20:6, 14, 21:8 (see the notes on those texts). It is also found in the Jewish paraphrastic translations of the Old Testament called Targums and in other ancient Jewish works.[25]

To the Church at Pergamum

2:12. **"To the angel of the church in Pergamum write:**

These are the words of him who has the sharp, double-edged sword. ¹³I know where you live—where Satan has his throne. Yet you remain true to my name. You did not renounce your faith in me, even in the days of Antipas, my faithful witness, who was put to death in your city—where Satan lives.

¹⁴Nevertheless, I have a few things against you: you have people there who taught Balak to entice the Israelites to sin by eating food sacrificed to idols and by committing sexual immorality. ¹⁵Likewise you also have those who hold to the teaching of the Nicolaitans. ¹⁶Repent therefore! Otherwise, I will soon come to you and will fight against them with the sword of my mouth.

¹⁷He who has an ear, let him hear what the Spirit says to the churches. To him who overcomes, I will give some of the hidden manna. I will also give him a white stone with a new name written on it, known only to him who receives it."

---

[25]An example, as translated and quoted in Charles (1.59) is from the *j Tg.* Deut 33:6, "Let Reuben live in this age and not die the second death [Aram. *bemôtānâ tinyânâ*] whereof the wicked die in the next world" (cf. *Tg.* Jer 51:39, 57; *Tg.* Isa 22:14, 65:6, 15; *b. Soṭa* 35a on Num 14:37; Ford 393-394).

2:12-17   **To the Church at Pergamum**   **Exposition**

Our Lord's letter to the believers at Pergamum was bittersweet. Like the Ephesian letter, there is first commendation, then warning of judgment. We have the Apostle Paul's reminder that "in a large house there are articles not only of gold and silver, but also of wood and clay; some are for noble purposes, some are for ignoble. If a man cleanses himself from the latter, he will be . . . made holy, useful to the Master and prepared to do any good work" (2 Tim 2:20, 21). Local churches, as suggested by the Parable of the Tares (Matt 13:24-30, 36-43) are often made up of some of each. The "gold" in Pergamum was modeled by Antipas, faithful to the point of death. Apparently, the majority remained true in extreme testing and did not renounce their faith. The ultimate test of genuineness is the God-given capacity to stand true under the pressure of Satanic influence. Pergamum was a great cult center for Satan worship. There the issues should have been painted black and white. Nevertheless, some, apparently in positions of influence, were willing to compromise like Balaam for a price. Idols' temples and sexual immorality in antiquity, as their counterparts today, were often found together. The fellowship of Christ and the fellowship of the world do not mix. Sexual immorality with its devastating consequences on home and family flies in the face of Jesus and repudiates our covenant relationship to God. When ancient culture took sexual license lightly and often even gave religious sanction, the biblical law of complete abstinence from sex outside of legitimate marriage reflects the fact that Christians live in a different realm, not under the dominion of Satan but in the kingdom of Christ. The "sword of his mouth" is not only his spoken or written word, but that word spoken with the authority that promises severe judgment to any who refuse to repent. The white stone, like the white robe, stands as a symbol of holiness and righteous conduct of which the master approves.

2:12-17 To the Church at Pergamum Notes

12. On the **angel of the church**, see 1:20. **Pergamum** was the capital city of the Roman province of Asia. It was an illustrious intellectual and

The archaeological remains of the Imperial Cult Temple in Pergamum where Christians were commanded to sacrifice to the Roman Emperor, Pontifex Maximus

cultural center, and the place where the Roman emperor was worshiped after the fashion of the ancient Babylonian mysteries. **13.** The Babylonian cult was for centuries prior to the writing of the Revelation a focal point for Satan worship, including sexual orgies and the veneration of the serpent. At the death of king Attalus III Philometer in 133 B.C., his will ceded Pergamum to the Romans. Attalus was the last to inherit the title, Pontifex Maximus, "Divine" high priest of the cult. After a time the Roman Emperor took to himself the local cultic function and the title, Pontifex Maximus.[26] In 29 B.C. the Imperial cult erected in Pergamum a

---

[26]This is documented by Alexander Hislop in *The Two Babylons; or Papal Worship proved to be the Worship of Nimrod and His Wife*, 3rd ed. (Edinburgh: J. Wood, 1862; reprinted by Loizeaux Brothers, New York, and A. & C. Black, London) 240-242. Although Hislop makes a strong case, he sometimes, as in the title of his work, overstates his conclusions or overextends evidence, especially when he draws conclusions from etymology, a not uncommon fault in the mid-nineteenth century. For the Babylonian origin of the cult at Pergamos, Hislop cites from Barker and Ainsworth's *Lares and Penates of Cilicia* (ch. 8, p. 232): 'The defeated Chaldeans fled to Asia Minor, and fixed their central college at Pergamos." He alludes also to statements from Pausanius, a second century Greek chronicler (*Phoc.* 10.15.833). According to this tradition, on the occasion of the Persian conquest the Babylonian Magi fled to Pergamos. There they invested the kings of that city state with the office of Pontifex Maximus previously held by Belshazzar and his Babylonian predecessors. For a list of the succession, see Ch. Rollin's *Ancient History* (New York: Leavitt & Allen, n. d.), 1.92, 93. On the probable identification of Semiramis of Greek tradition with the Babylonian queen, Sammuramat, of Mesopotamian inscriptions, see Sidney Smith, "The Foundation of the

temple to the Emperor Augustus. The provincial governor functioned as the local high priest of the cult. In the second century, a second temple was erected to Trajan and a third to Severus. (Charles 1. 60-61)

14. On **the teaching of Balaam**, see Num 31:1-16; cf. 25:1-3. Balaam, a false prophet of the LORD, offended the kings of Moab who had hired him by blessing Israel whom he had been hired to curse. Apparently, to regain their favor and perhaps collect his pay, he then advised the kings to use their Midianite women to seduce the men of Israel into attending temple banquets, practicing sexual immorality, and worshiping Baal of Peor.[27] Religious prostitution was common to much of the pagan worship in the ancient Mediterranean lands. It was practiced by the Nicolaitan cult in the name of Christianity (see Rev 2:15 and ftn. 20). **15. The Nicolaitans**, probably falsely, attributed their heinous doctrine to Nicolaus, the deacon of the Jerusalem church (Acts 6:5). Their error was a variety of Gnostic philosophy which held that, because the material and spiritual worlds are essentially separate, licentious conduct was not in conflict with the Christian faith. They therefore imported into Christian piety practices which were common to pagan temples (cf. Jude 3-16). **16.** The Lord's commandment was to **repent**. Sexual immorality is intolerable to the Lord. Repentance is essential to faith. Indeed, repentance and purity are frequently reiterated themes in our Lord's last prophecy. The Lord will **fight against** the unrepentant. He will bring judgment against those who deliberately violate his laws. The language of the text implies temporal as well as eternal judgment. For **the sword of my mouth**, see the note on 1:16. Through this text Christ speaks as the Divine judge with absolute authority.

Assyrian Empire," in *The Assyrian Empire* (ed. by J. C. Bury, S. A. Cook, and F. E. Adcook; *The Cambridge Ancient History*; New York: Macmillan, 1925), 3.27.

[27]That Balaam advised the Moabite kings so is not stated but this inference is highly probable. This understanding is documented in first century, A.D., authors (as cited by Charles 1.63: Ph. *Vita Mos.* 1.53-55; cf. Jos. *Ant.* 4.6.6. Also Origen *Num. Hom.* 20.1). Balaam, whose father was Beor of Aram Naharaim (Mesopotamia; Deut 23:4), attests the presence of prophets of Yahweh in the Land prior to the arrival of the Israelites, with whom he was not identified and whom he apparently did not know (Num 22:11). In spite of his obedience to Yahweh while under considerable coercion, there are several indications that he was indeed a false prophet. After Yahweh told him to go with the Moabite kings, He was nevertheless "angry with him when he went" (v. 22; not "because he went," *NASB*, RSV, KJV, since God had told him to go; the Hebrew כִּי, *kî* may be understood here as a temporal adverb). God's anger likely was caused by Balaam's insincerity and self-interest (cf. 2 Pet 2:15, Jude 11).

17. For **he who has an ear to hear** see the note on verse 11. The **hidden manna** had been placed in a golden pot and placed in the Ark of the Covenant so that future generations would remember God's gracious provision of food to Israel in their wilderness wanderings (Exod 16:32-34; Heb 9:4). A tradition recorded in 2 Macc 2:4-7 reports that, when Jerusalem was under siege by the Babylonians in 587/86 B.C., Jeremiah hid the ark with this pot of manna in a cave on Mount Nebo where it was to remain hidden until the Messianic rebuilding of the temple. The hidden manna is a symbol of the Messianic life of the Age to Come. The believer is given **some** of it in the sense that the "manna" is *shared among all who overcome* (Gk. τοῦ μάννα, *toû mánna*, a partitive genitive; BDF 93). The overcomer will also receive **a white stone**. This stone (Gk. ψῆφον, *psêphon*) is probably the stone used by a juror to indicate his vote in a jury trial, indicating by its white color that the accused is reckoned not guilty of his sin, for which Christ has made atonement. Brightman cites Ulpian *Demonsthenes against Timocrates* and Aristophanes in *PHEE* 10 (Brightman, p. 25). The stone was sometimes inscribed with the name of its designated recipient (Brightman, citing Plutarch, *Aristides 25). The new name written on it is the name of the believer. Leon Morris explains that in ancient times a person's name was taken as an expression of their character (69). The secret name (***known only to him who receives it***) is an indication of the indwelling Christ whose righteousness is imputed to the believer. Brightman asks why the Revelation gives three assurances of everlasting life to the overcomer. He responds, "though they should be cried down for guiltie upon earth by all mens[sic] voices, yet they should hereby know most certainly, that they are adjudged for guiltlesse before the heavenly *Tribunall of God*" (p. 25; italics and 17th century spelling his).

To the Church at Thyatira

2:18. "**To the angel of the church in Thyatira write:**

These are the words of the Son of God, whose eyes are like blazing fire and whose feet are like burnished bronze. [19]I know your deeds, your love and faith, your service and perseverance, and that you are now doing more than you did at first.

²⁰Nevertheless, I have this against you: You tolerate that woman Jezebel, who calls herself a prophetess, By her teaching she misleads my servants into sexual immorality and the eating of food sacrificed to idols. ²¹I have given her time to repent of her immorality, but she is unwilling. ²²So I will cast her on a bed of suffering, and I will make those commit adultery with her suffer intensely, unless they repent of her ways. ²³I will strike her children dead. Then all the churches will know that I am he who searches hearts and minds, and I will repay each of you according to your deeds. ²⁴Now I say to the rest of you in Thyatira, to you who do not hold to her teaching and have not learned Satan's so-called deep secrets (I will not impose any other burden on you): ²⁵Only hold on to what you have until I come.

²⁶To him who overcomes and does my will to the end, I will give authority over the nations—

²⁷ 'He will rule them with an iron scepter;
He will dash them to pieces like pottery—' [Psa 2:9]

just as I have received authority from my Father. ²⁸I will also give him the morning star. ²⁹He who has an ear, let him hear what the Spirit says to the churches."

2:18-29   To the Church at Thyatira   Exposition

The picture of the glorified Lord is quite unlike the compassionate Savior we find in the Gospels. His deity is clearly dramatized in the language of chapter one (vv. 14, 15), the particular figures showing that penetrating perception and holiness which makes the sinner tremble before the Divine Judge.

Difficult though it must have been for the Godly saints in Thyatira, they had learned to tolerate the heretical and immoral "Jezebel" rather than take that drastic disciplinary action. Such action would have offended many, not only her devotees and friends. The church today has difficulty accepting responsibility to discipline. There is a tendency to fear the opposition, to keep the peace, to maintain the numbers. We look for more positive ways to help the wayward. There are likely also to be those who are not ready to allow such authority to the responsible administrators. We grieve our Lord if we refuse to guard the holiness of His temple. We may forget that "the Lord disciplines those whom He loves" (Heb 12:6; cf. Deut 8:5; Prov 13:24). Like a good farmer, He prunes the vine that it may bear more fruit (John 15:2).

The Lord promised, nevertheless, to severely punish the wicked woman (22, 23). We have the solemn warning of Scripture that "if anyone destroys God's temple [the local church], God will destroy him" (1 Cor 3:17). To the Jezebel cult He says, "I will repay each of you according to your deeds" (v. 23). The punishment promised to "Jezebel" and her followers suggests that they were true heretics, impenitent, unwilling to abandon their erroneous, sinful ways. They had no rightful place in the Church for they belonged to the world.

The Lord enjoins the Thyatirans only to hold on to what they had (v. 25). Indeed, the church that must constantly fight against the forces of Satan within likely will be powerless to carry out a mission to the world.

Nevertheless, the one who conquers evil in this life is promised an opportunity to share Christ's rule in the Age to Come. He will also know the abiding presence of the Morning Star, the risen Savior, the Lord Jesus Christ.

2:18-29   **To the Church at Thyatira**   **Notes**

18. For our remarks on **the angel of the church**, see 1:20. **Thyatira** was located on the Roman Imperial Post Road connecting East and West. It lay in a valley east of Pergamum where its chief destiny was to serve as a rather vulnerable outpost to guard the capital city from invading armies. It was from the first a military colony, a garrison city founded to guard a passage between two great river valleys, but not from an easily defended location. Ramsay comments on its later history: "Its fate in the many centuries of fighting between Mohammedans (first Arabs, then Turks) and Christians must have been a sad one. Its situation exposes them to destruction by every conqueror . . . " (p. 323). One may imagine how our

Lord's prophecy in this letter may have been fulfilled, but history has not recorded the events. When the Revelation was given, Thyatira had been at peace for almost two hundred years. The city was small and a prosperity was setting in which lasted through the peaceful era of the second and third centuries. Its great commerce is illustrated by Lydia, who was found in Philippi, "a dealer in purple cloth from the city of Thyatira" (Acts 16:14). Lydia also may indicate a Jewish community in Thyatira, as she was a Gentile "worshiper of God." The term ordinarily describes a Gentile who attends synagogue worship. From coins we know that the local god of Thyatira was seen as united with the deities of Pergamum as well as with the Imperial cult (Ramsay 319-323).

The Son of God is a title that was taken by the Roman Emperor as an incarnation of the pagan god, Apollo, worshiped at Thyatira according to his traditional local name, as Tyrimnos. The title represented the Emperor's full claim to kinship with the gods. As applied to our Lord, it stands over against the false claims of the local religion as a clear statement of his Deity.[28] The description of Christ—**whose eyes are like blazing fire and whose feet are like burnished bronze**—quoted from 1:14, 15, is also found in Dan 10:6. In all of these passages the language indicates powers of the Deity which enable Him to make penetrating and pure judgments in every case, including that of the Thyatiran Jezebel. **19.** To the church, he says, **I know your deeds**. Christ knows and summarizes them in the four qualities which follow: **Your love and faith, your service and perseverance**. The first pair leads to the second—love is expressed in service, faith in perseverance. The Ephesians had lost their first love; the Thyatirans were doing more than at first. With such encouragement Jesus then introduces his criticism in vv. 20-23. This pattern of encouragement followed by criticism is found also in His letter to the Ephesians.

20. You tolerate that woman Jezebel. Probably this woman was called "Jezebel," not because it was her real name, but to associate her

---

[28]The full deity of Christ is necessarily implied in many passages of the Bible. It is plainly stated in several places: "He will be called . . . mighty God . . . " (Isa 9:6); "The Word was God" (John 1:1); "My Lord and my God" (John 20:28); "God was pleased to have all his fullness dwell in him" (Col 1:19); "In Christ all the fullness of the deity lives in bodily form" (Col 2:9); "About the son he [God the Father] says, 'Your throne, O God, will last for ever and ever'" (Heb 1:8). These passages are even more emphatically unambiguous when fully examined in their original languages and contexts.

with King Ahab's wife, who served the Canaanite god, Baal (1 Kgs 16:31). She was like Jezebel. Baal was served by priestesses who were religious prostitutes. The proceeds from these women supported pagan temples.[29] It is probable that similar rituals were practiced in the name of the local cult shrine and that "Jezebel" as a self-styled prophetess had brought such practices into the Christian community. Perhaps she was a former priestess converted to Christianity who after assuming the role of a prophetess sanctioned the blending of some of her former pagan ways with professed Christianity. We cannot know whether she was associated with the cult of the Nicolaitans, but as that "Christian" fertility cult seems to have been widespread, the inference is probable. As the Israelite Jezebel had been an evil influence on the Northern Kingdom in the ninth century B.C., so the first century prophetess, "Jezebel," had afflicted the Thyatiran church. The leaders stood under grave censure for being tolerant of her false doctrine and immorality (see Deut 29:16-21). Compare the Apostle's teaching regarding the Corinthian's toleration of their incestuous member: "Shouldn't you rather have been filled with grief and have put out of your fellowship the man who did this? . . . When you are assembled in the name of our Lord Jesus and I am with you in spirit . . . hand this man over to Satan, so that the sinful nature may be destroyed and his spirit saved on the day of the Lord" (1 Cor 5:2, 4, 5; see also Matt 18:15-18; 1 Tim 1:20; 2 Thess 3:14, 15; 2 Cor 3:5-11). **By her teaching she misleads my servants.** As a prophetess "Jezebel" misled many who served Christ in the Thyatiran church. Leaders have a grave responsibility to exercise biblical discipline. This is especially urgent when errant members presume to exercise "spiritual" gifts (1 Cor 14:32, 37). **Sexual immorality and eating foods sacrificed to idols** were the common practices of the contemporary first century culture, as they had been in the pagan culture of ancient Canaan.[30] On "sexual immorality," see

---

[29]See Oral Collins, "Prostitution in the Ancient Near East," *The Stem* ZNH *and Prostitution in the Hebrew Bible* (Ph. D. dissert.; Brandeis U.; Ann Arbor, Mich.: U. Microfilms, 1977) 26-60.

[30]Although the Bible does speak of spiritual prostitution and spiritual adultery, the reader should take this text literally. There is nothing in the letter to suggest otherwise. The Greek translated "sexual immorality" here and in v. 14 is the verbal form of the noun, πορνεία, "unchastity," "fornication," "harlotry." This Greek word is equivalent to the Hebrew word, זנות. For a thorough study of the use of the Hebrew word, זנות and its cognates, see Collins, *The Stem* ZNH, n. 28, above. A vast literature has been written about the biblical use of these terms, especially in those passages which make statements relative to divorce. There are two principles that are sometimes overlooked or even contradicted: (1) Words for sexual immorality, πορνεία/זנות, and for adultery,

"Jezebel," above. Animals ritually slaughtered were commonly served at special banquets conducted in honor of the gods. The Apostle Paul's limited permission to eat such food in Rom 14:2, 3, 22 and 1 Cor 8:8 was conditioned by the Christian's practical responsibility to avoid offending the conscience of the weaker brother, one who was likely to be present, at least on those public occasions when idols' food was served (Rom 14:20; 1 Cor 8:13). This responsibility presupposes that conscience is a Divinely ordained function which must be respected to preserve moral responsibility (see 1 Cor 10:28, 29; also Rom 2:15; 13:5; 1 Pet 3:16, 21). The believer whose conscience is weak must be discipled, so that his informed conscience will operate harmoniously with right conduct. **21. I have given her time to repent.** God exercises grace in his longsuffering (2 Pet 3:9). **22. I will cast her on a bed of suffering.** Jesus speaks here of temporal judgment (compare 1 Cor 11:29, 30). He draws out the analogy with Jezebel who suffered an untimely and horrible death (1 Kgs 21:21, 22, 2 Kgs 10:30-37). **Those who commit adultery with her** are those who follow Jezebel's doctrine. Although literal adultery probably was part of the apostasy, "adultery" here may have metaphorical overtones. The term is commonly used in Scripture for Israel's unfaithfulness to her "marriage" covenant with the Lord (Hos 1:2, 3:1; Ezek 16:8-17; 23:5-10; Matt 12:39; Mk 8:38; James 4:4; et al.). **23. I will strike her children dead** further extends the analogy with the Ahab-Jezebel story. Seventy sons of Ahab were killed so that this judgment of Ahab and Jezebel caused the royal line of Ahab to cease. Commentators incline to understand "children" in this text figuratively as referring to those in Thyatira who adopted the teachings of "Jezebel." This, however, may not be warranted in view of the biblical principle that is attached to the Lord"s covenant with Israel that the

---

μοιχεία/נאף, although sometimes used broadly as synonyms (cf. Hos 2:4, 4:14), nevertheless, as in those texts, always have distinctive meanings. Whereas πορνεία/זנות denotes unchastity, that is, illicit sexual intercourse outside of or without regard to a marriage relationship, adultery (μοιχεία/נאף) denotes specifically the violation of a marriage contract. Adultery has its root idea in the marriage covenant, not in the sex act. It is doubtful whether this distinction between the two word groups in biblical usage is ever lost. The word, "prostitute" is an apparent exception, as the general label serves whether or not the prostitute is involved as or with a married person. (2) In each text, context and especially genre must be considered carefully for their bearing on specific meaning. Jesus' use of πορνεία in Matt 5:32, 19:9 and parallels in His debate with Pharisaic rabbis must be understood from the standpoint of Hebrew Bible case law, as Jesus when He appealed for textual authority always appealed to the Old Testament (cf. Deut 22:13-21).

children do suffer, often fatally, from the sins of their parents (Lev 26:22, 29; Deut 28:32, 41; Ezek 23:25, 47). Ezekiel describes apostate Judah as an adulterous wife who by her adultery despises her children (16:45). **Then all the churches will know.** The Lord's judgment of Jezebel will be known among all the churches and be an example and a warning to any who act in disobedience as though he doesn't know their hearts and minds. **And I will repay each of you according to your deeds.** We learn from verse 24 that these words are addressed primarily to Jezebel and her followers, but the necessity for obedience in the face of judgment is clearly taught in other Scriptures (see Matt 25:31-46). **24.** The remainder of this letter to Thyatira is addressed to those who had not followed "Jezebel." The reference to **Satan's so-called deep secrets** has given rise to several interpretations: 1. Some understand the word, "so-called," in the sense that what they understood as "the deeper doctrines" were called "the deep things of Satan" by more orthodox believers. However, this interpretation is an unlikely reading of the word, "so-called," which when literally translated from the Greek must be rendered, "as they say." Most scholars believe that this probably refers to what the heretical Thyatirans themselves were saying. 2. Others say the expression is an ironic turn on the Thyatirans' use of the phrase, "deep things of God" (cp. 1 Cor 2:10) in which Christ substitutes "Satan" for "God" to indicate the true source of Jezebel's doctrine. 3. Alternatively, perhaps the followers of Jezebel, themselves, styled their doctrine as "the deep things of Satan." If the latter was true, they taught, as some Gnostics later did, that participation in pagan rites may be experienced by the spiritually mature without alteration of one's spiritual state or of one's relationship with God. Some Gnostics taught that one had not proven his maturity until he had experienced as a believer such pagan practices.[31] **I will not impose any other burden on you.** The burden of confronting "Jezebel" and her converts was enough. **25. Only hold on to what you have.** The necessity for the cleansing of God's house may prevent the progress of a church until the task is done. To hold strongly the Faith and to prevent further apostasy is the primary responsibility. **Until I come** points to the Second Advent, giving courage and hope.

---

[31] See Barnes, 85 (position 1); Mounce, 89 (position 2 or 3); William Barclay, *The Revelation of St. John* (Philadelphia: Westminster Press, 1960), 1.136-138 (position 3).

26. To him who overcomes: as in each of the letters a promise is made to the overcomer. Here only, perhaps as a reflex on the preceding verse, it is expanded with an explanatory clause, **and does my will to the end** (cf. 1 John 5:4, 5). The promised reward follows in two parts: first, **I will give authority over the nations . . . .** The Savior quotes Psa 2:9, which addresses the Messianic rule over the nations of the world. The participation of the saints in the power of Christ's throne is affirmed in the apocalyptic vision of Dan 7:27: "Then the sovereignty, power and greatness of the kingdoms under the whole heaven will be handed over to the saints, the people of the Most High." The theme is reiterated in Rev 5:10 and 20:4, 6. It is also found on the lips of Jesus in Matt 19:28 and from the pen of Paul in 1 Cor 6:2, 3. **27.** Christ's use of Psa 2:9 in Rev 2:27 implies that the authority ascribed to him in the Psalm is, as stated in Daniel, given also to the victorious saints. To **rule with an iron scepter** denotes absolute authority to enforce the law, such as must be ascribed to Christ and to those who rule with him. Also implied is a condition where there is a plurality of nations and where moral perfection has not yet been realized. The promise belongs to the millennial age following "the end" and the Second Advent mentioned in verses 25 and 26 (cf. our notes on Rev 20:1-6).[32]

28. The second reward promised to the overcomer is that Christ **will also give him the morning star.** The "morning star" is identified in 22:16 by Jesus, himself, where he says," I am the Root and the Offspring of David, and the bright Morning Star."[33] The Scriptural use of the figure is anticipated by Balaam's prophecy in Num 24:17, "A star will come out of Jacob; a scepter will rise out of Israel." In antiquity the power of the throne was commonly symbolized by heavenly bodies. In pagan thought these were also identified with the gods to whom kings attributed their source of authority. Such symbolism is common in the Bible and abounds in the book of Revelation. Here the Old Testament text, which historically found a measure of fulfillment in David, takes on Messianic significance from the Davidic Covenant which promised a Son who would come to rule perpetually on David's throne (2 Sam 7:12-17). So Jesus identifies

---

[32] The attempt of H. B. Swete and others to find fulfillment of this text in "the Church's influence upon the world" in the present age violates the explicit contextual indication that Christ was addressing the consequences of the Second Advent; Swete, 47.

[33] The morning star is of course in the most literal sense the planet Venus.

Himself as "the root and offspring of David."[34] The saint who is called upon to rule need not fear for Christ will be with him. Christ in his physical presence will personally be seated on his throne as king and His indwelling Spirit will fully empower those who assist Him in that rule (see 1 Cor 6:2). For the Thyatiran who had not adequately disciplined "Jezebel" and her followers, there was a certain irony in this promise of the iron scepter to the overcomers. It stands as a testimony to the grace of God as revealed in the Gospel as accomplished in the person of the messenger, the Lord Jesus Christ. **29.** See above, Notes on 1:7.

To the Church in Sardis

3:1. **"To the angel of the church in Sardis write:**

These are the words of him who holds the seven spirits of God and the seven stars. I know your deeds; you have a reputation of being alive, but you are dead. ²**Wake up! Strengthen what remains and is about to die, for I have not found your deeds complete in the sight of my God.** ³**Remember, therefore, what you have received and heard; obey it, and repent. But if you do not wake up, I will come like a thief, and you will not know at what time I will come to you.**

⁴**Yet you have a few people in Sardis who have not soiled their clothes. They will walk with me, dressed in white, for they are worthy.** ⁵**He who overcomes will, like them, be dressed in white. I will never blot out his name from the book of life, but will acknowledge his name before my Father and his angels.** ⁶**He who has an ear, let him hear what the Spirit says to the churches."**

3:1-6   **To the Church at Sardis**   **Exposition**

Faithful obedience signals life. A reputation for being alive is not enough. Christ calls the church to remember its source of

---

[34]The Essene sect of the Dead Sea Scrolls adduced from Num 24:17 that the Messiah would appear as the end-time warrior to deliver his people (F. F. Bruce, "The Revelation of John," *A New Testament Commentary,* p. 666; cited in G. B. Caird, *A Commentary on the Revelation of St. John the Divine* (New York, Harper & Row, 1966), 395.

power, the Holy Spirit, the Power of God, and to become spiritually alive. A church that only maintains programs dies. Obedience includes outreach, evangelism, and world mission. Sardis enjoyed a reputation for being alive in the sight of men, probably in the ecclesiastical world, but her deeds incomplete in the sight of God. If His people do not wake up, the Lord promises to come in an unexpected moment to bring them into judgment. Imagine yourself as one of the "faithful" few in the Sardis church to whom Christ makes his wonderful commitment, "They will walk with me in white, for they are worthy." Many of us have been in the place where we struggled with too few helpers, so it seemed just to keep the doors open. How wonderful to receive this letter from the glorified Lord Jesus assuring our sagging spirits before his Father and the holy angels.

3:1-6   **To the Church at Sardis**   **Notes**

1a. For **the angel of the church**, see above, the notes on 1:20. **Sardis** was located about thirty miles south-southeast of Thyatira on a ridge at the foot of Mount Timolus in the middle of the plain of the River Hermus. Once the great and wealthy capital city of Lydia under King Croesus, the city at the end of the first century lay in a degenerate state. Artemis, the nature goddess of the Greeks, reappeared as Cybele, the patron deity of Sardis. People attributed to her the power of healing and of raising the dead.[35] Ramsay says that "when the Seven Letters were written, Sardis was a city of the past, which had no future before it."[36] Its greatness did not survive the changes which occurred as empires passed. No one lives there now. All is gone but protruding stones to indicate the grandeur of its past. **1b.** The church at Sardis was dead. Jesus addresses this church as the One **who holds the seven spirits of God**, the One whose agency is the all powerful Holy Spirit.[37] This church must know

---

[35] William M. Ramsay, *The Letters to the Seven Churches of Asia* (New York: A. C. Armstrong, 1909), 354-368.

[36] Ramsay, 368.

[37] On the "seven-spirits" metaphor, see notes on Rev 1:4-5 above.

that Jesus Christ can by His Spirit make a dead church come to life (see above on Rev 1:4b). He also holds **the seven stars**, the messengers of the churches. Here the "messengers" must in some way be intrinsic to the welfare of the churches. This suggests that the messengers are either guardian angels or the administrative leaders of the several parishes (see above on Rev 1:16). **I know your deeds; you have a reputation of being alive.** Good works are sometimes done which are not the product of the Spirit of Christ. They may give the appearance of life, but they are not complete (cf. v. 2b) nor will they sustain a dying church. In spite of them Christ states, **You are dead**; that is, without the regenerating power of the Spirit of Christ.[38] **2. Wake up!** Death here, as nearly always in the Bible, is viewed as "sleep." **Strengthen what remains**: There were a few faithful people (v. 4), but they would die and nothing would be left without a renewing work of the Holy Spirit. **3. Remember** the words of this epistle. **Obey** its message. **Repent** of those sins of neglect and disobedience which have brought death to the church. **I will come like a thief:** Familiar words on the lips of Jesus (cf. Matt 24:43, Luke 12:39). **And you will not know at what time.** The New Testament employs the illustration of the thief to teach the uncertainty of the time of Christ's coming with the need to be watchful, prepared and occupied with serving our Lord.[39] **4. Soiled their clothes:** a metaphor expressing the negative of the "white garment" of righteousness (see further below). **They will walk with me.** "Walking with the Lord" is a common figure denoting obedience to and fellowship with God. **In white:** White means "righteousness," sometimes represented also as "fine linen" (cf. 3:5, 18; 4:4; 6:11; 7:9, 13, 14; 15:6; 19:8, 14). This righteousness is described both as the result of the saints having "washed their robes and made them white in the blood of the Lamb" (7:14, which see) and as "the righteous acts of the saints" (19:18). Righteousness results both from the atoning death of Jesus Christ, who as

---

[38] There is an apparent paradox here. Christ appeals to the will of the "dead" to wake up! The text is best understood to mean that the fruitless majority were indeed unregenerate and therefore spiritually dead. Brightman comments, "Christ calleth them dead, who were void of faith and knowledge of salvation, John 5:25. And the Apostle calleth the lascivious woman, *live-dead*, however she had given her name to Christ; I Tim, 5.6" (32). The exhortation with its appeal to the will implies, nevertheless, that in the mystery of Providence, prevenient grace could enable repentance and genuine, obedient faith (cf. Rev 3:19-21, John 6:37, Eph 5:14).

[39] Not the doctrine of a secret rapture. The meaning of the illustration is clear from each of the other contexts in which it occurs: Matt 24:25, Luke 12:39, 1 Thess 5:2, 4, 2 Pet 3:10, Rev 16:15.

man is the only one wholly righteous, and from personal obedience. By virtue of substitutionary atonement the believer in his imperfect righteousness is reckoned as perfect wholly on the ground of Christ's righteousness (Rom 5:18, 19). The promise that the saints will walk with Jesus in righteousness points to the Age to Come when the saints receive their covenant inheritance. **They are worthy** because they have been reckoned as righteous and have walked in the obedience of faith. **5.** The one who **overcomes** has been "washed in the blood of the Lamb" (7:14; cf. 14:4) and wages a victorious warfare against sin. To such a person Jesus says, **I will never blot out his name from the book of Life.** God's record indicates who will enter into the Age to Come (Exod 32:32f.; Psa 69:28; Isa 4:3; Dan 12:1; Luke 10:20 [cp. Acts 13:48]; Phil 4:3; Rev 13:8, 17:8; 20:12, 15; 21:27). **6. He who has an ear, let him hear:** See above, Notes on 2:7.

To the church at Philadelphia

3:7. "To the angel of the church in Philadelphia write:

These are the words of him who is holy and true, who holds the key of David. What he opens, no one can shut; and what he shuts, no one can open.[40] [8]I know your deeds. See, I have placed before you an open door that no one can shut. I know that you have little strength, yet you have kept my word and not denied my name. [9]I will make those who are of the synagogue of Satan, who claim to be Jews though they are not but are liars—I will make them come and fall down at your feet and acknowledge that I have loved you. [10]Since you have kept my command to endure patiently, I will also keep you from the hour of trial that is going to come upon the whole world to test those who live on the earth.

[11]I am coming soon. Hold on to what you have so that no one will take your crown. [12]Him who overcomes I will make a pillar in the temple of my God. Never again will he leave it. I will write on him the name of my God and the name of the city of my God, the new Jerusalem, which is coming down out of heaven from my God; and I will also write on him my new name. [13]He who has an ear, let him hear what the Spirit says to the churches.

---

[40]Isa 22:22.

| 3:7-13 | To the Church at Philadelphia | Exposition |

Christ addresses the church of Philadelphia as the One whose words are from "him who is holy and true" (7a). "Who is like you—majestic in holiness?" (Exod 15:11) "There is no one holy like the LORD" (1 Sam 2:2). "He who is holy and true" is a clear affirmation of the Deity of Jesus. The absolute holiness of Christ indicates that He is set apart as God from all imperfection and moral evil. As holy, His authority is unblemished and His promises sure.

Jesus walks among the churches as one who holds the keys to David's theocratic kingdom. The concept is covenant-oriented. Jesus is the true Davidic king and the fulfillment of the theocratic kingship by which God rules over the hearts of believing men. He absolutely controls their destiny regardless of Satan's opposing forces which have invaded the evil world, even at times Christ's church, as at Philadelphia.

Because Christ holds the keys, the same keys He delegated to Peter and the Apostles (Matt 16:19; 18:18), He has opened the door of opportunity to His church to be Christ's servant and messenger to the world. As Pergamum is the gateway to Phrygia, so every local church placed by Christ has neighboring peoples who need the Gospel. Philadelphia was not a strong church but, in the face of opposition and with the enablement of the Spirit of God, they had remained faithful. They had not denied their Lord. There is no higher calling of the church of Jesus Christ in any circumstance than to obey the Word of God. With obedience there is ultimate victory and vindication.

Christ is coming soon! Though the original readers in the Philadelphian church didn't live to witness that event, their next moment of consciousness beyond death will witness Christ in his glory and introduce them into that blessed age to come (1 Cor 15:18-23; 1 Thess 4:15). Then they with us will be made perfect (Heb 11:39), and we will be crowned with life and immortality, for "our citizenship is in heaven. And we eagerly await a Savior from there, the Lord Jesus Christ" (Phil 3:20).

3:7-13   To the Church at Philadelphia   Notes

7a. For **the angel of the church**, see the notes on 1:20. **Philadelphia** was about thirty miles east of Sardis on the ancient Roman Post Road and on the main route from western harbors to Phrygia and many points east. It was founded in the mid-second century, B.C., as a border town to the regions of Phrygia and Lydia in order to promote the Greek language and culture in those provinces. It was a missionary city for the Greek way of life" "the city of "the open door" (cf. v. 8), "the keeper of the gateway to the [Phrygian] plateau" (Ramsay 405). Beginning in A.D. 17, Philadelphia was terrorized by earthquakes. At first, the city was destroyed, then numerous aftershocks for many years frightened the people so that many took up residence outside the city. The church at Philadelphia maintained a strong witness for many years with the result that the city resisted the Turkish conquests until the mid-fourteenth century. More than forty years ago, William Barclay wrote, "To this day there is a Christian bishop and a thousand Christians in Philadelphia" (1.160). The city is now called Alashehir.

    7b. The words of him who is holy and true: This description of character is peculiar to the Deity (cp. 6:10). The "Holy One" meaning God the Father is found in Isa 40:25; Hab 3:3; Mark 1:24, 4:34; John 6:69 (NASB, NIV); 1 John 2:20. "Holy and true" (Gk: ʽο ʽάγιος ʽο ʼαληθινός, *ho hágios ho ʽaléthinós*) is best understood as an expansion on "the Holy One," a Messianic title in the New Testament as in Mark 1:24; Luke 4:34; John 6:69; 1 John 2:20; Acts 2:27 (cf. Psa 16:10); 3:14; and 4:27, 30. The expression probably means "the true Messiah" (cp. "the true light," John 1:9, "the true God" John 5:20; Beckwith, 478-450). Christ's message to the Philadelphians is the most positive of the seven letters. He writes to assure the faithful people of God that the rewards promised are certain to occur. Christ **holds the key of David.** As Messiah, the Son of David holds the key to the royal house, the Messianic Kingdom (cf. 2 Sam 7:11-16; Isa 22:22; Matt 16:19). The key symbolizes the King's authority to rule (cf. 1:18). **8. I know your deeds.** What follows indicates that the judgment is positive. **I have placed before you an**

open door. As the city of Philadelphia had been a missionary to carry the Greek culture to the plateau region to the East, so the church was to carry the Gospel through that door of opportunity (cp. Acts 14:27; 1 Cor 16:9; 2 Cor 2:12; Col 4:3).[41] **I know that you have little strength.** This enlarges on the introductory statement, "I know your deeds." The church at that time was not large nor of great influence. **You have kept my word and have not denied my name.** This highest complement recognizes their loving obedience to their Master Teacher. Moreover, their refusal to deny Jesus suggests that they had suffered persecution from the Jewish population (see below). **9. Those who are of the synagogue of Satan** appear to be unbelieving Jews. In view here is the concept of the two kingdoms, the Kingdom of Christ and the Kingdom of Satan. Those Jews who rejected Jesus as their Messiah and perpetuated their own synagogue in Philadelphia in opposition to the Christian assemblies are in their unbelief dominated by Satan. They **claim to be Jews though they are not.** The true Jews are those who receive Jesus, the true Jewish Messiah. Jesus promised, **I will make them come and fall down at your feet.** Jesus' words here are from Isa 60:14: "The sons of your oppressors will come bowing before you; all who despise you will bow down at your feet and will call you the City of the LORD, Zion of the Holy One of Israel." In this text Jerusalem is personified in the future era of everlasting peace when the Messiah reigns over the nations of the world (cp. Isa 2:1-5; 45:14; 49:23).[42] They will **acknowledge that I have loved you.** The words recall

---

[41]The idea suggested by Bousset, Beckwith, and others that the door represents entrance into the eschatological Messianic kingdom is less likely to be correct for the following reasons: the eschatological idea does not as well fit the context, which introduces the immediate struggle against the "synagogue of Satan," a discouraging situation which the church faced; (2) the pattern of the other letters suggests that the contemporary situation and the immediate future is addressed; (3) Jesus' teaching in the Gospels emphasizes entrance into the Kingdom in this Age (Matt 5:3-10, John 6:47, 51, 54, 10:7-9). There is nevertheless an inherent ambiguity in the Greek text which prohibits certainty in the matter (cf. Charles, 1.86, Beckwith, 480).

[42]One should not conclude with Barclay that Jesus intended by his use of Isa 60:14 that "the Jewish nation, as a nation, had lost its place in the plan of God," or "that all the promises that had been made to Israel had been inherited by the Church" (1.165), for in the very context from which Jesus quoted, the prophet said that "herds of camels will cover your ['Jerusalem's] land," and that "Foreigners will rebuild your walls, and their kings will serve you" (6, 10). The larger prophecy obviously pertains to the restoration of the Covenant nation in the covenant land as promised to Abraham, and as reiterated by many subsequent prophets (cf. Jeremiah 31-33; Ezekiel 36, 37; Joel 3; Amos 9:11-15; Micah 4-5, 7:8-20; Zeph 3:8-20; Zech 8:1-23; 9:9-10:12). Unbelieving Jews, with unbelieving Gentiles, will in that day bow down, but in the end, the nation Israel will have received a "new heart and ... a new spirit" after it has been gathered

our Lord's lament shortly before his crucifixion, "O Jerusalem, Jerusalem, you who kill the prophets and stone those sent to you, how often I have longed to gather your children together, as a hen gathers her chicks under her wings, but you were not willing" (Matt 23:37). **10.** Jesus' **command to endure patiently** is found in Matt 24:13. The believers are to persevere through tribulation.[43] **The hour of trial that is going to come upon the whole world:** This refers to the time of the "great tribulation" of 7:14, before which the 144,000 are sealed. The Last Days time of trial is mentioned frequently in the Scriptures: Dan 12:2 ("Jacob's trouble"); Zech 11:15-17; Matt 24:15-28; Mark 13:14-20; Luke 21:20-24; 2 Thess 2:3-12; 1 John 2:18; Rev 11:7-10; 13:5-18; 17:3-14. To these passages traditionally understood of the Antichrist, there probably should be added the associated prophecies of wars, calamities, and persecutions of the seal, trumpet, and bowl prophecies of Rev 6:1-16; 8:6-21; 11:15; 16:1-21, as well as the circumstances of the final battle of Armageddon predicted in Ezek 38, 39; Rev 19:11-18, and perhaps other Old Testament prophecies. An extended period and many events are implied by the these passages. Our Lord said in his prophecy of Matthew 24 that there would be wars, famines, and earthquakes which would be only the "beginning of birth pains" (vv. 4-8), "Then you will be handed over to be persecuted and put to death, and you will be hated by all nations because of me. . . . and many false prophets will appear and deceive many people . . . but he who stands firm to the end will be saved" (9, 11, 13). **Those who live on the earth**, in the context of what precedes and the above-mentioned prophetic passages, probably refers to believers who were to be tested.

"from all the countries" and brought back into its own land (Ezek 36:24-28). "They will live in the land I gave to my servant Jacob, the land where your fathers lived, they and their children and their children's children will live there forever, and David my servant will be their prince forever" (37:25). These are promises to the nation Israel which because they are unconditional and because they involve the physical and political dimensions of the nation in the inheritance land of Canaan can hardly be fulfilled by the Church universally in the world (cp. Rom 11:25-36).

[43]Leading versions illustrate two disparate translations of the Greek τὸν λόγον τῆς ὑπομονῆς: 1. "the word of my patience," KJV; "the word of my patient endurance," RSV; "my command to endure patiently," NIV; "my command to stand firm," (REB). 2. "the word of my perseverance," *NASB*; "my command to endure," TEV. Commentators likewise are divided: trans. 1: Charles, Ladd, Mounce (102 n. 22); trans. 2: Kiddle, Bruce. The Greek syntax is somewhat ambiguous but the predominant use of ὑπομονης is active rather than subjective (BAGD, 846). The *NASB* and the TEV should be preferred.

11. I am coming soon. Cf. 2:16, 22:7, 12, 20. Each of the seven letters ends with a reminder of circumstances which will accompany the Second Advent, a reminder of the emphatic and practical role given to this doctrine in the Scriptures. **Hold on to what you have:** Perseverance is a mark of genuineness in Christian experience. Jesus, in the Parable of the Soils, states that "the good soil" "stands for those with a noble and good heart, who hear the word, retain it, and by persevering produce a crop" (Luke 8:15). He nevertheless teaches here the necessity of personal commitment to maintain obedience and personal faith. The believers in Philadelphia have "little strength," yet they have reputation for faithful conduct (cf. v. 8). They must continue in order to obtain their promised **crown**. The "crown" (Gk. στέφανος, *stéphanos*) is that laurel wreath given to the winning contestants in the Greek games. Mounce points out that the crown "metaphor would be especially appropriate in this letter in that Philadelphia was known for its games and festivals" (104). In Scripture the word when so used refers not to a real crown but to the rewards promised to faithful believers: 1 Cor 9:25, "a crown that will last forever"; 1 Thess 2:19, Paul's "crown" will be his Thessalonian converts with him at the Judgment; 2 Tim 4:8, "crown of righteousness"; James 1:12; Rev 2:10, "crown of life"; 1 Pet 5:4, "crown of glory."[44] **11. For him who overcomes**, see notes on 2:26. The **pillar in the temple** draws figuratively from the biblical temple architecture. **I will write on him the name of my God and the name of the city of my God.** There were two named bronze pillars, "Jachin" and "Boaz," which were placed at the entrance in Solomon's temple (1 Kgs 7:13-22). The naming of pillars was common in antiquity as a means of memorializing donors or other persons of note. "Pillar" is a common symbol for a person of strength and stability (Gal 2:9; cp. 1 Tim 3:15). The figure of putting the name of God upon his people is found in the institution of the Aaronic benediction by means of which Aaron and his sons "will put my name on the Israelites, and I will bless them" (Num 6:27). In the Revelation, the 144,000 are sealed (7:3) with the name of the Lamb and the name of his Father on their foreheads

---

[44]Perhaps "crown of righteousness" may seem more naturally to mean a reward for righteous conduct or the righteous state by which the believer will be judged, that is, the imputed righteousness of Christ in which the believer stands by grace through faith (Rom 3:21-27). The alternate interpretation that righteousness is the reward in view is nevertheless consistently supported in Scripture where comparable language appears (in addition to the texts quoted above, see Psa 8:5 and 103:4). Righteousness is a gift to be realized fully in the experiential sense at the Second Advent (Gal 5:5; cp. Rom 5:19).

(14:1; cf. 22:4). **The city of God** here stands for the covenant concept of the Commonwealth of Israel in which the People of God hold their heavenly citizenship (Gal 4:23; Phil 3:20; Heb 11:10; 12:22). **Never again will he leave it:** This promise emphasizes the everlasting nature of the kingdom of God. **I will also write on him my new name** (cp. 2:17). Philadelphia had in its history several times been newly named. In his second Advent, Christ "has a name written on him that no one but he himself knows" (19:12). The name as written on the believer symbolizes that special relationship which by God's grace exists between the Savior and those who find his favor. **12.** See notes on 2:7.

The Church at Laodicea

3:14. **"To the angel of the church in Laodicea write:**

These are the words of the Amen, the faithful and true witness, the ruler of God"s creation. [15]**I know your deeds, that you are neither cold nor hot. I wish you were either one or the other!** [16]**So, because you are lukewarm—neither hot nor cold—I am about to spit you out of my mouth.** [17]**You say, 'I am rich; I have acquired wealth and do not need a thing.' But you do not realize that you are wretched, pitiful, poor, blind and naked.** [18]**I counsel you to buy from me gold refined in the fire, so you can become rich; and white clothes to wear, so you can cover your shameful nakedness; and salve to put on your eyes, so you can see.**

[45][19]**Those whom I love I rebuke and discipline. So be earnest, and repent.** [20]**Here I am! I stand at the door and knock. If anyone hears my voice and opens the door, I will come in and eat with him, and he with me.**

[21]**To him who overcomes, I will give the right to sit with me on my throne, just as I overcame and sat down with my Father on his throne.** [22]**He who has an ear, let him hear what the Spirit says to the churches."**

3:14-22   **To the Church at Laodocea**   **Exposition**

Jesus addresses the reader as "faithful and true," both obedient and genuine as a witness to the Faith and to ultimate realities. Not only is his Word altogether reliable, but he himself speaks with the authority of the Sovereign ruler and judge of all creation. The professed believer had best take warning and respond with humble repentance and a full commitment to righteousness. Jesus knows our deeds, both the collective actions of the local church and the personal deeds of every individual. To be "neither hot nor cold" is to be ineffectual, without practical value—mere nominalism (see notes, below). Many Christians, like the Laodiceans, are rich in their self-estimation and believe they "have need of nothing," unaware of their abject spiritual destitution. Yet as Jesus said, they are "wretched, pitiful, poor, blind and naked." The Laodiceans had material wealth from their garment industry and the manufacture of medicines, yet desperately needed the true riches, the garments of righteousness, and Spirit anointed vision.

Nevertheless the rebuke and discipline of our Lord is his expression of love. One should be moved to repentance by the knowledge that he stands at the heart's door and longs to come in, not as judge, but to enjoy fellowship with a repentant sinner.

The marvelous grace of our sovereign Lord is clear in the promise of future blessedness and meaningful service in the Age to Come.

3:14-22   **To the Church at Laodicea**   **Notes**

14a. For **angel of the church**, see notes on 2:1. **Laodicea** was located in the Lycus River valley on the primary ascent to the Phrygian plateau, central Anatolia, and points East. It lay at the crossroads of the two main highways, the other leading from the provincial capital, Pergamum, across the junction of the Meander-Lycus valleys southward to the seaport,

Attaleia, on the Mediterranean coast. Its location made it an important center of commerce, banking, and financial exchange (Cic. *Ep. ad Fam.*, 3.5), in Roman times the richest city of Asia. It was surrounded by fertile land where sheep with a distinctive black wool were raised for its garment industry (Str., 12.578). Also, medicinal powders and ointments were processed and marketed, as well as many other products. Laodicea grew up around the crossroads without a local water supply so that water had to be piped in from hot springs six miles to the north, arriving lukewarm. About ten miles up the road to the east of Laches lay the city of Colossae, to which the Apostle Paul wrote his epistle. About six miles north, on the opposite side of the valley from Laches, lay the city of Hierapolis, famous for its hot springs and health spas (cf. Col 4:13).

14b. The words of the Amen, the faithful and true witness are uttered with absolute authority. Isaiah 65:16 states that "Whoever invokes a blessing in the land will do so by the God of truth" (Heb. בֵּאלֹהֵי אָמֵן, *bē'lōhê 'āmēn*, "by the God of the amen"). Jesus in taking this name identifies himself with the God who is absolute Truth. As such he is "the faithful and true witness," a statement which explains the Hebrew allusion for the Greek reader. Moreover, he is **the ruler of God's creation** (cf. Col 1:15-18).[46] The Gk. 'αρχή, *'archē,* here means "first cause," thus the one who controls or exercises authority. The words give solemn authority to the pronouncements which follow. This letter is the only one of the seven that has no word of commendation, only warning and judgment. **15. The** Laodiceans were spiritually **neither cold nor hot. 16. Because you are . . . neither hot nor cold—I am about to spit you out.** The analogy of hot and cold is best understood of the medicinal hot springs at Hieropolis and the cold, pure water of Colossae. The point is not that the "spiritual temperature" of the Laodiceans is medium. Though they excelled in the material arts and commerce, spiritually they lacked any utilitarian value.

---

[46]The Greek,'αρχή *'archḗ,* may in other contexts mean either (1) "beginning" = "first-created," (2) "first cause," "source," or (3) "ruler." The apparent reflection of the language of Prov 8:22 should lead the reader to definition two. As the Divine Wisdom is reflected in God's creation, so Christ is also the source. In context, however, our text points not to the elements of design as does Proverbs, but to Christ's authority to make ultimate pronouncements to his church. To adopt definition 1 above would not only do injustice to the source text but would put the text in conflict the New Testament parallels referenced above.

To the church in Laodocea, 3:14-22

Their works were barren.[47] **17. You do not realize that you are wretched, pitiful, poor, blind and naked.** They had a reputation for their banking industry, their ointments and eye-salves, and their garment industry, but before God they were destitute beggars. **18.** The church that became wealthy in the money market is counseled to buy from Christ **gold refined in the fire.** The church that became rich through the merchandising of fine clothes is instructed to buy **white clothes to wear.** Both symbols speak of the need for righteousness, first reckoned to the believer, then realized through obedience. They are told to buy **salve** to put on their eyes to enable them to see. This speaks of that perception which comes only through the enlightenment of the Spirit (cf. 1 Cor 2:6-16; 2 Cor 4:4, 6). Their marketing of such medications had not given them spiritual discernment. **19. Those whom I love I rebuke and discipline.** This text reflects Prov 3:11-12, where, unlike the LXX which translates the Hebrew with the Greek verb, ἀγαπάω, *agapáō*, we find here the verb, φιλέω, *philéō*. Ἀγαπάω is more cognitive; φιλέω is more emotive. Φιλέω expresses the affection which our Lord feels toward wayward members of his church. (Charles, 1.99) **So be earnest, and repent.** In spite of the severity of the Lord's judgments stated earlier, there is an unmistakable genuineness in his call to repentance. **20. Here I am! I stand at the door and knock.** Our Lord is seen standing and ready, though outside. The unfruitful believer and the fruitless church must recognize that Jesus stands outside the door (cf. John 15:1-8) waiting and knocking to come in. **Anyone** indicates that the invitation is to individuals. The church must be restored through its individual members. To **hear** the **voice** of Jesus is to open the heart and to give over the will. As his Parable of the Soils teaches, one must take heed how one hears (Matt 13:1-23). The seed planted in that good soil bears fruit. **I will come in and eat with him, and he with me.** Eating together is the Oriental symbol of hospitality. Moreover, taking food to the ancient mind suggested the taking to heart of spiritual truth (cf. John 4:31-34). To enjoy this intimate relationship with the Son of God is the highest of honors available to man. Such fellowship implies a common commitment to holiness through obedience (cf. John 14:15-21).

---

[47]"The church in Laodicea 'was providing neither refreshment for the spiritually weary, nor healing for the spiritually sick . . . '" Mounce, 109, quoting Rudwick and Green, "The Laodicean Lukewarmness," *ET* 69 (1957-58), 176-178.

21. The one **who overcomes** obeys the Word of the Lord "to the end" (cf. 2:26). To such persons, Jesus said, **I will give the right to sit with me on my throne.** This is not an honorary position. The saints will actively participate in the judgment process (cf. Matt 19:28; Luke 22:30; 1 Cor 6:2; 2 Tim 2:12; Rev 20:4). Consistent interpretation will find the eschatological context of this and the related texts above-referenced in the millennial age of Rev 20:4. (see the notes on that text). **22.** On **He who has an ear**, see our notes on 2:7. Observe also that the singular number implies that this is given to the individual listener, for obedience must begin here. **To the churches** indicates that the message of this letter, as well as that of the previous six, where this expression is also found, is not only for the church addressed, but is applicable, to the members of all the churches.

Chapter Three

A DRAMA IN HEAVEN
Rev 4:1-5:14

Introduction

Chapters four and five introduce the series of predictions which follow throughout the rest of the Revelation. In appropriate imagery, chapter four presents the holy and sovereign God, the God of history, surrounded by the worship of his created heavenly beings. In chapter five, the Messiah Jesus, in the figure of the Lamb, is identified as the Redeemer. For this reason, he is the only one who is worthy to break the seals of the scroll and to establish the course of events leading from the time of writing up to the very end. This introduction closes proleptically with a climatic celebration of the exalted station of the Lamb as all creation sings his praise at the coming victory over the forces of evil—the grandeur of God the Son, whose Messianic reign is to be established for the Age to Come.

The setting is cast in the imagery of the heavenly sanctuary. In 1:12-16 Christ is seen in the Holy Place. Here, we have in apocalyptic description the inner sanctuary, the Most Holy Place—the very throne room of God.

The Throne in Heaven

4:1. **After this I looked, and there before me was a door standing open in heaven. And the voice I had first heard speaking to me like a trumpet said, "Come up here, and I will show you what must take place after this."** ²**At once I was in the Spirit, and there before me was a throne in heaven with someone sitting on it.** ³**And the one who sat there had the appearance of jasper and carnelian. A rainbow, resembling an emerald, encircled the throne.** ⁴**Surrounding the** throne were twenty-four other thrones, and seated on them were twenty-four elders. They were dressed in white and had crowns of gold on their heads. ⁵From the throne came flashes of lightning, rumblings and peals of thunder. Before the throne, seven lamps were blazing. These are the seven spirits of God. ⁶ᵃAlso before the throne there was what looked like a sea of glass, clear as crystal.

4:1-6a   The Revelation of Almighty God   Exposition

    Like the great prophets Isaiah and Ezekiel, our Lord began his prophecy with a revelation of the majesty and holiness of God (Isa 6:1-5, Ezekiel 1). To understand and act upon the subsequent forecast of events one must see God as both sovereign and holy. He has infinite power to rule over his creatures and the unique and unblemished purity that is inherent in his character and in his law. In this description of God, the stage is set for the scene of worship which follows.

    The manner in which his creatures in heaven and on earth must experience such awesome revelation of their Creator is suggested in the text which follows (vv. 6b-11).

4:1-6a   The Revelation of Almighty God   Notes

1. After this, I looked. This statement of the Seer (Gk., μετὰ ταῦτα εἶδον, *metà taûta eîdon*) occurs frequently in the Revelation as well as in extrabiblical apocalyptic literature.[1] The words convey the fact that the author was in the process of receiving a divine revelation while in a supernaturally gifted ecstatic state. The expression ordinarily (though not always) is introduced at an important transition point, indicating progress in the succession of events. To the above NIV translation the go Greek adds καὶ ἰδοὺ, *kaì idoú*, "and behold" to give further dramatic effect (KJV, NASV; RSV, "and lo!"). **There before me was a door standing open in heaven.** Again, the idea of an open door or gate in heaven through

---

[1]Cf. Rev 7:1, 9, 15:5, 18:1; 1 Enoch 85.1, 89.19,30, 54, 72, 90.2, et al. Cp. Rev 19:1, μετὰ ταῦτα ἤκουσα, "after this I heard." Μετὰ ταῦτα, "After this," occurs also in Rev 1:19, 4:2, 9:12, 11:11, 20:3.

which the seer is taken to receive revelation is common in apocalyptic literature (cp. 1 Enoch 14.15; T. Levi 5.1; 3 Macc. 6.18). An open door extends an invitation to enter—in this case, to view a marvelous revelation. The transition from earth to heaven also gives emphasis to the change in the content of the revelation from the earthly scene of the seven churches to the heavenly scene in chapters 4 and 5.[2] **The voice** John had heard speaking to him **like a trumpet** was the voice of Jesus (cf. 1:10). **"Come up here, and I will show you."** On the theory that this suggests the rapture and that the Revelation in the chapters following speaks of events subsequent to Christ's return for his Church, see the notes on 1:10 (with footnote 9). **What must take place after this**: This must be understood in relation to 1:19, "Write, therefore . . . what is now and what will take place later." Chapters two and three, addressed to contemporary (first century) churches, reflect the standpoint of the time of writing, "what is now." At 4:1, we arrive at the place in the book where the prophecy addresses "what will take place later," that is predictions of events future to the time of writing.[3] **2. At once** (NASV, "Immediately") is best understood as connecting what precedes with *the action* that follows. **I was in the Spirit.** The expression in apocalyptic writings denotes a condition in which the writer is conscous of being directed by the Holy Spirit. The text need not imply that this state begins or is heightened at this point. It simply reminds the reader of what had been stated earlier in 1:10 but had not been in focus during the progress of chapters two and three.[4] **A**

---

[2]"In heaven" appears here in the singular (ἐν οὐρανός), as also in 56 other occurrences in the Revelation. Only in 12:12 the plural, "heavens," appears, a quotation of a plural in Isa 44:23. As the plural form is the common idiom, such consistent use of the singular may suggest intent to give a generic or qualitative emphasis to the expression.

[3]See our explanation of the literary structure of the Revelation in the Introduction, "The Vision as a Whole." The importance of this chronological indicator is far reaching, as the reader is hereby led to expect that the subject matter which follows this point in the book will pertain to the times future from the standpoint of the author.

[4]For a discussion of several opinions, see R. H. Charles, *A Critical and Exegetical Commentary on the Revelation of St. John* (International critical commentary; Edinburgh: T. & T. Clark, 1920), 1.109-110; Isben T. Beckwith, *The Apocalypse of John* (1919; Limited eds. library; Baker, 1967), 495-96; George E. Ladd, *Commentary on the Revelation of John* (Grand Rapids: Eerdmans, 1972), 71. The idea that John had returned to normal consciousness while writing chapters two and three with the ecstatic state beginning again at this point is contrary to the structure of chapters 1-3. Christ's message to the churches in these chapters is a continuation of 1:19-20. Their reception by John presupposes the continuation of his "being in the Spirit." Charles' theory that John brought together material from several sources or that he combined records of several visions received on separate occasions, also perpetuated by some modern authors, violates the integrity of the historical revelation as the author reported its inception in chapter one. Swete's idea that "the state of spiritual exaltation" returned in

throne in heaven with someone sitting on it introduces in the aura of mystery the heavenly sanctuary of God. What follows is a magnificent description in apocalyptic language of the divine Presence in which his character is exalted both by the descriptive symbols and by the heavenly beings wholly absorbed with worship. **3. The one who sat there had the appearance of jasper and carnelian.** The description avoids the use of anthropomorphic language found in such passages as Ezek 1:26, 27; 2:9; Dan 10:5, 16. As Charles states, "No form is visible; only lights of various hues flashing through the cloud that encircles the throne" (1.113). We know from Rev 22:11 that this jasper of ancient times was "clear as crystal." It seems natural to see this stone as suggesting the brilliance of the Shekinah glory and the holiness of the Almighty. "Carnelian" (Gk., σαρδίον, *sardion*), a semiprecious stone named after the city of Sardis, is blood-red in color. One should see in the red carnelian the blood of the Covenant and the cognate theme of redemption. **A rainbow, resembling an emerald, encircled the throne.** Cp. Gen 9:12-17; Isa 54:9, 10; Ezek 1:28. In this beautiful representation of the Shekinah, one can visualize an iridescent green and be reminded of God's character as life-giver and his covenant remembered also by Isaiah in that prophet's glorious anticipation of the future restoration of the people of God:

> "Though the mountains be shaken
> and the hills be removed,
> yet my unfailing love for you will not be shaken
> nor my covenant of peace be removed,
> says the LORD, who has compassion on you" (54:10).

R. H. Charles points out that the throne of God is mentioned in each chapter of the Revelation except 2, 9, 10, and 15. The throne is implied, however, in 15:2 with its reference to the "sea of glass" (Charles, 1.111). God's sovereignty is central to the theme of the book. **4. Surrounding the throne were twenty-four other thrones** with **twenty-four elders.** The identity of the twenty-four elders has been subject to several interpretations: (1) The heads of the twelve tribes and the twelve Apostles, representing the ideal Church of the Old and New Covenants (Victorinus). (2) The heads of the tribes and the Apostles representing the raptured Church after the parousia and prior to the tribulation (Walvoord).[5] (3) The idealized heads of the twenty-four courses of the Levitical priesthood (1 Chr 24:1-19), representing God's Covenant people. (4) An order of

---

greater force is not implied by the text (Henry B. Swete, *The Apocalypse of St. John* (Grand Rapids: Eerdmans, pref. 1906), 66.

[5]This view is uniquely the understanding of the pre-tribulation rapture, futurist school.

angelic beings. The interpretation of the elders as symbolizing the Church, though attractive to many Christian minds, is dependent on the text of the King James version and does not bear up well under careful scholarship.[6] Even in the King James version, the elders are distinguished from the redeemed in 14:3 and 19:4. In the text accepted by the more modern translations, the elders are even more clearly differentiated from the redeemed. The elders say in 5:10, "You have made *them* [the redeemed] to be a kingdom of priests . . . and *they* will reign on the earth" (NIV; emphasis mine). In 14:3, the 144,000, "the firstfruits to God and to the Lamb," "sing a new song before the . . . elders." The number twenty-four does not appear elsewhere in the Scriptures as a symbol. The twenty-four elders are best understood according to interpretation (4) as angelic beings who sit as subordinate rulers enthroned and crowned in the court of heaven.[7] As angelic beings, they nevertheless stand before God as messengers who have representative status and authority connected with the Covenant People of God (see on 5:8, below). The number will then be especially appropriate as a typological reflex of the twenty-four courses of the Israelite priesthood.[8] **They were dressed in white**, indicating their righteous standing before God. They **had crowns of gold on their heads.** In the court of heaven only the twenty-four elders wear crowns. "For the

---

[6]The idea that the twenty-four elders represent the glorified saints in heaven, either during the intermediate state or in the future age is untenable for the reason just cited. The context here and in subsequent passages in the Revelation (4:10, 5:8, 11:16, 14:3, 19:4) suggests that they are a standard element in the heavenly court. The idea that the Apostles are represented as included at this time prior to the beginning of the events predicted is hardly agreeable to the fact that the Apostle is in all probability the living recipient and human author of the Revelation (see above, pp. 2-6).

[7]Walvoord's argument that the use of the laurel wreath crown (Gk., στέφανος) instead of the diadem implies that the wearers are victors and therefore redeemed saints rather than angels appears to overlook the fact that the diadem crown did not come into prominence in the Roman Empire until Diocletian in the late fourth century, A.D.; John F. Walvoord, *The Revelation of Jesus Christ* (Chicago: Moody Press, 1966), 106. The laurel wreath crown, though worn by the victors in athletic and military contests, was the standard crown of the Roman rulers in the first century. It was worn also by the kings of Macedonia and Greece.

[8]One may also see in the twelve heads of the twelve tribes when joined with the twelve Apostles as heads of the Messianic Assembly a reflex of the number twenty-four. On the question of the elders, see Beckwith, 498-499, G. R. Beasley-Murray, *The Book of Revelation*, Revised ed. (NCB; Grand Rapids: Eerdmans, 1978), 113-114, R. H. Charles, 1.129-130, and Swete, 68-69. The twenty-four member court has earthly parallels also in the Small Sanhedrin of ancient Judaism and in the Qumran sect of the Dead Sea Scrolls. See Joseph M. Baumgarten, "The Duodecimal Courts of Qumran, Revelation, and the Sanhedrin," *JBL* 95 (1976), 59-78. Beckwith's statement (p. 498) that "the number twenty-four has no parallel in Jewish literature" cannot now be sustained.

Lord takes delight in his people; he crowns the humble with salvation" (Psa 149:4). The high standing and authority given to the angelic beings who represent the People of God is indicated here, even as elsewhere the special status of God's people is indicated in Matt 19:28; Luke 22:30; 1 Cor 6:2; 2 Tim 2:12; and Rev 20:4. **5. Flashes of lightning, rumblings and peals of thunder** coming from the throne suggest something of God's awful power threatening retribution to those who offend his holiness. The language may be intended to remind the reader of the revelation to Moses at Sinai (Exod 19:16-19; cp. Psa 18:13-15; Ezek 1:13). The **seven lamps blazing . . . are the seven spirits of God.** See the notes on 1:46. **6a. Before the throne there was what looked like a sea of glass, clear as crystal.** Cp. 15:2. The appearance was not that of ordinary glass, which tended in antiquity to be only translucent, but transparent glass most pure and highly reflective of the Shekinah.[9]

The Throne in Heaven (cont'd)

7:6b. In the center, around the throne, were four living creatures, and they were covered with eyes, in front and in back. [7]The first living creature was like a lion, the second was like an ox, the third had a face like a man, the fourth was like a flying eagle. [8]Each of the four living creatures had six wings and was covered with eyes all around, even under his wings. Day and night they never stop saying:

> **"Holy, holy, holy is the Lord God Almighty,**
> **who was, and is, and is to come."**

[9]Whenever the living creatures give glory, honor and thanks to him who sits on the throne and who lives for ever and ever, [10]the twenty-four elders fall down before him who sits on the throne, and worship him who lives for ever and ever. They lay their crowns before the throne and say:

> **[11]"You are worthy, our Lord and God,**
> **to receive glory and honor and power,**
> **for you created all things,**
> **and by your will they were created**
> **and have their being."**

---

[9]For a summary of various interpretations, see Simon Kistemaker, *Exposition of the Book of Revelation* (New Testament Commentary; Grand Rapids: Baker, 2001), 189. Charles' suggestion that the "sea of glass" derived from Gen 1:7, the "waters above the earth" (cf. Psa 148:4; 2 Enoch 3.2; T. Levi 2.7) is unfounded (1.117).

Chapter Three	*The throne in heaven, 4:6b-11*	

4:6b-11 **The Worship of Almighty God** **Exposition**

Beyond the fact of the existence of the great God-King revealed in verses 4-6a, we have in these verses which follow an apocalyptic revelation of his relation to his created world and the appropriate response of his creatures to the King's rule.

In the four "living creatures" we have angelic beings who, as their description tells us, represent and are a counterpart to the entire roster of the animal and human creation in the natural world. Always in heaven these unfallen angels affirm god's holiness and sovereign power. The King controls destiny. He was, He is, and He is to be the Holy One. He was, He is, and He is to be the Almighty.

In "the twenty-four elders" we have angelic beings in heaven who represent the People of God on earth—the elect who in Christ will inherit all things, the elect for whose instruction and encouragement the message of the Revelation is given. These who represent God's chosen ones are crowned, enthroned, and stationed around the throne of God in intimate communion with the Sovereign Creator. Though distinguished by their privileged relationship to their Sovereign, they acknowledge their unworthiness and servanthood by casting their crowns at his feet and by their doxology of praise.

All who truly know God join this heavenly chorus, not only with words of praise but with obedience and holiness before the Judge of all the earth.

4:6b-11 **The Worship of Almighty God** **Notes**

6b. In the center, around the throne, were four **living creatures.** These "living creatures" (Gk.: ζῷα,, *zōa*, "living ones") appear as regular participants in the Apocalyptic court. See 5:6, 8, 14, 6:1, 3, 5, 6, 7, 7:11, 14:3, 15:7, 19:4. Probably the reader should equate them with the seraphim (literally, "the burning ones") of Isa 6:2 and the cherubim of Ezek 1:5-24, 8:4-10:22. Ezekiel specifically identifies the Living Creatures as cherubim (Ezek 10:20). In the Bible cherubim function as an order of spirit beings. In the various texts they have different characteristics and perform a variety of functions. We must understand the details as symbolic rather than literal.[10] **And they were covered with eyes, in front and in back.** (Cp. also Rev 4:8b.) 1 Enoch 71:7 describes the cherubim with the seraphim and the ophanim as "the sleepless ones who guard the throne of his glory"[11] The many eyes enable them to see all and to keep a perfect watch. **7. The first living creature was like a lion, the second was like an ox, the third had a face like a man, the fourth was like a flying eagle.** The symbolism, drawing upon prominent life forms, apparently intends to dramatize God's creative and sustaining power working to accomplish his ends throughout his creation. Whereas in Ezekiel the movement of the cherubim is given emphasis (1:10, 15-17, 19-21), in the Apocalypse they direct their energies to singing God's praise. The cherubim with their song speak as representatives of God's creation. Creation by design, if we will hear it, glorifies Him.[12] **8.** The **six wings** of the living creatures bring to mind the seraphim of Isaiah 6 where we are told that "with two they covered their faces, with two they covered their feet, and with two they flew" (tr. mine). In both passages their posture appropriately reflects the theme of their song. On their **eyes all around,**

---

[10]Two cherubim with flaming swords guarded the entrance to the Garden of Eden (Gen 3:24); two golden cherubim guarded the ark of the covenant (Exod 25:18-22; 1 Kgs 6:23-26; 2 Chr 3:10-13; Heb 9:5; Yahweh is described as dwelling or sitting between the cherubim, 1 Sam 4:4; 2 Sam 6:2; 2 Kgs 19:15; 1 Chr 13:6; Psa 80:1; 99:1; Isa 37:16); images of cherubim were embroidered on the curtains (Exod 26:1) and the veils of the tabernacle (Exod 26:31) and the temple (2 Chr 3:14) and they were carved on the doors (1 Kings 6:32, 34, 35) and on the panelled walls of the temple (1 Kgs 6:29; 2 Chr 3:7); the watercarts (lavers) also were decorated with cherubim (1 Kgs 7:29, 36). Ezekiel's new temple also was decorated with cherubim (Ezek 41:18-20, 25). In Ezekiel's vision of God, the cherubim seem to be conveying the assemblage on which rests the throne of Yahweh (1:19-21). A similar representation of two winged cherubim-like creatures were found by archaeologists on a relief supporting the throne of Hiram, king of Byblos (R. K. Harrison, "Cherubim," *The Illustrated Bible Dictionary* [Leicester, Eng.: Inter-Varsity Press, 1980], 1.264). For other references to cherubim not mentioned above, see 1 Sam 4:4; 2 Sam 6:2, 22:11; 2 Kgs 19:15; Pss 18:10, 80:1, 99:1; Ezek 41:18.

[11]Cp. Ezek 1:13, 18, 10:12; 1 Enoch 61:10, 71:7. James H. Charlesworth, *Old Testament Pseudepigrapha* (Garden City, N. Y.: Doubleday, 1983-1985), 1.50.

[12]See Ladd, p. 77. It is not necessary to answer the question as to whether they are only apocalyptic symbols or real spirit beings. In either case, their literary function is clear. The idea promulgated by the Early Church Fathers that they represent the four Gospels is clearly an example of allegorizing and has no foundation in legitimate interpretation (see William Barclay, *The Revelation of St. John* [Philadelphia: Westminster Press, 1960], 1.202-204; Robert H. Mounce, *The Book of Revelation* (Revised ed.; Grand Rapids: Eerdmans, 1998), 125.

see Rev 4:6, above.[13] **Holy, holy, holy is the Lord God Almighty:** Their message is an expression of God's design for his creation—its exaltation of his perfect holiness and unlimited sovereignty through eternity past, present, and future. Our understanding of past revelation as well as his present working prepares us for the future. The Revelation is about to introduce to the first century reader how that sovereignty will unfold through the course of the present age.[14] **9-10. The twenty-four elders,** another order of angelic beings representing the Covenant People (see above on v. 4), prostrate themselves in worship before God (cp. Rev 1:17). They **fall down before him**—the act of utmost humility before their Sovereign.[15] The Almighty is he **who lives forever and ever,** literally, "he who lives unto the ages of the ages" (Gk.: τῷ ζῶντι εἰς τοὺς αἰῶνας τῶν αἰώνων, *tō zōnti eis toûs aiōnas tōn aiōnōn*; cp. Rev 1:18 and refs. there). This forward looking perspective inherent in the very nature of God gives hope to his suffering people. **They lay their crowns before the throne** in humble recognition that their authority as representatives of the people of God wholly derives from the divine grace in his plan of redemption. By this act which introduces their doxology that follows, the elders show the submission of the People of God to the sovereignty of their Creator. **11.** The kingly rule of God over all things derives from his role as creator—**By your will they were created and have their being.** Therefore, all creatures great and small belong to him and owe him homage. **Glory and honor and power** belong to him. So the irrefutable fact of the sovereignty of God is fundamental to the message of the Revelation and, most immediately, to the great truth which is to be introduced in . The sovereign Creator-God controls the destiny of his creation and of all mankind.

---

[13]In Ezek 1:6, 10 each cherubim has four wings. Such differences tell us that the details of the symbolism have importance only as they contribute to our understanding of the particular text in its own context. If such describe real angelic beings, the details can hardly be taken as literal definition.

[14]The idea that a prophecy directed to the first century reader which pertains initially to times immediately to follow cannot have any relevance for the reader in the twenty-first century is unsound, as witnessed by the many other fulfilled prophecies of Scripture. See above, Introduction, Historicist School, and Append. 2.

[15]Cp. 2 Chr 20:18; Dan 3:7; Mark 3:11; Rev 1:17, 5:8, 10, 14, 7:11, 19:4, and 22:8.

The Scroll and the Lamb

> 5:1. **Then I saw in the right hand of him who sat on the throne a scroll with writing on both sides and sealed with seven seals. ²And I saw a mighty angel proclaiming in a loud voice, "Who is worthy to break the seals and open the scroll?" ³But no one in heaven or on earth or under the earth could open the scroll or even look inside it. ⁴I wept and wept because no one was found who was worthy to open the scroll or look inside. ⁵Then one of the elders said to me, "Do not weep! ⁶ See, the Lion of the tribe of Judah, the Root of David, has triumphed. He is able to open the scroll and its seven seals."**

5:1-5   **Christ Has Triumphed!**   **Exposition**

In this scene we have a most extraordinary situation. It is now disclosed that the great Creator-God-King as revealed and worshiped in the previous chapter holds in his hand a great scroll. The scroll is full of writing on both sides but securely sealed with seven seals. Moreover, it appears at first that no one in heaven or on earth is worthy to open it. The scroll apparently holds major revelations which chart the course of future events leading to the extinction of evil and the glorious establishment of the Kingdom of God (Rev 4:1).

When it appeared to the Seer that the scroll could not be read, he fell to protracted weeping. Then, one of the angelic "elders," disclosed dramatically that there was One who was indeed worthy! "The Lion of the tribe of Judah, the Root of David, has triumphed!" The Messiah has conquered! (see Rev 3:21) Not by military might nor by political genius but by his death and resurrection, Jesus is victor! Jesus by his triumph has determined the future destruction of God's enemies and the future glorious destiny of the People of God.

| 1-5 | **Christ Has Triumphed!** | Notes |

1. In symbolism, **the right hand** is the hand of strength. The **scroll** was in New Testament times the standard form for any extended writing. Scrolls were made of "pages" or leaves of papyrus or thin leather sewed together at the left and right margins so that as the document was read the pages could be unrolled from one side and rolled up on the other. Scrolls did not normally have writing on both sides. The exception was made when there was an excess of information (cp. Ezek 2:10). Here, we may infer, the reader is to understand that the message is extensive and therefore of great consequence.[16] In the first century, documents were **sealed** by tying with string and sealing with a lump of clay impressed with the sender's signet ring. The seal was comparable to the wax seals commonly used for letters and official documents as recently as the 19th century. The original copy of marriage contracts, wills, etc. was commonly sealed inside with a duplicate, accessible copy outside to protect the original from wear and tear. In such cases a flap was sewn into the document so that an inside seal could remain attached while the outer part could be unrolled. So perhaps with our seven-sealed scroll. After each seal was broken an additional part of the scroll could be unrolled and read. (See above, ch. 1, The Seven-Sealed Scroll.) The sealing of the scroll symbolizes the hidden or inaccessible nature of its predictions. Compare Dan 12:4, where the prophet is told, "Close up and seal the words of the scroll until the time of the end" (also Dan 8:26). The unsealing of the Revelation may in fact be a conscious allusion, the reverse of the sealing of the Daniel prophecies, for as we have seen above in chapter 1 on Daniel, the Revelation may be viewed as a commentary or explanation of the major visions of Daniel. The **seven seals** further

---

[16]The interpretation of Elliott that the writing on the back of the scroll is intended to suggest that the events predicted run parallel in time with those written on the front is ingenious but fanciful (E. B. Elliott, *Horae Apocalypticae* (5th ed.; London: Seeley, Jackson, and Halliday, 1862), 1.114. Without known ancient precedent to condition the original readers to such a device, this approach seems hardly creditable.

serve to lead up to the principal themes of the book. While they are one of the three main structural elements which include also the seven trumpets and the seven bowls, as seals they suggest what is in some sense preliminary. Moreover, the symbolic number seven always carries with it the idea of completion—the entirety of the matter under consideration. R. H. Charles well states:

> The roll ... deals with the things ἅ μέλλει γενέσθαι ["which are about to occur"]. With the loosing of each seal a part of its contents is revealed in symbolic representation. In other words, the Book is a prophecy of the things that fall out before the end. Owing to the solemnity with which it is introduced and the importance attached to it by the Seer, it should contain all the future history of the world described in the Apocalypse to its close; and so Nicolas de Lyra, Corn. a Lap., Bengel, Düsterdieck, Bousset, etc., explain. This appears to be the right view. . . . (1.138)

The scroll contains a prophecy of the whole course of history, not as Charles suggests, "all the history of the world" but events future to the Revelation that expand the Christ-Antichrist theme as introduced in the prophetic visions of Daniel.[17] **A mighty angel** speaks not only here but again in 10:1 and 18:21. In each instance, an announcement of utmost importance is made, one which has primary significance regarding the message of the Revelation. The first signals the role of the Lamb in opening the scroll; the second presents the Little Book message concerning the impending victory in the war with Antichrist. The Third announces the Fall of Babylon, the Antichrist power. **2. I wept and wept because no one was found who was worthy to open the scroll.** The apparent crisis for want of someone worthy to open the scroll serves to heighten the drama and appropriately focus on the Messiah-Victor. **5. "See, the Lion of the tribe of Judah, the Root of David, has triumphed. He is able to open the scroll . . . ."** The Messianic titles serve to bond the Christian revelation of Jesus as the antitypical Lamb with the historic Hebrew hope in the coming Messiah. The lion, Judah's tribal symbol (Gen 49:9, 10; 4 Esra/2 Esd 12:31-32) and king of beasts stands for the King-Messiah while the "Root of David," that is, the plant growing from the root, reflects the Messiah's covenant inheritance of the Davidic kingship (cp. Rev 22:16; 2 Sam 7:11b-16; Isa 11:1; 53:2). The long promised Davidic Son has come to

---

[17]Charles goes on to say that "it is hard to reconcile this view with the rest of the Apocalypse" (1.138). His own presuppositions about the nature of prophecy as an essentially humanistic enterprise may have hampered him in the effort.

reign. Paradoxically, the Lion **triumphed** as a Lamb, a point greatly emphasized in the Revelation. His triumph focused on His death, as indicated in the verses which follow, but there is much more to His victory to be learned from what follows.

The Scroll and the Lamb (cont'd)

5:6. Then I saw a Lamb, looking as if it had been slain, standing in the center of the throne, encircled by the four living creatures and the elders. He had seven horns and seven eyes, which are the seven spirits of God sent out into all the earth. ⁷**He came and took the scroll from the right hand of him who sat on the throne.** ⁸**And when he had taken it, the four living creatures and the twenty-four elders fell down before the Lamb. Each one had a harp and they were holding golden bowls full of incense, which are the prayers of the saints.** ⁹**And they sang a new song:**

"You are worthy to take the scroll
 and to open its seals,
because you were slain,
 and with your blood you purchased men for God
 from every tribe and language and people and
  nation.
¹⁰You have made them to be a kingdom and priests
 to serve our God,
and they will reign on the earth."

5:6-10 **Exposition**

What the elder proclaimed, John now saw through tearful eyes wonderfully dramatized in the heavenly scene. The Lion is a lamb! A Lamb-like being, scarred from mortal wounds, was nevertheless grandly alive and standing before Him in the throne room of heaven. The slain Lamb can represent no other than the One about whom Isaiah said, "He was 'led like a lamb to the slaughter, . . . cut off from the land of the living; for the transgression of my people he was stricken'" (Isa 53:7, 8). His seven horns and His seven eyes indicate His sovereign control over the destiny of His creation as well as His care for His people in "all the earth."

As the aged and suffering John was comforted, so we are to be comforted by this vision of the Victorious Lamb who is worthy not only to unveil the sealed prophecies, but to call forth the fulfillment of all the glorious predictions of all God's prophets, insuring that in His time His purposes for His world and for our redemption will be fulfilled.[18]

When the Lamb takes the scroll, the heavenly company falls prostrate in abject recognition of his Deity. They worship Him with a new song of praise and gratitude for those on earth for whom He made atonement, who now serve God and will one day reign with Him on a renewed earth. As a great antiphony, myriads of myriads of angels beyond number encircle the throne room of heaven to join in singing praise to the Lamb.

Then, as a marvelous proleptic view of a time when "every tongue will confess that Jesus Christ is Lord," every creature in all creation sings the grand hymn of praise to the Lamb.

With this high drama the Messiah Jesus is presented as the Book of the Revelation is about to be unsealed. The central place is given to Messiah Jesus, the Lamb of God. He is the victorious Savior, the one who will receive universal worship—"praise and honor and glory and power, for ever and ever!"

5:6-10   **The Worship of the Lamb**   **Notes**

5:6. John saw a Lamb. Jesus Christ is called the Lamb in the Book of Revelation 29 times, a point of emphasis in the book. The diminutive, ἀρνίον, *'arníon*, is used rather that ἀρνός, *àrnós*, which occurs elsewhere in the New Testament, to heighten the contrast with "the lion" of verse 5. **Looking as if it had been slain**: In the Old Covenant the lamb was the central sacrificial victim at the morning and evening sacrifices, at all the festal celebrations, and on the Day of Atonement. It was a symbol of innocence, purity, and gentleness, as well as of the efficacious sacrifice

---

[18]Thomas Goodwin, "An Exposition of the the Book of Revelation," *Works* (1639; Louisville: Mounts Publishing, 1979), 3.9.

which insured atonement.[19] The Lamb bears visible sacrificial death wounds but is nevertheless alive! (see Rev 1:18, 2:8) "The Lord has laid on him the iniquity of us all" (Isa 53:6). The Atonement has been accomplished by the resurrected Savior; so the destiny of God's people is assured. The Lamb is **standing in the center of the throne, encircled by the four living creatures and the elders.** The text is best translated "between the throne (with the four living creatures) and the elders" (NASB).[20] The Savior stands in an intermediary position as the victorious God-Man between the elders who are heavenly representatives of the redeemed and the Throne of Heaven (see Notes above, on Rev 4:5). His **seven horns** indicate omnipotence, universal and absolute authority. The number seven is, as always, a sign of completion or fullness. The horn as a symbol of power and authority is common in the Old Testament as well as in extra-biblical apocalyptic literature (Num 23:22; Deut 33:17; Psa 89:17; Dan 8:3; Zech 1:18; 1 Enoch 90:9; et al.).[21] His **seven eyes** indicate another quality of Deity, omniscience. They are identified with **the seven spirits of God**, apocalyptic language for the Holy Spirit, here as in Zech 4:6, 10 going **out into the whole earth**. The language is of course Messianic and is reminiscent of Pentecost, suggesting the role of the Spirit of Christ in and through the Church throughout the world and leading to the end-time restitution of all things (John 14:15-19; 16:7, 13; Matt 24:14; Dan 7:13, 27). 7. The Lamb now stepped forward **and took the scroll from the right hand of him who sat on the throne.** The enthroned God acts to delegate and transfer power, in this case, to the One who will unseal the scroll and unlock destiny of mankind. 8. The triumphant Lamb provokes the praise of all creation as the vision of the Lamb's sovereignty

---

[19]B. D. Napier, "Lamb," *IDB* (New York: Abingdon, 1962), 3.58, 59. The objection of some scholars that pre-Christian Jewish sources never characterize the expected Messiah as a Paschal lamb need not weigh against our interpretation. The OT Paschal lamb imagery itself and Isaiah 53:7 are sufficient to render the symbol appropriate in the Apocalyptic drama. The apparent omission of the Paschal lamb typology in pre-Christian Jewish messianism is nevertheless striking. (Of course, it could be explained as the result of anti-Christian editing during the conflict of Judaism with Christianity.)

[20]The RSV, NRSV, NEB, NASB, NIV, and REB each offer essentially different interpretations of this Greek text. The author's use of ἐν μέσῳ . . . ἐν μέσῳ may be understood to mean either "between the throne (with the four living creatures) and the elders," as we have represented it or alternatively, "in the midst of the throne (with the four living creatures and in the midst of the elders," in which case the two phrases with μέσῳ are understood as parallel. We follow Charles and others who see ἐν μέσῳ . . . ἐν μέσῳ as reflecting the Hebrew idiom, בֵּין וּבֵין, literally, "between [one place] and between [the other place]," meaning simply "between one place and the other" (cp. Gen 3:15, 9:16, 17, 13:3, LXX & MT; Charles, 1.140).

[21]Charles, 1.141

unfolds. **The four living creatures** representing the natural creation and **the twenty-four elders** representing the redeemed People of God prostrate themselves to worship the Sovereign Savior. **Harps** in the ancient culture were the appropriate instrument for enhancing the worship of God. The living creatures join also in celebration and praise of the Lamb because creation is also subject to redemption (see on v. 10, below).[22] The **golden bowls full of incense**, as in the Old Covenant temple (and later again in the Apocalyptic vision) bear upward with their aromatic smoke **the prayers of the saints**. The elders and the living creatures, after falling prostrate and worshiping, stand to sing (see v. 14). **9.** This **new song** of the "living creatures" and the "24 elders" addresses the Lamb and focuses on his redemptive work on behalf of his Covenant People. **With your blood you purchased men for God** reflects the ransom concept of the atonement for the sin of those chosen from Adam's race (cf. Gen 2:17; Matt 20:28/Mark 10:45; Rom 5:12-15; 1 Tim 2:6). The fact that the Lamb "purchased **men** [= 'people'; 'men' not explicit in the Gk. text] . . . **from** every tribe"; The Greek preposition ἐκ [ἐκ πάσης φυλῆς, *ek pásēs phulēs*, etc.] implies that the atonement was made not for all but for the elect. The preposition ἐκ implies *separation out of* the people groups enumerated (BAGD, 234 1.d). **Every tribe and language and people and nation** implies that all people groups of the earth are represented and probably, in the context of Scripture generally, also implied are all ages of redemptive history.[23] The enumeration of the populous probably is an allusion to Dan 7:14, which provides a prophetic substratum for verses 9 and 10.[24] **10.** The Lamb by His atonement has **made them to be a kingdom**, that is, to be subjects serving under the rule of God. The redeemed are **priests**—they are the true Israel, a nation called into a unique rela-

---

[22]Many scholars prefer to limit the pronoun to the elders, a less natural reading of the Greek, on the ground that the music and the presentation of incense are priestly functions inappropriate to the living creatures. However, the living creatures sing praise with the elders and others in v. 11 and as these represent the physical creation they are rightly seen as participants in the redemptive work of God.

[23]The alternate textual readings which in the KJV supply the first personal pronoun here and twice in v. 10 are inappropriate for several reasons: 1. As we have already noted above, the elders, though they *represent* the redeemed in the court of heaven, are in several places within the book differentiated from redeemed. 2. The textual authority for "us" (Gk. ἡμας) in v. 10 is too weak to sustain that reading (two 13th cent. mss., 792 and Codex Gigas, and a 16th cent. ed. of the Vulgate translation).

[24]In the Book of Revelation, such enumeration most often includes "tribes" (5:9, 7:9, 11:9, 13:7, 14:6; cp. 10:11, 17:15), probably intending to suggest inclusion of people from the tribes of Israel (Cf. also Dan 3:4, 5:19; 2 Esdr. 3:7.) The twenty-four elders represent the saints but are distinct from them. The elders refer to the saints in the third person, as "them" and "they." On the identity and role of the elders, see above on 4:4.

tionship with God (Exod 19:6). The words, **to serve**, are supplied in the NIV; the Greek simply reads, "priests to **our God**," emphasizing here the relationship. Ladd well states, "The idea of priesthood means full and immediate access into the presence of God for the purpose of praise and worship" (p. 92). That the Covenant People **will reign** is taught elsewhere by our Lord (Matt 19:28), by the Apostle Paul (1 Cor 6:2, 3), and again, in Rev 20:4. That the reigning saints will live **on the earth** is integral to the biblical message of redemption. As the earth is subject to the evil consequences of the Fall (Gen 3:17-18) and as the Promised Land suffered from the apostasy of the Covenant Nation (Lev 26:31, 33-35; Deut 28:38-42), so also will the earth be subject to restoration in the future redemption of the Lord's people. Redemption will include both the Covenant Land (Isa 35:9-13; 60:1-22; Jer 31:5-14; Ezek 36) and on a wider scale a renewed Earth (Isa 65: 17-25; 66:22; Rom 8:19-21; 2 Pet 3:13; Matt 5:5; Rev 21:1). This last is most beautifully stated by Paul in his Epistle to the Romans: "The creation waits in eager expectation for the sons of God to be revealed. For the creation was subjected to frustration . . . but . . . will be liberated from its bondage to decay and brought into the glorious freedom of the children of God" (8:19-21).

The Scroll and the Lamb (cont'd)

5:11. **Then I looked and heard the voice of many angels, numbering thousands upon thousands, and ten thousand times ten thousand. They encircled the throne and the living creatures and the elders.** ¹²**In a loud voice they sang:**

> **"Worthy is the Lamb, who was slain,**
> **to receive power and wealth**
> **and wisdom and strength**
> **and honor and glory and praise!"**

¹³**Then I heard every creature in heaven and on earth and under the earth and on the sea, and all that is in them, singing:**

> **"To him who sits on the throne and to the Lamb**
> **be praise and honor and glory and power,**
> **for ever and ever!"**

¹⁴**The four living creatures said, "Amen," and the elders fell down and worshiped.**

5:11-14 The Great Anthem of Praise Exposition

This great anthem of universal praise celebrates the completion of God's saving work. The earlier song (vv. 9, 10) celebrates Christ's work of redemption. The vision now looks to the finale when all creation rejoices and exalts in God and in the Lamb, the incarnate Son.

At first, myriads upon myriads of angels surround the elders and the living creatures around the throne to sing praise for the Lamb. He, though slain as the suffering and dying Servant (v. 9; cf. Isa 52:13-53:12), is worthy to be enthroned and to rule with all honor as Lord and King over the entire creation. All that is ascribed to the Father in 4:9-11 and more is now in 5:12 given to the Son.

This exaltation of the Son is further amplified in verse fourteen where every creature in all creation joins with the angels to swell the song with the fullest possible praise addressed both to the Lamb and to the Creator God, the One seated upon the throne.

This scene is the last of the "interlude" which introduces chapter six and the forecast of "things to come."

5:11-14 The Great Anthem of Praise Notes

11. Then I looked (Gk. καὶ εἶδον, *kaì eîdon*) introduces a change of perspective, a new scene in the vision (see note on 4:1). Whereas the preceding scene exhibiting the opening of the scroll is contemporaneous with the author, this scene is proleptic, as indicated by its allusion to the angelic host of Dan 7:10 and the universality of worship. It views the goal and end product of the Lamb's redemptive work in his restored creation. **The voice of many angels** is in context an antiphonal response to the song of the living creatures and the elders. The size of the angelic choir (**thousands upon thousands, and ten thousand times ten thousand**; Gk., μυριάδες μυριάδων καὶ κιλιάδες κιλιάδων, *muriádes muriádōn kaì kiliádes kiliádōn*) is beyond number, "countless thousands" (BAGD 529b; cf. 1 Enoch 40:1, 71:8). **12. "Worthy is the Lamb, who was slain."** This worship language is directed to Jesus Christ and corresponds to the language in 4:11 directed to God. The seven qualities given to

Christ are all ascribed to Christ elsewhere in the New Testament: **Power** (1 Cor 1:24), **wealth** (2 Thess 1:9), **wisdom** (1 Cor 1:24), **strength** (Eph 6:10; 2 Thess 1:9), **honor** (Heb 2:9), **glory** (John 1:14; Heb 2:9), and **blessing** (Mark 11:9, 10).[25] **The passage also has several notable parallels with Solomon's prayer in 1 Chr 29:10-13. 13.** In the final burst of praise, the angels are joined by all God's creatures in universal worship of the Creator God and of the Lamb. The two here are equally recipient of such praise language as properly belongs only to Deity. While we are not dealing with a chronological prophecy here, the scene is in vision only, but is such as will occur when the course of history finds fulfillment in the return of Christ, the resurrection of the dead, and the extinction of evil.[26] **14.** The concluding response of **the four living creatures** and **the elders** again focuses the drama on what is most central from the standpoint of the Lamb's great work to be carried out through the process of time according to the forecast to follow in chapters 6-19—that is, the redemption of the created world and the redemption of the Covenant people of God.

---

[25]Morris, 99. The last occurs as a different grammatical form in Mark, but the same idea is implied.

[26]is not necessary to understand with Barclay and others that "under the earth" pertains actually to the dead then in Hades. Barclay cites a list of biblical texts which affirm that the dead in Hades cannot praise God (Psa 6:5, 30:9; 88:10-12; Isa 38:18) and then concludes that this Revelation text "sweeps all this away" (228-229). The theological and hermeneutical principle of progressive revelation should not be so construed as to affirm that the New Testament contradicts clear, propositional statements of the Old. Such is an unworthy viewpoint, contrary to our Lord's affirmation that "the Scripture cannot be broken" (John 10:35). Moreover, the language of Rev 5:13 is hardly compliant with the concept of impenitent sinners eternally existent in hell.

Chapter Four
THE OPENING OF THE SEALED SCROLL
Rev. 6:1-17, 8:1

Introduction

The stage is now set in the drama of the Revelation. The throne of the Creator is displayed in chapters four and five where He is worshiped in the heavenly sanctuary. There the Savior is presented who alone can provide the key to redemptive history. The scroll is ready to be unsealed. The Apocalyptic drama is about to present the message of "things to come." As the church at the end of the first Christian century was persecuted by the Emperor Domitian, it may have fearfully anticipated the fulfillment of Daniel's prophecy—the Little Horn Antichrist and his terrible war against the saints (Dan 7:8, 21, 24, 25). Nevertheless, that same prophecy promised the Savior who would come to conquer evil and assure victory (Dan 7:13-17, 26, 27). Jesus had said, ". . . He who stands firm to the end will be saved. And this gospel of the kingdom will be preached in the whole world as a testimony to all nations, and then the end will come." (Matt 24:13, 14)

The Revelation provides in apocalyptic symbols a general guide to the faithful who look to see the hand of Providence in history. One should assume from the nature of ancient apocalyptic dream-vision prophecies, that for the original readers the vision would relate to the immediate future and then lead to Christ's victory over Antichrist and the glorious return of the Lord Jesus to establish His Kingdom (see above on Rev 4:1).[1]

---

[1]Historians of prophecy have found only one scholar prior to the rise of the Protestant-futurist interpretation in the nineteenth century who excluded the church age from the prophecies of Revelation. Hippolytus (died ca. A.D. 236) assumed there was a gap between the 69th and 70th "seven" of Daniel 9:24. His commentary on the Apocalypse has not been preserved. He is known to have been an allegorist in his approach to the interpretation of Scripture. Note his comments on Dan 9:24-27: "Then he says: 'After threescore and two weeks the times will be fulfilled, and for one week he will make a covenant with many; and in the midst (half) of the week sacrifice and oblation will be removed, and in the temple will be the abomination of desolations.' 'For when the threescore and two weeks are fulfilled, and Christ is come, and the Gospel is

Because of the function of seals and because they appear only in the first part of the book, the seal prophecies should be understood as introductory to the other prophecies which follow. Some ancient documents used multiple seals to provide the means of reading a preliminary copy of a text while preserving as unread and protected the official text (see ch. 1, The Seven-Sealed Scroll). Similarly here, the several seals introduce six brief sequences. When the seventh seal is opened the larger part of the book remains to be read. These pertain to the subjects of principal concern—the coming war of Antichrist against the church, Christ's victory in that war, and the glorious consummation of this age. The details of the six seal prophecies correspond so well with events of the first three Christian centuries that the reader familiar with that history should immediately see the correlation. This approach to interpreting the seals was followed by most of the leading Protestant interpreters at least from the seventeenth century until the preterist and futurist schools gained ascendancy in the twentieth century.[2]

---

preached in every place, the times being then accomplished, there will remain only one week, the last, in which Elias will appear, and Enoch, and in the midst of it the abomination of desolation will be manifested, viz., Antichrist, announcing desolation to the world. And when he comes, the sacrifice and oblation will be removed, which now are offered to God in every place by the nations." ("The Extant Works and Fragments of Hippolytus," *The Ante-Nicene Fathers,* [Grand Rapids: Eerdmans, 1986] 5.182.21-22.) See further Append. 1 and E. B. Elliott, *Horae Apocalypticae* (5th ed.; London: Seeley, Jackson, and Halliday, 1562), 4.283-286.

[2]Joseph Mede, *A Key to the Apocalypse, a translation of Clavis Apocalyptica* (1627; London: J. G. & F. Rivington, 1833), 68-114; John Trapp, "Revelation of St. John the Divine," *Commentary on the New Testament* (Evansville, Indiana: Sovereign Grace Book Club, 1958), 750-751; Thomas Goodwin, "An Exposition of the Book of Revelation," in *The Works of Thomas Goodwin* (1639; Edinburgh: James Nichol, 1861), 3.17-52; Jurieu (1687; see Elliott 4.496); Jonathan Edwards, "Notes on the Apocalypse," in *Apocalyptic Wriings*; *The works of Jonathan Edwards* (John E. Smith, ed.; New Haven: Yale University Press, 1977), 5.97-305; Ch. Daubuz, *Perpetual Commentary on the Apocalypse* (London: Benj. Tooke, 1720; from Elliott 4.513-514); Isaac Newton (1733; from Elliott 4.518-520), Th. Newton, *Dissertations on the Prophecies*. (1754; Repr., London: Crissy & Markley, 1850), 460-471; G. S. Faber, *Dissertation on the Prophecies* (4th ed.; London: F. C. and J. Rivington, 1810), 1.51, 54; Alexander M'Leod, *Lectures upon the Principal Prophecies of the Revelation* (New York: Whiting and Watson, 1814), 68-108; Adam Clarke, "Revelation of St. John the Divine," *The New Testament* (1826; New York: Carlton & Porter, n.d.), 2.993-996; Th. Scott, "Revelation of John the Divine," *The Holy Bible . . . with Explanatory Notes* (5th London ed.; Boston: Sam. T. Armstrong, 1831), unpaged; S. T. Bloomfield, *'H KAINH ΔIAΘHKH, The Greek Testament with English Notes, Critical, Philological, and Exegetical* (Boston: Perkins and Marvin, 1837), 576-578; Elliott (1st ed. 1844), 1.119-252; David Simpson, *A Key to the Prophecies* (London: Wm. Walker, 1847), 310; Albert Barnes, Notes on the New Testament: Revelation (1851; enlarged type ed.; Grand Rapids: Baker, 1949), 136-168; Wm. Hutcheson, *The Apocalypse Opened* (Glasgow: Wm. Collins, 1857), 73-95; B. W. Johnson, "Revelation," *The Peoples New Testa-*

Chapter Four *The opening of the sealed scroll, 6:1-17, 8:1* 121

The seal, trumpet, and bowl prophecies constitute the principal structural symbols for understanding the vision of Revelation. They present three distinct periods of divine judgment as occurring sequentially much as each of the individual scenes occur in the drama of the Revelation (see Append. 3).

SEVEN SEALS Ch. 6   SEVEN TRUMPETS Chs. 7-8, 11:15   SEVEN BOWLS Chs. 15-16

The Seals

6:1. **I watched as the Lamb opened the first of the seven seals. Then I heard one of the four living creatures say in a voice like thunder, "Come!" ²I looked, and there before me was a white horse! Its rider held a bow, and he was given a crown, and he rode out as a conqueror bent on conquest.**

³When the Lamb opened the second seal, I heard the second living creature say, "Come!" ⁴Then another horse came out, a fiery red one. Its rider was given power to take peace from the earth and to make men slay each other. To him was given a large sword.

⁵When the Lamb opened the third seal, I heard the third living creature say, "Come!" I looked, and there before me was a black horse! Its rider was holding a pair of scales in its hand. ⁶Then I heard what sounded like a voice among the four living creatures, saying, "A quart of wheat for a day's wages, and three quarts of barley for a day's wages, and three quarts of barley for a day's wages, and do not damage the oil and the wine!

⁷When the Lamb opened the fourth seal, I heard the voice of the fourth living creature say, "Come!" ⁸I looked, and there before me was a pale horse! Its rider was named Death, and Hades was following close behind him. They were given power over a fourth of the earth to kill by sword, famine and plague and by the wild beasts of the earth.

---

ment (ca. 1900; Nashville: Gospel Advocate, 1982); 433-440; E. P. Cachemaille, *XXVI Present Day Papers on Prophecy*. (London: Seeley, Service, 1911), 164-202; Basil F. C. Atkinson, *The War with Satan: an Explanation of the Book of Revelation* (London: Protestant Truth Society, 1940); 62-68; Harold Barton, *It's Here: the Time of the End* (New York: Exposition Press, 1963), 139-143; McKinley Ash, *Anti-Christ Past, Present, and Future* (n.p.: Osterhus, 1967), 175-181; S. H. French, *The Unsealed Book* (London: Prophetic Light Publications, 1968), 22-30.

6:1-8   The Four Horsemen   Introduction

The correspondence between the imagery here—wars, famines, pestilence, wild beasts, etc.—and the language of the Lord's Olivet Discourse (Matt 24:4-28; Mark 13:7-20; Luke 21:10-24) is sometimes explained as indicating John's dependence on the latter (as e.g., Charles 1.158-161). Better it is to see this as the rhetorical use of common prophetic language having its source in the Covenant curses delivered by Moses (Lev 26:14-43; Deut 28:15-68). This language is used in the Bible to mark such calamities as divine judgments— punishments which ensue from the violation of Covenant law (Jer 21:7; Ezek 14:21, et al.).

While such terms as "wars," "famines," "pestilence," and "wild beasts," have common meanings and relevance for understanding the divine providence, one may not assume that whenever they occur in biblical prophecy they refer to the same events. Historical and literary context must determine for each passage when the particular punishment will occur. This is illustrated by the fact that the Mosaic prophecies of doom in Leviticus 24 and Deuteronomy 28 had substantial fulfillment for the Israelite-Jewish nation in the pre-exilic and Roman destructions, whereas the Olivet discourse of Matthew 24-25 focuses on the period beginning with the Jewish-Roman wars and ending at the Second Advent.

As we will attempt to demonstrate below, the dramatic elements of these first four seals may be understood as aptly predicting the course of pagan Roman history as it was experienced in the second and third centuries by the Christian church. The negative progression corresponds exactly to the gradual deterioration of the Empire as it actually occurred in the second and third centuries.

We do not suggest, however, that the Book of Revelation gives either a full or a balanced history of the church, as some critics of the Protestant-historicist interpretation represent our approach. Historicist interpreters have understood that the Revelation focuses on the Fourth Kingdom, the Roman Empire—the unnamed beast of Daniel seven. In Revelation 11 and 13, this focus leads to the rise of the Antichrist power within the sphere of the Roman Empire, its war against the true church, and in subsequent chapters finally to Christ's victory over Antichrist and the end of this age.

The prophecies of the seals trace the course of the pagan Roman Empire to its eventual downfall under the heavy hand of God's judgment.

Chapter Four *The four horsemen, 6:1-8*

In consequence of the progressive deterioration of the Empire not only the pagans but the People of God were to suffer, both from the evils described by the horsemen and from direct, physical persecution. The persecution climaxed as symbolized by the fifth seal. The climax of God's judgments against the pagan Empire is described in the sixth seal.

During the period of the seals, the church grew immensely but became increasingly decadent, both by the influx of nominal Christianity and by the introduction of erroneous doctrines.[3] By these seal prophecies the Early Church, as well as the church of subsequent centuries, was warned of disciplinary judgments as well as of judgments to fall upon the pagan world.

The Revelation characteristically draws upon the Old Testament for most of its symbols. So with the horsemen, who appear here in a manner similar to the prophecies of Zechariah (1:7-11, 6:1-8) as bearing according to their colors such messages as peace and war.

With the church at the end of the first century, we identify the Fourth Beast of Daniel 7 with Rome—the fourth world empire in succes-

---

[3]The struggle against false doctrine was already obvious in the first century, as indicated in the letters to the churches in chapters 2-3. At first, the struggle was against Jewish legalism (Acts 15; Gal 1:6-9, 3:1-5, 6:12, 13; 2 Cor 11:1-15; et al.) and Gnostic-like heresies (Col. 2:1-8; 1 John 4:1-4; Rev 2:14-16, 20-24) which led either to asceticism or libertinism and to the degrading of the person of Christ. These two heresies in the second century took form in two branches of Ebionism and persisted more or less in various forms and in various parts of the Roman world into the third century (see Schaff 2.428-508). There were also doctrinal deviations which, though not so radical as generally to be treated as heresies, nevertheless gradually invaded orthodoxy so as to lead the church in the direction of paganism and what later was to become enshrined in sacramentalism and in the Roman Catholic Papacy. Specifically, one might mention infant baptism (late second century); see Paul Jewett, *Infant Baptism and the Covenant of Grace* (Grand Rapids: Eerdmans, 1978), 16-45; Johannes Warns, *Baptism* (Minneapolis, Minn.: Klock & Klock, 1980), 73-80), baptismal regeneration, Montanism (false prophecy and fanaticism), image worship, the intercession of dead saints, etc. To the foregoing one might add the allegorical method of Scriptural interpretation, which in subsequent centuries lent a false authority to many erroneous doctrines. The following statement from Joseph Milner regarding Iranaeus of Lyons speaks directly to the point of this note: "Violent persecution without, and subtle heresies within, called for the exertion, at once, of consummate dexterity and of magnanimous resolution. . . . . Heresy proved a more constant enemy than persecution. The multiplication of it, in endless refinements, induced Iranaeus to write his book against heresies . . . "; Joseph Milner, *History of the Church of Christ* (2nd ed.(Cambridge, Eng.: J. Burges, 1800), 1.306.

sion from Babylon (Dan 7:7,19-25).[4] In the Empire, the persecutions under Nero and Domitian probably put first-century believers in a state of expectancy. They may have wondered, "Is the stage now set for Daniel's Little Horn persecutor?" They would have looked to the Book of Revelation for answer to such questions.

The angelic introduction, "I must show you what must start to occur after this" (4:1, trans. mine) most naturally suggests the time immediately future to the seven churches of chapters two and three.[5]

While in the Fulfillment sections which follow we will show the appropriateness of our interpretation with regard to detailed history, we here address several general considerations which suggest that these four Seal prophecies focus on events immediately following the time of our Lord's revelation to the Apostle John:

1. The analogy of the dream-vision apocalypses of Daniel 2, 4, 7, 8, 10-12 and many of the pseudepigrapha should have prejudiced the original readers to expect the fulfillment of the vision to begin in the future near to the time of the author or, with regard to the pseudepigrapha, near the time of the alleged author.

2. The Jewish and Christian communities of the first century expected a deterioration of the Empire in the end time comparable to that portrayed in these symbols. They were suffering persecution at the hand of Rome and hoping for the soon appearing of the Messiah to deliver them. One should therefore assume that they would have looked to the near future and to Rome for the fulfillment of these Seal prophecies.

3. As we correlate this scene in the Apocalyptic dream-vision with the dream-visions of the book of Daniel, one should expect to view the horse as a symbol for the course of empire. There is an analogy between the parts of the human image in Daniel 2 or the beast in Daniel 7 and 8 and the horse in Revelation 6. As the beasts in Daniel's visions are each associated with a specific national power, one might expect that the

---

[4]*Barn.* 4.3-6; K. Lake, *The Apostolic Fathers* 1 (New York: Macmillan, 1912), 348-351; Le Roy Edwin Froom, *The Prophetic Faith of Our Fathers* 1 [Review and Herald, 1950], 210-214). Other veiled allusions in the Apostolic Fathers appear to identify Rome with the power out of which Antichrist was expected to arise according to Daniel 7:8. This is entirely according to reason, as the identification of Daniel's Fourth Beast with Rome and the Little Horn power with a Roman Antichrist had become standard eschatology in pre-Christian Judaism (Sib. Or. 5:162-165; 2 Bar. 39.5-40.2; 4 Ezra 15.40-45 ("Babylon"=Rome); Sigmund Mowinckel, *He That Cometh* (New York: Abingdon Press, 1954) 290-291; G. F. Moore, *Judaism* 2 (Cambridge, Mass.: Harvard University Press, 1966), 331-333.

[5]This, and the parallel reference in Rev 1:19, which reads "about to take place" (Gk., μέλλει γενέσθαι), may be understood as an ingressive aorist tense and translated, "start occurring." See my comment in Notes above on 1:19, with n. 16.

first-century reader should have understood the horses of the Revelation in a comparable manner.in Revelation 6.

Roman coin showing the horse sacred to the national god Mars

Illus. from Elliott 1.126

4. The horse as an imperial symbol in the first century has a suitable association with Rome. The Romans held the horse to be sacred to their national god Mars, the god of war. The horse was sacrificed to Mars annually. Images of the horse appeared on the verso of Roman coins which commemorated the god Mars.

We will address the seventh seal (Rev 8:1) in chapter five, as introductory to that chapter.

In our exposition to follow we assume that the four successive periods indicated by the horsemen are not strictly contiguous eras. While the succession of each horseman presupposes that the beginning of the period on which the seal focuses follows that of the preceding, one period does not necessarily end when the next begins. There is in fact in the actual history predicted by seals two through four a cumulative effect resulting in the eventual dissolution of the pagan Empire with the sixth seal. How this dissolution remarkably corresponds with the seal symbolism, we proceed to indicate.[6]

---

[6]Our treatment of the predictive portion of Revelation will usually be organized as follows: 1. Scripture text. 2. Introductory comments (as textual analysis may require). 3. Exposition offering practical application and inspiration. 4. Explanatory notes on details of the text. Here we will include prophetic fulfillment only in so far as we suppose the first century reader could have anticipated it. 5. Fulfillment. Here we will address fulfillment of the Apocalyptic prophecies from the vantage point of subsequent history. From our place in current history, we will point up prophetic fulfillment or want of fulfillment as it may appear to us that such may or may not have occurred. While these sections 1-4 follow the pattern established in chapters two and three, section 5 is made necessary by the introduction of prediction into the Apocalyptic drama, "the things which are to take place later" (1:19).

6:1-8   **The Four Horsemen**   **Exposition**

The first-century reader would probably have assumed quite correctly that the drama of the four horsemen portrays the dissolution of the pagan empire of their time. As those readers encountered the galloping horsemen, they could nevertheless not have known that these concise statements pertain to several centuries in time. But the prophecy should have led them to expect a period of relative peace in the Empire as indicated by the white horse and rider, then a downhill sequence—the gradual deterioration of conditions leading at length to the pale horse and rider named "Death."

As the action in the drama is controlled by each living creature who cries out from heaven, "Come," so the course of events on earth is controlled by our sovereign God. While He often permits evil men to pursue their wicked course, He nevertheless "works out everything in conformity with the purpose of His will" and ultimately will bring "many sons into glory" (Eph 1:11; Heb 2:10). He permits evil both as punitive judgment on the ungodly and as loving discipline of His children.

While we as believers must participate in the sufferings and experience many of the evils of this world, we take courage in the message of the Revelation—our God is sovereign and Jesus Christ is king! Evil governments will eventually fall. The kingdoms of this world will surely become "the kingdom of our Lord and of his Christ" (Rev 11:15).

The horsemen also provide an introduction leading up to the fifth seal, where with the dramatic presentation of the Souls of the Martyrs, a suffering church first comes into focus.

Chapter Four   *The four horsemen, 6:1-8*

6:1-2   The White Horse and Rider   Notes

1. On the **Lamb** as a symbol for Jesus Christ, see above, on 5:6-10. The complete number, **seven**, corresponds to the fact that these seals open the entire Revelation. The number "seven" also calls attention to the structural symmetry of the three series of Seals, Trumpets, and Bowls and signals their central role in indicating the sequential aspect of the events forecast by the three series. In view of the many chapters which follow in the Apocalyptic drama, one should assume that the message the Seals contain is in some sense introductory to the remainder of the drama. **The four living creatures** serve in the drama as agents of Providence (see Ezek 1:15-21 and above on Rev 4:6.) In this scene, the cherubim act to control the progress of the drama. **"Come!"** here and in vv. 3, 5, and 7 is best understood as the imperative call of Providence to the horsemen.[7] **2.** The **horse** here and in the three seals that follow represents the course of empire, in the context of the first century reader, the Roman Empire.[8] **The rider** then will represent the Emperor or the authority of his throne. The Emperor, as depicted here, often rode a **white** horse. The **bow** in Scripture represents militarism (Jer 49:35; Hos 1:5)—as our text indicates, **he rode out as a conqueror bent on conquest.** At the time the Book of Revelation was written the bow was associated especially with

---

[7]The idea that the call is to John, the Apocalyptist, to come and see is unlikely, as it is the function of the ζῶα, the living creatures, as the arm of Providence to control the action. The alternate view is represented, nevertheless, by several ancient manuscripts including Sinaiticus and Alexandrinus.

[8]The horse in each of the first four seal prophecies must have the same general meaning. Sound interpretation does not allow the idea that in the first seal prophecy the white horse and rider represent the triumphant church while the other three horses and horsemen in seals two through four represent the secular Roman Power or the temporal scene. The church and the Roman Empire are not analogous concepts. The difficulty is apparent in the commentary of George Ladd who identifies the white horse with the proclamation of the Gospel whereas his treatment of the other three horses is rather unclear (99-101). While all recognize that the figure riding the white horse in Rev 19:1-16 is clearly identified by the language of the text with Christ, the First Seal rider on the white horse is bent on conquest with the bow, a common weapon of temporal warfare. Moreover, the horse and rider are described in a fashion clearly parallel with the other three horsemen. Beasley-Murray says, "It is extraordinary how frequent and persistent is the identification of the first rider with Christ . . . . But this is to play havoc with the whole scheme of John's vision. The Lamb on the throne of God opens the seals . . . . It is a strange notion to make the Lamb one of the riders" (*The Book of Revelation* [New century Bible; Revised ed.; Grand Rapids: Eerdmans, 1978], 131).

either of two nations, the Parthians who ruled in the East beyond the bounds of the Roman Empire and the Cretans, who were famous as archers and extensively employed by Rome as mercenaries in Roman armies.⁹ If the rider represents the Roman power, the Cretan association alone is appropriate.¹⁰ The bow, then, may be taken to suggest that the Emperor signified was Cretan or otherwise associated with Crete. The rider is given **a crown**, indicating victory. Here, the Greek στέφανος, *stéphanos* denotes the laurel wreath crown awarded to athletes and worn by the Roman Emperor celebrating victory in battle. Thus, the White Horse and Rider point to an era of peace—a time of triumphant militarism. One of our illustrations shows Emperor Marcus Aurelius receiving the laurel crown at such a victory celebration. Another is a Cretan coin bearing the image of the god Mars on the face and on the verso an image of the sacred horse.

6:1-2   **The White Horse and Rider**   **Fulfillment**

The prophecy of the white horse and rider was remarkably and uniquely fulfilled in the era extending from A.D. 98-180. Historians have

---

[9]It appears that Cretan mercenaries are represented by the Kerithites in the personal body guard of King David, as mentioned in 1 Sam 30:14; 2 Sam 8:18; 15:18, etc. The targumists may not have been ignorant when they translated the Hebrew, כרתים, with "archers" (H. P. Smith, *A Critical and Exegetical Commentary on the Books of Samuel* [Edinburgh: T. & T. Clark, 1912], 309). The Kerithites are commonly identified with Cretans and the Cretans were famous in antiquity both as archers and as bow makers. As cited by Elliott (1.140, n. 4), Diodorus states that the Cretan Apollo was, in legend, the inventor of the bow and the instructor of Cretans in archery (D. S. 5.100.74). Elliott presents an instance of a bow inscribed on an ancient tombstone where the epigram expressly says it is presented to indicate that the deceased was a Cretan (1.142). Cf., as cited in Elliott (1.139-143): Hom. *Il.* 700.880; Pi. *Pyth. Od.* 5.54; Ar. *Ranae* 1356; Th. *Hist.* 6.43; Plu. *Life of Pyrrh*; Liv. *Hist.* 37.41; 38.21; Luc. 3.185; Hirt., *Bell. Alex.* 1; Treb. Pol. *Vit. Claud.* 100.16;.also Carl S. Ehrlich, "Cherethites," *The Anchor Bible Dictionary* (New York: Doubleday, 1992), 1.898-899.

[10]R. H. Charles and many preterist commentators identify the bow with the Parthians (see 1.163). Charles claim that "the very form of the words [ἐξῆλθεν νικῶν] favors this view" in that the aorist tense of the verb looks backward to the Roman defeat by the Parthians in A.D. 62! However, the Apostle is simply using the past tense to refer to what he had previously seen in the vision. This interpretation fails to recognize the Roman orientation of the prophecy, as the Parthian Empire lay outside the Roman Empire (for the Roman orientation, see above on 6:1-8, Introduction). When Cretan mercenaries commonly served as bowmen in the Roman army, it is a source of wonder that so many scholars completely ignore the substantial evidence for the Cretan character of this symbol.

identified this very time when the book of Revelation was first read as the most notable period of peace in world history. This period extended from the death of the Emperor Domitian in A.D. 96 to the death of Marcus Aurelius in A.D. 180. Gibbon says that this period is the time "during which the condition of the human race was most happy and prosperous."[11] Historians agree that this peace was maintained by strong emperors and the effective military control of Roman borders. Elliott points out that the Roman wars during this period were "all but uniformly triumphant"—outstanding were Trajan's celebrated conquests and additions to the Roman provinces, the victory against Bar Cochba and his Jewish messianists, the defeat of the barbarian invasions, and the Parthian War."[12]

Moreover, it is one of the currently uncelebrated wonders of prophecy that only one Emperor in the long history of Rome was born in Crete and that was Nerva, who ruled from A.D. 96 to A.D. 98. Though Nerva's reign was short, 16 months, he had had a distinguished

Coin showing Emperor Marcus Aurelius wearing a laurel-wreath crown

Emp. M. Aurelius celebrating victory

Coin showing Cretan bowmaker
Nests. from Elliott 1.137, 139, 140

---

[11]Edward Gibbon, *The History of the Decline and Fall of the Roman Empire*, with notes by H. H. Milman (New ed.; New York: Harper & Brothers, n.d.), 1.95. This statement is quoted also, from various eds. of Gibbon by Elliott, 1.131; Barnes, 143; and Cachemaille, 171. Such prophetic scholars expand and illuminate the remarkable correspondance between Gibbon's description and the implications of our text. Both ancient and modern historians have agreed that this time was outstanding for peace and felicity in the Empire. Boak states that "the long period between the death of Domitian in 96 A.D. and that of Severus Alexander in 235 A.D. falls naturally into two parts. . . . The first of these, closes with the death of Marcus Aurelius in 180 A.D. . . . ." Boak states further that during this period, "the Roman Empire reached its maximum in territorial extent, in population, and in material prosperity. This was due to the happy combination of internal peace and good government which produced for the Mediterranean area as a whole a degree of security and well-being otherwise unexampled in its history for so long a time and has caused this epoch to be looked upon as the golden age of Roman imperialism" (A. E. R. Boak, *A History of Rome to 565 A.D.* [4th ed.; New York: Macmillan, 1955], 313).

[12]See H. G. Wells, *The Outline of History* (Garden City, N. Y.: Garden City Publishing Co., 1921), 455-456; Boak, 313-327; or any good history of ancient Rome.

career as a Roman senator and he enacted several laws to inaugurate reforms designed to eliminate abuse and injustice. One of these was the *Fiscus Judaicus*, a law which put a stop to certain abusive practices connected with the collection of a tax the Romans imposed on Jews.[13] The symbolic allusion to the bow in the hand of the horseman is most appropriate, as Nerva, the first emperor in the succession after the author's time, called attention to his Cretan origin on his coinage.[14] What of Nerva's successors during this era and this era only? To maintain the succession each was chosen and legally adopted by his predecessor, with the result that each was legally and officially Cretan.[15]

6:3-4   **The Red Horse and Rider**   Notes

3. See above Notes on verses 1-2. **4. Then another horse came out.** This marks a new chain of events of a different character than the preceding. The color is changed from white to **fiery red**. The **red** color is universally understood to denote the bloodshed of warfare, as the **rider was given power to take peace from the earth and to make men slay each other.** In that the rider is "given power," the text emphasizes the divine providence which controls the forces of history. This seal clearly indicates a transition from the peaceful condition of the first seal to a time of war and bloodshed. The **large sword** given to this rider, though mentioned in the place of emphasis which concludes the description, may seem

---

[13]Nerva appears to have taken a much more peaceable approach toward Jews, as he not only enacted the *fiscus Judaicus*, but also eliminated defamatory imagery from coins commemorating the Roman conquest of Judea—the representation of a weeping Jewish woman and a victorious Roman soldier on either side of a palm tree representing Judea. The *fiscus Judaicus* is documented by Nerva's revision of one of these coins with the phrase, "Fisci Judaici Calumnia Sublata," translated "the calumny [i.e., defamatory false accusation] of the Jewish tax is lifted"; "Queries & Comments," *Biblical Archaeology Review*, 20.2 (Mar-Apr 1994), 73-81. Hebrew Christians must also have benefited from Nerva's reforms.

[14]Prior to this time each emperor had come from Roman or Italian families. After Domitian this no longer held true, as witnessed by the Roman historian, Aurelius Victor and cited in Elliott, 1.144, with n. 1.

[15]The Emperors of the White Horse period were Nerva, A.D. 96-98; Trajan, A.D. 98-117; Hadrian, A.D. 117-138; Antonius Pius, A.D. 138-161; Marcus Aurelius & Lucius Verus, A.D. 161-169; Marcus Aurelius, A.D. 169-177; Marcus Aurelius with Commodus, A.D. 177-180. Although there has been controversy regarding Hadrian's adoption by Trajan, this seems to have been the officially recognized position of the Senate (R. P. Longdon, "Nerva and Trajan," *Cambridge Ancient History* [Cambridge: University Press, 1936], 11.198-199; Elliott, 1.111-113).

somewhat superfluous after the preceding description. The sword (Gk., μάκαιρος, *mákairos*) was the common weapon of the military at the time of writing, especially of the Roman military. It was the short sword in distinction from the long broad sword (ῥομφαία, *hromphaía*) mentioned in a figurative sense as protruding from the mouth of Jesus (Rev 1:16; 2:12, 16; 19:15, 21; otherwise Rev 6:8, Luke 2:35). Both words may simply mean, "sword," but in the context, the first-century reader would have found very natural the association of the μάκαιρος *mákairos* sword with the Roman military. The adjective, "great," unusual as pertaining to the short sword, suggests the measure of power given with the weapon (cp. *1 Enoch* :19).[16] The bloodshed and the destruction will be extraordinary. **The earth** in this context denotes the world of the first-century reader, the Roman world and the people who live there.[17]

As the first horseman was given to portray a time of peace, so this horseman is given by Providence to indicate a subsequent time of strife and bloodshed in the Empire.

6:3-4   **The Red Horse and Rider**   **Fulfillment**

We have observed above that the period indicated by the white horse and rider forecasts a time when there was to be peace in the ancient Roman Empire. Looking at the time immediately following the writing of the Revelation for the fulfillment of this, the first of the seal prophecies, we observed that such an era began in A.D. 98 with the accession of the Emperor Nerva and lasted through the reign of Marcus Aurelius, ending in A.D. 180.

Assuming as our working model a continuous-historical fulfillment of the Revelation prophecy, what character do historians ascribe to the Empire for the times immediately following Marcus Aurelius? From the accession of the Emperor Commodus in A.D. 180 until the death of Carinus in A.D. 285 conditions existed which strikingly fulfill the

---

[16]The context here clearly disassociates this use of the sword from what Charles calls the eschatological tradition in Scripture, in which Yahweh wields the sword of judgment against His enemies (Isa 27:1; 34:5; 46:10; 47:6; Ezek 21:3-5; Charles, 1:165). In Revelation, the sword of Yahweh's judgment (ῥομφαία, *hromphaía*) is found in the mouth of the exalted Christ.

[17]"The earth" quite consistently has this meaning in the Apocalyptic drama, not as Rome is politically defined, but as that part of the planet Earth on which Daniel's fourth kingdom, the Roman Empire, operates. This usage is not unlike that of the Old Testament usage of the Heb. word אֶרֶץ (Gk., γῆ) meaning "earth," but frequently referring to the homeland of Israel and translated "land."

prophetic imagery of this second seal. When, Commodus, the son of Marcus Aurelius, succeeded his father as sole emperor in 180, all historians testify that a marked change occurred in the Empire. Boak described Commodus as "the ignoble son of a noble father"; he was "cowardly, cruel, and sensual" (327). After a brief, evil reign, Commodus died ignominiously by the hand of an assassin. He introduced an era aptly characterized by the dramatic imagery of our text—civil war and bloodshed.

The formerly happy condition of the Empire is now victimized by competing rivals from the military who ruled by the sword. With the assassination of Commodus, a series of usurpers one after another seized the throne. Over a span of about ninety years there were thirty-two emperors and twenty-seven pretenders who alternately claimed to be emperor, mostly by murderous coups.[18] It was the bloodiest period in the history of pagan Rome. Though civil warfare was the primary problem, this weakened the ability of the Roman Legions to defend its borders against the barbarians, who incessantly attacked and waged warfare on all the borders.

This era, which we may appropriately call the Era of the Red Horse, is unique in that it initiated the eventually fatal dissolution of the Empire. Elliott points out that this chain of events resulted almost inevitably in the other social and political evils predicted in the Revelation with the opening of the third and fourth seals. They accelerated the decline of the pagan Empire. The "'increase of the dangerous power of the army,'" and the subsequent policy of "'the house of Severus,' constituted, as Gibbon expresses it, 'an internal change which undermined the foundations of the empire' . . . ."[19]

This extremely unstable condition of civil warfare indicated by the red horse did not end until Diocletian became emperor and reorganized the Empire in A.D. 285.

6:5-6 **The Black Horse and Rider** Notes

6:5. See above on verses 1-2. The color **black** indicates that the condition of the Empire targeted by this seal was very bad. In the Bible as

---

[18]Barnes, 147 (citing the historian, Sesmondi 1.36); Cachemaille, 176.

[19]Elliott, 1.159, quoting Gibbon, 1.254. Elliott adds that the contemporary historian, Dion Cassius, writing in the early third century his *History of Rome*, gives strong support as agreeing with this conclusion (71.36-72.34).

in the ancient world generally, black was the emblem of mourning.[20] The details also suggest that the prediction not only indicates worsening conditions, but specific circumstances peculiar to the era forecast. Whereas the peace forecast when the First Seal is broken is said to be taken away by the forecast of the Second Seal, we need not infer that the bloodshed of the second Seal ends when the era of the third seal begins. The conditions forecast and the actual fulfillment will determine when each era ends. **The rider was holding a pair of scales in his hand.** The scales are balance scales. Beyond their use for measuring produce and for making payments, the balance scales were in antiquity a universally known symbol of justice. Job stated, "Let me be weighed in a just balance, that God may know my integrity" (31:6, NKJV; cp. NRSV). Many other Scriptures, as well as extrabiblical texts, could be quoted.[21] The balance scales were known to symbolize justice both in this life and in the life to come. The contextual significance of the scales in the hand of the rider is considered further in relation to verse six. **6.** John heard **what sounded like** a voice. The language of comparison ("like") is used here, as often in the Revelation, to remind the reader that John is reporting elements of a visionary experience rather than actual reality. The orientation of the unidentified voice as **among the four living creatures** may be intended to call attention to the divine providence which exercises control over events on the earth. The voice was heard to **keep saying**,[22]

> **A quart of wheat for a denarius,**
> **and three quarts of barley for a denarius,**
> **and do not harm the oil and the wine!** (6:6, NASB)

---

[20]One may cite Mal 3:14, ". . . going about like mourners . . . ." The Hebrew adverb, קְדֹרַנִּית translated here, "like mourners," is built on the Hebrew stem, קָדַר from which also the nouns, קֵדָר "black-skinned (Bedouin tribe)," and קַדְרוּת "black," and the verb, קָדַר "darken," "mourn," are constructed. See Ezek 31:15; Mic 3:6, Isa 50:3.

[21]Commentators allude to Ezek 4:16 and Lev 26:26, which predict famine conditions with the statement, "they shall dole out the bread by weight" (JPSV). However, the scales cast this passage in a different perspective from rationing—the perspective of regulating quantity against price. The popular interpretation that this seal predicts famine and that the balance here simply means measuring out food to famine victims bypasses the most common use of these scales as a symbol for justice, as found in many texts: Lev 19:36; Job 31:6; Psa 62:9; Prov 11:1; 16:11; 20:23; Ezek 45:10; Dan 5:27; Amos 8:5; Mic 6:11; also Sir 28:25; 42:2-4; 2 Ezdr 3:34. In pagan cultures as well as in Israelite life, balance scales were sometimes placed in tombs or shown in funerary inscriptions to indicate just judgment for the deceased in the future life. Further difficulty for the famine interpretation is encountered with the words spoken regarding oil and wine (see our discussion following).

[22]The Greek verb translated "saying" is in the present tense, implying continuing or repeated action.

This statement of the unidentified voice has been the subject of much discussion and controversy. One should recognize that the commodities—**wheat, barley, oil** and **wine**—were the principal staples of diet and of economics in the ancient Roman world.[23] Moreover, the statement clearly emphasizes the price of the commodities, not the fact that they were distributed by measure, as was always done.[24] The **quart** in the original language of the text is the *choenix*, a common measure of about one liter. The **three quarts** of **barley** simply reflects the fact that barley, for the poor man's bread, was ordinarily priced about one-third the price of **wheat**. For the wheat and the barley, then, we have, either for the purpose of information or for the intent to regulate, a statement of the value of these staples. The more interpretive translations render **denarius** "a day's wage(s)" (NEB, NIV, TEV, NAB) *or "a day's pay"* (NRSV). *The Greek original gives a monetary value,* δηνάριον, *dēnárion*, the amount paid in Jesus' parable of the laborers for a day's work in the field (Matt 20:2). The popular interpretation of these injunctions is that they indicate famine or near famine conditions but the evidence for this is commonly exaggerated and does not account fully for the language of our text.[25]

---

[23]"'Corn [i.e., cereal grain] and oil and wine' is the standing formula designating the nutritive products of the earth, whether with reference to times of plenty or dearth; *e.g.* Dt. 7^{13}, 11^{14}, 28^{51}; 2 Chron. 32^{28}; Neh. 5^{11}; Hos. 2$^{8, 22}$; Joel 2^{19}; Hag. 1^{11}. These were the staple food supplies grown in the biblical lands. They were all essential to the normal life of those countries, they were none of them really luxuries" (Isben T. Beckwith *The Apocalypse of John* [1919; Limited editions. library; Baker, 1967], 521). Olive oil was commonly used for cooking, for illumination, for medication, for cleansing of the skin, and other everyday functions. Cf. the references cited by Beckwith, above.

[24]Texts where distribution by measure indicates famine (Lev 26:26, Ezek 4:16) probably reflect the practice of rationing out grain in domestic situations rather than purchasing in the marketplace, as they do not mention price.

[25]For the famine interpretation, see e.g. R. H. Charles, *A Critical and Exegetical Commentary on the Revelation of St. John* (International critical commentary; Edinburgh: T. & T. Clark, 1920), 1.166-167; Ladd, 101; G. B. Caird, *A Commentary on the Revelation of St. John the Divine* (New York, Harper & Row, 1966), 155; William Barclay, *The Revelation of St. John*, (Philadelphia: Westminster, 1960), 6-10. Elliott (1.165, n.*) points out that the evidence for the famine interpretation, largely based on the value given to the δηνάριον, is commonly flawed by unduly inflating the price. G. B. Caird, for example, cites Cicero who lived in Sicily about a century before Domitian, as the standard: "The price appears to be ten to twelve times what it should have been (cf. Cicero, *Verr.* iii.8)," *A Commentary on the Revelation of St. John the Divine* (New York: Harper & Row, 1966) 395.155; so also Charles 1.167; Wm. Barclay, *The Revelation of St. John* (Philadelphia: Westminster Press, 1960), 2.9; Ladd, 100; Beasley-Murray, 133; et al.). The cheaper end of the scale, where the price of bread was 16-20 times cheaper than our text, appears to have been based on the conditions existing in the Carthaginian wars, some 300 years earlier. The famine interpretation may be motivated in part by a tendency to see the author as dependent for the seal prophecies on Matt 24:5-14 (Mark 13:6-24; Luke 21:8-26). This approach is addressed at some length by

Nevertheless, the price our text indicates for wheat and barley is two to three times higher than the price known from Domitian's time, clearly forecasting economically very hard times.[26] The instruction, **do not damage [or harm] the oil and the wine,** as translated, is unclear. While harming vineyards and olive groves is a natural concept, what is to be understood of harming oil and wine? Those who prefer this translation must understand it figuratively in terms of vineyards and olive groves. They often appeal to a decree the Emperor Domitian made on account of surpluses which at first ordered the destruction of vineyards.[27] But, as we are not given prices of "wheat fields" and "barley fields," we should understand the text in terms of the commodities, oil and wine. "Harming" should be understood in relation to the balance scales. Elliott rightly has pointed out that, given the scales and what they imply regarding the administration of justice, the Greek represented in the standard translations by "do not harm or damage," ἀδικησῃς '*adikēsēs*, should be translated according to the primary meaning of that verb, "do no injustice with regard to." This complements very well our understanding of the earlier lines as establishing prices for wheat and barley.[28] So here, the order is to establish a just price for the basic commodities of oil and wine. "Do not inflate them unjustly." What circumstance leads government to levy price controls on basic commodities? Generally, inflation caused by severe economic conditions.

John M. Court, *Myth and History in the Book of Revelation* (Atlanta: John Knox Press, 1979), 48-56.

[26]The calculation is based on Pliny *HN* 18.10, as quoted in Elliott, 1.164-165, where 3 δηνάρι is the average price of a *modius* of wheat. One *modius* = ca. 8 χοίνικες. Pliny wrote in the late first century.

[27]Favored by Charles (1.166-167) as having been advocated by Harnack (*TLZ* [1902], 591 sq.). Domitian issued the edict in A.D. 92 designed to curtail the production of wine but later he withdrew it. Harnack suggested that the author of Revelation was indignant and therefore prophesied a future time when oil and wine would be abundant. Though this fanciful approach to the prophecy hardly needs refutation, it is wanting also in that it fails to account for the inclusion of olive oil with the wine. Nevertheless, many commentators mention this as providing at least an historical rationale for their interpretation.

[28]Elliott documents this use of ἀδικέω carefully: "ἀδικεω is a *neutral intransitive verb*, as well as verb *transitive* and *active*; . . . in the case of intransitive neutral verbs generally there is frequently appended to them an *accusative of definition*, i.e. one defining the *object* to which the verb relates: in which case . . . the accusative usually precedes the verb, so as here"; 1.168; cf. BAGD. The verb in our text is such an intransitive with an accusative of reference. Several other examples of corresponding usage of this verb are given by Elliott.

6:5-6   **The Black Horse and Rider**   **Fulfillment**

We have observed that the Black Horse and Rider forecast an era of severe economic hardship in the Roman Empire. The balance scales and the voice speaking out indicate that justice is needed to correct unjust prices charged for basic commodities. We should expect to be able to identify a time when such conditions existed and to note an Emperor who attempted to administer justice by establishing price controls.

Assuming the sequential nature of the Seal prophecies, we should expect that the era predicted would begin to occur sometime after the inauguration of the civil warfare indicated by the Red Horse and Rider. As noted above, one need not assume that the era of these wars ceased when the Third Seal period begins.

Historians record that in the third century continual civil warfare in the Empire led to excessive taxation. Before this time, the principal revenues came from the tribute, a per capita tax required of Roman citizens, plus, particularly in the provinces, various taxes collected on produce, including excise taxes, customs, and taxes on harvests from the land. Enormous sums were demanded. This excessive demand for state monies was accompanied by severe depreciation of the currencies by which the taxes were paid. Ferrero, after an extensive discussion of this, remarks:

> From thence came a giddy augmentation and a wild irregularity of prices, which reduced the unfortunate peoples to despair and against which the Emperors contended in vain by issuing edicts. Then arose continual impoverishment of the most numerous and least wealthy classes aggravated by the order which several emperors gave that the taxes must be paid in gold. The State refused to receive the bad money with which it was inundating the Empire![29]

The intensifying hardship resulting from an irresponsible government bureaucracy combined with high level inflation and excessive taxation was even more greatly aggravated by the Emperor Caracalla. In the year A.D. 212, to secure more revenue he enacted his famous Edict, known as the Antonian Constitution, by which he gave to all the free people throughout the provinces of the Empire "free" Roman citizenship. They were now faced with the burden of paying to Rome, in addition to all their prior tax responsibilities, the tax mandated formerly only to the

---

[29]Guglielmo Ferrero, *The Ruin of the Ancient Civilization and the Triumph of Christianity* (New York: G. P. Putnam's Sons, 1921), 59-60.

privileged citizen class—the tribute (Boak, 335). Gibbon states, "He crushed alike every part of the empire under the weight of his iron scepter."[30] In addition to the tribute, he doubled the tax on legacies and inheritances from ten to twenty percent (Gibbon, 1.194). The Roman Imperial crisis of the third century focused on the excessive and unjust collection of taxes. Constant turmoil and continuing civil wars, as indicated by the red horse rider, placed great strain on the economy of the Empire. Large armies of mercenaries demanding ever higher pay, the enormous cost of military highways stretching out long distances into the provinces, the feeding and provision of troops, and great public works, demanded more and more taxation. Tax collectors brutally enforced collections, even with the aid of police and soldiers. Many farmers who experienced crop failure fled their land rather than face the tax collectors. Much land became unproductive and many small towns were abandoned (Boak, 367; Ferrero, 56-62). Ferrero continues:

> Exterminated, ruined, or dispersed, the aristocracy and the middle classes which had grown up during the first and second centuries throughout the Empire, which constituted the foundation of its organization,—political and social,—and which by the fusion of Hellenism and Romanism had carried the ancient civilization to its zenith now disappeared.
> ... The Empire sank back internally into barbarism ... [60].

Excessive taxation is recognized by historians as one of the main reasons for the economic decline of the Empire, a decline accompanied by severe hardships.

For collecting tax revenues, the praetors at Rome and the appointed governors in the provinces were the emperor's right arm. Returning to our text, we should not now be surprised to learn that the symbol of their authority for this, as commonly represented on their coinage, however ironic, was the balance scales (see illustrations below).[31]

---

[30]1.160, 194; for an extended discussion of taxes in the Roman Empire see Gibbon, 1.185-195. Caracalla ruled only five years and is remembered chiefly for this edict, which practically all historians note as an important contributing factor in the decline of Rome.

[31]Elliott states, "In imperial times indeed the supreme *judicial* and *financial*, as well as supreme *military* power, centered in *the emperors:* whence the ascription to them of the *balance of justice;* whether in historic writings, or on imperial coins, such as that of Alex. Severus ... , with the legend *Æquitas Augusti* around it. But the authority ... was delegated of course by them to their subordinate provincial and financial governors ... " (1.185-186). "Multitudes of Roman medals, of almost every emperor and every province of the empire, are extant, bearing the device of *a pair of balances*: and all, I believe, in symbolization of equity ... " (1.170, n. 2).

We will see below how these conditions led to the destitution and death depicted dramatically by the Apocalyptic pale horse and rider which follows with the opening of the fourth seal.

Regarding the voice which calls out from among the four living creatures—"A quart of wheat for a denarius, and three quarts of barley for a denarius; and do not harm the oil and the wine" (6:6, NASB)—taxes were most often paid in the produce of the land. The government set prices per standard measure for basic commodities to determine the tax due to Rome.[32] The balance scales and the directive, "Do no injustice with regard to the oil and the wine" (see our Notes, above), reflects the third century concern for just regulation in the collection of taxes, as is also conveyed by the balance scales on Imperial coinage. The symbol on the coins, however, was more fiction than fact. Injustice was common, though at times considerable effort was made to prevent it. Ironically, often the very officials who displayed the balance scales were responsible for the abuse.

Roman coin with modius, standard measure for establishing price of grain

Imperial coin of Alexander Severus illustrating the use of the balance scale as a symbol of justice

Coin showing table of a tax collector

Illus's. from Elliott 1.185

This black horse era produced a particularly remarkable illustration of the conditions dramatized by the symbols of the third seal. Emperor Alexander Severus (A.D. 222-235), an exceptionally judicious ruler, was instrumental in getting laws passed against extortion and injustice in the collection of taxes. In some cases, the official prices to be paid for the staple commodities were named, as in the language of our prophecy. Elliott has pointed out that even the amount stipulated by the voice from the Throne, when the deflation of the *choenix* in the period of

---

[32]As indicated above, the "quart" in the Greek is the *choenix* standard measure, about one liter. Roman taxes were more often measured in the *modius*, a measure of about eight liters. However, when the legislation placed stress upon a very exacting standard, the smaller measure was used (see the ancient Latin sources cited by Elliott, 1.183-184, n. 2).

Alexander Severus is factored in, accurately represents the prices then stipulated.[33]

Surely, the Apocalyptic prophecy has with wonderful brevity and precision targeted this, the second major contributing factor to the decline and fall of pagan Rome.

6:7, 8   **The Pale Horse and Rider**   **Notes**

6:7. See above on verses 1-2. **8.** The color **pale** (Gk., χλωρός, *chlōrós*) is often used of the face bleached by illness; it may as here be a color of a horse (Swete, 88; BAGD, 882). The **rider** of this horse is **named death**. The Greek θάνατος, *thánatos* may also be translated "pestilence," but the action subsequently attributed to the rider supports the common translation. One might be simplistic to suggest that because the rider has the name, "death," he no longer represents the Imperial power of Rome. The label may be intended to suggest that the Imperial power is the bearer of death, as conditions which were to develop in the Empire were largely the consequence of evils in government.[34] **Hades** seems to be walking behind the horse and rider. "Hades" follows behind

---

[33]This is calculated and documented from original sources by Elliott, 1.177-184. In the days of Cassius (d. 42 B.C.), the approximate price of wheat was one *modius* per *denarius*, with a *modius* being the equivalent of eight *denarii*. When these symbols are understood as having their fulfillment in the period of Alexander Severus (A.D. 222-235) some adjustments from the first-century B.C. values can be made. By the time of the Elder Pliny, the price of wheat had tripled to three *denarii* per *modus* (Elliott cites Pliny 18.10, and calculates to show that the average price of a *modius* of wheat in the late first century A.D. was three *denarii* [1.180, n. 4, 1.164-165, n. 2]). By the time of the Constantines (4th century), the price of a *modus* had declined to about one and one-half *denarii*. As the second century was relatively prosperous, it may be reasonable to suppose that only about one third of this decline had occurred by the second quarter of the third century, the time of Commodus. This suggests that Commodus' price would be about one-third of a *denarius*. However, in the third century the *denarius* had been devalued by two-thirds. This makes the true value for Commodus as viewed from the standpoint and language of the first century agree with the voice from the Throne, that is—"one *choenix* of wheat for a *denarius*." Although the general sense of the prophecy was clear to the first-century reader, as with many prophecies, the precise fulfillment could only be known during or after the predicted time!

[34]We have a similar situation in 12:9, where the Dragon is identified with the Devil, yet more than likely is to be identified with pagan Rome which in the setting of the Apocalypse humanly ruled Satan's Empire. Nevertheless, Elliott, with others, does opt for the simpler understanding of the Pale Horse, "The *rider* is not, as before, the representative of *human functionaries* and *rulers* . . . . It was the personification of DEATH!" (1.191).

Death as "death and the grave" are a common couplet. The presence of Hades makes the figure of Death more dramatic. The two **were given power**—again, the passive voice indicates that Providence was exercising control. **One fourth of the earth** probably means "one fourth of the population of the Roman world" (see Mounce, 145).[35] It could mean one-fourth of the area of that world.[36]

To kill by sword, famine and plague, and by the wild beasts of the earth clearly indicates the forecast of an era, as Elliott puts it, "of terrible mortality" (1.191). This formulary expression reproduces the "four dreadful judgments" of Ezek 14:21. As these in turn reflect the Covenant curses of Lev 26:14-39, one should recognize again a reference to the divine providence. In the light of the spread of the Gospel, the Revelation holds even the pagan world responsible to the divine covenant which it rejected with its rejection of Jesus Christ. Mounce points out that "death by wild beasts . . . is to be expected in a land decimated by war and famine" (145).

6:7, 8   The Pale Horse and Rider   Fulfillment

We have noted above that the white horse and rider indicated an era of peace and prosperity. Then the red horse and the black horse with their riders indicate successive overlapping stages with deterioration of the Empire, the second adding further calamity to the preceding. First civil warfare, then the breakdown of the economy with inflation and excessive taxation. Now the pale horse and rider with the name, "Death," suggests some terrible calamity accompanied by the massive loss of human lives.

---

[35]Elliott prefers to assume a Greek original no longer extant but witnessed by the Vulgate of Jerome, that is, τὸ τετράδιον τῆς γῆς, *tò tetrádion tēs gēs,* "the quadripartite earth," or "the four parts of the earth." To witness this syntax, he cites Petrus Siculus, chapter 13: "την του Ευαγγελιου τετρακτυν"; 1.201-202. Mede, in his 17th century commentary, while rejecting this understanding, nevertheless alludes to it as a "common interpretation" of τέταρτον τῆς γῆς of our text (92). This reading then is seen to attest to the division of the Empire into four parts—East, West, Illyricum, and Italy—under the Emperors Posthumous, Aureolus, and Zenobia (1.202). The reading, though attractive, has insufficient support for full confidence.

[36]Barnes, 155. This figure may be understood as metonymy—"the earth" standing for its inhabitants. The same figure is explained in the epexegetical expression, "the earth and its inhabitants" (13:12), where "the earth" is said to worship and therefore cannot be taken literally. Beckwith suggests that "the fourth part" means "a large but not unlimited part" (523, 253).

Chapter Four *The four horsemen, 6:1-8* 141

Our approach to the Revelation leads us to look for the fulfillment in the third century and sometime after the calling forth of the black horse rider, which we dated A.D. 212. Has this prophecy been fulfilled?

The period from A.D. 248 to about A.D. 270, beginning with the rule of the Emperor Philip and ending with the Emperor Aurelianus, is aptly characterized by the rider, "Death." Gibbon says, "During that calamitous period every instant of time was marked, every province of the Roman world was afflicted, by barbarous invaders and military tyrants, and the ruined empire seemed to approach the last and fatal moment of its dissolution" (1.279). Gibbon describes the power of death by the sword. Rampant civil war together with Gothic invasions from the North brought ruin. What about famine? He states, "A long and general famine . . . was the inevitable consequence of rapine and oppression . . . " (1.328-329). Was there also pestilence? Gibbon was not a believer and certainly was not writing a commentary on the Apocalypse but he gives the answer (1.329):

> Famine is almost always followed by epidemical diseases, the effect of scanty and unwholesome food. Other causes must, however, have contributed to the furious plague, which, from the year two hundred and fifty to the year two hundred and sixty-five, raged without interruption in every province, every city, and almost every family, of the Roman empire. During some time five thousand persons died daily in Rome; and many towns that had escaped the Barbarians were entirely depopulated.

Gibbon mentions documents which show that more than half the population of Alexandria perished (1.329; Eus. *Hist.* vii.21). Although we do not have comprehensive statistics, we may reasonably suppose that our prophecy of the death of one-quarter of the population of the Roman world was fulfilled in this epoch. Other historians witness the same. Solomon Katz writes that starting in A.D. 235,

> The Roman Empire was ruled for fifty years by a bewildering succession of soldier-emperors . . . . Of twenty-six reigning emperors . . . only one escaped violent death. A contemporary observer, St. Cyprian, . . . [stated in his *Letters* 1.6,] "Behold, the roads closed by brigands, the sea blocked by pirates, the bloodshed and horror of universal strife. The world drips with mutual slaughter, and murder . . . ."
> Famine and plague rode side by side with Rome's enemies. The scourge of epidemic disease raged for fifteen years, decimating whole regions and undermining the Empire's already weakened powers of resistance.[37]

---

[37]Solomon Katz, *The decline of Rome* (Ithaca, New York: Cornell University Press, 1955), 32-33.

What of the wild beasts? Cachemaille observes, "Where the reign of man fails, that of the wild beasts begins; they quickly occupy scenes of waste and depopulation." The ancient historian, Arnobius, testifies that this, indeed, was so.[38]

The four horses with their riders forecast for first-century and subsequent readers what later historians have seen. They tell us in dramatic symbols what were the most significant and central conditions for understanding the downward course of the Empire during the first two centuries after the Revelation. The horse eventually became inappropriate as a symbol, for the Empire was no longer unified under one head. In A.D. 293 Diocletian divided it into four parts under two senior *Augusti* each ruling with a junior *Caesar*. Augustus Diocletian ruled Asia, Egypt, and Thrace with Caesar Galerius ruling Illyricum and part of the East. Augustus Maximian ruled Italy and Africa (from Milan) with Caesar Constantius (after 297) ruling Gaul and Britain.[39] So, the Empire was divided into four parts and governed by four Emperors.

The Seals (cont'd)

6:9. When he opened the fifth seal, I saw under the altar the souls of those who had been slain because of the word of God and the testimony they had maintained. [10]They called out in a loud voice, "How long, Sovereign Lord, holy and true, until you judge the inhabitants of the earth and avenge our blood?" [11]Then each of them was given a white robe, and they were told to wait a little longer, until the number of their fellow servants and brothers who were to be killed as they had been was completed.

6:9-11   The Souls of the Martyrs   Exposition

With the opening of the fifth seal, the suffering of the church comes to the forefront in the focus on the outcry of martyred souls

---

[38]Cachemaille, 182. Elliott (citing Arnobius), "'Men complain, There are now sent us from the gods *pestilence, droughts, wars, scarcities, locusts,* hail, and other things noxious to man:' and then he asks,—'But was it not so in ancient times also?' . . . . 'Were there not wars with *wild beasts* and battles with *lions and destruction from venomous snakes,* before our time?'" (1.200; cp. Exod 23:29).

[39]Gibbon, 1.406-407; Robert M. Grant, *Augustus to Constantine* (New York: Harper & Row, 1970), 226 (Schaff, 2.65, n. 2). Schaff reports that Gibbon calls Diocletian "the founder of a new empire, rather than the restorer of the old" (2.65), an important observation to which we shall return later.

Chapter Four — The souls of the martyrs, 6:9-11

whose blood cries out from the ground for Divine vindication even as had the blood of Abel. Difficult it is for most Christians in the twenty-first century to comprehend martyrdom as it occurred in ancient and medieval times. There have been many martyrs in recent years, to be sure, but those earlier times excelled in specialized, exquisite ways of putting to death.

Under the ancient Roman Empire, Christians who refused to sacrifice to pagan gods were often tested by torture to induce them to repent—burning alive, impaling alive on sharpened posts, tearing limb from limb—to name a few. Only later, during the Inquisition was the technique of torturing more highly developed.

While many Christians compromised their faith, one must hold in awe the many stalwart believers who refused, though under great duress, to perform any worship ritual to a pagan god. Many died tortuously while many others, consigned to slavery under the most cruel conditions, were it not for their devotion would have preferred death.[40]

The mercifully brief glimpse of coming conflict presented with the opening of the fifth seal was a warning to the church at the beginning of the second century and to all of us even now not to become soft and flabby in faith but to know that this world is the kingdom of Satan. There are battles to be fought and lives to be lost, but also one needs to know that the battle is the Lord's and that life is to be lived and death is to be died not for this or that cause but for the Kingdom of God and for life in the age to come. We are reminded of the Apocalyptic promise, "Blessed are the dead who die in the Lord" (Rev 14:13).

Two institutions are targeted in the presentation of the martyrs—the Word and the Testimony (v. 9). Both are central to the message of our Lord in the Book of Revelation. As the martyrs teach us, both are worth living and worth dying for. To witness to the Word is to declare the presence and the program of the message of our Lord in the Book of Revelation. To witness to the Word is

---

[40]See the excellent work of W. H. C. Frend, *Martyrdom and Persecution in the Early Church* (Garden City, N. Y.: Doubleday, 1967).

to declare the presence and the program of the Sovereign Creator-God, to declare Jesus Christ as the living God-Man Redeemer and loving Savior. The Testimony here is the witness of the true believer, who knows by experience saving faith and the sanctifying presence of Christ through His Holy Spirit. That testimony by deed and by word of mouth is the living Gospel message to the lost world. It is the means of grace by which God most often calls men to Himself.

But there is apparent injustice to be experienced in this life. The martyrs cry out, "How long, Sovereign Lord, holy and true, until you . . . avenge our blood?" The message is to remind us that the witness is to continue. The Church must complete its mission to the world until the Day appointed for the final judgment.

6:9-11   **The Souls of the Martyrs**   Notes

9. He is again "the Lamb," Jesus Christ. See Rev 6:1-2, above. John saw the souls **under the altar**. The altar, unmistakably, is the great altar of sacrifice of the Israelite tabernacle and temple. We should not overlook the fact that, as in chapter one, where Christ as high priest walks among the sanctuary lampstands representing the churches, so here again we have Israelite imagery introduced.[41] As under the New Covenant the Church is the true temple, that is, the antitype of which the Old Covenant temple is the type, so the Church—Messianic Jews and believing Gentiles—is also the true Israel. The altar focuses on the Atonement, the antitypical atoning sacrificial death of Christ. As the animal victims blood

---

[41]It is a hermeneutical fallacy to infer from this symbolic representation of the altar in apocalyptic genre that an actual altar exists in heaven. Sufficient for the Apocalyptic imagery is the prior existence of the Israelite-Jewish altar, the meaning of which is well clarified in the Scriptures. To assume that this altar is to be perceived as existing in heaven (apparently, Charles, 1.172-173; Mounce, 146; Walvoord, 133; et al.) is to miss what is fundamental to the whole plan of the Apocalypse, that is, that the Temple imagery, as in the very first scene (1:12-20), is oriented with respect to the church on earth (cf. 11:1, 2). This corresponds to the biblical typology, central to the redemptive message of Scripture and expressed in the Apostle Paul's affirmation addressed to the church of Corinth, "You, yourselves, are God's temple" (1 Cor 3:16). For a thorough exegesis of the Apocalyptic scenery, see Elliott, 1.97-110; cp. Rom 12:1-2.

was poured at the base to flow under the Israelite altar (Lev 4:7), so in the Apocalyptic drama the souls of the martyrs cry out from that place. The language draws not only from ritual slaughter on the Temple altar but also from the Old Testament concept that the Hebrew נֶפֶשׁ, *nĕphĕsh* ("life," "soul," "living being") is inherent in the blood (Deut 12:23). As the blood of Abel cried out from the ground where he had been slain, the souls of the dead martyrs are seen under the altar (Gen 4:10). The **souls**, conceptually in the disembodied condition of the intermediate state, have aroused from their repose (see Rev 6: 11).[42] **10.** They call out **with a loud voice** to the Lord. Loudness probably is intended to put great emphasis on what follows. God is addressed here as **Sovereign Lord** (Gk., δεσπότης, *despótēs*), the strongest affirmation of the Divine authority. King of heaven and earth, His purposes will prevail. God also is **holy and true**, an affirmation giving character to his absolute authority. These qualities are fundamental to the nature of God and intrinsic to His redemptive work and His eternal kingdom. They are given great emphasis in Revelation (cf. 4:8; 14:4; 15:3; 19:8; 19:11, 21:2, 27; 22:14). The call to **avenge** is not for retaliatory vengeance but for vindication of God's justice in the martyrs' cause (Rom 12:19). **11.** The **white robe**, as always in the Book of Revelation, is a symbol of righteousness. Given to each of the martyrs, it should be understood as an emblem of the substitutionary atonement and of the imputed righteousness of Christ (Rom 3:21, 22; 5:18, 19; Gal 3:6, 7). Then, they were told to wait a little longer, until the number of their fellow servants and brothers who were to be killed as they had been was completed.[43]

At least two conclusions are implied by this text. First, the prophecy implies that we have in the message of the sixth seal only one link in a chain of predicted events. More is to follow. Second, this seal

---

[42]It would be hazardous to construct a doctrine of the nature of man from this highly symbolic passage. Nevertheless, the text appears to assume conceptually the existence of the soul independently of the body, though generally in a state of repose or rest. The intermediate state of death is most often described in Scripture as "sleep" (Deut 31:16; 2 Sam 7:12; 1 Kgs 1:21; Job 7:21; Psa 13:3; Jer 51:39, 57; Dan 12:2; Matt 9:24; Mark 5:39; Luke 8:52; John 11:11; 12; 1 Cor 11:30; 15:51; 1 Thess 4:14), a concept into which this text fits harmoniously, as the instruction to "return to their rest" seems to imply their having awakened from sleep.

[43]The verb translated here "to wait" ἀνάπαυσις, *'anápausis*, means literally "to rest" (BAGD, 59). Rev 13:14, "Write: Blessed are the dead who die in the Lord from now on.' 'Yes,' says the Spirit, 'they will rest from their labor, for their deeds will follow them.'" Thus, our text indicates that the intermediate state is a time of rest, a time to celebrate the righteous deeds of those who have died "in the Lord." Cp. Dan 12:13, "As for you [Daniel, now an old man], go your way till the end. You will rest, and then at the end of the days you will rise to receive your allotted inheritance."

prophecy is given not only to indicate theological truth or to teach principles which may be applied as appropriate throughout history—it points to a specific future time or era which will also be characterized by martyrdom. is a central theme in the Apocalypse (cf. 11:7, 8, 12:11, 13:15, 14:4, 17:6, 19:2, 20:4).

6:9-11   **The Souls of the Martyrs**   **Fulfillment**

Persecution and martyrdom, symbolized here with the opening of the fifth seal, was during the second and third centuries of the church occasional and sporadic, often existing in one location or another at the whim of local rulers. But new conditions came into play in the Roman Empire in the fourth century which brought the conflict into sharp focus and which accounts for the place of the altar of sacrifice in the number sequence in the opening of the seals.

Near dissolution in the era of the fourth seal, the pagan Roman Empire experienced brief recovery under the rule of several restoring Emperors, the most eminent and powerful of whom was the last, Diocletian. However, after the restoration had been accomplished, then Diocletian in A.D. 303 announced his determination to eliminate Christians and Christianity from the Empire.

So severe were Diocletian's edicts of extermination that his reign has come to be known by historians as the Era of the Martyrs. Churches were razed, libraries of sacred books were burned, and believers were tortured to death. Prior persecutions had been local and spasmodic—generally inconsequential against the spread of the Christian faith. Diocletian's war against the church is the outstanding exemplar of pagan fear and hatred of the true Faith.[44] At least two conclusions are implied by this text. First,

---

[44]The sacred symbolism mercifully fails to relate the details of the exquisite tortures by which these saints were put to death. In the carrying out of the destruction and slaughter, Diocletian was aided by his zealous son-in-law and co-ruler in the East, Galerius. While the truly faithful refused to recant or to sacrifice to pagan deities, many nominal believers did give in. Although historians generally are at a loss to know what provoked Diocletian and Galerius to turn against the Christians, Eusebius believed that the tragedy was God's judgment against excesses of the church: "When, by reason of excessive liberty, we sunk into negligence and sloth . . . , then the divine judgment . . . began to afflict its episcopacy . . . ." "Then, as Jeremiah says, 'The Lord in his anger darkened the daughter of Sion, and hurled from heaven to earth the glory of Israel." Eusebius cites envying, quarrels, threats, hatred, competition for high office, etc., most particularly among the clergy. (Eusebius *Eccl. Hist.* Bk. 8.1. For his treatment of the entire epoch, see Eusebius, *Eccl. Hist.* Bk 7.1-32; *Bk. of Martyrs* 1-8.) For an in-depth study of these persecutions with extensive bibliography, see Frend, 350-392, 548-554.

the chronological sequence of the seal prophecies appropriately targets Diocletian's persecution. Second, the message of the fifth seal also focuses more generally on suffering and martyrdom, a phenomenon which occurred in various locations and with various intensities throughout the entire earlier period of the seals, as well as after Diocletian until Constantine became sole emperor. The completion of the number of the martyrs mentioned in verse 11 was to await yet another era foretold in Revelation 13. The symbolic "Beast," an apostate church, was to conduct a war against the true faith which would dwarf the persecutions of the pagan Emperors (see below, on 13:1-10).

The Seals (cont'd)

¹²I watched as he opened the sixth seal. There was a great earthquake. The sun turned black like sackcloth made of goat hair, the whole moon turned blood red, ¹³and the stars in the sky fell to earth, as late figs drop from a fig tree when shaken by a strong wind. ¹⁴The sky receded like a scroll, rolling up, and every mountain and island was removed from its place. ¹⁵Then the kings of the earth, the princes, the generals, the rich, the mighty, and every slave and every free man hid in caves and among the rocks of the mountains. ¹⁶They called to the mountains and the rocks, "Fall on us and hide us from the face of him who sits on the throne and from the wrath of the Lamb! ¹⁷For the great day of their wrath has come, and who can stand?"

6:12-17   The Great Earthquake   Introduction

After the opening of the sixth seal, three scenes are introduced consecutively into the Apocalyptic narrative: 1. The Great Earthquake (6:12-17), 2. The Sealing of the 144,000 (7:1-17), and 3. The Great Multitude in White. The last is then followed by the opening of the seventh seal (8:1). At this juncture, it is essential that the reader understand the literary-dramatic structure of the Book of Revelation. Chapter seven, like chapters four and five, introduces an interlude, an excursus from the presentation of "what must take place after this" (Rev 4:1, which see). This excursus is indicated in 7:1 by the "four angels . . . holding back the four winds of the earth." This is an apocalyptic way of putting the passage of time on hold while the message of chapter seven unfolds.

The message of this excursus is preliminary to what follows, with the resumption of the prediction of earthly events in chapters eight through fourteen.

6:12-17.   **The Great Earthquake**   **Exposition**

When the Lamb opened the sixth seal, as earlier John had seen before him the temple sanctuary (1:12-16) and the altar of the altar court (6:9), he now saw spread out in front of him the Roman earth with its pagan populace, slave and free—the rulers and the ruled. Spread above he saw the heavens, that is, the sky. As he watched this scene intently, calamity struck. But, we are not to take the visionary description as physical reality. It would be impossible in the physical sense for the stars to fall to the earth, this to be followed by what is described in verses 15-17. We know that the immense size and intense heat of one star would evaporate the earth before it could reach our planet. It would be impossible for the sky to roll up like a scroll and the mountains and islands to be removed from their places while life continues on earth. The language here, as in most of the Apocalyptic drama, is symbolic. It must be understood as indicated by the use of such symbols as they occur elsewhere in the Bible.

We are not at a loss, however, to understand this seal. The rhetorical style and the figures of speech found here are all commonplace in the Old Testament prophets. There we can examine them in context and know their meaning. This approach to the symbols leads to the conclusion that this sixth seal does not describe literal celestial and terrestrial happenings but radical revolution of temporal government (see our Notes below).

In our exposition of the first four Seals, we have seen the pagan Roman Empire after an era of peace gradually disintegrate. Then, after a short-lived recovery, the Empire is bent on the destruction of the Christian Faith, as symbolized by the fifth seal. Now, if we allow the Apocalyptic message to unfold in the manner

Chapter Four *The great earthquake, 6:12-17* 149

natural to the original readers, we should expect that the government then forecast to collapse was the pagan Roman Empire and that the collapse will be due to the wrath "of him who sits on the throne" and "the wrath of the Lamb."

Christians can take heart from knowing that God, while permitting certain evils, nevertheless will not forever withhold His judgment nor forfeit His sovereign control.

Earthly potentates must learn that there is a sovereign and holy God who throughout history has exercised temporal judgments. Nevertheless, believers should exercise good influences, in so far as possible both locally and nationally, to purge evil and to establish sound, Godly governmental policies.

6:12-17   **The Great Earthquake**   **Notes**

12. I watched repeats the formula which introduced the First Seal, giving the renewed emphasis appropriate to this final and catastrophic episode of the seal prophecies. Regarding **as he [the Lamb] opened** the sixth seal, see above, p. 104-111. **The sixth seal** is the last Seal to disclose mundane events.[45] We must return to this later; see on 8:1, below. The **great earthquake** indicates an extraordinary and terrifying disturbance, especially in the political sphere.[46] The figure is frequently invoked by the Hebrew prophets to describe military conquest with its revolutionary and devastating disruption of life—of ruling powers and religious institutions. Jeremiah states regarding the impending Babylonian destruction of Judah, "I looked at the mountains, and they were quaking; and all the hills were swaying . . ." (4:24). Haggai presents both the figure and his own interpretation:

> In a little while I will once more shake the heavens and the earth, the sea and the dry land. I will shake all nations, and the desired of all

---

[45] The same appears to be true of the Trumpet series, as the seventh trumpet introduces an excursus with scenes which have their orientation in heaven (11:15-19). The seventh bowl, on the other hand, continues the sequence of bowl judgments, adding a seventh prediction to those that precede. This provides an important clue for understanding the chronological relationship of the seal, the trumpet, and the bowl judgments.

[46] This "earthquake" may be contrasted with another in 16:18, the latter to occur under the seventh bowl.

nations will come, and I fill this house with glory. . . . . . . Tell Zerubbabel . . . that I will shake the heavens and the earth. I will overturn royal thrones and shatter the power of the foreign kingdoms (2:6, 21, 22).

These are the words of the LORD regarding national powers impeding the future glory of the Second (i.e., post-exilic) Temple.[47] This prophetic use of terrestrial symbolism should warn us against interpretations which look for a literal earthquake.

Moreover, the end-time, literal interpretation now popular can hardly be sustained in view of texts which differently describe the final cataclysm. 2 Pet 3:10 states that "the heavens will disappear with a roar; and the elements will be destroyed by fire, and the earth and everything in it will be laid bare." Characteristically, terrestrial symbolism makes no mention of burning nor of fire.[48] **12-13. The sun,** like the **moon** and **the stars** which follow, should be understood as astral symbols in accord with their symbolic use in Hebrew poetry, as often in the judgment prophecies of the Old Testament. The celestial symbols represent ruling powers of

---

[47]Though one need not require that Haggai comprehended in advance the chronology of fulfillment, the "earthquake" of the prophecy must be understood to have been fulfilled primarily in the days of the second temple (see C. F. Keil, "Haggai," *Commentary on the Old Testament* [Peabody, Mass.: Hendrickson, 1989], 185-202). As indicated in Daniel's prophecies and by subsequent history, the Persian and Grecian powers were broken (2:39, 40; 7:6, 7; 8:5-12). The promise of greater glory to the temple was fulfilled both by the wealth of the nations brought to the Second Jerusalem Temple and by the grand remodeling by Herod by means of which the Temple complex was unrivaled in the ancient world (Carol Meyers, "Jerusalem Temple," *ABD* [New York: Doubleday, 1992], 6.364-365). The promise of peace (v. 9) may be understood of the Second Temple as the place where the Messiah was to be presented to the Covenant Nation.

[48]A correct hermeneutic will require that the language has one meaning, either literal or figurative. Many more examples of the figurative use of such apocalyptic symbols occur in Scripture. Isaiah, with reference to Yahweh's judgment against Babylon, states, ". . . The earth will shake from its place at the wrath of the LORD Almighty . . ." (13:13; cf. Hag 2:6, 7; Isa 24:18b-20; Amos 8:8; Joel 2:10; *T. Mos.* 2:4; 2 Esdr 9.3, et al.). Cuninghame, in *A dissertation on the Seals and Trumpets of the Apocalypse* (London: T. Cadell; Hatchard; and J. Nisbet, 1843), 16, states, "The natural universe is used as a symbol of the political world; whence it follows, that a great earthquake denotes a mighty revolution in the world politic."

various magnitude. Isaiah forecasts as follows the ancient destruction of Babylon by the Medes(Isa 13:10; cf. Jer 4:23):[49]

> The stars of heaven and their constellations
> will not show their light.
> The rising sun will be darkened
> and the moon will not give its light.[50]

As late figs drop from a fig tree reflects the language of Isa 34:4 and has no connection with Matt 24:32 (Charles 1.181). The effect is to make more dramatic the description of falling stars. **14. The sky receded like a scroll, rolling up.** Again the text reflects the language of Isa 34:4, "the sky rolled up like a scroll," referring here to "all nations" (cp. Psa 102:25, 26). The language should be understood as metaphorical rather than literal, predicting in the ancient metaphor the Divine destruction of earthly powers, perhaps together with their imagined astrological deities.[51] **Every mountain and island was removed from its place.** Again, apocalyptic metaphor derived from severe earthquake activity

---

[49]The rationale for the use of astronomical bodies as symbols for the powers of human rulers appears to have arisen originally in the pagan culture in which kings claimed to rule under the authority of gods who were believed to be represented in the pagan pantheon by heavenly bodies. From the appearance of the heavens, the highest god was represented by the sun, the spouse or consort by the moon, and lesser gods by the stars (cp. Gen. 37:9, 10). Thus the divine authority of kings in the pagan world was often symbolized on their monuments and stelae by representations of the sun, moon, and stars above their heads. See further for biblical and extrabiblical use: Isa 34:4a; Jer 4:23b; Ezek 32:7; Amos 8:9; Zeph 1:15; Joel 2:30, 31; Matt 24:29 || Mark 13:24 || Luke 21:25a; *T. Mos.* 10.5; 2 Ezdr. 5:4, 5; cp. 1 Enoch 2.1, 41.5.

Charles correctly states regarding the woes of the sixth seal, "They are not in our author the immediate heralds of the end . . . . The end cannot come till the great persecution and martyrdom of the faithful have taken place" (1.179). They are precursors of the end of the world only in the sense that they indicate that a sovereign Deity metes out judgment. Temporal calamities are portents of God's eventual end-time judgment—calamitous for the unregenerate. There is, nevertheless, a certain ambiguity in apocalyptic symbolism which should discourage dogmatism and encourage watchfulness for impending judgment, whether temporal in this age or end-time and final.

[50]So also we should expect that the celestial signs of Matt 24:29 (with Mark 13:24, 25; Luke 21:25, 26) forecast radical revolution among nations.

[51]The language of Isa 34:5-17 addresses Edom specifically, apparently as an exemplar for reason of which the other nations are to take heed. The prophecy has temporal dimensions—the wild desert creatures after the destruction will "dwell there from generation to generation" (vv. 14-17). We probably should understand vv. 9, 10 metaphorically. Edom will suffer a severe and permanent destruction comparable to that of Sodom and Gomorrah (vv. 9, 10; cp. Jer 49:18) followed by a long period of desolation (vv. 10-17). The prediction regarding Edom was fulfilled sequentially by the Babylonian and Moslem destructions.

speaks of Divinely instigated temporal disruption of seemingly permanent human institutions. Jer 4:24 reads, "I looked at the mountains, and they were quaking; all the hills were swaying . . ." (cf. 10:4). That the language cannot be taken literally is obvious from what follows in verses 15, 16.[52]

15. The kings . . . the princes, the generals [etc.] embrace all classes of people. The language here is literal and in part explanatory of what precedes (cp. Luke 21:26). "Kings" (Greek, βασιλεῖς, *basileîs*) reflects the Hebrew, מְלָכִים, *mᵉlakím*. In the Semitic idiom of the Apocalypse, the word may refer to any heads of state, an appropriate term for Roman emperors. **The earth**, here and throughout in both common and Apocalyptic metaphor, is the Roman world, that governed by the dragon and the beasts of chapters 12 and 13.[53] The symbols derive their political orientation both from Revelation's historical setting and from the fourth beast of Daniel seven (see on chs. 12-13, below). **16. They called to the mountains and the rocks, "Fall on us and hide us."** Cp. Hosea's warning of the impending destruction of Samaria, "Then they will say to the mountains, 'Cover us!' and to the hills, 'Fall on us!'" (10:8; cf. Isa 10:2, 19, 21; Luke 21:20; 23:30)[54] The extreme fear of the populace giving rise to their desire to hide in mountain caves is targeted here. Archaeological discoveries at Qumran and the Bar Kokhba caves of Murabbaʿat have illustrated the practice in the ancient biblical world of fleeing for cover to remote caves. **Hide us from . . . him who sits on the**

---

[52]Neither can the innovative interpretation of Albert Barnes be sustained. Barnes sees in the symbolism of the sixth seal "the impending judgments from the invasion of the northern hordes of Goths and Vandals, threatening the breaking up of the Roman empire—the gathering of the storm, and the hovering of those barbarians on the borders of the empire . . ." (166). The symbols indicate radical revolution, not merely the threat of invasions and a "gathering of the storm."

[53]The concept that the "world" was represented by that part governed by Rome was illustrated in the Early and Medieval Church by the use by the ecumenical councils of the term, οἰκουμένος, from which our word, "ecumenical," is derived. Its lexical meaning is "inhabited earth," "world," or "Roman Empire." The term was used with reference to the churches of the Roman world.

[54]Although the Isaiah passage appears to refer to the end time, one should not: assume that similar rhetoric in another place has the same chronological referent. Always the immediate context has priority for determining the larger meaning (here, the prophetic chronology), including the literary structure in which the text has its place. Luke 23:29, 30 reflects 21:23 and is best understood of the Roman destruction of Jerusalem; William Barclay, *The Gospel of Luke* (Edinburgh: Saint Andrew Press, 1953), 296; William F. Arndt, *The Gospel according to St. Luke* (St. Louis: Concordia Publishing House, 1956), 465-466); E. E. Ellis, *The Gospel of Luke* (London: T. Nelson & Sons, 1966; repr., Eugene, Oreg.: Wipf & Stock, 2003), 244-245, 266.

throne and from the wrath of the Lamb! Cp. Hos 10:8. The populace will view this revolutionary event as an act of God's judgment, even also a judgment of Jesus Christ. "The wrath of the Lamb" is an ironic use of the "lamb" symbol; nevertheless, Christ affirmed His wrath, as reported in Matt 25:41-46; cp. Luke 21:36. Moreover, that the Messiah would judge the ungodly was a standard doctrine of Judaism (cf. Charles 1.182-183). **The face of** God reflects the Semitic idiom indicating direct, personal communication, in this instance, negative (cp. Psa 10:11; 13:1; 17:15; et al.). **17. The great day of their wrath** refers to a time when those described in v. 15 fear they are being subjected to Divine judgment.[55] Contrary to many expositors, it should not be taken exclusively to refer to the end-time Day of the LORD. A proper understanding of the biblical use of "the day of the LORD" is of great importance to this text. The late J. Barton Payne stated accurately that "Zephaniah furnishes . . . a succinct Biblical demonstration of the comprehensiveness of this phrase, to identify that wide range of points in history at which God lays bare His holy arm to achieve His redemptive, testamentary goals."[56] Payne indicated that Zephaniah applies "the day of the LORD" in certain texts to his own time and in other texts to the future. Zephaniah's expression, "the great day of the LORD" (1:14a), Payne applies correctly to the days of Josiah and the impending destruction by the Babylonians which occurred in 586 B.C..[57] The text reads (Zeph 1:14a, 16, 18c, JPSV; cp. REB):

> The great day of the LORD is approaching—
> Approaching most swiftly.
> . . . .

---

[55]This text is better served by the variant reading, αὐτοῦ (i.e., His wrath), as the clause explains the motive of those who flee from the Divine wrath, and therefore is best understood as representing their thought rather than that of the author. See Charles, 1.183, *"This verse expresses the alarm of the conscience-stricken inhabitants of the earth . . . .* but our author teaches that the end is not yet; the roll of the martyrs is not yet complete; the unbelieving world has worse woes still to encounter." If the reading, αὐτων, is preferred, the plural pronoun may be understood to refer to God and the Lamb (Swete, 530).

[56]*Encyclopedia of Biblical Prophecy* (New York: Harper & Row, 1973) 440.

[57]Payne translates Zeph 1:2 and comments, "'I will utterly consume all things from off the face of the ground [Heb.,הָאֲדָמָה] . . . man and beast, birds and fish.' This might suggest . . . earth's final destruction. But the immediate context moves into the punishment of sinful Judah at the exile (v. 4[-13]) and concludes in v. 18 with the parallel words that therefore 'the whole land [Heb., הָאָרֶץ] shall be devoured . . . He will make an end of all them that dwell in the land [Heb., הָאָרֶץ].'" (Payne 439-443, cf. 131-133) Both Hebrew terms, הָאֲדָמָה and הָאָרֶץ, can be used either in the local sense, "the ground" or "the land" or more universally, "the earth" or "the world." Context must always be the determinant.

> A day of horn blasts and alarms—
> Against the fortified towns
> And the lofty corner towers.
> . . . .
> The whole land will be consumed;
> He will make a terrible end
> Of all who dwell in the land.[58]

Joel likewise describes the Day of the LORD as "great" and "dreadful," while applying the language to a contemporary locust plague in the days of ancient Israel (2:11, cf. v. 31). The context in every instance must indicate the point in time to which it refers. Moreover, the biblical prophets generally viewed every judgment of Yahweh as having both immediate relevance and ultimate significance. **Who can stand?** The question is rhetorical and the answer negative. No one can withstand the strong arm of Divine judgment. Cp. with Nah 1:6; Mal 3:2. The scene does not indicate the final eschatological event but suggests nevertheless the fear which accompanies such judgment.

6:12-17   The Great Earthquake   Fulfillment

As we have observed in our notes above, the celestial and terrestrial symbolism used in this text occurs frequently in prophetic passages of the Old Testament to describe the fall in ancient times of earthly kingdoms. Each is viewed by the prophets, not simply as the result of human failure in governance or in warfare, but as also the decisive hand of Divine providence. God chose to judge heathen nations for their idolatries and for their oppression of Israel. Moreover, He chose also in a similar manner to judge Israel for its apostasy.

Consequently, when we look for the fulfillment of this seal, we should look for a nation or government central to the unfolding revelation of this book which falls in consequence of a Divine judgment. Moreover, the chronology of the seal prophecies indicates that this judgment should have occurred soon after the persecutions of Diocletian predicted by the fifth seal.

Just such an event did in fact occur, an event historians are unanimous in identifying as a major turning point in history—the fall about

---

[58]The contextual references to the geography and political orientation of Judah in the day of the prophet clearly testify to a judgment which was to occur in the land of Israel in ancient times. One need not translate the terms more broadly to make a more universal practical application of the prophet's message.

A.D. 325 of the pagan Roman Empire. Contemporary historians recorded with great wonder this unanticipated and revolutionary event. The church historian, Eusebius, who lived to witness both Diocletian's persecution and Constantine's revolution from paganism to Christianity wrote,

> We . . . have been beyond measure astonished at the magnitude of the grace manifested by the author of our mercies, and . . . bear witness to the truth of those declarations recorded, where it is said, 'come hither and behold the works of God, the wonders that he hath done upon the earth . . . .' . . . All the race of the enemies of God were . . . thus suddenly swept away from the sight of men . . . (*Eccles. Hist.*, Bk. 10.1.).

Excursus on Celestial and Terrestrial Signs

Many contemporary commentators interpret the sixth seal prophecy as pertaining to the end of time—circumstances connected with the second coming of Christ. Often the passage is taken to indicate, literally, a celestial-terrestrial event. Several influences have come to bear upon current interpretation: 1. Internal elements in the text taken in the context of an assumed parallel or synchronous structure of the seals, trumpets, and bowls imagery (see Appendix 3). (Circular reasoning may be at work here.) 2. A superficial reading, when compared with other end-time prophecies may lead in this direction. 3. Our Lord's prediction concerning the "darkening of the sun," etc. (Matt 24:29; Mark 13:24, 25; Luke 21:25, 26) is often invoked as a chronological parallel, in spite of the fact that this kind of language is used of many different events, both fulfilled and unfulfilled, prophesied elsewhere in Scripture. Moreover, historicist scholars have understood the celestial signs of Matthew 24 as also pertaining to the fall of the pagan Roman Empire. 4. Commentaries that deny that the Revelation is predictive prophecy and that are devoted to finding only general principles for application seldom give due attention to structural elements and the chronology of prediction. 5. The influence of the popular eschatology of Scofield dispensationalism. 6. Scholars who reject the supernatural providential element as assuring the accuracy of biblical prediction incline to interpret prophetic pronouncements regarding events now historically and accurately fulfilled as evidence of an erroneous expectation of the end-time as near.

The language obviously intends to indicate a great revolution—a decisive and terrifying act of Divine judgment. Nevertheless, this text should derive its specific meaning from the use of such apocalyptic language in the Bible. What this implies may best be seen by examining the Old Testament occurrences of the symbols which describe this seal. Illustrative passages will be given in the notes below. Current commentators appear to neglect to consult the older post-Reformation divines on the Apocalypse, most of whom defended our view. Some of the post-Reformation apologists pursued the analysis of the Apocalypse systematically and thoroughly in the effort to refute Jesuit proponents of the preterist and futurist schools. Although these works must be understood in the light of their times, the authors were committed to the authority of the Scriptures and often displayed a more comprehensive and insightful understanding of biblical prophecy than the modern writers who have been influenced substantially by the preteristic and futuristic interpreters whom the Reformers opposed. See Appendix 1. Expositors who have held our view of the Sixth Seal include: Brightman, Mede, Trapp, Goodwin, Jurieu, Edwards, Daubuz, Isaac Newton, Thomas Newton, Simpson, Faber, M'Leod, Clarke, Thomas Scott, Hutcheson, Bloomfield, Elliott, B. W. Johnson, Cachemaille, Atkinson, H. Barton, Ash, French, and Caringola. Clarke quotes Dr. Dodd as follows, "The fall of Babylon, Idumea, Judah, Egypt, and Jerusalem, has been described by the prophets in language equally pompous, figurative, and strong" (Clarke 6.9).

As Joseph Mede in his ground breaking analysis of Apocalyptic structure indicated in 1632 (and many after him), such symbolism is a common way of referring to "the ruin of states and . . . their entire subversion" (99-100). Mede cites numerous parallels from the prophecies, including prophecies that were fulfilled in the ancient past (*ibid.*). Elliott writes, "From earliest times, the symbols of the sun, moon, and stars were used of rulers," a practice illustrated by Joseph's dream 1.247; Gen 37:9). Similarly, the earthquake, which had been experienced in antiquity to have destroyed entire civilizations, came to be a symbol for national calamity of whatever origin viewed as a judgment of God.

Those who assume an end-time understanding of the sixth seal sometimes hold that the language refers to literal astral, solar, and terrestrial events. Yet, in the natural order of creation, this is impossible. Literal stars cannot fall to a literal earth. The sky cannot roll up like a scroll. Were this somehow possible, humans could not remain on earth as described in vv. 15 and 16 to call for refuge from an angry God. If not literal, then the language must be apocalyptic symbolism. The reader must assume the meaning given to such language in other Scriptures. Though this by itself does not rule out an end-time interpretation, other factors lead in that direction.

There is a marked contrast between the language used to describe the event of the sixth seal and a comparable but subsequent event in the end-time as described in chapter 16. Here we have "a great earthquake." There we have "a severe earthquake. No earthquake like it has ever occurred since man has been on earth, so tremendous was the quake." There is in chapter 16 a deliberate contrast with what precedes.

Moreover, the final, end-time destruction with which commentators often identify the language of the sixth seal will be accompanied by fire, "'Surely the day is coming; it will burn like a furnace. All the arrogant and every evildoer will be stubble, and that day that is coming will set them on fire,' says the LORD Almighty. 'Not a root or a branch will be left to them . . . . they will be ashes under the soles of your feet . . .'" (Mal 4:1, 3); "The heavens will disappear with a roar; the elements will be destroyed by fire, and the earth and everything in it will be laid bare" (2 Pet 3:10).

Bloomfield, in his *Greek Testament* published in 1837, states that "this sixth seal is generally understood to refer to the downfall of paganism, and the

Chapter Four — *The great earthquake, 6:12-17*

establishment of Christianity in the reign of Constantine (2.577-578). The language of the sixth seal prophecy exactly describes an event now historical—the revolutionary fall of the pagan Roman Empire. This we will address in our fulfillment section below.

Several factors lead us to understand with the great majority of the older post-Reformation interpreters that the sixth seal is a fulfilled prophecy pertaining to the pagan Roman Empire: (1) The place of this prophecy in the general structure and plan of the Revelation, as both preceded and followed by prophecies relating to the progress of earthly events (see Append. 3). (2) The remarkable correspondence between the predictions of the first five Seals and the progress of Roman history, A.D. 96-312, as presented above. (3) The character of the sixth seal symbolism as commonly employed in the Bible with respect to prophecies fulfilled in ancient times. (4) The remarkable correspondence between the elements of the sixth seal prophecy and the events of the early fourth century A.D., as will be presented in the Fulfillment section to follow. As Adam Clarke stated, the fall of the pagan Roman Empire was one of the two greatest events that have taken place from the flood to the eighteenth century (the other being the Roman destruction of Jerusalem). Referring to our text, he stated that such an event would "well justify the strong figurative language used here."[59]

Elliott compares God's raising up of Cyrus as his agent to deliver the Covenant people from the Babylonian captivity to God's Providence through Constantine in saving His people from pagan Roman oppression.[60] William Jones says it this way, "The fall of paganism, which may be considered as having begun to take place in the reign of Constantine, and as nearly consummated in that of Theodosius, is probably one of the most extraordinary revolutions that ever took place on the theater of this world."[61] The pagan philosophers of the time, who viewed the demise of paganism as highly portentous, are quoted by Gibbon as having described this revolution "as a dreadful and amazing prodigy, which covered the earth with darkness, and restored the ancient dominion of chaos and of night" (3.155).

We can assume that the prophecy focuses not only on the revolution of the Empire at the time of Constantine and his contemporaries but, more broadly,
on the entire period of the conversion and establishment of the church-state alliance beginning with Constantine and ending with Theodosius, A.D. 325-550.

---

[59]Adam Clarke, "The Revelation of St. John the Divine," *The New Testament of Our Lord and Saviour Jesus Christ* (New York: Carlton & Porter, n.d.), 2.995.

[60]Elliott 1.583; note also Lact. *Instit.* 1.1 (cited in Elliott, 1.238).

[61]William Jones, *History of the Christian Church* (Louisville: Ephraim A. Smith, 1831), 193. Basil Atkinson notes that modern historians have recognized the revolutionary significance of the fall of the pagan Empire in that "the *Cambridge Ancient History* ends at the year 324, and the *Cambridge Medieval History* begins with the Emperor Constantine" (67).

Constantine's revolutionary victories over the heathen emperors with the ensuing Imperial policies which suppressed pagan religion satisfy the extraordinary imagery of the sixth seal. Even the details speak appropriately to specific conditions. The "kings of the earth" answer to the several rulers defeated by Constantine and his one-time co-ruler, Licinius.[62] Constantine viewed their violent deaths due to warfare or disease as judgments of God and of the Christ under whose banner he fought. Their superstitious fear of the Christian's God is aptly expressed (6:15).

Men of all classes "hid in caves and among the rocks of the mountains" (15b).[63]

The picture is one of great fear, a general and intense dread on the part of the pagan populous of what was happening in the Empire. This language is used in the Bible to describe the fears which accompanied war and political revolution, as seen in such passages as Judg 6:2; 1 Sam 13:6; 24:3; Hos 10:8; Luke 23:30.[64]

---

[62] In the Hebraic idiom of the book of Revelation, the word, "king" (Gk. βασιλεύς, *basileús*; Heb. מֶלֶךְ, *mĕlĕk*), is appropriate for "emperor," as it commonly means simply "ruler." The several Emperors during this era were Maximian (captured by Constantine in 309; died in 310), Galerius (died 311), Maxentius, successor to Maximian (defeated in 312), Maximin (defeated by Licinius; died in 313), Diocletian (retired and died in 313), Licinius (defeated in 314 and again in 323; died in 324).

[63] The appropriateness of such language is also illustrated by the caves of the Judean wilderness, which have been repeatedly inhabited when people believed their lives or their liberties were endangered. Although many Christian slaves were set free by Constantine, the majority of slaves in the Empire were pagans who would have shared the fearful anticipation of judgment at the hand of the Christian Emperors.

[64] Scholars who object to our understanding of the sixth seal sometimes state that Constantine's revolution was a relatively peaceful transition from paganism to a highly paganized Christianity. They advance at least two reasons for this: 1. Christian rulers generally exercised considerable restraint in carrying out the prescribed punishments for violation of the new laws against paganism. 2. The majority of pagans nominally converted rather than risk suffering and possible death as formerly many of the persecuted Christians had done. There is reason to believe, nevertheless, that pagans under Constantine and successive Christian emperors promulgated among their kind an atmosphere of fear.

When Constantine defeated Licinius and liberated the eastern provinces of the Empire in A.D. 324, he wrote an Imperial letter for publication throughout the East, apparently having the character of an edict, which included provisions to ensure the rights of Christians, including the restoration of the enslaved to free status, the restoration of confiscated properties without payment or compensation, the prohibition of

Chapter Four   *The great earthquake, 6:12-17*   159

From the post-Reformation scholar, Joseph Mede, in 1627, until the recent ascendancy of the Preterist and Futurist schools in the twentieth century (see Appendix 1), this understanding of the sixth seal was nearly unanimous among Protestant scholars who wrote on the Book of Revelation. Cuninghame, in his 4th edition of 1843, writes that this was at that time the judgment of "the great body of modern commentators" (18).

144,000 Sealed

7:1 **After this I saw four angels standing at the four corners of the earth, holding back the four winds of the earth to prevent any wind from blowing on the land or on the sea or on any tree.** [2]**Then I saw another angel coming up from the east, having the seal of the living God. He called out in a loud voice to the four angels who had been given power to harm the land and the sea:** [3]**"Do not harm the land or the sea or the trees until we put a seal on the foreheads of the servants of our God."** [4]**Then I heard the number of those who were sealed: 144,000 from all the tribes of Israel.**

---

pagan sacrifices, divination, and the dedication of new cult images, and with threat of punishment, either temporal or eternal, for any failure of compliance. The persecuting emperors all died, either through violence or physical affliction, by act of God. Constantine made clear his intention to treat Christians preferentially, including candidates for the imperial offices throughout the Empire. Pagans were to be tolerated but traditional forms of pagan worship prohibited. Timothy Barnes states that "a change so sudden, so fundamental, so total shocked pagans" (210). What was tolerated was not sanctioned. There was much reason for fear.

As the newly formed Christian Empire developed in the fourth century, the provisions and prohibitions of Constantine were further extended, especially under Theodosius and his successors. There were more threatening decrees under Theodosius I (A.D. 379-395) when all pagans and heretics deviant from the Nicene faith were condemned and many pagan temples were destroyed or confiscated. Pagan worship and sacrifice to the gods was banned on pain of death and these policies were continued by his two sons, Arcadius (in the East, A.D. 395-408) and Honorius (in the West, A.D. 395-423). See Jones 193-194; Schaff 3.63-71.

Gibbon quotes contemporary sophists who describe the ruin of pagan religion "as a dreadful and amazing prodigy, which covered the earth with darkness, and restored the ancient dominion of chaos and of night" (Eunapius, *Life of Aedesius*; Eunapius, *Life of Eustathius*, Καὶ τι μυθῶδες καὶ ἀειδὲς σκότος τυράννησει τὰ ἐπὶ γῆς πάλλιστα (Gibbon 3.155, n.68). One may conclude, moreover, that the Apocalyptic language was intended not only to prefigure such a condition, but also to convey the radical and ominous nature of the impending Divine judgment of the pagan world.

> ⁵From the tribe of Judah 12,000 were sealed,
> from the tribe of Reuben 12,000,
> from the tribe of Gad 12,000,
> ⁶from the tribe of Asher 12,000,
> from the tribe of Naphtali 12,000,
> from the tribe of Manasseh 12,000,
> ⁷from the tribe of Simeon 12,000,
> from the tribe of Levi 12,000,
> from the tribe of Issachar 12,000,
> ⁸from the tribe of Zebulon 12,000,
> from the tribe of Joseph 12,000,
> from the tribe of Benjamin 12,000.

7:1-8 The Sealing of the True Israel Introduction

    Chapter seven is one of the interludes which interrupts the progress of the prophetic drama of Revelation. The interlude follows the opening of the sixth seal and precedes the blowing of the first of seven trumpets. It has the effect of preparing the reader for the disclosure of the tribulation which is to fall upon the church (chs. 8-13). The first scene (vv. 1-8), the sealing of "Israel," is preparatory for the tribulation. "Israel" represents the Covenant Community of God's people, both believing Jew and believing Gentile.⁶⁵ The second scene (vv. 9-17), a "great multitude," represents those who have come victoriously out of the great tribulation (v. 14). The latter is proleptic, that is, it carries the reader to the end time for a glimpse of the future victory, while at the same time "the four winds" are being held back to delay the prophetic judgments to come. The fact that "the great tribulation" is yet to come when the winds are released and the prophetic drama resumes is strong proof against those who see in the sixth seal the end time and therefore adopt a parallel or synchronous understanding of the Apocalyptic structure. Both scenes in chapter seven are designed to encourage the faithful in the church as they are about to experience the judgments forecast in chapters 8-9, 16.

---

    ⁶⁵The New Testament church was keenly aware of its Israelite-Jewish roots and found such symbols entirely natural and appropriate as a means of conceptualizing the spiritual character of the People of God as having its identity in the Covenant nation of Israel (cf. Eph 2:12-19). As the Apostle Paul teaches, the non-Jewish element in the Church is adopted into Israel (Gal 4:5, *NASB*) or grafted into the olive tree that is Israel (Rom 11:17). The apparent reluctance of New Testament writers to refer to the People of God as "Israel" may have been due to the antipathy that existed between the church and the unbelieving nation of Israel whose official posture of that time was hostile to Christianity. A possible exception is Gal 6:16.

Chapter Four   *The sealing of the true Israel, 7:1-8*   161

Excursus on the 144,000 of Israel

In support of our understanding that "Israel" and that nation's tribes in the sealing episode represent the Church, including both Jewish and Gentile believers rather than *literally* the elect out of national Israel, I offer the following observations:

1. Apocalyptic dream-vision is drama, primarily symbolic in style (see above, pp. 11-15). We should assume, unless there are specific indicators otherwise, that the description of Israel here is to be read as symbol, rather than as literal description.

2. The artificial appearance of the round number, "144,000," the composite of 12,000 from each tribe argues for symbolic meaning. It would be unnatural to understand that the actual number of elect individuals from each tribe would be indicated by a round number equivalent to the product of multiplying 1000 by 12.

3. The omission of the entire tribe of Dan, when the text specifically states that *all* the tribes are represented (v. 4), indicates that the text cannot be taken literally. (Note that a territory is assigned for Dan in the end-time prophecy of Ezekiel 48:1).

4. Revelation is addressed to churches which are primarily Gentile in constitution (chs. 2 & 3). It is therefore most natural to assume that "Israel" here stands for the Church (or a part of it) as the Church is defined in the New Testament without ethnic differentiation—that it consists of Jews and Gentiles who believe in the Jewish Messiah, Jesus Christ.

5. At the very beginning of the revelation, the Apocalypse is both Gentile in its historical and geographical orientation and Israelite in its imagery. The correlation between the two is so intimate that one should not infer that Israelite symbolism denotes literal Israelite meaning. Revelation displays throughout a consistent use of Israelite symbolism: Jesus walking among the seven lamps (1:12-16), the sacrificial altar (6:9; 11:1; 14:18; 16:7), the altar of incense (8:3-5, 9:9-13), the tabernacle sanctuary (11:1, 19), the ark of the covenant (11:19; 15:5, 8), the incense bowls (16:1-17), the apostate harlot (ch. 17; cp. Ezek 16 & 23). The tribes and their numbers present a natural extension of this Israelite symbolism. One could extend this elaboration into much greater detail.

6. Were we to assume that "Israel" here is literal, then why, *before* the tribulation, (7:4-8; cf. 14:1), are national Israelites alone marked out to receive the seal bearing the name of God and of Jesus Christ? Other Scriptures teach that not only believing Jews but all believers bear the seal of God (2 Cor 1:21-22; Eph 1:13; 4:30). (Many futurist-dispensationalist interpreters escape this by placing the entire prophecy of chs. 4-19 in the context of the seventieth week of Daniel nine and by understanding it in terms of the Jewish nation after the rapture of the Church. This approach encounters even more serious problems. See my Notes on 4:1 and Appendix 1.)

7. Rev 14:2-5 states that the "144,000" are the only ones who can sing the song of redemption on account of their having kept themselves undefiled and pure. But this song can be sung by all the redeemed and, in fact, in chapter 7, essentially the same song is sung by "the great multitude from every nation" (9-17).

8. In Rev 11:2, we read that the outer court of the temple "has been given to the Gentiles." "Gentiles" here, as the context implies, means "heathen," requiring the reader to understand that the Revelation includes all believers in the covenant community of "Israel." The same word also appears in 20:3 where the NIV translators have rendered it "nations," but the meaning, "heathen," or "non-'Israelite'" again is implied from the context.

This New Testament doctrine is assuredly the perspective of the book of Revelation. The use of the covenant name, "Israel" and that nation's tribal names as symbols for the Covenant People as they consist of both believing Jews and Gentiles in the Christian Church should not be considered improbable or unnatural. Scripture teaches that Gentiles are "grafted in" to the Covenant Nation (Rom 11:17). God has destroyed "the dividing wall" and consequently Gentiles "are fellow citizens with God's people, Old Covenant Israel regardless of their tribe, and members of God's household" (Eph 2:14, 19). This language, used by Paul to address our standing before God is Israelite covenant terminology. The enumeration of the tribal names in our text renders the figure more emphatic, but need not be taken literally, as the round numbers suggest. Gentiles who find unnatural their close biblical association with the nation of Israel must remember the admonition of the Apostle Paul, "Do not boast.... ... You do not support the root but the root supports you" (Rom 11:18).

The great majority of scholars, the major exception being those in the futurist school who place the entire prophecy in the end-time "seventieth week" of Daniel 9, are in agreement with our interpretation.[66]

---

[66]The more literal interpreters of the futurist school include Joseph A. Seiss (*The Apocalypse*, 9th ed. [New York: Charles C. Cook, 1906], 1. 402-413); Walter Scott (*Exposition of the Revelation of Jesus Christ* [Westwood, N.J.: Revell, n.d.], 162); and Walvoord (p. 143). Of the parallel-historical school holding the figurative view identifying the 144,000 more broadly with all the redeemed are Cunningham (25-36); B. H. Carroll (*The Book of Revelation* [new ed.; Nashville, Broadman, 1947], 102); Philip Mauro (*The Pat*mos Visions [Boston: Scripture Truth Depot, 1925], 246); Hendriksen (132-133); A. B. Arnot (*Last Words to a Lost World* [New York: Carlton, 1975], 37). The preterist interpreters supporting the figurative view are Charles (1. 199-200); Beckwith (534-535); Martin Kiddle (*The Revelation of St. John* [London: Hodder & Stoughton, 1940], 133); M. Eugene Boring (*Revelation* [Louisville: John Knox Press, 1989], 129-131). Figurative interpreters of the futurist school include Ladd (111-117); Mounce (157-160); and Beasley-Murray (139-141). Most if not all continuous-historicist interpreters have held to a figurative interpretation. These include Mede (126-140); Brightman (79-80); James Durham (*A Complete Commentary upon the Book of the Revelation* [Falkirk: Robert Renny, 1799], 2.24-25); Th. Newton (472-474); Elliott (1.259-319); John Cumming (*Lectures on the Book of Revelation, 1st series* [Philadelphia: Lindsay and Blakiston, 1856], 57-70); Barnes (174); Cachemaille (209-211); Barton (147-148); Atkinson (70-72); McKinley Ash (185-186); and Lee (58-63).

7:1-8	The Sealing of the True Israel	Exposition

Chapter seven is an interlude in the drama of Revelation. Whereas the opening of each of the preceding seals introduces predictions of events which from the standpoint of the author and his original readers were to come in the future, here we see that the angels are "holding back" the winds of the Divine providence until the sealing and the celebration described here have been in dramatic form presented. With chapter eight, the seventh seal is broken and prediction resumes.

The four angels had been given power to harm "the earth and the sea" (7:2). But before Providence will permit this to occur, a heavenly messenger appears with "the seal of the living God" to secure the destiny of the His people. Later, as we read in the later part of the chapter (vv. 9-17), they will celebrate victory after having passed through "the great tribulation" (7:14).

The Covenant people of God are addressed in our text as "the 144,000 from all the tribes of Israel" (v. 4). However, in the context of our Lord's New Covenant revelation, it is a mistake to limit this text to the literal descendants from Jacob (see our Notes, below). As the Apostle Paul clearly teaches, the "olive tree" that is ethnic Israel has not only "natural branches" but it has also "unnatural branches" that are "grafted in" and "who share in the nourishing sap from the olive root" (Rom 11:17).

There is great encouragement for the believer in the reminder that the Lord knows those who are His. We are not left to the highly figurative language of Revelation to learn this truth. The Apostle Paul teaches in 2 Cor 1:21, 22, "Now it is God who makes both us and you stand firm in Christ. He anointed us, set his seal of ownership on us, and put his Spirit in our hearts as a deposit, guaranteeing what is to come." In another place, he states, "Having believed, you were marked in him with a seal, the promised Holy spirit, who is a deposit guaranteeing our inheritance until the redemption of those who are God's possession—to the praise of his glory" (Eph 1:13b, 14).

So throughout the centuries during which the church has endured persecution and even martyrdom, as well as at the specific times implied by the prophecies of Revelation 7-14, the destiny of the People of God is secured against all affliction so that we know, whatever we experience in this life, we shall with "the great multitude" celebrate victory in the Last Day!

7:1-8   The Sealing of the True Israel   Notes

1. For **After this I saw**, see notes on Rev 4:1 (cp. 7:9). What follows is a two-part interlude between the opening of the sixth and seventh seals. The interludes in the book do not predict future events but characteristically set the stage in the drama for understanding what follows. Here, after the catastrophic judgment of the sixth seal, the interlude is given to encourage the people of God in the face of new waves of persecution. The **four angels** are symbolic agents of God's providential, sovereign control over events on earth. The **four corners of the earth** represent the conventional language for the direction of "the four winds."[67] One need not assume that the ancients, much less the author of Revelation, believed the earth was square or flat. The **holding back** of **the four winds** suggests that the progress of the predicted events described by the blowing of the trumpets (chs. 8-9) is interrupted and postponed until after the interlude.[68] For "the winds" as representing the forces of war or

---

[67]Cp. Zech 2:6, "four winds of heaven"; Zech 6:5 ESV, "the four winds [from Heb.רוּחַ, *rûaḥ*, "wind" or "spirit"].

[68]The Greek πνέῃ is present tense, durative action, suggesting the translation, "continue blowing." This implies that the events represented by the winds have been in progress. The progress is now interrupted until after the sealing of the 144,000. This interruption argues against some historical interpreters who suggest that the calm introduced by the interruption of the winds forecasts a peaceful period in the Empire. Better it is to see the sealing scene simply as an excursion from the sequence of prediction given to teach that in spite of upcoming tribulation God's true people are secure.

calamity, see Jer 18:17; 49:36; 51:1, 2; Dan 7:2, 3. **On the land or the sea or on any tree,** that is, as Mede indicates, "those objects which the winds are wont to damage," symbolic of the Roman setting in which the trumpet judgments to follow would occur (124). **2. Another angel** suggests a different task from the four preceding. **The east,** we learn from ancient temple architecture, was conventionally associated with the rising sun and with the presence of God. Ancient temples usually faced east. The angel messenger comes from God. The **seal,** when used on the human forehead, was a mark of ownership, in this case, of Divine protection (cp. Ezek 9:1-4). Note Rev 14:1, which indicates that the seal imprinted the name of the Lamb and the name of his Father. The mark distinguishes the true believers and the true Church of Jesus Christ from Christians in name only. They stand in contrast to those who bear the mark of the beast (cp. Rev 13:16, 17; 15:2 (KJV); 16:2; 19:20; 20:4). **3. The location of the seal** mark **on the foreheads** was the conventional location of such marks of ownership. However, one should not infer that this mark is visible, as the action of the drama is symbolic and denotes God's sovereign, mystic knowledge of the redeemed whereby he insures their Providential care and eternal destiny. "The Lord knows those who are his" (2 Tim 2:19; Num 16:5, LXX); see Matt 13:24-30; 2 Cor 1:21-22; Eph 1:13; 4:30). **The servants of our God,** that is the "144,000," are described in Rev 14:4, 5 as "those who were purchased from among men and offered as firstfruits to God and the Lamb . . . blameless." There is, however, no hint of martyrdom in chapter seven. The numberless multitude (v. 9) suggests otherwise. The believer is to be a *living* sacrifice (Rom 12:1, 2). **4. The number of those who were sealed: 144,000** is, as nearly all commentators recognize, a symbolic number, the square of the 12, times 1000. It is also the number by which the tribes of Israel were conventionally counted—that is, by "thousands" (Heb. אֲלָפִים, *ªlaphím*; Gk., χίλια, *chília*). The number of the sons of Jacob, the number 12, became in Israel a sacred number, reiterated by our Lord in the naming of twelve apostles. In the New Jerusalem, the names of the patriarchs were written on the twelve gates (21:12), and the names of the apostles were written on the twelve foundations 21:14).[69] **All the tribes of Israel** in the list of verses 5-8 do not include Dan (as does Ezekiel 48) and Joseph is named in place of Ephraim. The omission of Dan whereas it is included in the prophecy of

---

[69]That the number is intended to indicate smallness in contrast to the large number of nominal converts which resulted from the fall of paganism cannot be sustained together with the identification of the 144,000 with the "great multitude" of 7:9 (see above).

Ezekiel argues for the symbolic nature of this list in Revelation.[70]

5. The tribe of Judah is placed at the head of the list, probably because it is the tribe from which Jesus, the Messiah, came. This tribe also was given first place in several of the arrangements at Sinai.[71] **5-6.** The identification and order of the remaining tribes, different than any other known list, has some interesting features.[72] **Reuben, Gad, Asher, Naphtali & Manasseh** were in the northern kingdom, their identity at the time of writing had been lost to historians (but known to the Divine author). Doubtless, descendants of these "lost" tribes through the centuries have had their number, along with Gentile believers, in the Messianic Community. This fact, though commonly overlooked, heightens the impact of the symbolism and may, perhaps, help to account for the prominent place which these tribes occupy in the list. (The force of this observation is somewhat weakened, however, by the placement of the lost tribes of Issachar and Zebulun near the end of the list.) **7. Simeon** is not mentioned in the Old Testament after the Babylonian exile.[73] Though the tribe of **Levi** is usually omitted in other lists, its inclusion here is appropriate as

---

[70]Though the numbers are surely symbolic and the correlation of Gentile believers with specific tribes appears likewise to be figurative, one might reason that at the particular time in the prophetic chronology of revelation, A.D. 4th century), Dan was omitted because the number of the elect who are Messianic Jews does not include any descendants from the tribe of Dan. Though the Jewish people have not preserved records of their lineage, God knows the Israelite tribal connection of every Jew. The suggestion is often made with reason that Dan may have been omitted because of the tribe's early apostasy or because in ancient Judaism and early Christianity it was believed that the Antichrist would arise from the tribe of Dan. For Jewish roots of the Antichrist doctrine, see Dan 7:8, 11, 24-36, and R. H. Charles, "Testaments of the Twelve Patriarchs," *Apocrypha and Pseudepigrapha of the Old Testament* (Oxford: Clarendon Press, 1913), 2.334, n. 6; Swete, 98; H. C. Kee, "Testaments of the Twelve Patriarchs," in *Old Testament Pseudeprigrapha*, James H. Charlesworth, ed.(Garden City, N. Y.: Doubleday, 1983), 1.809, n. 5b; Martin Rist, "Antichrist," *IDB*, 1.140-143.

[71]Out of 20 occurrences of the names of the tribes in the Old Testament, Judah is found first in four: at the arrangement of the encampment of the tribes around the tabernacle (Num 2:3) and the order for the bringing of offerings for the dedication of the tabernacle (Num 7:12), in the order of the Israelite march (Num 10:14), and in the enumeration of the tribal genealogies (1 Chr 2:3-4:23; for additional refs. see Swete, p. 98.).

[72]In part because the twelve tribes are specified by name, some scholars have inferred that the author drew the list of tribes from an earlier Jewish source (e.g., Charles 191-201; Beckwith 534, 535). This approach appears not to have due regard for the fact that the author attributes his source directly to his vision and to "a revelation of Jesus Christ" and to "the testimony of Jesus" (see above, on Rev 1:1-2).

[73]Probably Simeonites who had remained in their tribal territory were exiled with Judah in Babylon and some participated in the establishing of the post-exilic Jewish state but are lost historically.

material inheritance is not the focus of the symbolism but the personal protection of those whom God seals. **8. Joseph** is named instead of his son, Ephraim, to whom the inheritance was given (Gen 48:12-22). Because Manasseh is named earlier, one must assume that Joseph is given as the name for the tribe of Ephraim (cp. Amos 6:6). The unblemished character and prominent role of Joseph in the deliverance of the patriarchal family may have prompted his inclusion in the list.[74]

7:1-8   **The Sealing of the True Israel**   **Fulfillment**

In chapter six, we have expounded the prophecies of the first six seals to show their fulfillment in the progressive decay and eventual fall of the pagan Roman Empire, culminating with the sixth seal in the nominal conversion of the Empire under Constantine to Christianity. We saw that the dramatic presentation of images in Revelation correlated accurately, both chronologically and conceptually, with the major events of this period as historians have discerned them, even with the details in the drama.

Whereas the overthrow of paganism carried with it great foreboding for the pagans of the Empire, especially for those in positions of leadership in government and in the temples, it carried with it great release and hope for Christians and for the church. Nevertheless, during the first two centuries certain evils had crept into the church including Platonic and Gnostic philosophy, the allegorization of Scripture, sacramentalism (especially baptismal regeneration), veneration of dead saints, and the elevation of priesthood—all to be substantially enhanced in the newly Christianized Empire. These would bring upon the church Divine judgments to be disclosed in the chapters following.

The interlude of chapter seven has its chronological setting about the end of the fourth century A.D., near to the revolution indicated by the sixth seal.

The sealing of the elect, symbolized by so small a number, may well be intended to underline the larger extent of the nominalism that inevitably resulted from the mass conversions, at first permitted by Galerius, then encouraged under Constantine, and at length in the late fourth century, directed by Imperial law. Converts are reminded that

---

[74]One need not assume with Mounce that Manasseh as well as Ephraim is included in "Joseph" as used here (159).

"small is the gate and narrow the road that leads to life, and only a few find it" (Matt 7:14).

The message for the faithful of the ensuing tribulation was to ensure their protection, not from temporal suffering and possible martyrdom, but from Satanic delusion and want of eternal life. The two-fold reminder of the Apostle is appropriate here: "God's solid foundation stands firm, sealed with this inscription: 'The Lord knows those who are his,' and 'Every one who confesses the name of the Lord must turn away from wickedness" (2 Tim 2:19).

The Great Multitude in White Robes

7:9 After this I looked and there before me was a great multitude that no one could count, from every nation, tribe, people and language, standing before the throne and in front of the Lamb. They were wearing white robes and were holding palm branches in their hands. [10]**And they cried out in a loud voice:**

> "Salvation belongs to our God,
> who sits on the throne,
> and to the Lamb."

[11]**All the angels were standing around the throne and around the elders and the four living creatures. They fell down on their faces before the throne and worshiped God,** [12]**saying:**

> "Amen!
> Praise and glory
> and wisdom and thanks and honor
> and power and strength
> be to our God for ever and ever.
> Amen!"

[13]Then one of the elders asked me, "These in white robes—who are they, and where did they come from?"

[14]I answered, "Sir, you know."

And he said, "These are they who have come out of the great tribulation; they have washed their robes and made them white in the blood of the Lamb. [15]Therefore,

> "they are before the throne of God
> and serve him day and night in his temple;
> and he who sits on the throne will spread his tent over them.
> [16]Never again will they hunger;
>   Never again will they thirst.
> The sun will not beat upon them,

nor any scorching heat.
[17]For the Lamb at the center of the throne
will be their shepherd;
he will lead them to springs
of living water.
And God will wipe away every tear
from their eyes."

7:9-17   The Great Multitude in White   Exposition

Here we have before us in the drama of the Revelation our first glimpse of the glory of the world to come. Here the Revelator takes us to the very end when the redeemed of all ages stand before the throne of God and before our incarnate Savior, the Lord Jesus Christ. Here the myriads of angels, the heavenly elders, and the four living creatures interrupt their hymns of praise to observe the numberless host of the redeemed of all ages and all races take their stand before the throne and cry out in chorus, "Salvation belongs to our God . . . and to the Lamb."

Here in the face of pending tribulation, the testimony of Jesus interrupts the predictive sequence of coming calamities to remind His Church of its destiny in the age to come. As the Apostle states, "Neither death nor life, neither angels nor demons, neither the present nor the future . . . will be able to separate us from the love of God that is in Christ Jesus our Lord" (Rom 8:38, 39). Always amid the evils of this age, Scripture holds before the believer the resurrection, the return of Jesus and our gathering to meet him as our true destiny, our delight, and our source of strength.[75]

This company will include "every nation, tribe, people, and language," a universal company from every quarter of the earth. Surely, from the chosen nation, Israel (of whom we are informed in part in the great faith passage of Hebrews 11) and from every Gentile nation and language. This bears out the forecast of our

---

[75] 1 Cor 15:19, 22-25; 2 Cor 4:14, 5:1-10; 1 Thess 2:19; 3:13; 4:13-18; 2 Tim 4:6-8; 2 Pet 3:8-14.

Lord that before the end comes "this Gospel of the kingdom will be preached in the whole world as a testimony to all nations" (Matt 24:14). Though Jesus said that proportionately and at any particular time only a few enter by the narrow gate (Matt 7:13, the redeemed will be "a great multitude that no man can count" (Rev 7:9).

Believers will celebrate the great Creator-God who sits upon the throne and the incarnate Son, the Lamb, "at the center of the throne" (7:17). To the redeemed, Christ is always the Lamb—that is, the One who by his sacrificial and atoning death effected their salvation. The object of their praise and their focus is the grace of God in salvation: "belongs to our God . . . and to the Lamb" (7:10). The enthroned God is the sovereign Savior! "By grace you have been saved, through faith—and this is the gift of God—not by works, so that no one can boast" (Eph 2:8, 9). These whom God has saved are indeed the true saints—they are dressed in white (7:9) for "they have washed their robes and made them white in the blood of the Lamb" (14). Jesus died in their place and they stand before their Creator-Judge cleansed and spotless.

To this marvelous celebration, even the angelic creatures, whose home always has been in heaven, say "Amen!" Then, they affirm the praises of the redeemed earth-creatures, while at the same time continuing their eternal anthem of praise (7:12).

One of the heavenly elders, with a rhetorical question, identifies the numberless host of celebrants (7:13). They are, at least from the standpoint of the Revelator, "they who have come out of the great tribulation" (14). Many years of suffering and deprivation would contribute to so great a multitude but now they know that victory has come—never again will they hunger or thirst, nor suffer exposure to desert sun, for "the lord will spread his tent over them" (15b, 16). The enthroned Jesus will wipe away the tears and provide for them eternally pleasant places.

Let those who suffer for their faith take courage from this great Scripture of promise. The downcast, difficult days in the life of the believer can be more easily borne when buoyed up with this glorious promise of everlasting life on the new earth in the Kingdom of God. Then "there shall be no more delay" (Rev. 10:6) and we shall serve God "day and night in his temple."

Chapter Four *The Great Multitude in White, 7:9-17* 171

7:9-17   **The Great Multitude in White**   Notes

9. For **after this I looked**, see above, notes on 4:1. The formula implies an important disjuncture between what precedes and what follows. Whereas the sealing (vv. 1-8) is done *before* and in preparation for suffering, the multitude is seen *after* "the great tribulation"—the war against the saints described in the chapters following. **And there before me** gives emphasis to the supernatural, dramatic aspect of the vision; see above, "The Revelation as Drama" (see above, ch. 1, Understanding Apocalyptic Writing, The Revelation as Drama). Although some infer an intended contrast between **the great multitude** of this text and the "144,000" of 7:4 and 14:1, 3, given the obvious symbolic nature of that number of "Israel," this is not a necessary inference and is unwar-ranted.[76] The great crowd of people represents at the end of this age "those who have come out of the great tribulation" (7:14; see our note thereon below). The fact that **no one could count** the number need not be understood as an absolute but as the language of appearance or practicality, an idiom for which there are many examples in the Bible (Gen 41:49; Josh 11:4; Judg 7:12; Rev 20:8; et al.). The language may nevertheless be a reflex of the Abrahamic covenant (see Gen 13:16, 32:12). **Every nation, tribe, people, and language** describes the multi-ethnic nature of the elect (cp. Matt 24:14 and notes on Rev 5:10, above). The expression should not be understood to represent four mutually exclusive ethnic classes but rather any and all such classes.[77] This multitude is seen **standing before the throne and in front of the Lamb**, having arrived in the heavenly court and taken this station to worship their Creator and Redeemer. Their **white robes** indicate imputed righteousness (Rom 4:22-25). Their palm branches indicate a victory celebration, traditional in Judaism (John 12:13; cf. also 1 Macc 13:51; 2 Macc 10:7). **10.** They **cried out** is translated by the REB with better connotation, "shouted aloud." The context indicates not a burst of

---

[76]The "144,000," a round number and the square of 12 times one thousand (Heb., אֶלֶף, *'ĕleph)*, the tribal unit, indicates completeness. Because the number is a relatively small and limited number, one may infer a dimensional contrast with the remainder of "Israel" not sealed. These, however, cannot be included in "the great multitude" of the redeemed.

[77]This expression occurs with some variation elsewhere: Rev 5:9; 11:9, 11; 13:7; 14:6; 17:15; Dan 3:4, 7, 29, 31(LXX); 5:19; 6:25; 7:14; 4 Ezra 3:7. In the original texts there are always four members, though the order and sometimes one of the terms may differ.

emotion but a thoughtful, disciplined chanting of praise delivered with clarity and conviction. The chant proclaims **salvation belongs to our God, who sits on the throne, and to the Lamb.** Clearly, the twin doctrines of Divine sovereignty and grace are emphasized. **11.** For the identity of **the elders**, see the Notes on 4:4. Perhaps we may assume that, as in 4:4, the elders were seated on thrones surrounding the Deity. For the role of **the four living creatures**, see the notes on 4:6b. As John watched this joyous celebration, the angels **fell down on their faces before the throne and worshiped God.** The posture represents the appropriate humility of the worshiper before the holy God. Cp. Rev 4:10, 5:8; Ezek 2:28; cp. Isa 6:5; Jer 1:17. **12. Praise and glory and wisdom and thanks and honor and power and strength**—each of these key words of the angels' hymn is freighted with meaning. Barclay comments, "There is no greater exercise in the life of devotion than to meditate on the praise of the angels . . ." (2.34). **14. They who have come** (Gk., οὗτοί εἰσιν οἱ ἐρχόμενοι, *houtoi 'eisin hoi 'erchómenoi*) is constructed with the present participle but the participle reflects the aorist tense of the verb, ἦλθον *'ēlthon*. The subjects referred to need not, as some interpreters infer, be identified exclusively with the redeemed martyrs (Charles 1.211) or only with those who have come through a future tribulation (Mounce 173). Because the scene is proleptic, the dialogue regards it as having already occurred. **The great tribulation**, here with the definite article (Gk.,τῆς θλίψεως τῆς μεγάλης *tēs thlípseōs tēs megálēs*), cannot be understood of tribulation in general. As Charles correctly states, "It is quite wrong to take it as meaning generally the tribulation that the faithful must encounter in the world" (1.213). The expression requires a familiar antecedent known to the original readers. This particular tribulation must embrace that which follows in the ensuing chapters but probably takes its full character from Matt 24:21: "For then there shall be a great tribulation [*thípseōs megálēs*]. . . ." As the tribulation of Matthew 24 begins with the Roman destruction of Jerusalem in A.D. 70, the tribulation referred to here must already be in progress at the point at which it is intersected by our text. Our text nevertheless focuses on those who will have experienced the particular calamities forecast in the chapters which follow.[78] **They have made them white.** That

---

[78]Many historical interpreters have understood that Jesus' reference to "great tribulation" in Matt 24:21 and the parallel mention in Luke 21:22 of "the time of punishment" (KJV, "days of vengeance") and "the great tribulation" of Rev 7:14 pertain to the "desolations" of Dan 9:26. These, in turn, apparently have their antecedent in Moses' prophecy of Deut 32:43, to which Luke 21:22 appears to make explicit reference (refer to the LXX text of Deuteronomy and the author's "Two Difficult Readings," *Henceforth...* 1 [Fall, 1972].45-47). Gentile incorporation into the Covenant Nation has implications for both covenant blessings and covenant curses (Leviticus 26; Deuteronomy 28). The extension of the tribulation associated with the Roman destruc-

"white" results from washing "in the [red] blood" betrays the figurative nature of the language. The white robe is of course a symbol of righteousness before the great Divine Judge (see above notes on Rev 3:4, 18). **The blood of the Lamb** speaks of the atoning death of Jesus, the Messiah-Savior. No mystical power of this blood is implied, as with the blood bath initiation into the religion of Mithraism. The metaphor is derived from the Old Covenant typical sacrifice, which likewise pointed to the death of the Messiah—to substitutionary atonement, a legal, juridical concept rather than a mystical identification of the suppliant with the life-force of the victim. **15. He . . . will spread his tent over them** when literally translated reads, "He . . . will tabernacle or dwell over them" (cp. NKJV).[79] The verb, σκηνόω, *skēnóō* "to tent," which in its ordinary sense means to live in a tent or to live in a temporary dwelling, here takes its meaning from the throne room of the Israelite tabernacle and so carries with it the idea of God's abiding presence protecting and sheltering His people (see NRSV, REB). The thought is fleshed out beautifully in 9:16-17. **17. The Lamb . . . will be their shepherd.** The Savior is here presented as the Shepherd-King, the gracious and faithful sovereign who will everlastingly provide for His people. **Living water**, in the ordinary sense of the original, is running water or spring water in distinction from stagnant water. As in John 4, the figure stands for life in the Spirit and spiritual refreshment.

---

tion of Jerusalem in A.D. 70 and the ensuing afflictions of the Jewish Diaspora is implied by Luke 21:24 (cp. Matt 24:21, 22, 29), as well as by several Old Testament texts. The prediction by Moses in 26:27-39 and in Deut 28:49-68 requires the extension of the tribulation far beyond the Roman-Jewish wars. Surely, the Mosaic forecasts as well as the war against the saints by the Little Horn power of Daniel 7 (see vv. 21, 25; cp. 2 Thess 2:3) cannot otherwise be described than as a "great tribulation." Because Moses was the great lawgiver and the first and the greatest of the Old Covenant prophets, even a type of the Messiah (Deut 18:18, 19), it is most plausible that the subsequent prophets built on this foundation and that Jesus advanced this prophetic tradition in His prophetic pronouncements. We should, therefore, seek an integrated understanding of the several tribulation passages. See Birks 217-239; H. Grattan Guinness, *The Divine Programme of the World's History* (London: Hodder & Stoughton, 1889), 202-211, 378-383; Daniel T. Taylor, "The Great Tribulation," *The Great Consummation* (Boston: Advent Christian Publication Society, 1891), 53-74.

[79]The Greek construction appears only here (Charles 1.215).

7:9-17   The Great Multitude in White   Fulfillment

As indicated above, this scene is the second part of an interlude in the sequence of predicted events represented by the opening of the seven seals. As the sealing scene of 7:1-8 has its historical orientation prior to the tribulation forecast in the chapters which follow, this unveiling of the great multitude dressed in white robes is identified as "those who have come out of the great tribulation." Commentators quite universally recognize that the scene is proleptic, that it looks ahead to the time after the rapture (1 Thess 4:17) when all the saints of God, who have been sealed as insuring their everlasting destiny, are gathered around the throne praising God and celebrating his redemptive work. This great multitude is represented by the "144,000" of 7:1-7 who were sealed before passing through the tribulation forecast in chapters 8-16.

As the event forecast here is still future, the multitude, though ever growing through the evangelistic and missionary efforts of the church, remains still incomplete. The number, nevertheless, in the mystery of Providence, is fixed in heaven, as "the Lord knows those who are his" (2 Tim 2:19).

Chapter Five

THE SOUNDING OF THE SEVEN TRUMPETS

8:1-9:21, 11:15

Introduction

   The opening of the seventh seal completes the unsealing of the scroll. This suggests that the content of the first six seals can be considered introductory to the rest of the Book of Revelation. Beckwith points out that, as contrasted with the part sealed by the first six seals, the "main contents of the roll must include according to common apocalyptic expectation . . . a series of vast movements before the actual end . . . . We should expect then at this point not an immediate entrance of the end . . . but what we find, only the great movements more directly leading up to it."[1] This observation supports a consecutive relationship between the seal prophecies and the two sequences, the trumpets and the bowls that follow. The implications of this will be seen in the Fulfillment sections below, as well as in Appendix 3.
   With the opening of the seventh seal a transition occurs, for the seventh seal introduces the second major series of prophecies, those announced by the seven trumpets. The trumpets, like the seals which precede them, serve as a dramatic device to signal the reader and to give chronological structure to the elements of the prophecy.
   Before the first trumpet sounds, preparatory revelations occur. Then the trumpet judgments follow. The preparatory section, verses 1-5, introduces not only the trumpet prophecies but all the remaining judgments to be disclosed in the entire vision, for the final seal opens the rest of the scroll.[2]

---

   [1]Isbon T. Beckwith, *The Apocalypse of John: Studies in Introduction, with a critical and Exegetical commentary* (1919; repr. Grand Rapids: Baker, 1967), 549.
   [2]The seventh, being the last seal, is an element in the designed ambiguity of the book of Revelation which cloaks in mystery the chronology until after the fulfillment of the forecast events. This Providential characteristic of the book leads to the phenomenon

The Seventh Seal and the Golden Censer

8:1. **When he opened the seventh seal, there was silence in heaven for about half an hour.** ²**And I saw the seven angels who stand before God, and to them were given seven trumpets.**

³Another angel, who had a golden censer, came and stood at the altar. He was given much incense to offer, with the prayers of all the saints, on the golden altar before the throne. ⁴The smoke of the incense, together with the prayers of the saints, went up before God from the angel's hand. ⁵Then the angel took the censer, filled it with fire from the altar, and hurled it on the earth; and there came peals of thunder, rumblings, flashes of lightning and an earthquake.

8:1-5   Seven Trumpets and the Prayers of the Saints   Exposition

Before the seven angels were given their trumpets and before the angel with the censer appears, the writer observed an extraordinary phenomenon—"there was silence in heaven for about half an hour." As John experienced with his ears and eyes the awesome drama and as he recorded the mysterious prophecies, a half hour of silence must have seemed interminable. We have here a dramatic pause of considerable effect.

The reason for this dramatic pause may be that for the first time a major junction point has come in the predicted judgments. A new series of symbols with a different order is pending. When the action resumes, the angelic trumpeters appear. They receive their instruments but still another interruption prolongs the suspense.

For the reader, this announced silence offers an occasion for reflection, a time to consider God's sovereignty in judgment and in grace. As the exiled Apostle considered the meaning of this silence, so the reader of the Revelation should take pause to consider his or her relationship to a sovereign God who holds all men responsible to his Word. An angel at length appears and stands at the great

---

of progressive interpretation addressed in Appendix 1.

brazen altar of the tabernacle. He holds a golden censer, as had the earthly high priest to receive incense placed on burning coals. The high priest then carried this into the Holy Place to the golden incense altar before the throne. The fragrance of the incense rose to God, emblematic of the prayers of God's people.

Jesus Christ is the antitypical high priest who serves in the heavenly sanctuary (7:11-17; John 14:6; 16:24, 26; 1 John 2:1, 2; Heb 7:26-8:2). During life's battles, the believer is assured that God attends to the prayers of His people. He is with them to comfort and guide them and he will preserve their destiny even when conditions are devastating.

The censer served another function. It carried fire from the altar to be cast out on the earth. In the vision, this is the fire of Divine judgment as indicated by the resounding thunder, the lightning, and the earthquake. With this anticipatory warning, the trumpet judgments follow.

8:1-5. Seven Trumpets and the Prayers of the Saints Notes

8:1. At this place in the drama, the Lamb opened the seventh seal. Some scholars have understood **silence in heaven** with reference to the prior singing of the angelic choirs, so the Divine attention turns to the prayers of the saints (Charles, Barclay). It is better to understand "silence" as pertaining in a figurative sense to the natural heavens, that is, the setting of John's vision.[3] Chapter seven begins similarly with the "holding back of the four winds" (7:1) and 8:5 describes "peals of thunder" and "rum-

---

[3]It is possible, with E. B. Elliott (*Horae Apocalypticae* [5th ed.; London: Seeley, Jackson, and Halliday, 1862], 1.324-325), to understand "heaven" as the region of the four winds, thunder and lightning, etc., which in apocalyptic language denotes actions which play out on earth (cp. 7:1; 8:5b; 11:9b) and "silence" (Gk. σιγή) as denoting stillness from such activity, citing parallels: Plin. *HN*, 18.69, Ov. *Metam.*, 7.187; and Shakespeare's Hamlet, Act 2, Sc. 2:9

"Twas, as we often see against some storm,
a silence in the heavens; ...
The bold winds speechless, and the orb below
As hush as death: anon the dreadful thunder
Doth rend the region."

blings." The "silence" will then indicate a pause in the prediction of future events, producing suspense and heightened drama.[4] The silent period, **about half an hour**, in the context of the prophetic chronology indicates "a brief time."[5] As with the holding back of the winds in 7:1, this interval provides an appropriate window for viewing the heavenly interlude described in verses 2-5.

2. The seven angels who stand before God are the archangels known to Jewish tradition as Suru'el, Raphael, Raguel, Michael, Saraqa'el, Gabriel, and Remiel (1 Enoch 20.2-8; Charlesworth, 1.23-24). Michael and Gabriel only are identified by name in the Bible (Daniel 10:13, 21; 12:1; Luke 1:19, 26; Jude 9; Rev 12:7). They are known in Scripture as "the angels of the presence" (Isa 63:9; Luke 1:19). Barclay remarks, "In the heavenly order of things the greatest honour is to be ever ready to be sent on the service of God; and that is the honour these angels possessed" (2.51). There is no identification here or elsewhere of these archangels with the seven spirits of Rev 1:4; 4:5; and 5:6. The heavenly beings around God's throne are identified only as they come to function in the drama. The **seven trumpets** will announce later seven consecutive prophecies (8:6-9:19). The trumpet with its penetrating sound was in ancient times the common instrument for public announcement.

3. Another angel indicates that the censer-bearing angel was not one of the archangels. In Judaism and the Old Testament, Michael and other archangels mediate the prayers of the Covenant People (Dan 12:1; *1*

---

[4]H. B. Swete points out that, though a half hour is a relatively short time, it "is a long interval in a drama" (*The Apocalypse of St. John* [Grand Rapids: Eerdmans, pref. 1906], 107).

There is nothing in this silence to suggest to the reader a chronological retrogression so as to signal a parallel or synchronous relationship between the seal prophecies and those of the trumpets. This idea is imported to this text by those who regard the symbolism of the sixth seal as describing conditions of the Last Day preceding the second coming of Christ. That theory is further weakened by the absence of any such "silence" or comparable phenomenon introducing the bowl prophecies (15:1). For further discussion of the parallel interpretation of the seal, trumpet, and bowl series of prophecies, see above on the sixth seal (Rev 6:12-17) and Appendix 3.

[5]Elliott cites Menander (via Pollux and Grotius) for his use of ἡμίωριον as "pro minimo tempore" ("for a very brief time"; 1.325, n.4). Elliott, nevertheless, suggests that "one-half hour" "on the *year-day scale*, equals 7½ days, if we allow 24 hours to the day" (1.325, n. 4).

Chapter Five *The prayers of the saints, 8:1-5* 179

Enoch 68.2-5; cp. Tob 12:12-15; *1 Enoch 9:3; 89.76; T. Levi* 3:5; *T. Dan* 6.2). The one mediator under the New Covenant is Jesus Christ.⁶ How-ever, the angel is introduced here to facilitate the drama, not to identify the mediator (Mounce, 173, 174). The text emphasizes the prayers of the saints. A **golden censer** was used in the Israelite temple on the Day of Atonement.⁷ Gold was reserved for the most holy furniture and utensils. **The altar** at which the angel stood must then be the altar of sacrifice, as this is the altar from which the coals for burning incense were taken in the Israelite temple. They were carried in the censer from the altar of sacrifice in the courtyard to the golden incense altar in the Holy Place within the sanctuary. Incense could not be given at the incense altar, as that was accessible only to the officiating priest (Lev 16:12, 13; Num 16:46; Elliott 1.328-329). The prayers of the saints rose to God as holy, that is, as cleansed in type by the fire from the sacrificial altar and in antitype by the atonement symbolized.⁸ The angel **was given much incense to offer**. With the Old Testament tabernacle and the temple, the ingredients for the incense were given by the worshiping people (Exod 35:21, 29; Jer 41:5). Here, **the prayers of all the saints** are represented by the incense (cp. 5:8). Bruce explains the translation of the Greek dative, *taīs proseukeīs,*

---

⁶Th. Brightman comments, "His ministery[sic] is that of the High Priest, which *Angels* so properly called do never exercise, but the truth whereof belongeth to *Christ alone* . . ." (*The Revelation of Saint John* [Amsterdam: Thomas Stafford, 1644], 33).

⁷Brass censers were used in the wilderness tabernacle (Exod 27:3) but gold is most appropriate here for the heavenly sanctuary. The word, "censer" (λιβανωτός *libanōtós*) ordinarily means "frankincense." Here, because the word is modified by "golden," it must have reference to the container.

⁸"All access to heaven lies through the avenue of sacrifice. Whether it be the prayers of the faithful or the martyrs themselves, both alike must be presented or offered on the heavenly altar that they may be cleansed thereby . . . and made acceptable to God" (R. H.Charles *A Critical and Exegetical Commentary on the Revelation of St. John* [International critical commentary; Edinburgh: T. & T. Clark, 1920], 1.231).

The identification of the altar should be determined from the Old Testament prototype. Commentators who try to reconstruct a composite of the several descriptions of the "heavenly temple" sometimes try to avoid a more complex reconstruction by identifying this altar with the incense altar (see Charles, 226-227; Beckwith, 552-553; Barclay, 1.49). However, each passage should speak for itself without necessarily reflecting a composite view. Neither is it wise to infer, as does Charles, that the incense altar is intended because "there is no definite evidence in Jewish or Christian Apocalyptic of two altars in heaven" (1.227); Wm. Barclay states, "The altar cannot be the altar of burnt-offering, for there can be no animal sacrifice in heaven" (*The Revelation of St. John*. [2 vols; Philadelphia: Westminster Press, 1960], 1.49). The temple and its fixtures in the Revelation are metaphorical antitypes which correspond theologically to the Old Testament types. This antitypical altar and its burnt offering represent not the sacrifice of animals but the sacrifice of Christ. The intent of the apocalyptic language should be derived from this typological use of the symbol.

as reflecting the Hebrew preposition, ל, *le* (of definition), "consisting of the prayers of all the saints" (F. Bruce, 646, quoted from Mounce, 174). The prayers were offered **on the golden altar before the throne** (Psa 141:2; Eph 5:2). This altar is the incense altar, located in God's presence. In the earthly temple the incense altar was separated from the throne room (the Most Holy Place) by a curtain. The antitypical sanctuary has no veil, for the High Priest is sinless and has made atonement, once for all time (Matt 27:51; Mark 15:38; Luke 23:44; Heb 10:19-22). **4. The smoke of the incense** carries with it the prayers of the saints. In the tabernacle typology, the fire from the sacrificial altar produced the fragrant smoke which, as it ascended from the incense altar, represented prayers going heavenward. The trumpets are about to signal coming judgments, bringing catastrophe from which the saints are not to be spared (see 6:11); God receives their prayers in the throne room of heaven. The prayers may be understood as for assurance of the Lord's protection in the face of imminent danger (cf. James 5:16b). The angel again **took the censer** and **filled it with fire**. One need not infer that this action is a response to the prayers of the saints (*contra* Swete 109, Barclay 2.50). As noted above, **the altar** here is the one first mentioned, the great sacrificial altar, where all the ceremonial fire originated. The vision at this point is not dealing with prayer but with holiness and judgment. Cp. Ezek 10:2, 7. Taking the fire, the angel **hurled it on the earth**. The act introduces judgments which follow, not only those announced by the trumpets, but those of the remainder of the scroll, all of which is now unsealed and open (cf. 8:7; cp. 15:7; and 16:1). The **thunder, rumblings, flashes of lightning** and the earthquake are dramatic symbols indicating the Divine authority and the temporal effects of the censer fire on the nations and inhabitants of the earth (see Notes on 4:5).[9]

The Trumpets

⁶Then the seven angels who had the seven trumpets prepared to sound them.

⁷The first angel sounded his trumpet, and there came hail and fire mixed with blood, and it was hurled down upon the earth. A third of the earth was burned up, a third of the trees were burned up, and all the green grass was burned up.

---

[9]"The lightnings, thunders, voices, and an earthquake are not the precursors of the plagues that are about to ensue in connection with Trumpets, as has been assumed, but form the close of the introduction to the Seventh Seal, as they likewise do to the Seventh . . . Trumpet . . . , xi. 19, and to the Seventh Bowl, xvi. 18" (Charles 1.232).

⁸The second angel sounded his trumpet, and something like a huge mountain, all ablaze, was thrown into the sea. A third of the sea turned into blood, ⁹a third of the living creatures in the sea died, and a third of the ships were destroyed.

¹⁰The third angel sounded his trumpet, and a great star, blazing like a torch, fell from the sky on a third of the rivers and on the springs of water—¹¹the name of the star is wormwood. A third of the waters turned bitter, and many people died from the waters that had become bitter.

¹²The fourth angel sounded his trumpet, and a third of the sun was struck, a third of the moon, and a third of the stars, so that a third of them turned dark. A third of the day was without light, and also a third of the night.

8:6-12   The First Four Trumpets   Introduction

The trumpet was used extensively in ancient times as a signalling instrument. In Israel the priests blew trumpets to call worshipers to the festivals. Commanders used trumpets to signal the troops in warfare. The latter practice prevailed in Roman armies when the Revelation was written. This use probably provides the rationale for understanding the ominous signals in our text, as the destruction and horrors of warfare are appropriately suggested by the subsequent symbolic language of the drama.

One may logically infer that the three major series indicated by the seals, the trumpets, and the bowls forecast in symbol three successive eras, each having distinctive character and subject to Divine judgment.[10] We have seen in the Fulfillment sections how this approach to the seal prophecies may be understood. We will look to the fulfillment of the trumpets and later the bowls below.

The language of the trumpet prophecies, like that of the seals, draws upon the natural sphere—frightening abnormalities of earth and sky, of land and sea—storms, fire, flood, and shooting stars. Too literal interpretation may see in this only the sub-human phenomena of nature. However, such symbols are commonly used in biblical apocalyptic to represent human conditions and events. Nebuchadnezzar in his first dream was represented by the head of a man-made image (Dan 2:38), later by a tree (4:22). Daniel dreamed of Nebuchadnezzar and his Babylonian successors as represented by a lion (7:4) and of Alexander by a goat (8:5-8). In a

---

[10] The majority of scholars have understood the seal, trumpet and bowl prophecies in this linear fashion. For a defense of this approach, see Appendix 3.

vision Zechariah saw Joshua the High Priest and Zerubbabel as two olive trees (Zech 4:11-14). So here, with cosmic symbols and abnormalities of nature, the Trumpet prophecies represent Divine judgments to be executed by human armies with ordinary implements of warfare.

The use of the trumpet was an ordained function for warfare in Israel (Num 10:9). The battle of Jericho was commemorated annually at the Festival of Tabernacles by the blowing of trumpets. The miraculous conquest of Jericho was understood to point to the Messianic redemption at the end of time. Barclay appropriately suggests that in Biblical symbolism "the trumpet is always the symbol of the intervention of God in history"(2.51).

The trumpet sounded loudly when the Law was given at Sinai (Exod 19:16, 19). Isaiah forecast that when the end-time ingathering of Israel occurs "a great trumpet will sound" (Isa 27:13). Joel calls for repentance in anticipation of the coming Day of the Lord with the command "to blow the trumpet in Zion" (2:1, 15). "The last trumpet of God" will sound at the second coming of Christ to signal the resurrection of the righteous dead and the rapture of the saints (1 Cor 15:52; 1 Thess 4:16). Here the trumpets signal events future to John which our Lord in His Revelation views as Divine judgments leading toward the time of the end.

Most commentators point out marked similarities between the language of this section and the description of the plagues of Egypt (Exodus 7-11). The connection is not one of dependence, nor of a developing tradition, as some suggest.[11] From the standpoint of the Divine author of Scripture one should see the reintroduction of Exodus language as a reaffirmation of the Divine principles implicit in that event.[12] The hand of God is working supernaturally with miraculous signs as He did in the Exodus experience of the Covenant people to declare his sovereign authority in judgment. The Divine deliverance of the Israelite people from Egypt is repeatedly emphasized in the Psalms, especially with references to hail, lightning bolts, and fire (Psa 18:12, 13; 78:47, 48; 105:32). Similar use of Exodus phenomena occurs later in the bowl prophecies (ch. 16).

---

[11] An example of the naturalistic, developmental approach to the supernatural implications of such language is found in the commentary by John Court, who states, "It seems reasonable to see here a process of development from the formative traditions of the Exodus and in particular from Yahweh's 'signs and wonders' in Egypt. . . . The development of this tradition [in the Old Testament and Jewish literature] has made it eminently suitable for the use to which John applies it." (*Myth and History in the Book of Revelation* [Atlanta: John Knox Press, 1979], 76-77). This approach to our text appears to ignore and to controvert the supernatural, revelational character of John's Apocalypse.

[12] This phenomenon is called allusive reference.

The trumpet prophecies, like the seals, and in lesser degree the bowls, reflect a stylistic 4-2-1 formula. The first four are tersely presented, the fifth and sixth have more extended content, and the seventh, after interludes, is both terse and culminative, apparently introducing what follows after the series. This suggests corresponding degrees of emphasis and, perhaps, temporal extension in the events predicted. At least, this cryptic style enhances the mystique of the prophecy.

8:6-12**The First Four Trumpets****Exposition**

The first four trumpet judgments target metaphorically "the earth" (v.7), "the sea" (vv. 8,9), "the rivers and springs" (vv. 10, 11), and "the sun, moon, and stars" (v. 12). There is such brevity of language that these prophecies are peculiarly difficult to interpret. There is general agreement, nevertheless, that they describe judgments, which from the standpoint of the author, God in His sovereign providence would allow to afflict the Roman world.

"Hail and fire mixed with blood" suggests human warfare and death. This is accompanied by the burning of trees and other vegetation, such as often accompanied ancient war. Trees were cut, not only to build siege equipment, but to fire the walls of fortress cities in order to break down the fortifications. The prophecy is intended to incite the sinner to fear the retribution of an angry God.

The second trumpet prophecy introduces earthquake, another biblical emblem of Divine judgment. Here the imagery of war focuses on the sea, suggesting naval battles with severe consequences.

The third trumpet suggests another military scenario, which now is directed toward river ways and their source streams or "springs." Until modern times, such river ways were the primary means of access to inland cities, as well as to the surrounding river valleys, fertile lands for farming and settlement. Again, blood indicates human warfare and death.

From the language of this passage, we should expect to see human armies advancing over land, fighting battles in the sea, and advancing by means of the great rivers and river basins of the Roman earth.

The fourth angel brings with the announcement devastation on the sun, the moon, and the stars. In ancient literature and in the Old Testament these are used as symbols of human rulers. The "sun" suggests the highest ruling power. Because the Revelation was given during the rule of the Romans, we should expect that this prediction would have its fulfillment with regard to Rome and the Roman Empire.

These judgments are described in terms of one-third of the earth, one third of the sea, and one-third of the "rivers and springs." The destruction envisioned must be most severe and devastating.

The emphasis of the Revelation on suffering and martyrdom suggests to the reader that "the earth" or "Roman world" includes professing Christians and the world of the church. The prophecy reminds us of our responsibility before an almighty God and therefore of our liability to disciplinary and retributive judgment in the course of human events. God's sovereignty is a recurring theme throughout the Revelation.

8:6-12   **The First Four Trumpets**   Notes

8:6. On the **seven angels** and their **trumpets**, see above, notes on 8:2. This verse dramatizes with appropriate emphasis what follows.

7. The **angel sounded his trumpet** to announce the first in the series of judgments—**and there came hail and fire mixed with blood.** Hail is used in the Old Testament as an evidence of Divine punishment (Exod 9:23; Job 38:22, 33; Psa 18:13; Isa 30:30). As hailstorms in Canaan usually came from the north, so hail prefigures destruction by northern armies executing judgment (Isa 28:2, 17). That such is in our text **mixed with blood** speaks of the terror of war and human destruction. **The earth** here, as in other Scriptures (Luke 2:1) and commonly in Revelation (11:10; 13:8; 17:18), refers to the Roman world (see above on

6:4, with n. 18).[13] **One third** (of the earth, the trees, and the grass) probably denotes in a general manner the extent of the plague, referring either to a partial destruction or to a part of the Empire (cp. Zech 13:8, 9; Ezek 5:2).[14] The language of burning suggests a military invasion in which fire is used as a destructive weapon involving not only "the earth," but **the trees** and **the green grass**. "The trees" and "the green grass" probably should be taken literally. Whereas "the earth" in such contexts focuses on destruction of the inhabitants, "the trees" etc. focuses on the destruction of the vegetation and perhaps other valuable aspects of their habitation. Compare Ezek 20:47-48, "I am about to set fire to you, and it will consume all your trees, both green and dry. . . . Everyone will see that I the LORD have kindled it."[15] Such admixture of literal with figurative language is essential to the nature of symbolism. Otherwise, contact with reality is lost. If we may assume that the plague refers to an invading army, the burning of vegetation was sometimes a conspicuous circumstance.[16]

8. The words **something like** indicate analogical or symbolic language. **A huge mountain, all ablaze, thrown into the sea** indicates a city or nation destroyed, "the sea" being the nations or lands over which the city rules (cf. 17:15). Similar imagery is found in the Old Testament

---

[13]So also extrabiblical writers (as quoted in Elliott 1.359): Dionysius Halicarnassus, *Antiq. Rom.* 1.3, "Ἡ δε Ῥωμαίων πόλις ἁπάσης μεν ἄρχει γῆς, . . . ἐστί, πάσης δε κράτει θαλάσσης . . . , "The republic of the Romans, . . . rules both the entire earth and the entire sea . . . " (trans. mine); also Ovid. *Fasti*, 2.683, *Gentibus est aliis tellus data limite certo, Romanae spatium est urbis et orbis idem*, "The countries of other races have been given fixed boundaries; the dimension of the city of Rome and that of the earth is the same" (trans. mine).

[14]Elliott and some other subsequent commentators held that "the third part" refers to one of the three divisions of the Roman Empire, that is, the Western Empire. The other two, in his view, were the Eastern Empire and the central part, principally Illyricum (to the north of Italy), which was occupied by the Goths. While this may be for some a plausible interpretation, one need not insist upon it (1.358-365; also E. P. Cachemaille, *XXVI Present Day Papers on Prophecy*(London: Seeley, Service, 1911), 237-238. For the use of "earth" for the populace of the earth, see Isa 24:4, 6; 45:22; 52:10; 60:2.

[15]Jonathan Edwards, nevertheless, wrote in his "Notes on the Apocalypse," "'All green grass was burnt up"; that is, all the former glory and beauty of the empire was departed" (*Apocalyptic writings*: "Notes on the Apocalypse," *The works of Jonathan Edwards*, v. 5, edited by John E. Smith from unpublished mss. [New Haven: Yale University Press, 1977], 102). Green foliage was of course associated with beauty and well-being in the Mediterranean lands. Isaiah laments over God's judgment of Moab, "The waters of Nimrim are dried up and the grass is withered; the vegetation is gone and nothing green is left" (Isa 15:6). Cp. Psa 37:2; Isa 37:27; Jer 17:8.

[16]Much mixed figurative and symbolic language occurs in the Bible. Elliott cites Isa 21:1, Jer 1:13, 14, 18:17, Ezek 17:10, 19:12, 27:26, Hos 13:1, etc. (1.355-358).

prophets. Jeremiah prophesies of Babylon, "I will dry up her sea and make her springs dry" (51:36) and again,

> The sea will rise over Babylon; its roaring waves will cover her. Her towns will be desolate, a dry and desert land, a land where no one lives . . . . The nations will no longer stream [Heb. נהר, *nāhar*, "flow"] to him [the god, Bel] and the walls of Babylon will fall." (Jer 51:42-44)

The peoples over whom Babylon has ruled will no longer flow into her but foreign invaders will inundate her like a flood, even as the "roaring waves" of the sea. Revelation similarly identifies Rome with the sea—the Mediterranean, as surrounded by Roman Imperial lands. The seven-headed beast rises from "the sea" (13:1; cp. 17:8) and the prostitute sits on "many waters" (17:15a). The "many waters" are interpreted for us as "people, multitudes, nations and languages" (17:15a). Isaiah predicts the demise of an Egyptian empire in terms of the drying up of the sea: "I will hand the Egyptians over to the power of a cruel master . . . . The waters of the river [Heb. ים, *yām*, "sea"] will dry up, and the river bed will be parched and dry." (19:4-5). No doubt, in this text the "sea" is the Nile (see Isa 19:6-10) but the term *yām* identifies the river with the mystique anciently associated with great waters. The language cannot be taken literally as the prophecy does not address the total demise of Egypt but the fall of the Pharaonic empire as known in Isaiah's day: "I will hand the Egyptians over to the power of a cruel master and a fierce king will rule over them" (Isa 19:4).[17] The devastating destruction of the second trumpet prophecy is described also as a **burning mountain**. Jeremiah similarly represents ancient Babylon, "I am against you, O destroying mountain, I will . . . make you a burned-out mountain" (Jer 51:25). Battles involving burning and great destruction are in view. **9.** For **a third**, see above, 8:7. The sea **turned into blood** suggests massive slaughter. The language recalls the Egyptian plague (Exod 7:20-21). However, whereas the Egyptian plague was literal, the term here is an apocalyptic symbol.[18] The death of **living creatures in the sea** denotes mass destruc-

---

[17] The drying up of the Nile cannot be taken in the literal sense as without the river the desert could not sustain even the decadent life described as the predicted result.

[18] One should not assume as do many commentators that the writer is dependent upon earlier written sources. As symbols are to be understood by analogy, we must assume that the Divine author regards such community of language as an aid to the comprehension of the reader. The human author was instructed simply to write what he saw (1:11).

tion which in the context of warfare hints of human bloodshed (cp. Zeph 1:3). In this context the destruction of **ships** suggests naval battles.[19]
10. With the third trumpet, **a great star, blazing like a torch, fell from the sky.** The language describes literally a large falling meteorite. Astral symbols in apocalyptic literature usually denote ruling authorities (see above on 6:12-13, with n. 49). The king of Babylon is represented by Isaiah as a falling star (14:12; cf. also Num 24:17).[20] The meteor, commonly viewed as a falling star, is in this context a symbol of a fearsome, illustrious ruler who invades with a fast moving destructive army. The second trumpet judgment falls on **the rivers and on the springs of water.** These, in distinction from the second trumpet judgment, are land symbols. The springs (τὰς πηγάς *tàs pēgás*, "running water, streams") probably refers to the tributaries of rivers or of a river system.[21] **11.** The star is named **wormwood** to characterize the bitterness or suffering which resulted from its destructive power. **12.** When the fourth angel sounded **a third of the sun was struck.** "The sun" must represent the highest ruling authority, **the moon** and **the stars** lesser powers of the same kingdom.

8:6-12   **The First Four Trumpets**   **Fulfillment**

Among historical interpreters, the great majority after Joseph Mede's commentary have understood the first four trumpet prophecies as

---

[19]Brightman, writing in the early 17th cent., reverts to spiritualizing more characteristic of pre-Reformation interpretation, explaining the second trumpet prophecy as indicating the corruptions of doctrine in the church of the Nicene Fathers (87). The language, though surely figurative, hardly suggests this interpretation.

[20]The common interpretation of Isa 14:12 as having reference to Satan is not well founded, for it can only be maintained by giving two disparate meanings to the same text. The judgment is pronounced specifically against the king of Babylon (8:4). The translation of הֵילֵל, *hêylēl*, as "Lucifer" in the KJV has contributed to this error, as does now the NKJV. The Hebrew noun means "shining one," which term commonly referred in antiquity to the planet Venus, hence the parallel appellation in our text, "son of the dawn" (the alternate translation for "Lucifer" in the NKJV footnote, "Day Star"). The prophecy foretells that the "morning star" was to be "brought down to the grave," his body devoured by maggots and worms (v. 11), hardly appropriate of Satan or any angelic being. The king of Babylon cannot be a type of Satan, as a type by definition must precede its antitype. See A. Berkeley Michelsen, *Interpreting the Bible* (Grand Rapids: Eerdmans, 1963), 245-246.

[21]Henry G. Liddell and Robert Scott, *A Greek-English Lexicon* (New ed. revised and augmented throughout by Henry S. Jones; Oxford Clarendon Press, 1940), 1399. Such usage may be found in extra-biblical sources; cp. Hdt. 2.28; 4.53; Str. 17.1.52, "source(s) of the Nile." Cf. Psa 104:10.

forecasting the barbarian destruction of the old western Roman Empire.[22] Assuming a sequential understanding of the symbols, this conclusion follows naturally upon the common, historical interpretation of the seal prophecies as culminating with the fourth century conversion of the Empire by Constantine (see above, ch. 4, Rev 6:1-17).[23]

The Barbarian invasions of the Roman Empire are, indeed, the only suitable model for the fulfillment of the first four trumpet prophecies. This is supported by the following observations:

1. These wars followed directly upon the Constantinian era of the sixth seal, the close of which we have associated with the death of Theodosius (A.D. 395).

---

[22]Froom includes here Mede (1631), Goodwin (1654), Sherwin (1670), Jurieu (1687), I. Newton (1691), Horch (1697), Fleming (1701), C. Mather (1702), Crinsos de Bionens (1729), Pyle (1735), Edwards (1739), Th. Newton (1754), Langdon (1774), Bicheno (1793), Galloway (1798), Farnham (1800), Faber (1804), Th. Scott (1805), Fuller (1810), Cuninghame (1813), Gauntlett (1821), Fry (1822), Cooper (1825), Irving (1826), Keyworth (1828), Keith (1828), Henry (1829), Drummond (1830), Habershon (1834), Jenks (1834), R. Scott (1834), Ashe (1835), Gaussen (1837), Litch (1838), Elliott (1844), Jenkin (1844), Barnes (1851) [Froom, 2.786, 3.252-253, 744-745, 4.394]. To these may be added Whiston (1706 [Elliott 4.522]); Daubuz (1720; Elliott 1.514-515), Th. Newton, *Dissertations on the Prophecies* (1754; repr., London: Crissy & Markley, 1850.), 476-481; Alexander M'Leod, *Lectures upon the Principal Prophecies of the Revelation* (New York: Whiting & Watson, 1814), 126-140; John Cummings, *Apocalyptic Sketches: Lectures on the Book of Revelation, 1st series* (Philadelphia: Lindsay & Blakiston, 1856), 71-85; H. Grattan Guinness, *The Approaching End of the Age*. 1st ed., 1878. (8th ed.; New York: A. C. Armstrong and Son, 1884), 433; B. W. Johnson, *The People's New Testament . . . with Explanatory Notes* (Nashville, Tenn.: Gospel Advocate Company, 1982), 2.446; Cachemaille (1911), 237-245; Basil F. C. Atkinson, *The War with Satan* (London: Protestant Truth Society, 1940), 76-79; H. Barton, *It's Here: the Time of the End* (New York: Exposition, 1963), 149-153; and McKinley Ash, *Antichrist, Past, Present, and Future* (Robbinsdale, Minn.: Osterhus, 1967), 187-192; Foxe in 1856 identified the fourth trumpet with the Barbarian conquest of Rome (Elliott 4.462). More authors could be added, as many listed in Froom contained no information on these trumpets. Only for a very few others did he list alternate interpretations. Froom adhered to the Seventh-day Adventist parallel interpretation and his work appears to display a disinterest in documenting the continuous understanding.

[23]The reader should remember that the modern preterist and futurist schools, as well as the parallel-historicist school, are bound by presupposition regarding the general approach to understanding the Book of Revelation to ignore or disagree with this continuous-historicist approach to these prophecies (see above, Ch. 1, Approaches to Intepretation). Historicist interpreters have, nevertheless, introduced confusion by their division between parallel and continuous interpretation. Those who assume the parallel approach must extend each of the three major series over the entire church age, leading to a much more general application of the symbols, often resorting either to spiritualizing or to the ignoring of detail. See Appendix 3.

2. Assuming the common biblical use of celestial symbols as representing the powers of governing authorities (defended above, 6:12-17, with notes), the fourth trumpet concludes the four-trumpet series with a major diminution of such powers (8:12). This corresponds agreeably with the demise of the old Western Roman Empire, as we shall see below.

3. The sequence of four trumpets corresponds agreeably with the four major barbarian invasions often cited by historians of this period.

4. A correct understanding of the symbolic language should both recognize some consistency in the use of common symbolism in the several trumpet prophecies while allowing for distinctive implications where different symbols occur. Both the commonality of the symbols and the variation correspond well with the period of the barbarian wars against Rome.

The first major assault by a barbarian power against Rome and the power of the Empire was carried out principally by two barbarian generals, Alaric the Goth and Radagaisus, a pagan Vandal.[24] Alaric, who began his military career as a mercenary in the Roman army, became an officer and eventually a general in charge of the province of Illyricum. Taking advantage of political instability in the Empire after the death of Theodosius, Alaric marched his destroying army through what is now Yugoslavia, Macedonia, and Greece. In a temporary Imperial vacuum of power in the province, Alaric defied Rome by declaring himself King of the Goths. During the period from 408-410, he wasted Italy and laid siege to Rome three times. In the final devastation of 410 his barbarian army was given free reign for three days to pillage, rape, and destroy with unimaginable terror. Alaric died shortly after in southern Italy while on his way to planned military adventures in Africa.[25]

The barbarian conquest of Rome was a signal event, the first conquest of the Imperial City for more than six hundred years (Elliott, 1.372-

---

[24]The Goths, including Alaric, were Arian Christians, the tribe having been evangelized largely by the missionary, Ulfilus, ca. 311-381. See George P. Fisher, *History of the Christian Church* (New York: C. Scribner's Sons, 1916), 92-93; Elgin S. Moyer, *Who Was Who in Church History* (New Canaan, Conn.: Keats Publishing, n.d.), 414; *Mosheim's Institutes of Ecclesiastical History* (London: Wm. Tegg, 1859), 124-125, with n. 1; Kenneth Scott Latourette, *A history of the Expansion of Christianity* 1 (New York: Harper and Brothers, 1937), 230-235.

[25]Thomas S. Burns, *Barbarians within the Gates of Rome* (Bloomington, Ind.: Indiana University Press, 1994), 183-246; Edward Gibbon, *The History of the Decline and Fall of the Roman Empire*, with notes by H. H. Milman, (New ed.; New York: Harper & Brothers, n.d.), 3.190-293.

378; Gibbon, 3.244). As Elliott and others have indicated, the symbolic elements of the first trumpet prophecy were fully satisfied by this (see Notes, above). The destroying judgment as a hailstorm came from the north, from beyond the Danube River. The extraordinary burning of trees and vegetation is mentioned in the ancient sources describing the movements of the barbarian armies, as is the burning of conquered cities, including many stately mansions in Rome itself.[26]

Not only Alaric, but also at this time Radagaisus, who with his barbarian warriors was turned back from invading Rome, nevertheless ravished part of Italy as well as much of Gaul and Spain (Burns, 197-198; Elliott, 1.375-378).[27]

The period of the first trumpet aptly forecasts the initial barbarian invasion of Rome and the Western Roman Empire which occurred between A.D. 400 and 410, though the effects continued into the succeeding times of the second, third, and fourth trumpets.

The second trumpet signals that "something like a huge mountain, all ablaze, was thrown into the sea. A third of the sea turned into blood. A third of the living creatures in the sea died, and a third of the ships were destroyed." As we have seen above (see Notes), "the sea" in context is an appropriate apocalyptic symbol for the Roman Empire and the language otherwise suggests battle scenes involving burning, bloodshed, and great destruction. Historians are quite unanimous in noting the next major assault on Rome. Katz reports that "the Goths withdrew from Rome as quickly as they had come, but in 455 Rome was once more sacked by barbarians, this time by the Vandals from Africa."[28] They had in fact

---

[26]Regarding the plight of Jovinian, an old man banished to rural poverty, Gibbon quoting an ancient source, says, "His trees, his old contemporary trees, must blaze in the conflagration of the whole country" (Gibbon, 3.200). Of Alaric's Grecian campaign, Gibbon says, "The most fortunate of the inhabitants were saved, by death, from beholding the slavery of their families and the conflagration of their cities" (3.194); of his invasion of Rome, "The flames . . . consumed many private and public buildings . . ." (3.286). Of Radagaisus' campaign in Gaul, Gibbon says, "The scene of peace and plenty was suddenly changed into a desert; and the prospect of the smoking ruins could alone distinguish the solitude of nature from the desolation of man" (3.223-324). With reference to the Spanish campaign, Gibbon says, "The Barbarians . . . ravished with equal fury the cities and the open country" (3.309). Gibbon, when commenting on the seige of Florence, states, "The savage Radagaisus was a stranger to the manners, the religion, and even the language, of the civilized nations of the South. The fierceness of his temper was exasperated by cruel superstition; and it was universally believed, that he had bound himself, by a solemn vow, to reduce the city into a heap of stones and ashes, and to sacrifice the most illustrious of the Roman senators on the altars of those gods who were appeased by human blood" (Gibbon, 3.219).

[27]See also n. 22.

[28]Solomon Katz, *The decline of Rome* (Ithaca, New York: Cornell University Press, 1955), 92.

devastated much of Western Europe and Spain en route, occupying Spain in 409. Passing through the Straits of Gibraltar, they drove through North Africa, took Carthage, then launched their ships for Rome, burning the Roman navy at sea.

H. G. Wells gives this summary: "The Vandals of the south of Spain, under their king Genseric, embarked *en masse* for North Africa (429), became masters of Carthage (439), secured the mastery of the sea, raided, captured, and pillaged Rome (455) . . . ."[29]

When the third trumpet sounded, John saw a great blazing star fall from the sky on the rivers and their source streams so that the deaths of the victims turned the waters bitter (see Notes, above). The next great intrusion into the Roman Empire by the barbarian invaders was commanded by Attila the Hun. Attila, who later became known appropriately as "the Scourge of God," in A.D. 441 launched his campaign via the Danube River and its tributaries southward into Roman lands in a manner that rather exactly fulfills the imagery of the fourth trumpet.[30] He was king of the Mongol Huns, Scythians who had moved down out of the steppes and established themselves in Germany north of the Danube. It is said of Attila that he was viewed superstitiously by his subject princes, kings of the Ostragoths and Gepidae, as a superhuman representative of Mars, the Roman god of war. Gibbon relates that "the barbaric princes . . . could not presume to gaze, with steady eye, on the *divine majesty* of the king of the Huns" (Gibbon, 3.391, citing Priscus, 65). Barnes states that Attila's military career extended from A.D. 433 to A.D. 453.[31]

These barbarian assaults across the Danube into the Imperial City were so extraordinary in their severity that contemporary Christian preachers saw in them the fulfillment of Apocalyptic prophecies, omens of the end of the world.[32] Katz states that 'Far away in Bethlehem, St. Jerome lamented when he heard the news from refugees from Rome: "The lamp of the world is extinguished, and it is the whole world which has perished in the ruins of this one city." In Africa, St. Augustine wrote his greatest work, *The City of God*, to explain the disaster and to refute the charge that a city which had triumphed over its enemies as long as the

---

[29]H. G. Wells, *The Outline of History* (Garden City, N.Y.: Garden City, 1920), 482.

[30]Gibbon says that the title was applied to Attila by "modern Hungarians," 3.399.

[31]Albert Barnes, *Notes on the New Testament: Revelation*. (1852; Grand Rapids: Baker Book House, 1949), 205.

[32]The unbelieving Gibbon comments, "The clergy, who applied to recent events the lofty metaphors of oriental prophecy, were sometimes tempted to confound the destruction of the capital and the dissolution of the globe" (3.289).

pagan gods were worshiped had succumbed at last because its rulers had accepted Christianity' (92).

The fourth angel prophecy in which a third of the sun, moon, and stars were struck has correctly been understood by historicist interpreters to refer to the fall of the Western Roman Empire. As in astral symbolism, the sun represents the highest ruling authority, so Rome and the Western Empire is the logical referent of this symbol. As Elliott points out, the Empire earlier had been divided into three parts—the East, the West, and the central region north of Italy known as Illyricum. Though Constantine took the Imperial throne to Byzantium, later renamed Constantinople, a lesser emperor continued to govern the West from Rome up to the time targeted by this prophecy. The Western Empire fell in A.D. 476 at the hand of the barbarian chief of the Heruli, Odoacer.[33] Odoacer abolished both the name and office of the Roman Emperor and ceded the authority of the Western Empire to Constantinople (Elliott, 1.383). The last vestiges of the old pagan Empire, the Roman senate finally dissolved in A.D. 550.

One may infer that one of the factors prompting these judgments of the Almighty against Christian Rome and perhaps in part motivating the barbarian Gothic soldiers in the mass destruction of Roman Christian institutions was the increasing paganization of the church in the late fourth and in the fifth centuries. In contradiction of the Second Commandment, Constantine had even erected a statue of Christ in the forum at Constantinople.[34] The veneration of the relics and images of the saints as well as the transfer of other religious customs from paganism to the liturgy of Christian worship were outward signs of the nominalization of Christianity under the state church.

According to the contemporary historian, Sozomen, the moral decadence of the time was another reason for the Divine judgment— these calamities on the Romans were "indications of divine wrath sent to chastise them for their luxury, their debauchery, and their manifold acts of injustice toward each other, as well as toward strangers."[35]

---

[33]Tim Newark, *The Barbarians: Warriors & Wars of the Dark Ages.* (Poole, U.K.: Blandford, 1985), 64.

[34]Philip Schaff, *History of the Christian Church* (New York: Scribner's Sons, 1910; repr. Grand Rapids: Eerdmans, 1910), 3.565-566.

[35]*Eccles. Hist.* 9.6, quoted in Jaroslav Pelikan, *The Excellent Empire* (SanFrancisco: Harper & Row, 1987), p. 70.

Chapter Five *The three woes, 8:13* 193

The Three Woes

8:13. As I watched, I heard an eagle that was flying in midair call out in a loud voice: "Woe! Woe! Woe to the inhabitants of the earth, because of the trumpet blasts about to be sounded by the other three angels!"

8:13   **The Three Woes**   **Introduction**

The announcement of the three woes by the flying eagle introduces a marked distinction between the first four trumpet prophecies and the fifth, sixth, and seventh trumpets which follow.[36] The more severe judgments implied are reflected in the more lengthy descriptions given for the fifth and sixth trumpets (ch. 9). John's readers probably would have inferred that in fulfillment there would be a major historical transition that should occasion such alarm as the three woes suggest. The passing of the first and second woes is signaled in 9:12 and 11:14, respectively, heightening anticipation of the final crescendo of calamity which is to precede the end. The text does not identify the third woe except to indicate that it is to be announced by the seventh trumpet. When the seventh trumpet sounds, it is followed by an interlude (11:16-19), then by the Little Scroll message of chapters 12-14. Chapter 15-16 describe the seven bowl judgments. These are introduced as the seven last plagues—"last, because with them the wrath of God is finished" (15:1). "The last

---

[36]The KJV & NKJV reads "flying angel," after the Textus Receptus. 'Αετοῦ "is decisively supported by ℵ A 046 most minuscules . . ." (Metzger, 743). The substitution of "angel" for "eagle" could have been accidental (᾽αετου for ᾽αγγελου), but more likely an assumed correction to improve the sense. Swete suggests that had the Apocalyptist written "angel," the text probably would have read "another angel" rather than "an angel" (the text reads ἑνος ἀετου, literally, "a lone eagle").

Some historicist expositors have seen in the flying eagle a forecast of Gregory the Great (ca. 540-604), as e.g., Brightman who states, "The time and agreement of the matter do make me to think, that this *Angel is Gregory the great, the Bishop of Rome*; This man was one, as it were, excepted out of the rabble of many *Popes*, whose labour God would use to profit his Church" (90; emphasis his). So also Elliott, who marshals much evidence for Gregory's call of a great alarm at the fall of the old Roman Empire (1.399-404). However, identification of the flying eagle is hardly necessary to the text, no more than other messengers, which rather frequently appear.

plagues" are then most probably the principal message of the seventh trumpet and of the last or third woe of 9:12.[37]

8:13 **The Three Woes** Exposition

This verse marks a transition between what precedes and what follows while highlighting the importance of the latter. The reader is reminded of the supernatural character of the Revelation, while also being solemnly warned of Divine judgment. In principle, such judgment is inherent in the terms of the Lord's Covenant with his chosen people, whether Israelite, Jew, or Gentile.[38] This was given at Sinai as stated in Leviticus 26 and reiterated by Moses in Deuteronomy 28, as well as frequently by the prophets. The believer, who will stand before the Judge of all the earth can rejoice in his assurance of God's grace for salvation but must also stand in awe before God's Law and know that we must then give account to the Almighty "for the things done while in the body, whether good or bad" (2 Cor 5:10). The specific judgments here predicted fall upon the nations of that Roman world which provided the historical setting for our text, but the principle of judgment is applicable to all.

---

[37]If the pouring out of the seven bowls of wrath are in fact the last plagues, then they qualify as the final "woe" (see 15:1). Mounce objects that this "would separate in kind the first two (demonic assaults) from the third (judgments of God)" (183). But one need not assume either that the demonic assaults are not Providential judgments or that the bowl plagues are not demonic. Beckwith correctly addresses the woes from the standpoint of the overall structure of the book: "The important place which the three woes occupy in the author's plan is evident; they are the last three great calamities in the course of the 'tribulations' sent upon the world before the final issue. As the seventh trumpet is the last and ushers in the movements which are to follow to the end (107), so its 'woe,' the third, is to form the closing scene in the pre-messianic visitations" (669).

[38]The term, "Israelite," properly refers to the pre-exilic period, whereas "Jew" (from the Hebrew, יְהוּד, $y^e h u d$), pertains to the former inhabitants of the Southern Kingdom after they returned from Babylon in the sixth century and established the Jewish state.

| 8:13 | **The Three Woes** | Notes |

13. As I watched reminds the reader that John is observing a Divine revelation (see above Notes on Rev 1:2, 3). The **eagle** suggests three qualities: strength, speed in flight, and predation. On the last, see 19:17, 18. The first insures the characteristic loudness of this bird of prey. **Flying in midair** is characteristic of this bird while the position affords the cry maximum exposure. **Call out in a loud voice** may be freely translated "shrieking loudly."[39] **Woe! Woe! Woe . . . !** The three-fold repetition is surely emphatic but here, the text indicates that it also points to three distinct future judgments. The first two are represented by the fifth and sixth trumpets (cf. 9:12; 11:14). The third, one may infer, is the final trumpet announcing the seven bowls (11:15). This is confirmed when the bowl series begins, as they are called "the seven last plagues—last, because with them God's wrath is completed" (15:1).[40]

Beckwith states decisively, "The recognition of the bowl-plagues as the third woe has important bearing on the question of the composition of the Apocalypse. According to this interpretation the program of the three woes, interwoven with the trumpet-series which was introduced in chapter 8, is completed in a manner which accords with the first two. woes in nature and purpose, and which gives to the series the climax anticipated at the outset. Thus the bowl-series not only looks back to the members with which it is organically connected; it also looks forward to the two crowning events now to follow, the destruction of Rome and the battle of the Great Day" (671). The seven bowls (chs. 15, 16) are the culminating judgments which lead to Armageddon and the destruction of the forces of the Antichrist (chs. 17-19).[41]

---

[39] Ford, J. M. *Revelation.* (Anchor Bible; Garden City, NY: Doubleday, 1975), 134.

[40] Bp. Th. Newton says, 'How can it be said that "the wrath of God is filled up in them," if there are others besides them?' *Dissertations on the Prophecies* (1st ed. 1732; Repr., London: Crissy & Markley, 1850); 559-560. So also leading expositors Brightman (1644), 161; S. T. Bloomfield,'Η ΚΑΙΝΗ ΔΙΑΘΗΚΗ: *The Greek Testament with English Notes* (Boston: Perkins and Marvin, 1837), 2.593; Elliott (1862), 491-492; Cachemaille (1911), 374; Beckwith (1919), 559, 669-671; et al.

[41] See further our notes on chs. 15, 16 below. For more detailed interpretation of the third woe, see our discussion of the seventh trumpet prophecies in Chapter 9.

The Fifth Trumpet

9:1. **The fifth angel sounded his trumpet, and I saw a star that had fallen from the sky to the earth. The star was given the key to the shaft of the Abyss. ²When he opened the Abyss, smoke rose from it like the smoke from a gigantic furnace. The sun and sky were darkened by the smoke from the Abyss. ³And out of the smoke locusts came down upon the earth and were given power like that of scorpions of the earth. ⁴They were told not to harm the grass of the earth or any plant or tree, but only those people who did not have the seal of God on their foreheads. ⁵They were not given power to kill them, but only to torture them for five months. And the agony they suffered was like that of the sting of a scorpion when it strikes a man. ⁶During those days men will seek death, but will not find it; they will long to die, but death will elude them.**

⁷The locusts looked like horses prepared for battle. On their heads they wore something like crowns of gold, and their faces resembled human faces. ⁸Their hair was like women's hair, and their teeth were like lions' teeth. ⁹They had breastplates like breastplates of iron, and the sound of their wings was like the thundering of many horses and chariots rushing into battle. ¹⁰They had tails and stings like scorpions, and in their tails they had power to torment people for five months. ¹¹They had as king over them the angel of the Abyss, whose name in Hebrew is Abaddon, and in Greek, Apollyon.

¹²The first woe is past; two other woes are yet to come.

9:1-12   **The Fifth Trumpet**   **Exposition**

At the beginning of this chapter (9:1) we are introduced once again to apocalyptic symbolism in which astrological bodies represent ruling authorities (see above on 6:12-17). Here, the description of the angel as a "star that had fallen" apparently intends to identify the authority as Satan, a fact that is addressed at the conclusion of this passage (9:11).

To this evil angel authority "is given." From this (passive construction) we are to understand that even the evil at work in the world is operating within the permissive will of God, ultimately carrying out His purpose, in this instance, to exact judgment. There is in fact an invasive and overarching Providence in which even the evil acts of wicked people serve as agencies for an omnipotent and holy providence in the punishing of unbelievers (Psa 7:1-11; Ezek 35:1-9; Nah 1:1-8; Rom 1:18), the discipline of the church (Rev 2:5, 16; 3:16, 18), and the parenting of God's elect children (Job 5:17; Psa 94:12; Heb 12:5-11; Rev 2:19).

As believing members of the Family of God we may suffer, not entirely escaping such judgments, yet those sealed in 7:3 in the face of impending great tribulation are later described as having "come out" for celebration in 7:14. A parallel may be seen in Ezek 9:1-11 where "a man clothed in linen" is told to mark the foreheads of those who grieve over the sins of Jerusalem, in consequence of which they were to remain "untouched" by the ensuing slaughter (v. 6). Nevertheless, when Jerusalem fell to Nebuchadnezzar those saints did suffer with the others who were carried off to Babylon. Ezekiel's message indicated at least that their eternal destiny remained secure.[42]

"To open the Abyss" is to cause evil forces to come forth, as it were, from the underworld to do their destructive work. In a cloud of dense smoke locusts swarmed out of the Abyss (v. 2). The locust was a peculiarly destructive natural force in the Near Eastern world.

We are introduced to locusts in the prophecy of Joel, chapters 1 and 2, where locusts may represent invading armies causing great destruction. "Before them the land is like the garden of Eden, behind them, a desert waste" (2:3). "They have the appearance of horses; they gallop along like cavalry" (4). "They charge like warriors; they scale walls like soldiers" (7). "The LORD thunders at the head of his army; his forces beyond number, and mighty are those who obey his command" (11). Joel's description of a devastating locust plague as an invading army provides a Scriptural foundation by which we may understand the fifth trumpet imagery.

---

[42]Regarding this, Calvin states, "While God apparently sends trouble to his people in common with the wicked, there is still this distinction on the side of the former, that nothing befalls them but what shall turn to their salvation. When God, therefore, forbids the Chaldeans to touch his faithful servants, he does not mean that they should be free from all trouble and annoyance, but promises that matters should be ordered so differently with them, as compared with the wicked, that they should know in their own experiences God had not forgotten his faithful word." Quoted in Fairbairn, *Ezekiel* (4th ed.; Edinburgh: T. & T. Clark, 1876), 98.

When periodically the great swarms come out of Arabia and spread over the land, all vegetation falls victim to their voracious appetite. Paradoxically, however, in our text they were not to harm "the grass of the earth or any plant or tree" but only people, "people who did not have the seal of God on their foreheads." This indicates the focus of this Divine judgment, a judgment which was directed especially against unbelievers and nominal Christianity (see Fulfillment section below).

As believers, like the Apostle Peter, we need to make our "calling and election sure" (2 Pet 1:10). That is, as James enjoined, earnestly to demonstrate our faith by bearing the fruit of personal holiness and those good works that are commanded in Scripture and prompted by the Holy Spirit (2:17-19). By such means we have assurance of our election.

This, the first of the three great woes, indicates that the forces of evil are at the time of this woe's fulfillment working greatly in the world. The locust-like powers were to cause intense suffering but not "to kill," as even the forces of Satan are limited by the bounds of God's providential judgment (Job 1:12). Death when it comes brings release from torment only after the Divine judgment has accomplished God's purpose.

The detailed description of the locust-like forces (vv. 7-10a) and the "five month" interval (v. 10b) are given ultimately to provide clues for identifying the temporal fulfillment of the prophecy (see the Fulfillment section, below). The details suggest that they are not literal locusts but apocalyptic symbols involving human agencies.[43]

Verse 11 clearly indicates the responsible ruler who deploys the evil forces—the "angel of the Abyss," king of the underworld, Satan.[44] With this climactic announcement "the first woe is past; two other woes are yet to come" (v. 12).

---

[43] Enoch Pond, *The Seals Opened; or, The Apocalypse Explained* (Portland: Hoyt, Fogg, and Breed, 1871), 97.

[44] Though Satan is indeed a fallen angel, the common interpretation of Isaiah 14 as referring to the fall of Satan (vv. 12-15) is contrary to sound interpretation, as the text explicitly ascribes this fall to the king of Babylon (v. 3). Similarly, Ezek 28:12-19, predicting the fall of the king of Tyre (v. 12), is erroneously understood to refer to Satan.

9:1-12.   **The Fifth Trumpet**   Notes

9:1. The **star**, as in earlier references, denotes a ruling authority (cp. v. 11; also see 1:16, 20; 6:13; 8:10; 12:1, 4 and the Notes on these). Similarly, **sky** denotes the exalted sphere from which authorities rule, whereas **earth** indicates, from the perspective of the original recipients, the realm of the subjects, the lands of the Roman Empire (see Notes on 6:4, n. 17; 6:15, n. 53). **The Abyss** refers to the "underworld," the abode of fallen angels who await final punishment in "the lake of fire" (20:10, 14, 15; Charles, 1.240). Because such are inherently spirit beings, one need not think of it as a material realm but rather as an anthropomorphic expression calling attention to such evil forces. The **shaft of the Abyss**, also anthropomorphic, dramatizes the particular invasive advance of these forces. **2. Smoke rose like the smoke from a gigantic furnace.** Such furnaces operated in antiquity chiefly as brick and pottery kilns. As high-carbon fuels were burned and very high temperatures required, they produced great quantities of dense smoke. **The sun and sky were darkened** is probably intended here to indicate the great number and extent of the evil forces represented. **3. Locusts** invade with great destruction owing to their vast numbers. When invading the lands of the Near East, they normally came from Arabia, which might well have suggested to the original Eastern Mediterranean reader an enemy power from that place. They **were given** power: "The passive voice ... suggests that this plague ... is under the sovereign control of God (especially since they are not permitted to harm God's people!). Throughout the Apocalypse he is the "Lord God Almighty" (4:8; 11:17; 15:3; 16:7; 21:22)." (Mounce, 187) **Like that of scorpions:** Scorpions are lonely, isolated creatures which inflict their victims with painful venom. To give locusts with their vast hoards this power of the scorpion is to amplify to the extreme the force of this plague. **4.** The locusts **were told not to harm the grass of the earth or any plant or tree**, that is, they were not to do what by nature locusts are expected to do—destroy the vegetation—but only to attack people not sealed. **The seal of God on their foreheads** obviously refers to the sealing of the 144,000 described in 7:3, 4 (see above on 7:1-8).[45] **5. They were not given the power to kill them but only to torture them** reflects

---

[45]This reference to the sealing under the sixth seal while explaining an earlier event under the fifth trumpet is enough to refute the assumption of the parallel-historicist school that the events of the seals, trumpets, and bowls run in some manner parallel to one another. For our critique of the parallel school, see Appendix 3.

the nature of scorpions whose sting is not ordinarily fatal but extremely painful. **Kill** here may have a figurative sense and, as reflecting the nature of the scorpion's sting, be intended not absolutely but in contrast to the extravagant killing which was to occur under the sixth trumpet (cp. 9:18).[46] The text clearly places the emphasis on the painful conditions to be endured under the fifth seal. **Five months** must be understood consistently with other time references in Revelation to represent 150 days or, according to the prophetic year-day principle, 150 years). 6. **Men will seek death, but will not find it** suggests that there would be "such a condition of public suffering that men would regard death as a relief" (Barnes, 214).

7. What follows in vv. 7-11 is a description of the "locust" armies, apparently designed to aid in their identification in the era of fulfillment. They **looked like horses prepared for battle . . . and their faces resembled human faces** clearly recalls Joel 2:1-11 and indicates invading cavalry units. 8. **Like women's hair**, that is the riders were effeminate in appearance, probably with long hair. **Teeth were like lions' teeth** suggests power and ferocity. 9. **Breastplates of iron** suggests armored cavalry. **The sound of their wings** reflects the appropriateness of the locust imagery to symbolize the noise of moving cavalry. 10. **In their tails they had power to torment people**. See v. 3. Perhaps in light of the metaphor, one need not assume that the horsemen's power was in some figurative sense "in their tails," but the orientation may simply reflect the anatomy of the scorpion. **Five months**, see note on verse 5. 11. **The angel of the Abyss** must suggest a Satanic messenger and indicate the Satanic orientation of the invading armies. **Abaddon** and **Apollyon** both mean "destroyer" (see also v. 1).

12. **The first woe is past; two other woes are yet to come.** The identification of this plague as the first of three woes suggests that there is a particular significance to these three judgments in distinction from the first four trumpet prophecies (see above on 8:13).

---

[46]Brightman comments, "How can this agree to the Saracenes who spilled so much Christian blood? These things seeme to be spoken not simply, but by comparison. If the slaughter which these men made be compared with that which was to be made in the next Trumpet. The Saracenes may seem to pricke and to torture and not to kill" (p. 95).

9:1-12   **The Fifth Trumpet**   **Fulfillment**

As indicated above in our discussion of the Three Woes, and as anticipated by our exposition of the first four trumpets, we should expect this, the first of the three, to signal some major calamity to fall upon the nominally Christianized Roman Empire soon after the Barbarian invasions and the fall of Rome in the fifth and sixth centuries..

The church-state union under Constantine had over three centuries introduced many corruptions into the relatively pure church of the first three centuries. William Jones in his *Church History* states:

> Constantine the emperor . . . undertook to convert the kingdom of Christ into a kingdom of this world, by exalting the teachers of Christianity to the same state of affluence, grandeur, and influence in the empire, as has been enjoyed by pagan priests and secular officers in the state. . . . In the sequel, it will appear, that when the bishops were once exalted to wealth, power, and authority, this exaltation was of itself the prolific source of every corrupt fruit.

The corrupt fruit included the worship of images and many resulting idolatrous practices.[47] Moreover, early in the seventh century, Boniface, the Bishop of Rome, now exalted as the leader of the Catholic church received from the Byzantine Emperor, Phocus, the title of "Universal Bishop," which in a previously stated opinion of Gregory "the Great," marked him as "the forerunner of Antichrist." Such corruption within the church left it ripe for the judgments prefigured in the Apocalypse as the fifth and sixth trumpets.

One need not know in depth the history of that time to discover the obvious fulfillment of the Fifth Trumpet prophecy by Mohammed and the Saracen conquests. Until the advance of preterism and of futurism in recent times, this fulfillment was recognized by very nearly all the Protestant interpreters, even by many of those who held to a recapitulation or parallel structure for the seals, trumpets and bowls of the

---

[47] Wm. Jones, *The History of the Christian Church: from the Birth of Christ, to the XVIII century* (Conrad, Mont.: Triangle, 1993), 1.270-271.

Apocalypse.[48]

Mohammed first announced his mission in A.D. 612. In 629 he proclaimed war against Christendom. After his death in 632, his successors led an army of Saracen warriors into Syria and Omar subdued the Syrian province in 636.[49] Within eight years, Omar with his armies "had reduced to his obedience 36,000 cities or castles, destroyed 4000 churches, and built 1400 mosques for the exercise of the religion of Mahomet" (Elliott, 1.449). Subsequently Egypt, Cilicia, Asia Minor, North Africa, Spain, and southern France fell to the Moslems. Such continued until the middle of the eighth century when the Saracenic empire suffered from an internal change in the Caliphate—the fall of the Ommiades and the rise to power of the Abasides. When the deposed caliph fled to Spain where his authority was recognized, the Moslem world was split between east and west. In 762 the Abaside Caliph began to construct a new capital east of the Euphrates which he called *Medinat al Salem*, "City of Peace." This marked the beginning of an era when the caliphs pursued luxury and their military power declined. (Elliott, 1.459-462; Barnes, 224).

---

[48]Those of whom this author is aware include, in the 16th cent.—Bullinger (1557), Napier (1593); in the 17th cent.—Brightman (1614), Pareus (1618), Mede (1631), Trapp (1647), Durham (1657), Sherwin (1672), Goodwin (1683), Beverley (1684), Jurieu (1687), Cressener (1690); in the 18th cent.—Fleming (1701), Whiston (1706), Horch (1712), I. Newton (1727), Crinsoz de Boinens (1729), Pile (1737), Edwards (1742), Lowman (1745), Th. Newton (1754), Gill (1757), Daubuz (1770), Brown (1784), Wood (1787), Langdon (1791), Bichemo (1793), Simpson (1795), Gallaway (1798), King (1798), Durham (1799); in the 19th cent.—Farnham (1800), Whitaker (1802), Wm. F. Miller (1803), Faber (1804), Th. Scott (1805), Fuller (1810), Davis (1811), Smith (1811), Cuninghame (1813), Alexander M'Leod, *Lectures upon the Principal Prophecies of the Revelation*, (New York: Whiting & Watson, 1814); 126-140, Schmucker (1817), Haywood (1819), Bayford (1820), Irving (1820), Gauntlett (1821), Fry (1822), Reid (1824), Cooper (1825), Park (1825), Croly (1827), Keith (1828), Keyworth (1828), Addis (1829), Jones (1829), Drummond (1830), Cox (1832), Ashe (1835), Fry (1835), Habershon (1835), Bickersteth (1836), Bloomfield (1837), Gaussen (1837), Hinton (1842), Birks (1843), Cumming (1843), Elliott (1844), Junkin (1844), Lord (1847), David Simpson (1847), Barnes (1851), Garratt (1866), Thomas (1866), Steele (1870), Pond (1871), Craven (1874), Kelly (1874), Faldesius (ca. 1885), McIlvaine (1886), Johnson (1891), Guinness (1899); in the 20th cent.—Cachemaille (1911), Atkinson (1940), Harold Barton (1963), Ash (1967), Lee (2000). Also in the earlier 20th century A. B. Simpson, A. J. Gordon, Hudson Taylor, and James A. Nichols, Jr. were among the 20th century notables who are known by this writer to have held the above view, along with many others, though they may not have written commentaries. See Froom, vv. 2-4; Elliott, v. 4, et al.

[49]C. H. Becker, "The Expansion of the Saracens—the East," *Cambridge Medieval History* (New York: Macmillan Company, 1926), 2.342-346. Syria at this time included Palestine.

Chapter Five — The fifth trumpet, 9:1-12

The locust symbolism most appropriately describes the rapid and devastating Muslim conquests. Thomas Scott on Rev 9:3-5 (unpaged) gives the following description:

> Out of this smoke came ... locusts: that is, vast armies of Saracens were raised by means of Mohammed's imposture to spread desolations through the nations. They came from the same regions, whence the largest swarms of these destructive insects have in all ages arisen. Locusts are said to be bred in pits and caverns; and these proceeded from the smoke that came out of the bottomless pit. Yet at the same time they also resembled scorpions, whose sting gives extreme pain, and often proves mortal: and whilst locusts destroy the fruits of the earth, yet do not hurt the bodies of men; these mystical locusts were commanded not to hurt the grass, or other vegetable productions, but only those men who had not the seal of God upon their foreheads: and it is remarkable that the Saracen armies were expressly laid under a similar injunction. 'When Yezed was marching with his army to invade Syria, Abubeker charged him with this among other orders, Destroy no palm-trees, nor burn any fields of corn; cut down no fruit-trees, nor do any mischief to cattle, only such as you kill to eat' (*Bp. Newton*, 482).

How did three centuries of Protestant interpreters consistently identify Mohammed and his followers as the proper fulfillment of the first woe? First, predominant Protestant interpreters identified the sixth seal with the fourth century conversion of the Roman Empire under Constantine and his establishment of the church-state union. That logically led them to look for the next major historical event. For this, historians point to the Moslem conquests. But beyond this methodological consequence, there is the fact that they recognized *prima facie* the remarkable correspondence of the symbolism with the events.[50] One need not look farther than Mohammed to determine the next great revolution to follow upon the Barbarian invasions of the Roman-biblical world. Persia lay threatening to the east but succeeded only briefly and with little consequence in the Holy Land or in the Roman Empire.[51] Thomas Scott comments on vv. 7-9 as follows:

> The 'crowns on their heads like gold,' may denote the turbans which the Arabians have always worn; or it may refer to the many kingdoms which they subjected to their dominion. They had beards ... like men; but they wore their hair like women, plaited, or flowing down their

---

[50] See further Schaff, 4:171-174; Philip K. Hitti, *History of the Arabs* (London: Macmillan & Company, 1953), 111-122, 139-168. For an extended essay on the appropriateness of biblical symbols for indicating the local province of a particular text or prophecy, see Elliott, 1.420-431.

[51] The Persians laid seige to Jerusalem in 606.

backs; and the Arabians are known to have done this. The teeth, as of lions, ... represented their strength and fury to destroy.... The sound of their wings prefigured the fury, with which they assaulted their enemies, and the rapidity of their conquests.

The sacred text emphasizes principally two aspects of the "locust" plaque, destruction (as of lion's teeth) and the pain (as of the scorpion's sting) associated with battle. At the same time, there is in the locust symbolism a paradoxical prohibition against hurting "the grass of the earth, or any plant or tree." ("grass," Gk., χόρτος *chórtos,* "green grass," "stalks of grain in their early stages" [BAG, 884]); such normally provides the essential diet of locusts. This prohibition displaces the usual kind of devastation associated with locusts and substitutes for the material destruction the devastation and pain inflicted by the locust power on the people of the Roman world, "those people who did not have the seal of God upon their foreheads" (9:4).

A second restriction , that they should not kill men, but only torture them until they longed for death (9:5-6) probably alludes not to the battle scene but to conditions of life under Muslim oppression. Christians were known as "dogs" and subject to official, degrading policies tions"), which included prohibition of the use of arms, an annual "life-redemption" tax, distinctive dress, the obligation to stand deferentially in the presence of any Muslim, the prohibition against building new churches or chiming existing church bells, and the necessity to admit any scoffing Muslim into the sanctuary of any church. Moreover, the Muslims offered strong and largely effective inducement to apostasy with the death penalty for those who might afterward return to the Christian faith. Add to this the indescribable abuse of Christian women. (Elliott 1.450-451) Elliott concludes with this comment: "How could it be but that the bitterness of their lot should be felt, and the poison rankle within them, . . . so as to make life itself almost a burden?" As a parallel, Elliott further cites Jer 8:3 (the Lord's judgment in deporting Judah to Babylon), "Death shall be chosen , rather than life, by all the residue of them that remain of this evil family, which remain in all the places whiter I have driven them" (1.451, n. 1). He cites further Job 3:20, "Wherefore is light given to him who is in misery, and life unto the bitter in soul? Which long for death but it comes not, and dig for it more than for hid treasures:which rejoice exceedingly when they find the grave" (1.451, n. 1).

The "five months" during which the locust power had authority thus to torment people (vv. 5, 10), corresponds to the life cycle of the locust from the springtime hatching of the egg to the death of the locust in the fall. When calculated on the year-day principle, thirty days to each month according to the ancient Israelite calendar, the time period amounts to 150 years. Many scholars have noticed that this corresponds exactly to the period of the Saracen conquests, beginning in A.D. 612 when Mohammed publicly began his mission and ending in A.D. 762 when Caliph Almansor built Baghdad and removed the caliphate to that city on the Euphrates, thus ending the Saracen conquest period and beginning of the so-called "Golden Age" of Islam.[52]

The Sixth Trumpet

9:13. **The sixth angel sounded his trumpet, and I heard a voice coming from the horns of the golden altar that is before God.** [14]**It said to the sixth angel who had the trumpet, "Release the four angels who are bound at the great river Euphrates."** [15]**And the four angels who had been kept ready for this very hour and day and month and year were released to kill a third of mankind.** [16]**The number of the mounted troops was two hundred million. I heard their number.**

[17]The horses and riders I saw in my vision looked like this: Their breastplates were fiery red, dark blue, and yellow as sulfur. The heads of the horses resembled the heads of lions, and out of their mouths came fire, smoke and sulfur. [18]A third of mankind was killed by the three plagues of fire, smoke and sulfur that came out of their mouths. [19]The power of the horses was in their mouths and in their tails, for their tails were like snakes, having heads with which they inflict injury.

[20]The rest of mankind that were not killed with these plagues still did not repent of the work of their hands; they did not stop worshiping demons, and idols of gold, silver, bronze, stone and wood—idols that cannot see or hear or walk. [21]Nor did they repent of their murders, their magic arts, their sexual immorality or their thefts.

9:13-21   **The Sixth Trumpet**   **Exposition**

We have now arrived at the sixth in the intensifying series of judgments announced by the trumpet angels. Though this announcement corresponds to the previous one in length of text, the symbolic content suggests that this judgment is even more severe in its consequences than the previous one. When the trumpet sounded, the Apostle heard a voice "coming from the horns of the

---

[52]M'Leod, 163; Elliott, 1.463. See also Peter Mansfield, *A History of the Middle East* (New York: Viking, 1991), 14-18; Albert Hourani, *A History of the Arab Peoples* (Cambridge, Mass.: Harvard University Press, 1991), 32-37.

golden altar that is before God." This, the incense altar, which in the tabernacle-temple architecture stood at the very entrance to the Most Holy Place, represents the symbolic vehicle for communication with God (see above, on 8:3,4, exposition and notes), not only at the daily services but also at annual day of atonement ceremony. The prayers of God's people have been represented as ascending with the incense in 8:4; thus, the Word of God comes from the altar back to His people. The message (9:14-19) is one of retribution and judgment resulting from the particular idolatrous corruptions in the church during the era upon which the prophecy focuses (9:20, 21).

Verses 20 and 21 imply that the worship of the people in the nominal church was corrupted by the incorporation of elements from popular pagan religion which were directly contrary to the Word of God. For this reason the word from the altar is one of judgment, a judgment "to kill a third of mankind" (9:15).

The number of the "four angels" may suggest the universality of the Divine judgment, as in symbol, four often reflects the four directions—north, south, east, and west—meaning "the whole 'earth.'" The four angels may be either four literal angels assigned to carry out this judgment or they may perhaps be only part of the emblematic scenery intended to convey the idea of the release of the forces from beyond the Euphrates. These forces are to come from a site on or near the river Euphrates (9:14), a major international boundary dividing the Mesopotamian powers from the East Mediterranean world in ancient times.

While the details of the description will be explained in the Notes and Fulfillment sections below, the appearance of the fierce units of cavalry ("mounted horseman," NIV; 9:17-19) strikes terror in the mind of the reader who is unprepared to face the holy God, the God who offers grace but forecasts as a reward for impenitence and unbelief such awful judgment.

The number of the horsemen, "two hundred million," probably is intended to indicate an incalculable number (see Notes, below). This adds to the enormity of the predicted judgment.

While a specific event is forecast (see the Fulfillment section, below), the timeless message surely calls mankind to repentance from such idolatries as are mentioned in verses 20-21. The targeted sins of the ancient world are strikingly reiterated in the post-

Chapter Five   *The sixth trumpet, 9:13-21*   207

modernist, new age culture of the twenty-first century—not only their idolatries but "their murders, their magic arts, their sexual immorality or their thefts."

9:13-21.   **The Sixth Trumpet**   Notes

9:13. The sixth angel trumpets the second of the three woes. The **voice** speaks the Word of God. **The horns** focus the listener on the function of the altar, **the golden altar**, the altar of incense (Exod 30:1-11) by which the ancient worshiper in the Israelite temple communicated with God, after an annual atonement was made with a sacrificial victim at the altar of sacrifice. Elliott explains the function of these altars in the sin-offering ritual (1.483; cf. Exod 30:1-10; Lev 4:1-7):

> . . . The hands of the party seeking reconcilement and forgiveness were to be laid on the head of the victim, and his sins told over it; then, after the sacrifice of the animal victim [at the altar of sacrifice], its blood to be sprinkled by the priest seven times before the vail of the sanctuary, and then some of blood to be put upon the *horns* of the altar of incense. so was an atonement to be made for the sins of the transgressors, especially for their sins in respect of holy things . . . .

The above Messianic typology clearly point to the antitypical fulfillment of the sin offering ritual in the atoning death of Jesus Christ. Elliott calls attention to King Hezekiah's cleansing of the land from the sins of his father, Ahaz, through the conduct of this sin offering by which the blood was applied to **the horns of the altar**. By this means, as accompanied by the repentance of many people and fervent prayer, God defeated the forces of Sennacharib and sent his armies retreating back across the Euphrates (2 Chron 29-30; 32:20-23). In our text, the voice warns from **the horns of the altar** an unrepentant people of impending judgment from beyond the Euphrates.[53] The focus on **the golden altar that is before God** both serves to intensify the sense of God's presence and the function of that

---

[53]This striking parallel from one of the most commanding episodes of Old Testament history is one of many insightful comments by E. B. Elliott, whose commentary was the standard work through much of the 19th century. It is beyond my comprehension that the leading 20th century commentators choose to completely ignore Elliott, as well as other authors of the historicist school, the dominant approach to understanding Revelation in earlier times. This is illustrated by the 1245 p. work of G. K. Beale in the prestigious NIGTC series who neither includes Elliott among the 865 works in his bibliography, nor in his 15 p., 2 col. author index. Nor does it appear that any of the other major historicist works are referenced in his book, *The Book of Revelation* (NIGTC; Grand Rapids: Eerdmans, 1999).

altar, which is to facilitate communication with God through prayer (cp. 8:3, 4). God's response to the prayers of His people follows. **14.** The rationale for **four** angels is to be found in the representation of widespread forces in terms of the "four winds," as indicating the four points of the compass (cp. 7:1-2, where perhaps we have the same angels).[54] The angels are **bound** as awaiting the Divine command for their execution of judgment. The River Euphrates is called **great** because in ancient times it served as the primary boundary between the great threatening powers to the east and the more western world, including the Roman Empire. **15.** The extraordinary time designation, **for this very hour and day and month and year** (Gk, εἰς τὴν ὥραν καὶ ἡμέραν καὶ μῆνα καὶ ἐνιαυτόν, *eis tēn hóran kai hēméran kai mēna kai eniautón* is taken by those outside the historicist school as formulated to heighten the emphasis on a particular time known to the sovereign God only. Elliott points out, however, that the particular order of the formula has the opposite effect from intensification, as it widens the time designations from "hour" to "year" rather than narrowing them from "year" to "hour." The appropriate intensifying order for such a formula is illustrated by 2 Enoch 33:2, which emphasizes an unknown time in the Divine providence by moving from the general to the particular, "A time when there is no computation . . . neither years, nor months, nor weeks, nor days, nor hours" (quoted from Charles, 1.252).[55] As the Greek article appears only with "the hour," the first of

---

[54] Charles states that "no explanation or even parallel can be offered. We cannot discover 'the four angels' in other apocalyptic writings, nor can we even conjecture why the number is 'four'" (1.251). However, Swete offers the following regarding the four angels, "These angels are evidently the leaders of the invading host of horses, though not distinctly so designated; this is implied in their being loosed, and especially in the fact that the purpose for which they are said to be loosed . . ." (566). Nevertheless, we need not look for four cavalry divisions to fulfill this prophecy.

[55] Charles, while advocating the emphatic understanding of this text, calls attention to several instances in Scripture where time designations display this order from the particular to the general: Num 1:1, Zech 1:7, and Hag 1:15 (1.252). However, in each of these instances, a specific historical date is given, rather than an emphatic declaration of a particular time. Charles' interpretation (1920) is that of most critical and modern scholars. Among them Elliott identifies Vitringa (1705), Daubuz (1720), Heinrichs (ca. 1800), and M. Stuart (1845) (1.517, n. 1). To these may be added Swete (1906), Beckwith (1919), Walvoord (1966), Ladd (1972), Mounce (1977, Rev. ed., 1998), Hughes (1990), Beale (1999), et al.

Philip Edgcumbe Hughes while advocating the emphatic rationale for the formula, (inadvertently?) reverses the order of the progression: "These angels . . . are set free and activated at the precise moment determined by the wisdom and purpose of God . . . whose calendar sets not merely the **year, month**, and **day** but the very **hour** of the fulfillment of his will" (*The Book of Revelation: a Commentary* (Grand Rapids: Wm. B. Eerdmans Company, 1990), 113.

As an emphatic list, the nouns are listed in a backwards order. If indeed the sequence is to be understood as emphatic, there is no way to account for the reverse order. This has been admitted by a few leading commentators. Swete states, "The ascensive order . . . is difficult to explain . . . ." He then for support references Num 1:1,

Chapter Five   *The sixth trumpet, 9:13-21*   209

the nouns in the list, one may with most historicist commentators view the one article as governing all the nouns in the list so as to bind them together as a quantity equal to the sum of the parts. Such composite enumeration is also found in the expression, "time, times [i.e., *two* times; (Hebrew dual no.)], and half a time: for 3 $\frac{1}{2}$ years (1260 days) symbolizing 1260 years (Dan 12:7; Rev 12:14; cp. Rev 12:6; 13:5). An extra-biblical example of this composite method of indicating a span of time is found in the truce granted to Richard "the Lion-Hearted" by Saladin (A.D. 1187). The span of the truce was for *"three hours, three days, three weeks, three months, three years,"* all the times to be added together and taken as a whole.[56] Taking this as the only reasonable interpretation, most historicists have found here the time period which indicates the duration of the time during which the destroying angels would accomplish their task. Calculating this formula for the period on the year-day principle, the sum of the parts (hour + day + month + year) as based on the solar year adds up to 396 years + 118 days. The calculation runs as follows:

hour	=		30 days[57]
day	=	1 year	
month	=	30 years	
year	=	365 years	88 days (365 1/4 years)
Total	**=**	**396 Years**	**118 Days**

The solar year is preferred, as the Greek uses ἐνιαυτός, *'eniautós,* for "year," ἐν αὐτος, *'en 'autos,* literally, "that which returns into itself."[58]

Zech 1:17, and Hagg 1:15, all of which refer in a conventional, unemphatic manner to mundane events (122). Mounce passes off the problem with the assertion that "the ascending order . . . is of no particular significance" (195).

Regarding the emphatic interpretation, Elliott comments, " . . . it will be obvious that it explains the clause as made up of tautologies: tautologies such that every successive word after the first, instead of strengthening, only weakens the supposed meaning . . . (1.518). Robert Frew, in his essay on the year-day principle in the introduction to Barnes' commentary makes the following statement, 'It is said to mean only, "that at the destined hour, and destined day, and destined month, and destined year" the calamity should happen; that is to say, it should occur simply *at the appointed time.* We venture to say that such a periphrasis for an idea so simple has no parallel elsewhere' . . . . (Editor's Preface: "Year-day Principle," in Barnes, xxv).

[56] Quoted from Elliott 1.528-529, n. 3; as from Hume, *Richard I* 2.21 (italics Elliott's?). See Elliott's extensive remarks on the various reports of this truce and his attempt at determining the rationale for Saladin's unusual formulation (1.528-530, n. 3).

[57] The prophetic day is 12 hours (John 11:9); 1 day = 1 year; 1/12th of 1 year = 91 days less 3 days Gregorian correction = 88 (Elliott, 1.522).

[58] While one ordinarily should avoid etymologizing in determining the meaning of words, here we are dealing with a symbolic time designation, which we justify in order to differentiate from the use of the 360-day/year as apocalyptic symbol, by which 3$\frac{1}{2}$ years ("42 months" or "time, times, and half a time") = "1260 days" (cp. Rev. 11:2, 3, 11; 12:6, 14; 12:5; Dan 12:7).

This general approach to the time formula is adopted by most historicist interpreters, including Mede, Birks, M'Leod, Th. Scott, Elliott, Barnes, Guinness, Cachemaille, H. Barton, and Caringola.. The four angels were released **to kill a third of mankind.** This may be understood in the general sense or with reference to a third part of the Roman world. The latter interpretation can be accommodated by understanding the **third** as an "accusative of reference" (Gk. ‘ἵνα ἀποκτείνωσιν τὸ τρίτον τῶν ἀνθρώπων), and translating, "that they might kill with reference to the third [part] of mankind." The advantage of this understanding will be seen in the Fulfillment section, below. **16.** The **mounted troops** most probably represent cavalry, though in symbolic representation they have characteristics clearly not to be taken literally but rather to convey their power to effect destruction and death. There is nothing in the text to indicate that they are demons, as some suggest.[59] They should rather be seen as earthly and devastating agents of human warfare acting in the succession of events predicted by the trumpet announcements. Their **number, two hundred million** (Gk, δισμυριαδες μυριαδων), literally translated reads, "twice ten thousand times ten thousand." This symbolic language probably should be understood to mean "too many to count." Cp. Judg 6:5; 7:12; Jer 46:23; Judith 2:20; 24; 4 Ezra 13:8, 11, 34-36; Jos. and Asen. 16:17-19, "the cells [from which bees rise] were *innumerable, ten thousand (times) ten thousand and thousands upon thousands . . .*" (Beale, 510, emphasis his). Large numbers which in ancient times were beyond ordinary comprehension afford a natural circumstantial way to state emphatically their enormous quantity. This characterization should not be understood as the Apostle's own manner of describing what he saw, as perhaps drawing on a literary tradition, for he states, **I heard their num-**

---

[59]According to Beale, ". . . The piling up of monstrous metaphors underscores that the demons are ferocious and dreadful beings that afflict people in a fierce, appalling, and devastating manner" (510). This direct identifcation with demons is an unnecessary inference inappropriate to biblical apocalyptic which ordinarily addresses mundane powers, though surely in this and comparable instances such powers are energized by demonic agents of Satan. The distinction we make here is fundamental to the hermeneutic of apocalyptic prophecy, which historically takes as its model the visions of Daniel. When occasioally supra-mundane forces are part of the drama, they are nevertheless part of a chronological timeline, within a specific series of predicted events (see, e.g., Rev 19:14), or an interlude which gives perspective to the course of the prediction, such as Dan 10:4-11:1; Rev 4:1-5:19; or 19:1-8.

Chapter Five *The sixth trumpet, 9:13-21* 211

ber.[60] Apparently, the angelic messenger dictated the characterization. **17. The horses and riders** are introduced as a composite symbol. It is not clearly indicated whether **their breastplates** were seen as worn by the riders, the horses, or both. The colors, **fiery red, dark blue, and yellow**, appropriately reflect the "three plagues of fire, smoke and sulfur" (9:17b). The horses having heads that **resembled the heads of lions** adds to the terror by thus converting a domestic animal to a ravenous beast. Out of these lion-like mouths **came fire, smoke and sulfur.** This has been seen by some to suggest demonic activity associated with the Greek concept of Hades and the Satanic underworld,[61] or by others with warfare involving the use of gun powder.[62] The latter, though essentially incomprehensible to the first-century reader, could be a veiled allusion to a kind of warfare which would be prominent in later times. The passage does describe earthly events constituting judgments against impenitence (9:20-21). **18.** For **a third of mankind**, see above on 9:15. **Was killed** should be taken literally as implying temporal death. This sixth trumpet plague does not carry protection for believers from temporal death, as promised for the fifth trumpet plague. Each of the three plagues, **fire, smoke and sulfur**, carries with it in the original Greek the definite article, calling specific attention to each factor as contributing importantly to the devastation. Fire, smoke, and sulfur are associated with the destruction of Sodom (Gen 19:23-28) and suggest overtones of Divine judgment. **19. Their mouths**, seen here as "like lion's mouths," are viewed as the principal killing agents. Their **tails were like snakes, having heads with which they inflict injury.** Perhaps this fearsome feature is intended to show that death, which can be merciful in warfare, is not the only consequence to be

---

[60]I therefore reject Beale's suggestion after citing an illustrative parallel in Jeremiah that "Jeremiah appears to have been part of an OT tradition drawn on in Revelation 9 that formularically portrayed armies from the east or from beyond the Euphrates as uncountable (510). That Revelation 9 draws upon an oral or literary tradition runs counter to the Apostle's statement, not that he drew upon a tradition, or even that the number was his own expression, but that he "heard their number" as part of the revealed drama (9:16b).

[61]Beasley-Murray, 165-166. Beale, 510-511.

[62]Mede, Joseph. *A Key to the Apocalypse, a translation of Clavis Apocalyptica*; tr. by R. Bransby Cooper (1627; London, J. G. & F. Rivington, 1833), 204; James Durham, *A Complete Commentary on the Book of Revelation, Delivered in Several Lectures*. (2 vols.; Falkirk, Scotland: Robert Penny, 1799), 174; Th. Scott, "Revelation of John the Divine," in *The Holy Bible . . . with Explanatory Notes* (5th London ed.; v. 1, unpaged; Boston: Sam. T. Armstrong, 1831), on 9:16-19; Elliott 1.510, Francis Nigel Lee, *John's Revelation Unveiled*. (Brisbane, Australia: Queensland Presbyterian Theological College, 2000), 93.

suffered in this plague but that there are also to be painful injuries to be endured. **20. The rest of mankind** refers either to the two-thirds number who escaped death in the predicted event or to those in the two-thirds area where the scourge occurred (see on v. 15). That in consequence of this plague, those who survived did not repent speaks of the hardness of men's hearts during the era in focus. The **worshiping** of **demons** (Gk, τά δαιμόνια, *tá daimónia*), either "pagan deities" or "evil spirits," characterize the idolatrous era in focus here. The alternate concepts should hardly be sharply distinguished. The word is applicable to any spirit being or alleged spirit being inferior to God and therefore unworthy of worship.[63] The spirit beings here identified as δαιμονια ("demons") should probably be understood as those associated with the man-made idols which are the focus of the remaining part of the verse. See Deut 32:17, Psa 106:37, 1 Cor 10:20. This era is also described as worshiping **idols of gold, silver, bronze, stone and wood**. Such hand-made gods, of course, have no reality in the spirit world, as frequently pointed out by the biblical prophets (Deut 4:28; Psa 115:1-8; Isa 44:6-20; Jer 10:3-5, 8-9, 11, 14, 15). **21.** The idolatries of 9:20 lead to the kind of sins cataloged here: **murders, magic arts, sexual immorality,**[64] **and thefts**. Demons and idols leave no authentic revelation, in consequence of which the lifestyles

---

[63]See BAGD, 169: "**1.** *a deity, divinity* . . . . **2.** *Demon, evil spirit*, of independent beings who occupy a position somewhere between the human and the divine." BAGD classifies out text with category two, but our context does not indicate which of the two definitions is to be preferred. Category one is otherwise illustrated in the New Testament by Acts 17:18, as well as in other contemporary texts. One may assume, nevertheless, that any δαιμόνιον that is worshiped is from the standpoint of the Word of God an "evil spirit" and under the dominion of Satan.

[64]The Greek word here is πορνεία which in this context means, as the NIV translates it, "sexual immorality." The word is always used in the Bible and elsewhere in distinction from μοιχεία, translated "adultery." Adultery, rather than a sexual sin, per se, is a transgression of the marriage covenant. The distinction between the two terms is well illustrated by Hosea 4:13-14 (LXX), where the verbal form of πορνεία is paired with (unmarried) "daughters" and the comparable form of μοιχεία is paired with (married) "daughters-in-law."

The distinction is also maintained in sin catalogs, which often include both πορνεία and μοιχεία or their derivatives. Two exceptions are the seventh commandment (Exod 20:14), which forbids adultery, probably to highlight the most heinous sexual sin as emblematic of the larger category, and the law of the unchaste bride (Deut 22:21, LXX), where "being promiscuous" is in the Greek the verbal form of πορνεία. The apparent explanation for the adjudication of this case law on the ground of πορνεία is that in the nature of the case it is indeterminant whether the offence occurred before or after the effecting of the marriage covenant. This apparent exception in the use of πορνεία is the basis of Jesus reference to "*a case of* πορνεία" in Matt 5:32 (Gk: λόγου πορνείας). The use of λόγος with the noun is a legal idiom to indicate reference to a specific case law (Deut 22:21; cp. Matt 19:9, where the idiom is abbreviated).

Chapter Five — *The sixth trumpet, 9:13-21*

attributed to them are man-made and often reflective of basic human instincts, inherently sinful and contrary to the Word of God (cp. Isa 47:9-15; Dan 2:1-11; Mal 3:5; Mark 7:20-23; Gal 5:19-21; Eph 5:3-12).

9:13-21   **The Sixth Trumpet**   **Fulfillment**

The sixth trumpet or second woe prophecy forecasts a time following after the era of the fifth trumpet Saracen conquests when armies from the vicinity of the Euphrates river wage devastating warfare against lands to the west. We have seen above that the era of the fifth trumpet, first woe prophecy climaxed in A.D. 762 when Caliph Almansor built Baghdad and moved the Muslim Caliphate to that city near the Euphrates.

One may, with Elliott, pose a later date for the final demise of the Saracen power, a time in the late tenth century with the victory over the Saracens in Crete, Cyprus, Cilicia, and Antioch in the east Mediterranean world. In the west, the Moors in Spain were finally defeated in A.D. 998 (1.464-467, 469-470).[65]

After the demise of the Saracens, the Seljuk Turks captured Baghdad in A.D. 1050.[66] By 1071, the Seljuks had defeated a Byzantine army and captured the Byzantine emperor, which enabled them to settle in Asia Minor, constituting a very serious threat to Eastern Empire and its capitol, Constantinople. As the result of this threat, Pope Urban II launched the Crusades against the Muslims with the particular incentive to liberate Jerusalem and the Holy Land from Muslim control. The Crusaders were finally defeated at the Horns of Hattin by Saladin in 1187. Constantinople fell to the Ottoman Turks in 1453.[67] The epoch of Turkish Muslim conquest fulfills in a remarkable way the symbolism of the sixth trumpet, 2nd woe prophecy.

As the angels were released from "the great river Euphrates" (9: 14), so the Turks waged warfare westward from their capital in Baghdad, which lay a short distance east of the river.[68] "To kill a third of mankind,"

---

[65] See also J.B. Bury, 'The Struggle with the Saracens: Summary," *The Cambridge Medieval History* (Macmillan Company, 1927), 4.151-152.

[66] Peter Mansfield, *A History of the Middle East.* (New York: Viking, 1991), 20. Several older sources give 1055.

[67] Mansfield, 20-24. See Mansfield for a good summary of the above history.

[68] Bagdad was located at the place where the Tigris and the Euphrates converge most closely together, facilitating the construction of the irrigation canals required for the agriculture needed to support a large population. The Euphrates constituted a major international boundary between eastern and western powers.

as indicated in the above Notes, may be translated "to kill with reference to a third of mankind." This, as many scholars have indicated, may be understood to refer to the eastern third of the Empire, the Greek empire with its capital in Constantinople.[69] As the first four trumpets impacted the western empire, so the fifth and sixth trumpet should be understood to impact primarily on the east. It is possible, nevertheless to take "third part" in the more general sense of a large approximation, more than one-quarter but less than half. That such large numbers died in the Turkish wars is probable.

The description of the sixth trumpet forces as "mounted troops" (NIV) is most apt for the Turkish invaders, as they are well-known for use of horses in warfare. With the contemporary armies of Western Europe, the majority of the fighting men were foot soldiers, with a minority of knights as cavalry, whereas the Turkish armies consisted of cavalry and were therefore very swift and powerful (Elliott, 1.506).

The Turks were known more than others for counting their horses in *tomans* or *myriads* (10,000). 'Gibbon speaks of "the *myriads* of the (Seljukian) Turkish horse overspreading the Greek frontier, from the Taurus to Erzeroum" or of the cavalry of the earlier Turks of Mount Altai "being, both men and horses, proudly computed by *millions*."[70] The expression translated "two hundred million," as we indicated in our Notes, above, should be understood as an extremely large number, beyond counting, especially in the context of John's vision. It is a very significant indicator of Turkish superiority in mounted cavalry. The importance of the number as such is emphasized by John's statement, "I heard their number" (v.16).

Most historicist interpreters have noticed that the colors, "fiery red, dark blue, and yellow as sulfur," bear a striking resemblance to the conditions produced by the fact that the Turks introduced the use of gunpowder.[71] It was by their use of enormous cannon that they succeeded in 1573

---

[69] Τὸ τρίτον ("the third") may be read as an accusative of reference. The clause will then be translated, ". . . that they may kill with regard to the third (part) of mankind." For the view that this refers to the eastern Roman Empire, see Mede (197) and Elliott (1.17); Cachemaille (272); et al. M'Leod understands this as "the prophetical expression for the subjects of the great empire, the object of this wo[sic]" (169). Steele comments, "The object of the first woe is the nominally Christian Roman empire, which still stands in its Eastern section; and is to be totally demolished by the second woe-trumpet . . ." (116).

[70] Cited by Elliott from Gibbon, 7.287 and 10.351; 1.506, with n. 5.

[71] Mounce, citing Moulton & Milligan's *The Vocabulary of the Greek New Testament* (647), suggests that the color, "dark blue," probably is the "dusky blue colour as of sulphurouous smoke" (196). The Greek word translated "yellow as sulfur" (θειώδης) is sometimes rendered "sulphurous" (BAGD, 354), in this context meaning, "sulfur yellow."

in breaking down the great walls of Constantinople and taking both the city and the empire. Gibbon, as Elliott comments "always the unconscious commentator on the Apocalyptic prophecy," describes the battle, "The volleys of lances and arrows were accompanied with the smoke, the sound, and the fire of the musketry and cannon. . . . how, as from the lines, the galleys, and the bridge, the Ottoman artillery thundered on all sides, the camp and city, the Greeks and the Turks, were involved in a cloud of smoke . . . " (Elliott, 1.511). The historian Chalcocondylas states:

> Mechmet . . . ordered the largest cannon to be made, of a size which . . . we had never known to have existed. . . . . One of which was of such magnitude, that it was drawn by seventy yoke of oxen and two thousand men. To this, two others of the largest size were attached on either side, each of which sent forth a stone, whose weight was equal to half a talent. After these, came that wonderful mortar which threw a ball whose weight amounted to three talents, and threw down great part of the wall.[72]

A Turkish historian, Saadeddin, describes this battle:

> The Moslems placed their *cannon* in an effective position. The gates and ramparts of Constantinople were pierced in a thousand places. The flame which issued from the mouths of those instruments of warfare, of brazen bodies and fiery jaws, cast grief and dismay among the miscreants. The smoke which spread itself in the air rendered the brightness of day sombre as night; and the face of the world soon became as dark as the black fortune of the unhappy infidels.[73]

Thus we have a striking correspondence between the symbolic language of "fiery red, smoky blue, and sulfur-yellow" and the actual circumstances of the battle which ended the Eastern Roman Empire.[74]

---

[72]As quoted by Mede (206).

[73]From Elliott, 1.512, as cited by Keith (*Apoc.* 2.46) from the *Tadg al Tivarikh* ("Diadem of History"), "as translated in David's *Grammar of the Turkish Language."*

[74]Modern commentators tend to avoid looking for mundane fulfillment of such details but it is this writer's opinion that such a broadly sweeping approach to apocalyptic drama runs contrary to proper interpretation as established with the visions of Daniel. The modern approach appears to be fueled at least in part by an aversion to the approach of the historiicist school of prophetic interpretation. It is instructive to learn how the alternate schools originated—in part from the writings of Jesuit, counter-Reformational commentaries and in part from negative influences, sometimes subtle, of modern literary criticism.. Understanding that the identification of the fulfillment of prophecy must be based on analogy between the revealed text of Scripture, correctly understood, and a corresponding sequence of events, it is entirely reasonable to assume that the Divine author would have provided *in the details* correspondances with the unfolding history. The attempt to negate this historical, chronological approach to the Book of Revelation naturally tends to cause an aversion to such an hermeneutic.

216   *The sixth trumpet, 9:13-21*   Chapter Five

One of the most difficult elements in the sixth trumpet description is the horses tails. We read that "the power [ἐξουσία, *exousía*] of the horses was . . . in their tails, for their tails were like snakes, having heads with which they inflict injury" (9:19). Some have seen here an indication of Satanic power, while others suggest the aftermath of the Muslim conquests which did grave injury to Christian institutions in the eastern empire. Elliott has offered the explanation that the Turkish conquerors adopted horse tails for their standards, which represented the authority of their commanders, or "heads." The tails were tied to a small crossbar on the standard poles ("snakes"). The "heads," as commanders, were responsible for "killing a third of mankind."[75]

We have observed in the Notes above that the time formula, "this very hour and day and month and year" may be understood on the year-day principle as a composite period of 396 years, 118 days. Togrul Beg, the Seljuk Turk launched his campaign to conquer the Greek Empire from Baghdad on January 18, A.D. 1057, as prefigured by the loosing of the four angels (9:14, 15). To secure his base for westward conquest, he first marched his army victoriously eastward, in Iraq, then returned to Baghdad a year later for his ceremonious Coronation before proceeding westward. Several successors carried on the campaign until Jerusalem and all Asia Minor had fallen and Constantinople was seriously threatened. The situation in the east alarmed Pope Sextus II and caused him to launch the Crusades. The Crusades for two hundred years had the effect of suppressing Turkish Conquest, but after Saladin's truce, the effort was resumed by the Ottoman Turks. After a fifty-two day siege, Constantinople fell on May 29, 1453—396 years and 130 days, marking the end of the old Eastern Roman Empire and the beginning of a new era in the history of the Mediterranean and Middle Eastern world. The fall of Constantinople and the Eastern Roman Empire in 1453 was just 12 days more than the forecast period of 396 years and 118 days. Starting from Jan. 18, A.D. 1057, the forecast period ended on May 17, 1453. On the year-day time scale,

---

[75]1.512-513. Even Elliott remarks on this unlikely symbol— " . . . a *horse-tail* to indicate a ruler! Strange association! Unlikely symbol! Instead of symbolizing authority and rule, the *tail* is in other Scriptures put in direct contrast with the head, and made the representative rather of the subjected and the low [Deut 28:44]. . . . . And yet among the *Turks,* as we know,—i.e. among the Euphratean horsemen who were to kill the third part of men,—that very association had existence, and still exists to the present day. . . . And this as what was thenceforward—from the prime vizier to the governors of provinces and districts—to constitute each ruler's badge, mark his rank, and give him name and title. For it is the ensign of *one, two,* or *three horse-tails* that marks distinctively the dignity and power of the *Turkish Pasha.*—Marvellous prefiguration! And who but He could have depicted it, to whom the future is clear as the present; and who, in his Divine prescience, speaks of things that are not as though they were?" (1.513-515; cf. Rom 4:17)

Chapter Five   *The sixth trumpet, 9:13-21*   217

the fall of Constantinople exceeded this period by less than one-half hour!

Although one might well be satisfied with this as an adequate and remarkable fulfillment of the symbolic formula, Elliott takes this a step further and notes that if one subtracts 12 days of the siege, one arrives at the 40th day, about which Gibbon states, "After a siege of *forty days* the fate of Constantinople could be no longer be averted" (1.527). Thus, we can be satisfied that from God's point of view, the time formula may well have been fulfilled to the very day!

The importance of the fall to the Ottoman Turks of Constantinople for the Roman world of the sixteenth century can hardly be overestimated, thus the prophetic drama of history in the Revelation understandably targets this event. Jarolav Pelikan states accordingly that "the great trauma for the East . . . was not the decline and fall of Old Rome in the fifth century, but the fall of New Rome a whole millennium later in 1453."[76]

This brings us to the final verses expounding the sixth trumpet, verses 20 and 21. The text tells us that those not killed "did not repent of the work of their hands," i.e., their idolatries—"their worship of "demons, and idols of gold, silver, bronze, stone and wood." The period of the Turkish conquests bridged the centuries from A.D. 1057-1453. Such worship was strictly forbidden in the Moslem world, as well as of course also to Jews and Christians to whom the Bible and the second commandment more directly applied (Exod 20:4).

It is ironic to observe that as in the fourth century pagan ideas and practices tended to invade the church, the ecclesiastical leaders defended the worship of saints and their images until the practice became pervasive in the church, as well as in people's homes. Images of Jesus were also made. Though some councils vigorously condemned the use of images, others with equal or greater vigor condoned them until toward the end of the eighth century, Irene, the Empress of Constantinople, and her son, Constantine, convened "the seventh general council" at Nice, where they decreed that, whereas pagan Greek idolaters commonly invoked the spirits of their dead,

> . . . that holy images of the cross should be consecrated, and put on sacred vessels and vestments, and upon walls and boards, in private houses, and in public ways. And especially that there should be erected images of the Lord God, our Saviour Jesus Christ, of our blessed Lady, the mother of God, of the venerable angels, and of all the saints. And that whoever should presume to think or teach otherwise, or to throw

---

[76]Jaroslav Pelikan, *The Excellent Empire* (San Francisco: Harper & Row, 1987), 77.

away any painted books, or the figure of the cross, or any image or picture, or any genuine relics of the martyrs, they should, if bishops or clergymen, be deposed, or if monks or laymen be excommunicated.[77]

During the entire period of the fifth and sixth trumpet, the sixth through the fifteenth centuries, the worship of saints was widely practiced in both the Eastern and Western churches, as having its beginnings in the fourth century. Philip Schaff comments that the worship of saints "was a Christian substitute for heathen idolatry and hero worship, and well suited to the tastes and antecedents of the barbarian races, but was equally popular among the cultivated Greeks" (4.442).

In fact, the Greek term (δαιμονία, *daimonía*) "demons," the very term used by pagan Greek idolaters to invoke the spirits of their dead, was the appropriate term to refer to departed saints. The word is used in the Old Testament (Greek Septuagint version) with reference to heathen gods: "For all the gods of the nations are *idols* [δαιμονια]" (Psa 96:5), "They sacrificed to demons , which are not God . . . (Deut 32:17). Such worship of demons [δαιμονια] was integral to Baalism and the worship of the spirits of the dead, as indicated by several Old Testament texts (Psa 106:28; Num 25:2, 3; Isa 8:19; 65:4, 11). Likewise, the New Testament uses "demons" with reference to pagan gods: "He seems to be advocating *foreign gods*" ("strange demons," Ξένων δαιμονίων; Acts 17:18), ... The sacrifices of pagans are offered to *demons*, not to God" and ". . . You cannot have a part in both the Lord's table and the table of *demons*" (1 Cor 10:20, 21; cp. Isa 65:11, LXX). (Elliott 2.498-510)[78] (italics mine)

In the ancient world, demons were thought to be the spirits of the dead who functioned as intermediaries between living humans and the celestial gods. The Greek philosopher, Plato, stated this as follows:

> Demons [Gk: δαιμονία, *daimonía*] are middle powers, through whom both our desires and merits pass to the gods. They are carriers between mortals and the heavenly inhabitants, from hence of prayers, from thence of gifts; who bear to and fro from hence petitions, and from

---

[77]Quoted from Jones 2.402. See his discussion of the ecclesiastical wars over image worship on pp. 390-403; also Schaff 4.442-474.

[78]See also T. H. Gaster, "Demons, Demonology," *IDB* (Nashville: Abingdon Press, 1962) 1.817-824, especially 822-823. For an in-depth discussion of the use of δαιμονια in the Bible and in this prophecy, see Elliott 2.497-508 (Appendix I). Elliott, in his careful analysis of the biblical use of δαιμονια, indicates that in addition to the use of the term with reference to pagan gods, the New Testament also in other texts uses it with reference to evil spirits. The distinction requires careful attention to context, as well as the recognition the the alleged beneficent "demons" worshiped by pagans were themselves as objects of worship an evil to be repented of.

thence supplies; or, indeed, they are interpreters and ushers on either side. For it would not be suitable to the majesty of the celestial gods, to attend to these things.[79]

The Early Church took over this practice of praying to the dead as intermediaries from the heathen custom. The late fourth century theologian, Theodoret, writing to pagan Greek detractors, defends such saint worship with the following:

> If the poet [Hesiod] called good men, after their decease, guardians and preservers of men from evil . . . and would have their sepulchres respected and honoured, why then find fault with what we do? We do not call them *daemons*; God forbid we should be so mad! but the *friends* and kindly disposed *servants of God*. . . That the souls of holy men, even when out of the body, are in a capacity of taking care of men's affairs Plato affirms in the xith Book of his Laws. . . . The martyrs' temples are famous for their beauty and greatness. They . . . pray . . . : . . . not going to them (*the martyrs*) as gods, but making application to them as to *divine men*, and asking them to be advocates on their behalf. . . . . The Lord hath introduced his own dead (the martyrs) into the place of your gods; and the latter he hath dismissed, and hath given their honour to his martyrs.[80]

The practice of praying to Mary or to other "departed saints," as promoted in those early centuries and still presently by the Catholic churches, quite obviously displaces the sole mediatorship of Jesus, our Savior and conflicts with the clear teaching of Scripture as stated by the Apostle Paul, "There is . . . one mediator between God and men, the man Christ Jesus" (1 Tim 2:5). Though the Catholic churches distinguish between "veneration" and "worship," the verb used in Roman Catholic canon law legalizing and promoting such saint worship in the churches was the Latin equivalent of προσκυνέω, *proskunéō* the same verb as used in Rev 9:20.

This worship of departed spirits of the dead was ordinarily combined with their representation by images. The practice was hotly debated during earlier centuries but was officially certified by the Greek church early in the era of the sixth trumpet. It corresponds entirely with the prophetic description in Rev 9:20 where it is clearly labeled as idolatry.

The Apostle Paul stated in his first letter to Timothy, ". . . The Spirit expressly says that in later times some will fall away from the faith,

---

[79] As quoted in Mede, 209. See further, Mede, 208-211; and Mede, *Treatese on the Apostasy of the Last Times,* in his *Works,* 623ff (as cited in Elliott 2.497).

[80] As quoted in Elliott, 2.507.

paying attention to deceitful spirits and *doctrines of demons*" (1 Tim 4:1; NASB [italics mine]; cp. NKJV). "Doctrines of demons" should be understood to mean, "doctrines *about* demons."[81] This rather general prophecy reiterates the warnings of Jesus regarding the apostasy of the last days (Matt 24:4-6, 11, 23-26; Luke 21:8). These "last days" are the Messianic times, the age between the Advents, the age of the Christian church. The apostasy of the last days may have had its beginnings in the first century, perhaps even the Christian worship of "demons," the spirits of the dead.

Associated with our Lord's indictment of demon worship and idolatry in 9:20 we read also the catalog of moral sins listed in 9:21: "their *murders*, their *magic arts*, their *sexual immorality*, or their *thefts*" (italics mine). It is hardly necessary for those who know the history of the era in question to detail the excesses listed here. Murders were commonplace in Roman Christendom as part of the process of persecuting dissenters. Barnes, quoting Sismondi, states:

> It is supposed that in this crusade against the Waldenses a million of men perished. .... That this continued to be the characteristic of the Papacy after the judgments brought upon the Roman world by the Turkish invasion, or that those judgments had no tendency to produce repentance and reformation, is well known, and is manifest from the . . . . establishment of the Inquisition. One hundred and fifty thousand persons perished by the Inquisition in thirty years; and from the beginning of the order of the Jesuits in 1540 to 1580, it is supposed that nine hundred thousand persons were destroyed by persecution (244).

Fornication, a sin common everywhere, in this context must have some peculiar relevance to leaders and to the nominal church in the era addressed. Schaff states that "the Middle Ages [A.D. 590-1049] of Western Christendom resembles the period of the Judges . . . when 'every man did that which was right in his own eyes'" (Judg 21:25; 4.327). Clerical immorality sank to its lowest depth in the middle of this era (10th-11th cents.) but continued throughout the era, as illustrated by the frequent legislation of the synods. Gibbon states regarding this period that "it

---

[81]I have preferred the *NASB* to the NIV which reads, "things taught by demons." The Greek genitive, δαιμονίων should be understood as an objective genitive, "Things taught *about* demons." There are two reasons for preferring this: 1. The alternate translation, as a subjective genitive, "things taught *by* demons" (NIV, et al.) creates a redundancy as sequel to "deceiving spirits." 2. The Apostle indicates in the text following that such doctrines are not taught by men (as deceived by demons) but by hypocrites whose consciences have been seared (v. 2). Though the prophecy apparently was fulfilled in Timothy's parish, our Lord's prediction forty years later provides a striking parallel, a prediction for a later time, the era of the sixth trumpet.

would be difficult to find anywhere more vice or less virtue."[82] This disregard of ordinary morality extended even to the Papacy, itself. To illustrate the fact that this sordid state of affairs continued without abatement, as our text indicates, after the Turkish invasions, Barnes mentions among other popes Alexander VI, "who at the close of the fifteenth century stood before the world a monster, notorious to all, of impurity and vice." According to the historian Infessura, "Most of the ecclesiastics had their mistresses; and all the convents of the capital were houses of ill fame" (Barnes, 246). In return for monitory compensation, licenses were commonly issued by the church to "celibate" clergy giving permission to live in fornication with concubines (Elliott, 1.473, n.1; 2.14).

Next in the list of vices, *magic arts,* likewise flourished in Catholicism in the era of the sixth trumpet. Puppets, relics, images of the saints and other paraphernalia were commonly alleged to perform miracles in exchange for payment. Hallam states, "It must not be supposed that these absurdities were produced by ignorance. In most cases they were the work of deliberate imposture" (cf. Rev 18:23).[83]

The last in the sin list of verse 21 is *theft.* The era of the sixth trumpet witnessed the development of several institutions designed to extort payments of money for alleged favors from ecclesiastical officials. Among these were the elevation of individuals to sainthood, the creation of new images, the enshrinement of relics, the institution of penance, and the sale of indulgences. All of these alleged means of divine grace were designed to bring money into the hands of clerics and the papal treasuries. Add to this the developed sacramentalism and the doctrine of purgatory, and you have a complex engine to bring power and wealth into high places as well as to deceive and impoverish the common people; worse, to estrange them from the true Gospel of Jesus Christ.

We have now completed our review of the circumstances in the Middle Ages, specifically the period we have correlated with the sixth trumpet—A.D. 762-1453. Our text clearly indicates that the terrible plagues of the sixth seal are providential judgments directed against "a third of mankind." We have seen that this prophecy, "the second woe," corresponds remarkably and uniquely to the period of the Turkish conquests which resulted in the fall of Constantinople, the capital of the Eastern Roman Empire. Moreover, we are informed in 9:21 that "the rest of mankind that were not killed by these plagues did not repent of the work

---

[82]As quoted in Shaff, 4.328, n. 1. Schaff adds in this note, "The judgments of Hallam, Milman, and Lecky [well-known church historians] are to the same effect."

[83]As quoted in Elliott, 2.16.

of their hands." The period embraced by this era is uniquely the time when most of the excesses targeted in verses 20-21 were institutionalized in the Catholic churches, largely in the Western church but to a considerable degree also in the Eastern church. We can marvel at the detailed correspondence between the prophecy of the sixth trumpet and the period of Turkish conquest, a correspondence which has been recognized by most all Bible-believing interpreters from Reformation times through most of the nineteenth century.[84]

While lamenting the tragic excesses targeted in Revelation 9, we should, nevertheless keep in mind that throughout this era there was a faithful remnant, a witnessing martyr church, which will be addressed as our prophecy unfolds, and which will, with all the faithful, arise victorious in the first resurrection (Rev 20:5).

---

[84]The principal exception to this was the embryonic beginnings of the futurist school in the 1830's with its relegation of the Apocalyptic prophecies to the last seven years of this age, a movement which gained great impetus when embraced by Moody Bible Institute near the end of the nineteenth century, then later also by MBI's many satellite schools.

Chapter Six

THE LITTLE SCROLL
THE TEMPLE
AND THE TWO WITNESSES

10:1-11:19

Introduction

At this point, we begin a rather elaborate excursus in the structure of the seven-sealed scroll prophecy. This excursus, which extends from chapter 10:1 through chapter 14:20, is placed in the center of the book and plays a prominent role in the message of the prophecy (see above, ch. 1, Structure and Theme).

This part of the Book of Revelation begins in chapter 10 with the introduction of a "little scroll" and ends in chapter 14 with the climactic harvest scene of final judgment. The excursus divides naturally into eight sections:

(1) The Angel and the Little Scroll. ch. 10
(2) The Temple and the Two Witnesses. 11:1-13
(3) An interlude: first, a brief excursus on the passing of the second woe and the sounding of the seventh trumpet (11:14, 15a), second, a proleptic scene showing the 24 elders in heaven celebrating victory (11:15b-18), and third, the opening of God's Temple followed by fearsome signs (11:19)
(4) The Woman and the Dragon. Ch. 12
(5) The Beast from the Sea and the Beast from the Earth. ch. 13
(6) A proleptic scene showing the Lamb and the 144,000 celebrating victory on Mount Zion . 14:1-5
(7) Three Flying Messengers and a voice from heaven. 14:6-13
(8) The End-time Harvest of the Earth. 14:14-20

These eight sections are best understood as follows:

Section one, here an extraordinary angel introduces a Little Scroll to the Apostle John. This, after the analogy with Ezek 2:9-3:9, presupposes (a) that the Little Scroll contains its own message which is structurally independent (except for section 3), from the principal prophetic sequence indicated by the Seven-sealed Scroll, and (b) that the message of the Little Scroll will be found in the text which follows, prior to the actual resumption of the seventh trumpet with the pouring out of the seven bowls (ch. 15).

Section two, The Temple and the Two Witnesses, chapter 11:1-13, sets the stage for chapters 12-14 by introducing the war between the Beast and the People of God in its setting, the antitypical temple of God.

Section three is an interlude which consists of three parts, 11:14, a structural indicator, 11:15-18, a proleptic announcement and celebration of the sounding of the seventh trumpet, and 11:19, a transitional statement regarding God's "Temple" and a warning of further judgments to come. The passing of the second woe and the sounding of the seventh trumpet function to fix the prophetic chronology of the Little Scroll and to connect it with the sequence of predicted events in the Seven-sealed Scroll. The time at which the prediction of 11:13, the "great earthquake," occurs is the same as the time of the passing of the second woe and the sounding of the seventh trumpet, events chronicled in the Seven-sealed Scroll. This indicates also that we are to understand the Little Book message as constituting supplemental chronological predictions. The second part of chapter 11, verses 15-18, is a heavenly scene similar to that of 7:9-17 in which the "twenty-four elders" (see above, on 4:4) celebrate future victory around the throne. Here again we have a proleptic view, on this occasion presupposing the victorious culmination of the seventh trumpet prophecies by the celebration of victory over the Antichrist powers. This part of the interlude ends with verse 19, which by thunder and lightning, earthquake and hailstorm, brings the reader back to the series of judgments which are yet to be disclosed in what follows.

Section four, chapter 12, The Woman and the Dragon, introduces the war of the dragon power against the People of God, represented as the "woman clothed with the sun."

Section five, chapter 13, has two parts. The first, verses 1-10, describes the war of a "beast from the sea" against the People of God, here identified simply as "the saints" (v. 7). The second part, verses 11-17, describe another beast, a "beast from the earth," which functions in a complementary manner to assist the "beast from the sea." This section, with sections three and four, constitute the bitter antichrist message of the Little Scroll.

Section six, chapter 14:1-5, follows the fearful message of chapters 12 and 13 with yet another proleptic assurance of future victory, Christ "the Lamb" over Antichrist, the 144,000 saints sealed in chapter 7:1-8, over the dragon and the two beasts. This brings to a climax the Little Scroll message regarding Christ and Antichrist. The remaining two sections are transitional, leading to the end-time and returning the reader to the primary structural series with the final, third woe-seventh trumpet message.

Section seven, 14:6-13, introduces The Three Angelic Messengers. These flying angels make announcements designed to prepare the reader for understanding the period yet to be played out in the final seventh trumpet message to follow in chapters 15-18.

Section eight, 14:14-20, The Harvest of the Earth, provides a fitting conclusion to the Little Scroll with two symbolic descriptions of the final judgment. Both scenes reflect Joel 3:13, "Swing the sickle for the harvest is ripe. Come trample the grapes, for the winepress is full." This harvest is emblematic of the everlasting destruction of the wicked. This rather obvious end-time judgment signals the end of the Little Book chronology and the return to the events announced by the seventh trumpet. There we will encounter the final in the three series of sevens alternately described as the "seven last plagues," or the pouring out of the seven bowls of wrath.

The recognition of the above-described structure of chapters ten to fourteen provides a suitable rationale for understanding how these chapters interrupt the sequence of the three major series of symbols—the seals, the trumpets, and the bowls. The Little Book message is primarily a message regarding the Antichrist, the one to fulfill Daniel's Little Horn prophecy, the one expected both by Jews and Christians of the first century still to arise out of the Roman beast of Daniel seven. Our Lord, nevertheless, sweetened this bitter message for the Apostle and his readers by a foreglimpse of the blessed state of the redeemed as they afterward will gather to sing the praise song of redemption around the white throne.

How these prophecies unfold and the logic which transports the reader through the content of the Little Scroll will be addressed in the commentary to follow.[1]

---

[1]Our understanding of chs. 10-14 differs from many historicist commentators in our identifying the Little Book with with the content of chs. 11-14. Many commentators have preferred to understand the Little Book as the Bible, or as the message of the Gospel as revealed in the Reformation movement. There are several difficulties with this interpretation: 1. The term, "*little* scroll" (Gk. diminutive, βιβλαριδιον) has obvious connotations with reference to the seven-sealed scroll with seven seals and "writing on both sides" (5:1), an uncommon characteristic which indicates a large and very full scroll. This correlation and contrast is enhanced by the fact that the little scroll like the seven-sealed scroll is associated with a "mighty angel" (5:2). (The only other occurrence of a mighty angel is in 18:21, where "a mighty angel" is instrumental in picking up "a stone like a great millstone" to throw it into the sea.) In both 5:2 and 10:1, the mighty angel apparently is so described because in the symbolic language of the revelation he is a direct representative of Deity (see our commentary below). 2. The Little Scroll is to be eaten by John in a manner which is obviously allusive to Ezek 3:3. In both passages the command to eat the scroll is followed by a directive to prophesy. Eating the scroll with the effects obviously has reference not to the physical scroll but to the message it contains. Scholars usually recognize that the content of the prophet's message is given in the text following; this also should be our understanding of the same motif in Revelation. 3. Recgnition of this principle also has the effect of providing a rationale for understanding the relationship of chs. 10-14 to the larger structure of the seven-sealed scroll. This is indicated especially by the final judgment scenes in ch. 14, in spite of the resumption of the seven-trumpets chronology in chaps. 15-16. 4. This interpretation of the Little Scroll provides a rationale for the obviously different structure of these chs. of Revelation from the three series of seals, trumpets, and bowls.

For examination of many of the alternate approaches to understanding the Little Scroll and its structural relationship to the Seven-Sealed Scroll, see E. B. Elliott, *Horae Apocalypticae* (5th ed. London: Seeley, Jackson, and Halliday, 1862), 1.105, 3.1-5, Isben T. Beckwith, *The Apocalypse of John* (1919; repr., Limited eds. library; Baker, 1967), 578-579, and G. K. Beale, *The Book of Revelation* (Grand Rapids: Eerdmans, 1999), 526-527. Some of the problems these approaches face follow: 1. Those historicist commentators who take the Little Scroll as the Bible or the message of the Gospel as preached in the Reformation movement divorce it from the standpoint of literary structure from the content of the texts following. This hardly does justice to the symbolism in which the Apostle is directed to eat the scroll with the resulting effects on his stomach. This has allusive reference to Ezek 1.3. In both texts the apparent implication is that the message subsequently delivered to the prophet is that to be "eaten." 2. Beckwith, on the other hand concludes that the scroll "contains [only] God's command to prophecy" (576). This, like item 1, above, hardly does justice to the figure, nor the analogy with the Seven-sealed Scroll which clearly contains revelation. 3. R. H. Charles and others held that the message of the Little Scroll is found in 11:1-13 (*A Critical and Exegetical Commentary on the Revelation of St. John* [ICC; Edinburgh: T. & T. Clark, 1920], (1.260). This, in itself, is attractive but does little to resolve the question of the structural relationship of chs. 12-14 to the larger context. 4. G. K. Beale extends Charles' approach to include at least chs. 12-16 and perhaps even chs. 17-22 (526-527). Others have taken the Little Scroll to contain all the rest of the book, chaps 11-22. Any interpretation which separates the Seven Bowls (equals the Seventh Trumpet and the Third Woe) from the Seven-sealed Scroll and the earlier elements of the primary symbols of that scroll does excessive violence to the prophetic vision. One may object to this writer's understanding on the ground that it makes the Little Scroll part of the larger

Chapter Six — The angel and the little scroll, 10:1-11

The Angel and the Little Scroll

10:1. Then I saw another mighty angel coming down from heaven. He was robed in a cloud, with a rainbow above his head; his face was like the sun, and his legs were like fiery pillars. ²He was holding a little scroll, which lay open in his hand. He planted his right foot on the sea and his left on the land, ³and he gave a loud shout like the roar of a lion. When he shouted, the voices of the seven thunders spoke. ⁴And when the seven thunders spoke, I was about to write; but I heard a voice from heaven say, "Seal up what the seven thunders have said and do not write it down."

⁵Then the angel I had seen standing on the sea and on the land raised his right hand to heaven. ⁶And he swore by him who lives for ever and ever, who created the heavens and all that is in them, the earth and all that is in it, and the sea and all that is in it, and said, "There will be no more delay! ⁷But in the days when the seventh angel is about to sound his trumpet, the mystery of God will be accomplished, just as he announced to his servants the prophets."

⁸Then the voice that I had heard from heaven spoke to me once more: "Go, take the scroll that lies open in the hand of the angel who is standing on the sea and on the land."

⁹So I went to the angel and asked him to give me the little scroll. He said to me, "Take it and eat it. It will turn your stomach sour, but in your mouth it will be a sweet as honey." ¹⁰I took the little scroll from the angel's hand and ate it. It tasted as sweet as honey in my mouth, but when I had eaten it, my stomach turned sour. ¹¹Then I was told, "You must prophesy again about many peoples, nations, languages and kings."

10:1-11   **The Angel and the Little Scroll**   **Exposition**

Chapter 10 introduces a major transition in the unfolding drama of the Revelation. Another "mighty angel" appears before the apostle in the drama in the heavens reminiscent of the previous mighty angel of 5:2, and in his hand another scroll brings to mind

---

book. The objection suffers from an excessive concreteness, as the scrolls are to be seen only as elements in a dramatic vision to communicate rationally the message of the Apocalyptic vision, rather than as concrete entities. The Little Scroll is presented both to give an emphatic place to its message and to introduce prediction of a complementary and supplementary series of chronological prophecies.

the scroll of 5:1. But before we take a closer look at this second scroll, we must confront the commanding figure of the angel.

We have seen this sort of "angel" before. Compare the description of the "one who looked like a man" who appeared to Daniel (10:5-6, 16), or the "one like a son of man" who appeared to the Apostle John on Patmos at the beginning of the dramatic vision we now address (Rev 1:13-16).

Dan 10:5-6	*Rev 1:13-16*	*Rev 10:1-3*
	someone like a son of man	
dressed in linen	**a robe reaching down to his feet**	**he was robed in a cloud**
		a rainbow above his head
belt of the finest gold	**a golden sash around his chest**	
	his head and hair white like wool, as white as snow	
body like chrysolite		
face like lightning		
		his face was like the sun
eyes like flaming torches	his eyes were like blazing fire	
his legs like the gleam of burnished bronze	his feet were like bronze glowing in a furnace	his legs were like fiery pillars
		he planted his right foot on the sea and his left foot on the land
voice like the sound of a multitude	his voice was like the sound of rushing waters	he gave a loud shout like the roar of a lion

The common elements suggest that all three messengers represent deity. They speak for God. In all three of these texts the extraordinary description is intended to make most emphatic the angel's Divine authority.

Having highlighted these heavenly messengers, one should not overlook the distinctive character in each text. The one who "looked like a man" (Dan 10:16) held the office of Captain of the Lord's Armies, in Daniel's vision a very real heavenly being (cf. Dan 10:13, 20; Josh 5:14, 15). The messenger in Revelation 1 is described as "someone like a son of man" (v. 13). "Son of man" in the original language simply means "human being," but in the apocalyptic context, it carries with it the connotation of the messianic figure of Dan 7:13, understood in Jewish and early Christian circles to be the coming Messiah. Moreover, in Rev 1:18, He identifies Himself as the resurrected Savior, surely not merely a symbolic element in the drama. In Revelation 1, we have the appearance in vision of the real person of Jesus Christ, the divine author of the prophecies to follow. Nevertheless, one perhaps should not assume that in the drama of the Revelation that all the messengers, even the extraordinary figure in chapter 10, are real beings. They may be only functional elements in the symbolic language and presentation of the vision.[2]

Surely the Apostle, when impacted by this colossal figure must have been struck with awe! Surely this messenger standing on sea and land, swearing with courtroom solemnity, loudly like the roar of a lion, speaks for the Lord Jesus Christ. Let us be reminded of the great importance of this, His revelation, which comes to us as the "testimony of Jesus," His final revelation to His Church.

This message of Christ was two-fold:

1. " In the days when the seventh trumpet is about to sound . . . the mystery of God will be accomplished" (10:7).
2. "Take the Little Scroll and eat it . . . . "You must prophesy again about many peoples, nations, languages, and kings" (10:8-11).

We infer from this that the Little Scroll message (chs. 11-14) addresses the mystery of God" and forecasts its accomplishment.[3]

---

[2]Beale comments, "It is possible that the angelic figure of Rev. 10:1 is merely an angelic representative of Christ who therefore possesses Christ's traits" (526). He makes further a comparison with 12:7-9 and suggests that Michael, who represents Christ in that text, would be a good candidate. However, the purpose of our text in ch. 10 is satisfied with no personal identification of the messenger. It is enough that the dramatic description conveys with great emphasis the sovereign authority of the message. One may thereby assume that Jesus, the One whose testimony is the Revelation, the Sovereign Christ, is the author of the message.

[3]Our identification of the Little Scroll message with chs. 11-14, I have since discovered, was anticipated in the sources at our disposal by G. S. Faber, apparently on chronological grounds (*Dissertation on the Prophecies* [4th ed.; London: F. C. and J. Rivington, 1810], 2.47). We will address this further below.

What is this "mystery of God"? We remember that Jesus spoke of the "secret of the kingdom of God" (Mark 4:11), by which he referred to the gradual introduction of God's rule in this age in which the church must co-exist with the forces of evil. We have observed in reviewing Daniel (ch. 1) that the Book of Revelation is an expansive commentary on Daniel's vision of the four beasts (Daniel 7). A major concern of the New Testament churches as they experienced persecution and awaited the return of Christ was that fourth Roman beast with its Little Horn who was to wage war against the saints (Dan 7:8, 20, 21; above, ch. 1, Apocalyptic and the Book of Daniel). We understand, both from this historical background and from what follows in chapters 11-14, that the "mystery of God" to which the messenger referred is the disclosure of the Roman Antichrist and his predicted war with the saints.[4]

When the colossal messenger shouted, "the voices of the seven thunders spoke" (10:3b). We are left with the impression that the thunders were in some sense an echo of the "angels'" loud shout. Not a mere echo but intelligible speech, for what they spoke, John was "about to write" until told to "seal up what the seven thunders have said and do not write it down" (10:4). Whatever the thunders said appears to have been in response to the majestic pronouncement of the mighty angel. Who the thunders represent or what they said the church was not permitted to learn, at least not before the time of fulfillment.

In the final section of this passage, 10:9-11, the text reaches its climax. Here the Apostle in his vision was given the Little Scroll and told to eat it. When he did, it tasted sweet in his mouth but

---

[4]We are comfortable with the traditional use of the term, "Antichrist," for the Little Horn of Dan 7:8, as we consider it highly probable that this antichrist power is that to which the Apostle Paul referred as the "Man of Lawlessness" in 2 Thess 2:3 and the same power mentioned by the Apostle John in his first epistle when he stated that his readers had "heard that the antichrist is coming" (1 John 2:18). The generic meaning of the term "Antichrist" lends itself suitably as a label for the Little Horn seen in the Danielic context of its war with the saints. Apparently, by the end of the first century this use of the term had become conventional in the New Testament church. For a more systematic exposition of the Antichrist theme, see Appendix 4.

turned his stomach sour! His experience was like that of Ezekiel, who on the occasion of his call to the prophetic office was given a scroll to eat containing "words of lament and mourning and woe" (Ezek 2:9-3:3). These words described the content of the judgments Jeremiah was to deliver to a rebellious Israel.

The parallel suggests that the Little Scroll of Revelation 10 contained prophecies of judgment to be meted out, even on the People of God. Though it is "sweet" to know that a sovereign God exercises oversight over his chosen people, even for them, there are "words of lament and mourning and woe." Ezekiel was a young man with the vigor and courage of youth (Ezek 1:1), but the message must have been bitter indeed for the Apostle John

The believer in the twenty-first century can take courage, in spite of the evils that surround us, in the fact that our God rules over land and sea. He exercises sovereign dominion over even the evil affairs of mankind so as to accomplish His purpose to bring to an end the mystery and to establish with His redeemed saints His everlasting kingdom.

The colossal stature of the angel when combined with his extraordinary qualities indicates not only that he is a unique messenger from God but also that he announces a major excursus in the structure of the drama. When we remember that the entire Apocalyptic drama is presented as if written on both sides of the seven-sealed scroll, such dramatic presentation of a little scroll suggests that in this way the Apostle was given a supplementary message, a prophecy which is not part of the connected chronology indicated by the seals, trumpets, and bowls, but one which must stand out with its own structure and emphatic message to present.

This message, in focusing on the war of the dragon and the two beasts against the saints supplements the message of the Seven-sealed Scroll, which is devoted more generally to the fourth beast of Daniel 7, the prediction of the course of events in the Roman Empire, the world of the Asian churches to which the Apocalypse was first delivered.

The excursus of the Little Scroll is, like the rest of the Apocalypse, rather complex. After the Little Scroll's introduction in chapter 10, 11:1-13 introduces a description of the war of Antichrist against the saints (cp. Dan 7:21). This is followed by the announcement of the passing of the second woe and the sounding of the seventh trumpet, an interruption that correlates the chronology of the predicted war with the message of the seven-sealed scroll (11:14, 15). This bitter message is then mitigated by a proleptic scene celebrating the ultimate victory of Christ and his church (11:15b-19). This is followed by an extended expansion of the war of 11:1-13 in 12:1-13:18 and another proleptic scene of victory in 14:1-7. The Little Scroll is concluded with a series of three angelic messages relating to the seventh trumpet period, 14:8-13, and scenes depicting the end-time final judgment, 14:14-20, the decisive event marking the end of this age and the entrance of the age to come.

Thus we see that the Little Scroll message speaks to the mystery of the Little Horn Antichrist power of Daniel 7:8, 20, 21, 24b, 25, providing further description and chronological orientation as well. It also reiterates Daniel's assurance of victory for the saints of the Most High (Dan 7:22).

10:1-11   **The Angel and the Little Scroll**   Notes

1. Then I saw reminds the reader that the Apostle is not composing in the normal manner from literary sources or from creative thought but watching the revelation unfold before his eyes in dramatic vision (see 1:11). The **mighty angel** is one of three angels so described in the Revelation (cp. 5:2, 18:21). **Angel** (Gk. ἄγγελος, *ángelos*) means "messenger" (BAGD, 7). Though this "angel" is sometimes identified with Christ (as Elliott, 1.41) or with the angel Gabriel (as Charles, 1.258), it may not necessarily have real existence but serve only as a functionary in the symbolic drama. The appropriate question, then, is not "Who *is* this angel?" But, Who does the angel represent? Clearly, the angel speaks on behalf of "the Faithful Witness," Jesus Christ. The angel was seen **coming down from heaven** indicating that the Apostle had at this point in the vision returned to his

Chapter Six   *The angel and the little scroll, 10:1-11*   233

station on earth. **Heaven** here, given context and the character of the mighty angel, indicates not the symbolic realm where earthly powers are represented by astral symbols (see above on 6:12-14) but the third heaven where God dwells. **Robed in a cloud** (περιβεβλημένον νεφέλην, *peribeblēménon nephélēn*) may be translated, "surrounded by a cloud." It is reminiscent of Dan 7:13, Rev 1:7; 14:14, and many other passages where the Deity is associated with a cloud or clouds are associated with Deity (Exod 13:21, 22; et al.; Deut 31:15; 2 Sam 22:12; Isa 4:4-6 [cp. Psa 78:14]; Ezek 1:4; and many others; see Beale, 525-526). Swete comments that the cloud is the vehicle "in which heavenly beings descend and ascend" (Psa 104:3; Dan 7:13; Acts 1.9-11; I Thess 4:17; Rev 1.7; 11:12; 14:14-16) (Swete, 126). The **rainbow above his head, his face . . . like the sun,** and **his legs . . . like fiery pillars** again reinforce the messengers divine authority. The many colors of the rainbow may result from the reflection from the angel's brilliant face (Swete, 126). **2.** The size of the **little scroll** is rendered emphatic by the use of the Greek, βιβλαρίδιον, *biblarídion,* the diminutive form of βιβλίον, *biblíon.* Βιβλίον, itself a diminutive of βίβλος, *bíblos,* had nevertheless become the ordinary word for "scroll" or "book" (BAGD, 141). The fact that this is the only occurrence of βιβλαρίδιον in the Bible (with vv. 9 and 10) may suggest that this scroll is emphatically small, probably to present an obvious contrast with the seven-sealed scroll introduced in 5:1. The fact that the scroll **lay open in his hand,** the entire text exposed, also suggests its relatively small size.[5] **His right foot on the sea and his left foot on the land** indicates the

---

[5]Such a diminuative scroll does not appear to this reader as an apt symbol for the entire Bible (as per Basil F. C. Atkinson, *The War with Satan: an Explanation of the Book of Revelation* [London: Protestant Truth Society, 1940], 87; Albert Barnes, *Notes on the New Testament: Revelation.* [1852; repr., Grand Rapids: Baker Book House, 1949], 752; Elliott 1.43; or Leon Morris, *Revelation* [Revised ed. Grand Rapids: Eerdmans, 1987], 137-138; et al.) nor for chs. 11-22 of the Revelation, as per Swete, 146; et al.; nor the message of the Gospel (Simon Kistemaker, *Exposition of the Book of Revelation* [New Testament Commentary; Grand Rapids: Baker, 2001] 309, et al.), which properly understood, is implicit in the Old Testament as well as explicit in the New. Neither does the view offered by Beckwith that the message of the little scroll is simply the command to John to prophesy appear convincing for the opposite reason; 576-579. It hardly justifies the highly dramatic manner by which this scroll is introduced. This expositor is inclined to think that the first two of the above interpretations are motivated more by the desired fulfillment (correlation with the Reformation period) than by contextual interpretation. The view expressed above that the message of the scroll is given in the text following is aptly suggested by comparison with Ezek 2:9-3:4, which provides a rather exact parallel with our text. The Apocalypse frequently draws upon such texts, not as the author's source, but as an aid to the understanding of those who receive the revelation. Several distinquished scholars have subscribed to this approach: Faber, 2.47, Charles, 1:258, 260; Martin Kiddle, *The Revelation of St. John*

universality of the domain to which the authoritative message is addressed. The size thus implied for the messenger is reminiscent of the colossal images often erected by ancient kings to emphasize their sovereign authority (cp. Dan 3:1). **3.** The authority of the message is also implied by the messenger's **loud shout like the roar of a lion**. "Lion of the tribe of Judah" is a title of the Messiah in Rev 5:5.[6] Compare Amos 1:2, 3:8, Joel 3:16, where the LORD roars his judgments against Judah, and Hos 11:10, where the LORD's forecast "roar like a lion" causes the dispersed of Israel to return trembling to their land. **The seven thunders** may reflect a subsequent voice of the Lord in some sense a reflex of the first. Compare Joel 3:16, "The LORD will roar from Zion and thunder from Jerusalem." In Joel "roar" and "thunder" are used as synonyms in the poetic structure so that they both refer to the same action. In our text, likewise, neither the **shout-roar** nor the **thunders** are recorded. The message of the angel is introduced solemnly and explicitly in verse 5 but the

---

(London: Hodder & Stoughton, 1940), 133; Matthias Rissi, *Time and History: a Study on the Revelation* (trans. G. Windsor; Richmond, Va.: John Knox, 1966), 43; Beale, 526-527; G. R. Beasley-Murray cites also Lohmeyer, Behm, and Lohse (*The Book of Revelation* [NCB; Revised ed.; Grand Rapids: Eerdmans, 1978], 171, n.2) but most have with Charles limited the scope of the Little Scroll to 11:1-13. Many have recognized that chaps. 12 & 13 expand on 11:1-13 and therefore might be included in the Little Scroll message, while ch. 14 provides a suitable conclusion to this. The problem identified with our view is 11:14 and 15, which mentions the passing of the "second woe" and "sounding of the seventh trumpet." These events appear integral to the structure of the seven-sealed scroll. Their omission of these vv., which requires also the exclusion of the text following through ch. 14, from the Little Scroll, I see as a too objective understanding of the two scrolls as symbols. The scrolls serve in the dramatic form of the revelation to give struc-ture and chronological perspective for understanding the forecast events. The Seven-sealed Scroll through its three-fold structural symbols outlines and gives order to the general course of events. It reveals God's sovereign control in the course of empire (as introduced by Daniel 7), whereas the Little Scroll retraces much of this history with particular focus on that power represented by Daniel's Little Horn (7:8, 21-25), surely addressing what must have been the greatest apprehension of the churches at the end of the first century. Thus, the two scrolls represent two parallel chronologies and 11:14, 15 (with 10:7) provide the key that connects and synchronizes the two time-lines. The intrusion of 11:14, 15 into the Little Scroll is not a problem to the recipient of the message because he has already learned their significance from the larger scroll. The two scrolls are designed to be read together as they were presented in the dramatic vision.

[6]In 2 Ezdras 11:37-46, a lion representing the Messiah addresses the Eagle (Rome, "the one that remains of the four beasts") and pronounces its doom "so that the whole earth, freed from your violence, may be refreshed and relieved, and may hope for the judgment and mercy of him who made it." (11:46; James H. Charlesworth, *Old Testament Pseudepigrapha* (Garden City, N. Y.: Doubleday, 1983), 1.549. 2 Ezdras (= 4 Ezra) is believed to have been written about 100 A.D.; Charlesworth, 1. 520.

Chapter Six   *The angel and the little scroll, 10:1-11*   235

thunders, though apparently intelligible to John are not to be recorded (v. 4). Perhaps, then, one should assume that the "shout/roar" and the "thunders" were the same message. **4. I was about to write** indicates that the "seven thunders" were intelligible to John. These words also indicate, contrary to the speculations of many critical scholars, that the Apostle wrote the Revelation in the manner directed in 1:19—that he wrote it as it was dictated to him, either by what he heard or by what he saw. Although this does not preclude subsequent editing of hastily written notes, it does rule out the concept that in writing he was dependent on previously written secondary sources. **The voice from heaven** probably should be understood (with the majority of commentators) as the voice of Jesus. Why the thunders were not to be written, we are not given to know. The command to **seal up** the words of the thunders reflects the fact that seals were used not only to authenticate but also to seal or lock a document so that it could not be opened without authorization to break the seal. Though the Revelation unveils much that was mystery, there remains in God's secret counsel that which we are not permitted to know (Rom 11:33-36).

5. We have in 10:5-6 the language of the courtroom. By raising **his right hand to heaven**, the angel standing on sea and land appeals to God above for the authority of his proclamation. **6.** With dramatic oath the angel **swore by him who lives for ever and ever.** Clearly, here we have the messenger differentiated from the Creator God, and therefore from the person of Jesus Christ (John 1:3; Col 1:16). God's sovereignty is clearly affirmed by His act as **creator** of all things, **the heavens . . . the earth . . . and the sea,** and "all that is in them." As creator, He has full authority over His creation and therefore governs even the flow of history. The messenger's pronouncement delivered from heaven with solemn oath follows. **"There will be no more delay!"** (NIV; Gk. χρόνος οὐκέτι ἔσται, *krónos oúkéti éstin*) Here, the King James Version (not NKJV) translates as "there should be time no longer." In our text, χρόνος, *chrónos*, has the sense of an interval of ongoing time, in distinction from καιρός, *kairós,* which would indicate specific or appointed time. What is not to be delayed? Charles aptly points out that the language of this verse as it describes the oath of the angel reflects exactly the angel's oath in Dan 12:7 (cp. Dan 7:25) regarding the time of the war with Antichrist, the period of "time, time, and half a time." Though Daniel's forecast refers to the period as in progress and alludes to its completion, our text addresses the beginning of this time. Charles continues (1:263):

> The reign of the Antichrist *has not yet begun in the visions of the Seer.* All the evils and plagues . . . are only forerunners of that period. But the

hour for the reign of the Antichrist has all but struck. There will be no further delay . . . . The evil of the world must now culminate in the revelation of the Antichrist . . . .[7]

7. In the days when the seventh angel is about to sound his trumpet, the mystery of God will be accomplished. Here our text indicates that the mystery will be accomplished when the angel is "*about* to sound" (μέλλῃ σαλπίζειν, *méllē salpízein*) (emphasis mine), indicating that the war with Antichrist will begin *prior to* the sounding of the seventh trumpet.[8] This will occur **just as he announced to his servants the prophets** (cp. Dan 9:6, 10). By this it is implied that the doctrine of a particular Antichrist who will wage war with the saints is an Old Testament doctrine, as the prophets so identified in the New Testament church did not contribute to the writing of Scripture. The Daniel texts cited are one example, as Daniel, though grouped with the Writings in the Jewish canon, is called a prophet by Jesus (Matt 24:15).[9]

8-9. **The voice** that John heard again **speak from heaven,** as in verse 4, was probably the voice of Jesus. The voice instructs the Apostle to **take the scroll** and **eat it** (Cp. Jer 15:16-19; Ezek 2:9-3:3). Ezek 3:3 adds, "Fill your stomach with it." The Word of God must be ingested fully. **It will turn your stomach sour, but in your mouth it will be as sweet as honey.** Here, the text emphasizes the negative effects of this Antichrist message, while nevertheless assuring the faithful of ultimate

---

[7]Charles continues, erroneously I think, to state that "The reign of the Antichrist which is about to begin is to be introduced by and embraced in the third Woe . . . " (1.263). See our discussion of the third woe following.

[8]The translation, "about to sound," in distinction from the KJV, "begin to sound," was anticipated by Elliott, though he renders it slightly differently, prior to its introduction in the RV and the ASV (2.125). Elliott suggests "a certain dubiousness only being made to attach to the time of the seventh Angel's sounding, and its results; though an event apparently not very distant" (2.127). All the subsequent versions now translate it "about to sound" or equivalent, including the NKJV.

As indicated above, we understand "the mystery of God" to be the war with Antichrist during the "time, times, and half a time" of Dan 7:25 and 12:7 (cf. Rev 11:3, 12:7, 14). The expression "time, times, and half a time," must be calculated as follows: "time" = one year, "times" (Hebrew dual) = two years, "half a time" = one-half year. This results in a total period of three and one-half years. The year on the ancient calendar of 360 days gives a total of 1260 days (11:3, 12:7).

[9]References to a coming Antichrist in the Old Testament in books other than Daniel are difficult to find as they are veiled at best. An example of this may be the allusions to the LORD's slaying, "in that day" when he will redeem his covenant people, Israel, of "Leviathan the gliding serpent" and "the monster of the sea" (in the parallel lines of Isa 27:2). The text, which has obvious parallels with Revelation 11-12, is otherwise rather obscure.

redemption. **11.** After in the context of the Apostle's vision, he had "eaten" the scroll, he was instructed, **"You must prophesy again about many peoples, languages and kings"** (cp. Ezek 3:4). "Many peoples, nations, languages and kings" indicates that the message to follow will have widespread implications in the multi-ethnic Roman world.

The Two Witnesses

11:1. **I was given a reed like a measuring rod and was told, "Go and measure the temple of God and the altar, and count the worshipers there. ²But exclude the outer court; do not measure it, because it has been given to the Gentiles. They will trample on the holy city for 42 months. ³And I will give power to my two witnesses, and they will prophesy for 1,260 days, clothed in sackcloth." ⁴These are the two olive trees and the two lampstands that stand before the Lord of the earth. ⁵If anyone tries to harm them, fire comes from their mouths and devours their enemies. This is how anyone who wants to harm them must die. ⁶These men have power to shut up the sky so that it will not rain during the time they are prophesying; and they have power to turn the waters into blood and to strike the earth with every kind of plague as often as they want.**

11:1-6   **The Two Witnesses**   **Exposition**

At this point, John in vision is called to be actively involved in the drama. The angel hands him a measuring reed and tells him to take measurements of the temple and the altar and to count the worshipers as he sees them in the dramatic scene before him. We should remember that this for the Apostle was an extra-sensory visionary experience which as a process of supernatural revelation was playing out in his mind, and that we are still dealing with the symbolic language of apocalyptic.

Moreover, as we have observed in our introduction to the Little Scroll above, we make at this point in the text the transition from the introduction to the scroll in chapter 10 to enter upon the content of the scroll itself. We should then expect that chapter 11 consists of event-oriented prediction. Let us now examine the symbols and attempt to understand how they might have been understood by the original recipients of the prophecy in John's day.

The focus here is on "the temple of God," "the altar," and "the worshipers there"; further in verse 2 on "the outer court." Though it is obvious that the imagery is that of the actual building as it had been known in Jerusalem, as symbol we should understand that a metaphysical meaning is intended. This may be suggested as well by the fact that the Greek word "temple" here is not the word for the building, per se, but the more abstract word that is often translated "sanctuary" (Gk. ναός, *naós*) with reference to God's dwelling place. Even before the A.D. 70 destruction of the Jerusalem temple, the Church was understood to be God's "temple" (sanctuary), as taught by the Apostle Paul in 1 Cor 3:16, 17 and 2 Cor 6:16.

The reader at the end of the first century should have understood that the Lord Jesus in our text made reference by means of the "temple" imagery to the church, that is, the visible church as it existed and continues to exist in the world. In measuring the "temple," John was not to calculate the physical dimensions of a building but to indicate the true dimensions of the church as it would exist at the time predicted in the future.

The "outer court" in the Jewish temple to which verse 2 refers was the Court of the Gentiles. Between that court and the Court of Israel there was a barricade with signs at the points of passage warning on pain of death against the entrance of uncircumcised Gentiles into the Court of Israel. Many devout Gentiles worshiped the God of Israel but could not go beyond this point to participate in the worship by sacrifices and offerings.

In contrast to this restriction, the Apostolic doctrine of the Church as the sanctuary of God is spelled out beautifully in Eph 2:11-22, which we now quote in part:

> For he himself [Christ] is our peace, who has made the two one and has destroyed the barrier, the dividing wall of hostility . . . . His purpose was to create in himself one new man out of the two, thus making peace, and in this one body to reconcile both of them to God through the cross.
>
> Consequently, you are . . . fellow citizens with God's people and members of God's household . . . . In him the whole building is joined together and rises to become a holy temple [ναός] in the Lord. (14, 15b, 16a, 19, 21)

The Apostle John is instructed not to measure "the outer court" because it has been given over to the Gentiles. The "outer court" was well known to have been "the Court of the Gentiles," where those outside of God's covenant were permitted to gather. The metaphor suggests that there would be, even in the church of Christ, those outside of the God's covenant who were not to be reckoned as God's People. Those "outside" in terms of the metaphor are here called "Gentiles," in distinction from the People of God who are the true "Israel," and who, metaphorically speaking, have entrance into the inner court. The instruction to "count the worshipers" is better translated, "measure . . . those who worship" (NASB), as the apparent intent is to determine their status, whether "Israelite" or "Gentile."[10]

"To measure" in our text is to indicate the true dimensions in the abstract sense of determining the true people of God. As many commentators point out, the function here is similar to the sealing of God's people in 7:1-7, but here an emphasis is placed on who is to be included and who is to be left out. The outer court with its worshipers was to be excluded.

How should one understand the command to "measure" the altar? (v. 1) The distinction between the two courts in the temple with their occupants has much to do with this altar, as the altar is the type of the antitypical atonement accomplished for God's covenant people by the death of Christ. This is clearly indicated in the passage quoted above from Eph 2:15-16a. "His purpose was to create in himself one new man out of the two . . . and in this one

---

[10]Such a distinction within the visible church is found also in Christ's parable of the Wheat and the Tares, where the " tares" (a weed, darnel, which mimics wheat) must be left until harvest, when the difference in the color of the grain enables the harvester to sort out the grain produced by the poisonous weed. The parable teaches that within the sphere of the Kingdom (visible church) there are pretenders who do not have true faith. Scholars who understand the "outer court" as referring to such nominal believers within the visible church include: R. H. Charles (1.274-278); Kiddle (189); Wm. Hendriksen (*More Than Conquerors* [7th ed.; Grand Rapids: Baker, 1954], 152-155), R. C. H. Lenski (*The Interpretation of St. John's Revelation* [Columbus, Ohio: Wartburg, 1943], 329-330); J. M. Ford (*Revelation* [AB; Garden City, NY: Doubleday, 1975], 176-177); Swete (133); and Rissi (96-98).

body to reconcile both of them to God *through the cross* . . . ." To measure the altar may then suggest the determination of the effect of the atonement in the church. Because a part of the sanctuary, the outer court, is not to be measured but "given to the Gentiles," we may understand that for those left unmeasured in the outer court the atonement will not be effectual.[11] The prophecy thus implies the existence of a future apostate church which, though outwardly viewed as "God's Temple," is not to be numbered with the elect.

For 42 months the "Gentiles" will trample on the Holy City (v. 2). Continuing with the metaphor of the former Jerusalem temple as a type of the true visible church as it existed in the churches of the Roman world, the Holy City cannot symbolize the literal city of Jerusalem but the province of the antitypical temple, the world as the sphere of the church. To "trample" (NIV) or to "tread under foot" (NASB) indicates, at least, abusive treatment and desecration (cp. Dan 7:7). "Forty-two months," as calculated by the ancient calendar with 30 days to the month, is 1260 days or three and one-half years, the same time period found in the prophecy of the Little Horn Antichrist in Dan 7:25.

Though the churches to which the Revelation was delivered would not likely have been disposed to understand this prophecy according to the year-day principle, that principle was nevertheless not unknown to them. It was witnessed by Israel's 40 years of wandering in the wilderness, punishment for each day of the spies unbelieving exploration in Canaan (Num 14:34), from Ezekiel's use of this principle in demonstrating the punishments to ensue for the southern and northern kingdoms of Israel (Ezek 4:5, 6), and even from Daniel's seventy-week prophecy of chapter 9, which had been fulfilled as 490 years with the accomplishment of the Messiah's mission.[12]

---

[11]As in the Apocalypse the covenant people of God are the antitypical "Israel" (Rev 7::1-7), and the church is the antitypical "temple," so the anti-Christian peoples are the antitypical "Gentiles" (= "heathen"). Cp. Rev 20:3, where Satan is bound "to keep him from deceiving the nations." Both "Gentiles" and "nations" are translations of the same Greek word, ἔθνοι. Satan when unbound deceives the unregenerate, the heathen.

[12]For Daniel 9, see above in ch. 1.

Such use of mysterious numbers contains a built-in ambiguity so that the people of God could not forecast accurately in advance when the prophecies would be fulfilled but would wait in constant anticipation for God to bring about the promised consummation—victory over Antichrist and evil. From our perspective, with the passage of almost two millennia since the writing of Revelation and with the precedent in Daniel 9, the figurative understanding, "years," remains a desirable option, especially in the light of the fact that the other elements in the passage must be taken figuratively.

The correlation between the "42 months" of the "trampling" and the "1260 days" of the witness and the "time, times and half a time" of Dan 7:25 should lead the reader to notice other correlations between Revelation 11 and Daniel 7.

The two witnesses are to prophesy for "1260 days clothed with sackcloth" (v. 3). How would the first century reader have understood the number "two"? The next few verses provide some clues. First we are told, "These are the two olive trees and the two lampstands that stand before the Lord of the earth" (v. 4). The allusion is to Zech 4:2-6, 11-14.

> "I see a gold lampstand with a bowl at the top and seven lights on it with seven channels to the lights. Also there are two olive trees by it, one on the right of the bowl and the other on its left." I asked the angel . . . , "What are these, my lord?" . . . . "So he said to me, "This is the word of the LORD to Zerubbabel. 'Not by might nor by power, but by my Spirit,' says the LORD Almighty. "What are these two olive branches beside the two gold pipes that pour out golden oil?" He [the angel] replied, . . . "These are the two who are anointed to serve the LORD of all the earth."

In the historical and textual context of this passage, the two men were Joshua, the high priest, and Zerubbabel, the princely leader of Judah. In the face of local opposition, these men were called by God to lead the rebuilding of the nation after the return from Babylonian exile. Clearly, the main point of Zechariah's vision was that these men were empowered for their task by God's Holy Spirit—Zerubbabel as the one who would be enabled to accomplish his task of rebuilding the temple and Joshua, as the spiritual leader of the newly established nation. Similarly, the promise for these witnesses to be empowered by God's Spirit is the central truth conveyed by Rev 11:3-6.

The allusion to Zechariah also provides a rationale in Revelation for the number, "two" (note v. 4). Joshua and Zerubbabel function as types of the "two witnesses" in our text.

Moreover, there is another more important rationale. In this passage, as throughout the Revelation, the word "witness" is used in a juridical sense. People are called to account for their witness to Jesus Christ and his Gospel. In such contexts "witness" carries with it the biblical principle that two witnesses are required to give authority to the truth of a testimony (Num 35:30; Deut 17:6; 19:15; Matt 18:16).

The question remains—Are two *individuals* forecast? The passage suggests rather that the metaphor refers to the witnessing church as a corporate body of believers. Unlike the vision in Zechariah, where we find a menora, that is a single stand with seven lamps on it, the two witnesses are called "two lampstands." As in Revelation 2 and 3, the lampstands are seven churches, so here the lampstand should suggest a plurality of individual witnesses, rather than single individuals.[13] One should note also that the temple menora was a type which has its New Covenant fulfillment in the community of believers, the Christian church. As indicated in Rev 1:12, 13, 20 above, the antitype of the light source in the temple could not be symbolized by a menora, as each of many local churches was a luminary. Thus, the seven churches of chapters 2-3 are seven single lampstands (1:20).

Similarly, if one considers Zerubbabel and Joshua as types of the two witnesses in our text, one should note that their royal and priestly functions in Zechariah's prophecy would likewise have their antitype in the collective body of believers. This is illustrated in Rev 5:9-10, where in this proleptic scene the Lamb is celebrated as having by his atoning sacrifice "purchased men for God . . . *to be a kingdom and priests . . .* " (italics mine). The fact that after the

---

[13]Kittle states, "While it is natural—indeed, inevitable—to use a variety of symbols to express one complex idea, it is a defiance of common sense to use the same distinctive symbol for two different ideas, within the compass of one book" (181).

death of the witnesses their bodies will be seen by "men from every tribe, language, and nation" (v. 7) also suggests a larger body of witnesses.[14] This writer inclines to agree with Beale who states. "The 'two witnesses' are not two individual prophets . . . . Rather, they represent the whole community of faith, whose primary function is to be a prophetic witness" (572-573). Their prophetic power (v. 3) is the power of Spirit-inspired preaching of the Word of God in the tradition of Elijah and Moses (v. 6). The fire from their mouth (v. 5) is a symbolic indication of the authority of the Gospel message, which renders those who reject it liable to divine retribution.

Surely, apart from the predictive intention of this passage, the timeless application is evident, as indicating that God has an essential role for his church in the world, and that is to witness to the true Gospel of the grace of Jesus Christ in making substitutionary atonement once for all time by his death on the cross, and that this task can only be accomplished by the power of his indwelling Holy Spirit.

11:1-6   **The Two Witnesses**   **Notes**

1. The reed was a long grass stalk commonly used for measuring, perhaps six to eight feet long (Barclay, 2.81). The fact that John was told to **go and measure the temple of God** is in no way disadvantaged by the fact that the temple had been destroyed by the Romans about twenty-six years earlier, as he experienced this in vision only. A vision is not necessarily a representation of objective reality. To **measure** the temple here must be understood in the figurative sense of determining the true nature of the thing, as not only the inner courts and the altar were to be measured but also the people. The NIV translation, "count the people," is more literally translated "measure the people." What is essential to the metaphor is their spiritual standing, not their number. **2. The outer court** is excluded to indicate a time when a part of the church is cut off from its God-given role as God's sanctuary. This court is **given over to the Gentiles.** "Gentiles," is used here as the antonym of "Israel." "Israel" is

---

[14]Beale offers several additional arguments (574-575).

in the Revelation the Covenant people of God (see note 10, above). Although we may infer here that those representing the outer court are in some sense to be identified with the trampling Little Horn in Daniel 7, whom we have chosen with the earliest Christian expositors to label the Antichrist, much greater detail is later revealed in chapter 13. **Trample** (Gk., πατέω, *patéō*), commonly has the ordinary sense, to "tread on," as to tread on grapes to extract the juice for wine-making. As applicable to humans, it carries the connotation of contemptuous, abusive treatment (BAGD, 634-635). The **holy city** is the antitypical "Jerusalem," that is, "the world," or in the more focused sense of the exposition regarding the role of the Little Horn power of the fourth beast, "the Roman world" as the realm of God's true witnesses, the church. The period of **forty-two months**, at thirty days to a month, is equivalent to the "1260 days" (see verse 3). God will empower his two witnesses **to prophesy**. "Prophesy" here means to preach the Gospel, rather than to utter predictions. **3.** Again, **I will give power** emphasizes the necessity of God's Spirit to accomplish his work. The witnesses will prophesy for **1260 days** (cp. 12:6). This is the same time as "42 months" (v. 2), and "time, times and half a time" (3½ years; Rev 12:14; Dan 12:7). The reiteration of this number in its several formulations heightens the sense of the mystery conveyed.[15] Its representation as 1260 days argues for the specific numerical value, rather than a more abstract concept. The reader at the end of the first century would have been left to decide whether the number should have been understood as three and one-half literal years or as 1260 years as suggested by the prophetic use of numbers for the time of God's retributive judgments in Num 13:33, 34 and in Ezek 4:5, 6. In these Old Testament passages each day symbolized one year. The dominance of Israelite symbolism in the Book of Revelation suggests that this ultimately

---

[15]The number is sometimes taken as a reflex of the approximately 3½ years during which the Jerusalem temple had been desecrated during the period of the Maccabean wars. As thus understood, it becomes an abstract symbol of warfare, desecration, and suffering of God's people. That the number is symbolic in an abstract sense hardly accounts for its enumeration as "1260 days." Those who hold to the Maccabean date of the Book of Daniel (ca. 165 B.C.) think that the Little Horn antichrist in Daniel 7 refers to Antiochus IV Epiphanes, a theory that is clearly contrary to the evidence of history and Scripture regarding the date of the Book of Daniel, as well as the authority of the Book of Revelation, which as predictive prophecy must refer to events future to the Apostle John.

is the correct way to understand these mysterious numbers.[16] **4. The two olive trees and the two lampstands** is an obvious allusion to Zech 4:2, 3:

> "What do you see?"
> I answered, "I see a solid gold lampstand with a bowl at the top and seven lights on it, with seven channels to the lights. Also there are two olive trees by it, one on the right of the bowl and the other on its left."

When Zechariah asked the angel for the meaning of this, he replied,

> "This is the Word of the LORD to Zerubbabel. 'Not by might nor by power, but by my Spirit,' says the LORD Almighty. What are you O mighty mountain? Before Zerubbabel you will become level ground."

Zechariah asked for a further point of clarification,

> What are these two olive trees on the right and the left of the lampstand?" (4:11)

And again,

> "What are these two olive branches beside the two golden pipes that pour out golden oil?" The messenger answered, "These are the two who are anointed to serve the LORD of all the earth" (4:12, & 14).

Two points are clear from the Zechariah passage. 1. The power for the task facing Zerubbabel was not intrinsic in the man but in God, the Holy Spirit (vv. 2, 3). 2. The olive trees represent the men God had anointed for the task, Zerubbabel the prince and Joshua the high priest (cf. Zech 3:1-7). The task of these leaders in the rebuilding of the restored community of Israel was great, as indicated in the post-exilic books of this period,[17] both for leading the Jewish returnees from Babylon and for contending with the surrounding enemy nations. An essential aspect of their ministry was their witness to the Word of God. Their work was Messianic, as the restored community was to be motivated by the expectation of the coming Messiah and the Messianic age. Witness God's instructions to Joshua:

> "Listen, O high priest Joshua and your associates seated before you, *who are men symbolic of things to come*. I am going to bring my servant, the Branch. See, the stone I have set in front of Joshua! . . . I will

---

[16]The first century believer would hardly have distanced himself from the glorious hope of Christ's return by positing that a 1260-year war must precede that event. This reminds us that the church's understanding of how the Revelation prophecies would be fulfilled must by Providential design be progressive. Otherwise, the imminency of the Advent would have been lost and complacency would have prevailed. Those who reject the supernatural character of the Revelation, on the other hand, must of necessity reject any such definitive prediction.

[17]Nehemiah, Ezra, Haggai, and Zechariah.

engrave an inscription on it," says the LORD Almighty, "and I will remove the sin of this land in a single day. (italics mine)

"In that day each of you will invite his neighbor to sit under his vine and fig tree," declares the LORD Almighty." (Zech 3:8-10)

As mentioned above, the Apocalypse views the New Covenant community, the Church of Jesus the Messiah, as the fulfillment of both the royal and the priestly offices of the Old Covenant (Rev 5:10). Those believers who would witness to that true Gospel, both Jew and Gentile, and who would function within that sphere of the Roman world indicated by the fourth beast of Daniel 7 are represented by the "two olive trees and the two lampstands"—the "two witnesses" of Rev 11:3.[18] **5. The fire which comes from their mouths** draws imagery from the word of God to Jeremiah (5:14), "I will make my words in your mouth a fire and these people the wood it consumes" (cf. also 2 Kgs 1:10, 12). **6.** The witnesses' **power to shut up the sky** is from the prophet Elijah's command of the dew and the rain (1 Kgs 17:1, 18:41-45). To **turn the waters into blood**, and **to strike the earth with . . . plague** reminds the reader of God's sovereign power as demonstrated through the prophet, Moses. These vivid allusions underscore God's promise in Rev 11:3, "I will give power to my two witnesses."[19]

---

[18] It is not necessary to press the analogy beween Zechariah and Revelation to account for the fact that in Zechariah the witnesses are identified with the olive trees and in Revelation with the lampstands. Zechariah's vision is ordered on the analogy of the menora familiar to the post-exilic audience, whereas Revelation is ordered on the typical concept of the the menora and its antitypical fulfilment in the people of God as represented in local churches (Revelation 2-3).

[19] The Apocryphal book of Sirach provides commentary on these allusive references. "They [the Ephraimites] sold themselves to (do) all manner of evil, until there arose a prophet like fire, whose word was like a burning furnace. . . . By the word of God he shut up the heavens" (37:24b; 38:1, 3); quoted from R. H. Charles, *Apocrypha and Pseudipigrapha of the Old Testament* (Oxford: Clarendon Press, 1913), 1.499-500.

Rev 11:1-6 **The Two Witnesses** **Fulfillment**

The Little Book section of the Apocalypse introduced in chapter 10 follows the era of the sixth trumpet forecast in 9:13-21. We concluded our comments on the sixth trumpet prophecy by observing with most historicist interpreters that it had its fulfillment in the period of the Seljuk and Ottoman Turkish conquests and that it ended with the fall of Constantinople in A.D. 1453.

We must now consider how the forecast given in Rev 11:1-6 may have been fulfilled in the progress of the history of the church. The following conclusions have been drawn from our above examination of the text as we believe it was to be understood by readers at the end of the first century:

1. The orientation of our text is the antitypical temple, that is, the visible church of Jesus Christ. The temple as a type contained both the court of Israel and the court of the Gentiles; so the antitypical church visible includes both those who profess the true Gospel and those whose profession is false.
2. The antitypical "Jerusalem" and "the Holy City" is the locale of the antitypical temple in the context of the historical "earth" to which the Revelation was originally given, that is the Roman or western world.
3. The measurement of the temple is to determine who within its structure constitutes the true visible church, as that church which proclaims the true gospel.
4. The measurement of the altar indicates that the true church is determined by its witness to the true function of the antitypical altar, that is the centrality of the true nature of the atonement in the church's experience and proclamation of salvation by faith alone.
5. We infer from the correlations with Daniel that the metaphorical use of the word, "Gentiles," as identified with the "outer court" and with their " trampling down" of the witnesses, is to be identified in some sense, at this point not entirely clear, with the Antichrist power called the Little Horn.
6. The symbolic numbers of the "42 months" and the "1260 days," as understood according to the Old Testament use of chronological numbers as symbols of the duration of divine judgment, indicate a period of 1260 literal years.
7. The antitypical function of the "two witnesses" is the witness to the true Gospel within the sphere of the visible church.
8. The number "two" of the "two witnesses" has its primary function as indication of a creditable witness according to the biblical law (Deut

19:15, Matt 18:16), and secondarily, it may correlate with two major bodies of faithful witness within the church.
9. The witness implied in the above is the testimony to the true saving Gospel as accomplished by the atoning death of Jesus Christ and experienced by divine grace through faith alone.

The above conclusions regarding our text are very largely accepted by continuous-historicist commentators, as well as, with respect to most of the seven points, by commentators of the several other schools. Items 1-4 are the result of presuppositions implicit in our general approach to the Apocalypse, as expounded in earlier portions of this commentary. The specific implications of these for our treatment of this passage will unfold more fully as we progress in the chapter beyond these verses.

We proceed, therefore, to examine item 6, the question of the fulfillment of the predicted 1260 years of the preaching of the witnesses.

This chapter introduces the "Two Witnesses" (11:1-13) before the passing of the sixth trumpet era, also called the Second Woe (11:14). For this reason, we look for the beginning of the period of the witnesses during, rather than after, the sixth trumpet era, a period of witnessing which was to continue for 1260 years.

As observed in our exposition above, the 1260 years corresponds to the "time, times, and half a time" during which the Little Horn power of Daniel 7 wages war with the saints and the "42 months" during which the world of the Roman Empire is "trampled down" by the "Gentiles" occupying the "outer court" of the "temple" (11:2). As the "temple" here represents the visible church, and the measured inner court of Israel (11:1) the true visible church, the outer court not measured must be an apostate church which wages war in Roman Christendom. By analogy with Daniel seven, we conclude that the apostate church is governed by the "Little Horn" power.

That the trampling Antichrist power would be an apostate Christian ruler arising within the church was recognized by Apocalyptic interpreters soon after the conversion of the Empire by Constantine and his establishment of the state church. As early as the fourth century, this was the view of Athanasius (296-372), Hilary of Poitiers (c. 300-367), Cyril of Jerusalem (c. 315-386), and Jerome (c. 340-420).[20] This view of Antichrist appears also to have been perpetuated subsequently by Primasius of Carthage (c. 553), the Venerable Bede (c. 700), and Ambrose Anspert (c.

---

[20]H. Grattan Guinness, *History Unveiling Prophecy* (New York: Revell, 1905), 59-60; Elgin S. Moyer, *Who Was Who in Church History* (New Canaan, Conn.: Keats Publishing, n.d.), 21, 110, 196, 217.

765). Though there was an understandable reticence during these centuries directly to label the Papacy as Antichrist, several of these writers identified the two-horned beast of Revelation 13 as "ecclesiastical rulers," "pseudo-Christian false prophets," or "the preachers and ministers of Antichrist." Berengaud in the late ninth century understood the beast-riding harlot of Revelation 17 as Rome (Guinness, *History*, 74-76).

With the Imperial certification of the universal authority of the Roman Papacy, the identification of the Papal Antichrist was soon to follow. This was further enhanced by the Pope's acquisition of temporal dominion over the city of Rome and the Exarchate of Ravena (c. 757).[21] Charlemagne in A.D. 800 further enlarged the Papal dominion to include all of Italy and later the entire Empire, renaming it the Holy Roman Empire (Guinness, *History*, 65).

Cotemporaniously with the development of the temporal authority of the Papacy were many abusive practices, as well as extravagant claims to exclusive spiritual authority over Christendom. When the Papacy took to itself the claim to exercise the prerogatives of God, ruling in three worlds—heaven, earth, and hell—and teaching with absolute authority on matters of faith and morals, dissenting expositors of the Word began to identify it with the Antichrist.[22]

What was the biblical basis for this identification of the Roman Papacy with the Antichrist of Scripture?[23] In the preceding chapters we have observed that the Apocalypse is devoted largely to an exposition of Daniel 7. This prophecy of the "Two Witnesses" alludes to that text with its reference to the "forty-two months" of the "treading down" of the people of God by the "Gentiles" and to the "1260 days" of the witness. There is further a correspondence between the war against the Witnesses and the war of the Little Horn of Daniel 7 "against the saints" (Dan 7:21), later expanded in Revelation 13. The several formulations of the time period calculate to the same length of time as "the time, times, and half a time" of Dan 7:25. These correspondences would suggest to the reader that Revelation 11 is an expansive commentary on Daniel 7.

As the Christians at the end of the first century were experiencing persecution under the Roman Emperor Domitian, this Little Horn

---

[21]G. I. Burr, "The Carlovingian Revolution, and Frankish Intervention in Italy," in *Cambridge Medieval History* (ed. J. B. Bury; New York: Macmillan, 1926), 2.589-591. The Exarchate of Ravenna, as under Papal authority, was a substantial territory in north-central Italy.

[22]Guinness, *History*, 67. Guinness attributes these last blasphemous pretensions to Boniface VIII, who acceded to the Papal throne in 1294.

[23]For a more full examination of this question, see Append. 4.

Antichrist text in Daniel 7 with its war against the saints would have been a matter of great concern.[24] Those readers were well aware that the four world empires of Daniel 2 and 7 were Babylon, Persia, Greece, and Rome. That Rome was that terrible beast that trampled the saints could hardly be denied from the actual sequence of empires and from the realities of the Imperial persecution under Nero and Domitian.[25] It follows further that the Little Horn Antichrist power must be Roman from the fact that in the symbol the horn grows out of the fourth Roman beast. Believers aware of this prophecy would have viewed the rather local persecutions of Domitian as "the tramplings" of the beast and precursors of the Little Horn yet to arrive. Expositors generally agree that the Apostle Paul, when he spoke of "the man of lawlessness" in 2 Thess 2:3, referred to the Little Horn of Daniel 7. Regarding this he said that before the "man of lawlessness" comes one who restrains must first be taken out of the

---

[24] The term, Antichrist, of course, means "anti-Messiah," that is, one who puts himself over-against the Messiah, Jesus Christ, usurping his place and his authority. The word is not used in either Daniel or Revelation, but only in the Johannine Epistles (1 John 1:18, 22; 2 John 7). We should not attach our understanding of the functionary to the term, per se, as in the course of historical interpretation its use has been extended far beyond the evidence of Scripture. But we should look to the Word of God to understand the concept as there defined. It seems highly probable to this writer that when the Apostle wrote in his first Epistle, "You have heard that the Antichrist is coming" (1 John 1:18), he referred to that power which appeared to Daniel as "the Little Horn." The Apostle Paul's reference to "the rebellion" and to "the man of lawlessness . . . doomed to destruction" in 2 Thess 2:3, which must come before the Day of the Lord, appears also to be a reference to Daniel 7, as several elements in the Apostle's description (v. 4) correspond to characteristics of the Little Horn. The origin of the term, "antichrist," nevertheless remains to us obscure, though probably it was coined by the Apostles, perhaps even by John, himself, while with the Asian churches. Nevertheless, the Apostle Paul had ministered to the Asian churches during his three-year stay in Ephesus on his second missionary journey and may have coined the term while teaching Daniel 7.

[25] The four empires were Babylon, Persia, Greece, and Rome. The modern theory that these four empires were Babylon, Media, Persia, and Greece rests upon the fallacious assumption that Daniel was written in the second century B.C. as a reflex of the Maccabean Wars and Antiochus IV's desecration of the temple. This pattern of thought assumes that the detailed predictions in the visions of Daniel were written after the events and that the Book of Daniel, like the many non-canonical apocalypses is a pseudepigraphon. Such scholars assume that the author of Daniel was ignorant of the actual course of history, so he mistakenly inserted Media into the sequence of nations. Several of the assumptions originally believed to support this theory have since been proven false by archaeology. The Dead Sea Scrolls indicate that Daniel was believed to be canonical as early as fifty years after its alleged pseudepigraphic and erroneous publication. Given the rigid criteria for determinining the canonicity of biblical books, this seems hardly possible.

way.

What is this that restrains and when was it to be taken away? We know that there was an era of peace and relative calm in the Empire as Nerva followed Domitian in A.D. 96. Following the understanding of the early fathers who lived under the Empire, we take this to be the power of the Roman state, itself. As F. F. Bruce suggested,

> No more convincing account of the restrainer has been suggested than that put forward by Tertullian [ca. 200 A.D.] (*De resurr. carn.* 24). "What is this but the Roman state, whose removal when it has been divided among ten kings will bring on Antichrist?" Similarly Chrysostom *(Hom. 4 on 2 Thessalonians)* says of ὁ κατέχων, "some interpret this of the grace of the Spirit . . . , but others of the Roman Empire, and this is my own preference. Why? Because, if Paul had meant the Spirit, he would have said so plainly and not obscurely, . . . but because he meant the Roman Empire, he naturally glanced at it, speaking covertly and darkly. . . . So . . . when the Roman Empire is out of the way, then he [Antichrist] will come."[26]

The Roman Empire fell in the West in A.D 476 with the deposition of Romulus Augustus. The times were turbulent as Rome was repeatedly ruined by competing forces. In A.D. 607, shortly after the "restraining power" came to an end, the Eastern emperor, Phocas, enhanced the authority of the Roman bishop by officially recognizing him as "Universal Bishop," thereby authorizing him to wield the "keys of the Kingdom" over all Christendom.[27]

With the universal authority of the Papacy, there arose the persecution of dissidents who rejected the abuses of the Roman Church. This brings us to the question of the identify of these Witnesses.

Subsequently, with the Protestant Reformation, scholars researched the earlier history of the church and produced several major works. These include: *Image of Both Churches* (c. 1545) John Bale,[28] *Catalogus*

---

[26]Bruce comments further, "Paul viewed established government as imposing a salutary restraint on evil (Rom 13:3, 4), and in his mission field established government meant effectively the Roman Empire (τὸ κατέχον), personally embodied in the emperor (ὁ κατέχων)." F. F. Bruce, *1 & 2 Thessalonians* (Word Biblical Commentary; Waco, Texas: Word Books, 1982), 171-172. Paul wrote to the Thessalonians under the reign of the Emperor Claudius (A.D. 41-54), a generally tolerant ruler.

[27]See Elliott, 3.302-304; Wm. Jones, *History of the Christian Church* (Conrad, Mont.: Triangle, 1993), 2. 380-387; Schaff, *History of the Christian Church* (1910; repr., Grand Rapids: Eerdmans, 1994), 4:221-225; John L. Mosheim, *Institutes of Ecclesiastical History* (London: William Tegg, 1859), 245-246, and primary sources referenced therein.

[28]Elliott, 2.143, 204, 4.450-457; L. E. Froom, *The Prophetic Faith of Our Fathers* (Washington, D.C.: Review and Herald, 1950), 2.395-401.

Testium ("Catalog of Witnesses") by Flacius Illyricus (1556),[29] Martyrology ("Book of Martyrs") by John Foxe (first edition, 1556). These works cataloged a valiant line of heroes, evangelicals many of whom died for their witness to the Gospel of salvation by faith alone and to the excesses of the Roman church. Though the first two works are now generally unknown, Foxe's work has remained in print as a great Christian Classic. Also very important as early works on this subject are *Churches of Piedmont* (1690) and *Churches of the Albigenses* (1692), both by Peter Alix.[30]

The witnesses were evangelical believers who fled from the persecution of the Roman church into remote regions high in the mountains of southern Europe and Asia Minor. These Christians have come to be known by historians by several sectarian names.

The Paulician sect was founded by one Constantine, a Greek Christian in the mid-seventh century to whom was given a copy of the Four Gospels and the fourteen epistles of Paul, after which he set about to establish churches. His strong emphasis on the Pauline Gospel probably gave rise to the name "Paulician." As the Paulicians rejected the errors of the Catholic church, their doctrines were caricatured by those ecclesiastics who alone recorded their history, with the result that their founder and hundreds of others were cruelly put to death. J. A. Wylie, in his *History of Protestantism*, states the following:

> They occupy an analogous place in the East to that which the Waldenses held in the West. Some obscurity rests upon their origin . . . but a fair and impartial examination of the matter leaves no doubt that the Paulicians are the remnant that escaped the apostacy[sic] of the Eastern Church . . . . They have been painted as a confederacy of Manicheans . . . but . . . an examination of the matter satisfies us that these imputations had no sufficient foundation, that the Paulicians repudiated the errors imputed to them, and that as a body their opinions were in substantial agreement with the doctrine of Holy Writ.[31]

Wylie's opinion is shared by Elliott. The doctrines of the Paulicians, on the basis of which they were condemned as heretics by the Catholic

---

[29] Illyricus was assisted in this research by Nicholaus Gallus, Johannes, Wigandus, Matthias Judex, all of Magdeburg, Germany (Elliott, 2.203,204).

[30] Second eds. were published in 1821 (Oxford: Clarendon Press), which were reprinted as two books in one as *Some Remarks upon the Ecclesiastical History of the Ancient Churches of Piedmont* (iii, 361 pp.) and *Remarks upon the Ecclesiastical History of the Ancient Churches of the Albigenses* (xiii, iii, 282 pp.) (both by Gallatin, Tenn.: Church History Research & Archives, 1989); also Ronald N. Cooke, *Antichrist Exposed* (Max Meadows, VA: Truth International Miistries, 2006), 1.93-103.

[31] (1878; repr., Kilkeel, N. Ireland: Monroe Missionary Trust, 1990), 1.32-33. 3 vols. bound in 2. This major, llustrated work runs to 1344 pp.

Church, were recorded by Photius, Patriarch of Constantinople and by Petrus Siculus, both enemies of the Paulicians for their opposition to errant tenets of the established church. In order to cast the sect in a bad light for the purpose of prosecution, it was in their interest to caricature their doctrines.[32] The Empress Theodora exceeded her predecessors in her opposition to the Paulicians in Asia Minor and, as reported by historian William Jones, she is "computed to have killed by the gibbet, by fire, and by the sword, A HUNDRED THOUSAND PERSONS" (1.428; emphasis his). It is significant to note that the Paulician sect arose shortly after the A.D. 607 decree of the Emperor Phocas elevating the Papal office to the rank of Universal Bishop, marking according to many interpreters the beginning of the temporal power of the Papacy.[33]

In the Western church, the dissenting evangelicals came to be known as Waldenses, after the name of one of their leaders, Peter Waldo. However, Peter Allix argues convincingly that before Waldo, they were known as Valenses, from the name of their habitat. Before the Valenses there were the Berengarians, the Patarines, the Cathari, and many other groups of Christians who took their names from their location, their leaders, or the label given to their piety. Ordinarily these were people who based their faith on their understanding of Scripture rather than on the ecclesiastical authorities of a corrupt established church.[34]

Elliott in his *Horae Apocalypticae* documents extensively the testimony of two Medieval sects who maintained witness to the true Gospel and resisted the evils of the Roman Church. These he identifies as primarily the Paulicians and the Waldenses. With these conclusions we incline to agree as to the principal identity of the Two Witnesses in the Medieval period.

The Two Witnesses (cont'd)

11:7. Now when they have finished their testimony, the beast that comes up from the Abyss will attack them, and overpower and kill

---

[32] Elliott, 2.248-268, basing his work on the original writings of Photius and Siculus; also Jones, 419-424.

[33] The enemies of the Paulicians consistently called them Manicheans though the evidence indicates that they were dedicated to Pauline Christianity in opposition to the extra-biblical practices that had crept into the Catholic churches (Wylie, 1.34, n. 6; also see Albert Henry Newman, *A Manual of Church History*, Rev. & enlarged ed. [Philadelphia: American Baptist Publication Society, 1931], 1.282–86.

[34] See Wylie, 1. 18; Alix, 121 and following; Schaff, 5.461-470; and Jones, 1.312-319.

them. ⁸Their bodies will lie in the street of the great city, which is figuratively called Sodom and Egypt, where also their Lord was crucified. ⁹For three and a half days men from every people, tribe, language and nation will gaze on their bodies and refuse them burial. ¹⁰The inhabitants of the earth will gloat over them and will celebrate by sending each other gifts, because these two prophets had tormented those who live on the earth.

11:7-10   **The Death of the Witnesses**   **Exposition**

This remarkable statement indicates that at the time when the witness of the evangelical church to the true Gospel of grace and against the evils of the Roman "beast" would reach its culmination, the Satan-inspired "beast" would attack and kill them. This difficult prophecy is encrypted with symbolic language which must be understood from the perspective of the first century New Testament church. We have explained above that the "two witnesses" represent the true testimony to the Gospel of grace. "The beast," introduced here in the Apocalypse for the first time, is presented as a known entity, as indicated grammatically in the Greek text by the definite article. This entity was known to the original readers from the prophecy of Daniel 7:7-28:

> ... In my vision at night I looked, and there before me was a fourth beast—terrifying and frightening and very powerful. It had large iron teeth; it crushed and devoured its victims and trampled underfoot whatever was left. It was different from all the former beasts, and it had ten horns.
> While I was thinking about the horns, there before me was another horn, a little one, which came up among them, and three of the first horns were uprooted before it. This horn had eyes like the eyes of a man and a mouth that spoke boastfully. ....
> As I watched, this horn was waging war against the saints and defeating them .... (Dan 7:7, 8, 21)

The original readers at the end of the first century understood from the sequence of the four kingdoms of Daniel 2 and 7 that the fourth beast was Rome. With rising persecution under the Emperor Domitian, and with the arrest and exile of the last of the Apostles, the beloved disciple John, they had every reason to anticipate with apprehension and wonder the power prefigured by Daniel's Little Horn. Our Lord's merciful response to this circumstance in the Asian church is this dramatic vision given to John to assure God's people of His providential provision and certain victory as they faced this terrifying prospect. So we must conclude that the "beast" represents a real historical world power, fourth in Daniel's sequence of world empires—Rome.

Our Lord's prophecy states that this beast will "attack" the Witnesses, "overpower them, and kill them" (11:7). Moreover, it appears from Daniel that this was to be accomplished through the agency of the "little horn" power.

The bodies of the dead witnesses were to "lie in the street of the great city" (11:8). To what "city" does this refer? The identification of "the beast" with Rome naturally leads to the conclusion that this reference is to Rome. Rome, moreover, was commonly known in antiquity as "the great city."[35] In the Apocalypse alone, according to historicist and preterist interpreters, it is so called in six other passages (16:19, 17:18, 18:10, 16, 18, 19, 21).[36] This city also is "figuratively called Sodom and Egypt, where also their Lord was crucified." Sodom stands in Scripture as a symbol of immorality and damnation, Egypt as a symbol of idolatry and enslavement of the Covenant people. "Jerusalem" here as the same place identified as "Babylon," "Sodom," and "Egypt" can hardly stand for the literal "holy city." "Where their Lord was crucified" appears rather to refer in figure to "Rome." Kistemaker comments (p. 334),

> The great city where their Lord was crucified is not an earthly city called Jerusalem; rather, it is contrasted with the holy city where God's people reside. The great city is the place where people contrary to the will of God have crucified and continue to crucify the Lord all over again (Heb. 6:6).

One should not identify "the great city" literally with the city of Rome but rather with the larger sphere dominated by Roman authority, the province of Daniel's fourth beast.

---

[35] Elliott cites Manilius, Lib iv (2.434, n. 2).
[36] Beale comments, "All other uses of 'the great city' in the Apocalypse refer to 'Babylon the Great,' not Jerusalem . . . " (591).

The death of the witnesses forecasts a time when the testimony to the true Gospel would be silenced. The reference to their dead bodies as prohibited from burial suggests, as does Daniel's description of the war with the beast, that literal death as well as cessation of witness is in view. The celebration of their death throughout the Roman world indicates the radical apostasy that was to occur in Christendom in that era. A truly evangelical witness is torment to an apostate church and a degenerate people.

How should the reader understand the "three and a half days" during which the bodies of the witnesses would lie in the streets? In keeping with the other time periods encountered in the Apocalypse, one should expect that a period of three and a half actual years is in view.

11:7-10   **The Death of the Witnesses**   Notes

7. "When they have **finished** their testimony" may suggest the end of the "1,260 days" of v. 3. However, the word translated "finished" (Gk. τελέω, *teléō*) may also be rendered "accomplished" in the sense of having reached a climax. Elliott comments as follows. "And since (to use the words of the Lexicographers Scott and Liddell) 'the strict signification of τελος is not *the ending of a departed state,* but *the arrival of a complete and perfect one,*' therefore τελέω signifies most properly *to bring to such a state of completion and perfection . . .*" (2.416).[37] This is an instance where only a suitable fulfillment will resolve the ambiguity. One need not assume that the death of the witnesses was to occur after 1,260 days or years. **The Abyss** (Gk. ἄβυσσος, *'ábussos)* refers to the underworld as the abode of Satan and his demons (Rev 20:3) and is comparable to Dan 7:3; Rev 9:1; and 13:1, which last represents the beast as "coming up out of the sea." The sea was understood in ancient times as a means of entrance into the Abyss. **Kill them** in view of the prohibition of burial must be taken as implying literal death. However, primary in our text is the implied temporary cessation of the witness. **8. Their bodies will lie in the street** indicates a condition which dishonors the dead. **9.** The **three and a half**

---

[37]See Elliott further, 411-423; also Barnes, 288 and Francis Nigel Lee, *John's Revelation Unveiled* (Brisbane, Australia: Queensland Presbyterian Theological College, 2000), 118.

days during which the bodies would remain unburied should be reckoned according to the "1,260 days" of 11:3, that is, as 3½ years. These time periods should be understood as part of the encryption of the prophecy which would only be so interpreted with the passage of sufficient time. **Will gaze on their bodies and refuse them burial** implies a common disdain for the witness and a deliberate dishonor in their death. **10. The inhabitants of the earth** has reference to the people of the Roman world according to the use of the term "earth" in this prophecy to refer to the domain of the fourth kingdom of Daniel seven. That the inhabitants should celebrate in such manner the death of the witnesses is a truly remarkable prediction, the fulfillment of which one should expect to be conspicuous.

11:7-10   **The Death of the Witnesses**   **Fulfillment**

We have identified the Two Witnesses with the evangelical sects who proclaimed the biblical Gospel and opposed the errors of the Roman Church. Although these in the Medieval period are known principally as the Paulicians in the East and the Waldensians in the West, they were known by many other names at various times and places. In order to prosecute these people for heresy, the Roman Church consistently caricatured their doctrines.[38]

How shall we find the extraordinary circumstances surrounding the death of the Witnesses fulfilled? Throughout their history the evangelical sects opposed fearlessly the errors of the Roman Church, even identifying it with the Harlot Babylon and the Antichrist. For this they were often aggressively persecuted and put to death. However, through numerous centuries their witness continued.

The prophecy requires that the death of the witnesses occur "when they shall have completed their testimony" (ὅταν τελέσωσιν τὴν μαρτυρίαν, *hótan telésōsin tēn marturían*). Their testimony reached such a climax in the years just prior to the Protestant Reformation, when the Roman Church decided to make a full end of their conflicting witness. Though the stage was set for the temporal power of the Papacy by the establishment of the state church under Constantine in the early fourth century, it was not until the Emperor Phocus in A.D. 607 granted to the Pope the title of Universal Bishop that the papal institution came to be generally recognized for its temporal authority. The process of gaining

---

[38]For a thorough defense of this assertion, see Elliott, 2.314-344, 385-408.

control of secular governments so as to conduct an all-out war against "heresy" took much longer.

Elliott documents this in detail and states, "Not until its religious supremacy was established over each *state* in Christendom, and the temporal power subjected to the spiritual, could it command the secular sword to strike down what it called heresy or heretic" (423-427, italics his). With this fuller establishment of Papal power in the twelfth century, the voice of the Witnesses turned from protesting specific doctrinal errors of the church to focus on Papal Rome, itself. When this occurred, "the Wild Beast, now thoroughly prepared, turned . . . his fierce rage against these Witnesses for Christ, and made war upon them" (Elliott 424). In the Council of Tours (A.D. 1163), Pope Alexander III forbade giving refuge to the Albigensian "heretics," forbidding buying or selling, or otherwise communicating with them. The Third Lateran Council (A.D. 1179) pronounced an anathema against Cathari, Patareni, Publicani, and other "heretics," forbidding the provision of harbor to them or even Christian burial. In 1183, Pope Lucius III pronounced anathema against Cathari, Patareni, Arnaldistae, and Humiliati (the "Poor Men of Lyons"), using the word "inquisition" for the first time for their detection and suppression. In 1198, Pope Innocent III called on the prelates to act, using the arms of people and prince as necessary to stamp out "heresy," establishing through the Spanish *Dominie* the Inquisition.

The Fourth Lateran Council (A.D. 1215) reiterated "all the former plans for the extirpation of heresy. the secular powers being expressly subordinated to the spiritual for the purpose . . . and crusaders rewarded with every . . . indulgence and privilege as the Crusaders to the Holy Land" (Elliott, 426). The Councils of Narbonne (A.D.1227) and Toulouse (1229) followed, which required even the children to denounce any whom they know to be "heretics" and prohibited the Scriptures to the laity. More councils directing the war against the Witnesses followed. Arles (1234), Narbonne (1235), Tarragona (1242), with Papal bulls of Gregory IX (1236) and Innocent IV (1244). The last provided that the Bishops might show mercy to those sentenced to burn, providing that their tongues be cut out to prevent further blasphemy.[39]

This war continued against all who witnessed for the true Gospel against the heresies of Roman Catholicism through the fourteenth and most of the fifteenth century, including Wycliffe in England and Huss in Bohemia (now part of the Czech Republic), and their followers. How can it be said that the Witnesses were "killed"? Of course millions actually

---

[39]Elliott fully documents the above, 2.423-427.

Chapter Six *The death of the witnesses, 11:7-10* 259

died but the figure speaks primarily of the cessation of their witness.[40] Elliott, citing historians Comenius (2.39) and Bost (2.430), indicates that when the surviving Bohemian churches sent deputies to search throughout Europe to find other churches of kindred spirit, there were none. The *Roman Catholic historian*, Cardinal Pallavicini reported, "In the West the true faith flourished, with scarce an contamination attaching to it. there remaining only, *almost invisible*, certain minute stains of ignoble and despised heresies, followed by a little flock of rustic and rude men, the remnant either of the Waldenses, or of the followers of John Huss, who had been condemned and burnt a century before, in the council of Constance."[41] The Protestant historian, Mosheim, states:

> As the [16th] century began, no danger seemed to threaten the pontiffs. For those grievous commotions which had been raised in the preceding centuries by the Waldenses, Albigenses, Beghards, and others, and afterwards by the Bohemians, had been suppressed and extinguished by the sword and by crafty management. The Waldenses who survived in the valleys of the Piedmont fared hard, and had few resources . . . . Those Bohemians who were displeased with the Romish doctrines, from their want of power and their ignorance, could attempt nothing; and therefore were rather despised than feared. (558)

On May 5, 1514, at the Ninth Session of the Fifth Lateran Council, the following announcement was proclaimed to Pope Leo X. "'There is an end of resistance to the Papal rule and religion. Opposers there exist no more." . . . "The whole body of Christendom is now seen to be subjected to its *Head*, i. e. to *Thee*.'"[42] Thus stands the remarkable fulfillment of the predicted "death" of the Witnesses.

Our prophecy continues, "Their bodies will lie in the street of the great city . . . . For three and a half days men from every people, tribe, language and nation will gaze on their bodies and refuse them burial" (11:8-9).

As indicated above, with the passage of centuries, the reader should expect the time numbers in the Apocalypse to be understood according to the year-day principle used in several Old Testament prophecies (Num 14:34; Ezek 4:5; Dan 9:24); that is, "three and a half days" will then mean "three and a half years." This is exactly the period of time during which the witness of the true church to the true Gospel was silenced—the period

---

[40] As "Two Witnesses" is a symbol, their "death" must also be understood in a figurative sense.

[41] As quoted by Elliott 2.430 (emphasis his?).

[42] As translated from the Latin and quoted by Elliott, 2.450.

from May 5, 1514 to Oct. 31, 1517, the date when Martin Luther started the great Protestant Reformation by posting his ninety-five theses.[43]

The punishments for "heresy" decreed by the Council included all the measures imposed by former Papal bulls and councils including the prohibition of burial. Bodies were left to the ravishes of wild beasts or, if burned, sometime the ashes were cast into lakes or rivers (Elliott, 2.451-452).

The last element of our text is found in verse 10. "The inhabitants of the earth will celebrate by sending each other gifts . . . ." This is exactly how Roman Christendom regarded the cruel suppression of dissidents. Barnes quotes Pareus commenting on Luke 15:32. "When heretics are burnt, Papists play at frolicsome games, celebrate feasts and banquets, sing *Te Deum laudamus* and wish one another joy" (291). At the close of the Fifth Lateran Council, there was great celebration. Elliott quotes Pope Leo X as follows. "All which [actions of the Council] considered, our soul exults in the Lord. and we judge that thanks should be given to God for it; and that, among all the faithful in Christ, there should be those signs of joy which on similar occasions are want to be observed." This was followed by a plenary Papal indulgence, the singing of the Te Deum, and lavish banqueting. (2.455).

We have observed that this very extraordinary and unique prophecy regarding the "death" of the Two Witnesses was fulfilled with great exactitude. What remains of the Two Witnesses for us to consider is their "resurrection" and ascension to "heaven."

The Two Witnesses (cont'd)

¹¹**But after the three and a half days a breath of life from God entered them, and they stood on their feet, and terror struck those who saw them. ¹²Then they heard a loud voice from heaven saying to them, "Come up here." And they went up to heaven in a cloud, while their enemies looked on.**

¹³**At that very hour there was a severe earthquake and a tenth of the city collapsed. Seven thousand people were killed in the earthquake, and the survivors were terrified and gave glory to the God of heaven.**

---

[43]The period is calculated as is the other such prophecies on the basis of a 360 day *symbolic* year. This is indicated by the fact that "three and one half" *symbolic* years (Dan 7:25) are also indicated as "1260 days" (Rev 11:3) and "42 [30-day] months" (13:5).

11:11-13   The Resurrection of the Witnesses   Exposition

As the "Two Witnesses" is a symbol for the true church as it witnesses to the true Gospel, and the death of the Witnesses is a figure for the cessation of the witness, so must the resurrection be a figure for the resumption of that witness. We have concluded above that the "three and a half days," also a figure, must be reckoned as three and one-half years.

The voice from heaven represents the Divine Providence, the voice of God, the instrument which effects the marvelous "resurrection." The "enemies" who look on are apparently powerless to deter the miraculous resumption of the witness, as the true church springs to life.

Once again, Jesus testifies to God's sovereignty in history. Even the acts of Satan against His church are limited by His providential control so that His promise that "the gates of Hades will not overcome it" (Matt 16:18) remains always true.

As the celestial bodies stand as symbols for human governments in the prophecy of the sixth seal, so "heaven" here represents the sphere of authority of earthly governments (cp. 12:4, 5). The "severe earthquake" and the collapse of "one-tenth of the city" likewise should be taken to represent some revolution in government in the Roman world. The city here, as in the reference to "the great city" suggests some event within the sphere of Roman government.

11:11-13   The Resurrection of the Witnesses   Notes

11. Three and one-half days according to the year-day principle means three and one-half 360-day years, totalling 1260 days (see comment on 11:9 in the Fulfillment section above). This corresponds to the period from the 9th Session of the Fifth Lateran Council (May 5, 1514) to Luther's posting of his ninety-five theses (Oct 31, 1517). The calculation of the 180 days is as follows:

Month	Days	Month	Days	Month	Days
May 5-31	27	July	31	September	30
June	30	August	31	October	31
Total	57	Total	119	Total	180

Add three years (3 x 360 = 1080 days) and the total is 1260 days. The period of time predicted is fulfilled exactly, *to the very day*! The **breath of life from God entered them** is the language of creation and of resurrection (Gen 2:7; Ezek 37:5). The life function, to witness, is thus restored to the witnesses.[44] **12.** The **loud** voice gives great emphasis to what follows, the **voice** speaks "**from heaven.**" "Heaven" here is used in the metaphorical sense for a position of political authority. This cannot be understood as their final reward because the Two Witnesses are already resurrected to life (v. 11) and the literal resurrection of the righteous is still future. The 1260 years forecast for their witness have not yet expired. In context, their "resurrection" as well as "Heaven," must be understood figuratively as a reflection of the ancient metaphor—ascendancy to the realm of authority to govern. "**Come up here**" indicates a call from someone in authority to give sanctuary to the witnesses. **While their enemies looked on** also indicates a circumstance in the temporal sphere to be observed by the opponents of the witnesses .

13. Hour (Gk. ὥρα, *hŏra*) is used here in the sense of "time" (BAGD, 896³, "*the time* when something . . . will take place."). The **severe earthquake** indicates political upheaval, revolution. **The city** in context should probably have been understood in the first century as the sphere of Roman authority, that is, the Roman Empire.

11:11-13   The Resurrection of the Witnesses   Fulfillment

How may it be said that the true evangelical church after three and one half years was restored to life and to witness? As we have seen above, this period began with the 9th Session of the 5th Lateran Council on May 5, 1514 and ended on October 31, 1517, the very day on which Martin Luther posted his 95 theses, calling for reforms within the Roman Catholic Church, the beginning of the Protestant Reformation. With the Reformation was the translation of the Bible from the original texts into the common languages, the English by William Tyndale and the German

---

[44]For several instances of resurrection used by extra-biblical writers as a figure for revival, see Elliott, 2.460, with n. 1.

by Luther, himself. As the Bible was read for the first time in many centuries by the common people and Gospel preachers sprang up in support of reform, grass-roots revival broke out across Europe. Public opinion in Germany largely supported Luther against the decrees of the Papal Church, including many in high office of government.

How may it be said that the Witnesses were "caught up to heaven"? As we understand "heaven" to refer here to the sphere of political authority, this had its fulfillment as the Reformation movement gained independence from the Roman Church. As Elliott points out, clearly an act of Providence provided for the unification of the Holy Roman Emperor and German Diet, as the Emperor and some of the states had supported the Papacy against the Reformers and others of the states supported the Reformation. However, when confronted with the threat of an invasion by the Turkish sultan, Suleiman the Magnificent, in 1534 they passed a decree called *The Pacification of Nuremberg*, which accorded full toleration to Protestantism (2.467). This was followed on August 12, 1542, by another, the Peace of Passau, later confirmed in Augsburg in 1555.[45] (Though these decrees gave political ascendancy to Protestants in part of Germany, soon to be followed in other countries, the Witnesses were still in sackcloth, as the inquisition still continued in Italy, Spain, and Portugal. Likewise it continued in France until 1598, and in Austria until 1783.) Thus, the Witnesses in the Holy Roman Empire gained a political status which to a large extent protected them from the Papal inquisitors whose practice it was to rely on the civil authorities to carry out their prescribed punishments.[46] The Witnesses ascension "in a cloud" suggests the Divine presence and the providential provision which enabled the Reformation to continue with power.[47]

The "severe earthquake," which occurred at that time is not difficult to identify. In the symbolic language of the Apocalypse, "a severe earthquake" indicates a great revolution (cp. 6:12). This is the political revolution that accompanied the Protestant Reformation. "A tenth part of

---

[45] E. P. Cachemaille, *XXVI Present Day Papers on Prophecy* (London: Seeley, Service & Co., 1911), 354-355.

[46] Barnes understood the witnesses "ascension to heaven" to mean simply their public recognition as approved by God (281). This alternate interpretation is not contextually implausible. Beale takes a similar position on this figure but looks for fulfilment "at the end of the age" (600).

[47] Beale calls the reader's attention to the article in the expression "in the cloud" (Gk. ἐν τῃ νεφελῃ, *en tē nephelē*), suggesting that it refers back to 10:1, where the mighty angel is "robed in a cloud." This is the same expression, except without the article (599). In the ancient tradition reflected in the Bible and in Jewish literature, the cloud is a symbol of the Divine presence (Ezek 1:4; Dan 7:13; Acts 1:9; Rev 14:14).

the city" suggests one of the ten kingdoms represented in Dan 7:7 by the "ten horns" of the Roman "beast."[48] Up to this time those countries which had withdrawn from Papal dominion lay outside the boundaries of the old Roman Empire, but England, one of the ten, by act of parliament withdrew in 1534.[49] One of the effects of the earthquake was "The seven thousand people killed" (11:13, NIV). The Greek states, καὶ ἀπεκτάνθησαν ἐν τῷ σεισμῷ ὀνόματα ἀνθρώπων χιλιάδες ἑπτά, *kaì apektánthēsan en tô seismô chiliádes heptá*. Literally translated, the text reads, "And there were killed in the earthquake seven *thousands* of men." As in Mic 5:2 (LXX), χιλιάδες, *chiliádes* "thousands," may be translated "tribal districts," as the number indicating divisions of the Israelite tribes apparently came to represent the territory assigned for their residence in Canaan. So here, the term may mean "districts" (note the plural, which with the specific number suggests a collective entity). The prophecy is understood by several leading commentators to point to the seven districts which formed the Dutch Union of Utrecht in 1579—Holland, Zealand, Utrecht, Frieseland, Groningen, Overyssel, and Guiderland.[50]

So we have observed how this extraordinary and mysterious prophecy was wonderfully fulfilled in the circumstances leading up to and resulting in the great Protestant Reformation era and the world missionary enterprise which was to follow.

In concluding this section on the Two Witnesses, allow me to quote the following from Cachemaille:

> Not only do these twenty-verses [10:1-11:13] furnish an admirable and trustworthy epitome of the history of the Reformation period; but also—what is far more important—all this is given as from God's point of view. It is the history inspired by His Spirit, and revealed by His Son, and therefore true and reliable . . . . (368)

---

[48]Cachemaille suggests that as the tithe (one tenth) is an acknowledgement that the whole belongs to the Lord, so here the tenth part may be intended to indicate God's right to the entire "city," according to the angel's planting "his right foot on the sea and his left foot on the land" (356-357; Rev 10:2).

[49]This was occasioned by the English king, Henry VIII, who believing his marriage to Catharine of Aragon to be unlawful, petitioned the Pope for a divorce. When dissatisfied with the response, Henry divorced Catharine and married Anne Boleyn. Parliament abolished Roman authority and declared the king head of the English church. This political conversion, nevertheless, hardly extended to the king, as his subsequent conduct hardly reflected the principles of the Reformation (Mosheim, 591-592).

[50]Elliott, 2.475-482, Cachemaille, 365-366.

Chapter Six *The passing of the second woe, 11:14* 265

The Two Witnesses (cont'd)
11:14 **The second woe has passed; the third woe is coming soon.**

11:14   **The Passing of the Second Woe**   **Exposition**

As observed above, verse 14 functions in the Little Scroll message to indicate the synchronism between the time of the "great earthquake," a political revolution that was to occur within the territory of ancient Rome, and the end of the sixth trumpet prophecy. This is an indication that the chronological sequence of events forecast in the Little Scroll runs parallel with some of the events predicted in the big seven-sealed book.

11:14   **The Passing of the Second Woe**   **Notes**

14. The second woe is part of a series of three "woes," the first of which is identified with the fifth trumpet prophecy (9:1-11). The formula in 9:12, "The first woe is past; two other woes are yet to come," corresponds with 11:14. "The second woe" is identified with the locust-like hoards of the sixth trumpet prophecy (9:13-21). **Yet to come,** the **third woe** is not so explicitly identified, but as indicated above, the bowl prophecies, which follow immediately after the Little Scroll excursus (chs. 15, 16), is the apparent candidate. The bowl prophecies are there described as "the seven last plagues—last, because with them God's wrath is completed" (15:1).

11:14   **The Passing of the Second Woe**   **Fulfillment**

We have identified the second woe with the Ottoman Turkish conquests which climaxed with the fall of Byzantium in A.D. 1453. Nevertheless, the Muslim Turkish armies continued to enlarge their empire until a decisive sea battle, the Battle of Lepanto. This occurred in 1571, about the time of the insurrection of the seven Dutch provinces described above in the Little Scroll prophecy which precedes this verse. (Elliott, 2.490-491) This striking synchronism between the major series of forecasts in the Seven-sealed Scroll and the events predicted in the Little Scroll lends credence to our structural analysis, as well as to our historicist interpretation, and to the apparent fulfillments propounded.

The Seventh Trumpet

11:15. The seventh angel sounded his trumpet, and there were loud voices in heaven, which said:

> "The kingdom of the world has become the kingdom of our Lord
>   and of his Christ,
> and he will reign for ever and ever."

[16]**And the twenty-four elders, who were seated on their thrones before God, fell on their faces and worshiped God,** [17]**saying:**

> "We give thanks to you, Lord God Almighty,
>   who is and who was,
> because you have taken your great power
>   and have begun to reign.
> [18]The nations were angry;
>   and your wrath has come.
> The time has come for judging the dead,
>   and for rewarding your servants the prophets
> and your saints and those who reverence your name,
>   both small and great—
> and for destroying those who destroy the earth."

11:15-18 **The Seventh Trumpet Sounded** **Exposition**

The Apocalyptic vision of the Revelation at several junctures looks ahead to the end-time culmination, the victory of Christ and His church over the Satanic forces of Antichrist and evil men. We have seen this in the "great multitude" choir of 7:7-12 and will see it again in celebration of the wedding of the Lamb in 19:1-8. Here in 11:15-18, two hymns are given to encourage God's people as they face further suffering to focus on a sovereign God and the ultimate and glorious victory of Christ and His Church. The sounding of the seventh trumpet occurs immediately after the announcement of a "third woe." This ominous anticipation of judgment warrants these hymns of praise and promise. As is often the case in prophecy, this future victory is stated in the past tense to indicate that the promise is as certain as if it had already happened.[51]

"The kingdom of the world" is the kingdom of Satan (see Psa 2:8, 9; Matt 4:8; Luke 4:5; John 12:31), nevertheless subject to God's overarching sovereignty and destined to become in the absolute sense "the Kingdom of our Lord and of his Christ" (Dan 7:13, 14) and "He will reign forever and ever." The anonymity of the voices serves to focus on the message and make that more wonderfully emphatic.

The second hymn is sung by the twenty-four elders, angelic beings representing the saints of both Testaments (see above on 4:10). Unlike the first, this hymn is addressed as an act of worship to God. It is a hymn of thanksgiving for a sovereign eternal God, "the Lord God Almighty, who is and who was" (11:17). Note that the familiar formula omits the final element, "and who is to come." This of course is not to diminish God's eternal nature but rather it reflects the proleptic orientation of the hymn at the time of the consummation of all things, when His people no longer need to look forward to his redemption. The hymn carries the reader to that very time when "there shall be no delay" (Rev 10:6)! This is the time of judging the resurrected dead, for rewarding the prophets, as well as all God's covenant people, those who reverence the Lord. The hymn ends with the promise of the destruction of "those who destroy the earth." The final extinction of evil from God's creation is part of the wonderful hope of the saints! (1 Cor 15:24-28)

The Temple and the Ark of the Covenant

11:19. Then God's temple in heaven was opened, and within his temple was seen the ark of his covenant. And there came flashes of lightning, rumblings, peals of thunder, an earthquake and a great hailstorm.

---

[51]In the Hebrew grammar of the Old Testament, this figurative construction is called the "prophetic perfect." See, e.g., Isa 53:1-9.

11:19   The Temple and the Ark of the Covenant   Exposition

We last encountered the Temple of God in 11:1, where John the Apostle was given a measuring reed to measure it and "to count the worshipers there." This he did according to Divine instruction, leaving out the court of the Gentiles. In this antitypical temple, we have learned that within the larger temple, the visible church, there are the true People of God, as represented by the court of Israel and others only nominally Christian, as represented by the court of the Gentiles (see above, on 11:1-2). The task of those represented by the inner court (the "Two Witnesses") is to witness to the true Gospel to those without. Thus the true "Temple of God" is the true witnessing Church identified with the antitypical "court of Israel."

The orientation of the antitypical Temple as "in heaven," as suggested by verse 12, probably indicates the church's political elevation (Cachemaille, 386). The Temple "was opened" probably is intended to represent the manifestation of the true church in distinction from that which was represented by the "court of the Gentiles."

The ark of God's covenant in the antitypical Temple draws attention to the true Gospel, as represented in the New Testament. The New Covenant is the Old revealed. While embracing the Gospel of grace, it also embraces the covenant law as reiterated by Christ and His Apostles.

The lightning, thunder, earthquake, and hail indicate that the sounding of the seventh and last trumpet, while it highlights the consummation, also must announce further judgments to play out in the final era of this age.[52]

---

[52]While I have preferred with Charles (1.297-298), Elliott (2.495), Beckwith (611), and Cachemaille (386) to understand 11:19 as a transitional link between the preceding passage on the Two Witnesses and the era of the seventh trumpet, some take this verse as belonging with chapter 12 (Barnes, 298). Beckwith states, "This verse is often taken as introductory to chapt. 12; but, its connection with that scene . . . is much less immediate than with the preceding" (611).

11:19 **The Temple and the Ark of the Covenant** **Fulfillment**

As indicated in our Exposition, "God's Temple" must be understood in the antitypical sense. The literal temple, destroyed by the Romans in A.D. 70, was a type of which God's elect people are the antitype as stated by the Apostle Paul in 1 Cor 3:16, "Do you not know that you, yourselves, are God's temple and that God's Spirit lives in you? So the high priest was a type of Jesus Christ, and the altar with its sacrifices a type of His atonement. (Heb 7:26-28). The Temple "opened in heaven" has its fulfillment as a result of the public elevation of the evangelical and reformed Church (11:12) which resulted from the Protestant Reformation movement in the 16th century. One should not underestimate the importance of this revolution in the church after a thousand years of dominance by the Roman Papacy and the nominally Christian nations largely within the boundaries of the old Roman Empire which gave allegiance to Rome and enforced the Papal decrees. The Reformation was not only a correction of erroneous theology and ecclesiastical practice but it was also a great revival movement in which people were converted to the true Gospel experientially, a movement which having begun, was to continue to spread around the world. The revealing of the antitypical ark of the covenant has its fulfillment in the revelation of the true New Covenant Gospel in the Reformation movement.

The latter part of verse 19 with the ominous symbols warned the reader of those judgments which were to follow as the seven bowls would be poured out.

Verse 19 is a transition statement thus connecting the prophecy of the Two Witnesses with the sounding of the seventh trumpet. This transition is preceded by the outburst of heavenly voices (11:15b-18) celebrating the victory implicit in the announcement of the last trumpet. It is as though they could not be restrained!

Chapter Seven

THE WOMAN
THE DRAGON
AND THE TWO BEASTS

12:1-13:18

Introduction

In this chapter we consider parts four and five of our outline of The Little Scroll message introduced above in chapter six:

(4) The Woman and the Dragon (ch. 12)
(5) The Beast from the Sea and the Beast from the Earth (ch. 13)

Jesus, the faithful witness, directed the message of Revelation to persecuted Christians at the end of the first century who had reason to fear the predicted war of the Little Horn Antichrist power forecast in Daniel 7. With the presentation of the Little Book in chapter 10 and a general introduction to the war of the Beast against the saints in chapter 11, we have arrived at the crux of the matter with the disclosure, however veiled, of the nature of the evil forces represented by the Little Horn, as well as some indication of the course of the battle.

Chapters 12 and 13 from the literary, structural point of view constitute an excursus which expands on chapter 11. Chapter 12 introduces the Satanic Dragon power which chronologically precedes the rise of the Little Horn-Beast, but which at length gives its power and authority to the Beast (13:2).

Chapter 11 ends with a proleptic song of praise by the twenty-four elders (11:16-18), heavenly beings which represent before the throne of God the covenant saints (see above on 4:4). Then follows the opening of the ark of the covenant (11:19). Both serve to give hope to believers facing inevitable struggle against the powers of evil encountered in chapters 12 and 13.

The Woman and the Dragon 12:1.

A great and wondrous sign appeared in heaven: a woman clothed with the sun, with the moon under her feet and a crown of twelve stars on her head. ²She was pregnant and cried out in pain as she was about to give birth. ³Then another sign appeared in heaven: an enormous red dragon with seven heads and ten horns and seven crowns on his heads. ⁴His tail swept a third of the stars out of the sky and flung them to the earth. The dragon stood in front of the woman who was about to give birth, so that he might devour her child the moment it was born. ⁵She gave birth to a son, a male child, who will rule all the nations with an iron scepter. And her child was snatched up to God and to his throne. ⁶The woman fled into the desert to a place prepared for her by God, where she might be taken care of for 1,260 days.

12:1-6   **The Woman and the Dragon**   **Exposition**

In our exposition we aspire to read the prophecy as it should have been understood by Christians when it was written at the end of the first century. What should the church have seen as predicted? What practical principles might they have mined from this text? Later, in the Fulfillment section, we will pursue questions of actual fulfillment as viewed in the light of history.

The message is presented as "a great and wondrous sign"! Surely, what is forecast is extraordinary. The prophecy is complex and its interpretation controversial, but nearly all expositors agree that the "woman" is a symbol of the church. Both the Old and New Testaments represent the covenant people as a woman, the bride of Yahweh and of Christ (Isa 54:5; Jer 3:6-8; Ezekiel 16; Hos 2:19-20; Gal 4:26; 2 Cor 2:2; Rev 19:7; 21:9). This is confirmed contextually in Rev 12:17, where offspring of the woman are identified as "those who keep the commandments and hold to the testimony of Jesus." The bride metaphor is entirely appropriate to the

Chapter Seven *The woman and the dragon, 12:1-6*

Antitypical symbolism common to the Apocalypse, as Old Testament Israel has as her antitypical correlative the Messianic community, that is, the assembly of professing believers—the church.[1]

The woman appears "in heaven . . . clothed with the sun, with the moon under her feet." The fact that the woman is clothed with the sun indicates that she is associated with the highest sphere of temporal authority, whereas the moon indicates a lesser sphere.[2] Beale sees in this language a reflex of Joseph's dream, in which he saw his father as the sun, his mother as the moon, and the stars as representing the tribes of Israel (Gen 37:9)[3]. *The Testament of Abraham*, a Jewish writing dated about A.D. 100, relates a dream of Isaac in which Abraham is represented as the sun and Isaac as the moon. In the dream, Isaac has the sun with its rays resting on his head. The dream forecasts the ascension of Abraham, whereby Isaac cries,

> 'I beseech you, my lord, do not take off the glory of my head and the light of my house and all my glory.' The sun and the moon and the stars mourned, saying, 'Do not take off the glory of our power.' (*T. Ab.* B 7:7, 8).

Here, the authority of Abraham which accompanies his reception of the covenant promises for Israel rests upon the head of Isaac and Isaac is fearful as he contemplates Abraham's departure that this inherited glory may be lost.

---

[1] Greek, ἐκκλησία, *ekklēsía*, "assembly." The corresponding term in the Old Testament is the Hebrew עֵדָה, *'ēdah*, "assembly," "congregation."

[2] Eusebius, in a speech recorded in his *Eccles. Hist.*, bk. 10, ch. 4, addresses the ecclesiastical revolution which occurred with Constantine and the Edict of Toleration as follows: "Those that were of his friends and of his household, he [the great Captain and Leader of the armies of God] advanced not only to glory with all men, but now also, with celestial powers, *the sun, the moon, and the stars*, the whole heavens and the world. So that now what never happened before, the supreme sovereigns [Constantine and Licinius], sensible of the honour conferred upon them by him . . . ridicule the ancient delusion of their ancestors, and acknowledge only the one and true God . . . " (italics mine). The translator, C. F. Cruse, appended the following footnote regarding the italicized words, "These expressions . . . may be regarded as oriental hyperbole, for the 'powers that be.' What immediately follows, shows that Eusebius means the reigning emperors" (410).

[3] G. K. Beale, *The Book of Revelation*. (Grand Rapids: Eerdmans, 1999), 625.

In Revelation 12, from the standpoint of the first century reader, a future time is predicted for the people of God, now outcasts from Judaism and from Rome and undergoing persecution, when the church will come into a new and radiant standing by association with a high governmental power. This must be a time future to the writing of Revelation, not the time of Christ's birth, as many expositors have postulated. Our Lord is instructing John regarding "what must take place *after this*," that is, after the Revelation on Patmos in A.D. 96 (4:1; italics mine).[4]

The twelve stars which crown the woman's head in Joseph's dream and in Jewish apocalyptic literature represent the heads of the twelve tribes. Here, they indicate the heads of antitypical "Israel," the angelic messengers which in heaven represent the churches.[5]

The representation of the moon as under the woman's feet indicated to the first-century reader that the woman was to exercise authority or influence over whatever is indicated by the moon. It was a convention of ancient rulers to represent conquered peoples as "under their feet."

The subjection of the moon to the authority of the woman complements the view that the sun represents temporal authority,

---

[4] E. B. Elliott comments with regard to understanding this prophecy as a prediction of the birth of Jesus, "In such a view . . . it must have retrograded to figure not, as the revealing angel said, 'things which are, or things to happen afterwards,' but things past 100 years before the vision in Patmos, in a manner quite unparalleled in the whole of the rest of the Apocalyptic prophecy"; *Horae Apocalypticae* (5th ed. London: Seeley, Jackson, and Halliday, 1862), 3.11. A careful expositor should recognize also that the state of the Jewish covenant people at the time of Jesus' birth hardly accounts for the radiant imagery in our text. Neither is it appropriate as symbol to indicate that a corporate body gave birth to a literal Jesus. Much less can one say that the antitypical Israel, the Christian church gave Jesus birth; the opposite is true (see R. H. Charles, *A Critical and Exegetical Commentary on the Revelation of St. John* (ICC; Edinburgh: T. & T. Clark, 1920), 1.299-300, n. 1).

[5] For the stars as symbols for the twelve tribes of Israel or their heads, see in addition to Gen 37:9, 10, also *Midr. Rab.* Num 2:13, *Midr. Rab.* Deut 1:14, *Midr. Rab.* Exod 15:6 (cited in Beale, 625-626). For the transferral of this motif to the churches, see Rev 1:16, 20, where the seven stars are the angel-messengers of the seven churches of chs. 2-3. Here the antitypical number 12 must stand for all the churches, that is, the local churches as they were to exist at the time of fulfillment.

the primary authority in the temporal sphere. She is "clothed with the sun," suggesting that in some sense she is associated as the recipient or benefactor, a temporal condition that would reverse that state of the church which existed at the end of the first century, when she was experiencing persecution and without status under Rome. What power or powers is symbolized as under the authority of the woman? What does the moon prefigure? We can only conclude, some lesser power or temporal sphere of authority.

The state of the woman as suffering the pains of childbirth (v. 2) is a common figure (Isa 26:17; 66:7-8; Hos 13:13; Mic 4:9, 10). Here it represents a future time of severe persecution of the people of God, as indicated by her "crying out in pain."[6]

In 12:3 we are introduced to "another sign," "an enormous red dragon with seven heads and ten horns and seven crowns on his heads." Given the relationship of the Apocalypse to Daniel 7 (see above, ch. 1), we should take note of the fact that this dragon has ten horns like the fourth Roman beast in Daniel's prophecy. Those who first read the Apocalypse would have identified this evil power with Rome and therefore also with the beast of Daniel 7:7, 19-21, out of which the predicted Little Horn would arise to wage war against the saints.

The seven heads of the dragon (12:3b), as identified with Rome, suggest seven consecutive governments, which as we learn from Rev 17:10 five had already fallen, one was current when the prophecy was given, and one at that time was still future.[7] Roman

---

[6]This condition of the "woman" does not suitably represent the circumstance preceding the birth of Jesus, as the covenant people were not undergoing severe persecution or suffering at that time. In spite of the discomfort and agitation of the Jewish community under Roman rule, the Jews were then allowed by the Romans to live in peace. See further note 2 above.

[7]With regard to the use of the term, "heads" Elliott comments, "That the chief executive authorities were named *heads* may be illustrated from Livy xxvi.16 and 40; 'In cos qui capita rerum erant animadversum.' Now wherever such is the symbol, the verb *fallen* may fitly be used of the thing's abolition. That this figurative term may be applied not to fall of *empires,* or *individual rulers* only, but also to *constitutional changes of forms of government,* I may illustrate from Cicero, *De Off.,* ii.13; *'Ea tua laus pariter cum Republicâ cecidit'* The Roman empire then still continued; but the *Republican form of government* had fallen." (3.117, n. 1; italics Elliott's).

historians at the end of the first century knew that five constitutional governments had passed and the sixth was in progress, as inaugurated by Octavian Augustus Caesar. This is witnessed by the historian, Livy (59 B.C.-A.D. 17), as well as by Tacitus (ca. A.D. 55-ca.117).[8] These six were:

1. Kings, 753-ca. 509 B.C.
2. Consuls, ca. 509-ca. 498 B.C.
3. Dictators, ca. 498-451 B.C.
4. Decemvirs, 451-443 B.C.
5. Military Tribunes, 443-31 B.C.
6. Emperors, 31 B.C.-A.D. 96+[9]

The identification of the seventh head, still "not yet come" (17:10) when the Revelation was given, must remain for our Fulfillment section, but because the heads had been identified with Rome's constitutional governments, the original readers will have been conditioned to look for a seventh revision of its constitution.

Much the same understanding of the heads of the dragon are those of the earliest known Protestant interpretations, as witnessed by Osiander (1544), Aretius (1581), Fulco (1587), Napier (1593),

---

[8]Titus Livius, *"Quae ab condita urbe Roma ad captam eandem Romani sub regibus primum,consulibus deinde ac dictatoribus decemuirisque ac tribunis consularibus gessere...,"* "The history of the Romans from the foundation of the City to its capture, first under kings, then under consuls, dictators, decemvirs, and consular tribunes...," *History* 6.1, ed. rev. Canon Roberts, n.p. (cited 3 Dec. 2002). On line: http://www.perseus.tufts.edu.

Tacitus, *Ann.* 1.1, *"Vrbem Romam a principio reges habuere; libertatem et consulatum L. Brutus instituit. dictaturae ad tempus sumebantur; neque decemviralis potestas ultra biennium, neque tribunorum militum consulare ius diu valuit. non Cinnae, non Sullae longa dominatio; et Pompei Crassique potentia cito in Caesarem, Lepidi atque Antonii arma in Augustum cessere, qui cuncta discordiis civilibus fessa nomine principis sub imperium accepit,"* "Rome at the beginning was ruled by kings. Freedom and the consulship were established by Lucius Brutus. Dictatorships were held for a temporary crisis. The power of the decemvirs did not last beyond two years, nor was the consular jurisdiction of the military tribunes of long duration," edited by Moses Hadas (Modern library ed.; New York: Random House, 1942), p. 3. (cited 3 Dec. 2002) On line: http://classics.mit.edu/Tacitus/annals.html (The Internet Classics Archive).

[9] Carl Ploetz, *Ploetz' Epitome of History*, 7th ed., trans. & enl. by William H. Tillinghast and Harry Elmer Barnes, ed. (New York: Blue Ribbon Books, 1925), 88-137; H. Barton, 178-79.

Chapter Seven   *The woman and the dragon, 12:1-6*   277

Brightman (1600), Pareus (1618), and Mede (1648).[10] So also the main line of Protestant-historical interpreters since Mede.[11]

Such detailed reflection of the ancient history of Rome as implied in the first six heads of the dragon should excite appreciation for the Divine origin and character of the Revelation given to John on Patmos. The omniscient God who gave the Revelation will insure ultimately its entire fulfillment in detail.

The dragon also has "ten horns and seven crowns on his heads" (12:3b). Horns were in ancient times conventional symbols of authority. The ten horns correspond to the ten horns on the Roman beast of Daniel 7:7. The interpretation of the horns in Daniel would have been familiar to the first century readers of the Apocalypse, as their meaning is given in Daniel. They represent "ten kings who will come from this [Roman] kingdom" (Dan 7:24). The reader will recall we observed above (pp. 22-23) that the Apocalypse is in many respects an expansion of the prophecy of Daniel 7. The word "kings" in the Aramaic of Dan 7:24 (מַלְכִין, *mălkhin*) should be understood to mean "kingdoms," as in 7:17.

The "seven crowns on his heads" are diadem crowns. The diadem had come to symbolize the absolute power of the oriental despot, consonant with the implied character of Daniel's terrifying Roman beast with the insolent Little Horn who would wage war against the saints. For the first-century readers it would have pointed to a time not past nor present but future when the Empire would assume this diadem symbol of the Oriental monarch.

We now must consider the action of the dragon as described in 12:4a, "His tail swept a third of the stars out of the sky and flung them to the earth." As indicated above, we understand the sky here

---

[10]See the discussion by Elliott, including answers to his critics, and sources indicated there, 3.116-120. Beginning dates for the 7th head by scholars not indicated by Elliott may be found in Froom, *The Prophetic Faith of Our Fathers*. (Washington, D.C.: Review and Herald, 1950-1954): for Aretius, 2.348; for Napier, 2.457; for Brightman, 2.512; for Pareus, 2.518; for Mede, 2.542.

[11]The tendency of recent commentators is to generalize such symbols and thereby to avoid the detailed historical prediction characteristic of supernaturally inspired apocalyptic prophecy. Witness, e.g., the detailed prediction of Dan 11:2-12:4.

to represent the sphere of temporal authority and the stars to function as emblems of the antitypical Israel—the Christian church. So our text indicates a time when the Satanic power of the Roman dragon wars against the church in one-third of the Empire. For the remarkable fulfillment of this prediction, see below, our Fulfillment section.

In 12:4b-5a, we read that "The dragon stood in front of the woman who was about to give birth, so that he might devour her child the moment it was born. She gave birth to a son, a male child, "who will rule all the nations with an iron scepter." The birth of the child who will rule with an iron scepter brings to mind the birth of Jesus, but as observed above, this rather too superficial identification ignores the fact that we are expounding events which must take place after this" (4:1), that is, *after* the giving of the Revelation to John on Patmos in A.D. 96. The language is fully capable of this alternate understanding. In fact, the language reflects the imagery of Isa 66:7-16, where the prophet addresses the deliverance of his people, Israel, excerpts from which follow:

> "Can a country be born in a day
>   or a nation be brought forth in a moment?
> Yet no sooner is Zion in labor
>   than she gives birth to her children
> . . . .
> Rejoice with Jerusalem and be glad for her,
>   all you who love her;
> rejoice greatly with her,
>   all you who mourn over her."
> For this is what the LORD says:
> "I will extend peace to her like a river,
>   and the wealth of the nations
>   like a flooding stream" (8b-c, 10, 13a)[12]

---

[12]Another possible figurative use of the childbirth imagery, in this case perhaps indicating the end-time rebirth of the nation of Israel, is found in Mic 5:3, "Therefore Israel will be abandoned until the time when she who is in labor gives birth and the rest of his brethren return to join the Israelites." This "abandonment" follows the birth of the Messiah in Bethlehem (v. 2). The "birth" in v. 3 is followed by the time of Israel's abandonment, during or after which "the rest of his brothers return" from dispersion. Verses 4-5a indicate that this culminates in the peaceful rule of the Messiah whose "greatness will reach to the ends of the earth." The figure is taken of the rebirth of Israel by Calvin, von Orelli, Wolfe, Marsh, and Renaud (Leslie C. Allen, *The Books of Joel, Obadiah, Jonah and Micah* [NICOT; Grand Rapids: Eerdmans, 1976], 345, n. 32).

Chapter Seven — *The woman and the dragon, 12:1-6*

In respect for the verbal accuracy of the Apocalypse, the "childbirth" metaphor must refer to an event future to the Patmos revelation and not to the historical birth of Jesus, which occurred more than 100 years earlier. This being so, the Isaiah prophecy offers the appropriate analogy to Rev 12:5a. We must understand the "birth of the child" as the establishment of some corporate entity analogous to Isaiah's forecast of the Messianic rebirth of Covenant nation of Israel. Beale comments cogently (640-641):

> Specific allusion to Isa. 66:7 is evident from the verbal similarity between Rev. 12:2, 5 (ὠδίνουσα ... τεκεῖν ... καὶ ἔτεχεν υἱὸν ἄρσεν) and Isa. 66:7 (ὠδίνουσαν τεκεῖν ... καὶ ἔτεκεν ἄρσεν; this clause is repeated in v. 8, with ἄρσεν replaced by τὰ παιδία) and from the combination of "son" and "male" in Rev. 12:5, which is based, at least in part, on the close parallelism of Isa. 66:7 with 66:8 in the MT:

Isa. 66:7	Isa. 66:8
She travailed, she brought forth ... she gave birth to a *male* (*zākār*)	Zion *travailed, she also brought forth* her *sons* (plural of *bēn*)

> The singular "male" and the plural "sons" both apparently refer to Israel.[13]

But what of the forecast that the "child" would "rule the nations with an iron scepter" (12:5b)? Psalm 2:9 applies this metaphor to the Messianic King, the Son of David and Rev 19:15 likewise attributes this to the commander of "the armies of heaven," the rider on the white horse. However this language may be applied to the church, as it is in Rev 2:27, suggesting for Rev 12:5b that the church would be "reborn" as a political entity that would come to exercise absolute authority as a sovereign state.

For the Messianic interpretation, see C. F. Keil and F. Delitzsch, *Minor Prophets* (COT; Peabody, Massachusetts: Hendrickson, 1989), 482–84.

[13] In spite of Beale's conclusion that the child forecast in Isa 66:7-8 was Israel and that Rev 12:2 is a specific allusion to that Isaiah text, he nevertheless concludes that the Isaiah text is applied to Christ in Rev 12:2 as an individual, "presumably because he is ideal Israel and represents the nation as their king ... " (641). Perhaps to accommodate his parallel analysis of Revelation, Beale makes this prediction into an historical allusion subject to the objections mentioned above.

Our text continues with the statement that "the child" was "snatched up to God and to his throne" (5c). Given the archetypal prophecies, Isa 66:7 and Rev 2:27, the reader would have needed to understand this "male child" in the metaphorical sense of the temporal sphere. The child is "snatched up to God."[14] This suggests that the newly born corporate entity destined to rule with authority would be elevated to a position recognized by a government dedicated to God and to His church, that is, by a theocratic kingdom (cp. 1 Chr 28:5, 29:23). The "snatching up" of the "male child" to this new sphere of authority would save it from being devoured by the dragon. That is exactly what was to happen, as we shall show in the Fulfillment section below.

What practical principles might the Apostle John's readers have mined from this text? Surely, believers experiencing or expecting persecution would see in the birth and elevation of the "male child" hope for deliverance from persecution, as well as grounds for confidence in the sovereignty of God in history. The woman's flight into the "desert" (v. 6) implies the opposite of the catching up to "heaven." That is, the authorities within the true visible church, at least in general, were to reject the position of authority indicated by "heaven."

12:1-6   **The Woman and the Dragon**   **Notes**

12:1. The terms **great and wondrous** translate for the NIV a single Gk. word, μέγα, *mega,* "great." The **crown** with 12 stars was the diadem (Gk., διαδήμα, *diadēma*). The diadem consisted of two strands of braided gold adorned with pearls and precious gems. The adjective as well as the description which follows suggests that the "sign" thing signified would indeed be highly extraordinary and unanticipated. This is the first revela-

---

[14]That the male child "is snatched up" is further evidence that this does not refer to the ascension of Jesus. The verb, "to snatch" (Gk., ἁρπάζω, *árpazō*), here in the passive voice, conveys the idea of taking up by an outside force or even by aggressive action in which the subject is passive (BAGD, 109). The ascension of Jesus is described in the Gospels as a deliberate and voluntary act of our Lord, surely not suitably described by the passive mode.

tion in the Apocalypse to be characterized as a **sign** (Gk. σημεῖον, *sēmeîon*), i.e., a miraculous sign or portent. Σημεῖον appears subsequently in 12:3; 13:12, 14; 15:1; 16:14; 19:20; the last two refer to false signs of demonic forces. The second or cosmic **heaven** is indicated by the luminaries, and this in the figurative sense is observed earlier in the Apocalypse where cosmic symbols represent human governmental powers (see above, ch. 4, on 6:12-17 with note 49 and the refs. there).[15] The figure, **under her feet** occurs frequently in Scripture, as in Psa 47:3, "He [the Lord] subdued nations under us, peoples under our feet"; more often of the sovereignty of Christ, "He must reign until he has put all enemies under his feet" (1 Cor 15:25; see also 15:27; Eph 1:22; Heb 2:8; Psa 8:6).[16] **2.** The **dragon** or sea serpent (Gk. δράκων, *drákōn*), sometimes named Leviathan or Rahab, is in the Bible a symbol of the evil powers that oppose God (Psa 74:13, 14; Job 3:8; 7:12; 9:13; 26:12, 13; Isa 27:1; et al.).[17] **3.** The **seven crowns** were diadem crowns (Gk. διάδημα, *diádēma*). The diadem crown was oriental in origin, in use by Persian monarchs at the end of the first century. Roman Emperors at this time wore a gilded laurel-wreath crown, an adaptation of the laurel wreath in its natural state awarded to victors in the athletic games or in warfare. **5.** The **scepter**, an ancient symbol of kingly authority, was an adaptation of the shepherd's crook, as illustrated by the numerous gilded examples found in the tomb of King Tutankhamen of Egypt. Normally, these were purely ceremonial but they could be used to beat a victim. An **iron** scepter is thus prepared to execute with absolute authority, including the most severe punishment.

---

[15]Beale cites Isa 60:19-20 and the Song of Songs 6:10, suggesting that the imagery in our text enhances the idea of the church's "incorruptible latter-day faithfulness and relationship with God," 626. However such imagery may enhance the stature of the church, the further description of the "stars" in v. 4 requires that they be identified more objectively with temporal powers understood in a manner comparable to our exposition of 6:13.

[16]An illustration of this can be seen in the temple at Luxor, where the seated statues of Ramses II show his feet resting on footstools on which are engraved images of bound captives of war.

[17]The symbol is found in several of the literatures of the ancient Middle East—Greek mythology as well as Babylonian and Ugaritic texts. See John Day, "God's Conflict with Dragon and Sea," *ABD* (New York: Doubleday, 1999), 228-31.

12:7. **And there was war in heaven. Michael and his angels fought against the dragon, and the dragon and his angels fought back. ⁸But he was not strong enough, and they lost their place in heaven. ⁹The great dragon was hurled down—that ancient serpent called the devil or Satan, who leads the whole world astray. He was hurled to the earth, and his angels with him.**
¹⁰**Then I heard a loud voice in heaven say:**
"Now have come the salvation and the power and the kingdom of our God,
and the authority of his Christ.
For the accuser of our brothers,
who accuses them before our God day and night,
has been hurled down.
¹¹**They overcame him by the blood of the Lamb**
and by the word of their testimony,
they did not love their lives so much as to shrink from death.
¹²**Therefore rejoice, you heavens and you who dwell in them!**
But woe to the earth and the sea,
because the devil has gone down to you!
He is filled with fury,
because he knows that his time is short."

¹³**When the dragon saw that he had been hurled to the earth, he pursued the woman who had given birth to the male child. ¹⁴The woman was given the two wings of a great eagle, so that she might fly to the place prepared for her in the desert, where she would be taken care of for a time, times and half a time, out of the serpent's reach. ¹⁵Then from his mouth the serpent spewed water like a river to overtake the woman and sweep her away with the torrent. ¹⁶But the earth helped the woman by opening its mouth and swallowing the river that the dragon had spewed out of his mouth. ¹⁷Then the dragon was enraged at the woman and went off to make war against the rest of her offspring—those who obey God's commandments and hold to the testimony of Jesus.**

Rev. 12:7-17.   The Woman and the Dragon   Exposition

Verses 1-6 give in concise, cryptic form a summary forecast of the war between the woman and the dragon which is reiterated in more detail in verses 7-17 (cp. vv. 6 & 14).

The casting down of the dragon from "heaven" to "earth" indicates that the Satanic Roman power would lose its position of dominion over the Empire and that Satan would have to resort to other means to continue to war against the church (vv. 8-9). The song which follows presents a three-fold message:

1. The casting down of the Satanic power (pagan Rome) is cause for great rejoicing (vv. 10, 12a).
2. The birth pangs of the woman (v. 2) represent the sufferings of a persecuted church during the period immediately preceding the birth (v. 11).
3. When cast down, Satan will continue his warfare against the people of God (12b)

In characteristic fashion, the song emphasizes the great victory achieved for the church in the birth of the child and the casting down of the Satanic power.

This song is pregnant with theological implications which have profound practical consequences. The angelic singer celebrates the great power of God and the authority of the ascended Christ to exercise providential control of history, to effect salvation, and ultimately to establish His eternal kingdom (12:10). This includes even the control of Satan and his angels so as to limit and ultimately to bring about their defeat (cf. Rev 20:2). Even the martyrs overcome Satan's designs by bearing witness unto death!

12:13-14 pick up on the third part of the song, verse 12:12b. The dragon now pursues the woman who gave birth to the child. The "woman" is providentially enabled to flee to "the wilderness" (cp. v. 6), where she would be protected from the dragon for "a time, times, and half a time" (1260 "days"). This introduction of the "1260 day" motif ties the chronology of this passage with that of Dan 7:25, and also with Rev 11:3. This is the period of the war of the Little Horn against the saints, as well as the prophecy of the Two Witnesses and their war with the Beast (see above, ch. 6, on the Two Witnesses). These verses strongly indicate the Divine providence in providing for the survival of God's true church during the long struggle against the Antichrist power. The "two wings of a great eagle" are promised to her to enable her to fly to "a place prepared for her" where "she would be taken care of" during this bitter time. How precious are such promises of God to His faithful servants during times of persecution! This language recalls Israel's escape from Egypt into the Sinai wilderness where she was to be nurtured by God with manna from heaven (Exod 19:4, Deut 32:11; see further on the metaphor, Beale, pp. 669-671).

In the context of the Apocalyptic metaphor, "the wilderness" probably suggests a state rather than a physical location. In the larger context it is an antonym of the term "heaven" in verse 3. Physical persecution was one of Satan's tactics even before he was thrown down (6:9-11, 12:11), and probably would have been understood to continue from verses 15-17, as later under the beast (ch. 13). The association of John the Baptist and the Qumran covenantors with the desert may have suggested to the original readers that the true church would flee from doctrinal or liturgical excesses that might invade the newly elevated church, disassociating from them and preserving a true witness to the Gospel.[18]

The next ploy of the Serpent is to spew water like a river and so to sweep her away, destroying her with the torrent (12:15). "But the earth helped the woman by opening its mouth and swallowing the river . . . " (v. 16). This strange language appears to indicate that the Satanic power represented by the serpent would continue its warfare against the woman. Beale, after giving extensive documentation from the Old Testament, the Dead Sea Scrolls, and rabbinic texts, states, " . . . OT and Jewish use of the flood waters metaphor and the use of mouth metaphors in the Apocalypse indicate that the image of the flood proceeding from the serpent's mouth portrays his attempt to destroy the church by deception and false teaching . . . " (p. 673). However, by some remarkable providence "the earth would swallow the water" so that Satan would be rebuked and the church spared. This would provoke the Dragon to great rage in which he would go "off to make war against the rest of her offspring—those who obey God's commandments and

---

[18]The Apostle John and other believers in the churches of the Roman province of Asia would remember the Qumran convenanters of the Dead Sea Scrolls who fled from Jerusalem into the Judean wilderness to escape the corruptions of the Jerusalem establishment and to preserve the true doctrines and priestly rites as they understood them. For these Essenes "the desert" became of symbol of their perceived orthodoxy.

hold to the testimony of Jesus."[19] Here we have a fine definition of the covenant people of God of both Testaments. We may rightly view the Old Testament law, both moral and ceremonial, as revealed and fulfilled in the testimony of Jesus, both in His teaching and in His life (cp. 14:3-5).

The distinction between the woman and "the rest of her offspring," given that the woman is a symbol for the church at the time of her giving birth to the "male child," must be understood as those who had subsequently been "born" to the woman.[20] Their description as "those who obey God's commandments and hold to the testimony of Jesus" suggests faithful believers in distinction from merely nominal Christians who would not have embraced the true Gospel.[21]

The drama of chapter 12 concludes as John sees the dragon standing on the shore of the sea (13:1). Apparently this Satanic power waits ominously for the scene recorded in chapter 13 to transpire.

---

[19]The reference to *the rest of the woman's offspring* in distinction from the male child (v. 5), would be hardly appropriate were the male child a reference to the birth of Jesus. If the woman were the literal mother of Jesus, the partitive expression would require that "rest of her offspring" also be literal children born to Mary. If the figure conceives of Jesus as having been given birth by the church, the partitive expression is hardly more appropriate. Moreover, the church did not give birth to Jesus but Jesus gave birth to the church.

[20]Were the "male child" to be understood of Jesus' birth, would not "the rest of her offspring" demean the uniqueness of Jesus' birth by putting the "male child" in the same category as ordinary human beings?

[21]We reject the sabbatarian doctrine that this text describes true believers as those who keep Saturday as the true Sabbath. Hebrews 4:9 teaches that the Old Testament sabbath law has its fulfillment in the atoning work of Christ: "There remains, then, a Sabbath-rest for the people of God, for anyone who enters God's rest also rests from his own work, just as God did from his." This indicates that the Sabbath, as a commemoration of God's creation rest, has its fulfillment for the believer in his appropriation of Christ's atonement. So also the Apostle Paul states, "Do not let any man judge you by what you eat or drink, or with regard to a religious festival, a New Moon celebration or a Sabbath day. These are a shadow of the things that were to come; the reality, however, is found in Christ" (Col 2:16, 17). We are dealing here with type and antitype.

12:7-17.   The Woman and the Dragon (cont'd)   Notes

12:7. War in heaven indicates conflict between the forces of good and evil. **Heaven** here indicates the sphere of political ascendancy. The figure derives from the common association of the cosmic bodies with the pagan gods and with the authority of human rulers (see above, p. 151-154 with notes 74, 75). We assume that Christians living under Domitian's persecutions should have identified the Satanic power with Rome, so a time is predicted when Rome would abandon her oppressive dominance over the people of God. Michael is the archangel who protects the covenant people (Dan 10:21, 12:1). The Bible sometimes represents such battles as fought both in heaven and on earth, by spirit beings and by human earthly forces. **8.** The dragon and his angels lost **their place in heaven**, that is, the pagan dragon forces lost their political dominance in the Empire. **9. The great dragon** was **hurled to the earth**. This cannot apply to the primordial fall of Satan or to some other event already history when the Apocalypse was written, as Satan was operative *on earth* when the prediction of "things to come" was given. We must take "heaven" and "earth," therefore, in this context as figurative expressions in harmony with the ancient use of such celestial and terrestrial terms as authority metaphors.

10-12. The musical interlude celebrates the great victory of the church over the forces of evil forecast in the preceding verses. **11.** The song refers to the past victory of saints who had at the time of the event predicted in the preceding verses **overcome by the blood of the Lamb** and by their valiant witness to the Gospel, even to the extent that they did not **shrink from death**. We are reminded of Rev 6:9-11, the souls of the martyrs crying out from under the altar in the fifth seal (Cp. Rom 12:1). **12. The earth and the sea**, in distinction from "the heavens" must in this context indicate that temporal sphere in which Satan must act while deprived of the authority of a temporal state. **The devil has gone down**

to you reiterates the "hurling down" of the dragon in v. 9 while focusing on the Devil's on-going war to be described in vv. 13-17.

13. The two wings of a great eagle indicate God's powerful providence in enabling his true church to find wilderness sanctuary. The **torrent** reflects the rather common circumstance in the eastern Mediterranean world in which a dry stream bed which offers convenient camp site or travel lane may with some distant rain become a deadly flood, sweeping all in its path.

12:1-17.   The Woman & the Dragon   Fulfillment

In our exposition above, we concluded our analysis of the Little Scroll message by observing that its chronology is in general independent from the message of the Seven-sealed Scroll. Chapter 11, with its message regarding the witness of the faithful martyr church during many years of apostasy, ends with both an anticipatory song by the twenty-four elders celebrating the eventual victory of God's people and a somber warning of judgments still to come with the pouring out of the seven bowls of wrath (chs. 15-16).

Thus, we have in chapters 12-13 another interlude which conditions the reader for understanding the rise of the Antichrist power and the conduct of its war against the saints.

To understand the fulfillment of the events forecast in 12:1-17, one needs to focus on the time when the dragon power, that is the pagan Roman Empire, wore the diadem. This period in Roman history began when the Emperor Diocletian introduced the diadem as his Imperial crown in the year 293 (Katz, p. 45; Ferrero, pp. 91-92). Prior to that time the laurel wreath crown was ordinarily used. The appearance of the diadems on the heads of the dragon is clear indication of the detailed accuracy of this temporal prophecy. In the symbolism of the first seal, which as we have seen clearly points to the Cretan dynasty of emperors in the late first and second centuries, the laurel wreath crown is worn (see above on Rev 6:1-2).

The introduction of the diadem crown was part of a new constitution introduced by Diocletian which was far reaching in its effects, so far reaching in fact that this newly constituted empire appears to be the seventh head of the dragon which at the time of the Revelation was "yet to come" (Rev 17:10).²²"Gibbon calls him [Diocletian] a second Augustus, the founder of a new empire, rather than the restorer of the old."²³ R. A. G. Carson thus describes his reorganization of the crumbling Empire: "The reign of Diocletian is one of the last great milestones in the history of Rome, for there was hardly one aspect of imperial civilization that the reforming hand of Diocletian left untouched, and what he created or refurbished provided the political, military and economic institutions by which the empire survived in the West for close on another two centuries . . . ." The appearance of the diadem on the dragon at this juncture is a remarkable confirmation of our continuous-historicist understanding of the Revelation, as this New Imperial constitution indicated by the "seventh head" had shortly before the birth of the state church under Constantine been introduced by Diocletian. It was the Imperial philosophy of his successor, Constantine, as well.²⁴

We have seen that the church's being "clothed with the sun" (12:1) indicates her recognition by the governing power, the Roman State, by which she was to be emancipated from bitter persecution (above on Rev 12:1). This came about as the four emperors established by Diocletian' reorganization of the Empire fought out their rival interests until Constantine eventually became sole emperor.

---

²²Apparently the diadem was first worn as a Roman ensign by the Emperor Aurelian (A.D. 270-275; Elliott, 3:537-538) and was subsequently ten years later institutionalized for emperors of the rank of Augustus by Diocletian. The identification of the first six heads and the eighth (see above on Rev 12:3) was correctly made by many commentators from Reformation times. They include Osiander (1544), Fulco (1573), Aretius (1581), Eicasmi (1587), Napier (1593), Brightman (1644), Pareus (1644), as documented by Elliott, 3.116, n. 2. To these may be added Mede (1648), Durham (1799), Scott (1808), M'Leod (1814), Elliott (1844), Wordsworth (1849), Barnes (1852), Guinness (1878), Cachemaille (1911), Barton (1963), Vandervaal (1971), Lee (2000).

²³Philip Schaff, *History of the Christian Church* (Grand Rapids: Eerdmans, 1950), 2.65, from Gibbon, *The History of the Decline and Fall of the Roman Empire* (New ed.; New York: Harper & Brothers, n.d.) 1.403.

²⁴ R. A. G. Carson, "From Tiber's Seven Hills to World Dominion," in *The Birth of Western Civilization: Greece and Rome* (ed. Michael Grant; New York: McGraw-Hill, 1964), 240. Carson's description includes the following: "In an overhaul of the provincial system, the provinces were reduced in size, and the consequently increased number of 101 provinces organized in larger units called dioceses, of which there were twelve, each in charge of a *vicarius*. Military command was now removed from the governor of a province and entrusted to an independent commander with the title of *dux*. The distinction between offices which could be held by senators and equestrian officers disappeared; there remained now only the one imperial civil service with it strictly ordered hierarchies." (240)

Chapter Seven *The woman and the dragon, 12:7-17* 289

Verse 4a states that the tail of the dragon swept "a third of the stars out of the sky and flung them to the earth." At this time, the Roman Empire was divided into three parts. Constantine and Licinius ruled Britain, Gaul, Spain, much of North Africa, and Italy. Galerius ruled the Eastern third (Egypt, Syria, and Asia Minor). Licinius, with Galerius and Constantine published an edict of toleration April 13, A.D. 311, thus giving official Imperial recognition to Christianity and putting for that time an end to persecution. However, when Galerius died the following month, he was succeeded as Emperor in the East by Maximin. As a final thrust in the dragon's war, Maximin resumed the persecution and deprived the church in his third of the empire of their newfound Imperial status. As a remarkable fulfillment of prophecy, the Dragon's tail swept a third of the stars out of the sky and flung them too the earth" (12:4).

The conversion of the Emperor Constantine to Christianity occurred as a result of his famous victory over Maxentius under the sign of the cross at Milvian Bridge, Oct 28, 312. As the war between rival emperors continued, Licinius defeated Maximin April 30, 313. Licinius became Emperor in the East and for a time restored there the status of Christianity. The Milan Edict of Toleration followed, giving to Christians and to the churches freedom to worship and to practice their faith, ending the severe birth pangs which had climaxed under the Emperors Diocletian and Galerius with their attempt to eradicate Christianity. (Subsequently, Licinius, himself, apostatized and again disenfranchised the Eastern churches, renewing persecutions [Eusebius, 433; bk. 10, ch. 8; Elliott, 3.22]).

Constantine transferred his authoritarian concept of government, as established for the new Empire by Diocletian, to the Catholic Church, giving birth to the "male child," a new state church "caught up" to the "heaven" of Imperial authority and power. As stated by Philip Schaff, the Constantinian toleration "opened the door to the elevation of Christianity, and specifically of Catholic hierarchical Christianity, with its exclusiveness towards heretical and schismatic sects, to be the religion of the state" (3.30-31). This state-church was to rule the nations of the Roman Empire with a "rod of iron," claiming and exercising absolute power in league with the "ten horns"or "kings" (see below on 13:1) during the time of the 1260 years.

The "war in heaven" between Michael and the dragon and their angels had its counterpart with the competing generals of the Empire— Constantine under the banner of the cross against the pagan forces. Diocletian had committed suicide; Galerius had died of a loathsome disease. Maxentius was killed near Rome in the famous battle of Milvian Bridge.[25]

After Constantine's victory over Maxentius, the pagan emperors Maximin and Licinius remained. Maximin, after taking Byzantium, was defeated by Licinius. He died in the summer of 313. The following year, Licinius gave rise to a dispute over the status of Illyricum, a territory claimed by Constantine north of the Adriatic Sea between the Eastern and Western Empires. Constantine went to battle to retain the territory and won. Licinius, after another rebellion, was put to death in 325.[26]

Thus, Constantine gained supremacy over the entire Roman Empire and "the great dragon was hurled down—that ancient serpent called the devil or Satan" (v. 9). Satan lost the means of Imperial Rome to wage his war against the church.

The Apocalyptic drama celebrates this forecast victory with a heavenly choir (12:10-12). It announces that "salvation and the power and the kingdom of our God" have come in this casting down of the pagan Satanic forces by Constantine and it lauds the martyrs who had not shrunk from death in their witnessing to the truth of the Gospel of Jesus Christ (cf. 11:3-10). The deliverance from the persecuting power of pagan Rome in the fourth century was indeed a great deliverance which enabled the church to freely proclaim the Gospel. The choir also warns of woes to come for the Devil is angry and "knows that his time is short" (12:12).[27]

The Devil, though not now dominating the powers of state, is on the loose in the "earthly" realm. The woman flies into the wilderness, where she is to remain for "a time, times, and half a time," or 1260 years. On the fulfillment of the mysterious time period, see below, our commentary on 13:5. It is important at this point to remind the reader that the "woman" represents the true visible church. While the "male child" is "caught up to heaven," the "woman" is not. The true visible church is distinguished in this passage from the newly born state church.

The newly born state church was of very different character from the "woman" from whom it was born. Constantine, as stated by William

---

[25]H. M. Gwatkin, "Constantine and His City," in *The Cambridge Medieval History* (New York: Macmillan, 1924), 1.4–5.

[26]Gwatkin 1.5–8

[27]This warning at the end of the choral interlude (12:10-12) should caution the reader not to assume that the introduction of a heavenly chorus celebrating the arrival of the kingdom indicates that the end has arrived at this point in the prophecy. The interlude divides the Apocalyptic vision into several parallel historical predictions. These proleptic announcements which point to the end-time celebration are intended to heighten the believer's hope during times of suffering. 19:1-8, the last of such interludes is the exception, as the end is at this point about to occur!

Jones, "produced an entire change in the whole of the Christian profession" (284). The restraint which resulted from the persecuting power of Rome "was wholly taken off by Constantine, the churches endowed, and riches and honours liberally conferred on the clergy . . . " (Jones, 285). The government of the church was reorganized after the model of the state with the status and authority of the bishops greatly enhanced. Constantine even took to himself the title of bishop and exercised authority over the external affairs of the church (Jones, 286). In the wake of the Arian controversy, he even required the death penalty, not only for pagan idolaters but even for Christian dissidents.

During the second and third centuries, Christians under persecution had been driven to the simplicity of the Gospel, seeking through patient humility and love to participate in Christ's sufferings and to realize their hope for life and immortality in the future kingdom. With the newly established state-sponsored church in the fourth century there was both an influx of nominally converted pagans and a tendency among all believers toward a formal externalism, as exhibited especially by the newly exalted bishops. This condition created a gulf between the Male Child, the catholic state church, and the Woman, the true visible church. Thus, she was given "the two wings of a great eagle, so that she might fly away into the desert" (v. 14).

We have observed above that the image of a flood proceeding from the serpent's mouth indicates a Satanic attempt to destroy the true church by deception and false teaching (Jones, 286). This is commonly understood by historicist interpreters as having been fulfilled by the intrusion of Arianism into the Empire. After the defeat of Arianism at the Council of Nicea in A.D. 325, Arianism still tended to dominate in the Eastern Church, and with the establishment of an Arian Emperor in the person of Constantine's son, Constantius, it came to prevail in the Western Church as well. Constantius ruled in the East from 337-353, then as sole Emperor from 353 until his death in 361. As the fourth century progressed, there was also an influx of Arian barbarians. After the death of Constantius, the Emperor Valens (364-378) continued vigorously to promote Arian doctrine. It remained for the powerful emperor, Theodosius I, to take strong actions officially to purge the Empire of Arianism, including the convening of the Council of Constantinople, where it was formally condemned in A.D. 381. Nevertheless, Arianism continued among the barbarians who invaded the Empire in several regions well into sixth century. (Schaff 3.632-641)

"The earth helped the woman by opening its mouth and swallowing the river" from the dragon's mouth (v. 16b). Cachemaille offers this explanation (421):

Superstitious and earthly-minded though the Roman population had become, they did service to Christ's Church in her present need. There was an absorption of the invading barbaric flood into the old settled Roman population; and not only were much of their original institutions, customs, and languages absorbed, but also their religion altogether. They were converted, at least nominally, to the Christian faith. Instead of barbaric paganism or Arianism, the Christian Trinitarian creed was at last universally adopted . . . .

Now in John's vision he saw that the dragon, enraged by his defeat "went off to make war against the rest of her offspring—those who obey God's commandments and hold to the testimony of Jesus" (v. 17). This characterization of the Woman's offspring suggests a distinction between the "run of the mill" in the true visible church and those who are seen as genuine believers. Jesus taught that in his kingdom there must grow together both "good seed" (wheat) and "weeds" (darnel).[28] There will always be professing Christians who will not pass muster in the final judgment (Matt 13:24-30). The characterization of 12:17b implies those whose faith is committed obediently to the true Gospel. This text leaves this effort of the dragon unexplored. The implication, as he stands on the shore of the sea (13:1), is that this will be addressed in what follows in chapter 13.

We have now arrived at section 5 of our outline of the Little Scroll (see above, Introduction to ch. Six): "The Beast from the Sea and the Beast from the Earth."

*The Beast out of the Sea*1

3:1. **And the dragon stood on the shore of the sea.**

And I saw a beast coming out of the sea. He had ten horns and seven heads, with ten crowns on his horns, and on each head a blasphemous name. ²The beast I saw resembled a leopard, but had feet like those of a bear and a mouth like that of a lion. The dragon gave the beast his power and his throne and great authority. ³One of the heads of the beast seemed to have had a fatal wound, but the fatal wound had been healed. The whole world was astonished and followed the beast. ⁴Men worshiped the dragon because he had given

---

[28]Darnel is an eastern weed that mimics wheat until it ripens, when it turns gray instead of the golden color of wheat. As it is poisonous, it cannot be milled with the wheat. Jesus taught that this is like the kingdom, as both must be left to grow together until harvest when the "wheat" will be separated from the "darnel."

authority to the beast, and they also worshiped the beast and asked, "Who is like the beast? Who can make war against him?"

13:1-4   **The Beast from the Sea**   **Exposition**

As the Apostle John watched the Apocalyptic drama unfold before him, the dragon came to stand on the shore of the sea, as if in anticipation of the arrival of his accomplice from the Satanic underworld. Then John saw rising out of the sea a beast with ten horns and seven heads (v. 1). On his horns were ten crowns and on each of his heads a blasphemous name. The ten horns suggest identification with the ten-horned beast of Dan 7:7, as well as the ten horns of the dragon. The seven heads suggest that the beast, like the dragon, is a symbol representing the Satanic power of the Roman Empire (on this identification, see above on Rev 12:1-6). The diadem crowns are located on the horns, whereas the dragon was seen wearing them on his heads. This suggests a time for the rise of the beast when the ten kingdoms have been established with their rule in place.[29] The blasphemous names on the heads of the beast reflect the fact that the Romans exalted their emperors as gods and had created an imperial cult which required their worship.

The beast is further characterized as "resembling a leopard," but having "feet like those of a bear," and a mouth "like that of a lion"(v. 2a). This allusive language proves the identification of this beast with the fourth beast in Daniel 7, except that here the fourth beast has characteristics of each of the previous three. One need not

---

[29]Those scholars who advocate a trans-temporal interpretation of such symbols in the Apocalypse appear to be influenced by the modern disaffection for the detailed prediction of temporal events which characterized the divinely interpreted visions of Daniel (Dan 2:37-45; 4:19-33; 7:17-27. Note Daniel's testimony to Nebuchadnezzar: "The great God has shown the king what will take place in the future. The dream is true and the interpretation is trustworthy" (2:45b). Rev 4:1 states, "Come up here and I will show you what will take place after this." Given the comparable apocalyptic style of the visions of Daniel and the vision of Revelation and the instruction that the Revelation is given "to show what must take place after this," one should not dismiss as inappropriate the understanding that specific mundane occurrences with their definition and frequency are indicated by the details of the symbolism.

assume that this is to indicate the continuing coexistence of those earlier world kingdoms (Greek, Persian, and Babylonian).[30] It rather suggests that the fierce powers of this fourth beast include the speed to the kill of the Greek "leopard," the powerful feet of the Persian "bear," and the ravenous mouth of the Babylonian "lion."

We next learn that "the dragon gave the beast his power and his throne and great authority" (v. 2b). Because, as was apparent to the original readers, the beast is the fourth beast of Daniel 7 and therefore represents the Roman Imperial government, this statement indicates that the beast is to operate as an agent of Satan. This should be understood from the standpoint of the teaching of our Lord that there are two kingdoms, the kingdom of God and the kingdom of Satan (Matt 12:26). The beast belongs to the latter. As the pagan Roman Imperial throne was the agent through which the dragon operated prior to his being cast down (12:9, 13), so this Roman throne was to be given to the beast.

"One of the heads of the beast seemed to have had a fatal wound, but the fatal wound had been healed" (v. 3). As observed above on 12:3, the heads of the beast represent successive constitutional governments, five of which had existed as "heads" of the Roman Empire when the Apocalypse was written. The sixth was at that time currently in existence, ruled by the Emperor Domitian. The "fatal wound" which appeared on one of the heads apparently indicates a time which at the end of the first century had not yet occurred, a time when the Roman Empire would fall, but later would be reconstituted when the "fatal wound" was "healed." This resurrected "head" is referred to in 17:11 as an "eighth king," that is, kingdom. The resurrection of the seventh head to become an eighth was envisioned as having occurred when the beast arose from the sea, as the text states, "the fatal wound *had been* healed" (italics mine). Thus, the beast from the sea must represent an eighth Roman Imperial government which would arise after the fall of Rome as represented by the seventh head which "suffered a mortal wound."

---

[30]The unhistorical order in which these characteristics are introduced also argues against an intention to indicate the coexistence of these kingdoms.

Our text states that "the whole world was astonished and followed the beast" (3b), worshiping both the beast and the dragon from whom the beast had received his authority. The new Rome empowered by Satan, was to capture the wonder of the Roman world for its irresistible authority and power (4).

The depravity of the human race is reflected in verse 4, which states that men "worshiped the dragon because he had given authority to the beast and they also worshiped the beast" because they admired his great power: "Who is like the beast? Who can make war against him?"

13:1-4	The Beast from the Sea	Notes

1. In the ancient world **the sea** was commonly regarded as "the habitat of evil deities that ruled the world. Storms at sea were an expression of the wrath of the sea gods. In the Semitic world there was a belief that the sea personified the power that fought against the deity.[31] In the highly figurative language of the Hebrew poetry, Yahweh is sometimes represented as defeating Rahab, probably a mythological symbol of the power of a raging sea: "You rule over the surging sea; . . . . You crushed Rahab like one of the slain . . . (Psa 89:9a, 10a). **2.** The dragon gave **his power** and his throne and great authority to the beast. "His power" (Gk. τὴν δύναμιν αὐτοῦ, *tēn dúnamin aútoû*), here when associated with his authority, probably indicates his ability to do miracles (cp. 1 Cor 12:10, "the ability to do miracles" [Gk. ἐνεργήματα δυνάμεων, *energēmata dunámeōn*]). Paul describes the coming of the Antichrist as "in accordance with the work of Satan, displayed in all kinds of counterfeit miracles, signs and wonders . . . " (2 Thess 2:9). **His throne** indicates that the dragon rules over Satan's kingdom and gives that rule to the Antichrist beast (John 12:31, 14:30, 16:11; 2 Cor 4:4; Eph 2:2). Our Lord's letter to the church in Pergamum indicates that Satan's throne was located in that city (Rev 2:13), probably a reference to the fact that the headquarters for the Roman Imperial cult of Pontifex Maximus was located there. The ruins of that Imperial cult center-temple can be seen to this day outside the wall at the

---

[31]*IBD*, 3.1406; cited in G. B. Caird, *A Commentary on the Revelation of St. John the Divine* (New York, Harper & Row, 1966), 244, n. 6.

east entrance to the city (see illus., p. 76). Rev 16:10 indicates that when the fifth bowl was to be poured out it would be on the throne of the beast, or Rome. Satan's **great authority** is described in Luke 4:5-6, where it states that Satan led Jesus "up to a high place and showed him in an instant all the kingdoms of the world. And he said to him, 'I will give you all their authority and splendor, for it has been given to me . . . .'" This authority he was to give to the beast. **3.** Which **one of the heads** was to suffer the **fatal wound** is not indicated but the mysterious formula introduced in 17:8 and 11 appears to indicate that it was to be the seventh. The formula reads, "The beast . . . was and is not and is about to rise up out of the abyss" (τὸ θηρίον . . . ἦν καὶ οὐκ ἔστιν, καὶ μέλλει ἀναβαίνειν ἐκ τῆς ἀβύσσου, tò thēríon . . . *hên kaì oúk 'éstin kaì méllei 'anabaínein 'ek tēs 'abússou;* 17:8). The formula is repeated in verse 11 but with the beast from the abyss identified as "an eighth king." The formula functions as descriptive of the beast as he is defined by his several heads or constitutional governments (see above, p. 284).[32] "The beast who was and is not" is a cryptic allusion to the "fatal wound" of the seventh head and the beast "that is to come up from the abyss" (17:8) is "an eighth" (17:11)." The eighth "belongs to the seventh and is going to his destruction" (17:11; cp. Dan 7:11, 26). Because the eighth "belongs to the seventh," we know that the beast from the abyss is another manifestation of the Roman government. **The whole world** here as in previous references refers at least primarily to the Roman world or the world as known at the end of the first century.

The Beast from the Sea (cont'd)

13:5. The beast was given a mouth to utter proud words and blasphemies and to exercise his authority for forty-two months. ⁶He opened his mouth to blaspheme God, and to slander his name and his dwelling place and those who live in heaven. ⁷He was given power to make war against the saints and to conquer them. And he was given authority over them. And he was given authority over every tribe, people, language and nation. ⁸All inhabitants of the earth will worship the beast—all whose

---

[32]Note that the formularies for the beast who "is not" and "is about to arise" are both gnomic presents, as is appropriate for such a mystic, descriptive formula.

names have not been written in the book of life belonging to the Lamb that was slain from the creation of the world.

⁹He who has an ear, let him hear.

¹⁰If anyone is to go into captivity,
into captivity he will go.
If anyone is to be killed with the sword,
with the sword he will be killed.

This calls for patient endurance and faithfulness on the part of the saints.

13:5-10   The Beast from the Sea (cont'd)   Exposition

The Beast from the Sea of Revelation 13 (cf. Dan 7:7) is a reincarnation of the Dragon (12:3). Both have seven heads and ten horns. Both are agents of Satan, expressions of his power and authority. Several conclusions regarding this beast were reached in our exposition of verses 1-4. *First*, it is to be identified with Rome, specifically, the Roman Imperial government. *Second*, it is described as the successor to the dragon, which as we concluded earlier represents pagan Rome as animated by Satan (see above on 12:3). *Third*, Rome under its seventh head was to have suffered a fatal wound, suggesting the temporary demise of the Empire known to the recipients of the Revelation near the close of the first Christian century. *Fourth*, with the rise of the beast from the abyss as the eighth head (constitutional government) with its seat in Rome, Satan was to have a new agency to which he was to give his authority to carry on his antichristian war against Christ and His church.

This beast is characterized by his proud words and blasphemies. This serves as commentary on Dan 7:8, 20 which states that the Little Horn "spoke boastfully" as well as the Apostle Paul's commentary in 2 Thess 2:4: "He exalts himself over everything that is called God or that is worshiped . . . ." So Rev 13:6 states that the beast was "to blaspheme God, and to slander his name, and his dwelling place, and those who live in heaven."

The beast was to be given power to make war against the saints (v. 7). The question naturally arises as to who was to give this power to the beast. The answer may be found in verse 4 where it states that the dragon "had given authority to the beast." Nevertheless, within the larger context of the Revelation, we are informed that it is God who is "the Alpha and the Omega . . . who is, and who was, and who is to come, the Almighty" (1:8) and it is Jesus Christ who is "the First and the Last" and who holds "the keys of death and Hades." As with Job, the Sovereign God permits Satan and his agents to wage this war but only within His providence and greater purpose.

The authority of the beast to wage war was to last for "forty-two months." This is the same period of time that is assigned in Daniel as "time, times, and half a time" (7:25), in Revelation for the nations to "trample down the Holy City" (11:2), for the "two witnesses" to prophesy" (11:3), and for the "woman" to be nourished in the wilderness" (11:6, 14). These time periods are all the same length, 1260 days, or according to the symbolic use of this time period on the year-day principle, 1260 years (see our remarks on 6:2-3 above, and in Appendix 2).

This war is the Apocalyptic commentary on the war of the little horn of the fourth beast described in Dan 7:21. In Daniel, he is distinguished by his boastful speaking against the Most High and his trying to change the set times and the laws (7:25). The Apostle Paul in 2 Thess 2:3 calls this horn "the man of lawlessness."[33] The Apostle refers to the war as "the rebellion" (Gk. ἡ ἀποστασία, *he*

---

[33] We believe, with most all historicist commentators that when the Apostle appeals to the coming of the man of lawlessness as an established authoritative doctrine that must be fulfilled before the second advent of the Lord, he is appealing to the prophecy of the Little Horn Antichrist of Daniel 7. This is borne out not only from the assertion that revelation of the man of lawlessness must occur but also by the correspondences between the description of the little horn in Daniel 7 and that of the man of lawlessness in 2 Thessalonians 2. Both are described as boastful, blasphemous, as waging war against the saints 1260 "days," and destined to destruction by the Lord at his coming.

apostasía). The occurrence with the article indicates a known entity. The word may also mean "apostasy." Whether the Apostle meant to describe the war more definitively as apostasy will be addressed in the Fulfillment section below.

Whether the predicted Little Horn, the Man of Lawlessness, was to be a single person or an institutional government is a much debated question among the several schools of Apocalyptic interpretation. Because the Little Horn is the basis of Paul's description, we should look to Daniel for any clue that might help us answer the question. In the visions of Daniel 2 and 7, the symbols usually represent national powers rather than individuals. The exception is Daniel 4, a vision which pertains to the personal history of Nebuchadnezzar, there represented as a "tree." In Daniel 2, Nebuchadnezzar is said to be "the head of gold." The head of the image is succeeded by "the chest and arms," representing Persia. No mention is made in the vision of the historical fact that included in the "head" were several more kings—Evil-Merodach, Neriglissar, Labashi-Marduk, and Nabonidus. The same multiplicity of rulers remains true for the rest of the kingdoms represented by the image, except of course for the fifth kingdom, the stone cut from the mountain, whose sole king is Messiah Jesus. The same multiplicity of rulers are indicated by the emblems of the four beasts in Daniel 7. What shall we say of the ten horns on Daniel's fourth beast? The horns are identified in the interpretation of the vision as "ten kings" (Dan 7:24). As the Little Horn symbol, so also the ten horns represent kingdoms rather than ten individual kings. As these horns arise "out of" the fourth kingdom, they must represent a subsequent or later stage in the development of the Roman Empire.[34]

---

[34]Keil commenting on Dan 7:17-18 states, "The kings are named as founders and representatives of world-kingdoms. Four kingdoms are meant, as v. 23 shows, where the fourth beast is explained as מַלְכוּ, [*malkhû*] 'dominion,' 'kingdom,'" Compare also ch. viii.20 and 21, where in like manner kings are named and kingdoms are meant. (Keil, *Daniel*, 238). Pusey states, "Throughout these prophecies the king represents the kingdom, and the kingdom is concentrated in its king. *The kings* then or *kingdoms* which should *arise out of* this kingdom, must, from the force of the term as well as from the context, be *kings* or *kingdoms* which should arise at some later stage of its existence, not those first kings without which it could not be a kingdom at all. For these do not arise out of it, but are a part of it" (79).

As the Little Horn is described in Dan 7:8 as arising among them, they must represent Roman kingdoms which were to be in place contemporaneously with the eighth head.

The beast "was given authority over every tribe, people, language and nation" (7). In the context of the first century Roman world, one need not understand this as referring to the entire globe but it is a statement that more probably has as its referent the world of the Roman Empire with its ten kingdoms.[35]

"All the inhabitants of the earth" again refers most probably to the Roman world. With the introduction of worship in v. 8, we are reminded of the Apostle's statement, a statement with which the first readers of the Revelation probably were aware, in 2 Thess 2:4 that the man of lawlessness even "sets himself up in God's temple" and therefore makes himself an object of worship. The word, "Temple," occurs with the article, ὁ ναός, *hò naós*, "the sanctuary." After the Roman destruction of the Jerusalem temple in A.D. 70, there was only one "temple" familiar to the readers of the Revelation that could be called "the sanctuary of God" and that was the church of Jesus Christ, as Paul had stated to the Corinthians, "You yourselves are God's temple [ναὸς θεοῦ, *naòs theoû*] . . . (1 Cor 3:16)." The original readers had sufficient information to infer from Scripture that the coming Antichrist would conduct his war from within the sanctuary of the Christian church.[36] There is a significant qualification to the multitudes who worship the beast. They consist of "all whose names have not been written in the book of

---

[35]Cachemaille states accordingly, "There must be limitation of these expressions according the context and the facts of history. Absolute universality cannot be insisted on. . . . . The 'people, tongues, and nations' are, as comparison with Daniel's prophecy proves those represented by the Ten Horns" (452; see Dan 3:4, 29; 4:1; 5:19; 6:25; 7:14]). The references in Daniel illustrate the bearing of context on the expression. All except 7:14 are limited to the particular kingdom in view. In this last instance, the expression is qualified by the interpretation, "Then the sovereign power and greatness of the kingdoms under the whole heaven will be handed over to the saints, the people of the Most High" (Dan 7:27).

[36]This conclusion should also have been implicit in the "harlot" motif of Revelation 17, as the Old Testament prophets had developed this extensively relative to the apostasy of Israel, the Covenant People, the bride of Yahweh (cf. Ezek 16:1-43; 23:1-49, et al.) See below on Ch. 17.

life belonging to the Lamb that was slain from the creation of the world." They do not include those who were sealed in 7:1-8 in anticipation of the tribulation and who are seen by John proleptically in 7:13-17 standing before the throne of God and before the Lamb, "a great multitude that no one could count, from every nation, tribe, people and language" (v. 9). They appear again in 14:1-5 singing the song of redemption as "purchased from among men" and "offered as firstfruits to God." The remainder of the "harvest" appears in chapter 19 singing the Halelujah Chorus!

So the first readers of the Revelation who faced the prospect of the Roman Beast, as well as those through the centuries following, have had in this great book a sure hope of their redemption and eternal glory. We can read today the witness of many who died in this war singing hymns of praise and confidence in God and in their eternal reward.

This section of our text ends with a solemn announcement, "He who has an ear, let him hear":

> If anyone is to go into captivity,
> into captivity he will go.
> If anyone is to be killed with the sword,
> with the sword he will be killed (vv. 9, 10a).

We are reminded here that it may be the destiny of some of us who are numbered among the redeemed even to be enslaved or to lay down our lives in testimony to the Lamb. The call is "for patient endurance and faithfulness on the part of the saints" (v. 10b).

13:5-10   The Beast from the Sea (cont'd)   Notes

The text here draws on Daniel 7 in such a way as to provide an expanded commentary:

Dan 7:8 LXX	Rev 13:5
There before me was another horn, a little one . . . . This horn had . . . a mouth that spoke boastfully [Gk., στόμα λαλοῦν μεγάλα].	The beast was given a mouth to utter proud words and blasphemies [Gk., στόμα λαλοῦν μεγάλα].
Dan 7:25b	Rev 13:5
He will . . . oppress his saints . . . . The saints will be handed over to him	He was given power to make war against the saints and to conquer them.
for a time, times and half a time [3½ years, or forty-two months; cp. 12:6, 7].	The beast was given . . . to exercise his authority for forty-two months [cp. 11:2, 3, 12:6, 14b]
Dan 7:10b	Rev 13:8
The court was seated, and the books were opened.	All the inhabitants of the earth will worship the beast—all whose names have not been written in the book of life . . . .

13:5, 7. The passive voice, **the beast *was given* [Gk. ἐδόθη, *edóthē*] a mouth**, emphasizes the permissive Providence in allowing the Satanic power to blaspheme and oppose God. This passive construction is repeated in v. 7, **he was given power to make war** (literally, "it was given to him to make war" [Gk., ἐδόθη αὐτῷ ποιῆσαι πόλεμον, *edóthē autǭ poiēsai pólemon*]), and **he was given authority [ἐξουσία, *exousía*]. 8. All the inhabitants of the earth,** literally translated, reads, "all those dwelling upon the earth." "All" is delimited by what follows, "All whose names have not been written in the book of life . . . ." Perhaps the reader might further be justified in understanding this as a generalization rather than an absolute statement.

9. He who has an ear, let him hear echoes the earlier statements of Jesus in Matt 11:15; Rev 2:7, 11, 17, 29; 3:6, 13; and 22. **10.** The dual couplet in this verse exists in three textual variants, the preferred of which, attested by the manuscript Alexandrinus, reads:

If anyone [goes] into captivity,	If anyone is killed by a sword,
εἴ τις εἰς αἰχμαλωσίαν,	εἴ τις ἐν μαχάιρῃ ἀποκτανθῆναι·
'eí tis eis aichmalōsían	'eí tis en macháirē apoktanthênai
Unto captivity he is going away.	He is to be killed by a sword.
εἰς αἰχμαλωσίαν ὑπάγει.	αὐτόν ἐν μαχαίρῃ ἀποκτανθῆναι.
'eis aichmalōsían upágei.	autón en machairē apoktanthênai. (trans. mine).³⁷

Kistemaker comments appropriately, "This reading of the Greek text stresses the inevitability of persecution and death for the faithful. This appeal to loyal endurance suits the context and tone of the entire Apocalypse and, further, is supported by Jer 15:2 and 43:11." (253)

13:1-10   **The Beast from the Sea**   **Fulfillment**

Before proceeding with the fulfillment of the prophecy of the Beast from the Sea, it will be helpful to review our observations regarding fulfillment of chapter 12. We outline our principal conclusions as follows:

1. "The woman clothed with the sun" (12:1) represents the state of the true visible church at the time of the recognition of Christianity by the Emperors Constantine and Licinius in the Edict of Toleration, A.D. 313.³⁸ The "sun" represents the authority of the Roman State, the moon civil authorities, the stars the People of God.
2. The "enormous red dragon" (12:3) represents the Satanic power of the pagan Roman Empire. The "heads" represent seven successive constitutional governments, the seventh of which was established by Diocletian, as symbolized by the diadem crowns. The ten "horns" represent ten kingdoms that were destined to rule with the beast of chapter 13:1-10.
3. The dragon's tail sweeping "a third of the stars out of the sky" (12:4) represents the Covenant People's loss of their newfound Imperial protection under the Emperors Maximin and Licinius, A.D. 311-313, 314-324.
4. The birth of the male child (12:5) represents the elevation of the catholic church to a position of political status and authority in the Roman Empire by Constantine, A.D. 313-325.

---

³⁷This reading is defended by Charles (1.355) and accepted as preferred by most subsequent commentators. It is followed by the NIV, the NCV, the REB, and the ESV. The alternate reading, ἐν μαχαίρῃ ἀποκτενεῖ, "If anyone will kill by the sword," is followed by the KJV, the NRSV, the NASV, and the NKJV.

³⁸We remind the reader that we use the term "true visible church" to indicate the church that consists of local congregations that adhere to and proclaim the true Gospel of justification by faith alone.

5. The flight of "the woman" "into the desert" (12:14) represents the separation of the true visible church from the newly formed state church.
6. The hurling down of the great dragon (12:9) represents the overthrow of the pagan imperial rulers by Constantine and the establishment of Christianity.
7. The dragon's pursuit of the woman (12:13, 15) represents the Satanic influx of heresy, especially Arianism, into the churches with the barbarians and the Arian emperors, Constantius (337-361) and Valens (A.D. 364-378).
8. The earth swallowing the river (12:16) represents the eventual assimilation of the heretical populace into the popular culture of Roman orthodoxy.
9. The war with the rest of the woman's offspring (12:17) represents what is revealed in chapter 13, explanation to follow.

With this review of the principal fulfillments of chapter 12, we now resume our comments on the fulfillment of Rev 13:1-10. We have observed in our Exposition above, as based on information available to the original first century readers, that the Beast from the Sea (13:1) is an incarnation of the Satanic dragon of 12:3. It has the same seven heads. The ten horns identify it with the fourth beast of Daniel 7:7, that is, the Roman Empire. When considering the fulfillment of the seventh head of the dragon, we found that a seventh constitutional government was established by Diocletian in the year 293.[39] This head (constitutional government) is described as suffering "a mortal wound" which indicates that the Empire under its seventh head ended. This occurred in A.D. 476 when the barbarian chief of the Heruli, Odoacer, deposed the last Roman Emperor, Romulus Augustulus. The Beast is identified in 17:11 as the eighth head. With the rise of the beast from the abyss as the eighth head (constitutional government) with its seat in Rome, Satan was to have a new agency to which he was to give his authority to carry on his antichristian war against Christ and His church.

How is the reader to identify the beast as it operates under its eighth head? We are informed in 13:3 that "the fatal wound was healed" and in 17:11 that the eighth head "belongs to the seven." Both of these texts seem to imply that this beast is a reincarnation of the Roman Empire. Tra-

---

[39]The identification of the "seventh head" among commentators of the historical school has been a sticky point until Elliott. For a review of the proposed solutions to the problem beginning with Mede (1627), see Elliot 3.120-121. Elliott makes a rather conclusive case for the identification of the 7th head with the new Roman constitution introduced by Diocletian, which government continued under Constantine and his successors until the fall of Rome in 476 (3.121-127).

ditional Protestant interpretation from pre-Reformation times has seen the Roman Papacy as the only qualifying candidate.

When Constantine converted to Christianity in A.D. 312, he set upon a course of converting the Roman Empire. He saw the newly liberated church as a potential force for control and stability in the empire and proceeded to encourage his authoritarian principles of government in his dealings with the bishops of the church and especially with the bishop of Rome. The new prestige and authority given to the church resulted in far-reaching changes. The historian, Jones, states that the government of the church

> was, as far as possible, arranged conformably to the government of the state. The emperor himself assumed the title of bishop—and claimed the power of regulating its external affairs; and he and his successors convened councils, in which they presided, and determined all matters of discipline. The bishops corresponded to those magistrates whose jurisdiction was confined to single cities; the metropolitans to the proconsuls or presidents of provinces. Canons and prebendaries of cathedral churches took their rise from the societies of ecclesiastics, which Eusebius, bishop of Verceil, and after him Augustine, formed in their houses, and in which these prelates were styled their father and masters.[40]

This authority structure was a far reaching change from the humble status of the church in the first three centuries. Many of the bishops became wealthy, solitious of honors, quarrelsome, and less capable of countenancing contradiction. Constantine had sown the seeds of this condition by his endowment of the churches and by the wealth and honors lavished upon the bishops. (Jones, 289). The new authoritarian structure and the authority given by the state to bishops included civil as well as ecclesiastic jurisdiction.

This alliance with Rome was especially beneficial when Constantine moved his capital to Byzantium in A.D. 330, for he could then rely on the Bishop of Rome with his subordinate bishops in the West to help to maintain both ecclesiastical and civil order. As tensions increased between Christendom in the East and in the West, between Greeks and Latins, there nevertheless persisted an aura surrounding Rome and the Roman bishops. When the barbarians wreaked havoc in the "eternal city," pagans argued that Rome perished when she turned from their ancestral gods to Christ. Augustine wrote *The City of God*

---

[40]1.286 (from Priestley's *History of the Corruptions of Christianity* 2.342).

to answer the obvious objection that Rome . . . perished only when she turned to Christ. True it was that the City of the World had fallen: but it had fallen in the Divine providence, when the times were ripe for a new and higher order of things to take its place. The reign of the City of God had been ushered in.[41]

So the preeminence of Rome and the Roman bishop, even the resurrection of the Roman Empire, was seen as destined to follow the demise of the old pagan Imperial institution. It remained with the interplay between East and West for Providence to permit the ascendancy of the authority of Rome over that of the Byzantine bishop.

The process was gradually coming into place from the time of Constantine, as indicated above. A major incident affecting the relationship between the East and the West focused on the use of the title, Universal Bishop. The bishop of Constantinople, John, known as "John the Faster," took to himself the title, implying that his position exceeded that of the other four leading bishops, the bishops of Rome, Jerusalem, Alexandria, and Antioch. A controversy over the Eastern bishop's right to the title, Universal Bishop, had long been going on. Gregory I, who came to be known as "Gregory the Great," beginning in 590 had issued numerous letters to the Patriarchs of Constantinople, Antioch, and Alexandria, and to many others.

One of Gregory's letters to the emperor, Maurice, reads in part as follows:

> Our most religious lord, whom God hath placed over us . . . to preserve peace and charity among the clergy. Every man who has read the gospel knows that, even by the very words of our Lord, the care of the whole church is committed to St. Peter . . . . and yet he is not called "Universal Apostle"—though this holy man, John, my fellow priest labours to be called "Universal Bishop!" . . . . It [that title] was offered to the bishop of Rome by the reverend council of Chalcedon [A.D. 451], in honour of St. Peter . . . but none of them either assumed or consented to use it . . . . This man (John) . . . . should be chastised who does an injury to the holy catholic church![42]

---

[41] C. H. Turner, "The Organization of the Church," in *The Cambridge Medieval History*, ed. J. B. Bury (New York: Macmillan Company, 1924), 1.170. It was in this context that Augustine introduced his allegorical, spiritualizing interpretation of Revelation 20 which has become known as amillennialism. During Augustine's millennium, Christ reigns through His church during the "church age," with the bishop of Rome, the successor to Peter, as its head (see Chapter XII).

[42] *Eps. Greg. Mag. Ep.* 32, from quotation by William Jones, *History of the Christian Church* (Conrad, Mont.: Triangle, 1993), 1.376-379; cf. Schaff, 4.218-225.

Gregory's petition seems to have been ignored by the emperor, as both John and his successor, Cynacus, continued to use the title. In a subsequent letter to emperor Maurice, Gregory stated further,

> I am bold to say that whoever adopts, or affects the title of "Universal Bishop," has the pride and character of Antichrist, and is in some manner his fore-runner in this haughty quality of elevating himself above the rest of his order. And, indeed, . . . as pride makes Antichrist strain his pretensions up to Godhead, so whoever is ambitious to be called the only or Universal Prelate, arrogates to himself a distinguished superiority, and rises, as it were, upon the ruins of the rest. (*Eps. Greg.* 1.6. Ep. 30; Jones, 1.380-381)

Not long after the above communications, the emperor Maurice with his entire family was viciously murdered by a centurian, Phocas, who by means of this treachery took the Imperial throne for himself. Responding to this rise to power, Gregory sent Phocas a long congratulatory letter, from which we have exerpted the following:

> Glory to God in the highest; who, according as it is written, changes times and transfers kingdoms. . . . In the abundance of our exultation, on which account, we think ourselves the more speedily confirmed, rejoicing to find the gentleness of your piety equal to your imperial dignity. Let the heavens rejoice and the earth be glad; and, for your illustrious deeds, let the people of every realm, hitherto so vehemently afflicted, now be filled with gladness. May the necks of your enemies be subjected to the yoke of your supreme rule, and the hearts of your subjects, hitherto broken and depressed, be relieved by your clemency.
>
> (Jones, 1.385)

The distinguished church historian, Philip Schaff, comments on this episode as follows:

> When Phocas an ignorant, . . . vulgar, cruel . . . upstart, after the most atrocious murder of Maurice and his whole family (a wife, six sons and three daughters), ascended the throne, Gregory hastened to congratulate him and his wife Leontia . . . in most enthusiastic terms, calling on heaven and earth to rejoice at their accession, and vilifying the memory of the dead emperor as a tyrant, from whose yoke the church was now fortunately freed.[43]

The emperor Phocas rewarded Bishop Gregory by a decree in 606 or 607 acknowledging, against the claims of the Eastern bishop, that the Roman

---

[43] Schaff, 4.221. See further in Schaff his footnote 3, in which he quotes similar comments of several notable historians but also offers charitably with Roman Catholic historians the possibility that Gregory " knew only the fact and not bloody means of the elevation" (221-222).

Church "was head of all the churches" (Schaff, 4.222). Thus the title, "Universal Bishop," no longer belonged to the Patriarch of Constantinople but only to the Bishop of Rome.

By 606-607, Gregory had died and Pope Boniface III had no scruples about accepting the newly authorized authority of the infamous Emperor, claiming the title Universal Bishop for himself and his successors. About this time also the designation, "Pope" became a common label for the Roman bishop.[44]

Many expositors from Reformation times and later have understood the "1260 days" in 12:6 and the "forty-two months" in 13:5 as 1260 years and counted their beginning from Phocas' official elevation of the Bishop of Rome in 606-607 to the position of Universal Bishop, claiming his rule over the entire world, both East and West. Those who fixed this date before those years expired could not know that 1866 or 1867 would prove to be the year when the temporal power of the Papacy would be rejected by the kings of Europe. Nevertheless, many of the Protestant expositors have identified the beginning of the period with the decree of Phocus and confidently marked the end as occurring 1260 years later. The date of Phocus' decree is not exactly indicated. Many assume it occurred in 606 and thus date the end of the Papacy's temporal power in 1866. Others have dated the decree from Phocus' death in 610.[45] Most prob-

---

[44]The word "Pope" is derived from the Old Latin, *papa*, meaning "father." In the Western Church this title is used exclusively for the bishop of Rome. In the Eastern Church it has been used more widely of the patriarch of Constantinople or of the head of the Coptic Church in Alexandria, Egypt.

[45]Expositors who have identified the Papacy's temporal power with the decree of Phocus and either explicitly or by implication forecast the 1866-1870 date include Chytraeus (1571) [H. Grattan Guinness, *History Unveiling Prophecy* (New York: Fleming H. Revell Company, 1905), 346], Bullinger (1573) [Guinness, *Hist.*, 346], Bale (1550) [Guinness, *Hist.*, 347], Pareus (1643) [Guinness, *Hist.*, 347-348], Holland (1650) [Guinness, *Hist.*, 348], Gill (1746) [Guinness, *Hist.*, 349], Reader (1778) [Guinness, *Hist.*, 349], Edwards (1782) [L. E. Froom, *The Prophetic Faith of Our Fathers.* (Washington, D.C.: Review and Herald, 1950), 3.184], Jn. Brown (1784) [*Harmony of Scripture Prophecies* (Glasgow [Scotland}: John Bryce, 1784), 411], Hopkins (1793) [Froom, 3.219], Bacon (1799) [Froom, 4.73] Galloway (1802) [Guinness, *Hist.*, 349], Faber (1805) [Guinness, *Hist.*, 349], Smith (1811) [Froom, 4.191], Kinne (1813) [Froom 4.190], Frere (1816) [Guinness, *Hist.* 349], Holmes (1819) [Guinness, *Hist.* 349], Gauntlett (1821) [Froom, 3.430], Bickersteth (1823) [Guinness, *Hist.* 349], Park (1825) [Froom, 3.535-536], Keyworth (1828) [Froom, 3.552], R. Scott (1834) [Froom, 4:399], Campbell (1837) [Froom, 4.399], Winthrop (1843) [Froom, 4.353] Elliott (1844) [Guinness, *History*, 349–50], Junkin (1844) [Froom, 4.363], Burder (1849) [Guinness, *Hist.*, 349], Steele (1870), *Notes on the Apocalypse...* (Philadelphia: Young & Ferguson, 1870), 133–34 (Steele comments, "We cannot know *with certainty....*" "Of all transactions recorded in history, however, that between Phocas and Boniface appears most like 'giving the saints into the hand of the little horn'"; p. 134); Guinness (1878) [*The Approaching End of the Age*, 8th ed. (New York: A. C. Armstrong and Son,

ably, the decree occurred sometime in 606 or 607, which gives a terminus of 1866-1867.

Some of the earlier commentators dated the 1260 "days" starting with 533 (Emperor Justinian's Imperial Law recognizing the Papal claims to supremacy) and ending in 1793, when the Roman Church was abolished in France. Some chose 538 (Justinian's law enforced) and 1798 (Napoleon had the Pope arrested and put in jail!).[46] As time passed and the 1866-1870 terminus came nearer, interpreters understandably tended to prefer the later date as most creditable. Some, such as Elliott and Guinness, allowing multiple fulfillments, credited both. (For the Providential character of progressive revision in interpretation, see Appendix 2) Note that all but 5 of the 33 commentators listed above gave preference to the decree of Phocus before the expiration of the 1260 year era in 1867-1870.

The First Vatican Council in 1870 witnessed *formally* the end of the Vatican's temporal power, a fact documented even by Roman Catholic historians.[47] This fact was occasioned by significant events in Europe which Cachemaille summarizes as follows:

> The battle of Sadowa, 1866, settled the ascendancy in central Europe in favor of Prussia and Protestantism. The Franco-Prussian war followed; after the disasters of Sedan, Rome was evacuated by the French troops, and the Papal government fell, to rise no more. In October, 1870, Rome was incorporated into the kingdom of Italy. (128)

Guinness comments similarly:

> Reckoned in full solar years, 1,260 years from the decree of Phocus terminated in 1866-67. The years 1866-1870 witnessed the overthrow of Papal Austria by Protestant Prussia [July 3, 1866]; the Spanish Insurrection [1868], and deposition of the [Roman Catholic] Queen; . . . the overthrow of the Imperial power of Papal France in its conflict with Prussia [Sept. 19, 1870]; and the rise of the Kingdom of United Italy [Sept.-Oct. 1870], and of the Protestant Empire of Germany [Jan 28, 1871]. (*History*, 343)

In contrast to previous councils, no secular princes were invited to the Vatican Council in 1870.[48] This, no doubt, was prompted by the fact that

---

1884), 612–13; Cachemaille (1911), 127-129; Atkinson (1940), *The War with Satan*, 93; H. Barton (1963), *It's Here: The Time of the End*, 73-74.

[46] See Elliott, 3:298-305; also Francis Nigel Lee, *John's Revelation Unveiled* (Brisbane, Australia: Queensland Presbyterian Theological College, 2000), 113.

[47] Philip Hughes, *A Popular History of the Catholic Church.*. (Garden City: Doubleday, 1947) 241-242; Martin, *Decline & Fall*, 247-258.

[48] Kenneth Scott LaTourette, *A History of Christianity* (New York: Harper Brothers, 1953), 1094.

the Papacy could not countenance rejection by those nations that had broken their concordats with Rome (LaTourette, 1094), governments which were represented in Daniel 7 and Revelation 12, 13, and 17 as the ten horns of the beast.

The decree of Papal infallibility appears to have precipitated the final, formal events which disposed of the temporal power. On July 18, 1870, the decree was adopted by the Council. It proclaimed, "It is a dogma divinely revealed that the Roman Pontiff, when he speaks *ex cathedra*, that is, . . . by virtue of his supreme apostolic authority he defines a doctrine regarding faith and morals to be held by the universal Church, is possessed of that infallibility with which the divine Redeemer willed that his church should be endowed . . . and that therefore such definitions of the Roman Pontiff are irreformable of themselves, and not from the consent of the Church (LaTourette, 1095).

> "It is said that arrangements had been made to reflect a glory around the person of the Pope by means of mirrors at noon when the decree was made. But the sun shown not that day. A violent storm broke over Rome, the sky was darkened by tempest, and voices of the council were lost in the rolling of thunder." (Guinness, *Hist.* 321, quotation marks his; source unindicated)

The very next day the Franco-German war was declared which led to the fall of the Roman Catholic French Empire of Napoleon III. (Guinness, 324, LaTourette, 1105). At that time Napoleon's troops, which had been protecting the Pope, withdrew and in September of that year an Italian army entered Rome and annexed the city to the Republic of Italy. This confined the Papal territory to the present area of the Vatican and formally brought to an end the temporal authority of the Papacy over the nations of Europe represented by the ten horns of the beast.

We conclude, therefore, that the "forty-two months" of Rev 13:5 equals 1260 days and is a symbol for 1260 years. It is the same period as in Rev 11:3, the time of the witness of the true church.. The same "1260 days" in Rev 12:6 is the time that the true church is consigned to the "wilderness" state. Here in Rev 13:5 it indicates the duration of the temporal power of the beast, the period from the decree of Phocus, A.D. 606-607, to the end of the Papacy's temporal authority over those nations indicated by the "ten horns" of Daniel 7 and Rev 12:3, 13:1, and 17:7,

A.D. 1866-67.⁴⁹ Events close to these termini served further to clarify the significance of these dates.⁵⁰

As indicated in our Exposition above, the first-century reader would rely on Daniel's interpretation: "The ten horns are ten kings who will come from this kingdom" (i.e., the fourth or Roman kingdom; Dan 9:24). Also, that the word "kings" in the Aramaic of Dan 7:24 (מַלְכִין, *mălkhin*) should be understood to mean "kingdoms," as in Dan 7:17. The number ten is not absolute but average. It is an appropriate symbol for these nations which more often that not have numbered 10 through the course of their history.

Starting at the year 476 when Odoacer defeated the last Roman Emperor and established himself as king of Italy, we have the following list of existing barbaric kingdoms made up of nations that had invaded and occupied territories within the boundaries of the old Roman Empire, ten in all:

1. Anglo-Saxons (conquest 449-582), Britain
2. Franks; later became France
3. Allemani; capitol Metz (both sides of the Rhine R.; German Switzerland in southern to French Netherlands)
4. Burgundians (King Gundobald; south of Allemani; Duchy of Burgundy, French Switzerland, Savoy, southern France within the Rhone)
5. Visigoths (southwest half of France between the Loire, Rhone, and Pyrenees between the Franks and the Burgundians, all Spain except Gallicia)
6. Suevi (Gallicia and most of Portugal)
7. Vandals (northern Africa from Gibraltar Straits to the Gulf of Sidra [now in Libya], as well as the islands of Sicily, Sardenia, and Corsica)
8. Heruli (Italy, including beyond the Alps, Noricum [S. of Danube R. in S. Austria and southern Germany] and the Tirol [eastern Alps, mostly in Austria])
9. Bavarians (southern Germany bordering on Austria and Czechoslovakia)
10. Ostrogoths (Pannonia) (Elliott, 3.135-137)

---

⁴⁹Commentators who avoid chronological, historical interpretation are at a loss to interpret such numbers. For example, Simon Kistemaker, much of whose work I admire, appeals to Matt 28:19-20 and states that the 1260 days in Rev 11:3 "is the period from the Great Commission to the consummation" (329-330). He gives no explanation for the significance of the particular number, "1260," nor why it is an appropriate symbol for the church age. Neither does he make any reference to the traditional Protestant Reformed interpretation that it is a symbol for 1260 years, nor to the prophecies of corresponding and similar numbers in Daniel (the Dan 12:7, 11).

⁵⁰On this, see Elliott, 3.302-303 and Guinness, *Approaching End*, 375.

By 532 and the time of the rise of the eighth head of the beast, certain changes had occurred, but again they totaled ten. Elliott concludes his discussion of the ten horns with the following: "So Gibbon [lists ten], with reference to the 12th century; Daubuz to the time of the Reformation; Whiston to the commencement of the 18th century; and finally Cuninghame (1843) to the regal governments at the last great settlement of Europe, A.D. 1815" (142). In addition to the above, Atkinson lists ten for A.D. 814, 1047, 1360-1400, 1740, 1871-1938, and 1958 (155-156). The number ten might be justified as the number of kingdoms at the time the horns are introduced in history.[51] Regardless, when the number ten is introduced as a symbol for these kingdoms, that number is the only one that could accurately function as standard.

Similarly accurate is the detail in the description of the horns which shows them crowned with the diadem, the official crown of Roman Emperors since Diocletian (see above on 12:3, Notes). As these barbarian kingdoms arose during the final era of the Old Roman Empire, to show their allegiance to Rome they stamped their coinage with the image of the emperor wearing the diadem crown. After a century or so, and with the fall of the Old Roman Empire and the empowerment of the Roman bishop, the barbarian kings resorted to printing their own images on the coins, but still crowned with the Roman Imperial diadem, in effect, asserting their independent and absolute authority. (Elliott 3. 142-147, 535-547, including folded illus. plate). So again we see that the prophecy accurately describes a particular era in history with every detail of the symbolism appropriate to that time.[52] Another characteristic of the beast is its

---

[51]So Isaac Newton (quoted in Elliott 3.141), and others, citing John 20:24 and 1 Cor 15:5, where the Apostles are called "the twelve," though their number had been reduced to eleven by Judas' defection.

[52]Contrast our historical interpretation with the popular philosophy of history method which struggles to account for the relevance of such details as the eight heads, the ten horns, or the diadem crowns—sophisticated spiritualizing explanations which would never have occurred to the original readers at the end of the first century, who had the visions of the Book of Daniel as their primary model.

The 1260 days during which the two witnesses prophecy is understood to refer to the entire church age period. Why the particular number, "1260"? and how can this method account for the added 30 days in Daniel 12:11 or the added 75 days of 12:12?.

Moreover, what right do we have to interpret "what must take place *after this*" as what had already taken place many years *before* this—the time the vision was given (Rev 4:1)? This so-called "transtemporal" understanding of the Book of Revelation is foreign to the first-century understanding of dream-vision apocalyptic, including the visions of Daniel as well as the other dream-vision apocalypses current at that time. Those extra-biblical, pseudepigraphic apocalypses claimed falsely ancient authors in order to present historical and current events as future to the time of the alleged author. As an example of transtemporal interpretation, Beale finds a rationale for understanding the seven heads of the beast in the fact that Daniel's 4 beasts in Ch. 7 have compositely

Chapter Seven   *The beast from the sea, fulfillment, 13:1-10*   313

propensity to blasphemy (13:5a, 6; cp. Dan 7:25, 2 Thess 2:4). We have defended the position of the Reformers that the eighth head of the beast represents Papal Rome. How does Papal Rome blaspheme God? The Papal claims to Divine authority are well documented, and this not in the sense in which clerics legitimately speak for God when expounding Sacred Scripture, but in the sense that the Papacy is uniquely ordained to represent God on earth. Many Popes have not only claimed to take the place of God on earth, but to be equal to God, and even to be God. Note the following quotations:

> **We hold the place of Almighty God on earth** (Apostolic Letter of Pope Leo XIII, June 20, 1894).
>
> **You know that I am the Holy Father, the representative of God on the earth, the Vicar of Christ, which means that I am God on the earth** (Pope Pius XI in the Vatican throne room, April 30, 1922, as reported in *The Bulwark* [October, 1922] 104).
>
> **I am the Way, the Truth, and the Life** (from a speech of Pope Pius IX, as attributed to himself and reported by Lord Acton in his *Quirinus— Letters on the Council*, p. 285.[53]

Cardinal Manning with regard to such statements said, "This is the doctrine of the Bull Unam Sanctam, and of the Syllabus, and of the Vatican Council. Any power which is independent, and can thereby fix the limits of its own jurisdiction, and can thererby fix the limits of all other jurisdictions, is (ipso facto) supreme. But the Church of Jesus Christ [that is the

---

seven heads: Lion - 1 + Bear - 1 + Leopard - 4 + Unnamed fourth beast - 1 = 7, a fact that no ancient reader, not having been exposed to modern theories, would have given significance (Beale 683, 871). The modern hermeneutic in interpreting apocalyptic fails to distinguish adequately between meaning, fulfillment, and application. The first century reader to whom the prophecy was first given would (1) have assumed that the entire vision from Rev 4:1 predicted events future to his time. (2) He would have understood the predictions according to the common, mostly Old Testament use of the symbols, and would have been able to derive the direction and meaning of the predictions without knowing specifically when or by whom they would be fulfilled. (3) He would have been able to derive transtemporal principles for practical application without that knowledge of fulfillment. As time and generations passed, the Apocalypse continued to be relevant for its practical implications as well as for its ongoing stimulus to discern the signs of the times by attempting to determine how and when the predictions may have been fulfilled. Thus, contrary to what is commonly alleged against the historicist approach, the book has always had meaning and relevance for the original readers and for every succeeding generation.

[53]These and many other comparable documentations are given in *The Antichrist: His Portrait and History*, by Baron Porcelli. 2nd American ed. (El Paso, Texas: Lamp Trimmers, 2001), 28, 29, 31 and context. See also his Appendix C, "He That Exalteth Himself," 96-101.

Papal Church] . . . is all this or is nothing, or worse than nothing, an imposture and a usurpation—that is, it is Christ or Antichrist."[54]

He was given power to make war against the saints and to conquer them. In 2 Thess 2:3-12, the Apostle Paul refers to the antichrist power as "the man of lawlessness" (v. 3). Most commentators have recognized that he refers to the Little Horn of Dan 7:25, about whom it is said that "he will speak against the Most High and oppress his saints and try to change the set times and the laws." To the Thessalonians living in the mid-first century, the Apostle states, "That day [the day of the Lord] will not come until the rebellion occurs and the man of lawlessness is revealed, the man doomed to destruction" (cf. Dan 7:11, 26). The word translated "rebellion," (Greek, ἀποστασία, *'apostasía)* in the context of "the lawless one" taking his seat in "the temple of God" (that is in the church), may better be translated, "apostasy."[55]

The Papacy has openly claimed to be a law unto itself and to have authority to change existing laws, whether ecclesiastical or civil, even the laws of Christ. Pope Gregory IX, in his *Decretals* , writes that the Pope

> is said to have a heavenly power: and hence he changes even the nature of things, applying the substantials of one thing to another, and can make something out of nothing; and a judgment which is null he makes to be real; since in the things which he wills his will is taken for reason; nor is there anyone to say to him: 'Why dost thou this?' for he can dispense with the Law; he can also turn injustice into justice by correcting and changing the Law, and he has the fulness[sic] of power. (Porcelli,

42-43)

The Vatican Council of A.D. 1870 stated that "such definitions of the Roman Pontiff . . . are irreformable" (Porcelli, 43). Pope Nicolas (A.D. 1447-1455) decreed the following: "Wherefore, no marvel if it be in my power to change times and laws, to alter and abrogate laws, to dispense with all things, yea, with the precepts of Christ" (Porcelli, 43). We conclude that the Roman Papacy speaks clearly as Antichrist.[56]

In verses 1-10 of chapter 13 we have predicted what is described in symbol as the beast from the sea which is represented as having seven heads and ten horns. The beast is a reincarnation of the seventh head and

---

[54]Henry E. Manning, *The Present Crisis of the Holy See* (London, 1861), p. 73, as cited in Porcelli, p. 30.

[55]BAGD, 98.

[56]That is, a substitute Christ, one who takes the place of Christ. For more extended documentation on the identification of the Antichrist with the Roman Papacy, see Porcelli, 42-46.

so constitutes an eighth. As such, it represents a Satan-empowered Roman government. This Roman government is to exercise temporal rule for 1260 years during which it wages war against "the two witnesses," that is, the true witnessing church, which though for a short time had been elevated to high status under Constantine and his successors (Revelation 12, above) before the fall of the old Empire, is now "in the wilderness," having fled from the established apostate church with its Satanic forces. We have shown how this has been fulfilled by the Roman Papacy operating as a temporal government. The "ten horns" of this "beast" have their literal counterpart in the ten Roman kingdoms which arose in the territory of the Western Roman Empire as a result of the barbarian conquests. There will be more to say about these kingdoms when we comment on chapters 16 and 17.

The Beast out of the Earth

13:11. **Then I saw another beast, coming out of the earth. He had two horns like a lamb, but he spoke like a dragon. ¹²He exercised all the authority of the first beast on his behalf, and made the earth and its inhabitants worship the first beast, whose fatal wound had been healed. ¹³And he performed great and miraculous signs, even causing fire to come down from heaven to earth in full view of men.**
¹⁴Because of the signs he was given to do on behalf of the first beast, he deceived the inhabitants of the earth. He ordered them to set up an image in honor of the beast who was wounded by the sword and yet lived. ¹⁵He was given power to give breath to the image of the first beast, so that it could speak and cause all those who refused to worship the image to be killed. ¹⁶He also forced everyone, small and great, rich and poor, free and slave, to receive a mark on his right hand or on his forehead, ¹⁷ so that no one could buy or sell unless he had the mark, which is the name of the beast or the number of his name.
¹⁸This calls for wisdom. If anyone has insight, let him calculate the number of the beast, for it is a man's number. His number is 666.

13:11-18   **The Beast from the Earth**   **Exposition**

Unlike the first beast, seen to arise out of the sea, this beast rises "out of the earth." He had two horns like a lamb, but he spoke like a dragon" (13:11). This beast's lamb-like character, without question, suggests his pseudo-redemptive priestly role in imitation of the true Lamb, that is, Jesus, the Messianic redeemer of God's people. That he "spoke like a dragon" suggests the Satanic deception inherent in his true role in making "the earth and its inhabitants worship the first beast" (v. 12). The reference to "the inhabitants of the earth" provides the context for understanding this beast's rise "out of the earth."

The first century reader should have understood the above meaning of this prophecy. Moreover, the description of this beast would have reminded them of the Imperial cult and its priesthood which made the people worship the Roman Emperor. Ancient sources say this cult was transferred from Babylon to Pergamum, where for a time the kings of Pergamum were worshiped as gods in their temple by means of its priests. When Pergamum fell to the Romans, their worship was transferred to the Roman emperors, so that the Roman Imperial Cult became the official state religion.

However, the first-century readers could have understood that they were living under the sixth head of the beast and that this prophecy looks to a future reincarnation of the seventh head which in fact would be an eighth (17:10). They could have concluded, therefore, that the implied priesthood, though comparable to their current Imperial cult, pertained to some future time.

The reader in any generation is warned to beware of deception, especially with reference to the Lamb of God and His revealed plan of redemption. Jesus had in His earthly ministry warned of such:

> Watch out that no one deceives you. For many will come in my name, claiming, 'I am the Christ' and will deceive many. (Matt 24:4, 5)

> For false Christs and false prophets will appear and perform great signs and miracles to deceive even the elect—if that were possible. (Matt 24:24).

As the first century church was warned by Jesus during His earthly ministry and here in His final testimony, so today the people of God should be on the alert to detect deceptive false doctrine. This is particularly vital in matters pertaining to the redemptive work of Jesus Christ as the Lamb of God.

In 13:12, we are informed that this beast "exercised all the authority of the first beast on his behalf, and made the earth and its inhabitants worship the first beast. So, like the first beast which functions as an instrument of Satan, so also this beast exercises that same Satanic power. He functions in an intermediary priestly manner between the first beast and the people. 13:13: He was seen to perform "great and miraculous signs, even to causing fire to come down from heaven to earth in full view of men." The fact that "he was given power" to do this indicates that this apparently supernatural ability was derived from Satan. "Given power," on the other hand, may refer to God's providential permission, as with Job (1:12). The miraculous signs are a principal instrument by which this beast deceives the people.

One should note that the apparent miracles of the beast from the earth mimic those of the true witnesses. As "fire" is associated with God's people, so also the counterfeit uses "fire" to deceive. We should be cautious at this point of drawing a close analogy or of taking the fire literally. The "fire" of the two witnesses comes "from their mouths to destroy their enemies." As we have seen above in our comment on 11:5, this apocalyptic fire draws from Elijah's contest with the priests of Baal and for the true witnesses it refers to the Word of God and to the retributive judgment which will result for those who reject their message. The reader should assume that the fire deceptively displayed as brought down from heaven to earth by the false prophet likewise draws upon the Elijah episode.

The false prophet was seen to order "the inhabitants of the earth" "to set up an image in honor of the [first] beast" (13:14b), and "to give breath to the image . . . so that it could speak and cause all who refused to worship the image to be killed" (13:15). The idea was made clear to the first-century reader because the priests in the Imperial cult did require the people in Ephesus to worship the likeness of Domitian in the form of a colossal statue (J.

M. Ford, 214).[57] However, because dream-vision apocalyptic characteristically communicates with symbolism,[58] the reader should not have expected the language to predict a literal statue-image, but rather an instrument that *reflects the beast's character*. That the image of the beast could breath so as to speak simply indicates that this instrument would be able to communicate effectively for the false prophet in requiring the worship of the first beast.

The mark of the beast on the right hand or on the forehead is the sign of ownership. In Roman times such a mark was a brand or tattoo. The prime significance here is that this mark is the alternative to the seal that in chapter 7 identifies the covenant people of God (7:3, 4). One belongs either to God's kingdom or to the kingdom of Satan, to the kingdom of light or the kingdom of darkness. Again, a historical exegesis of this apocalyptic vision should lead the reader to understand the mark, not in the concrete, literal sense as do many futurists, but as a figure for ownership. The first-century reader would have understood from this that the coming Antichrist would claim ownership of those who are deceived by the false prophet. Ownership implies obedience and servanthood. How precious is the truth that those who have been called out of Satan's kingdom into the kingdom of truth and light are sealed by God's Spirit, protected from antichrist powers, and are destined for God's eternal kingdom! As Jesus taught, "My father's will is that everyone who looks at the Son and believes in him shall have eternal life, and I will raise him up at the last day" (John 6:46).

The mark of the beast "is the name of the beast or the number of his name" (13:17). The compound expression is epexegetical; that is, explanatory—the number *is* his name (see Charles 1.364).

---

[57] J. M. Ford, *Revelation* (Anchor Bible; Garden City, NY: Doubleday, 1975), 214.

[58] The primary analogies should be found in Daniel 2 and 7. Daniel 7 is especially relevant, as we have seen earlier, and although there is no image in that vision, the dream consists almost entirely of metaphorical language, the exceptions being "the saints, the people of the Most High" and the conclusion in vv. 26, 27. God is described as usual by anthropomorphisms and the Messiah is called "one like a son of man," i.e., a human being (v. 13).

Verse 18 is an authoritative statement and therefore should be understood, not as the Apostle John's comment on what precedes, but as part of the ongoing testimony of Jesus:.

> This calls for wisdom. If anyone has insight, let him calculate the number of the beast, for it is man's number. His number is 666.

The instruction to *calculate* the number suggests what is called gemetria, a figure of speech where the numbers are understood as corresponding letters; the name is hidden in the numbers. The Greek word translated "let him calculate" (ψηφισάτω, *psēphisátō*, is from ψηφίζω, *psēphízō*}. Ψηφίζω means literally "to calculate with stones,"[59] implying an arithmetical procedure. The same verb is used in Luke 14:28 where the man in Jesus' parable who prepares to build a tower must first *calculate* the cost. The solution should be one which could have been easy for first-century readers to find, given the disposition and insight that the Holy Spirit provides to those who believe. Iranaeus in the second century suggested as one possibility, *LATEINOS*, "The Latin Man," from the following:[60]

λ = 30, α = 1, τ = 300, ε = 5, ι = 10, ν = 50, ο = 70, σ = 200, Total = 666

The language of the emperor and all official Roman affairs, including the army, was Latin, whereas the common language in the provinces and the lingua franca of trade and commerce was Greek. The Latin Man would be one way of referring to the Emperor or to anyone who represented the authority of the Roman Empire. Iranaeus did not consider this interpretation as authoritative, but he did suggest that this is "a very probable [solution] this being the name of the last kingdom [of the four seen by Daniel]" (1.559). By Irenaeus' time (the latter half of the 2nd century), the question appears to have been controversial and much discussed. Whatever may be the correct explanation, to be valid it must have a connection with

---

[59]BAGD, 892. Charles records a suggestion of Prof. J.A. Smith that the abacus was in common use and that this would imply a decimal approach to the calculation which would greatly limit the number of possibilities which could result (1. 366).

[60]Iranaeus, *Against Heresies*, 5.30; The Ante-Nicene Fathers (Ed. A. Roberts and J. Donaldson (Grand Rapids, Mich.: Eerdman's, 1981), 559. For a extended defense of this suggestion by Iranaeus, see Elliott, 3.345-260.

Rome, as the prophecy requires that Antichrist arise out of the Roman Beast and constitute its eighth head.[61] Furthermore, Antichrist at the time of the Revelation, is predicted as yet future, so his name should point forward to a future Roman head of state rather than backward to such as Nero or Titus.[62] With these considerations in mind, Iranaeus may have hit upon the most plausible Interpretation of 666—code for *Lateinos*, "the Roman man."

13:11-18   The Beast from the Earth   Notes

11. That this beast comes **out of the earth** rather than the sea probably is intended to emphasize the false prophet's close association with people, as the context following emphasizes.[63] The beast's **two horns** may simply be intended to indicate its lamb-like appearance. The words **like a lamb** may

---

[61]Hundreds of candidates have been proposed. For a catalog of the several approaches to solving the riddle, see Osborne, 519-521. Osborne states that the best option is Nero Caesar, but this, as most other suggestions, is highly problematic, reasons for which are well stated in Kistemaker, 395. Charles offers a cogent observation that "the Beast and one of its heads, though conceived separately in xiii. 1, 3, are subsequently in xiii. 12, 14 treated as identical. The man here, *i.e.* one of the heads of the Beast, is himself the Beast. If we discover the name of the man it is for the time the name of the Beast. This conclusion is of paramount importance in the interpretation of the verse as a whole," 1.365.

[62]The Apostle John in his first Epistle states that "You have heard that antichrist is coming, so now, many antichrists have come" (2:18, ESV). In 4:3, he states, "Every spirit that does not confess Jesus [as having come in the flesh] is not from God. This is the spirit of the antichrist, which you heard was coming, and now is in the world already." (ESV) Again, in his second Epistle, he states that "many deceivers have gone out into the world, those who do not confess the coming of Jesus Christ in the flesh, such a one is the deceiver and the antichrist" (7, ESV). In these texts the Apostle, in confronting deceptive Gnostic teachers in the church alludes to the coming Antichrist (note singular no.), then indicates that such a teacher is "*the* Antichrist" in the generic sense of the word, that is he has the deceptive and misleading character of the Antichrist who is coming. It should be obvious that the italicized article is used in the generic sense because it is singular in number but plural in application. This is supported also by the fact that the Antichrist *is coming* whereas the *many antichrists* have *already come*. For more on this subject, see Appendix 4.

[63]This is in contrast to the first beast, which rises out of the sea (13:1; "the Abyss" in 17:8) to emphasize his Satanic character. The abyss, the home of Satan, was conceptualized as under the sea. In another context, the harlot Babylon is described as "sitting on many waters" (17:1) and the "waters" are peoples, multitudes, nations and languages" (17:15). Each figure must be understood in its own context.

be inserted simply to make this point. The reader would not need to infer that two governing powers are indicated. Similarly, Jesus, who is portrayed as a lamb in chapter five, is represented as having seven horns, again probably not to indicate a specific number of powers but to indicate full or absolute authority.[64] That this lamb **spoke like a dragon** simply and forcefully indicates the deceitful appearance of this beast. **12.** Mention that **the fatal wound had been healed** emphasizes the fact that this eighth beast is a reincarnation of the seventh and therefore has the character of the seventh. **13. The great and miraculous signs** (Gk., σημεῖα μεγάλα, *sēmeia megála*), such as were characteristic of the pagan priests of the Imperial cult, were also to be characteristic of the Antichrist false prophet.[65] **14.** In the statement, "he deceived the inhabitants of the earth," **earth** should be understood, as with previous references, in terms of the Roman earth, that is, of the territories of the then known Roman world. **15. Everyone small and great, rich and poor, free and slave** embraces all classes of society. "Everyone" need not be taken in the absolute sense, as is obvious from the fact that some are sealed as the people of God. **17.** That **no one could buy or sell** without the mark of the beast deprives them of the basic necessities of life. Scholars have pointed out that the Roman government, though persecuting, did not use economic sanctions against Christians. However, local authorities sometimes did so. (Osborne, 518) First century readers would understand that the coming False Prophet would do so in the name of the Roman Antichrist. Such pressure would encourage the weak in the community of believers to apostasize. **The mark** should not be understood in a concrete, material sense (cp. 7:1-8), but in those actions or characteristics which would indicate one's identification with Antichrist. **18.** The **wisdom** called for is not the esoteric and often fanciful profundities of philosophers but that knowledge and particular insight which is available to the ordinary person and derives from a Spirit-enlightened, common sense approach to the Word of God (see Dan 12:3, 10. The angel put it plainly to Daniel, "None of the wicked will understand, but those who are wise will understand" (12:10). These are also described as those "who sleep in the dust of the earth" and

---

[64]One need not adduce subtle reasons such as suggested by Beale that the two horns mimic the two witnesses, the two lampstands, and the two olive trees. From a first century point of view, such hidden dimensions are unlikely, as dream-vision apocalyptic was event oriented, witness the several visions of Daniel. What do horns have in common with witnesses, lampstands, or olive trees?

[65]For copious references, see Aune, *Revelation* (Word biblical commentary; Nashville: Nelson, 1997-1998), 2. 758-760.

"who will awake to everlasting life . . . . Those who are wise will shine like the brightness of the heavens . . . (12:3).

13:11-18. The Beast from the Earth — Fulfillment

We have seen in the Exposition section above that the Beast from the Earth, otherwise known in the Apocalypse as the False Prophet (19:20), is presented to the reader to a considerable degree after the image of the priest of the Roman Imperial cult. Though preterists usually claim our text refers to this cult as it existed prior to the writing of Revelation, this cannot follow from the text, as both beasts are presented as future to the time of the vision (4:1).[66] Most historicist interpreters from pre-Reformation times have identified the Roman Catholic priesthood as fulfilling the functions attributed to the beast from the earth. This conclusion follows from several apparent observations:

First, the text requires that this power functions contemporaneously with the beast from the sea. This is evident from the fact that this beast is invested with the authority of the first beast (v. 12), so as to make "the earth and its inhabitants" worship the first beast.

Second, this lamb-like appearance of the beast from the earth suggests that its priestly function imitates the Hebrew-Christian atonement as accomplished by Jesus Christ. This suggests a deceptive entity which could be mistaken for a legitimate Christian priesthood. Barnes adds regarding the lamb-like image that it "seemed to be a mild, gentle, inoffensive animal" (326).

The Roman Catholic priesthood, even while insuring the torture and death of countless witnesses to the true Gospel, has generally maintained the office and demeanor described above.Third, "The image of the beast" (13:14, 15) like the other visuals in the drama, must be understood figuratively for something which is a representation of the character of the first beast, the beast from the sea. E.B. Elliott has made a strong case for the fulfillment of the image prophecy in the Papal general councils of the western Roman church (3.219-239).

As an image *represents* the original of which it is a likeness, the papal councils were *representative* in nature. Elliott quotes Gibbon who says that it was

> established as a custom and a law, that the Bishops of the independent churches should meet in the capital of the province, at the stated periods

---

[66]Exception to this statement will apply to those who date the Book of Revelation during the reign of Nero in the 60s, contrary to the witness of the early church.

of spring and autumn. These deliberations were assisted by the advice of a few distinguished presbyters, and moderated by the presence of a listening multitude. Their Decrees, which were styled Canons, regulated every important controversy of faith and discipline. (3.222)

The General Councils were constituted along similar lines but on a much larger scale in the establishment of the church under Constantine. Some seven or eight councils were under the auspices of the Emperors. All the provinces of the Roman world were represented by their bishops. Then with the division of the eastern and western Churches, twelve councils were held in the West over four centuries, 1123-1545, "all under the sanction and presidency of the Popes of Rome" (Elliott 3.222-223). It is these councils of the western Roman world that constitute the image of the beast. This concept of the word "image" is used of the British House of Commons and the French National Assembly.[67] It is found as well in a Patristic source and in the language of the church councils, them-selves.[68]

Four things are stated in Rev 13:14b-17. *First*, that the beast from the earth was to make an image of the beast from the sea. *Second*, that the beast from the earth was to give breath to the image that it should speak. *Third*, the image was to be worshiped. *Fourth*, that those who refused to worship the image should be killed.

1. To make the image, the Pope acted, not as temporal ruler but as head of the Roman priesthood, to call for the convening of a general council. Letters of announcement and invitation were sent to the kings of the Western World. Other letters were sent to archbishops and abbots of the monasteries charging them to communicate the same to their subordinate bishops and monks. Elliott concludes his review of this process with the following statement:.

> The whole preparatory process . . . was assigned to the Papal Clergy, even as to the Apocalyptic lambskin-covered Beast, or False Prophet, to say to them that dwelt on the earth that they should form an Image, or representative Council, to the Papal Anti-Christendom and Antichrist (3.227-229).

2. To "give breath to the image" is to enable it to speak. In the decision making process, only the clergy were allowed to vote regarding any matters ecclesiastical. The decisions of the councils were called canons

---

[67]Elliott quotes Burke, "The virtue, spirit, and essence of a *House of Commons* consists in its being *the express image* of the feelings of a nation" ("On the Present Discontents," *Works* 2.288 [8 vol. ed.] and Sir James Graham, speaking of the Reform Bill, which was "to constitute the House of Commons a *real and express image* and *representation* of the country" (*Evening Mail,* May 31, 1841). Italics Elliott's, 3.225.

[68]Documented in Elliott 3.225-226.

and the councils were said thus "to speak" them. These canons spoke what the Pope wanted to hear, as he had great authority and influence over them. So, it was an image of the pope that spoke. (Elliott 3.230-231) "From the first Lateran Council in 1123 down to that of Trent, the Western General Councils, while professing to be the representation and image of *Western Christendom*, were, to every . . . important intent and purpose, (above all on questions of faith and heresy,) the representation and image rather of the *Papal mind*" (Elliott 3.332).

3. How was the Image to be worshiped? (v. 15) The Roman General Councils produced canons on matters of faith with authority independent of the Scriptures. Such tradition was elevated above the Word of God, always to be venerated and given reverent obedience.[69]

4. The beast from the earth was to "cause all who refuse to worship the image to be killed" (v. 15). Those who rejected Canons of the councils were to be anathematized and excommunicated as heretics. By Canon Law, any person excommunicated was outside the protection of the law as administered by magistrates loyal to the Papacy. Anyone could kill them. Moreover, most of the general councils of the West made specific provision for extermination of heretics:

> The *extirpation of heretics* was a professed object in almost all of the convocatory Bulls of the Councils General of the West; and by the Canons, or voice of the Councils, their death was decreed, and provision made for accomplishing it. Thus in the 3rd Lateran Council there was a decree respecting *Cathari, Publicani*, and other like heretics; pronouncing anathema against them, and forbidding that any should harbour them while alive, or when dead give them Christian burial. (Elliott 3.238; italics his)

As suggested above, we do not understand the mark of the beast as a literal mark (see above on 13:16). With regard to the prohibition against buying or selling, trade with "heretics" has been prohibited by Canon Law. The Third Lateran Council (1179) "commanded that no man should entertain or cherish them in his house

---

[69]For more full discussion and documentation, see Elliott 3.234-238.

or land, or *exercise traffic* with them"; so also the Synod of Tours (1163) (which specifically forbade "buying or selling" with "heretics"), as well as the bull of Pope Martin at the Constance Council (1414-1418).

Thus, all that is predicted of the making of an image has been fulfilled by the priestly institution of the Roman Catholic Church.

Chapter Eight

THE LAMB WITH THE 144,000, THE FLYING ANGELS, AND THE HARVEST

14:1-20

Introduction

Revelation 14 is the concluding message of the Little Scroll introduced in chapter 10. Chapter 14 presents three scenes in the drama: 1. The Lamb and the 144,000 (vv. 1-5), 2. The three flying angels (vv. 6-13), and 3. The wheat and the grape harvests (vv. 14-20). We understand that the first message is another proleptic interlude which looks ahead to the culmination of history, to the celebration of the Messiah's second advent. We have seen that the content of the Little Scroll begins with the prophecy in chapter 11 regarding the measuring of the Temple to indicate the true church, and the prophesying of the Two Witnesses. Chapters 12 and 13 are an excursus on the Satanic triumvirate, the Dragon, the Beast, and the False Prophet with their war against the true people of God. Chapters 11-13 contain mysterious chronological indicators which provide clues for understanding the times of fulfillment, such as the 1260 days when the witnesses prophesy (11:3), "3½ days" of the death of the Witnesses (11:9), the passing of the "Second Woe" (11:14), the "1260 days" or "time, times, and half a time" of the woman's sojourn in the desert (12:6, 14). With the exception of the passing of the Second Woe (11:14), these function independently from the chronology of the Seven-sealed Scroll, but in a complementary manner.[1]

---

[1] See our introduction to the Little Scroll message (on chs. 10-14 above, including n. 1).

What follows in 14:6-20 are the two final scenes of the Little Scroll. These serve to inform and to warn regarding the end-time judgment, especially in the light of the message regarding Antichrist which precedes.

The Lamb and the 144,000

14:1. Then I looked, and there before me was the Lamb, standing on Mount Zion, and with him 144,000 who had his name and his Father's name written on their foreheads. ²And I heard a sound from heaven like the sound of rushing waters and like a loud peal of thunder. The sound I heard was like that of harpists playing their harps. ³And they sang a new song before the throne and before the four living creatures and the elders. No one could learn the song except the 144,000 who had been redeemed from the earth. ⁴These are those who did not defile themselves with women, for they kept themselves pure. They follow the Lamb wherever he goes. They were purchased from among men and offered as firstfruits to God and the Lamb. ⁵No lie was found in their mouths; they are blameless.

14:1-5   The Lamb and the 144,000   Exposition

After the dreadful revelation of the two beasts and their deceptive, Satanic war against the saints, the drama with a grand proleptic interlude shifts to bring to view the redeemed saints in their post-resurrection state, glorified and celebrating their redemption with harps and song. Viewing this dramatic revelation, as we have endeavored to do, from the standpoint of the first-century reader, this scene could mean no other than that final victory.[2]

---

[2]Here, I part company with Elliott's exposition, as he saw this scene as prefiguring the Reformation era (see E. B. Elliott, *Horae Apocalypticae*. [5th ed.; London: Seeley, Jackson, and Halliday, 1862], 3.305-317. The Reformation did not end the 1260 years of warfare and martyrdom of the saints. As the 144,000 in ch. 7 embrace all those who would experience this warfare, so here this victory celebration for this entire number can only occur in the age to come when the warfare has ended.

Chapter Eight   *The Lamb and the 144,000, 14:1-5*   329

Commentators usually point out the many implied allusive references found in this scene. Where we have the lamb-like Beast from the Earth in chapter 13, we have here the Lamb of God, the true Redeemer-Messiah. Where we have in chapter 13 the many who worship falsely both the Roman Dragon and the Papal Beast, we have here a majestic scene of the true worship of God by the redeemed. Whereas here the redeemed are described as having kept themselves pure and blameless, those in Revelation 13 who worship the Satanic triumvirate are subject to Satan's wiles. Whereas the 144,000 in chapter 7 are those who were marked for divine protection, the followers of the Beast are marked with his name, 666, and are subject to everlasting destruction.

The setting of the vision here is "Mount Zion,"the earthly Jerusalem. The angels testified that Jesus would return as he was seen to leave, from the Mount of Olives, an apparent allusion to Zech 14:4-11. First century readers would have reason to take this setting literally and to understand the passage eschatologically, in terms of their Messiah-King as having begun his millennial reign.[3] Beckwith cites the following texts from the writings of the prophets and apocalyptists as providing the historical and textual background of the eschatological Mount Zion: Joel 2:32; 2 Esdr 2:42f.; 13:35ff.; Isa 24:23; Mic 4:7; and Jub 1:28. He then comments insightfully:

> *Mount Zion*, synonymous with Jerusalem, is one of the standing terms to designate the central seat of the eschatological kingdom; and like Jerusalem, it sometimes has an ideal, though earthly, significance not identical with the local Zion of history; it belongs to the *renewed* earth as the holy place in the new kingdom; but its location is thought of vaguely, cf. 2 Es. 10$^{53f.}$, 13^{36}; En. 90.^{29} . . . . Much as Christian thought, especially Christian hymnology, has identified new Jerusalem and mount Zion with heaven itself, these terms are not used in the Scriptures and [by

---

[3]Simon Kistemaker and others of the amillennial and postmillennial schools understand "Mt. Zion" in this text symbolically, that is, as denoting "the place of God's dwelling as a symbol of safety and stability for his people," *Exposition of the Book of Revelation* (New Testament Commentary; Grand Rapids: Baker, 2001), 401. This interpretation accommodates their transtemporal understanding of the chronological prophecies in the Revelation.

> extra-biblical] apocalyptic writers to denote the celestial abode of God. The 'mount Zion . . . the heavenly Jerusalem in Heb. 12^{22}, the 'Jerusalem that is above' in Gal. 4^{26}, denote the perfect archetype or pattern of the earthly, which in Heb. thought now exists in heaven, and in the end is to descend in full realization; they are not designations of heaven the place of God and his hosts. (p. 647)

Together with the eschatological understanding of this glorious passage, there is implicit the practical truth that throughout history, the Lamb is victor and He reigns with his people. The *Geneva Bible* comments that

> "Jesus Christ rules His Church [on Mt. Zion] to defend and **comfort**," alias to strengthen her. The 'hundred and forty-four thousand' implies "**a great and ample Church**."[4]

The sound that the Apostle John heard of the singing multitude is compared to the roar of rushing waters and like a loud peal of thunder.[5] The statement that "no one could learn the song except the 144,000 who had been redeemed" should be received at its face value, and if so, the angels could not learn it. Only those who could learn it could sing it. In the eschatological setting, the saints could sing it on Mount Zion, even "before the throne and before the four living creatures and the elders" (v. 3), for in that time "God himself will be with them" (20:3) and "the throne of God and of the Lamb will be in the city, and his servants will serve him" (22:3).

The enormous number of the celebrants with the loudness of their song is compared to "the roar of rushing waters" and "a loud peal of thunder"! John also compared the sound to that of harpists playing on their harps so as to indicate something of the exquisite beauty of their music. I am reminded of the words of the old Gospel song:

---

[4]Lee, Francis Nigel, *John's Revelation Unveiled* (Brisbane, Australia: Queensland Presbyterian Theological College, 2000), 194; quotation marks and bold emphasis his.

[5]"From heaven" need not indicate the third heaven, which would then imply that the song being song was not by the 144,000 *on Mount Zion*, but by angels (as suggested by Swete and others), as all the saints are represented by the 144,000. "Heaven" here in context must be the first heaven, the sky in which the drama of the Revelation is being presented to the Apostle John (cp. 14:6).

> Holy, holy, is what the angels sing,
>   and I expect to help them make the courts of heaven ring,
> But when I sing redemption's story, they will fold their wings,
>   for angels never felt the joy that my salvation brings!

The "new song" of the redeemed host could only be sung by those who had experienced redemption through the atoning sacrifice of the Lamb of God. No one else could learn that song, not even the angelic beings who attended the Throne (v. 3).

The 144,000 are described as "Those who did not defile themselves with women, for they kept themselves pure" (14:4). In 7:14, these same people are described as "they who have come out of the great tribulation; they have washed their robes and made them white in the blood of the Lamb." Again, in 12:17, the holy people are described as "those who obey God's commandments and hold to the testimony of Jesus." Rev 14:5 states that "no lie was found in their mouths; they are blameless." Personal commitment to obedience, to personal purity, and holiness of life are implied in the statement, "They follow the Lamb wherever he goes" (v. 4b). "They were purchased from among men and offered as firstfruits to God and the Lamb" (4c). As the firstfruits selected for the offerings were required to be unblemished, so the people of God have been cleansed and given the disposition to obey and to serve the Lord (cf. Rom 12:1, 2).

14:1-5   The Lamb and the 144,000   Notes

1. I looked and there before me was . . . . This and comparable introductory expressions are intended to remind the reader that John is writing what he saw in dramatic form in his vision. One should resist the temptation to find in them some more subtle meaning. One should also remember that the conceptual content of the Revelation is not in the ordinary sense a literary composition of the Apostle but a transcription of what the Lord Jesus revealed to him in visionary form. This should rule out the apparent assumption of many commentators that John based his writing of the Revelation primarily on literary sources such as the Old Testament. One should assume, nevertheless, that he may have been influenced in his choice of words or expressions, or in matters of style by familiar passages in the Bible, or by the idioms of his native Aramaic language.[6] **His [the Lamb's] name and his Father's name** indicates that the name of the Lamb is added to expand on 7:2, which refers only to the seal of the living God. The name of the Lamb reflects the emphasis here on the redemption of God's people. **2.** The **sound** (φωνήν, *phōnēn*, "*sound*"; BAGD 870) John heard is sometimes translated "voice" (KJV, ESV). "Voice," if taken literally, is inappropriate, as the sound is that of many voices, whereas φωνήν is singular. **The roar of rushing waters** may have been suggested to John by the coursing of flood waters through the dry wadis of the semi-arid lands of the Middle East. **3.** The song of the redeemed host was a **new song** because it could never have been sung previously—God's plan of redemption will then have been accomplished. Another "new song" in Rev 5:9-14, addressed to the Lamb is sung in commemoration of His redemptive work, this time sung by the four living creatures and the 24 elders, then joined by "the voice of many angels, numbering thousands upon thousands, and ten thousand times ten thousand" (v. 11). **4.** The statement, **These are they who did not defile themselves with women,** is usually taken figuratively of spiritual adultery, but it may well stand more literally as a common example of unlawful conduct along with lying, as in verse 5. The sexual orientation should not be understood narrowly. **5.** They follow the Lamb should be understood in terms of an obedient and devoted life style—"walking in the way of the Lord."

The Three Angels

14:6. **Then I saw another angel flying in midair, and he had the eternal gospel to proclaim to those who live on the earth—to every nation, tribe, language and people. [7]He said in a loud voice, "Fear God and give him glory, because the hour of his judgment has come. Worship him who made the heavens, the earth, the sea and the springs of water.**

[8]A second angel followed and said, "Fallen, Fallen is Babylon the Great, which made all the nations drink the maddening wine of her adulteries."

---

[6]John may also have known Hebrew, as indicated by his knowledge of the Hebrew Bible, the Old Testament, as well as his having spent many years in Jerusalem, where Hebrew was commonly spoken.

⁹A third angel followed them and said in a loud voice: "If anyone worships the beast and his image and receives his mark on the forehead or on the hand, ¹⁰he, too, will drink of the wine of God's fury, which has been poured full strength into the cup of his wrath. He will be tormented with burning sulfur in the presence of the holy angels and of the Lamb. ¹¹And the smoke of their torment rises for ever and ever. There is no rest day or night for those who worship the beast and his image, or for anyone who receives the mark of his name." ¹²This calls for patient endurance on the part of the saints who obey God's commandments and remain faithful to Jesus.

¹³Then I heard a voice from heaven say, "Write: Blessed are the dead who die in the Lord from now on."

"Yes," says the Spirit, "they will rest from their labor, for their deeds will follow them."

| 14:6-13 | The Three Flying Angels | Exposition |

Three angelic messengers appear, each with a dramatic entrance and a distinctive message to convey. The messages of these angels form a contrast with the proleptic scene of celebration which precedes them in verses 1-5. Whereas that post-resurrection scene envisions all the redeemed people of God celebrating Jesus, their Lamb and sacrificial Savior, these angels sound the warning regarding this sovereign God that "the hour of his judgment has come" (v. 7), and certain responses are mandated. These messages are especially appropriate to the conclusion to the Little Scroll, the theme of which is the disclosure of Antichrist.

The first angel is described simply as "another." Numerous angels have served to deliver the several messages in the drama. It is best not to assume some particular contrast between this and previous angels, but to take the adjective simply in its ordinary sense. This first angel and three others (14:8, 9, 17) bring the Little Scroll to a conclusion. This angel is seen "flying in midair," like the eagle of 8:13, apparently to insure that he is seen and that his important message is heard by all. His message, "the eternal [i.e., everlasting] gospel," in the original Greek text appears without the article, probably indicating the generic sense; that is, focusing on the intrinsic, theological meaning of the term. The adjective, "everlasting" indicates effect or consequence rather than an everlasting process. "Gospel," here serves both as a final invitation and, as indicated in verse 7, a warning (cp. 11:9; 13:7; and 17:15). This message is proclaimed "in a loud voice, 'Fear God and give him glory, because the hour of his judgment has come. Worship him who made the heavens, the earth, the sea and the springs of water'" (v. 7). Those who fear God and give Him glory must, as the Little Scroll context of this message requires, respond by recognizing the Creator's sovereignty over all people—His creation. They must respond in humble obedience to His Word. They must reject the Antichrist and his antichristian priesthood. They must accept by faith alone the pure Gospel regarding the Lamb of God and His accomplished redemptive work on Calvary. They must prepare for imminent judgment by a sovereign God.

The solemn message of the first angel is followed by the damning announcement by the second: "Fallen! Fallen is Babylon the Great, which made the nations drink the maddening wine of her adulteries" (v. 8). From the standpoint of the first-century reader, this statement is a prediction of an event to occur at some time in the future, but as emphatically as if it were already accomplished. The deceptive tactics which deceived the nations are to end with the judgment of the Almighty. Antichrist is a lost cause from which all are to flee. Chapters 17 and 18 resume this judgment theme in the context of the seven-sealed scroll message.

The third angel expands on the messages of the first and second by elaborating on the "judgment of Antichrist" message. The destiny of any unrepentant person is described as vivid warning:

> If anyone worships the beast and his image and receives his mark on the forehead or on the hand, he, too, will drink of the wine of God's fury, which has been poured full strength into the cup of his wrath. He will be tormented with burning sulfur in the presence of the holy angels and of the Lamb. And the smoke of their torment rises for ever and ever. There is no rest day or night for those who worship the beast and his image, or for anyone who receives the mark of his name. (14:9-11)

Here for the intoxicating wine of Antichrist's deception is exchanged the wine of God's fury in judgment—not diluted but "poured full strength into his cup of wrath" (v. 10a). What this means is further described in the statement which follows: "He will be tormented with burning sulfur" (10b), with "no rest day or night" (11). This allusion to the fires of Gehenna is applicable not only, as here indicated, to the followers of Antichrist, but as we know from our Lord's teaching in the Gospels, it is applicable to all who do not believe and receive the Gospel.

Mention of the burning sulfur could remind a first-century reader of the statement of the Apostle Peter in his second epistle, that "the present heavens and earth are reserved for fire, being kept for the day of judgment and destruction of ungodly men" (3:7). "The heavens will disappear with a roar, the elements will be destroyed by fire, and the earth and everything in it will be laid bare" (3:10).

The duration of this burning is not explicit, but our text implies that alternate days and nights are involved. We may rest assured that the punishment will be sufficient in any individual case to satisfy the justice of a sovereign and holy God. The statement of the Apostle Peter that "the earth and everything in it will be laid bare" (3:10) may be taken to imply that the conflagration will cease when the fires have accomplished their mission, which includes the "destruction of ungodly men." This accounts well for the description of the final punishment by the prophet Malachi:

> "Surely the day is coming; it will burn like a furnace. All the arrogant and every evildoer will be stubble, and that day that is coming will set them on fire," says the LORD Almighty. "Not a root nor a branch will be left to them. . . . . Then you will trample down the wicked; they will be ashes under the soles of your feet on the day when I do these things," says the LORD Almighty (4:1, 2a, 3).

The reference to "the smoke of their torment rising forever and ever" should not be taken to indicate that the fires continue to burn everlastingly, which would contradict the prophet Malachi. The imagery is taken from the Lord's judgment of Edom, about which Isaiah stated,

> Edom's streams will be turned into pitch, her dust into burning sulfur; her land will become blazing pitch! It will not be quenched night and day; its smoke will rise forever. From generation to generation it will lie desolate; no one will ever pass through it again. The desert owl and screech owl will possess it; the great owl and the raven will nest there. (34:9-11a)

Clearly, the language is used to describe temporal punishment, everlasting in effect not in process. The figure of smoke rising forever and ever is used to indicate the permanence of the destruction. Scripture says that the temporal destruction of "Sodom and Gomorrah . . . serve as an example of those who suffer the punishment of everlasting fire" (Jude 7; tr. mine). The fire that destroyed Sodom and Gomorrah like that of Edom was everlasting in its effect. The figure of smoke rising "forever and ever" indicates a permanent memorial. The expression "forever and ever" may perhaps be considered an emphatic idiom for permanent effect, as neither the figure nor the memorial hardly lends itself to the endless ages of the future kingdom. So the Apostle Paul speaks,

> Then the end will come, when he hands over the kingdom to God the Father after he has destroyed all dominion, authority and power. For he must reign until he has put all his enemies under his feet. The last enemy to be destroyed is death. (1 Cor 15:24, 25)

Verse 13 records an anonymous voice which John heard from heaven which pronounced a blessing on "the dead who die in the Lord from now on." The Spirit responds and adds, "Yes, . . . that they may rest from their labor, for their deeds follow with them" (NASB). The message shifts from the bitter description of the everlasting punishment of those associated with Antichrist to the blessed state of the righteous dead. They are beautifully described as at rest with their righteous deeds continuing in their effects.

14:6-13   **The Three Flying Angels**   **Notes**

6. The message described as **eternal gospel** is the message clarified in verse 7. "Eternal gospel" occurs without the article. The anarthrous εὐαγγέλιον may be taken simply as "good news," the content of which must be determined from the context (Beale, 748). The content is given in verse 7. It is a call to prepare for judgment and wrath, as spelled out in verse 7 and the messages of the second and third angels (14:8-12). **7.** The call to **fear God and give glory** is addressed primarily to unbelievers in the light of imminent judgment. It is a call to repentance.[7] **Has come** addresses the future emphatically as if it were present.[8] **Worship**, Greek, προσκυνέω, *proskuneō*, conveys the respect and abject humility once commonly given to ancient gods and kings in the act of falling prostrate or bowing down before them (BAGD, 716). Worship is due to God as Creator, the one **who made the heavens, the earth, the sea and the springs of water.** "Springs of water" refers to fresh water of rivers and streams in distinction from the great bodies of the salt water oceans. **8. Fallen, Fallen,** by repetition enhances the emphatic quality of the second angel's message. "Fallen" (ἔπεσεν, *'epesen*) is a prophetic aorist reflecting the language of Isa 21:9 where Isaiah uses a past tense to emphasize the certainty of a future event:

> 'Babylon has fallen, has fallen!
> 'All the images of its gods
>   lie shattered on the ground.'[9]

Babylon the Great is found in the Old Testament only in Dan 4:30, where King Nebuchadnezzar boasted,"Is this not great Babylon I have built . . . by my mighty power and the glory of my majesty?" Immediately, "while the words were still on his lips his

---

[7]See Isben T. Beckwith, who cites the following texts: John 9:24; Josh 7:19; Jer 13:16; 1 Pet 2:12; & Rev 16:9; *The Apocalypse of John* (Macmillan, 1919 (Limited eds. library; Grand Rapids: Baker, 1967), pp. 655, 604.

[8]ἦλθεν, an aorist indicative, may perhaps be a gnomic aorist, in this case indicating a constantly pending condition (see F. Blass and A. DeBrunner, *A Greek Grammar of the New Testament and Other Early Christian Literature* [Chicago: University Press, 1961], 171).

[9]Beckwith, 656.

royal authority was taken from him (v. 31). Later, "Babylon" became an apocalyptic symbol for the city of Rome, as witnessed by the Sib. Or. 5:143, 159; the 2 Apoc. of Bar. 11:1; 67:7, 1QpHab 2:10ff.; Pss Sol 8:14-20, and probably by 1 Pet 5:13. In the Book of Revelation, Rome is so referenced here (14:8; also 16:19; 17:5; 18:2, 10, and 21), always as "Babylon the Great." The identification with Rome is clearly indicated by Rev 17:8, where the woman named Mystery Babylon the Great is seated on the seven-headed beast and the seven heads are identified with seven hills. (Beckwith 656). The angel also told John, "The woman that you saw is the great city that rules over the kings of the earth" (17:18). For the readers of the first century, this must have meant Rome.[10] Nevertheless, in principle, the practical application of this prediction should lead any wicked person to repentance. The deceptive nature of the Antichrist power is described as **maddening wine**. The use of wine to intoxicate and thereby to deceive was commonplace in ancient times, as it is today. To make it more effective, it was sometimes mixed with other mind-altering drugs. Deception is one of the defining characteristics of Antichrist. Although homosexual and bisexual temple-oriented prostitution was commonplace, the NIV **"adulteries"** is a free translation of the (Gk., πορνείας, *porneías*, "fornications," "harlotries." This occurrence, no doubt, refers to spiritual defection and reflects the language of the prophets with regard to apostate Israel (see Ezek 16:15-22; 23:5-21; Hos 1:2; LXX). Πορνεία literally translated means "prostitution" or "unchastity," but when such conduct violates a marriage covenant, it is also adultery. The concept of Πορνεία on the part of a married woman and the conspicuous use of this metaphor by the Israelite prophets favors our understanding of "Babylon" as referring to an apostate church as an alleged spouse of Yahweh. **9. Worships the**

---

[10] It is hardly adequate for those who insist on a transtemporal interpretation to take the reference to Rome as referring to "all wicked world systems" (as Beale, p. 755). To do so would have been entirely foreign to the mindset of the author and the original readers. Moreover, a transtemporal interpretation of an apocalyptic dream vision appears to confuse interpretation with application. Of course, the application of such a passage is transtemporal, as the predicted indictment of Rome for her wickedness is in principle applicable to any wicked world system.

beast and his image presents the opposite of the worship commanded in verse 7. One may understand the beast's **mark on the forehead or on the hand** as a figure for any action that identifies the worshiper with Antichrist. Ultimately, God is the judge of who is so identified as He also knows those marked as the 144,000. **10. The wine of God's fury** is the rhetorical equivalent of the intoxicating wine of "Babylon" (v. 8). **Poured full strength** indicates that it is undiluted, in this case not a means to deceive but a symbol for the unrestrained punishment that the justice of a holy God requires. The figure is commonplace in the Old Testament: Job 21:20; Psa 75:8; Isa 51:17, 22; Jer 25:15, 49:12. Undiluted wine is in these Scriptures a symbol for ruin and devastation, something that should give pause to those who intemperately indulge in alcoholic beverages. For the figure to have relevance and spiritual meaning, there must be a correlation between the material and the spiritual. **Tormented with burning sulfur** hardly suggests nor is it compatible with the interpretation that the punishment of gehenna fire is only a figure for severe mental anguish.[11] In none of the texts or their contexts dealing with punishment is it suggested or implied that the fire is not literal.[12] Osborne explains that "'Sulfur' or 'brimstone' [Gk., θεῖον, *theîon*] was a type of asphalt found particularly in volcanic deposits and produced both intense heat and terrible smell."[13] Fire is often in Scripture indicated as the punishment

---

[11]Beale states, 'As throughout the Apocalypse, fire is figurative for judgment (1:14, 2:18, 3:18, 4:5, 8:5, 7-8[sic, 8:7], 15:2, 19:12..... Unbelievers minds are "tormented" by their hopeless spiritual plight, which will result in extreme depression,' 759-760. Mounce states with reference to the fire and brimstone of gehenna that "we are dealing with a rather obvious symbol," which, nevertheless, he emphasizes is not to be taken lightly; 273. However, one should note that whereas the Apocalyptic references cited are either explicitly ["like fire"] or otherwise might be understood as obviously figurative, the allusions to gehenna reference a well established concept of literal fire from earlier Scriptures as well as earlier apocalyptic works. For a more literal view "everywhere supported in apocalyptic literature," see Beckwith, 657.

[12]The figurative intepretation of "fire" in such passages is probably inferred on the Platonic assumption that the human soul is indestructible and being incorporeal cannot burn eternally. Jesus stated plainly, "Do not be afraid of those who can kill the body, but cannot kill the soul. Rather, be afraid of the One who can destroy both soul and body in hell" (Matt 10:28).

[13]Osborne, Grant R. *Revelation* (Grand Rapids: Baker, 2002), 541.

to be suffered by unbelievers (Deut 32:22; Isa 33:14; 66:24; Matt 13:30; 42, 50; 25:41; Mark 9:44; Rev 19:20; and 21:8. The scene is descriptive of the wicked as being included in the cleansing of the earth by fire described explicitly by Peter:

> The present heavens and earth are reserved for fire, being kept for *the day of judgment and destruction of ungodly men.* . . . . The heavens will disappear with a roar, the elements will be destroyed by fire, and the earth and everything in it will be laid bare. (2 Pet 3:7, 10; italics mine)

. One should not assume that the destruction of the wicked will occur quickly, but rather as the justice of a holy God determines the intensity and duration of their punishment. **13. A voice from heaven** may be the voice of the Lord Jesus, Himself, though that is not indicated (cp. 10:4, 8, 11:12; 12:10; 16:1; 18:4; 21:3). "Heaven" most probably should be understood as the first heaven, the sky, as locus of the drama which John is experiencing. **From now on** (Gk., ἀπ' ἄρτι, *ap' ărti*) is somewhat ambiguous, but the first-century reader would likely understand it to mean, "from the present time (as you face future persecution from Rome). The blessing will have had added meaning, however, during the "1260 day" war with Antichrist.[14] This blessing has general application, nevertheless, not only to the persecuted and the martyrs but to all who face death with the "blessed hope" (Tit 2:13). Daniel expresses this hope in terms of the resurrection: "As for you, go your way till the end. You will rest, and then at the end of the days you will rise to receive your allotted inheritance" (12:13). Wherever the hope of the believer is addressed explicitly in Scripture it refers to the second Advent and the post-resurrection state.

---

[14]Beale reviews several possible interpretations: 1. "From now on" in distinction from times previous. 2. "From now on" beginning at the time of death, for which he cites 4 Ezra 7:92-99. 3. "From now on" referring to the *now* of Christ's redemptive work [an option which appears to strike at the unity of the Old and New Covenants]. 4. "From now on" as referring prophetically to time of the consummation. (769-770) Beale appears to leave the question open but prefers option 2 as based on Dan 12:12.

Chapter Eight   *The three flying angels, 14:14-20*   341

The Harvest of the Earth

14:14 **I looked, and there before me was a white cloud, and seated on the cloud was one "like a son of man" with a crown of gold on his head and a sharp sickle in his hand.** [15]**Then another angel came out of the temple and called in a loud voice to him who was sitting on the cloud, "Take your sickle and reap, because the time to reap has come, for the harvest of the earth is ripe."** [16]**So he who was seated on the cloud swung his sickle over the earth, and the earth was harvested.**

[17]**Another angel came out of the temple in heaven, and he too had a sharp sickle.** [18]**Still another angel, who had charge of the fire, came from the altar and called in a loud voice to him who had the sharp sickle, "take your sharp sickle and gather the clusters of grapes from the earth's vine, because its grapes are ripe."** [19]**The angel swung his sickle on the earth, gathered its grapes and threw them into the great winepress of God's wrath.** [20]**They were trampled in the winepress outside the city, and blood flowed out of the press, rising as high as the horses bridles for a distance of 1,600 stadia.**

14:14-20   **The Harvest of the Earth**   **Exposition**

This passage concludes the Little Scroll message with two-harvest scenes, a wheat harvest and a grape harvest. Commentators sometimes interpret the wheat harvest scene (1) as depicting the ingathering of the saints in distinction from the grape harvest as describing the harvest and judgment of the wicked (Swete, Ladd, Ford, Kistemaker). Others (2) see the first scene as general, including both good and evil, the second as evil (Beckwith, Mounce). A third alternative (3) sees both scenes as describing the harvest and judgment of evil (Elliott, Cachemaille, Hendriksen, Morris, Michaels, Beale). The reader should understand these scenes on their own terms and as they are commonly used in Scripture.

The message of the three angels which immediately precedes this harvest is a final appeal to the followers of the beast to receive the Gospel and escape the judgment of the beast in the fires of gehenna. This should lead the reader to anticipate "the harvest of the earth" (14:15b) in terms of the gathering of the wicked. There are other considerations internal to the passage which also lead to this last conclusion.

First, there is in both scenes reference to a "sharp sickle" (14:14b, 17, 18), as Elliott suggests, a strange emphasis for "a painless and most blessed" gathering of the elect people of God, 4.9. Second, there is the reference to the harvest as being "withered," (NASV, NIV, "ripe"; Gk., aor. pass. of ξηραίνω, *xērainō*, "dried up," "withered" [BAGD, 548]). This is not the normal way to describe good grain that is ready to reap, as it has in context a pejorative sense. Third, the two harvest scenes appear to be expanding on Joel 3:12-16, the only other text in the Old Testament where the sickle is included in the harvest metaphor. In Joel, the context clearly indicates that both the harvest and the treading the winepress are figures for the judgment of the wicked:

> "Swing the sickle, for the harvest is ripe.
> Come, trample the grapes, for the winepress is full and the vats overflow—so great is their wickedness!" (3:13)

The wheat harvest is a common metaphor for the final judgment of the wicked. (See Isa 17:5; Jer 51:33; 2 Bar 70:2; Kistemaker, 774-775.) We conclude that harvest scenes in verses 14-20 refer to the judgment of the wicked, primarily in terms of those who have worshiped the beast. The two scenes may perhaps best be understood as first a general overview in which the role of the Son of Man is explicit, then a more graphically detailed depiction in terms of "the winepress of God's wrath (v. 20). This structure—general overview, then more detailed description—is found in many prophetic passages.

The "one 'like a son of man,'" is an allusive reference to Daniel 7:13. The expression probably had become a Messianic title by the time of Jesus (cf. John 12:34). Jesus used it authoritatively as His favorite self-designation. In verse 14, the "son of man" figure is seated on a cloud and wearing a golden crown. The cloud reflects Dan 7:13 and the crown suggests His kingly authority and that He is victor. The seated position is an appropriate expression of His sovereignty.

The "temple" (ναός, *naós*, "sanctuary") in this context is the throne room of God, whose justice is being satisfied by the punishment implied by the "harvest of the earth." The angel from the temple, identified only as "another angel," who announces to the Son of Man that the time of harvest has come is simply part of the dramatic symbolism required to display this message which describes the action to follow.[15]

The statement that "the earth was harvested" must be understood contextually, as the first century reader would have understood it, that is, as the Roman earth.[16] As the Roman Empire developed under its eighth head (cf. 13:3; 17:11), the Papal kingdom, the harvest here may be understood as primarily focused on those territories where the Beast was worshiped. We know, nevertheless, from other texts including Revelation 19-20, that the final judgment will be universal, in the broadest sense. The book of Revelation serves as Christ's final warning to all who have not received Him as their savior and lord that their future judgment is certain.

Verses 17-20 focus more specifically on the process of this judgment. Here, the metaphor is the grape harvest for wine production. The announcing angel came from the great sacrificial altar as the one who has charge of the altar fires (v. 18). The altar is a symbol of God's justice. This reminds the reader of the fifth seal, which focuses on the souls of the martyrs who cry out to God to avenge their death (Rev 6:9; cf. Gen 4:10). At that time in the chronology of the Revelation, they are instructed to "wait [literally, 'rest'] a little longer until the number of their fellow servants and brothers

---

[15] This expositor does not think that the first century lay readers would have been likely to find the mystic numbers that some modern commentators are prone to explore—particularly, the many "sevens" in the Revelation, and in this instance, that there are seven "angels" or messengers, if one includes the "one like a son of man." While I do not rule out some hidden designs of the Divine Architect, such surely must be of secondary importance to the plain sense of the text.

[16] This contextual limitation of the word "earth," as was common in antiquity, we have defended above (see on 6:4, with nn. 13 and 17).

who were to be killed as they had been was completed" (6:11).[17] Even the first century reader would have understood this to refer to those who were to be martyred for their witness to the Gospel under the Antichrist eighth head of the beast. The altar angel indicates the justice of a holy God in punishing those who worship Antichrist.

The "winepress of God's wrath" is vivid imagery depicting the severity of impending judgment. The vine as an object of judgment is an appropriate symbol for unfaithfulness or apostasy from Israel's Covenant God, as witnessed by many texts from the Old Testament: for example, Isa 5:1-7; 7:23; 32:12; Jer 2:21; 6:9; Ezek 15:6; 17:5-10; 19:10-14; and Joel 1:7, 11.

As we may experience God's grace and His love poured out on the redeemed community of His people, we should not underestimate the inviolability of His holiness nor the severity of His wrath, as it is held in store for the unfaithful and ungodly.

The winepress is to be located outside "the city" (20). The city is Jerusalem. As Scripture elsewhere indicates, the location of this final destruction of the forces of evil is the Valley of Jehoshaphat, the valley of the Kidron on the east side of the Holy City (Joel 3:2, 12-16). As mentioned above, Rev 14:20 appears to be expanding on Joel 3:12-16.

The statement that the blood was "rising as high as the horses bridles for a distance of 1600 stadia" is best understood as hyperbole intended to express the never before encountered severity of the final slaughter. 1600 stadia is about 180 miles, equivalent to the entire south to north dimensions of the land of Israel. One might understand it to indicate that the battle will encompass the entire land. In the symbolic apocalyptic language, the "horses" represent cavalry. Until the twentieth century, horses were the cavalry instruments of warfare. Indeed, the ancient Greek or Hebrew had no words with which to refer to modern mechanized war machines.

---

[17]The Gk., ἀναπαύσονται, middle of ἀναπαύω, characteristically means "rest." Comparable passages are Rev 14:13 and Dan 12:13, in both of which it appears to refer to the sleep of death in the intermediate state.

This battle is mentioned again in the context of the seven-sealed scroll, the sixth bowl, in 16:14-16. Ezekiel 38-39 may also be a description of this future great battle.

| 14:14-20 | The Harvest of the Earth | Notes |

14:14. One like a son of man should be understood as a direct allusion to Dan 7:13 where One "like a son of man" appears on the clouds of heaven to receive His kingdom. The term, "son of man," a Semitic idiom, generically means "human being" (cf. Psa 8:4). The word "like" suggests that to Daniel the Son of Man looked human. However, the context in both Daniel and Revelation also suggests that that person's appearance was not *merely human*, but the glorified God-man who became flesh to dwell among us and to effect our redemption (Col 2:9; John 1:1, 14). The "one like a son of man," in context, is a Messianic figure to whom the sovereign power and everlasting dominion of God's kingdom is given. He is revealed to Daniel as God in the fact that He is to be universally worshiped (Dan 7:14). He serves also a priestly function, as apparently He gives His kingdom over to "the saints of the Most High" (Dan 7:18, 27; 1 Tim 2:12; Rev 5:9-10; 20:4; 22:5). The term, "Son of Man" became Jesus' favorite self-designation. It served to indicate both His identification with humanity and His Messianic office as Savior (Matt 8:20; 10:23; 11:19; 12:8, 32, 40; 13:37, 41; 16:13; 17:9, 22; 24:27, 30, 44; 25:31; 26:24; et al.) The **crown of gold** is the laurel wreath crown conventionally worn by the victors in athletic competition and by most of the Roman emperors before Diocletian. The gold laurel wreath crown was commonly awarded to the emperors as victors in battle (see above on 6:2). Here it symbolizes the royalty of the Son of Man and his victory over the forces of evil. The **sickle** was the common implement for cutting grain in the field or for harvesting clusters of grapes in the vineyard. It is described here and in verse 18 as **sharp** perhaps to suggest speed and efficiency, or even severity in the conduct of the "harvest." **15.** The harvest of the earth is described in the NIV as **ripe** (Gk., ἐξηράνθη, *exēránthē*). Charles comments, "ξηραίνω means 'to dry up,' as in xvi.12, or 'to wither' when used of plants (cf. Matt xiii.6, etc.) or of crops (cf. Joel i.17ff.), but not 'to ripen'" (2.22). There are no other known examples of this word being used to mean ripe or fully ripe. "Withered" suggests "overripe" (RV).[18] Swete comments, "Ἐξηράνθη . . . properly of the drying up of the juices of the wheat plant; in Joel i.17 ἐξηράνθη σῖτος refers to premature desiccation, but here that which indicates perfect ripeness is probably intended" (189). **19. The great winepress of God's wrath** may remind the reader that the grapevine was the national symbol of the covenant nation, Israel. Because in the book of Revelation "Israel" represents the entire Messianic community of believing Jews and Gentiles (see above on 7:4-8 and 14:1-5), the use of the vine and the winepress to symbolize the beast and his worshipers is appropriate to point to Antichrist as an apostate church.

14:1-20.   **The Lamb with the 144,000,**   **Fulfillment**
The Flying Angels, and the Harvest

Shifting our perspective from that of the original readers to our current place in history, again we raise the question of fulfillment. According to our Protestant historicist understanding, whereas the fifth seal refers to the martyrs under pagan Rome, the subsequent martyrs for whom retribution must wait are those martyred by Papal Rome (cf. Rev 6:11). We distinguish these martyrs from others, such as those martyred under twentieth-century communism or under the Nazis, because the Revelation focuses on the *eighth head* of the *Roman* beast and its war with God's covenant people. As we have reasoned, the eighth head should be identified with Papal Rome.

Chapter 14 begins with a proleptic interlude in which the Covenant People rejoice and celebrate by singing a new song, the song of redemption from earth's fallen state, and this on the occasion of their entrance into the Age to Come. This celebration marks the end of the tribulation anticipated by the sealing of 7:2-8, which sealing assured their ultimate destiny. Chronologically, chapter 14:1-5 is contemporary with 7:9-17, a previous proleptic glimpse into a glorious future age.

The inscription borne by the seal with which the 144,000 are sealed in chapter 7 is indicated in 14:1. It bears the names of the Lamb and of God His Father, to whom the redeemed belong. Were 666 to be literally

---

[18] All the common English translations render this "ripe" or "fully ripe."

Chapter Eight *The harvest of the earth, 14:1-20, fulfillment*

inscribed on the foreheads of those who worship the beast or his image, then one would expect that the seal of the redeemed would be so literally inscribed. It is better to understand the seal as a figure for the Providential certification of the identity of those who belong to one or the other of the two kingdoms and not to interpret the seals physically.

The first of the three flying angels "had the eternal gospel to proclaim to those who live on the earth—to every nation, tribe, language, and people." The second angel announced the fall of Babylon, the Roman Papal Antichrist power. The third angel announces that the wrath of God will be poured out on any who worship the beast or his image. The messages of the second and third angels are clearly dependent on the foregoing chapters, chapters 11-13 of the little scroll. For this reason we should understand that the messages of these angels pertain to a period in history after the historical identification of the beast and his image predicted in those chapters. As seen in the previous Fulfillment section, we identified the beast with Rome and the eighth head of the beast with Papal Rome. The instrument which Providence provided for making this identification widespread and public was the Protestant Reformation. The Reformation renewed the preaching of the Gospel and launched what became a worldwide missionary movement. Implicit in this movement was also the judgment predicted by the second messenger which would eventually bring about the fall of Antichrist and those who identify with it.

The messages announced by the three flying angels are particularly applicable to what church historians have called the modern period, the time from the Reformation to the return of Jesus Christ. The three messages constitute a unity, for one in the Roman church who receives the true Gospel must learn that the Roman Catholic Church is destined to fall, and that this prophecy instructs him to come out of her and not to participate in her sins.

We thus conclude that the era of the three flying angels is the period in the history of the church that began with the Protestant Reformation and that it leads to the judgments of 14:14-20, associated with the second advent of Christ.

As we indicated in our exposition of 14:14-20, we understand the two harvest scenes as forecasting in symbolic language the end-time harvest and judgment of the wicked at the time when Jesus Christ returns to begin His glorious reign on the earth. This prophecy thus remains unfulfilled, but it provides (1) a suitable warning against rejection of

God's plan of redemption, as well as (2) an appropriate and unambiguous end to the message of the Little Scroll which was introduced in chapter 10. This also serves (3) to return the reader to the interrupted sequence of the seals, trumpets, and bowls. Of these major structural symbols, only the bowls remain to be set forth in Revelation, chapters 15-16, the subject of our Chapter 9, which follows.

Chapter Nine

THE THIRD WOE
OR THE
POURING OUT OF THE SEVEN BOWLS

15:1-16:21

Introduction

As we begin this chapter on the pouring out of the seven bowls, we remind the reader that the seven bowls are the third and final series of judgments which govern the general chronological structure introduced with the presentation of the seven-sealed scroll in chapter five. Each of these series focuses on a particular stage in the ongoing life of the fourth beast, that is, the Roman government, so conspicuously present in the lives of the first readers near the end of the first Christian century. Each of these three stages helps to bring about the eventual and final fall of Rome as it is presented in the prophecy as a Divine judgment. This judgment in its culminating stage is dramatically portrayed in chapters seventeen and eighteen as the fall of "Babylon the Great."

The seals of the first series predict the major episodes which led to the demise of the old pagan Roman government. The trumpets of the second series in a similar fashion predict the destruction of the remaining "Christian" Empire, first by the Barbarians, then by the anti-Christian Muslim forces from Arabia and the East. These anti-Christian attacks which brought down the old empire are called the first and second woes. With the fall of the old imperial system, the Roman beast under its seventh head lay dead. It remained for the Little Scroll (1) to chronicle with considerable detail the resurrection of the Roman beast under its eighth head, Papal Rome. The Little Scroll (2) forecasts the elevation of this resurrected Roman beast to a position of great power from which it wars against the Covenant people of God, leading up to the awful judgments which must follow. These judgments are styled the Third Woe and are the subject of this, the ninth chapter of our commentary (15:1-16:21).

Seven Angels With Seven Plagues

15:1. I saw in heaven another great and marvelous sign: seven angels with the seven last plagues—last, because with them God's wrath is completed. ²And I saw what looked like a sea of glass mixed with fire and, standing beside the sea, those who had been victorious over the beast and his image and over the number of his name. They held harps given them by God ³and sang the song of Moses the servant of God and the song of the Lamb:

> "Great and marvelous are your deeds,
>   Lord God Almighty.
> Just and true are your ways,
>   King of the ages.
> ⁴Who will not fear you, O Lord,
>   and bring glory to your name?
> For you alone are holy.
> All nations will come
>   and worship before you,
>   for your righteous acts have been revealed."

15:1-4 **The Seven Last Plagues** **Exposition**

The Apostle John saw in the vision spread before him in the sky another great and marvelous sign! Marvelous because of the magnitude of its implications. The angels bore seven last plagues, "last, because with them God's wrath is completed" (v. 1). The outpourings of Divine wrath he had in vision already witnessed were now to be climaxed with God's final, devastating judgments on an apostate church—marvelous also because with these the wrath of God is completed. Every devout believer longs for the day when wrath will end and a new world will usher in an everlasting and blessed peace!

Chapter Nine   *The seven last plagues, 15:1-4*

Then a glorious scene spread before John's eyes, for there before him the vision presented a view of the throne-room of God—a great expanse, a "sea of glass," like a mirror reflecting the glory of God, and standing beside this "sea" were the victorious saints who had not worshiped the beast nor his image. God had given them harps and they were singing the song of Moses and the Lamb! Here we have another view into the future life and the victory celebration which will occur after Jesus returns to reward his own. These saints are not now in heaven, for the assembly had to keep growing in number over centuries until the end of the age, when it will constitute a great singing choir. The scene is proleptic. It envisions these saints as resurrected and celebrating in the future kingdom after the evils of this world have been done away. That celebration is introduced in advance here to give hope to a suffering church facing the announcement of future judgments to be forecast in the pouring out of the bowls. It was originally delivered to believers who in the late first century were experiencing persecution under the emperor Domitian, as well as to all suffering saints in every generation since. There is a glorious future which lies beyond the evils of this age!

The song of Moses and the Lamb reminds us that there is no conflict between the two Testaments of God's Word. The song celebrating grace and redemption is identified with Moses as well as with the Lamb! The song celebrates the glory of God, who though He permits his chosen people to suffer, is nevertheless just and true with respect to all his deeds. He alone is to be worshiped as sovereign and holy, and in His time, all nations will come to worship Him

But the glory reflected in the sea of glass was mixed with fire. Here we have an indication that the wonderful celebration of victory expressed in the song cannot be realized until the bowl judgments have been poured out on the Beast and the Third Woe has been accomplished. God's celebrated in the song requires this. Though first-century believers could not have known how this was to play out in a distant future, the imagery clearly indicates both the severity and the redemptive significance of the forecast events. Also indicated is their finality.[1]

15:1-4   **The Seven Last Plagues**   Notes

1. The word **sign** (Greek, σημεῖον, *sēmeîon*) here simply denotes an apocalyptic symbol. However, when accompanied by the adjectives, "great" and "marvelous," the language indicates a revelation of great importance and consequence. This, of course, refers to the seven last plagues. The **seven last plagues** are to be identified with "the third woe" (see above on 11:14). **2.** On the **sea of glass**, see 4:6, "Before the throne there was what looked like a sea of glass, clear as crystal" (literally, "like crystal", Greek, ὁμοία κρυστάλλῳ, *hómoía krustállō*). It appears likely that luminescence is intended, as reflecting the Shekinah glory and greatly enhancing the ambience of the scene. The reiteration of the "sea of glass" functions as an allusive reference to the scene in 4:2-11, and the description of the throne room given there. Beside the sea were those **who had not worshiped the beast**, *etc*. We are not to assume that this body of redeemed saints consisted only of those described here, as we know that all the redeemed will appear at this post-resurrection event, many of whom lived at times other than those of the reign of the beast. The text identifies those who lived under the beast because the Revelation focuses on the rule and destiny of the beast in response to the concerns of the original readers of the first century. On **the beast and his image and . . . the number of his name**, see above on 13:14-18. **3-4.** The language of the song emphasizes the sovereignty of God with the titles **Lord God Almighty** and **King of the ages**. God's sovereignty as well as His must be recognized in the context of the severe judgments which are to follow in the pouring out of the seven bowls. His severe judgments are **righteous acts** which are consequent of His.

---

[1]To state, as is often done by those who desire to dismiss the credibility of the historicist interpretation of the Revelation, that the prophecy was meaningless to first century believers if it was not to be fulfilled in their time is a caricature which should be obvious to the thoughtful reader. The power of the apocalyptic language to speak for itself quite irrespectively of the fulfillment of predicted events is a fact recognized by all schools of interpretation.

Seven Angels with Seven Plagues (continued)

15:5. **After this I looked and in heaven the temple, that is, the tabernacle of the Testimony, was opened. ⁶Out of the temple came the seven angels with the seven plagues. They were dressed in clean, shining linen and wore golden sashes around their chests. ⁷Then one of the four living creatures gave to the seven angels seven golden bowls filled with the wrath of God, who lives for ever and ever. ⁸And the temple was filled with smoke from the glory of God and from his power, and no one could enter the temple until the seven plagues of the seven angels were completed.**

15:5-8. The Seven Last Plagues (cont'd)   Exposition

At this point, the scene in the Revelation changes and open before John was the temple, not a view of the external architecture, but the sanctuary (Greek, ναός, *naós*), the holy dwelling place of God. The sanctuary is also called "the tent (tabernacle) of the testimony," as it was here that the ten commandments were enshrined in the ark, bearing witness to the Lord's covenant with his people (see Exod 40:20-21). This suggests to the reader that the bowl judgments to follow result from the violation of this covenant.

Out from this holy sanctuary John saw seven angels dressed in shining white linen with golden sashes bearing the bowls of God's wrath to be poured out. The garments worn by the angels are appropriate to their priestly station as coming out from the sanctuary and the presence of God. The dress is strikingly similar to that of the figure in Dan 10:5 and of Christ in Rev 1:13 (cp. Ezek 9:2). Apparently, these are the same angels who in 8:2 were given the seven trumpets to announce the judgments recorded in 8:6-9:21. They are introduced as "the seven angels who stand before God" (8:2).

Seven golden bowls filled with the wrath of God are given to the seven angels by one of the four living creatures. The bowls represented here are most probably the saucer-shaped bowls used to carry live coals from the sacrificial altar to the incense altar and to dispose of the coals from the incense altar. To dispose of such coals, the priests would fling out the hot, burning coals from such vessels onto the ground. Notice the symbolic demonstration of this in 8:5: "Then the angel took the censer, filled it with fire from the altar, and hurled it on the earth . . . ."

The agency of one of the four living creatures in giving the bowls to the seven angels reflects the earthly orientation of the bowl judgments. On the four living creatures (Greek, ζῷα, zôa) see above, ch. 3, on 4:6-8). The God of wrath who commissioned the angels is described as the one who "lives for ever and ever." This heightens the sense of the infinite authority of the Covenant God in duly punishing His apostate people. The smoke-filled temple probably indicates in this context that no one can escape from the impending bowl judgments, nor can they prevent their occurrence. The die is cast and it cannot be altered.[2]

15:5-8   The Seven Last Plagues (cont'd)   Notes

5. It is this writer's opinion that one should not infer from such expressions as **After this I looked** that they are indicators of rather elaborate literary structures. The original readers would have understood them simply as indicators of the sequence of scenes in John's vision. Such expressions do serve, nevertheless, to indicate transition and to give a certain emphasis to what follows. **7.** The **bowls** should be identified with the shallow, broad dish used by priests for libation offerings. The Greek φιάλη, *phiálē*, translates in Septuagintal texts the Hebrew noun, מִזְרָק, *mizqar,* from the verb, זָרַק, *zāqar,* "to toss, splash, or scatter."[3] When

---

[2]See Exod 40:35; 1 Kings 8:10-13; Isa 6:4; Ezek 10:4; R. H. Charles *A Critical and Exegetical Commentary on the Revelation of St. John* (ICC; Edinburgh: T. & T. Clark, 1920), 2.39-40; and David E. Aune, *Revelation* (Word biblical commentary; Nashville: Nelson, 1997-1998), 2.880-882.

[3]Aune, 2.879.

used by the priests to dispose of hot coals from the altar, the contents were flung so that they were splayed out over the ground. This use of the bowls drawn from the temple imagery offers a suitable analogy for illustrating the meting out of God's wrath in the bowl judgments. **8.** The temple was filled with **smoke** rather than cloud apparently to heighten the negative character of these judgments (cp. Exod 40:34, 35; Aune 880-881). That **no one could enter** further emphasizes God's wrath and the severity of the judgments.

The First Four Bowls of God's Wrath

16:1. **Then I heard a loud voice from the temple saying to the seven angels, "Go, pour out the seven bowls of God's wrath on the earth."**

²**The first angel went and poured out his bowl on the land, and ugly and painful sores broke out on the people who had the mark of the beast and worshiped his image.**

³**The second angel poured out his bowl on the sea, and it turned into blood like that of a dead man, and every living thing in the sea died.**

⁴**The third angel poured out his bowl on the rivers and springs of water, and they became blood.** ⁵**Then I heard the angel in charge of the waters say:**

"**You are just in these judgments,**
you who are and who were, the Holy One,
because you have so judged;
⁶**for they have shed the blood of your saints and prophets,**
and you have given them blood to drink as they deserve."

⁷**And I heard the altar respond:**

"**Yes, Lord God Almighty,**
true and just are your judgments."

⁸**The fourth angel poured out his bowl on the sun, and the sun was given power to scorch people with fire.** ⁹**They were seared by the intense heat and they cursed the name of God, who had control over these plagues, but they refused to repent and glorify him.**

16:1-9   The First Four Bowls of God's Wrath   Exposition

The "loud voice" from the sanctuary indicates the great importance of this series of judgments, especially inasmuch as it is coming out of the sanctuary, apparently as the voice of God.[4] The severity of the judgments is indicated by the reiteration in verses 5-7 of God's justice in pouring them out upon "the people who had the mark of the beast and worshiped his image."

The symbols used to convey the nature of the judgments make allusive reference to the ten plagues of Egypt: the sores (Rev 16:2; Exod 9:9), water turned to blood (Rev 16:3-4; Exod 7:20-21), the hail (Rev 16:21; Exod 9:23-25). The analogies, though striking, are not thorough-going, nor are they very helpful in indicating the figurative meaning of the language in Revelation. The plagues in Egypt were literal, whereas the language in Revelation is symbolic. The allusive reference does nevertheless remind the reader that God is sovereign and will carry out his purpose for His people as He did for the Israelites whom He delivered from Egypt.

The first angel "poured out his bowl on the land and ugly and painful sores broke out on the people who had the mark of the beast and worshiped his image" (2). The first-century reader would have been conditioned by his present situation to assume that the beast was a future Roman government and that those worshiping its image were at the least adopting Roman, pagan ways—perhaps even worshiping in Roman temples. Contrary to those who claim that a historicist interpretation would have been meaningless at that time, the message regarding God's eventual sovereign judgment of the Roman Antichrist would be very clear and profoundly encouraging.

The question remains as to how they might have understood the plague of "ugly and painful sores." The same type of sore was experienced by the Egyptians as one of the ten plagues, which sug-

---

[4]See also 16:17; Simon Kistemaker refers the reader to Isa 66:6 and further states, "In a typical Jewish manner John avoids using the name of God, so here and in verse 17 he mentions a loud voice coming from the temple and he intimates that God speaks. . . . . The voice came forth from the Holy of Holies and is none other than the voice of God, who fills the inner sanctuary with his glory and now sends forth his seven angels." *Exposition of the Book of Revelation* (New Testament Commentary; Grand Rapids: Baker, 2001), 439.

gests that there may be here an allusive reference to that Egyptian plague. Nevertheless, here we have metaphorical language—we are dealing with a symbol; in Egypt they had literal sores. Beale points out that "just as the pouring out of the bowl and 'the mark of the Beast' . . . are figurative, so also the bowl's effect of producing "a bad and evil sore" . . . should be taken metaphorically."[5] A precedent for the use of "sores" as a metaphor for the apostasy of the covenant people is found in Isa 1:4-6:

> [4]Ah, sinful nation,
>   a people loaded with guilt,
> a brood of evildoers,
>   children given to corruption!
> They have forsaken the LORD;
>   they have spurned the Holy One of Israel
>   and turned their backs on him.
> [5]Why should you be beaten anymore?
>   Why do you persist in rebellion?
> Your whole head is injured,
>   your whole heart afflicted.
> [6]From the sole of your foot to the top of your head
>   there is no soundness—
>   *only wounds and welts and open sores,*
>   not cleansed or bandaged
>   or soothed with oil.

The language of Isaiah may also be intended to remind the reader of the Egyptian plague of boils. Boils begin as painful welts, then break into open sores, as described in 5b above. The first-century reader who reflects on the imagery might well expect the prophecy to refer to a spiritual defection which would grow gradually to the point of bursting out into a more general and devastating condition.

"The second angel poured out his bowl on the sea, and it turned into blood like that of a dead man, and every living thing in the sea died" (16:3). This second judgment reminds the reader of

---

[5] G. K. Beale, *The Book of Revelation*. (Grand Rapids: Eerdmans, 1999), 814.

the first plague that turned the waters of Egypt into blood so that all the living creatures in the waters died, even the waters stored in "wooden buckets and stone jars" (Exod 7:19). Like imagery is found in the second trumpet judgment of 8:8-9, where it states that "a third of the sea turned into blood, a third of the living creatures in the sea died, and a third of the ships were destroyed." This bowl judgment uses the same image, the sea turning to blood, but here not a third but all the sea is embraced in the figure.[6] In Rev 8:9, the mention of ships suggests that either naval battles or commerce is involved. Both may be, as control of the sea which permits commerce is accomplished by naval warfare. Beale comments, "The bowls generally are linked to the judgment of Babylon, as implied from the connection of 14:8, 10 with 15:7 and 16:1. The seventh bowl makes the link with 14:8, 10 explicit, especially in 16:19: 'Babylon the Great was remembered before God, to give her the cup of the wine of his fierce wrath.'" (815) Beale continues, "The second bowl is either a figurative parallel with or an anticipation of the dissolution of 'Babylon the Great' as the source of prosperous maritime commerce in Revelation 18. As a result, all those who make their living on the 'sea' become impoverished (18:17, 19)." (815) We conclude that one should expect fulfillment in terms of some catastrophic events causing death and destruction on the Roman seas.

"The third angel poured out his bowl on the rivers and springs of water, and they became blood" (4). The parallel here with the third trumpet is obvious, as in both texts the judgment

---

[6]However, we need not with Kistemaker absolutize "the sea," as he states, "God judges the entire world, and by having the angel pour the bowl of wrath into the sea, the food supply from the sea is taken away from the human race" (441). As "the earth" in the Revelation generally refers to the Roman earth, the world of the first-century readers, so "the sea" refers to the Roman seas, those seas serving the interests of the Roman State, the state identified with "Babylon," as referenced above. Charles addresses the case for universal application with this, "It is natural to assume that the first Plague is of the same character as in the second, third, and fourth, *i.e.* universal in its incidence." Then he follows with: "If the above conclusion is not valid, then we must assume that only the adherents of the Roman Empire, and not the rest of the heathen, are affected by the first Plague." (*Commentary*, 2.43)

affects "the rivers and springs of water." As with the second bowl, we should see blood here as an indication of human death and in that part of the Roman world where the rivers and their tributaries ("springs") play a predominant role. As previous judgments have involved warfare, the reader may well have expected that here, too, the killing mechanism is the devastating advance of human armies. The divine justice, as announced by the angel of the waters in verse six, is retribution for the deaths Rome has exacted on God's covenant people. The altar responds from the sanctuary (cf. 15:5). Most likely this is the altar of sacrifice. The response may be an allusive reference to 6:9, 10, where the souls of the martyrs cry out to God to avenge their blood. The altar now testifies, "Yes, Lord God Almighty, true and just are your judgments . . . " (16:5-7).[7] Mounce comments appropriately:

> The judgment of God is neither vengeful nor capricious. It is an expression of his just and righteous nature. All caricatures of God that ignore his intense hatred of sin reveal more about human nature than about God. In a moral universe God must of necessity oppose evil. 'Righteous are you, O LORD,' declared the Psalmist, 'and your laws are right' (Ps 119:137).[8]

"The fourth angel poured out his bowl on the sun" (8a). This continuing series of judgments is now focused on "the sun," with the result that the angel "was given power to scorch people with the intense heat" (8b).[9] As we have observed above, the sun as a

---

[7]E. B. Elliott, *Horae Apocalypticae*. (5th ed; London: Seeley, Jackson, and Halliday, 1862), 3.382, n. 1.

[8]Robert H. Mounce, *The Book of Revelation*. (Rev. ed.; Grand Rapids: Eerdmans, 1998), 294.

[9]The NIV, most modern translations, and many commentators read καὶ ἐδόθη αὐτῷ καυματίσαι to mean "and it [the sun] was given power to scorch . . . ." The KJV and the NKJV, on the other hand, translate "and power was given to him [the angel] to scorch." The latter is preferable as indicated by the fact that the sun is the object rather than the acting subject of the principal action of this judgment. Elliott comments, "The *sun* is surely the recipient and sufferer, under the vial poured out upon it, precisely as the *earth, sea,* and *rivers,* under the vials poured on them:—just too as the *sun* was described as the object of judgment in the fourth Trumpet. It seems to me quite extraordinary that commentators should so generally have been drawn aside, from what both the figure itself of receiving a vial of wrath poured on it, and analogy of every parallel without exception, show to be the true meaning: and that, in consequence simply of *scorching heat*, an effect of the *literal* sun, being the result of the Vial, they

celestial symbol represents a primary ruling power in the political heavens. Ironically, the prophecy seems to indicate that those people would receive as Divine retribution the punishment that ordinarily would be that power's prerogative to give. On the other hand, a beneficent ruler has it in his power to provide those blessings for his people that correspond to the normal function of the sun (cf. Psa 84:11).

Verse 9 states that in figure the angel seared the people with the intense heat. In spite of the severity of this Divine punishment, "they cursed the name of God, who had control over these plagues" and "refused to repent and glorify him." Thus we are reminded of the rebellious nature of the natural man, which though rightly attributing his suffering to the providence of God, still stubbornly rejects His Gospel invitation to repentance (cf. Rom 1:18-23). In the light of the preceding chapters of the Revelation, the first-century reader would have understood that those who suffer these bowl angels' judgments are the followers of the Antichrist.[10]

16:1-9 The First Four Bowls of God's Wrath Notes

1. Earth (Greek, ἡ γῆ, *hē gē*) need not mean the global earth, but often, especially in the Hebrew idiom, "land," or some local sphere defined by context. Here, because the bowls are poured on both land and sea, and because the province of the beast is indicated, "earth" should be understood as "the Roman earth." **2.** Again, **earth** should be defined as in v. 1, "the Roman earth" (see above, Notes on 6:4, with n. 17). **3.** Blood **like that of a dead man** need not indicate the color nor the character of the blood (contra Barnes, 360, from Stuart). The comparison is better understood to indicate to the reader that the "blood" which colors the sea results from human death. **Every living thing** (Greek, πᾶσα ψυχὴ ζωῆς, *pâsa psuchè zōês*, literally "every living soul"), in context may bet-

---

should have supposed the *symbolic sun* of this vision, and not the *outpouring angel*, to be the agent that caused it" (3.391-392, italics his).

[10]Wm. Hendriksen, *More Than Conquerors*. (7th ed.; Grand Rapids: Baker, 1954), 445.

ter be translated, "every living person." That human death is indicated by the bloody sea is supported by the angel's response regarding God's justice in "these judgments" (vv. 4-6) answering man's anticipated complaint that God's severity is unjust.[11] With regard to **every**, Osborne observes what must be recognized, that "hyperbole/overkill is characteristic of apocalyptic," 580. Taken literally, the killing of all life in the sea with the sea turned into blood would destroy the ecosystem and result in the end of civilization. The context implies that life on this planet goes on with the 3rd through the 7th bowl judgments. **4.** The expression **springs of water** (Greek: τὰς πηγὰς τῶν ὑδάτων, *tàs pēgàs hudátōn*) refers to the streams that flow into and provide source waters for the rivers. As with the third trumpet (8:10), the springs of water in distinction from the sea (cp. 8:8b, 9; 16:3) suggests an inland location. Again, **blood** is the blood of dead men, as indicated from context (vv. 3, 6). **5-7.** For the unregenerate, God's holiness and justice requires blood for blood.

The Fifth and Sixth Bowls of God's Wrath

16:10. The fifth angel poured out his bowl on the throne of the beast, and his kingdom was plunged into darkness. Men gnawed their tongues in agony [11]and cursed the God of heaven because of their pains and their sores, but they refused to repent of what they had done.

[12]The sixth angel poured out his bowl on the great river Euphrates, and its water was dried up to prepare the way for the kings from the East. [13]Then I saw three evil spirits that looked like frogs; they came out of the mouth of the dragon, out of the mouth of the beast and out of the mouth of the false prophet. [14]They are spirits of demons performing miraculous signs, and they go out to the kings of the whole world, to gather them for the battle on the great day of God Almighty.

[15]"Behold, I come like a thief! Blessed is he who stays awake and keeps his clothes with him, so that he may not go naked and be shamefully exposed."

---

[11]This interpretation is a more direct understanding and, in this writer's judgment, more to be preferred than the view that the text focuses on the commercial contribution of the sea principally in terms of the fishing industry (Beale, 815; Kistemaker, 441; Grant R. Osborne, *Revelation* (Baker Exegetical Commentary on the New Testament.; Edited by Moises Silva; Grand Rapids: Baker, 2002), 580).

The fifth and sixth bowls of God's wrath, 16:10-16   Chapter Nine

¹⁶**Then they gathered the kings together to the place that in Hebrew is called Armageddon.**

Chapter Nine *The fifth and sixth bowls of God's wrath, 16:10-16*

16:10:16.   The Fifth and Sixth Bowls of God's Wrath   Exposition

"The fifth angel poured out his bowl on the throne of the beast, and his kingdom was plunged into darkness" (10a). Clearly, this indicates a circumstance that brings an end to the Antichrist's temporal power. First-century readers would not have understood this as a transtemporal prediction; that is, a forecast of Satan's world-wide influence over the nations of the world always and everywhere. They would have expected a particular power corresponding to the Little Horn of Daniel 7 and the Eighth Head of the Beast (Rev 17:11).[12] From their perspective, the primary focus of these final bowl judgments, with which "the wrath of God is completed" (15:1) should be poured out on a specific Roman governmental power that was to arise as the Man of Lawlessness and wage war against the saints (Dan 7:21).

As with the pouring out of the fourth bowl on the sun, men's obstinate rebellion against God is indicated by their response: "Men gnawed their tongues in agony and cursed the God of heaven because of their pains and sores, but they refused to repent of what they had done" (10b, 11).

"The sixth angel poured out his bowl on the great river Euphrates, and its water was dried up" (16:12a). The biblical use of this figure is to identify a nation by the major river system associated with it. The prophecy reverses that of 9:14 where the sixth trumpet angels are released from "the great river Euphrates." One should expect that the national power instrumental in the trumpet judgment is forecast to come to its end in this sixth trumpet. Support for this is found in the further statement that this is to "prepare the way for the kings of the east" (16:12b). "The kings of the east" from a biblical perspective were kings east of the Euphrates river.

---

[12]The first-century reader on the basis of Daniel's visions and other comparable apocalyptic writings were conditioned to view dream-vision prophecies as event oriented.

The symbolic use of a river flooding to represent a conquering power from the vicinity of that river can be illustrated from several biblical texts: "The LORD is about to bring against them the mighty flood waters of the River—the king of Assyria . . . . It will overflow all its channels, run over all its banks and sweep on into Judah . . . " (Isa 8:7). "Who is this that riseth like the Nile, like rivers of surging waters? Egypt rises like the Nile, ... She says, 'I will destroy cities and their people.'" (Jer 46:7, 8) Given such prophetic imagery, it will be natural to understand "the drying up of the great river Euphrates" as indicating the fall of a nation associated with that great boundary between west and east. This nation before its "drying up" is viewed as having hindered or prevented the eastern kings from moving their armies westward.[13] The apparent purpose of this invasion of the kings from the east is to participate in "the great battle on the great day of God Almighty" (16:14).

"The kings of the whole world" are to be gathered for that battle at "the place that in Hebrew is called Armageddon" (14-16). In the light of such passages as Ezekiel 38-39; Zeph 3:8; Zech 14:1-4; and Rev 19:19-21, there is reason to understand that this alludes to a literal battle, a battle which is to be interrupted by the coming of the Lord Jesus (Zech 14:4; Rev 19:11-13, 19).

With the "drying up of the Euphrates," there also appeared before the Apostle John "three evil spirits that looked like frogs; they came out of the mouth of the dragon, out of the mouth of the beast, and out of the mouth of the false prophet. They are spirits of demons performing miraculous signs . . . " (13, 14a). This prediction references the leading Satanic characters from the Little Scroll, chapters 10-14. The Dragon is identified with Satan (12:9; 20:2), but as Satan does not ordinarily operate in a vacuum, we may infer, as the first-century church would surely have done, that the Dragon was associated particularly with the pagan Roman Empire (see

---

[13]Beale makes a plausible case for the "drying up of the Euphrates" here to refer to the fall of metaphorical "Babylon," i.e., Rome, which he understands as "the wicked world system" (828). This interpretation is perhaps an alternate possibility when "Babylon" is understood as the Papal Roman power.

above, ch. 7, on 12:3). This is implied by the apparent identification with the fourth beast of Daniel 7, as both have ten horns. The Beast also has roots in Daniel, where, as we have seen, the Beast of Revelation 11 and 12 corresponds with the Little Horn of the Beast in Daniel 7. The False Prophet, who is called by that name first in Rev 16:13 and again in 19:20, is first introduced as the Beast from the Earth in 13:11. Their identification as "like frogs" probably indicates primarily their loquacious nature, although commentators frequently mention their characterization as unclean (Gk, ἀκάθαρτος, *àkathartos* [see Lev 11:9-12]; NIV, "evil"). Their unclean characterization probably is intended to qualify the deceptive role they play as spirits of demons drawing the nations to the great end-time battle against the Almighty. The miraculous signs which they perform (v. 14), though demonic, may nevertheless be deceptive trickery, as suggested by 2 Thess 2:9, 10: "The coming of the lawless one will be according to the work of Satan with all kinds of powers, signs, and counterfeit wonders, and with every deception for those who are perishing" (trans. mine). Each of the frog-like spirits will reflect the character of its host. The Dragon speaks for paganism, the Beast for Antichrist, and the False Prophet as the agent of Antichrist.

The announcement of Jesus Christ (v. 16) following the gathering of the nations to Armageddon and "the great day of God Almighty" (v. 14) regarding His coming "like a thief" implies that Jesus' second coming is closely tied to that final great battle (cf. Zech 14:1-4; Rev 19:11-19). His coming "like a thief," as always where that metaphor is used, indicates the suddenness of the Advent, so as to caution against the neglect of spiritual preparation.[14] The Apostle Paul expands on the practical applica-

---

[14]The idea that the illustration of the thief teaches that Christ's coming and the rapture will be secret is nowhere indicated where the illustration is used. A secret parousia is in fact contradicted by our Lord in Matt 24:30, 31: "They [the nations] will see the Son of Man coming upon the clouds of the sky with power and great glory. And he will send his angels with a loud trumpet call and they will gather his elect from . . . one end of the heavens to the other." Also this is reiterated by the Apostle Paul in 1 Thess 4:15-17: According to the Lord's own word . . . we who are still alive, who are left till the coming [Gk., παρουσία, *parousía*] of the Lord, will certainly not precede

tion of this metaphor in 1 Thess 5:1-11.

16:10-16   The Fifth and Sixth Bowls of God's Wrath   Notes

10. Darkness in this context suggests loss of political authority, but it may also suggest accompanying evils which come to fill that vacuum. The statement that **men gnawed their tongues in agony**, taken literally, is of course an indication of great pain. Because here we are dealing with symbolic language, the figure may indicate some kind of extreme inner pain and suffering due to some circumstance, perhaps including the terrors of war. **12.** The **great river Euphrates** was in most of ancient times a major international boundary between the Middle East and the Near East and points further west. **13-14. Evil spirits that look like frogs**, more literally translated from the Greek (πνεύματα τρία ἀκάθαρτα ὡς βάτραχοι) should read "unclean spirits like frogs." The spirits probably are described as being "like frogs" not because they look like frogs but because frogs are known to be loquacious. They tend to communicate incessantly and loudly. They suggest the spread of false, deceptive doctrines which were to have widespread influence on the orientation of nations at the end-time, resulting in major political alignments of those nations for the great war of Armageddon. **15.** The illustration of the **thief** occurs frequently in the New Testament. It always is used to teach the sudden, unexpected arrival of the intruder rather than his secret arrival. As here, the point is precaution against such an event. So one should always be alert and prepared in expectation of our Lord's return. To **go naked** is a figure for moral and spiritual unpreparedness. **16. Armageddon** may perhaps be used figuratively as reflecting the legendary locale of the final battle between the forces of good and evil (see 4th Ezra 13:34-

---

those who have fallen asleep. For the Lord himself will come down from heaven, with a loud command, with the voice of the archangel and with the trumpet call of God , and the dead in Christ will rise first. After that, we who are still alive and are left will be caught up [Gk., ἁρπαγησόμεθα, *árpagēsómetha*, "to be caught up, to be raptured] with them in the clouds to meet the Lord in the air."

Chapter Nine   *The fifth and sixth bowls of God's wrath, 16:10-16*   367

35; *1 Enoch* 56:7; *Sib. Or.* 3:663-668). Joel 3:2 locates the end-time battle in the Valley of Jehoshaphat; Zech 14:2 locates it similarly in Jerusalem. The Valley of Jehoshaphat is generally identified with the Kidron Valley, the eastern boundary of the city. As these place names should from context be taken literally, this location may answer for both. The Kidron Valley is overlooked by the Mount of Olives, to which Zech 14:4 states the LORD will return, apparently during the midst of the battle. Another mention of the end-time battle is found in Ezek 38-39. Here the scene of the battle is the reinhabited mountains of Israel (38:8, 9). It is said of Gog that on this occasion, "You will advance against my people Israel like a cloud that covers the land." (38:16). In the light of the Ezekiel text, one may well take the reference to Armageddon literally and understand this as perhaps the opening stage of this invasion which later will climax in Jerusalem. The final reference to the battle described in Ezekiel is found in Rev 19:11-21, to which we shall return later.

16:1-16   The First Six Bowls of God's Wrath   Fulfillment

It was expedient to postpone consideration of the fulfillment of the first six bowls of wrath until we completed our exposition and notes on all six. We now turn to consider the fulfillment of these prophecies.

Before attempting to identify some comparable circumstances in history, we must take note of the place of the bowl prophecies in the sequence of the major chronological symbols of the Apocalypse. We have given evidence for adopting a continuous interpretation of the seal, trumpet, and bowl prophecies with the conclusion that the seventh trumpet with its seven bowls addresses a time subsequent to the sounding of the sixth trumpet. We have concluded that the fifth and sixth trumpet prophecies forecast the Muslim conquests by the Mohammedans and Turks, concluding the period with the Turkish conquest of Constantinople in A.D. 1453. Therefore, we should expect the bowl prophecies to begin to have their fulfillment in the later 15th or 16th centuries.

The Fulfillment of the First Bowl Prophecy

We have observed above on 16:2 that the "ugly and painful sores" of the first bowl should be understood as metaphor, with the result that we see predicted a time and circumstance when growing apostasy and moral corruption gradually produced a climactic outburst of evil. Such a condition is comparable to the manner in which a boil, such as the plague of boils in Egypt, gradually and painfully festers until it erupts with its discharge of infected matter. The "ugly and painful sores" symbolize conditions which developed in the Roman earth during the 15th-17th centuries and eventually erupted in the 18th century French Revolution. Several factors may be identified which contributed to this catastrophic event:

1. The growing moral and spiritual decadence of the Papacy and its established church during these centuries.
2. The extreme atrocities authorized by or committed by the Roman Church with its persecution and slaughter of dissenting Christians, Jews, and other "heretics," sufficient to turn thinking people against religion and belief in God.[15]
3. The advocacy and growing popularity of enlightenment philosophies with their inherent humanistic atheism.
4. The French Revolution, with its adoption of inhumane and murderous suppressive tactics in the interest of advancing the overthrow of totalitarian political structures and establishing democracy.

We proceed to address each of these items.

1. The moral and spiritual decadence of the Papacy in this period of the first bowl is reported by all historians. Temporal and spiritual authority rested absolutely in the Papal throne. This had been buttressed with the forged document called The Donation of Constantine. This led to extreme license, which expressed itself in the accumulation of wealth though the sale of spiritual favors, as well as all kinds of personal indulgences. Guinness, quoting Pennington, states:

---

[15]By "dissenting Christians," we refer primarily to those who adhered to the doctrines of grace and rejected the sacramental system of the Roman Church.

"The vice, flagrant sins, and public crimes of the popes of the last half of the fifteenth century, and the early part of the sixteenth, gave them a conspicuous place in the annals of infamy" (*History*, 82; quoting Pennington's *Epochs of the Papacy*, 151).

This, Guinness proceeds to illustrate from the lives of several of the leading popes, who practiced drunkenness, fornication, greed, and murder. Alexander VI, who secured the Papal office through bribery, fathered several illegitimate children, and even programmed Bacchanalian orgies in the Papal palace.[16] Because the Roman Church was generally recognized as the official, established Christianity, it is no wonder that many dismissed the Christian religion as unauthentic and false, while the less thoughtful derived from it license for their own immoral and even violent behavior.

2. The 15th-17th centuries also witnessed great atrocities committed on the authority of the Roman Church, especially in its pursuit of and attempted elimination of "heresy." The principal victims of these tactics were Christian believers who rejected the Papal claims and doctrines as unbiblical. The doctrines of these sects were commonly misrepresented to enhance the allegations of heresy.[17] The victims of these persecutions were subjected to extreme forms of torture in the attempt to induce them to recant, and many, if not otherwise tortured to death, were burned at the stake. Such evangelical Christians were known by many sectarian names, as derived from the names of their leaders or from their geographical location, as for example, the Waldenses, the Albigenses, the Paulicians, the poor men of Lyons, the Bohemian Brethren, the Wycliffites, the Taborites, the Calixtines, the Valenses, the Vaudois, and the Hussites.[18] The savage

---

[16]*History Unveiling Prophecy; or Time As an Interpreter* (New York: Fleming H. Revell Company, 1905), 82, 83; Schaff 7.8-12.

[17]See Peter Alix, *Some Remarks upon the Ecclesiastical History of the Ancient Churches of the Piedmont*, 200-216, and *Remarks upon the Ecclesiastical History of the Ancient Churches of the Albigenses*, 109-204 (bound in 1 v.; Oxford: Clarendon Press, 1821; reprinted, Gallatin, Tenn: Church History Research & Archives, 1989). On the history of the evangelical sects, see William Jones, *History of the Christian Church* (Conrad, Mont.: Triangle, 1993), 1.425-444, 472-501; J. A. Wylie, *History of Protestantism* (Kilkeel, N. Ireland: Mourne Missionary Trust, 1990), 1.28-44.

[18]H. Grattan Guinness, *History Unveiling Prophecy* (New York: Revell, 1905), 103-111. Although the elimination of "heretics" is not commonly addressed by the institutions of our contemporary culture, nor by most modern historians, there are ample authorities which can be consulted by the interested reader. In addition to Guinness' *History* cited above, note the following: J.H. Ignaz von Dollinger, *The Pope and the Council* (London, 1869); John Foxe, *Book of Martyrs* (Grand Rapids: Baker Book House reprint, n.d.); Juan Antonio Llorente, *A Critical History of the Spanish Inquisition* (John Lilburne Company, 1967; reprint of 1823 English ed.); D. M. Loades, *The Oxford Martyrs* (New York: Stein and Day, 1970); Samuel Moreland, The History of

treatment of millions of people must have further contributed to the antireligious enlightenment spirit which developed during these centuries.

3. **The growth of Renaissance humanism,** augmented by materialistic science and antichristian philosophy had a marked effect, especially in France and western Europe during these centuries. The writings of such men as Descarte, Locke, Voltaire, and Rousseau produced a spirit of independence from the established institutions of church and state. Rationalism encouraged the enthronement of human reason and discouraged belief in God or Divine revelation.[19] These trends encouraged rebellion against the absolutism of both church and state and eventually broke out in the French Revolution.

4. With the French Revolution what had festered and inflamed like a boil broke out in violent warfare in 1789. The event had great importance, not only for France, but "was of major importance for the world."[20] The effects were especially devastating for the Roman Catholic Church. Its sources of revenue were undermined, its administrative control over its dioceses was lost, and its property confiscated. The atrocities that had formerly been committed by the Roman Church against "heretics" were now done to Papal priests and those who adhered to the Church in opposition to the revolution.

> Precedents were but copied therein of similar atrocities practiced in earlier days by the Papal clergy . . . . These precedents were . . . held out to public notice and execration, at the time. . . . The horrid Hugonot[sic] massacre of St. Bartholomew's day was represented in the theater . . . . At Paris . . . at Lyons, in La Vendée, and elsewhere, the examples thus set before them were copied too faithfully:—copied by a populace again "drunk with fanaticism;" . . . . The *shootings*, the *drownings*, the *roastings* of the Roman Catholic loyalists, both priests and nobles, (not to speak of other injuries great, yet less atrocious) . . . (Elliott, 3.371-372).

---

the Evangelical Churches of the Valleys of the Piemont (London: Adoniram Byfield, 1658; reprint, Dallas Texas: Baptist Standard); Samuel Smiles, *The Huguenots in France* (New York: Harper, 1874); David Steele, *The Two Witnesses* (Cincinnati: Times Steam Printing Establishment, 1859; reprint Edmonton, Alb.: Still Waters Revival Books); A. S. Turberville, *Mediaeval Heresy & the Inquisition* (Hamden: Archon, 1964); Daniel T. Taylor, *The Great Consummation* (Boston: Advent Christian Publication Society, 1891; publication on demand Charlotte, NC: Advent Christian Publications), 85-120.

[19]See Kenneth Scott LaTourette, "Preparation for Revolution: 'The Eve of the Nineteenth Century," *Christianity in a Revolutionary Age* (Grand Rapids: Zondervan, 1969), 1.27-119; Paul Johnson, *The Intellectuals* (New York: Harper & Row, 1988).

[20]Kenneth Scott LaTourette, *A History of the Expansion of Christianity* (New York: Harper Brothers, 1937), 1008.

Elliott further states that the figure of the ugly and painful sores indicating previously existing corruptions that break out in ulcerations is amply fulfilled in the French Revolution. "Whether we consider the horrors and sufferings arising out of the national atheism, licentiousness, revolutionary democratism, or bloodthirstiness of spirit then exhibited, they were but the evolution into violent action of the corrupt principles, religious, moral, social, and political, existent long before in the nation: and which had been indeed in no little measure infused and cherished, as part of Rome's religious system, by the Papal Beast that it worshiped" (3.372-373).

"The Revolution was aimed at the power of the Papacy, and in five years two million people were slain, including 24,000 priests. Forty thousand churches were made into stables. The power of the popes in France was shattered."[21]

The Fulfillment of the Second Bowl Prophecy

The second bowl was poured out on the sea, with the result that the sea was turned into blood and every living thing in the sea died (16:3). Analogy with our understanding of the Second Trumpet prophecy (8:8, 9) suggests that we should expect fulfillment that will focus on a time of major maritime battles, the difference being that in the trumpet prophecy only one third of the sea was affected, whereas here it appears to affect the entire sea. As Genseric and his Vandals targeted Rome, so we should expect also that Rome or Papal Christendom will be targeted in the second bowl prophecy.

If we look for such an event following the French Revolution, we are led to consider the Roman Catholic maritime powers of France, Spain, Portugal, and Holland, and their war with Protestant England.

The war started in February 1793 and lasted over twenty years (Elliott, 3.378). The following victories are listed by Cachemaille:[22]

1793. Lord Hood. Destruction of the French fleet at Toulon.
1794. Lord Howe at Ushant. Taking of Corsica, and of nearly all the smaller Spanish and French West Indian Islands.

---

[21]Steve Gregg, ed., *Revelation: Four Views, a Parallel Commentary* (Nashville: Thomas Nelson, 1997), 356; Kenneth Scott LaTourette, *Christianity* (Grand Rapids: Zondervan, 1958), 1. 220-233.

[22]E. P. Cachemaille, *XXVI Present Day Papers on Prophecy* London: Seeley, Service & Co., 1911), 517-518.

1795. Lord Bridport [Defeat of French fleet off L'Orient. Admiral Ephistone's] Taking of the Cape of Good Hope.[23]
1797. Mutiny of the English fleet at Spirhead and the Nore; general consternation.[24]
1797. Victory over the Spanish fleet off Cape St. Vincent, and over the Dutch off Camperdown.
1798. [Lord] Nelson and the Nile. 1801: Copenhagen. 1805: Trafalgar.

Elliott gives this summary: "Altogether in this naval war, from its beginning in 1793 to its end in 1815, it appears from James' Naval History that there were destroyed near 200 ships of the line, between 300-400 frigates, and an almost incalculable number of smaller vessels of war and ships of commerce (3.379)."[25] By this means the world power of the Papacy was greatly weakened.[26] The war resulted in the loss to Papal France of colonies in the West Indies and in South America. Harold Barton states that "with what is now Haiti, France had commerce which required 1,600 ships and 27,000 sailors. All this trade was lost to Papal France" (192).

The Fulfillment of the Third Bowl Prophecy

"The third angel poured out his bowl on the rivers and springs of water, and they became blood" (4). As indicated above, "rivers and

---

[23]Two events appear to be conflated by Cachemaille here. See William James, *The Naval History of Great Britian* (London: Richard Bentley, 1837), 1.245-247 (L'Orient), 301-302. Cited 15 Dec 2004. On line: http://www.pbenyon.plus.com/Naval_History/Vol_II/Contents.html.

[24]Odd that Cachemaille lists these mutinies as victories; the positive results are that they were effectively settled. The demands of the sailers at Spirhead (Apr 15, 1797) were reasonable and so granted. The mutiny at Nore (the mouth of the Thames; May 22, 1897) was forcibly settled and the ringleader hanged; Carl, Ploetz's *Epitome of History*, 7th ed., tr. & enl. by W. H. Tillinghast and H. E. Barnes, eds. (New York: Blue Ribbon Books, 1925), 535-536.

[25]Elliott appends this note: "This total destruction of the French marine and commercial power is the more remarkable from the circumstance of Buonaparte's sense of its importance, and craving after *'Ships, colonies, and commerce.'* But all-powerful on land, where he had to fulfil prophecy, he was impotent in what prophecy denied him."

[26]With our interpretation of the fulfillment of the second bowl prophecy agree Faber, Keith, Elliott, Lord, Cuninghame, Barnes, Guinness, Cachemaille, Atkinson, Harold Barton, and others. Because the bowl prophecies indicate the final series of judgments leading to the return of Christ, scholars in the earlier Reformation period attempted to understand them in terms of their own time, so as not to encourage the postponement of the end into the more distant future. Lee, whose work was published as recently as 2000, appears to have been influenced by them in his adoption of the Reformation interpretation of several of these bowl prophecies; 212-213.

springs" echoes the third trumpet prophecy (see on 8:10, Notes) and probably points to the Danube, the Rhine, and the Po Rivers, their tributaries and surrounding territories. In contrast to the second bowl which focuses on maritime warfare, this third bowl suggests warfare on land. One should view this as a consequence of the French Revolution. The French waged wars around Roman Europe and what may be most significant, Napoleon launched in 1796 his first Italian campaign. He directed his armies into the Alpine territories of northern Italy. Barnes points out that

> this was the very region where the persecutions against the Waldenses and the Albigenses had been carried on—*the valleys of the Piedmont.* In the times of Papal persecution these valleys had been made to flow with the blood of the saints; and it seemed, at least, to be a righteous retribution that these desolations of war, these conflagrations, and these scenes of carnage, should occur in that very land, which had before been turned into blood by the slaughter of the friends of the Saviour, should now be reddened with the blood of men slain in battle. (364)

Napoleon marched his army southward through Italy. Barnes comments that "a blow was struck [to the Papal power] . . . from which Rome has never recovered, and sentiments were diffused as the result in favour of liberty [from Papal authority] which it has been difficult ever since to suppress . . ." (364).

The Fulfillment of the Fourth Bowl Prophecy

"The fourth angel poured out his bowl on the sun." As indicated in our exposition, we prefer to translate the following statement differently from the NIV, "and he (the angel) was given power to scorch people with fire."[27] The sun here, as elsewhere in the Apocalypse, signifies the highest level of temporal authority, which from the time of Charlemagne for a thousand years had been invested in the head of the Holy Roman Empire. Napoleon was instrumental in ending this German confederation starting in 1806 with the limitation of the authority of the Emperor Francis to his hereditary province of Austria. As Elliott states, "within two short years after, most of the other once independent sovereignties of Western Europe were revolutionized, and their *light eclipsed* in the political heaven" (3.390). Historians have recorded the extreme carnage of these

---

[27]Quoted in Elliott 3.393, where the translation is based largely on a comparison with the fourth trumpet prophecy of 8:12; see Elliott 3.389-395.

Napoleonic wars, whereby entire villages were destroyed by burning involving the deaths of many thousands of villagers as well as soldiers killed in battle. William Cuninghame records extensively from official reports, including the following:

> The destruction and distress which marked the countries through which the French army fled from the bloody fields of Leipic were altogether indescribable. Dead bodies covered the roads. Half-consumed French soldiers were found in the ruins of the villages destroyed by the flames. Whole districts were depopulated by disease. For a month after the retreat no human being, no domestic animal, no poultry, nay, not even a sparrow was to be met with: only ravens in abundance were to be seen, feeding on corpses.[28]

By such means the people were "scorched with fire" and "were seared by the intense heat." (8b, 9)

Nevertheless, in spite of these excruciating judgments, "Men . . . cursed the name of God, who had control over these plagues, but they refused to repent and glorify him" (9). Atheism and Roman Papal Catholicism continued to prevail.

The Fulfillment of the Fifth Bowl Prophecy

"The fifth angel poured out his bowl on the throne of the beast, and his kingdom was plunged into darkness" (10). The throne of the beast is Rome and the beast, now under its eighth head, is the temporal power of the Papacy—the Antichrist, as represented by the reigning pope. This fifth bowl prophecy was dramatically fulfilled in the circumstances which resulted from the French Revolution and culminated in 1866-1870 with the Vatican's loss of temporal power.

During the period of the fourth bowl, the legal status of the Papal church was severely restricted. Even the physical properties of the church were confiscated, churches destroyed, and many of the priests in France were massacred. The wealth of the Vatican was either paid to France, or later, stolen by military force. On February 15, 1798, the Pope was arrested, his ring signifying his office as husband of the Church removed from his finger, and he was carried off as prisoner to France. Elliott com-

---

[28]William Cuninghame, *A Dissertation on the Seals and Trumpets of the Apocalypse* (London: T. Cadell; Hatchard; and J. Nisbet, 1843), 282, selected from many such quotes from Cuninghame, 281-285.; quoted in Elliott, 3.393, n. 2.

ments, "The Vial had thus touched the *throne of the Beast*, just in Apocalyptic order, after their first and earlier sprinkling of each of the four preceding Vials: and the confiscation of all territorial possessions of the Church and monasteries, and the pillage of the Popes's library, museum, furniture, jewels, and even sacerdotal robes . . . " (3.401).[29]

The final stage of "the darkening of the sun" is to be identified with the ending of the 1260 days in 1867, when the kings of Europe for the first time were not invited by the Vatican to attend the Vatican I Council, as they had rejected the Vatican (see above on 13:5).[30] In 1870, the temporal power of the Papacy over the kingdoms of Roman Europe officially ended with the Kingdom of Italy established in Rome (Atkinson, 134).

The Fulfillment of the Sixth Bowl Prophecy

The pouring out of the bowl of the sixth angel resulted in "the drying up of the Euphrates River to prepare the way for the kings of the east" (v. 12). As observed in the Exposition section above, the drying up of a river, like the flooding of a river, is used in prophecy as symbol for the country associated with that river. In the sequence of the bowl prophecies, we should look in the 19th century for such a Middle Eastern nation that suffered great loss of power or falls. Historicist scholars have not been slow to recognize that exactly that condition occurred with the Ottoman Turkish Empire. Even Elliott, who wrote before that power's final demise arrived at that conclusion, largely from biblical texts:

> It seems to me manifest that the same Turkish power is here intended that was described under the sixth Trumpet as loosed from the Euphrates. [see   Isa 8:7; Jer 46:7] Like the Assyrian power of old, when Providentially employed to desolate Judah, it had overflowed from its Euphratean river-banks over Grecian Christendom. And now the Apocalyptic vision represented that its symbolic river-flood was to be dried up:—dried up, as the next great event after the outpouring of the fifth Vial on the seat of the Beast, that is, on Rome. (3.422-423)

The "drying up" of the Turkish Empire can be traced as a gradual process through the nineteenth century until its power in the Middle East

---

[29]For a detailed summary of the effects of the Napoleonic period on the Vatican and its fulfillment of the 5th bowl prophecy, see Elliott, 3.389-410.

[30]The probable reason the Vatican did not invite the kings is because it did not want to suffer the indignity of their refusing the invitation.

was broken and it was reduced in 1918 to the current boundaries of Turkey, confined to the sub-continent of Asia Minor.

Internal revolt against the Sultan in 1820 by Ali Pasha precipitated the Greek insurrection, which at length led to the battle of Navarino on September 1827, in which Turkish and Egyptian fleets were defeated by an alliance of Greece with British, French, and Russian forces. The Turkish fleet was destroyed (Cachemaille, 542-543). Cachemaille wrote the following summary of the Turkish losses between 1820 and 1911 (544-545):

> From 1820 to 1897 Turkey has lost Greece, Servia, Moldavia, Wallachia, Morocco, Algeria, Egypt, Bosnia, Herzegovina, Bulgaria, and Crete. These have emerged as islands from the subsiding flood, as Christian principalities or provinces, and the professedly Christian population in them has again become dominant.
>
> Nor has the drying up ceased. Everywhere the process of internal decay and depopulation goes on . . . .

On December 11, 1918, the process was brought to a conclusion when General Allenby with the help of Arabian Bedouin forces conquered Palestine and Damascus. Allenby marched into Jerusalem celebrating the British conquest of the Ottoman Turks. Britain and France came to control the entire Middle East, which subsequently was partitioned as we now know it. The predicted "drying up of the Euphrates" was thus remarkably fulfilled.

The elimination of the Turkish Empire in the Middle East has served "to prepare the way for the kings from the east" (Rev 16:12). Several kings and their kingdoms were established as the result of the circumstances surrounding the League of Nations' partition of the Ottoman territories and the subsequent dissolution of the British Empire in the Middle East. In distinction from the reborn nation of Israel, they are the Arab Muslim nations of Jordan, Syria, Iraq, Iran, Saudi Arabia, and Egypt. Most of these lie to the East of Jerusalem, the focal point for the battle of Armageddon, and these now appear to be the probable candidates for "the kings of the east." Harold Barton summarizes this well as follows (195):

> The preparation for the kings of the East" we believe to have been accomplished in 1917, when the Turk was forced out of Jerusalem and the Jews permitted to go back and establish themselves as a nation, with power and wealth. This is what provides the kings of the East, as well as

the Power of the North, with an incentive to invade for the last time the "Holy Land." The Power of the North will come for spoil and those from the East for revenge and the gratification[sic] of long-standing hatred of God's chosen Old Testament people.

The "three unclean frog-like spirits" each have a specific province. Their fulfillment must reflect conditions existing at the time of or subsequent to the "drying up of the Euphrates," that is, as this author and many historicist interpreters see it, the later 19th century to the present. These spirits are "unclean" in the sense that they are demonic. They promote ideologies that oppose the true Gospel and the People of God.

The spirit "from the mouth of the dragon" suggests atheism or some pagan ideology. In the mid-twentieth century many identified it with atheistic communism. Much of this Marxist philosophy still prevails in the institutions of education today. We see this in the prevalent existentialism and relativism of post-modernist philosophy, which rejects absolute truth. Today, we must consider the Satanic spirit of Islam, most noticeable in radical Islam.

The spirit "from the mouth of the beast," from the standpoint of historicist interpretation, focuses on the Vatican and the Papal Antichrist. As a political power, the Papacy is inherently fascist. The Vatican has fostered the ecumenical spirit which has led to the rejection of the Papal Antichrist doctrine, the doctrine which helped to fuel the Protestant Reformation. Today, the Pope is exalted even among many Protestants as an exemplary representative of Christianity, in spite of his advocacy of the antichristian doctrines of the Roman Catholic Church (cf. Gal 1:6-9).

The spirit "from the mouth of the false prophet" points to the Roman Catholic priesthood. Revelation 13:11 indicates that this false prophet has "two horns like a lamb" but he speaks "like a dragon"; that is, he speaks as an agent of Satan. The message of the priest is to promulgate the doctrines of the Papal Church and to disciple converts in those disciplines. Jesuits were responsible for introducing both the futurist and the preterist alternatives to the Protestant historicist understanding of prophecy.

In the post-Reformation period, in 1833, Jesuit priests launched the Tractarian Movement, a movement designed to restore Roman Catholic doctrine and practice in the Anglican churches of England. This was intended to counteract the Protestant eschatology with its Roman Antichrist doctrine by teaching that the Antichrist and the events associated with him would occur as a future end-time event. This doctrine was imbibed by some Protestants in England in the 1830s and quickly spread to the United States and other countries, where it has become a common evangelical teaching among many believers. See Appendix 4.

Some Roman Catholics are also fostering the belief that a new European or World Confederacy will be headed by the Papacy.[31] The Jesuit-originated preterist interpretation of prophecy, which identifies the Antichrist with an ancient Roman emperor, has become attractive to many Revelation scholars, at first mainly to German rationalists, but more recently even to many evangelicals, as well as to humanistic scholars.[32] Largely in consequence of this Roman Catholic anti-Reformation movement, the Protestant historicist understanding of Revelation has been abandoned and largely ignored by many expositors.

The radical errors which currently accompany the interpretation of prophecy may well be attributed to the demonic influence of the three unclean spirits of Rev 16:13-14.[33]

---

[31] See the work of the Roman Catholic scholar, Malachi Martin, *The Keys of This Blood: the Struggle for World Dominion Between Pope John Paul II, Mikhail Gorbachev, and the Capitalist West* (New York: Simon & Schuster, 1991).

[32] Preterist interpreters include Grotius (1644), Eichhorn (1791), Ewald (1828), Stuart (1845), DeWette (1848), Milligan (1889), Holtzmann (1891), Swete (1906), Beckwith (1919), Charles (1920), Barclay (1959), Adams (1966), Ford (1975), Chilton (1987), Boring (1989), and Gentry (1997).

[33] I describe the errors as radical because they lead to several mutually exclusive interpretations of the Book of Revelation, which has discouraged many from making a serious study of the book, the book which contains our Lord's final biblical message to His Church.

The Seventh Bowl of God's Wrath

16:17. **The seventh angel poured out his bowl into the air, and out of the temple came a loud voice from the throne, saying, "It is done!"** [18]**Then there came flashes of lightning, rumblings, peals of thunder and a severe earthquake. No earthquake like it has ever occurred since man has been on earth, so tremendous was the quake.** [19]**The great city split into three parts, and the cities of the nations collapsed. God remembered Babylon the Great and gave her the cup filled with the wine of the fury of his wrath.** [20]**Every island fled away and the mountains could not be found.** [21]**From the sky huge hailstones of about a hundred pounds each fell upon men. And they cursed God on account of the plague of hail, because the plague was so terrible.**

16:17-21. The Seventh Bowl of God's Wrath   Exposition

With the pouring out of the seventh bowl, we have arrived at the last element of the last of the three major structural symbols of the book of Revelation—the seals, the trumpets, and the bowls. This emphatic ending is punctuated with a loud voice, the voice of God from the throne, saying, "It is done!" (16:17; cf. 15:1) One can hardly imagine the patience of the God who created mankind. He endured man's sinful rebellion and the apostasy of those who purport to be His chosen people. But the end of patience will surely come. God will act with final punitive judgment and He will reward his elect!

"The seventh angel poured out his bowl into the air" (16:17). One must conclude from what is subsequently described that the language of this passage is highly metaphorical (see below). It could hardly be fulfilled literally. Cities, though devastated by earthquake, do not split into three parts, islands do not fly away, and mountains do not get lost (16:19-20). The focus of this judgment is on "the great city," "Babylon." "Babylon" as a symbol for Rome stands not for the literal city but for Rome as the now global

Antichrist power. Babylon and its destruction is further described in chapters 17 and 18, where that city is identified also as "the great prostitute" (17:1, 5, 18). The implications of that characterization will be discussed later. We should understand the "earthquake" and the other terrestrial phenomena as figures for the overthrow of the political authority of the power represented. The theme of this passage is the destruction of Antichrist, the culminating event in the great series of Divine judgments addressed in the Revelation. This is the message the churches of Asia were waiting to hear when the apocalyptic vision was given! In God's time, Rome and the Roman Antichrist introduced in Daniel 7 will fall and Christ will reign as victor! Further explanation of this theme consumes the remaining chapters of the Revelation.[34]

What might the first century reader have learned from the fact that this final bowl is poured out upon the air? It would hardly be surprising, in the light of the bloodshed indicated in the previous bowls, if they assumed that some kind of human warfare was implied. The Romans were adept in the use of ballistic missiles hurled through the air by great catapults. Moreover, they would have remembered similar language in Old Testament warnings of end-time judgment, such passages as Ezek 38:22-23 (italics mine):

> I will execute judgment upon him with plague and bloodshed; *I will pour down torrents of rain, hailstones and burning sulfur on him and on his troops and on the many nations with him.* And so I will show my greatness and my holiness, and I will make myself known in the sight of many nations. Then they will know that I am the LORD.

The prophetic use of such symbols as earthquake and hail in the Old Testament is predominantly figurative, indicating the defeat and overthrow of national powers undergoing the judgment of God (see above, ch. 4 on 6:12-14). So the reader should under   stand

---

[34]One need not assume with Beale (p. 841) that the events described in chs. 17-21 follow "on the heels of the battle of Armageddon." 16:16 introduces the gathering of "kings" to the place called Armageddon. This is followed by the seventh bowl judgment as a precurser to that event. Likewise, 17:1-19:10 further prepares the reader for understanding seventh bowl conditions, the whole leading up to climax with Armageddon in 19:11-21.

Chapter Nine — *The seventh bowl of God's wrath, 16:17-21*

Rev 16:17-21. The language of these verses with its exaggerated style is highly emphatic—the greatest of all earthquakes and "huge hailstones weighing about a hundred pounds"! The focus is on the "Great City, Babylon," the Antichrist power that is represented by the Fourth Beast of Daniel 7 with its Little Horn. "The great city split into three parts, and the cities of the nations collapsed. God remembered Babylon the Great and gave her the cup filled with the wine of the fury of his wrath" (16:19). Antichrist is described earlier in Revelation 12 and 13, as well as in the subsequent chapters, 17 and 18.

There is great comfort for the church in knowing that the time is coming when the evils of this world will be destroyed. God will act to insure that His creation will be restored to its original holiness and glory!

16:17-21.   The Seventh Bowl of God's Wrath   Notes

17. The **loud voice from the throne**, the voice of God, speaking loudly, that is, with great authority (cp. 14:10). The language is metaphorical. The voice at this point should not be understood as a literal sound to be heard by all, but as auxiliary to what follows, so as to render emphatic the message which follows for those who would read. **18. A severe earthquake** unlike any that **has ever occurred** is an appropriate way to describe the final destruction of the powers of Antichrist. **19. The great city** is described in context as "Babylon." The description in chapter 18 favors the assumption that not only a city is described but an empire. Note 17:18, "The woman you saw is the great city *that rules over the kings of the earth*" (emphasis mine). **The cup filled with the wine of the fury of his wrath**: cp. 14:8, 10; here in 14:8 the wine cup is filled by Babylon "who made the nations drink the maddening wine of her adulteries." In 14:10, "anyone who worships the beast . . . will drink the wine of his [God's] fury, which will be poured full strength into the cup of his wrath" (cp. Rev 19:15). To "drink the cup" is an ancient idiomatic expression meaning to experience some awful destiny or judgment. (BAGD, 695; See Isa 51:17, 22; Lam 4:21; Matt 20:22; et al.) **20.** Compare **Every island**

fled away and the mountains could not be found with Rev 6:14, "Every mountain and island was removed from its place." This exaggerated earthquake imagery denotes the demise of a prominent world power. **21. Hailstones of about a hundred pounds** translates the Greek ὡς ταλαντιαία, *hōs talantiaía*, "weighing about a talent," or about 100 pounds (RSV, NASV, ESV). Exact weight is not intended; nor is it possible to determine from the archaeological evidence. The enormous size heightens the effect of the metaphor.

16:17-21 The Seventh Bowl of God's Wrath Fulfillment

We have observed in following the traditional historicist interpretation of Revelation that the province on which each bowl is poured out has indicated the location of the judgment. The bowl poured on the land focused on the Papal countries of Roman Europe; the bowl poured out on the sea focused on maritime warfare. This seventh bowl is poured out "upon the air" [Gk. ἐπὶ τὸν ἀέρα, *epì tòn aéra*]. This would appear to suggest a rather universal locale and perhaps aerial warfare. At no time in the history of the world has aerial warfare occurred as in the twentieth and the twenty-first centuries. The twentieth century witnessed the invention of the airplane and its use in warfare starting in World War I, also extensive use of aerial bombs and missiles, even inter-continental missiles. Nuclear warfare was demonstrated in the bombing of Nagasaki and Hiroshima. Two world wars fulfill the universal dimension of this prophecy. National upheaval has characterized these centuries. Empires have collapsed, governments have fallen. Many nations having been reconstituted. It may be said that "no earthquake like it has ever occurred since man has been on earth, so tremendous was the quake" (v. 18).

"The great city split into three parts" points to a time when the Antichrist power, the Papal empire, will suffer a three-fold political division. This may already be in progress with the reorganization of Roman Europe. Harold Barton, writing in the mid-twentieth century, comments:

> This was the result of the earthquake, which indicates a most remarkable change in the European commonwealth, and is the final breaking up of the Papal Empire into three parts, quite different from what has characterized it for about thirteen hundred years. The tenfold division has come to an end, and those who look for a restored tenfold Roman

> Empire will find only three divisions at the end time. When we see these three parts, . . . we shall know that the long-delayed judgment on Babylon is in remembrance before God, and His wrath will accomplish her final doom. (197)

Atkinson, writing about 1940, could see fulfillment of the three-fold division in terms of Communism-socialism, Nazi-fascism, and democracy. The political power of the Roman Church has already fallen as of 1870 with the expiration of the 1260 years a thing of the past. Yet, the countries of Roman Europe are still largely Roman Catholic in character. Catholic authorities look to the future for a time when the Pope will be at least the symbolic head of a renewed Europe, if not a universal one-world government.[35] From the standpoint of prophecy, this very doubtful. We must wait to see how the circumstances of our times play out.

The fall of "the cities of the nations" must also await further clarification from historical fulfillment. The context suggests that the cities probably refer to Roman Catholic entities in league with Rome.

The "huge hailstones" may well refer to the bombs and missiles characteristic of modern warfare.

There is difficulty in extending these last plagues beyond our present time. We have arrived at the final installment of the three major symbols—seals, trumpets, and bowls—which provide the chronological framework for the events predicted in the book. We believe we have identified plausibly, with a large degree of concurrence among historicist scholars, the fulfillment of each of the seven seals, the seven trumpets, and the seven bowls, and find that we are living in the era of the seventh bowl. This seventh bowl is God's final act of temporal judgment before the return of our Lord Jesus Christ. The odds that so detailed and complex a series of chronological fulfillments could be arbitrary and therefore fallacious are very great, indeed. Fulfilled prophecy should lead us to look up, for our redemption draws very near!

---

[35]For an extended Roman Catholic treatment of this theme, see Malachi Martin, *The Keys of This Blood: the Struggle for World Dominion Between Pope John Paul II, Mikhail Gorbachev, and the Capitalist West* (New York: Simon & Shuster, 1990). This teaching is the Roman Catholic version of Dominion Theology introduced in the fourth century with the exaltation of the Papacy under Constantine, which taught that Christ came to reign in the person of the Pope, and that through his reign the church would ultimately be victorious and rule over the world to establish Christ's kingdom.

The events addressed here immediately precede Armageddon and the return of Christ. The remaining chapters of the Revelation are commentary and explanation of that event.

Chapter Ten

THE FALL OF THE HARLOT BABYLON

Rev 17:1-18:24

Introduction

With the introduction of this chapter, we are starting our exposition of Revelation, chapters 17-18. The Vision has advanced through the major chronological indicators of the seven-sealed scroll: the seven seals, the seven trumpets, the little book, and the seven bowls of wrath. We have witnessed (1) in the six seals a forecast of the decline and fall of the pagan Roman Empire, in seal seven the introduction to the seven trumpets, and (2) with the six trumpets a prediction of the conquest of the Old Roman Empire by the barbarians in the West and the Muslims in the East. In chapter ten, a new parallel prophetic chronology (3) is presented in the form of a Little Book, with its presentation in chapters 11-13 of the Satanic triad as the Dragon, the Beast, and the False Prophet, their antichristian war against the covenant people of God, and in chapter 14 their final judgment. To show the chronological relationship of the two scrolls, the seventh trumpet is announced in 11:15 to indicate the time for the beginning of the seven-bowl final judgments against the Antichrist power. In chapters 15 and 16, (4) those judgments are described.

Chapters 17 and 18 are an extended excursus which enlarges on the seventh bowl and the fall of the Antichrist power. In context, this serves at least four purposes:

1. The introduction of the Antichrist as now not the controlling eighth head but as riding on the beast (17:1-6).
2. Clarification of certain details regarding the Antichrist symbolism (17:7-13).

3. The provision of a fitting climax to one of the overarching themes of the book by showing God's sovereign control of history, culminating with His judgment against the Antichrist power (17:14-18).
4. The excursus concludes with a poetic display which dramatizes the magnitude of this Antichrist power in its great defeat (ch. 18).

Chapter 19 appropriately follows this solemn judgment with a proleptic scene of the multitude of the heavenly beings joined by the great host of the redeemed and singing the Hallelujah Chorus!

The Woman on the Beast

17:1. **One of the seven angels who had the seven bowls came and said to me, "Come, I will show you the punishment of the great prostitute, who sits on many waters. ²With her the kings of the earth committed adultery and the inhabitants of the earth were intoxicated with the wine of her adulteries."**

³Then the angel carried me away in the Spirit into a desert. There I saw a woman sitting on a scarlet beast that was covered with blasphemous names and had seven heads and ten horns. ⁴The woman was dressed in purple and scarlet, and was glittering with gold, precious stones and pearls. She held a golden cup in her hand, filled with abominable things and the filth of her adulteries. ⁵This title was written on her forehead:

> **MYSTERY**
> **BABYLON THE GREAT**
> **THE MOTHER OF PROSTITUTES**
> **AND OF THE ABOMINATIONS OF THE EARTH.**

⁶I saw that the woman was drunk with the blood of the saints, the blood of those who bore testimony to Jesus.

   When I saw her, I was greatly astonished.

17:1-6a   The Woman on the Beast   Exposition

As observed in our introduction above, these first six verses serve as an introduction to chapters 17 and 18.

One of the seven bowl angels introduces the message of chapter 17 by inviting the Apostle John to come to see the judgment of "the great prostitute who sits on many waters." The definite article indicates to the reader that this prostitute is known from what precedes in the book. That fact is significant as that Antichrist power is not previously described in the figure of a "prostitute."

In the context of the message of Revelation, which draws heavily upon the Israelite covenant symbolism, the word implies that the woman does not represent a pagan or secular power but the unfaithful spouse of Yahweh, an apostate church.[36] That the prostitute riding the beast conveys the image of an apostate church is also suggested by the antithetic correspondence of this image with the positive image of the church as a woman in chapter 12, where, as we have seen in our comment on 12:1, she represents the true visible church. Whereas the woman of chapter 12:1, 6 is protected by Providence, the woman of chapter 17 is subject to God's judgment. We are reminded of our Lord's promise regarding His true church at Caesarea Philippi, "On this rock I will build my church and the gates of Hades will not overcome it" (Matt 16:18).[37]

The use of the label, "prostitute" (Heb. זוֹנָה, *zōnāh*; LXX Gk, πόρνη, *pórnê*) and its cognates as a metaphor for the unfaithful among the covenant people Israel is addressed in the prophetic

---

[36]Note also the priestly imagery in the description of the false prophet in ch. 13. The preterist interpretation that this represents the pagan priesthood of the Roman Imperial cult ignores the O. T. background of the symbolism in Revelation and requires a rejection of the year-day principle for understanding the 1260 day prophecies associated with the Antichrist. Moreover, the preterist interpretation usually rejects the testimony of the Apostolic church to the Domitianic authorship of the Book in identifying the Antichrist of Revelation 12 with Nero. See our Appendix 1.

[37]When speaking of the true Church, that is, those whose names are written in the book of life in heaven, we capitalize the word "Church," but when referring to the visible, local church, whether true or apostate, we use lower case. The exception, of course, is when the word is the name or part of the name of a specific entity, such as the Roman Catholic Church.

books of the Old Testament and therefore familiar to the Bible student, including the reader at the end of the first Christian century.[38] As the Covenant nation of Israel committed spiritual harlotry by her alliances with foreign kings (Ezek 16:26, 28, 29), so the prostitute of Revelation 17 engages in adulterous alliances with "the kings of the earth" (vv. 2, 12, 13).

The prostitute is described as "one who sits on many waters" (v. 1), later as "sitting on a scarlet beast" (v. 3). In the figure, the idea of "sitting" implies some kind of relationship, probably in view of what follows something less than the control that a rider normally exercises over his steed.[39]

"The inhabitants of the earth were intoxicated with the wine of her adulteries" (17:2). The figure of intoxication is part of the imagery of prostitution and suggests the lack of normal reserve and rationality (cf. v. 4b).

The woman is in a desert (Gk., ἔρημος, 'erêmos). This is the same figure found in 12:6 and 14, the place to which the woman representing the true visible church flees. The common "location" supports the historicist understanding that the figure represents dislocation from political status rather than a literal geographic loca-

---

[38]The KJV usually translates the noun as "harlot" or "whore." Cf. Isa 1:21; Jer 2:20; 3:1, 9; Ezek 16:15-22; 23:5-8; Hos 1:2; 3:3-5.

[39]Beale states "that sitting connotes sovereignty is clear," alluding to numerous verses where this appears to be true. However, context, rather than statistics, takes priority in determining meaning. What follows in v. 16 suggests the prostitute's lack of control. Further, Beale's suggestion that the seer's description of the woman's "sitting on many waters" is "taken from" Jer 51:13 (LXX 28:13) appears to imply that the author of Revelation was composing his text by expounding O. T. sources, rather than writing a description of what he saw and heard in the Patmos vision (G. K. Beale, *The Book of Revelation*. [Grand Rapids: Eerdmans, 1999], 848). Moreover, though Jer 51:13 refers to the literal inhabitants of Babylon as "dwelling on many waters," the statement should be understood as a literal geographical description regarding the waters of the Euphrates river and the connected irrigation canals, whereas the language of Rev 17:1 is metaphorical, as explained in v. 15. Further, it is the people of Babylon who dwell on "many waters," whereas in our text the "many waters" *are* the people. Nevertheless, this is not to reject Beale's main point in calling attention to the parallel between the literal Babylon in Jeremiah and the metaphorical Babylon in Revelation, both as victims of God's judgment. This is one of the many instances when the Divine author of Revelation introduces what are sometimes called allusive references.

tion. Though here in chapter 17 the woman characterized as a prostitute is still pretentiously dressed as royalty in purple and scarlet and adorned with gold and precious jewels (v. 4), ironically, she is found in the "wilderness." In the historical setting when this image is fulfilled, the time of the seventh trumpet and the fall of "Babylon," the woman is no longer ruling the beast as its eighth head but is riding on it (17:3). This should be understood to imply her loss of temporal power over the world of the Ten Kings. (How this fall from power will come about is addressed later in vv. 16 and 17.) The woman bore "a golden cup in her hand, filled with abominable things and the filth of her adulteries" (4b). The imagery should suggest the sinful deceptions with which the kings were intoxicated (v. 2).

The woman is further described as bearing her characterizing name on her forehead: "Mystery Babylon the Great, the mother of prostitutes and the abominations of the earth" (v. 5). The word, "mystery," suggests those aspects of this Apocalyptic imagery which for the first century reader must remain unexplained, specifically, how the rather complex imagery associated with this Antichrist power would later come to be fulfilled.

The characterization of the woman as "Babylon the Great" reminds the reader of the words of Nebuchadnezzar, "Is this not great Babylon that I have built, by my mighty power and for the glory of my majesty?" (Dan 4:30) The voice of God responded from heaven, "Your royal authority has been taken from you." So even the title of the woman, "Babylon the Great," is pregnant with Divine judgment. We remember that boasting is one of the characteristics of Antichrist in the character of the Little Horn ("The horn had . . . a mouth that spoke boastfully"; Dan 7:8) and the Apostle Paul's Man of Lawlessness ("He . . . exalts himself . . ."; 2 Thess 2:4).

The woman is also "The Mother of Prostitutes." As mother, she will bear apostate children who abandon the covenant of the Lord and resort to pagan idolatries. The final element of her title is

Mother "of the Abominations of the Earth." What is prohibited to the covenant people, Scripture describes as "an abomination" (NIV, "detestable") e.g., unclean food (Lev 7:18), idolatry (Deut 7:25), sexual immorality (Lev 18:26, 27), etc. Prostitution in the sense of spiritual unfaithfulness to the Lord is associated with the idolatries of the heathen and is particularly characterized as abomination by the prophets (Jer 13:27; Ezek 16:22, 36). Clearly, the woman riding the beast in chapter 17 represents a power or entity that is a "mother of abominations."

A practical application of this text warns us against assimilating attitudes and practices which characterize the pagan secular culture that surrounds us. Much of what we confront from this source is in God's eyes idolatry and spiritual prostitution.

The description of the "Great Prostitute" ends with the observation that the woman whom John saw "was drunk with the blood of the saints, the blood of those who bore testimony to Jesus" (17:6). This statement indicates that the woman is to be regarded as in some way closely identified with the beast on which she rides, for the beast in chapter 11:7-9 and 13:7 is the power conducting the war against God's people. As Revelation represents the evil powers as a triumvirate (the Devil, the Beast, and the False Prophet), rather than a foursome, it is best to see the woman and the beast as a complex representation of that one Antichrist power represented by the beast in chapter 13.

In chapter 13 and in 17:11, the Antichrist power is presented as the eighth, resurrected head. "One of the heads of the beast seemed to have a fatal wound, but the fatal wound had been healed" (13:3). The use of the past tenses (Greek perfect and aorist indicative) is to be understood as reflecting the Hebraic prophetic perfect, which envisions future events as certain as though they had already occurred.[40] Compare 17:11: "The beast . . . is an eighth

---

[40]For the prophetic perfect tense, see *Gesenius' Hebrew Grammar*. 2nd ed. (Oxford: Clarendon Press, 1910) §106.3, p. 312.

king. He belongs to the seven and is going to his destruction."[41] The difference indicated in symbol is that in chapter 17, the Antichrist power is represented by the woman who is riding. At the time on which this prophecy focuses, the time of the Seventh Bowl, she is no longer the head or governing power of the beast. Therefore, we conclude that the Antichrist, Mystery Babylon, has now lost temporal power over the nations symbolized by the ten horns (Cachemaille, 590-591).

17:1-6a. The Woman on the Beast — Notes

1. The prostitute is described as one who **sits on many waters**. This imagery is explained in v. 15 as "peoples, multitudes, nations and languages." This indicates her widespread association with many ethnic groups. **3.** "On many waters" appears to disagree with her location as in **the desert** (v. 3). The apparent discrepancy highlights the metaphorical nature of the language. As we have observed above on 12:6, "desert" in the Apocalypse is used to denote a condition remote politically from the established government. The beast is now first described here as **scarlet** (Gk., κόκκινος, *kókkinos*, "red"), probably to identify this "beast" as having the Satanic qualities of the red dragon of 12:3 and 13:2. Alternatively, the color may be intended to suggest the bloodshed occasioned by the beast. The **blasphemous names** allude to 13:5, 6 as well as to Dan 7:20, 25 and 2 Thess 2:4. On the **seven heads and ten horns**, see above on 12:3 and 13:1 and 3. **4. Purple and scarlet** were the colors worn by royalty in the Roman world. Kistemaker states, "Royalty wore garments of those colors, as did members of the Roman senate, dignitaries, and wealthy people" (464). The garments together with the adornment with **gold, precious stones and pearls**, gives a picture of great, ostentatious wealth. The **golden cup**, likewise, is a symbol of wealth and ostentation, but instead of offering wholesome beverage, it is full of **abominable things and the filth of her adulteries**. The language must be understood

---

[41]We will comment below on the omitted part ("who once was, and now is not").

as metaphorical elements of the prostitution symbolism. "The word abomination denotes the objects and practices that are acutely offensive to God. Among others, they include the worship of idols (Deut 18:22; 20:13); homosexual acts and all sexual perversions (Lev 18:22; 20:13); witchcraft, casting spells, and divination (Deut 18:10, 11)."[42] "The filth of her adulteries" points in the symbolism to the woman as the unfaithful spouse of Yahweh, that is one who has violated the redemptive covenant God has made with His people.[43] **5.** Her title, **Mystery**, may be intended to suggest only that the woman is to be understood as symbol rather than as literal Babylon.[44] This then will also apply to the harlot figure with her elaborate description. The reader may also be reminded of the Apostle Paul's allusion to the coming of the Man of Lawlessness as "the mystery of lawlessness" (Gk., μυστήριον . . . τῆς ἀνομίας; *musterion . . . tês ánomíos*, 2 Thess 2:7; trans. mine). The mystery is potentially revealed when the prophecy is fulfilled. **Babylon the Great** suggests judgment comparable to the destruction of ancient Babylon. This symbolic use of "Babylon" draws on the language of Dan 4:30, "Is not this the great Babylon that I have built as the royal residence, by my mighty power and for the glory of my majesty?" The pretentious character of the Little Horn (Dan 7:8, 20) and the Man of Lawlessness (2 Thess 2:4) is analogous to Nebuchadnezzar's bold statement, this to be followed by his abject humiliation. On **Babylon** as an apocalyptic symbol for the city of Rome, see above on 14:8. The destruction of the Roman Antichrist as "Babylon"

---

[42]Simon Kistemaker, *Exposition of the Book of Revelation* (New Testament Commentary; Grand Rapids: Baker, 2001), 465.

[43]Prostitution was rampant in the ancient world as always, even to our day. As a literal institution, it is offensive to God because of its corrupting effects on the principles of moral purity, marriage, and family life inherent in the laws which were given to govern God's people. The prostitute (πόρνη, *pórnē*) is characterized by the fact that her conduct (πορνεία) violates her personal *chastity*. *She becomes also an adulteress* (μοιχαλίς, *moichalís*) if she is married or if she has sex with married persons, as she inevitably does. The two terms are consistently used distinctively in the Bible, as *adultery* is not, per se, a sexual act, unchastity, but is by definition the violation of the marriage covenant. Both terms are so used in the LXX and reflect the biblical use of the Hebrew terms זְנוּת, *zenût*, "prostitution," זֹנָה, *zônah*, "prostitute," and נָאַף, *ni'uph*, "adultery."

[44]R. H. Charles, *A Critical and Exegetical Commentary on the Revelation of St. John* (International critical commentary; Edinburgh: T. & T. Clark, 1920), 2.65.

Chapter Ten   *The woman on the beast, 17:1-6*a   393

draws conceptually from the prophecies of ancient Babylon's destruction in Isa 13:1-32, 14:4-23; 21:1-12; 47:1-15; and Jer 50:1-51:64, as well as from extra-biblical usage as evidenced from Jewish literature.[45] Peter's reference to the church from which he writes as "She who is in Babylon" quite likely also is a reference to the church at Rome (1 Pet 5:13). The description of the woman as **The Mother of Prostitutes** brings to the forefront the figurative use of "prostitution" as spiritual adultery, i.e. violation of the exclusive spiritual marriage commitment of the covenant people to Yahweh (see especially Ezek 16 and 23, as well as the book of Hosea). This prophetic background anticipates that the Antichrist would be, in New Testament terms, an apostate church. The characterization as the "mother of prostitutes" views Antichrist as giving birth to many apostate offspring. She is also characterized as the mother of **the abominations of the earth,** which suggests that many other sins result from her apostasy. **6.** That the woman was **drunk** expands on the motif of prostitution, as alcohol, then as now, was used to release inhibitions and strictures of conscience. The figure also carries the connotation of irresponsible activity in the murder of **the saints**, who are described as **those who bore the testimony to Jesus.** This characterization alludes to 12:17, where the 144,000 are identified with "those who obey God's commandments and hold to the testimony of Jesus."[46]

The Woman on the Beast (cont'd)

17:6b. When I saw her, I was greatly astonished. ⁷Then the angel said to me: "Why are you astonished? I will explain to you the mystery of the woman and of the beast she rides, which has the seven heads and ten horns. ⁸The beast, which you saw, once was, now is not, and will come up out of the Abyss and go to his destruction. The inhabitants of the earth whose names have not been writ-

---

[45]For Jewish works, see *Midr. Rab.* Num 7:10; *Midr.* Pss. 137:1, 8; *Sib. Or.* 5.143, 159 (ca. A.D. 90); 2 *Apoc. Bar.* 10:2; 11:1; 33:2; 67:7; 79:1 (late 1st-early 2nd cent. A.D.); 4 Ezra 3:1-2, 28-31; 16:44, 46 (early 2nd cent.). David E. Aune, *Revelation* . (Word biblical commentary; Nashville: Nelson, 1997-1998), 2. 830; Beale, 755.

[46]This unambiguous identification of this formulary with the saints martyred under Antichrist would appear to be sufficient to refute the claim of some Seventh-day Adventists that 12:17 refers to Saturday-sabbath keepers.

ten in the book of life from the creation of the world will be astonished when they see the beast, because he once was, now is not, and yet will come.

⁹"This calls for a mind with wisdom. The seven heads are seven hills on which the woman sits. ¹⁰They are also seven kings. Five have fallen, one is, the other has not yet come; but when he does come, he must remain for a little while. ¹¹The beast who once was, and now is not, is an eighth king. He belongs to the seven and is going to his destruction.

¹²"The ten horns you saw are ten kings who have not yet received a kingdom, but who for one hour will receive authority as kings along with the beast. ¹³They have one purpose and will give their power and authority to the beast. ¹⁴They will make war against the Lamb, but the Lamb will overcome them because he is Lord of lords and King of kings—and with him will be his called, chosen and faithful followers."

17:6b-14   The Woman on the Beast (cont'd)   Exposition

The angel asks a rhetorical question, "Why are you astonished?" (6b). He then proceeds in this entire section to answer by explaining the mystical character of both the beast and the prostitute woman. Perhaps the Apostle's astonishment was due to the enormity of the woman's "drunken" slaughter of God's people, which may well have far surpassed his anticipation. Perhaps it was the shift in the metaphor from the eighth head of the beast to Antichrist as a *harlot*, an image new at this point in the Apocalyptic vision.

By analogy with the harlot metaphor as used of the Old Testament covenant people, Israel (Ezek 16:15-22; 23:2-21), John could hardly have missed the implication that the harlot represented an adulterous church. From our perspective in history, that implication should be rather obvious, but for John near the end of the first century, the idea that Antichrist was not the pagan Roman power probably had not been anticipated. At any rate, the angel proceeds to explain the mystery both of the woman and of the beast she rides. At this point, John had had little opportunity to reflect on the significance of what he had seen and written.

Much of what the angel says has been anticipated in the previous scenes of the vision. The angel calls attention to the fact that the beast has seven heads and ten horns. This must have reminded John that he has seen this beast before (13:1; cp. Dan 7:7, 24).

The angel explains the beast (v. 8) as the one "who was, is not, and is about to come up out of the abyss" (NASV, cp. RSV, NRSV, REB, ESV).[47] This mystical formula had in John's time much the character of a riddle. It pertains to the sequence of the eight heads of the beast. The beast that "is not" must be the old seven-headed beast when it was to suffer a mortal wound (13:3). It nevertheless would arise out of the abyss in the form of the eighth head. The eighth king "belongs to the seventh," as he is the resurrected seventh, and therefore participates in the seventh's character, that character described so graphically in Daniel 7. We will comment further on this in the fulfillment section below. The repeated declaration that this eighth head will "go to his destruction" (vv. 8, 11) emphasizes the eventual destiny of this Antichrist power (see 19:20).

The unusual ascription of double meaning to the seven heads of the beast in verse 9 has the effect of identifying the Antichrist beast with Rome while also explaining them as seven "kings," that is, kingdoms or governments.[48] Rome has been known from ancient times as the city on seven hills. This meaning would have been obvious to the first readers of this text. The explanation of Rome as a series of constitutional governments (i.e., kingdoms) was explicit in the ancient Roman historians (see above on 12:3), and therefore accessible to the informed reader at the end of the first century. For the identification of the eighth Antichrist head, see our Fulfillment

---

[47]The NIV translation inserts the word "now," reading "now is not." This changes the meaning of the formula, as the beast existed in John's day. See the comments following. The Greek formula reads, ἦν καί οὐκ, καὶ μέλλει ἀναβαίνειν ἐκ τῆς αβύσσου, ên kaí oúk 'éstin, kaì méllei 'anabaínein ek tês 'abússou. The verb ἔστιν should be understood as a gnomic present.

[48]It is of course an axiom of hermeneutics that a given word or expression can only have one meaning unless otherwise indicated in the context. This is an essential characteristic of language which normally must be unambiguous to convey meaning.

section below. However, as the prostitute is riding on the beast when this scene is to be fulfilled, her headship as the eighth head appears to have been replaced by the headship of the ten rebellious kings (see 17:16).

Regarding the ten horns, they are identified in 17:12 with ten kings "who have not yet received a kingdom." This prophecy cannot be transtemporal, as the language requires that it pertains to a time future to the time of writing. As in Daniel, the word "kings" refers to kingdoms, that is, nations as governmental institutions. The same ten horns appear on the fourth beast in Dan 7:7 and 24, on the dragon in Rev 12:3b, as well as here in Rev 17:3 and 12. The seven-headed dragon in 12:3b wore diadem crowns on its heads, whereas the beast in 13:1 wore diadem crowns on its horns. For the first-century reader, the diadem crown was not worn by Roman rulers but by the Persians. It was known as a sign of the despotic authority of the Persian kings, and thus an obvious evil omen when here associated with the Roman beast and his ten allied kings. Conditions could only go from bad to worse.

The ten horns are described in 17:12 as "ten kings who have not yet received a kingdom but *they will receive authority as kings at one time with the beast* [italicized trans. mine]." "At one time" translates the Greek original, μίαν ὥραν, *mían hōran*, an accusative of time (BAGD, 231a). Apart from the larger context, the phrase is ambiguous, as it may be translated "one hour" as in the common versions, or "at one time" as in my translation above. For the first-century reader, the ambiguity may be one of the mysteries inherent in the Apocalypse, which nevertheless should resolve itself for the discerning reader when fulfilled. For further comment, see the Fulfillment section below.[49]

---

[49]See E. B. Elliott, *Horae Apocalypticae*. (5th ed.; London: Seeley, Jackson, and Halliday, 1862), 3:81. The unanimity of the modern translations may reflect a common bias, and perhaps even ignorance of the particulars of historicist interpretation. The suggestion of ignorance is based on the fact that recent commentators, even those who write rather extended expositions such as Aune (1998), Beale (1999), and Osborne (2002) in their exegesis evidence no awareness of the interpretations of such historicist scholars as E. B. Elliott (5th ed., 1862). Elliott points out that if taken as "one hour," this text will conflict with any systematic exposition of other time references in the

Chapter Ten   *The woman on the beast (cont'd), 17:6b-14*   397

"They [v. 13a] have one purpose" refers to the relationship between the Ten Horns and the Beast. They will constitute an alliance in which the Horns will cooperate with the Beast in waging war against the Lamb (v. 14). Because the Lamb, Jesus Christ, is the head of the true visible church,[50] the war in the temporal sphere was to be directed against Christ's faithful Covenant people, as previously indicated in 11:7 and in chapter 13.

The Antichristian war is reintroduced here in this excursus (chs. 17-18) not to reiterate the terrible consequences of the war but to assure the reader that "the Lamb will overcome them because he is Lord of lords and King of kings—and with him will be his called, chosen and faithful followers"! (v. 14b)

17:6b-14   **The Woman on the Beast (cont'd)**   Notes

6b. When John saw the prostitute he was **greatly astonished**. The expression in the Greek is highly emphatic. Literally translated it reads, "I wondered [in] great wonderment" (ἐθαύμασα . . . θαῦμα μέγα *'ethaúmasa . . . thoûma méga*). θαῦμα with its derivatives has a variety of nuances which must be determined from context, whether negative or positive, whether denoting surprise or evoking wonder or amazement. Here, perhaps one should infer both amazement and, in the light of the mystery

---

prophecy. Elliott's work was declared by the late eminent bibliographer, Wilbur Smith, as "in some ways the most learned of all English works on the Apocalypse to appear in the 19th century. His knowledge of history is astonishing. . . . . His 400-page [sic; read 286-page] survey of the history of the interpretation of the book of Revelation is the most exhaustive in our language." (Wilbur M.Smith, *Preliminary Bibliography for the Study of Prophecy* (Boston: W. A. Wilde, 1952), 28) Nineteenth century interpretation predominantly followed Elliott. Another eminent and popular historicist scholar likewise ignored by more recent commentators is the great prophetic and missionary statesman, H. Grattan Guinness. Guinness followed and developed Elliott. He published six major works on biblical prophecy, most of which went through several editions.

[50]We remind the reader that we use the term, "true visible church" in distinction from "apostate visible church." The term "visible church" denotes the church as it exists organized in locality. Thus, the true visible church is a church, or collectively churches, which conforms to the essentials of biblical doctrine. Such churches will include both genuine and false believers, as Jesus taught in his parable of the Wheat and the Tares (darnel; Matt 13:24-30).

associated with the prostitute, also wonder. John from the perspective of the first century was probably amazed that a future Roman Antichrist should be presented as a prostitute, a figure which, as indicated above, was dominantly associated in their prophetic Scriptures with apostates among God's covenant people. Perhaps for him at this time, the priestly imagery of the Beast from the Earth (ch. 13) took on new light. Wonder in the sense of a need for explanation is served by the explanatory nature of the context to follow. **7.** The word, **mystery**, is commonly used in the pagan mystery religions of the New Testament period to indicate knowledge reserved for the initiates but kept from outsiders. The New Testament, however, uses the word to emphasize the public nature of the truths of the Gospel, including the revelation that is publicly declared by Christ and His Apostles and mediated to all who believe and follow Jesus. This usage in contradistinction from the pagan mysteries is illustrated by such passages as 1 Cor 15:51, "Behold, I tell you a mystery . . . " (NASB), and Rom 16:25-26, ". . . According to the revelation of the mystery . . . now revealed and made known . . . so that all nations might believe . . . ."[51] In our text, this usage of "mystery" is applied in a narrower sense to the woman—the angelic messenger proceeds to explain the mystery. As with all prophecy, an element of mystery remains, at least until its fulfillment.

The Woman and the Beast (cont'd)

17:15. Then the angel said to me, "The waters you saw, where the prostitute sits, are peoples, multitudes, nations and languages. ¹⁶The beast and the ten horns you saw will hate the prostitute. They will bring her to ruin and leave her naked; they will eat her flesh and burn her with fire. ¹⁷For God has put it into their hearts to accomplish his purpose by agreeing to give the beast their power to rule, until God's words are fulfilled. ¹⁸The woman you saw is the great city that rules over the kings of the earth."

---

[51]Occasionally the mystery concept is used in a manner more like that of the mystery religions: Mark 4:11, "To you has been given the mystery of the kingdom of God, but those who are outside get everything in parables . . . " (NASB).

Chapter Ten — *The woman on the beast, 17:15-18*

17:15-18 **The Woman on the Beast (cont'd)** **Exposition**

In the foregoing passage, 17:1-14, our Lord explains certain details concerning the "prostitute woman," the Antichrist Power, her relationship with the peoples of the Roman world, their governments as "the ten kings," and the antichristian war to be conducted against the true Covenant People of God. This war, both for the churches who first received this prophecy and for the church through the centuries since, was surely through much suffering to result in victory for Christ and for His people.

In 17:15-18, we have an explanation of the "waters" on which the prostitute sits, as well as the surprising revelation that the "beast and the ten horns" will eventually rebel against the Antichrist Woman and bring her to ruin. The statement concludes with the identification of the woman with Rome, "the great city that rules" even at the end of the first century "over the kings of the earth."

In this dramatic scene, the woman is seen sitting on "many waters" (17:1, 15). In 17:3 and 7 she is described as sitting on "the scarlet beast." How is the reader to understand this? The apparent discrepancy becomes clear when we read that the "many waters" are "peoples, multitudes, nations, and languages." The people are governed by the "beast" with its "ten horns," who carries the woman and over which the woman exerts her influence. The people are the victims of both.

The expression, "peoples, multitudes, nations, and languages," is not inappropriate as descriptive of the peoples governed by the ten-horn nations of the Roman world. It has a universal flavor which may have suggested, even in the first century, a more universal world power.

In this passage, the headship has shifted from the woman to the beast with its ten horns. In distinction from chapter 13 where Antichrist is represented as the eighth head of the Roman beast, here in chapter 17 Antichrist is represented as an evil woman. She at first is borne along by the beast, then subsequently brought to ruin by its ten horns or kings. The Beast's apparently temporal ruin of the Antichrist Woman is to be carried out by the very nations that had earlier allied with Antichrist in the conduct of the war against God's Covenant People.

17:17 indicates that the attack against the Woman by the ten-horns of the beast was ordained by God, "who put it into their hearts to accomplish his purpose . . . until God's words are fulfilled." The allusion to the fulfillment of God's words probably refers to Dan 7:11 and 15, where the text predicts Antichrist's final destruction. One may compare this with numerous passages in the prophets of the Old Testament which represent God as using foreign nations to wage war against Israel to purify the nation in preparation for her Messiah. See, for example, Isa 10:1-11 and Jer 34:12-22.

17:15-18.   The Woman on the Beast (cont'd)   Notes

15. The formula, **Then the angel said to me**, reflects the visionary character of the revelation, as introduced in 1:11, 19; 4:1, and subsequently with "I watched," "I saw," "I looked," "I heard," and in 17:1, "Come, I will show you . . . ." John actually experienced the drama unfold before his eyes, and in his consciousness seemed actually to move from one place to another to get a particular orientation for the message he was told to write.[52] The expression **peoples, multitudes, nations, and languages** in this context probably reflects Dan 7:14. Daniel says that "all

---

[52]Our literal understanding of the text as the Word of God precludes the apparent conclusion of some commentators that the writer in using such formulae was merely casting his own ideas in dramatic literary style to pursuade his readers of their Divine origin. See, e.g., Aune, 3.956 and his comment on v. 15, "Though the author-editor uses the stereotypical interpretation formula ἃ εἶδες, "that you saw," which is part of the structure of Revelation 17 (8, 12, 15, 18), v 15 is an interjection into the text that has no organic relationship to the preceding or following context . . . ." It should be obvious to the reader, however, that the explanation of the "waters" is provided here because it is a detail of the symbolism that had not previously been explained.

peoples, nations, and languages" (ESV) should serve the Son of Man in His kingdom reign. The formula appears in many places with minor variations in Daniel and Revelation. However, it occurs here as the words of the angel, not as originating with John. **16.** The angel's word regarding the devastation of the prostitute reflects Ezekiel's prediction of the destruction of Jerusalem in Ezek 23:25-29:

Rev 17:16	*Ezek 23:25-29*
They will . . . leave her naked	They will leave you naked and bare and the shame of your prostitution will be exposed (v. 29)
They will . . . burn her with fire	Those of you who are left will be consumed by fire (25b)

It is probable that the metaphorical language draws upon common law and biblical practices for punishing prostitutes, suggesting that prostitutes when punished were sometimes paraded naked in the streets (cf. Hos 2:3), or in more aggravated cases put to death by burning (cf. Lev 21:9). These metaphors suggest the consumption of the assets and the economy of the Antichrist power as indicated by the imagery in Revelation 18, as well as its ultimate destruction altogether. That **they will eat her flesh** may be understood metaphorically to indicate the destruction of her economic power, a subject expanded in chapter 18. One may also observe that the probable allusion to Ezekiel's apostate Jerusalem appears to function as a metaphor for an apostate Antichrist power, the Woman on the Beast. **17.** To **put it into their hearts** (ἔδωκεν εἰς τὰς καρδίας αὐτῶν, *'édōken eis tàs kardías aùtōn*) is a Semitic idiom (cp. Exod 35:34; Ezra 7:27; Neh 2:12, 7:5; Aune 3.958). **Their royal power** (τὴν βασιλείαν αὐτῶν, *tēn basileían aùtōn*), more literally, "the authority of their kingdom" or perhaps, "the territories of their kingdoms" (BAGD, 135). The phrase **until the words of God are fulfilled** implies the fulfillment of a previous prophecy, as in 10:7b, which reads "the mystery of God would be fulfilled, just as he announced to his servants the prophets" (ESV).

17:1-18.   The Woman on the Beast   Fulfillment

As explained in the introduction to this chapter above, chapter 17 is part of an extended excursus embracing chapters 17 and 18, which enlarges on the bowl prophecies and their prediction of the fall of the

Antichrist power. We pointed out that, in context, 17:1-18 serves at least three purposes:

1. The introduction of the Antichrist as now not the controlling eighth head but as a rider on the beast (17:1-6).
2. Clarification of certain details regarding the Antichrist symbolism (17:7-13).
3. The provision of a fitting climax to one of the overarching themes of the book by showing God's sovereign control of history, culminating with His judgment against the Satanic Roman Antichrist (17:14-18).

Most of the interpretive questions raised by this chapter and its fulfillment are answered either in our Exposition above or in the earlier commentary on the previous chapters of Revelation. These include (1) the identification and character of the woman and of the beast, (2) the nature of the woman's "adulteries," (3) the identification of the seven heads and ten horns of the beast, and (4) the war of Antichrist with the saints.

The major issue remaining is the chronological implication of the fact that Antichrist is presented here for the first time, not as the beast or one of its heads, but as a harlot riding on the beast. Antichrist is no longer the controlling eighth head of the beast. When in the process of prophetic fulfillment does this change occur, and when should we look for the attack of the ten horns on the woman?

The apparent rationale for the distinction between the beast and the prostitute woman is the implication that a time was to come when Antichrist would lose control of the Roman beast, and therefore no longer could appropriately be symbolized as its head. We can with some confidence therefore date the woman's dethronement and mounting of the beast at or shortly before 1870. This is illustrated dramatically in the fact that the "ten horn" kings who allied with the Antichrist beast to wage war against the saints (17:13-14) now turn against the Antichrist woman as instruments of Providence to ruin her (17:16). This loss of headship of the Roman Beast corresponds well with Papal Rome's loss of temporal power addressed in our previous chapter. We have seen above how the ten horns of the Beast aptly serve as a metaphor for the nations of Roman Europe. With the advance of Renaissance humanism and the rise of the nationalistic spirit in those nations, augmented by the corruptions of Papal Rome, they threw off the yoke of Papal sovereignty, as forecast in the pouring out of the first six bowls. The subsequent status of Antichrist as "sitting on the scarlet beast" (17:3), while nevertheless "dressed in purple and scarlet" and "glittering with gold, precious stones and pearls" corresponds with Papal Rome in the post-1870 era. Though without temporal power and divested of the Papal territories, she maintains the pretense and aura of her assumed royalty.

When 17:12 states that "the ten horns . . . are ten kings who have not yet received a kingdom," it speaks from the standpoint of the late first century when Revelation was written, not from the modern reader's time. The ten "Kings" came into their kingship as the Barbarian nations of Roman Europe. They gave "their power and authority to the beast" when they allied with the Papacy after the 5th-century fall of the old Roman Empire. They ruled "at one time" (see Exposition above) as kings together with the beast.

17:16 states that "the beast and the ten horns . . . will hate the prostitute," "bring her to ruin and leave her naked." The prediction that they will "eat her flesh and burn her with fire" has been understood by historicist interpreters to have been fulfilled during the era of the bowls. This conforms well to the circumstances occurring under the fourth and fifth bowls (see above), when the Papacy was assaulted by Napoleonic armies and deprived of much of her power and her physical territories in Italy. Many Papal properties were burned and great economic loss suffered. The Pope was taken prisoner to France. The ruin resulted in the Papacy's loss of temporal power, which climaxed in 1870 with her loss of political authority over the "ten kings," the nations of Roman Europe. Thus the metaphorical language of 17:16 was satisfied. Deprived of most of her properties, including extensive geographic territories, as well as many of her churches and priests, her political power, and her prestige, her "flesh" was "eaten" and she was left "naked." The presentation of the harlot as riding on the beast reflects the culmination of the process anticipated in the detailed explanations offered in the remainder of chapter ten.

18:1-24   **The Fall of Babylon**   **Introduction**

Chapter 18 is entirely devoted to the theme of "Babylon's" fall. Babylon here, as in chapter 17 is a symbol for the Roman church as Antichrist. The chapter divides into two parts: First, verses 1-8 announce with great intensity the fall of the Antichrist power, while warning her inhabitants to come out of her in order to escape her devastating judgment. The second part, 18:9-24 consists of a lengthy lament on the part of the kings and the merchants who witness her doom.

Throughout this chapter, Antichrist is viewed as a great city taking the name of ancient Babylon, whereas in chapter 17, Antichrist is presented in the figure of a harlot. Each metaphor carries with it a distinctive aspect of Antichrist's character, while both predict its destruction. There is left to the reader no question but that we are presented with two ways of looking at the same Antichrist power. The harlot is named "Babylon the Great, the mother of prostitutes" who holds out "a golden cup" "filled with abominable things" (17:4), and in chapter 18 it is stated that "all the nations have drunk the maddening wine of her adulteries. The kings of the earth committed adultery with her . . ." (18:3a).

In chapter 17, an apostate church is like a prostitute unfaithful to her covenant marriage to the Lord. Chapter 18 focuses on this "woman's" indulgence in commerce and wealth and the great sense of loss at her ruin on the part of those who had profited from her. Those who had been consorting with her should leave her lest they experience with her her punishment (18:4-5).

The fall of Babylon

18:1. After this I saw another angel coming down from heaven. He had great authority, and the earth was illuminated by his splendor. ²With a mighty voice he shouted:

> "Fallen! Fallen is Babylon the Great!
> She has become a home for demons
>   and a haunt for every evil spirit,
>   a haunt for every unclean and detestable bird.
> ³For all the nations have drunk
>   the maddening wine of her adulteries.
> The kings of the earth committed adultery with her,
>   and the merchants of the earth grew rich from her excessive luxuries."

18:1-3   **The Fall of Babylon**   **Exposition**

The introduction of this scene in John's vision by another angel from heaven having great authority, the earth made light by his splendor, and shouting with a mighty voice is obviously intended to give great emphasis to his message, as coming from God Himself. The message is the fall of the Antichrist power,

"Babylon the Great." The emphasis is further heightened by the repetition of the verb, "fallen," a typically Semitic manner of expression (cp. Isa 21:9). The word "fallen" (Gk, ἔπεσεν, *epesen*) is in the past tense (2nd aorist indicative), which reflects the Hebrew prophetic perfect. This construction, common in the Hebrew prophets, is an emphatic means of addressing a future event as certain to happen. It was essential, even for the first century readers, to learn that this persecuting Roman power was doomed to fall as an act of Divine judgment.

The language which follows in verse 2 further emphasizes the certainty and the extremity of this judgment by enriching the Babylon metaphor from the historical destruction of ancient Babylon, the literal city (cf. Isa 13:19-22). Isaiah predicted the desolations of that city in similar language (Isa 13:21-22a):

> Desert creatures will lie there, jackals will fill her houses; there the owls will dwell, and there the wild goats will leap about. Hyenas will howl in her strongholds, jackals in her luxurious palaces."

The rationale for this devastating judgment is the adulteries and excessive luxuries of the Antichrist power, thus returning to the harlotry motif of chapter 17.

18:1-3   **The Fall of Babylon**   **Notes**

1. Heaven in this context clearly represents the third heaven, the dwelling place of God. The **splendor** of the angel which **illuminated** the earth need not to be understood to indicate that the angel is Christ, but it does indicate that this angel came from the throne of God and thereby reflected the Divine radiance (cp. 10:1 and our Exposition above on that text). **2.** The repetitious **fallen, fallen** is in the Semitic languages the means of indicating the superlative mode, for which there were no inflectional forms. Here, it is clearly for purpose of emphasis. Compare Jesus' use when introducing His authoritative statements with "truly, truly" (ἀμην, ἀμην, *amēn, amēn*). Babylon **has become a home for demons**, etc., reflects the desolation motif found regarding the judgment of Babylon in Isa 13:21-22a; Jer 50:39-40; 51:17; and of Edom in Isa 34:13-15. The word translated "demons" (Gk. δαιμόνιον, *daimónion*) occurs also in Isa 13:21 (LXX), where it is often translated as "wild goats," but sometimes "satyrs" or "goat-demons."⁵³ **3. Adultery** is an NIV mistranslation of the Greek, πορνεύω, porneúō, "to commit sexual immorality" (cp. also NIV 14:8). "Commit adultery," μοιχεύō, *moicheúō*, always has a distinctive meaning in Scripture, as it denotes the violation of the marriage covenant and is not necessarily sexual. The use of the prostitution motif with זָנָה, (LXX πορνεύō) in such passages as Ezekiel 16 and 23 and Hosea where the focus is on Israel's violation of her covenant marriage to Yahweh is probably intended to indicate her chronic and mercenary unfaithfulness, as characteristic of the professional prostitute. The prostitution motif may also suggest the alluring attraction of Antichrist Rome to the ten kings. **Earth** here in the context of "Babylon" as Rome refers to the Roman earth as the territory ruled by the "ten horn" kings.

The fall of Babylon (cont'd)

18:4-8. Then I heard another voice from heaven say:
"Come out of her, my people,
   so that you will not share in her sins,
   so that you will not receive any of her plagues;
⁵for her sins are piled up to heaven,
   and God has remembered her crimes.
⁶Give back to her as she has given;
   pay her back double for what she has done.
   Mix her a double portion from her own cup.
⁷Give her as much torture and grief
   as the glory and luxury she gave herself.
In her heart she boasts,
   'I sit as queen; I am not a widow,
   and I will never mourn.'
⁸Therefore in one day her plagues will overtake her:
   death, mourning and famine.
She will be consumed by fire,
   for mighty is the Lord God who judges her."

---

⁵³"Wild goats": NIV, NKJV, ASV; "shaggy goats," NASB; "he-goats": NEB & REB, ESV; "satyrs": KJV, RSV, NAB, JPSV; NRSV translates as "goat-demons". BAGD offers only "demons," 169. The corresponding Hebrew word, שָׂעִיר, *sa'ir*, means "hairy creature," i.e. "male goat" (BDB, 972). Codex Vaticanus renders the Hebrew with δαιμόνιον; both Aramaic and Syriac translate as "demons" (Edward J. Young, *The Book of Isaiah* (Grand Rapids: Eerdmans Publishing Company, 1965) 1.428, n. 49). The Revelation passage (18:2), as it draws its language from God's judgment of ancient Babylon, strongly supports the understanding of Isa 13:21 as referring to demonic creatures.

18:4-8   **The Fall of Babylon (cont'd)**   **Exposition**

This second section of chapter 18 is introduced by "another voice from heaven." Whether the Deity or an angel is not indicated, but as it calls to God's people with the personal possessive pronoun, it must be God who issues the gracious call: "Come out of her, my people . . . (v. 4), a call to come out of "Babylon"—Antichrist Rome. Two reasons are given for the call to separate from "Babylon": (1) "so that you will not share in her sins," and (2) "so that you will not receive any of her plagues." As the past tense of verse 2 ("fallen, fallen") is a prophetic perfect, pointing to a future punishment, there is at this point in our text still time for God's people to take warning. The warning is a gracious provision of potential salvation for those who would flee "Babylon." Today there is still opportunity for the believer to escape the judgment of the Almighty by disassociation from Antichrist, as well as from other sinful beliefs and practices.

The remaining part of this section, verses 5-8, is devoted to indicating reasons for the justice of the promised severe judgment. The sins of "Babylon," Antichrist Rome, have reached heaven. "God has remembered her crimes"; they will have consequence as Divine judgment. She is to be paid back double "from her own cup" (v. 6). The reference to her cup identifies again the city "Babylon" with the prostitute of 17:4, who holds "a golden cup in her hand," a cup filled with "abominable things." She is to be paid back by receiving the punishment a just God requires for these sins.

The forecast destruction of Apocalyptic Babylon is stated in language reminiscent of God's judgment of literal Babylon, as predicted in Isaiah:

Isaiah, on Babylon	Revelation, on Antichrist Rome
I am, and there is none besides me. I will never be a widow or suffer the loss of children" (47:8b).	I sit as a queen; I am not a widow, and I will never mourn (18:7b).
Both of these will overtake you in a moment, on a single day: loss of children and widowhood (47:9a).	Therefore in one day her plagues will overtake her: death, mourning and famine (18:8a).
Surely, they [your astrologers] are like stubble; the fire will burn them up (47:14).	She will be consumed by fire, for mighty is the Lord God who judges her (18:8b).

As surely as ancient Babylon had been destroyed, so also will Antichrist Rome suffer destruction.

18:4-8   The Fall of Babylon (cont'd)   Notes

4. Not another angel but **another voice**, the voice of God addressing His people. The angel of 18:1 pronounces a message of doom, whereas this is the voice of grace mercifully calling God's people to come out of Babylon. **5.** "God has **remembered** her crimes." For God to "remember" is not to imply that there is anything that an omniscient God ever forgets. This Hebrew idiom simply means that He will act to judge those crimes. In contradistinction, for his believing covenant people, He "will remember their sins no more" (Jer 31:34b; Heb 8:12). **Crimes** is from the Greek, ἀδίκημα, *adíkēma*, "a wrong," "a crime," or "a misdeed." **7. I am not a widow** implies Babylon's contention that she is the true spouse of Yahweh. What follows in verse 8 implies that her claim is false. **8. In one day**, ἐν μιᾷ ἡμέρᾳ, *en mią̃ hēmérą̃*, literally, "at one time" implies suddenness; it is represented by "in one hour" in verses 10 and 17. It is an allusion to Jer 47:9, cited above. (Beale, 904)[54]

The fall of Babylon

18:9-17a. When the kings of the earth who committed adultery with her and shared her luxury see the smoke of her burning, they will weep and mourn over her. [10]Terrified at her torment, they will stand far off and cry:

> **"Woe! Woe, O great city,**
> **O Babylon, city of power!**
> **In one hour your doom has come!"**

[11]The merchants of the earth will weep and mourn over her because no one buys their cargoes any more—[12]cargoes of gold, silver, precious stones and pearls; fine linen, purple, silk and scarlet cloth; every sort of citron wood, and articles of every kind made of ivory, costly wood, bronze, iron and marble; [13]cargoes of cinnamon and spice, of incense, myrrh and frankincense, of wine and olive oil, of fine flour and wheat; cattle and sheep; horses and carriages; and bodies and souls of men.

[14]They will say, 'The fruit you longed for is gone from you. All your riches and splendor have vanished, never to be recovered.' [15]The merchants who sold these things and gained their wealth from her will stand far off, terrified at her torment. They will weep and mourn [16]and cry out:

> **"Woe! Woe, O great city,**
> **dressed in fine linen, purple and scarlet,**
> **and glittering with gold, precious stones and pearls!**
> **[17]In one hour such great wealth has been brought to ruin!"**

---

[54],Beale adds, "Possibly the historical fact that Babylon was conquered in a single night could be part of the typological image behind 'Babylon the Great's' rapid future demise (see Dan 5:30)." In a footnote, Beale credits Craig S. Keener, *IVP Bible Backgrounds Commentary: New Testament* (Downers Grove, Ill.: InterVarsity Press, 1993), 808.

| 18:9-17a | The Fall of Babylon (cont'd) | Exposition |

Here the commercial aspect of Antichrist Rome is targeted metaphorically by a lament of the merchants who have been enriched by trading with her. A rather comprehensive list of merchandise is listed which ends dramatically by including "the bodies and souls of men" (v. 13b).

Again, we have use of the Hebraic prophetic perfect—prediction of a future event as if it were past. The lament builds upon verse 3, "The merchants of the earth grew rich from her excessive luxuries." Now their source of wealth has been taken from them with the fall of Babylon.

The merchants are represented as "terrified at her torment." The finality as well as the torment in this scene should probably be understood as representing the end-time judgment, rather than such temporal losses as are represented by the poured out bowls of chapter 16. Such great wealth and ostentation will come to nothing "in one hour" (v. 17).

| 18:9-17a. | The Fall of Babylon (cont'd) | Notes |

9. The kings of the earth are identified by the clause "who committed adultery with her" (NIV) with the ten horn kings of 17:10-14. Adultery, again, is a mistranslation of the Greek, πορνεύω (see above on 18:3). The fact that they stand afar off to weep and mourn and are terrified at her torment (vv. 9, 10, 15) appears to indicate that the great fall of Babylon they lament is not the ruin they committed against her (17:16), but the final demise of Babylon as the beast and the false prophet described in 19:20. That **they stand afar off** must not be understood literally but as part of this apocalyptic funeral metaphor to dramatize the fall of Babylon. In the final event of 19:19, it is probable that they are joined with the other kings of the earth who ally with the beast in that great war. **11-13.** The merchandise enumerated in verses 11-13 indicates that Antichrist Rome was heavily involved in the traffic of goods of all kinds, including **the bodies and souls of men.** This last, at the place of emphasis in the long list, underscores the gravity of the Divine charge against her and the justice of her severe punishment. The specific items listed otherwise reflect those which were more or less commonplace in the economy of the first century, especially among those who marketed to wealthy customers.

The fall of Babylon (cont'd)

18:17b. Every sea captain, and all who travel by ship, the sailors, and all who earn their living from the sea, will stand far off. [18]When they see the smoke of her burning, they will exclaim, "Was there ever a city like this great city?" [19]They will throw dust on their heads, and with weeping and mourning cry out:

> "Woe! Woe, O great city,
>   where all who had ships on the sea
>   became rich through her wealth!
> In one hour she has been brought to ruin!
> [20]Rejoice over her, O heaven!
>   Rejoice, saints and apostles and prophets!
>   God has judged her for the way she treated you."

[21]Then a mighty angel picked up a boulder the size of a large millstone and threw it into the sea, and said:

> "With such violence
>   the great city of Babylon will be thrown down,
>   never to be found again.
> [22]The music of harpists and musicians,
>   flute players and trumpeters,
>   will never be heard in you again.
> No workman of any trade
>   will ever be found in you again.
> The sound of a millstone
>   will never be heard in you again.
> [23]The light of a lamp
>   will never shine in you again.
> The voice of bridegroom and bride
>   will never be heard in you again.
> Your merchants were the world's great men.
>   By your magic spell all the nations were led astray.
> [24]In her was found the blood of prophets and of the saints,
>   and of all who have been killed on the earth."

18:17b-24.   The Fall of Babylon (cont'd)   Exposition

In this, the final scene in the drama of "Babylon's" fall, the motif shifts from the lament of the merchants to a lament of the sea captains who have been similarly enriched by the merchant trade of "Babylon." That trade is envisioned as widespread and the grief is experienced by "all who had ships on the sea" (v. 19). Though the seamen are represented as losing their source of wealth with the fall of Rome, they also recognize the justice of Rome's plight by calling Heaven to rejoice, with also the saints, apostles, and prophets who had been victims of Rome's ill treatment (v. 20): "God has judged her for the way she treated you." The chapter ends with a dramatic declaration by a mighty angel who, picking up a large millstone and casting it into the sea, declared, "With such violence Babylon will be thrown down, never to be found again" (v. 21). All gaiety, all trade, and commerce, and even the ordinary pursuits of everyday life will cease. The angel addresses "Babylon" directly with the second personal pronoun to declare that even the sound of a millstone, the light of a lamp, or the voice of the bridegroom and bride will never occur again (vv. 22-23).

The angel's climatic announcement ends with an allusion to Antichrist's war against God's true people: "In her was found the blood of prophets and of the saints, and of all who have been killed on the earth" (18:24). The inclusion of "all who have been killed" must be understood in the context of the foregoing message as referring, not to all those slain in the course of history, but to those killed by Antichrist Rome, as the Little Horn prophecy in Dan 7:21 and the prophecies of the Beasts in Rev 11:7 and 13:15 indicate. "The earth" refers to the Roman earth, that is, that part of the earth over which the Antichrist power would exercise sovereignty.

The destruction of Antichrist Rome is complete and final. It appears to point to the culmination of that final battle forecast in Rev 19:19-20.

18:17b-24. **The Fall of Babylon (cont'd)** Notes

17b. The prominence of **all who earn their living from the sea** reflects the primary role of seafaring in interstate commerce in the first Christian century. In spite of the relative limitations of ancient seafaring, the transport of large cargoes was most readily accomplished by that means. Roman roads were relatively well developed but they were in no way comparable to our modern interstate highways, nor were there multi-ton, diesel-engined trucks to transport freight. All was limited, quite literally, to horse power. **18.** The metaphorical description of Antichrist Babylon with **"Was there ever a city like this great city?"** builds on the fact that, in the first century, though the Mediterranean was rimmed with several great cities, such as Alexandria, Antioch, Tarsus, Athens, and Carthage, nevertheless, Rome stood out among them and embraced them all as central and foremost, as the capital of the great and powerful Roman Empire. Antichrist Rome, here presented in context as the eighth head of the Roman Beast, was to maintain much of the traditional power and prestige of Rome as it existed near the end of the first century. **20.** The fact that **apostles** and prophets are included among those who were ill-treated and therefore are to rejoice at Babylon's fall (cp. v. 24a), indicates that Rome as Antichrist includes the earlier as well as the eighth head of the Roman beast. This is indicated also by the fifth seal which, as we have seen, refers to martyrs under pagan Rome as headed by such emperors as Nero, Domitian, Decius, and Diocletian. Tradition informs us that several of the Apostles were martyred by Rome, most principally, James, Peter, and Paul, but also probably many or most of the others.[55] **21.** The **large millstone**s can still be seen in many places in the world of ancient Rome. They measure about four feet in diameter and 10-12 inches thick. A boulder of this size would make a very emphatic statement when thrown into the sea! **23.** "Babylon's" **magic spell** probably alludes to her harlot image as the one with a golden cup "filled with abominable things" (17:4), making the nations drink "the maddening wine of her adulteries" (18:3). **24. The blood of the prophets and the saints** reiterates 17:6, "I saw that the woman was drunk with the blood of the saints, the blood of those who bore testimony to Jesus" (cp. 18:13).

---

[55]John Foxe, *Book of Martyrs* (ed. W. G. Berry; Grand Rapids: Baker Book House, 1992), 6-11. Several of the traditions reported by Foxe remain otherwise undocumented, so as perhaps to raise questions regarding their reliability, but one might well conjecture the probability that they are in general factual.

18:1-24   **The Fall of Babylon**   **Fulfillment**

Chapter 17 presents Antichrist Papal Rome as a harlot riding on the beast, reflecting her loss of political authority over the nations of Roman Europe. It further describes judgments which those national powers themselves executed against the Papacy, while nevertheless maintaining the semblance of association with her, as indicated by her representation as a rider. Chapter 18 pronounces Antichrist's final doom utilizing the imagery of ancient Babylon's destruction as announced by Israel's prophets Jeremiah and Isaiah.

While we in the beginning of the twenty-first century could address chapter 17 as a largely fulfilled prophecy, chapter 18 appears to forecast "Babylon's" ultimate and permanent doom, a destiny which awaits our Savior's return as "the rider on the white horse" forecast in 19:11-16. This is corroborated by the Hallelujah Chorus which appears immediately thereafter in 19:1-9, praising God for His judgment of the "great prostitute" and celebrating the arrival of the great wedding festival and the marriage supper of the Lamb!

One should resist a too literal understanding of the elements of the funerary motifs found in 18:9-19, as the graphic scenes are designed to enhance the emphatic announcement of Babylon's fall. Yet there is an unmistakable emphasis here which is implicit also in chapter 17 with its harlot motif on the commercial aspect of Antichrist's reign.

As we have identified the "great harlot Babylon" with the Roman Papacy, it is appropriate to point up the degree to which this institution has been involved in commercializing the operation of the Roman Church. We submit the following excerpts from the official year 2000 annual report, Vatican City, July 6, 2001:

> Being a consolidated financial statement, this represents the sum of all the expenses and the income of the diverse Vatican administrations which enter into the consolidation: the Administration of the Patrimony of the Apostolic See (APSA) which is the largest; the Congregation for the Evangelization of Peoples; the Apostolic Camera; Vatican Radio; Osservatore Romano—Vatican Press (incorporated into one with regard to administration); the Vatican Television Center; and the Vatican Publishing House.
>
> For the eighth consecutive year, the operating statement for fiscal year 2000 for the Holy See closes with a net gain of 17.720 billion [lira], equal to $8,516,000 US at the exchange rate at the end of the year of

Chapter Ten		*The fall of Babylon, 18:1-24*		415

2,080.89 lire per dollar. The total expenses were 404.378 billion and the total income was 422.098 billion [lira. U.S. $202,844,936.54].[56]

During two subsequent fiscal years, the Vatican reported an annual deficit of several million U.S. dollars, but, nevertheless, the amount of financial activity remained and still remains strong. The above states only the Vatican's administrative budget, but the Vatican is heavily involved financially in a maze of business enterprises and industries, including the banking industry. Rupert Cornwall, a former correspondent of the *Financial Times* of Italy, writes:

> Of all the mysteries of the Eternal Church, few are greater than that of its finances. The sheer geographical extent of the institution is part of the difficulty, but a bigger reason is the Vatican's obsessive secrecy. Clearly its possessions are huge, in terms of land, art and property.[57]

Some of the properties of the Vatican were documented in considerable detail by the journalist and reporter, Nino Lo Bello, in his work, *The Vatican Empire* (c. 1968).[58] The book jacket summarized Lo Bello's work as follows:

> Mr. Lo Bello describes in . . . detail Vatican investment in real estate—one-third of Rome is owned by the Holy See—electronics, plastics, airlines, and chemical and engineering firms. He also gives evidence that the Vatican is heavily involved in Italian banking and that it has huge deposits in foreign banks. Some of these accounts are in America, many are in Switzerland. . . . In addition, the author establishes that the Vatican is one of the world's largest shareholders, with a portfolio that can conservatively be estimated [in 1963 dollars!] in billions.[59]

Apart from the current immense temporal commercial activities of the Vatican, through many centuries the church has been involved with the sale of indulgences and other exchanges of money for dispensations of

---

[56]Vatican Code: ZE01070622, Date: 2001-07-06, Economic Report of the Holy See for 2000, as presented at a press conference by Cardinal Sergio Sebastiani, president of the Prefecture for the Economic Affairs of the Holy See. Cited 2 Dec 2004. On line: http://www.zenit.org/english /visualizza.phtml?sid=7818.

[57]"God's Banker" (New York: Dodd, Mead & Company, 1984) 55.

[58]New York: Trident Press, c. 1968. 186 pp. See especially Chs. 7 & 8, 89-124.

[59]A well-known work on this subject is *The Vatican Billions* by Avro Manhattan (London: Paravision Books, 1972). The Vatican has maintained connections with the Mafia, as documented by Richard Hammer throughout his work, *The Vatican Connection* (New York: Rineholt and Winston, 1982). The book documents a billion-dollar counterfeit stock deal heavily involving the Mafia and the Vatican Bank.

"divine grace." Revelation 18 is couched in the language of the first century, but it is no less relevant in the twenty-first. Though this commerce is largely hidden, those who benefit from it would have ample reason to lament its loss.

Chapter Eleven

THE GREAT DAY OF THE LORD

19:1-21

Introduction

With the foregoing judgment of Babylon we have reached a major transition in the sequence of prophetic time and have arrived at that great series of culminating events called in the book of Joel, "that great and dreadful day of the LORD" (2:31). These include: (1)the second coming of Jesus Christ (19:11-16),(2) the battle of Armageddon (19:17-19), and (3) the defeat and destruction of the Antichristian powers (19:20-21). One might add to these the events of Revelation 20: the first resurrection (20:4), the millennial age with the establishment of Christ's temporal reign (20:1-6), the Gog and Magog insurrection (20:7-9), the destruction of Satan (20:10), the second resurrection (20:12a), the Great White Throne Judgment (20:12b-13), and finally, the everlasting destruction of evil (20:11-15). We have chosen to include the events of Revelation 20 in our next chapter, chapter 12.

To introduce 19:1-21, the dramatic disclosure of the events leading to the glorious return of Jesus Christ, we have another proleptic scene, 19:1-8, looking forward into the time after the resurrection of the people of God and their rapture "to meet the Lord in the air" (1 Thess 4:17). Antichristian Rome has suffered her temporal ruin (chs. 18:16-19:24) and only the final victorious battle of Christ against the ten-horned beast remains (19:11-18) before the judgment of the evil forces and Christ establishes His eternal reign on earth, as in ch. 20:4-15.

The drama in 19:1-10, before the bitter play-out of the battle of Armageddon, once more introduces the proleptic celebration of promised victory which has come to be known as The Hallelujah Chorus!

Hallelujah!

19:1. After this I heard what sounded like the roar of a great multitude in heaven shouting:

"Hallelujah!
Salvation and glory and power belong to our God,
²for true and just are his judgments.
He has condemned the great prostitute
who corrupted the earth by her adulteries.
He has avenged on her the blood of his servants."

³And again they shouted:

"Hallelujah!
The smoke from her goes up for ever and ever."

⁴The twenty-four elders and the four living creatures fell down and worshiped God, who was seated on the throne. And they cried:
"Amen, Hallelujah!"

⁵Then a voice came from the throne, saying:

"Praise our God, all you his servants,
you who fear him, both small and great!"

19:1-5   **The Hallelujah Chorus**   **Exposition**

Appropriately, the revelation turns from the dramatic and awful destruction of the apostate power which had stood against the true people of God to a scene of celebration in heaven. We must first recognize that, in spite of its great severity, God's condemning judgment is just. Salvation, glory, and power belong always to God. His truth and justice remain indelibly ingrained in his character. Like Edom, "Babylon's" destruction is permanent,

"Its smoke will rise forever" (Isa 34:9, 10). When injustice seems to prevail, we do well to worship God and know that not only in God's future but always, "True and just are his judgments." When hope seems distant, we can claim this promise that victory will surely win over evil. The Day of the Lord will come. Then the people of God, both the poor or oppressed and the eminent, will praise him.

19:1-5. The Hallelujah Chorus   Notes

This passage, like several before, is proleptic; from the standpoint of the prophetic chronology, it looks forward to a future event. That occasion is the glorious ingathering of the saints "caught up . . . to meet the Lord in the air" (1 Thess 4:17), a time when heaven will join earth in celebration. The passage is a transitional interlude between the foregoing description of "Babylon's" fall and the events which follow in 19:11-21.

1. The **roar** ("loud voice," NASB) of the multitude dramatizes the vast number (see 7:9, 10 and 14:2, 3).

One should distinguish the "great multitude in heaven" of 19:1 from the second "great multitude" of 19:6. The first is not identified except for its location in heaven, whereas the second is identified as the bride of Christ who wears "fine linen"—the righteousness of the saints. One need not look far in Scripture to identify the first multitude. Hebrews 12:22 identifies "thousands upon thousands of angels in joyful assembly" along with "the church of the firstborn whose names are written in heaven." The author of Hebrews appears to be thinking of the same event described here in Revelation, as he addresses his readers as having come "to the spirits of righteous men made perfect" (v. 23). The structure of this passage suggests that the first chorus is made up of those angelic beings described in Heb 12:22 and the second, called upon to praise God in verse 5, is the host of the redeemed.[1]

The shouting of the great multitude is described in verse 6 as **the roar of rushing waters** and **like loud peals of thunder** (see 7:9, 10 and

---

[1]Each multitude is introduced and described independently, the first is identified as "a great multitude in heaven." The second in a subsequent scene introduced by "Then," and identified by the dress in "fine linen" as the redeemed saints (cf. 7:9).

14:2, 3). **Hallelujah**, "praise Yahweh," occurs only here (with vv. 3, 4) in the New Testament. The word is derived from the Hebrew, הַלְלוּ יָה, *hăl°lū yāh*, the imperative of the verb, "to praise," with an abbreviated form of the covenant name of God, "Yahweh." Many have pointed out that Jewish interpreters of the Old Testament prophecies expected the restoration of Israel to follow upon the destruction of Babylon (Rome) and that they noted the first occurrence of the Hallel in Scripture at the end of Psalm 104, where they observe "that the Hallel comes not till there be tidings of the destruction of ungodly men."[2] The last third of the nineteenth century witnessed the end of Papal Rome's temporal power in 1870 and the beginning of the restoration of the Jews to Palestine. The twentieth century saw the restoration of the state of Israel in 1948 and the beginnings of grass roots Hebrew-Christian Messianism in Israel and elsewhere. **Salvation and glory and power** echo the words of 12:10, where "the kingdom of our God and the authority of his Christ" appear instead of "glory." Both texts focus on the God's sovereign power to deliver His people from Satanic forces to the end that His glorious reign may be accomplished. **2.** Two reasons are given for God's judgment of **the great prostitute**, her **adulteries** (more accurately translated "fornications" (ESV; Gk.: πορνεία, *porneía*; see on 9:21; 17:1) and her persecution and slaughter of saints (see on 18:23). **He has avenged on her the blood of his servants** indicates that with the judgment recorded in chapter 18, the cry of the martyred souls of 6:10 is satisfied (see that text). God always vindicates in due time His righteousness against evil. **3.** The smoke of "Babylon's" burning "goes up for ever and ever." Like incense it goes up, a perpetual testimony of God's justice (see 14:11). The language is quoted from Isa 34:10, where Edom's projected destruction is held up as an example of the Lord's wrath against all the ungodly nations who wage war against His people. From such prophecies the ancient rabbis saw Edom as a type of Rome, their present antichrist.

4. On **the twenty-four elders and the four living creatures**, see our Notes on Rev 4:4, 6. This is not referring to the saints as having gone to heaven, but to the elders as representing in heaven the saints of past ages who received the Gospel in advance by faith. The author of Hebrews has already stated with reference to those dead saints that "only together with us [the still living] would they become perfect" (11:40). The perfection of the saints is promised only at the resurrection.

---

[2]E. B. Elliott (quoting Lightfoot), *Horae Apocalypticae* (5th ed. London: Seeley, Jackson, and Halliday, 1862), 4. 49, 50.

Hallelujah (cont'd)

19:6. **Then I heard what sounded like a great multitude, like the roar of rushing waters and like loud peals of thunder, shouting:**
   "Hallelujah!
      For our Lord God Almighty reigns.
⁷Let us rejoice and be glad and give him glory!
   For the wedding of the Lamb has come,
      And his bride has made herself ready.
⁸Fine linen, bright and clean, was given her to wear."
(Fine linen stands for the righteous acts of the saints.)

⁹Then the angel said to me, "Write: 'Blessed are those who are invited to the wedding supper of the Lamb!'" And he added, "These are the true words of God."

¹⁰At this I fell at his feet to worship him. But he said to me, "Do not do it! I am a fellow servant with you and with your brothers who hold to the testimony of Jesus. Worship God! For the testimony of Jesus is the spirit of prophecy."

19: 6-10   The Hallelujah Chorus (cont'd)   Exposition

The angelic choir of verses 1b-5 is joined in verse 6 with the second great multitude "like the roar of rushing waters and like loud peals of thunder." The emphasis upon the loudness of the sound suggests that the significance of this multitude is even greater than that of the first. This choir is described as the bride of Christ. It was the custom in ancient times as it is today to make great celebration at weddings. One indication of this is found in Jesus' participation in the wedding at Cana (John 2:1-11). Such feasts lasted for several days—Samson's for seven days (Judg 14:12). Tobias in Tobit 8:20 was directed by his father-in-law to celebrate by feasting 14 days.[3]

---

[3] Frank Zimmermann, *The Book of Tobit: an English Translation with Introduction and Commentary* (New York: Harper & Brothers, 1858), 97. The date of the Apocryphal book of Tobit is uncertain, but it is believed to be approximately contemporary with the New Testament.

For millennia, the people of God have looked forward to the celebration of the final victory over evil in the great Marriage Supper of the Lamb. In ancient Israelite imagery, the Revelation sees the people of God as the bride of Christ, our Messiah-Savior. From the day of our election, when the marriage contract was written, till our wedding day, the time of betrothal passes. The wedding feast introduces and celebrates the wonderful consummation of the marriage, when the Bridegroom take His Bride into His home to live in union with her forever.

In this passage, the holiness of God and the purity of the bride stand in contrast to the adulterous prostitute who had "corrupted the earth by her harlotries." During the present betrothal days, the figure suggests that we must keep ourselves pure and live in anticipation of that great day when Messiah comes and of that new, unending life with Him. It is worthy of reiteration that "fine linen purity" here is defined as "the righteous acts of the saints." It should be obvious that the saints are not those whom the church may have canonized, but those who have been betrothed to Christ, set apart for that occasion. Though the Lamb has made atonement with its imputation of righteousness to the people of God, they are nevertheless here called to obedience, in that most practical manner to wear "garments of white."

Even the messenger angel stands with John and with all the people of God as a fellow servant who holds to the prophecy, "the testimony of Jesus" (v. 10). In this proleptic scene, God's people are given a foreglimpse of the great reunion to enliven their hope, to encourage them to the obedience of faith, to stand in awe of their great Creator King, sovereign Lord over the destiny of all His works.

19:6-10   **The Hallelujah Chorus**   Notes

6. In addition to the great multitude of angelic beings celebrating the redemptive work of God in verses 1-3, another **great multitude** of the redeemed celebrates in chorus in verses 6-8. Jesus taught that relatively few would enter the narrow gate to eternal life (Matt 7:13). Nevertheless, the aggregate of the people of God is "a great multitude that no one could count, from every nation, tribe, people and language" (7:9). **7. Let us rejoice and be glad.** Notice that the rejoicing does not focus on the rewards about to be received or the happiness of the kingdom age about to be experienced, but upon the more perfect reign of God and the glory he deserves (6b, 7a). **The wedding of the Lamb has come.** The focus on the marriage feast symbolism further expands the Israelite covenant theme so prominent in this book. The Lord's covenant marriage to Israel is described in Isa 54:6; Ezek 16:7; and Hos 2:16. It is expounded at length in these and other passages. The Isaiah and Hosea texts both speak of the last day restoration of that broken union. Brought to fruition by Israel's Messiah, the Gentile church is grafted in and numbered with the redeemed of Israel. The total covenant people will celebrate the union. Jesus said that the saints would eat and drink in the Kingdom of God (Matt 8:11; 26:29). **8.** The bridal gown, **fine linen, bright and clean**, is explained to mean, **the righteous acts of the saints**. The explanation may be regarded as a comment by John, the human author. The wearing of these garments is **given her**—"the righteousness that comes from God and is by faith" (Phil 3:9).

9. These are the true words of God. The words of the chanting multitude are so described because the entire vision of the Revelation is **the testimony of Jesus** (see on 1:2).

10. The testimony of Jesus is the spirit of prophecy: This is capable of various interpretations, but with Mounce, I believe it is most consistent with the several other occurrences of the phrase, "the testimony of Jesus" (1:2, 9; 12:17; cp. 22:20) and the present context to take the entire expression to mean that the testimony which Jesus, himself, bears is the essence of true prophecy. (The phrase should be understood as a subjective genitive).[4]

The Rider on the White Horse

---

[4]Robert H. Mounce, *The Book of Revelation* (Revised ed.; Grand Rapids: Eerdmans, 1998), 349.

19:11. **I saw heaven standing open and there before me was a white horse, whose rider is called Faithful and True. With justice he judges and makes war.** [12]**His eyes are like blazing fire, and on his head are many crowns. He has a name written on him that no one but he himself knows.** [13]**He is dressed in a robe dipped in blood, and his name is the Word of God.** [14]**The armies of heaven were following him, riding on white horses and dressed in fine linen, white and clean.** [15]**Out of his mouth comes a sharp sword with which to strike down the nations. "He will rule them with an iron scepter." He treads the winepress of the fury of the wrath of God Almighty.** [16]**On his robe and on his thigh he has this name written:**

KING OF KINGS AND LORD OF LORDS.

19:11-16 **The White Horse Rider** **Exposition**

This passage begins with the Apostle's description of the final event anticipated throughout the New Testament, the second coming of Jesus Christ! This dramatic scene describes in metaphorical language the fact that Christ at His return will appear, not only as Savior of the Redeemed, as anticipated in the foregoing proleptic prophecy of the Marriage Supper of the Lamb, but here He is described as a militant warrior who will be victorious over evil, including evil incarnate in the Antichrist powers. This event will bring this age to a sudden end and introduce the long-awaited Age to Come when Christ will establish His everlasting reign.

The white-horse Rider called Faithful and True comes from the opened heaven metaphorically riding on a white horse to judge and make war (v. 11). In the first century, the white horse was associated with generals, high officials, emperors, and kings, as in Rev 6:2. In 6:2, the rider carried a bow, in the Roman world the weapon of a temporal warrior, and wore the laurel-wreath crown as worn at that time by the emperor. However, this Rider wears many diadem crowns, indicating total sovereignty over the nations of the world. His piercing eye like "blazing fire" conveys to the reader both His penetrating gaze and His insightful judgment.

The awesome description continues with the striking fact that the Rider, whose robe one might think should have been white (cp. v. 14b), nevertheless wore a robe "dipped in blood."[5] The text directs the mind of the reader to Isa 63:1-6, which passage, though directed to the Divine judgment of Edom, illustrates also the final judgment of the Antichrist powers at the end of the age.[6] Observe the correlation between the two passages:

Isa 63:1-6	Rev 19:12, 13
[1]Who is this coming from Edom, from Bozrah, **with his garments stained crimson**? Who is this, robed in splendor, striding forward in the greatness of his strength? 'It is I, speaking in righteousness, mighty to save." **[2]Why are your garments red. like those of one treading the winepress?** **[3]I have trodden the winepress alone**; from the nations no one was with me, I trampled them in my anger and trod them down in my wrath; **Their blood spattered my garments, and I stained all my clothing.** [4]For the day of vengeance was in my heart, and the year of my redemption has come.	[12]His eyes are like blazing fire, and on his head are many crowns. He has a name written on him that no one but he himself knows. [13]**He is dressed in a robe dipped in blood,** and his name is the Word of God. [14]The armies of heaven were following him, riding on white horses and dressed in fine linen, white and clean. [15]Out of his mouth comes a sharp sword with which to strike down the nations. "He will rule them with an iron scepter." **He treads the winepress of the fury of the wrath of God Almighty.** [16]On his robe and on his thigh he has this name written: KING OF KINGS AND LORD OF LORDS.

---

[5]A rather prominent textual variant reads, "sprinkled with blood," with the Greek βεβαμμένον (perf. pass. part. of βάπτω) replaced mainly with ἐρραμμένον (from ῥαίνω), but the ms. evidence favors βεβαμμένον (Bruce Metzger, *A Textual Commentary on the New Testament.* [New York: United Bible Societies, 1971], 763-764.

[6]Lowth goes so far as to see the primary reference of the Isaiah passage to the event predicted in Rev 19:1-6 with the Isaiah text an emblematic anticipation of that event: "The period to which it refers is probably the same with that predicted in the 19th chapter of the Revelations[sic], some parts of which (13, &c.) are expressed in the same terms with this, and are generally understood of the fall of Antichrist and his followers, of which the destruction of Babylon, Edom or Bozrah, may be considered as an emblem." (Robert Lowth, *Isaiah: a new translation . . . with a summary view and explanation of the same* [London: C. Paramore, 1791], 92.)

The Isaiah passage, with its striking figure of the Lord returning from Bozrah, the capital of Edom, with blood-stained garments as a sign of Edom's certain judgment, serves to enhance by historical precedence the inevitable judgment to ensue on antitypical, Antichristian Rome. Edom alone is not the object of Isaiah for verses 5 and 6 extend his message to "nations" in general:

> ⁵"I looked, but there was no one to help,
> I was appalled that no one gave support;
> so my own arm worked salvation for me,
> and my own wrath sustained me.
> ⁶I trampled the nations in my anger;
> in my wrath I made them drunk
> and poured their blood on the ground."

The first-century reader when informed of Jewish interpretation could have understood the typology, as rabbinic teaching had identified Edom as well as Babylon with the Antichrist motif.

19:11-16   The White Horse Rider   Notes

11. The formula, **I saw** (Gk. Καὶ εἶδον, *Kaì eîdon*, "And I saw") is generally taken by commentators as introducing a new vision.[7] However, as we have previously pointed out, the Revelation is introduced in chapter 1:10-11, 19 as a single vision received by John as a unified whole on one occasion. It is therefore better to address the many scenes in the one vision, appropriately recognizing the unity and continuity of the whole. The introductory καί, untranslated in the NIV, may be understood as a Hebraism, reflecting the comparable use of the Hebrew copulative ו, *waw*.[8] The description of the **heaven standing open** is found in Scripture

---

[7]As e.g., G. K. Beale, *The Book of Revelation*. (Grand Rapids: Eerdmans, 1999), 949; David E. Aune, *Revelation* . (Word Biblical Commentary; Nashville: Nelson, 1997-1998), 3.1052.

[8]*Gesenius' Hebrew Grammar* (ed. and enl. by E. Kautzsch; revised in Accordance with the 28th German Ed. of 1909 by A. E. Cowley; 2nd ed.; Oxford: Clarendon, 1910), 484-485. The meaning of the Hebrew ו must be inferred from context and is sometimes considered, as may be the case with the NIV translators, untranslatable.

only in Ezek 1:1 where it introduces a series of Divine revelations. A comparable metaphor occurs in Rev 4:1, in which the Apostle saw "a door standing open in heaven," marking the beginning of the revelation of events which for John were to take place in times which were still future. Aune catalogs several occurrences of this figure in rabbinic and Jewish apocalyptic writings (3.1052). The idea that the Jewish Messiah would come as a warrior appears to have been common during the Roman period, as illustrated by Rabbi Akiba's identification of Simon bar Kokhba, the leader of the second revolt against Rome (A.D. 68-70) as Messiah.[9] For the distinction between this white horse rider and the one in 6:2, see above my Exposition section and commentary on 6:2. Aune states that "the appearance of the rider on the white horse accompanied by an angelic cavalry is generally, and probably correctly, understood as a dramatization of the Parousia of Jesus" (3.1053). **12. His eyes are like blazing fire** reiterates 1:14 and indicates that piercing perception by which the Divine judge "always knows the spiritual condition of the ungodly" (Beale, 951) whether they profess belief (1:14) or unbelief. The **many crowns** on the Rider's head are diadem crowns (Gk. διαδήματα, *diadēmata*) indicating absolute authority (see above, on 12:1). The "many crowns" indicate authority beyond comparison with that of earthly kings. The **name** that **no one but he himself knows** has given rise to many pages of discussion (see e.g. Beale, 953-957). Perhaps it is best to understand the formula simply in its generic sense to indicate that no mortal comprehends fully the character of the God-man Jesus. His inscrutable name indicates His uniqueness as sovereign judge.[10] **13.** In addition to His inscrutable name, **his name is the Word of God**. The Rider as Messiah is the incarnation of Truth and the teacher of all that God has revealed. As the Word, He is absolutely qualified to judge. **14. The armies of heaven** are angelic beings well-known even to the first-century reader from Jesus' own teaching (Matt 13:40-42, 16:27, 24:31, 25:31-33; Mark 8:38; Luke 9:26; cf. also 2 Kgs 6:17; Zech 14:5; 1 Thess 3:13; 2 Thess 1:7; Jude 14-

---

[9]Marinus de Jonge, "Messiah," *ABD* (New York: Doubleday, 1992) 4.786.

[10]Beale states that "the confidential nature of the name here . . . alludes to Christ being absolutely sovereign over humanity's experiential access to his character" (955). Beale indicates his indebtedness to M. G. Kline, *Images of the Spirit* (Grand Rapids: Baker, 1980), p. 130, where Kline argues that the verb, "know," here means "own" (Beale, 955, n. 366).

15.)[11] **White horses**, as well as **fine linen, white and clean** give emphasis by their whiteness to the justice with which they are to carry out judgment. **15.** The **sharp sword** protruding **out of his mouth** further emphasizes the justice by which the Rider by His Word exacts punishment (cf. Isa 49:2). **Nations** (Greek, ʾέθνοι, *ʾéthnoi*, "Gentiles") in the covenant imagery of the Book of Revelation means "heathen," in distinction from the Covenant People (cp. 11:2, 20:3). The **scepter** was in ancient times the symbol of the king's authority. Adapted from the wooden shepherd's crook, when made of **iron** it could function as a weapon and symbolized absolute if not violent authority. **He will rule them** as judge with **the fury of the wrath of God Almighty. 16.** The third name addressed in our text, **KING OF KINGS AND LORD OF LORDS** dramatizes the Rider's sovereign mission to pronounce judgment upon all heathen kings, nations, and peoples on earth.

The Rider on the White Horse (cont'd)

19:17. And I saw an angel standing in the sun, who cried in a loud voice to all the birds flying in midair, "Come, gather together for the great supper of God, [18]so that you may eat the flesh of kings, generals, and mighty men, of horses and their riders, and the flesh of all people, free and slave, small and great."

[19]Then I saw the beast and the kings of the earth and their armies gathered together to make war against the rider on the horse and his army. [20]But the beast was captured, and with him the false prophet who had performed the miraculous signs on his behalf. With these signs he had deluded those who had received the mark of the beast and worshiped his image. The two of them were thrown alive into the fiery lake of burning sulfur. [21]The rest of them were killed with the sword that came out of the mouth of the rider on the horse, and all the birds gorged themselves on their flesh.

---

[11]Comparable extra-canonical sources dating after the Book of Revelation include T. Levi 3:3; Apoc. El. 3:4; 1 En. 102:3; 2 En. 17.1; 1 Thess 3:13, which reads "holy ones" (Gk. ʿαγίοι) is sometimes understood to mean "saints," but there is no compelling reason to distinguish it from the parallel passages, which read "angels" (Gk. ἄγγελοι).

19:17-21   **The White Horse Rider (cont'd)**   **Exposition**

This final battle is mentioned in Rev 16:16 as the battle of Armageddon. The kings gathered for this battle include the "kings from the east" (16:12). These kings appear as distinct from the ten kings allied with the Beast. Armageddon may be metaphorical for a location other than the present Tell Megiddo, as in the first century, the site was already legendary as a site for memorable battles. If the place name is to be taken literally, than the reader is to understand that the end-time battle will be multi-focused geographically. The battle may begin at Megiddo and terminate in the Valley of Jehoshaphat, the Kidron east of Jerusalem (Joel 3:2), A metaphorical understanding of Megiddo will give emphasis to the decisive nature of the end-time battle occuring in the Kidron.

The prophets also announce this as an end-time battle: Dan 2:44; Dan 7:11, 26; Zech 14:1-6; Mal 4:1-3. Our Revelation text is Christ's final warning of their destiny to the Antichrist powers, as well as to all the unfaithful, who are promised coming judgment.

Verses 20-21 bring to a climax the Satanic war between Christ and Antichrist and prepare the reader to understand the ensuing reign of Christ in union with His chosen people, as about to begin, that beginning described in Rev 20:1-4.

19:17-21   **The White Horse Rider (cont'd)**   **Notes**

17. The angel's position, **standing in the sun**, should be understood as emphasizing his authority (cp. 12:1). His location also facilitates his mission in calling to the birds. The **great supper** stands in contrast to the Marriage Supper of the Lamb introduced so shortly before in verse 9. **18. Eat the flesh** is a clear allusion to Ezek 39:17-20.

19. The beast understood in the context of the preceding, Rev 13:1-10, as the Roman Antichrist power, united in some sense with **the kings of the earth**, that is, the nations of the Roman earth of Daniel's fourth world empire to conduct war against the Rider and His angelic hosts. **20.** With the beast in his defeat was **the false prophet** of 13:11-17. **The two**

of them were thrown alive into the fiery lake of burning sulfur, a metaphorical description of their summary defeat and destruction. **21. The rest of them were killed** refers to the armies that allied with the Beast and the False Prophet in the war. That this is the case is indicated by the battle scene described in the context, including the final allusion to Ezek 39:17-20. The **sword** is the sword of justice executing punishment, and should not be construed here as accomplishing any of the redemptive mission of the Word of God.

19:1-21   The Great Day of the Lord   Fulfillment

This chapter divides into two sections: first, a proleptic vision of the celebration of the victory of Christ over the evil Satanic forces by a great multitude of heavenly beings (19:1-4), followed by a call from the throne to all God's servants (19:5), answered by another great multitude of the shouting saints (19:6, 7) in what has come to be called the Hallelujah Chorus, announcing that "the wedding of the Lamb has come, and his bride has made herself ready." This glorious celebration reflects the ancient Israelite wedding tradition, in which perhaps as much as a year elapsed between the enactment of the wedding covenant and the consummation of the marriage. At the time of the consummation, the groom ordinarily would go to the home of his bride and bring her to his house where a great celebration would be in progress. This sometimes lasted for a week or more. After this joyous celebration, the bride and groom would begin their life together.[12] The Marriage Supper of the Lamb represents the wedding celebration at the end of the long betrothal period during which Christ has entered into a contractual relationship with His bride, the Covenant People known in the New Testament as His Church (cf. Eph 5:25-32). This celebration anticipates the actual union of Christ with His Chosen People immediately to follow, when subsequent to His return to earth, He begins His everlasting reign as indicated in Revelation 20.

Before this glorious occasion, however, the predicted events of 19:11-21 must transpire. This great end-time battle, the battle of

---

[12]Alfred Edersheim, *Sketches of Jewish Social Life* (London: Religious Tract Society, n.d.), 148-155; J. A. Thompson, "Marriage," *The Illustrated Bible Dictionary* (Wheaton, Ill.: Tyndale House Publishers, 1980), 2.955-957.

Armageddon, in which Jesus Christ will appear as conqueror and defeat the Antichristian powers, is now apparently due to occur.

If our understanding of the Bowl prophecies is correct, and there are sufficient correspondences between them and the flow of historical events for some confidence, then the world has experienced much that is predicted of the pouring out of the seventh Bowl (16:17-21, with 17:1-18:20), and only the final event of this age remains to be fulfilled (19:11-21) before the celebration occurs and the marriage is consummated!

One should question whether the elaborate and rather detailed series of chronological events envisioned in our continuous-historicist interpretation together with the correspondences of the symbols with actual history can rationally be considered capricious and arbitrary. What are the odds that these numerous correlations extending over nearly two millennia could be accidental and erroneous, as sometimes charged? While this writer makes no claim to absolute truth in prophetic interpretation, he stands in a long line of historicist interpreters who have progressively advanced the line of continuous-historical interpretation to arrive at the above conclusions.

We have reason to expect that soon the great end-time battle will occur and our Lord will return as He was seen to go. His feet will take their stand once more upon the Mount of Olives (Zech 14:4; Luke 24:50-51; Acts 1:9-12).

Excursus on the Restoration of Israel

The physical and spiritual restoration of national Israel in the Land is not a theme treated in the Book of Revelation but it is unambiguously forecast in both the major and the minor prophets of the Old Testament. Chief among these are the following: Jer 30-33; Ezek 36-37; Amos 9:11-15; Zech 12:7-14:21. It may also be seen as implied or affirmed in Luke 13:35 (cp. Psa 118:22-27; Matt 21:9; Mk 11:9); Rom 11:26-29; as well as Gal 6:16.[13] The restoration promise is clearly unconditional (Ezek 36:22-23; Rom 11:29); the people of Israel will be regathered from the Diaspora and returned to the Land (Ezek 36:24); the covenant land of Israel will be restored, the cities rebuilt, and the fields made fruitful (Ezek 36:8-11); both northern and southern kingdoms

---

[13] On the last reference, see Burton, Ernest DeWitt, *A Critical and Exegetical Commentary on the Epistle to the Galatians* (Edinburgh: T. & T. Clark, 1921) 357-358.

will be restored (Ezek 37:15-22); the people will be regenerated by the Holy Spirit so as to be in covenant reunion with God (Ezek 36:25-28); the Davidic King Messiah will reign from Jerusalem in perpetuity (Ezek 37:22, 24-25).

It is the understanding of this writer that there is no Scriptural warrant for allegorizing these promises so as to exclude the very people and nation to which they were addressed by the inspired prophets, so as to apply them only to the Church to the exclusion of their national, geographical, and temporal elements. The return to the land and its restoration with the reunion of the Northern and Southern Kingdoms can hardly be understood as referring in an exclusively spiritual sense to the Church at large. To treat these detailed promises as pertaining only in a non-literal sense foreign to the original audience is to violate the hermeneutical principle of grammatico-historical exegesis. The Book of Revelation assumes the New Testament doctrine that Gentiles are adopted or grafted into the covenant Israelite nation as taught by the Apostle Paul in Rom 11:11-29, but not in such a manner as to void or give new meaning to the unconditional promises made by the Israelite prophets.

Zechariah 12 appears to indicate that Israel's national repentance will occur in the context of the final battle against Jerusalem:

> On that day, when all the nations of the earth are gathered against her [Jerusalem], I [the LORD] will make Jerusalem an immovable rock for all the nations. All who try to move it will injure themselves . . . . . And I will pour out on the house of David and the inhabitants of Jerusalem a spirit of grace and supplication. They will look on me, the one they have pierced, and they will mourn for him as one mourns for an only child, and grieve bitterly for him as one grieves for a first born son. . . . . On that day a fountain will be opened to the house of David and the inhabitants of Jerusalem, to cleanse them from sin and impurity. (12:3, 10, 13:1)

And again in Zechariah 14:

> A day of the LORD is coming when . . . I will gather all the nations to Jerusalme to fight against it . . . . Then the LORD will go out and fight against those nations, as he fights in the day of battle. On that day his feet will stand on the Mount of Olives, east of Jerusalem . . . ." (14a, 3, 4a)

These two oracles of Zechariah appear to indicate that Israel's national repentance will occur in the context of the great final battle which the Book of Revelation calls the battle of Armageddon. Their interpretation allows for two possible understandings: 1. That their repentance will occur during this battle, perhaps when victory otherwise seems hopeless.

This requires that their looking on "the one they have pierced" is to be understood metaphorically, rather than as a result of their seeing their Messiah after His advent. 2. That this vision of Christ is to be understood literally and their repentance occurs after His second advent.[14] This writer prefers interpretation number one as the more likely of the two.

Returning to our exposition of the description of the end-time battle, this battle is mentioned in Rev 16:16 as the battle of Armageddon. The kings gathered for this battle include "the kings from the east" (16:12). These kings appear as distinct from the ten kings allied with the Beast. Armageddon may be metaphorical for a location other than the present Tell Megiddo, as in the first century, the site was already legendary as a site for memorable battles. If the place name is to be taken literally, than the reader is to understand that the end-time battle will be multi-focused geographically. The battle may begin at Megiddo and terminate in the Valley of Jehoshaphat, the Kidron east of Jerusalem (Joel 3:2), A metaphorical understanding of Megiddo will give emphasis to the decisive nature of the end-time battle occuring in the Kidron.

The prophets also announce this as an end-time battle: Dan 2:44; Dan 7:11, 26; Zech 14:1-6; Mal 4:1-3. Our Revelation text is Christ's final warning of their destiny to the Antichrist powers, as well as to all the unfaithful, who are promised coming judgment.

Verses 20-21 bring to a climax the Satanic war between Christ and Antichrist and prepare the reader to understand the ensuing reign of Christ in union with His chosen people, as about to begin, that beginning described in Rev 20:1-4.

---

[14]Some even place the spiritual ingathering of the Jewish people in the millennial age.

Chapter Twelve

THE MILLENNIAL REIGN AND THE GREAT WHITE THRONE JUDGMENT

20:1-15

Introduction

In the foregoing chapter, Revelation 19, we have witnessed a proleptic celebration of the final victory of Christ over Antichrist with the anticipation of the consummation of the long-anticipated marriage of Christ with his bride, the Covenant community of both Testaments. The Antichrist beast and his false prophet were cast into the lake of fire for their everlasting destruction. Only the Devil remains of the Satanic triumvirate which allied against Christ and His people. The time for Christ's eternal Kingdom reign has come. The Devil remains to be vanquished. At this point the first-century reader is prepared to anticipate a particular sequence of events immediately to follow, as shown by several clear passages in the Gospels and the Epistles. These passages include Matt 24:30-31; 1 Cor 15:22-23; 1 Thess 4:16-17.

Matt 24:30-31	1 Cor 15:22-23	1 Thess 4:16-17
At that time the sign of the Son of Man will appear in the sky, and all the nations of the earth will mourn. **They will see the Son of Man coming on the clouds of the sky**, with power and great glory. ³¹And he will send his angels with a loud trumpet call	[Cp. Dan 7:13: "Before me was **one like a son of man, coming with the clouds of heaven**."]	¹⁶For **the Lord himself will come down from heaven**, with a loud command, with the voice of the archangel and with the trumpet call of God,
	²²For as in Adam all die, so in Christ all will be made alive. ²³But each in his own turn: Christ, the first fruits; then, **when he comes, those who belong to him.**	and **the dead in Christ will rise first.** ¹⁷After that, **we who are still alive and are left will be caught up together with them in the clouds to meet the Lord in the air.** And so we will be with the Lord forever.
and **they will gather his elect from ... one end of the heavens to the other.**		

In the above passages the coming of the Son of Man results first in the resurrection of the faithful dead. It is then followed by the gathering of the elect from all over the earth to meet the Lord in the sky. First Thessalonians chapter 4 concludes verse 17 with the result that "we will be with the Lord forever." Several other passages deserve treatment, some of which we shall take up in our Exposition below. But these are sufficient to illustrate the heritage of even the earliest readers of the Book of Revelation by which they were aided in their understanding of its chronological continuity and its eschatology.

One contributing factor to the diversity of opinion regarding the doctrine of the millennium is the brevity with which the matter is presented. This can best be accounted for by the fact that the concept was a familiar part of the Jewish Messianic expectation. The church was born in Judaism and its leading Apostles were instructed by the Jewish Messiah as well as, in the case of the Apostle Paul, one thoroughly educated in the principal rabbinic school. The fact that the chronology of the Millennium is spelled out in Scripture only in the twentieth chapter of our Lord's prophecy should not blind us to the facts that the millennium is part of the historical background of the text and that the leading other concepts wheter explicit or implicit are amply taught elsewhere in Scripture.[1]

Chapter Twelve		*The millennial reign, 20:1-6*		435

The Thousand Years

20:1. **And I saw an angel coming down out of heaven, having the key to the Abyss and holding in his hand a great chain. ²He seized the dragon, that ancient serpent, who is the devil, or Satan, and bound him for a thousand years. ³He threw him into the Abyss, and locked and sealed it over him, to keep him from deceiving the nations anymore until the thousand years were ended. After that, he must be set free for a short time.**

⁴I saw thrones on which were seated those who had been given authority to judge. And I saw the souls of those who had been beheaded because of their testimony for Jesus and because of the word of God. They had not worshiped the beast or his image and had not received his mark on their foreheads or their hands. They came to life and reigned with Christ a thousand years. ⁵(The rest of the dead did not come to life until the thousand years were ended.) This is the first resurrection. ⁶Blessed and holy are those who have part in the first resurrection. The second death has no power over them, but they will be priests of God and of Christ and will reign with him for a thousand years.

20:1-6		**The Millennial Reign**		**Exposition**

The first order of business in introducing the millennial reign of Christ is to deal with the fact that chapter 19 ends with Satan still at large. In 20:1, the angel is seen coming down from heaven carrying the key to the Abyss and a great chain. He comes to seize the dragon, whom he identifies as Satan, and to bind him and to cast him into the Abyss. The "great" chain should be understood to bind him securely. The Abyss is then locked and sealed over him. The language, though metaphorical, makes it very clear that Satan is totally incapacitated and therefore prevented from deceiving the nations during the period of the thousand years (vv. 2 & 3; cp. 9:1-

---

[1] Although various Rabbis posited different lengths for this temporal Messianic reign, it nevertheless was a doctrine widespread in Judaism. A literal thousand year reign was held by some prestigious rabbis. With the influence of Revelation 20, this became common doctrine in the early church until the rise of the allegorizing interpretation with Origen (ca. 185-ca. 254). (J. Massyngbaerde Ford, "Millennium," *ABD* (New York: Doubleday, 1992) 4.832-834).

2). This is further indicated by the statement which follows, which indicates that after the thousand years, he is to be set free for a short time. This implies that he was not free to deceive the nations during the millennial age.[2]

The meaning of "one thousand years" may be open to question. If the number is to be understood on the year-day principle, that historicist interpreters apply to time periods prior to the Second Advent, then the millennial kingdom may be expected to last 360,000 years. While this is not inconceivable, given that the millennium functions as the first period in Christ's *eternal* reign, most premillennial historicists have preferred to believe that the length of the millennial era, because it occurs after the return of Christ when there is no need for ambiguity, should be calculated either in literal years or as a symbol for a rather long, indefinite period of time. Here it is wise to remember that the first century reader to whom the Revelation was originally written as a supplement to the earlier teaching of Jesus and His apostles would have been informed by the common Jewish-Christian millennial expectation.[3]

Now with Antichrist destroyed and Satan imprisoned, the major events which in previous biblical texts are associated with the return of Christ begin to unfold. As we have illustrated with the quotations above, the next event to occur after the Second Advent of Christ is the resurrection of His people who are represented as

---

[2] Amillennialists identify the millennium of ch. 20 with the church age, and therefore have to understand that Satan is only partially bound and therefore presently active outside of the Abyss. That contradiction with the language of these verses should be sufficient to indicate the erroneous nature of the amillennial interpretation.

[3] Hermann Gebhardt in his work, *The Doctrine of the Apocalypse*, states, "Eminent Rabbis fix the duration of the Messianic kingdom; and they do so according to a combination of Isa. lxiii.4 and Ps. xc.4 (comp. 2 Pet. iii.8), probably in union with the reasons adduced by Barnabas, that as God in six days created the world, and rested on the seventh, so in six thousand years . . . all will be finished, and on the seventh . . . thousand, a great world-Sabbath (the Messianic reign) will be celebrated. From the brevity with which the seer treats of this period, it seems to follow that he regarded it as well known, and that it had for him a symbolic value, and signified a long but limited period of time" (Clark's Foreign theological library; New Series 58; Edinburgh: T. & T. Clark, 1878), 277-278.

"asleep" (Dan 12:2). The scene is prepared for the judgment of those who had survived the destruction forecast in 19:20-21.[4]

The Apostle "saw thrones on which were seated those who had been given authority to judge" (v. 4). The prominence of these thrones, especially in view of the economy of words which characterizes this passage, suggests that the process of judging is to be a prominent characteristic of the millennial era. This reminds us that Jesus had told His Apostles (Matt 19:28/Luke 22:30) that "when the Son of Man sits on his glorious throne" they would "sit on twelve thrones, judging the twelve tribes of Israel."[5] Because verse four later informs us that all who are raised in the first resurrection will rule with Christ, we should understand this first sentence as introductory and the following statements as explanatory. Those who rule with Christ and serve as judges must in fact include those who have participated in the first resurrection. As the Apostle Paul stated, "The saints shall judge the world" (1 Cor 6:2, 3; cp. Rev 2:26, 27; 3:21; 2 Tim 2:12). The multiplicity of judges in the world after the resurrection suggests that perhaps many will serve Christ in the millennial era as civil servants and judges, as well as perhaps as other local officers and priests (cf. 20:6; cp. 1:6).

Included in the first resurrection are those who had been martyred for their testimony. As we are to understand and know from history that the death of the martyrs was literal (cf. Rev 2:13, 6:9-11; 11:7-10; 13:7, 15; 14:4; 17:6; 18:13, 24), contextual interpretation should lead us to understand the resurrection of the

---

[4]The "rest of them" described as killed (19:21) refers to the members of the armies gathered to war against the Rider (v. 19). One may not assume that the total world population of unbelieving people was wiped out.

[5]Though Judas was still numbered among the Apostles at this time, we must assume that Jesus was using the number twelve in the general sense, and that Judas, the "one doomed to perdition" (John 17:12), would be excluded. We do know that Matthias took his place (Acts 1:26).

martyrs (20:4) as a literal resurrection.[6] The theme of witness and martyrdom in the literal sense is central to the message of Revelation. We should expect the book to be faithful in forecasting the fulfillment of the martyrs' promised hope.

Although "those who had been beheaded because of their testimony" are specific in 20:4, all schools of interpretation that believe in the authority of Scripture recognize that the martyrs are representative of the full body of the faithful. Perhaps we may assume that the text by this means gives special honor to the martyrs.

We infer from the distinction between the resurrected saints in verse 4 and "the rest of the dead" which were to "come to life" after the 1000 years that two resurrections are necessarily implied (cp. John 5:28-29).

That the resurrection of believers who arise in an immortal state should be separate from the resurrection of unbelievers to be raised in their fallen, sinful condition is most logical and in keeping with the sanctity of this glorious event. It is also supported by the fact that in several passages where the resurrection of the saints is addressed by the Apostle Paul, no mention is made of the condition of the wicked dead. This is best explained by the assumption that the common Apostolic teaching, probably inferred from Jesus own instruction, and in harmony with the predominant belief in Judaism, was that the just would be raised independently of the wicked. We should expect that the teaching of Jesus as the Messiah would provide here this chronological indicator, as explicitly stated in Rev 20:5.

Jesus had addressed the resurrection as the fulfillment of the believer's hope for eternal life in John 6:40, "My Father's will is

---

[6]The martyr theme, so prominent in the previous chapters, can hardly be understood in terms of spiritual death, a condition existing prior to their resurrection, as these subjects are described as faithful witnesses. It is therefore clearly unacceptable hermeneutics to make the resurrection of those "who had been beheaded because of their testimony for Jesus and because of the word of God" refer to the spiritual regeneration of those who had previously been spiritually dead. Yet this appears to be fundamental to postmillennial and amillennial interpretations, so popular today.

that everyone who looks to the Son and believes in him shall have eternal life, and I will raise him up at the last day" (cp. John 6:39, 44, 54). The implication is that the unbelievers will not participate in this resurrection. Such statements from Jesus may underlie the teaching of Paul to the Thessalonians (1 Thess 4:15-17):

> According to the Lord's own word, . . . we who are still alive, who are left till the coming of the Lord, will certainly not precede those who have fallen asleep. For the Lord himself will come down from heaven, with a loud command, with the voice of the archangel and with the trumpet call of God, and the dead in Christ will rise first. After that, we who are still alive and are left will be caught up together with them in the clouds to meet the Lord in the air. And so we will be with the Lord forever.[7]

Although the unbelieving dead are not raised at the beginning of the millennial age, there are several indications that unbelievers will survive Christ's second advent. One may well infer that all earth's inhabitants will not be warriors involved with the battle of Armageddon and therefore will not be subject to that destruction. Moreover, Scripture teaches that subsequent to the establishment of Christ's reign, the saints will reign with Christ over the nations (Gk. ἔθνοι, *éthnoi*). As we have seen from Rev 11:2, the "nations" (there translated "Gentiles") are unbelievers, outside of the true church and not numbered with God's Covenant people. This indicates that there will be unbelievers surviving into the millennial age who will be subjected to Christ's judgment, as assisted by immortal saints.[8]

---

[7]One should not assume that either Jesus or Paul was presenting a defense against a general resurrection, as the contextual question in each case seems to have been otherwise. But those passages do seem to imply belief in a particular resurrection for believers who rise in immortality for eternal life.

[8]Some, including Seventh-day Adventists, have maintained that the entire unregenerate population of the earth will be destroyed in the events associated with Armageddon and the destruction of the Antichrist powers, as described in Rev 19:19-21. However, in the statement, "The rest of them were killed . . . ," "them" refers to its contextual antecedent, "the beast and the kings of the earth and their armies" (v. 19), probably not to the entire world populous. For this understanding, cf. I. C. Welcome and Clarkson Goud, *The Plan of Redemption by our Lord Jesus Christ* (Boston: Advent Christian Publication Society, pref. 1867), 425-445; for Seventh-day Adventist interpretation see *The Seventh-day Adventist Bible Commentary* (Washington, D.C.: Review and Herald, 1957) 7.879-880. However, this understanding has the limitation of not providing a suitable setting for the fulfillment of some of the Messianic prophecies of

Viewing our text chronologically, we note that those who participated in the first resurrection "reigned with Christ" during the thousand years. "Reigned" means to rule, we must assume as agents of Christ, who will be king over the nations during the millennial age. In the ancient world, the office of king always included the function of judge. We learn from other texts that, indeed, "the saints will judge the world" (1 Cor 6:3; cp. Matt 19:28). Given the great economy of words with which the Revelation is given, we are left to use our imagination to understand how this may be carried out. A very realistic approach may infer that immortal believers will function as civil servants at various levels of government throughout the world.[9] The process of making such assignments must

---

the Old Testament, such as Ezek 37:26-28:

> "I will make a covenant of peace with them [the northern and southern kingdom Israelites (v. 19)]; it will be an everlasting covenant. I will establish them and increase their numbers, and I will put my sanctuary among them forever. My dwelling place will be with them; I will be their God, and they will be my people. Then the nations will know that I the LORD make Israel holy, when my sanctuary is among them forever.'"

"Forever," in context need not extend the temple beyond the millennium into the new earth, as it may be understood in a Hebraic sense (עוֹלָם, *hōlam*) meaning "continuously" or "age-lasting" (BDB, 762.2b).

Other questions may be raised regarding the viability of this millennial concept. If the Jewish people experience a mass conversion to Jesus as Messiah, during or before their desperate time at Armageddon, as one may expect and hope (Rom 11:26), or when Jesus returns to accomplish victory, when will the predicted massive return to the land occur (Isa 43:6-11; Jer 31:7-14; Ezek 37:1-14, 21-22; et al.)? Another question for the empty millennium theory is the meaning of the statement that "they will be priests of God and of Christ" during the millennial age (v. 6). By definition, priests must be intermediaries, implying a constituency to whom the priests can minister. If the redeemed saints are priests, then one should infer that there will be others to whom they will minister the Gospel during the millennial age. While this writer inclines toward this understanding, he does not hold it dogmatically to the exclusion of possible alternatives.

[9]Because we have never experienced such a condition, the situation involving immortals mixing socially with mortals may seem very strange. However, we need not assume that immortals will look or function differently in the sensory world, except that imortals will have greatly enhanced capacities. They will have freedom from disease, the effects of depravity, and from other weaknesses of the flesh. Even the unregenerate in the millennial age, though still mortal and subject to their Adamic nature, will be greatly advantaged from the beneficent rule of Christ and the prevalence of worldwide justice administered with "an iron rod" (Rev 2:26, 27; 12:5, 19:5).

include our Lord's judgment of the individual saints as they first appear before him. This may take some time.[10] Our understanding incorporates an extension of the Gospel of grace and the operation of the Holy Spirit into the millennial age. Jesus demonstration of His Divine character during His first-advent ministry, including His glorious resurrection, did not result in "automatic conversions," nor should we expect this in the millennial age.[11]

20:1-6. The Millennial Reign — Notes

1. The angel holds the key to the **Abyss (Gk.** ἀβυσσος ,'*ábussos*). The word is found in Luke 8:31, where the demons of the demoniac healed by Jesus begged Him repeatedly not to order them to go into the Abyss. In Rev 9:1, an angel unlocks the Abyss so that demonic "locusts" could come out to kill and torture (v. 5). The beast described in 13:1 as "coming out of the sea" is said in 11:7 to come up from the Abyss. The ancients thought of the sea as an entrance into the Abyss (Psa 107:26). The word denotes the underworld either as the grave (cf. Rom 10:7) or as the abode of demons The **great chain** (Gk. ἅλυσιν, *hálusin*) is described as "great" (μεγάλην, *megálên*) to indicate strength sufficient for binding Satan securely. **2-3.** It is apparent here that the angel as God's agent exercises total control over Satan as he seizes, binds, and throws him into the Abyss. The Abyss is then **locked** and **sealed**. If language here is allowed any meaning, it indicates the total incapacitation of Satan during this confinement. Both here and in 9:1 an angel exercises control over the Abyss, as indicated apocalyptically by his unlocking and locking with a key. Thus God indicates that He exercises providential control over the forces of evil in the world (cp. Job 1:6-12). **4. Thrones** are for those who rule, implying that the resurrected saints will be given authority to assist Christ in his kingly reign. This is clarified at the end of the verse. **Authority to judge**

---

[10]Premillennialist historicists who have believed that all the unsaved in the world will be destroyed in connection with the battle of Armageddon and that therefore only the immortal saints will live in the millennial age usually defend this with the assumption that Christ when he returns to earth will "leave his mediatorial throne," and that in consequence there can be no salvation in the millennial age. Cf. e.g., Welcome and Goud, 304-305.

[11]For a defense of this understanding of the covenant of grace by a Reformed theologian, see D. H. Kromminga, *The Millennium*: *Its Nature, Function, and Relation to the Consummation of the World* (Grand Rapids: Eerdmans, 1948), 71-73.

was in Bible times always the prerogative and responsibility of the king. Here it is delegated to the resurrected saints. **Souls** as used here means persons (cf. BAGD, 894.2). That they are not disembodied spirits is indicated by their resurrection. That they are the souls of the martyrs, in the light of the prominent role of literal martyrs in the book, requires that the term must be understood literally. The translation, **They had not worshiped** (NIV) obscures the pronoun in the original text, which is more literally translated in the KJV, the NASB, ESV, et al. The Greek text reads, καὶ οἵτινες οὐ προσεκύνησαν, *kai hoitines óu prosekunēsan*, "*and those who* had not worshiped . . . (NASB). While it is true that the indefinite relative pronoun, οἵτινες often functioned in koiné Greek in place of a definite relative, the context here favors the broader interpretation: Not only the martyrs but all believers unallied with the Beast will experience resurrection.[12] **5.** The parenthetical statement that **the rest of the dead** were not raised until after the thousand years introduces the second resurrection. "The rest of the dead" is a partitive concept, in that the text views the dead collectively, then divides their resurrection into two temporally separated events. The grammar requires that those who are raised at each time were "dead" in the same sense. If the first resurrection is literal, the resurrection of the rest must also be literal, and vice versa.[13] This second resurrection is not mentioned again until verse 12 where it is implied, as the dead are seen standing before God in the judgment. **6.** Those who participate in the first resurrection are especially blessed, as they escape the second death (everlasting punishment which follows the

---

[12]The Augustinian, amillennial view requires a convoluted logic which transposes the order of the phrases in v. 4, so that the souls "came to life" spiritually (i.e., were regenerated) before death, before their literal testimony and martyrdom, though our text presents the temporal sequence the other way around. Beale comments, "This understanding of the text demands that the three clauses be read in a temporal order opposite to what appears most natural . . . " (though he appears later to adopt this unnatural reading as necessary to his amillennial theology; p. 1012).

[13]This is contrary to amillennialists and most postmillennialists, who make the first resurrection figurative and the second literal. Henry Alford in his *Greek Testament* has cogently stated, "If in a passage where *two resurrections* are mentioned . . . the first resurrection may be understood to mean spiritual rising with Christ, while the second means literal rising from the grave;—then there is an end of all significance in language, and Scripture is wiped out as a definite testimony to anything" (4.732, as quoted in Beale, p. 1004). Beale counters this with the observation that spiritual resurrection and physical resurrection are in fact found in the same context, as e.g. Rom 6:4-13, but he does not address the partitive nature of the expression, "The *rest of the dead*," and therefore these examples have no weight. The contexts of such passages as Rom 6:4-13 clearly differentiate between what is spiritual and what is literal.

final judgment; v. 14) and **reign** with Christ a thousand years.[14]

Satan's Doom

20:7. **When the thousand years are over, Satan will be released from his prison** [8]**and will go out to deceive the nations in the four corners of the earth—Gog and Magog—to gather them for battle. In number they are like the sand on the seashore.** [9]**They marched across the breadth of the earth and surrounded the camp of God's people, the city he loves. But fire came down from heaven and devoured them.** [10]**And the devil, who deceived them, was thrown into the lake of burning sulfur, where the beast and the false prophet had been thrown. They will be tormented day and night for ever and ever.**

20:7-10   **Satan's Destruction**   **Exposition**

These verses describe the final effort of Satan to attack and destroy the work of Christ and His kingdom. It is remarkable that in God's inscrutable providence, Satan was permitted to escape from total confinement at the end of the millennial age and to resume his nefarious activities. God has something to demonstrate in that He will be the ultimate Victor over the powers of evil and the actions of the unbelieving and evil populous that will persist even through the thousand-year rule of Jesus Christ. One can discern this high purpose of the millennial era and its aftermath in that it demonstrates the radical nature of human depravity which persists even with Satan bound and under the optimum circumstances of a just and beneficent world government. Even with the continuing gracious offer of the eternal Gospel, mankind apparently is eager to accept Satan's invitation to war. Unregenerate humanity will be fully capable still at this time to respond to Satan's deception, and

---

[14]Oddly, those who see the first resurrection as figurative find no explicit mention of the resurrection of the righteous dead in Revelation 20, though it is the resurrection of the righteous that is distinctively emphasized as the hope of God's people in both Old and New Testaments.

to the belief that wicked men can muster armies sufficient to put an end to Christ and His kingdom.

The description indicates a world-wide, organized military campaign, with immense numbers, and we may assume now with the best of modern military equipment. It would appear that many of God's people in this situation may have resorted to Jerusalem and its environs, whether they will be a military camp we are not told, but the destruction to follow will not require arms. The enemy will surround the encamped people of God and the Beloved City, where those evil forces will be summarily destroyed with fire from heaven!

As the death of the great army by fire from heaven is differentiated from that of Satan and his cohorts (19:20, 20:10), we may infer that the destroyed army suffered what Scripture calls "the first death." This argues for the view that this battle called "Gog and Magog" precedes the second resurrection implied by verses 5 and 12.[15]

The term, Gog and Magog, is used here as a symbol for this great battle, while alluding to the previous battle of Armageddon where the two terms appear. However, both the terms and the battles have different meanings. The battle of Armageddon draws upon Ezek 38-39 where Gog is described as "the chief prince of Meshech and Tubal, and Magog is the name of the land from which he comes, accompanied by many nations, to attack Jerusalem (Ezek 38:2-3). The term, "Gog and Magog," functions only as a name for the battle in Rev 20:8, perhaps to call attention to certain similarities between the two battles. One obvious difference between them is that following Armageddon as described in Ezekiel, there is an extended work to clean up the scene of the battle and to purify the land, implying a continuation of the historical process, whereas with the "Gog and Magog" battle it is followed by a general resurrection, the judgment, and the new heavens

---

[15]As indicated above (notes 8 & 10), some commentators, including Seventh-day Adventists, have understood that the battle of Gog and Magog is to be fought by wicked men raised in this second resurrection.

and the new earth (20:11-15; 21:1). The earlier battle ends with the destruction of the Beast and the False Prophet; the later battle ends with the fiery burning alive of the armies Satan recruited. Satan is then thrown into the lake of fire to suffer eternal destruction with the Beast and the False Prophet.

What is meant by the expression, "forever and ever"? To understand this, we should do as Jesus commonly did while teaching—look to the Old Testament, where it occurs rather frequently. The Greek reads, εἰς τοὺς αἰῶνας τῶν αἰώνων, *eis toùs aiōnas tōn aiṓnōn*, literally translated "unto the ages of the ages." The same expression occurs in 19:3 and in 14:11, though in the latter without the articles. In both of these the expression applies to the smoke going up. These in turn reflect the Hebrew idiom which occurs in Isa 34:9-11a:

> Edom's streams will be turned into pitch,
>   her dust into burning sulfur;
>   her land will become blazing pitch!
> It will not be quenched night and day;
>   *its smoke will rise forever.*
> From generation to generation it will lie desolate;
>   no one will ever pass through it again.
> The desert owl and the screech owl will possess it.
>   (italics mine)

Here we have the three elements found in the Revelation texts—burning sulfur, night and day, and smoke rising forever. It is apparent from history that the eternally rising smoke is not literal but meant as a symbol to indicate to posterity the devastation and its permanence. Much of this land can be seen by travelers to this day, but they will not see any smoke from that burning. The Hebrew words used here to express the duration of the desolation, עוֹלָם, *holam,* "forever," and נֵצַח, *nēzaḥ,* "ever again," may be understood in a finite sense, "for a long time," "having endurance in time," or "for a lifetime" (BDB, 664.3; 762.2.a). The meaning is determined from context. When describing God or other immortals, the meaning is infinite duration.

Given the Hebraic character of the Greek language in the Book of Revelation, one should interpret in terms of equivalent

Hebrew usage. Moreover, because only God and saints who participate in the future resurrection are described in the Bible as having immortality (1 Tim 6:16; 1 Cor 15:53), we should not take license to impute immortality to angels or to other created beings. The Hebrew Scriptures (the Old Testament) are very clear regarding the destiny of the wicked and the extinction of evil. These Scriptures are the authority to which Jesus appealed and about which He said, "The Scriptures cannot be broken" (John 10:35). Other texts clearly indicate that the destiny of the wicked is "death" and "destruction":

> The soul who sins is the one who will die. . . . A righteous man . . . will surely live, declares the Sovereign LORD. (Ezek 18:4b, 5, 9b)

> "Surely the day is coming; it will burn like a furnace. All the arrogant and every evildoer will be stubble, and that day that is coming will set them on fire," says the LORD Almighty. "Not a root nor a branch will be left to them. . . . . Then you will trample down the wicked; they will be ashes under the soles of your feet on the day when I do these things," says the LORD Almighty. (Mal 4:1, 3)

> "The day of the LORD is near for all nations. As you have done, it will be done to you . . . . They will . . . be as if they had never been." (Obad 15a, 16b)

> . . . Rebels and sinners will both be broken, and those who forsake the LORD will perish (Isa 1:28).[16]

Jesus and the Apostles reaffirmed this message. Jesus clearly differentiated between the death common to all and the eternal death of the wicked:

> Do not be afraid of those who kill the body but cannot kill the soul. Rather, be afraid of the one who can destroy both soul and body in hell (Matt 10:28).

The apostles likewise speak of eternal punishment as death:

> The wages of sin is death, but the gift of God is eternal life (Rom 6:23).

---

[16]Those who teach that the torments of hell will continue forever sometimes reject the plain sense of these Old Testament statements by appealing to the doctrine of progressive revelation, implying that what was taught in the Old Testament is superseded by a different view of the sinners destruction in the New. In effect, this implies that on account of progressive revelation the teachings of Jesus and the New Testament corrects the teachings of the Old. Our understanding affirms the integrity of the Old Testament and the unity of the Old and New Covenant Scriptures.

These men blaspheme in matters they do not understand. They are like brute beasts, creatures of instinct, born only to be caught and destroyed, and like beasts they too will perish (2 Pet 2:12).

Peter clearly indicates here that wicked men will perish as do beasts—they will suffer death and extinction of being. This being so, we must understand the expression, "for ever and ever," when used of mortals as in Rev 20:10, as a figure of speech, an intensive form of αἰῶνα, *aiōna*, meaning age-lasting or a long time.[17] Rev 20:10 must be understood, nevertheless, to indicate tortuous burning in Gehenna. This process will end with literal death and destruction of body and soul, as Jesus stated, but it nevertheless teaches that the agonies to be experienced in the process will be intensive and extended as long as God's justice requires.

20:7-10   **Satan's Destruction**   **Notes**

8. The **nations** (Gk. τὰ ἔθνη, *tà ĕthnē*, i.e., "the Gentiles") are in 11:2 not included in the "Israel of God," God's covenant people (cf. Rom 11:26). The term is used figuratively for the unregenerate in distinction from "Israel," which denotes the covenant people of God. (See above on Rev 11:2.) The **four corners of the earth** is an expression equivalent to "the four directions of the compass," meaning from all directions or perhaps the entire earth. The ancients did not believe the earth was square so the expression cannot be taken literally. The expression **Gog and Magog** builds symbolically on the battle of Ezekiel 38-39 to indicate a battle of world forces of evil against the Covenant people of God. The number of the forces **like the sand on the seashore,** a common idiom in Scripture, indicates an immense number beyond counting (cp. Gen 22:17; 32:12; 41:49, et al.). **9. The city he loves** refers to Jerusalem. We may imagine the city as having been rebuilt during the millennial reign of the Messiah, as indicated in Isaiah 60:10-14; 62:1-12; Jer 31:38-40, et al. **10.** The devil, with the Beast and the False Prophet, are thrown into the lake of burning sulfur, where they are tormented day and night **forever and ever**. This expression, though uniformly translated throughout the Bible, varies in its original language forms. Most often it reads in Greek (LXX and N. T.) εἰς αἰῶνα αἰῶνος, *'eis 'aiōna 'aiōnos*, literally, "unto [the] age of [the]

---

[17]See Edward William Fudge, *The Fire that Consumes* (Houston, Texas: The Providential Press, 1982), 289-307.

age" (e.g., Psa 20:5, LXX (21:4, NIV), both words singular in number). Psa 9:6, LXX (9:5, NIV) reads, εἰς τὸν αἰῶνα καὶ εἰς τὸν αἰῶνα τοῦ αἰῶνος, *'eis tòn 'aiōna kaì 'eis tòn 'aiōna toū 'aiōnos*, "unto the age, even unto the age of the age" (Again all singular number, but note the addition of the articles, ἅ & τοῦ as well as the redundant αἰῶνα.). If the expression were to be understood literally, one should expect "the age of the ages." Sometimes the entire expression is in the plural, as it is in Rev 20:10, εἰς τοὺς αἰῶνας τῶν αἰώνων, *'eis toùs 'aiōnas tōn 'aiōnōn*, "unto the ages of the ages." Jews and Christians in the first century believed in only two ages, "this age" and the "age to come." It is therefore hardly possible to understand 20:10 literally as "ages of the ages," though it may well be hyperbole. Moreover, many references in the Bible indicate that the wages of sin is "death." This death is called "the second death," in distinction from the common destiny of all, and this second death is also described as "destruction" or "perishing." In this light, "Forever and ever" in its varieties of expression appears to be an idiom which as applied to mortals means something less than "unending life." "Tormented day and night" may then mean torment without respite during the process of dying, whereas "forever and ever" may mean an extraordinarily long time. Perhaps one should also understand that a "long time" of torture is not necessarily as long as more tolerable experiences. Nevertheless, the justice of a holy God must thereby be satisfied. We are dealing in 20:10 with the devil, who we must assume is a mortal creature, for Scripture states propositionally that God alone possesses immortality (1 Tim 6:16).[18] When Satan is cast into the lake of fire, he will experience the second death (20:14). The Beast and the False Prophet, had been cast into the Lake of Fire, as described in 19:20. Now this fate is attributed to Satan. In the Revelation the Beast and the False Prophet may be symbols for institutions, rather than only individual persons, but they too will meet their demise.

---

[18]For the mortality and death of Satan, see Gen 3:15 (where Satan's head is to be *crushed* (whether "bruised" (KJV, RSV, *NASB*, ESV), "crushed" (NIV), or "struck" (REB, NRSV, JPS), it appears obvious that the normal sense as directed to the head rather than the tail denotes killing the serpent. Basil Atkinson states, "Whatever the exact meaning of the verb, the picture seems to be clear. To bruise the head is a picture of fatal and final destruction. To bruise the heel is a picture of damage, which is neither fatal nor final." *The Book of Genesis* (The Pocket commentary of the Bible; Chicago: Moody Press, 1957) 51.

Chapter Twelve   *Second Resurrection and Judgment, 20:11-15*   449

The Dead Are Judged

20:11. **Then I saw a great white throne and him who was seated on it. Earth and sky fled from his presence, and there was no place for them.** [12]**And I saw the dead, great and small, standing before the throne, and books were opened. Another book was opened, which is the book of life. The dead were judged according to what they had done as recorded in the books.** [13]**The sea gave up the dead that were in it, and death and Hades gave up the dead that were in them, and each person was judged according to what he had done.** [14]**Then death and Hades were thrown into the lake of fire. The lake of fire is the second death.** [15]**If anyone's name was not found written in the book of life, he was thrown into the lake of fire.**

20:11-15   The Second Resurrection and Judgment   Exposition

The next scene in John's vision is a description of what has come to be called The Great White Throne Judgment. It is the culminating and final judgment which brings this age to a close and introduces the age to come. Jesus' reign will begin at His second advent and will continue through the millennial kingdom. This intermediate kingdom with His *temporal* reign will terminate with this final great event to be followed summarily with the total destruction of evil in the "lake of fire," but Christ's reign will continue into the Age to Come and throughout eternity. Perhaps the previously resurrected saints who have reigned with Christ as judges during the millennial age will also participate then, but our text focuses only on the One who sits upon the throne. This event is anticipated graphically by our Lord himself in Matt 25:31-46, the "sheep and goats" judgment.[19] The setting for this scene is supra-mundane. The statement that "earth and sky fled from his presence, and there was no place for them" is a description of John's visionary experience rather than of literal, physical phenomena. It does, nevertheless, suggest that this judgment introduces a new order. Metaphorically,

---

[19]Jesus' Sheep and Goats" portrayal of the final judgment may in fact coalesce the judgments following the first resurrection and during the millennial age with this final great judgment event.

it appears to mean that the old order consisting of humanly administered governments which had had to be ruled with "a rod of iron" were at this time to pass away, along with any astral symbols which earthly rulers may have claimed to represent them. The astral metaphor, so understood, would reflect the mentality of the ancient pagan world rather than that of the time of fulfillment.[20]

This passage expounds the dramatic vision of Daniel 7, where it states:

> thrones were set in place, and the Ancient of Days took his seat. His clothing was as white as snow; the hair of his head was white like wool. His throne was flaming with fire, and its wheels were all ablaze. A river of fire was flowing, coming out from before him (vv. 9, 10a). The court was seated and the books were opened. . . . I kept looking until the beast was slain and its body destroyed and thrown into the blazing fire" (10b, 11b).[21]

The supra-mundane setting of the white throne judgment accounts for the fact that the physical process of resurrection is not described. The scene is not envisioned as taking place on earth—John saw "the dead . . . standing before the throne." One must assume that the implied resurrection includes those mentioned in verse 5 as "the rest of the dead," as well as any who died during the millennial period and those destroyed by the fire from heaven as a result of the battle of Gog and Magog (v. 9). Assuming that mortals may have become believers and died during the millennial period, this will include both believers and unbelievers.

The mention of the books is anthropomorphic, as there is no requirement for the omniscient God of heaven to keep physical records. These books inform the reader that the Triune God knows each person to be judged both with respect to his works and with regard to his standing in the Gospel of grace (the Book of Life). Verse 13 addresses the resurrection as including all the remaining dead, whether they died and were buried at sea or were buried on

---

[20] See above on Rev 6:12-13.

[21] The inclusion of the beast in Daniel's judgment scene argues for his coalescence of the two judgments recorded in Rev 19:20 and the white throne judgment of 20:11-15.

Chapter Twelve   *Second resurrection and judgment, 20:11-15*   451

land. "Death and Hades" appear to be personified here, as John uses the plural pronoun to refer to them. Of course, "death" is actually a condition and Hades is a place, often in Scripture simply the place of burial, the grave. As personification, Hades is subject to and contingent upon death. Their giving up of their dead renders them no longer functional, except in terms of the "second death (cf. v. 14)."[22]

The finale for the evils of this world order is forecast in verses 14 and 15. Death and Hades, still personified, along with all whose names are not recorded in the Book of Life are cast into the lake of fire, the symbolic representation of the permanent end of "death" and "Hades" and the final punishment of all who are found guilty of unbelief in God's great plan of redemption.

20:11-15   The Second Resurrection and Judgment   Notes

11. The **great white throne** is described as "great" to reflect the magnitude and power of the sovereign God. It is "white" to communicate the absolute holiness of the One seated on it. **Him who is seated on it** is best understood as a symbolic representation of the Triune God. In Dan 7:9, the occupant of the throne is the Ancient of Days, who in context is differentiated from the Messianic Son of Man figure (7:13) representing the Messiah, God the Son. **12.** The description of the dead as **great and small** has not to do with their physical stature but more probably with their reputation, as kings and slaves will stand equally before the great white throne. It does not mean "children and full grown," as one should expect also that infants and grown-ups will be raised as mature adults. (On the opening of the heavenly **books**, see Dan 7:10; also Isa 65:6; Mal 3:16; cf. Psa 69:28; see also numerous references in the Apocrypha and Pseudepigrapha [Aune 3.1102]). The books indicate that God knows all the deeds of those whom he judges. That "Books" is plural may reflect the Jewish tradition that God has one book for the deeds of the righteous and another for the deeds of the wicked (Aune 3.1102). **13.** Commentators point out that this verse appears to be out of order, as it should precede

---

[22]For a thorough discussion of the expression "death and Hades," see David E. Aune, *Revelation* (Word Biblical Commentary; Nashville: Nelson, 1997-1998), 3.1102-1103.

verse 12. However, barring textual evidence for such a transposition, one should understand it simply as explanatory of what precedes. The distinction between **the sea** and **Hades** addresses the Hebrew understanding that those buried at sea were not usually thought of as being in Hades, the more conventional place of land burial. The sea was feared and "burial" at sea was undesirable.[23] **15.** We have here an instance where an apocalyptic symbol is explained for the reader: **"The Lake of fire** is the second death." With the passing of the final judgment and the destruction of evil with **the second death**, we will reach the culmination of this temporal age. The living righteous, though unmentioned, as mortals must be included as participants in the final judgment. They, with the resurrected dead, are to be caught up to the judgment scene while the old earth "passes away" (21:1b) and the creation is prepared for the New Heavens and the New Earth (ch. 21).

20:11-15. The Second Resurrection and Judgment Fulfillment

Though the prophecies we are dealing with are currently unfulfilled, it may be appropriate to comment briefly by way of summary of the above in concluding this chapter. Our understanding presupposes that belief in a future temporal reign of the Messiah over the nations was a common belief in Judaism and in the church when our Lord gave His testimony as recorded here in this chapter.[24] One should understand that this revelation, cryptic as it is, should be fleshed out from the prophetic preaching of the Old Testament prophets, as well as from the earlier teaching of Jesus and His apostles. There is much more to be harvested from these sources than we have addressed in our commentary above. Further, we may expect some element of mystery regarding everyday life in the millennial age until there is opportunity to experience it. This should in no way deflect us from reading the text of this chapter in its plain and ordinary

---

[23] Aune 3.1102-1103. The idea that Hades was commonly associated only with earth burials supports its Hebrew definition as "grave," or "place of burial."

[24] The fact that Jewish teachers independently from Christianity came to believe in an intermediate age when the Messiah would reign suggests that the premillennial doctrine really is implied in the Old Testament Scriptures. For discussion of millennial ideas in pre-Christian Judaism, see Daniel T Taylor, *The Reign of Christ on Earth: or the Voice of the Church in All Ages*. (Boston: H. L. Hastings, 1893), 13-24; Kromminga, *Millennium*, 25-26.

sense, without resorting to the allegorizing interpretation of Augustine and his fourth-century contemporaries.[25]

We should assume that the condition of believers during the millennium will be most happy. They will have responsibilities globally in both church and state that will be personally fulfilling. Justice will prevail, personal enterprise will be rewarded, and Godly families will flourish. The effects resulting from man's fallen state, though not eliminated in mortals, will be minimized through the just and beneficent rule of the King of kings. Yet one of the presumed reasons God in His providence has ordained the millennial age is to demonstrate that depravity still induces mankind to sin, even when Satan is not in the picture.

We now look with great anticipation to the concluding chapters of Revelation, which address the Age to Come and the eternal order, the restoration of God's creation to its edenic state.

---

[25]Constantine's establishment of a new and revolutionary state church with the bishop of Rome as its head provided a rationale for the concept of a a spiritualized millennium which was to a large extent political as well as ecclesiastical. In this radical new idea, Christ reigned as represented by the bishop of Rome. Augustine refined this concept by making Christ's spiritual reign contemporaneous with the entire church age. Augustine thus gave rise to amillennialism.

Chapter Thirteen

THE NEW HEAVENS AND THE NEW EARTH

21:1-22:21

Introduction

We have now arrived at the culminating chapters in the Book of Revelation, chapters 21 and 22! With chapter 20, the prophetic timetable of the book has reached from the end of the reign of Domitian in A.D. 96 to the end of the millennial era. The sequence of fulfilled prophecies in chapters 4 through 16 is too lengthy and complex to indicate arbitrary interpretation. In any case, we are now at the place where there should be more agreement regarding the relevance and in general the meaning of the vision.[26]

The forecast of the new heavens and the new earth is in 2 Pet 3:13 associated with the second coming of Christ, an event which in our understanding of Revelation 20 is to occur prior to the millennial age, whereas we now indicate its occurrence subsequent to the millennium. How are we to understand this apparent inconsistency? The apostolic writers when addressing the second coming commonly coalesced the final events so as to point to the practical dimensions of the subject, principally the necessity of preparing for the judgment. This is illustrated by Jesus, Himself, in Matt 25:31-46, where He addresses the Great White Throne judgment as consequent upon his second coming (v. 31), though in Rev 20:11-15, He indicates that this will occur at the end of the millennial age. Similarly, the Apostle Paul addresses the events subsequent to the future resurrection in

---

[26]We allude to the disparity that exists between the several schools of interpretation. See above, ch. 1.

1 Cor 15:24-28 in terms of Christ's reign and judgment without indicating the millennial age as such (note v. 25).[27]

Chapters 21 and 22 begin with the revelation of the new heavens and the new earth predicted in Isa 66:22 and end with a final warning from the Lord Jesus Himself of the sacredness of the words of the prophecy and the danger to anyone who adds or detracts from them (21:18b-19). With this Jesus reaffirms that these prophecies are His testimony as His Faithful Witness to His people (21:20).

The New Jerusalem

21:1. Then I saw a new heaven and a new earth, because the first heaven and the first earth had passed away, and there was no longer any sea. ²I saw the holy city, the new Jerusalem, coming down out of heaven from God, prepared like a bride beautifully dressed for her husband. ³And I heard a loud voice from the throne saying, "Now the dwelling of God is with men, and he will live with them. They will be his people, and God himself will be with them and be their God. ⁴He will wipe every tear from their eyes. There will be no more death or mourning or crying or pain, for the old order of things has passed away."

Rev 21:1-4   The New Home of the Bride   Exposition

The expression, "Then I saw" reiterates the manner in which this prophecy was given to the Apostle on Patmos—that is, he experienced it as a Holy Spirit-inspired revelation which came to him in vision, as it were, displayed in the heavens. At this point, we do well to remember that the prophetic message of the Book of

---

[27]Nevertheless, he speaks only of the resurrection of "those who belong to him [Christ]" (v. 23), a forecast agreeable with Jesus' testimony in Rev 20:4, 5). Again in 1 Thess 4:16, the Apostle Paul speaks of the "dead in Christ" only as they who will arise from death at the time of Christ's second advent. In Phil 3:11, he refers to his goal "somehow, to attain to the resurrection from the dead" (Gk. εἴ πως καταντήσω εἰς τὴν ἐξανάστασιν τὴν ἐκ νεκρῶν, literally translated, "if somehow I might attain the resurrection *out from among* the dead"; emphasis mine.) Clearly, the Apostle refers here to a partial resurrection consisting only of believers, as in Rev 20:4.

Revelation is introduced as the testimony of Jesus Christ, the Second Person of the Godhead, the Messiah, the Savior of God's People of both Testaments—the redeemed Covenant community of Israel and the Church. The promise of the new heavens and the new earth is as certain as the integrity of God!

The reference to "heaven" does not refer to heaven as the place in which God dwells, but to the atmospheric heavens and to the cosmos we see when we look into the sky. This is the marvel of our Creator's handiwork, defectively preserved after Adam's fall in the original paradise, but destined to be restored to its pristine state in the new heavens and the new earth. We are assured that the old, sin defaced earth which had been subjected to the curse (Gen 3:14-19) will pass away and be forever gone.

The absence of the sea described in verse 1b reflects the fact that the ancients in Israel, and even more generally during the Roman era when the Revelation was written, knew the sea was much to be feared. The Mediterranean, though smaller than the great oceans, was subject to severe storms which caused the loss of many seamen (cf. Acts 27:1-44). As we have seen above (cf. on 9:1-3 and 13:1), the region beneath the sea was associated with the Abyss, the underworld where demonic forces ruled. In the new world such evils will be forever gone.

The Apostle next saw the Holy City, the New Jerusalem "coming down out of heaven from God" to the new earth. The city is described as "prepared as a bride beautifully dressed for her husband." The strong physical implications of verse 1 suggests that what follows regarding the city might be understood in terms of a physical place. This is enhanced by the description which follows in verses 9-27. But the descent should be understood not as a physical reality but from the standpoint of the Divine architect. The significance is to be found in the marriage metaphor, as expanded further in verse 3: "The dwelling of God is with men, and he will live with them. They will be his people, and God himself will be with them and be their God." This reflects the ancient marriage covenant formula, "You are my wife and I am your husband." Such covenants were intended to imply that the husband would be the loving provider who would ensure the welfare of the wife and provide for her a happy habitat where she could assume for him her domestic duties of home and family.[28] God will forever wipe away the tears often occasioned in this evil world through disappointment and dying and again insure for His "bride," both men and women, a happy, eternal home. "There will be no more death or mourning or crying or pain, for the old order of things has passed away" (13:4).

21:1-4   The New Home of the Bride   Notes

1. The reference to **the new heavens and the new earth** are reminiscent of Isa 65:17 and 66:22-23. Isaiah 65 and 66 are remarkable in several respects. As we reflect on Revelation 21:1, Isaiah illustrates the unity of the Old and New Covenants. What is promised to the faithful in the eighth-century B.C. nation of Israel on the authority of Jesus will be fulfilled for all of God's people in God's time. What was degraded in the original creation by sin and its curse will be recreated in its original perfection in the future kingdom with the reign of Jesus Christ. Isaiah looked through the prophetic telescope and predicted what will happen in the distant future, so that the faithful saints more than twenty-eight hundred years ago had the same hope as we who believe in the twenty-first century A.D. The chronology that is implicit in Revelation is telescoped in Isaiah, so that some of the promises may appear to us as millennial and others as post-millennial. Isaiah's prophecy highlights what is essential for all—those who persist in unbelief will suffer just punishment (66:3-6, 14b-17, 24), and the faithful will live happily in God's peaceful kingdom in a restored Jerusalem (65:19) and a restored Israel (66:7-9) in which Jerusalem will flourish (66:10-14a). Most fundamentally, the redemption of the entire creation is assured in the promise of the new heavens and the new earth. The fact that the bride was seen **coming down out of heaven from God** does not indicate that those believers have lived in heaven during their intermediate state, as the bride includes those living at Christ's return as well as those who have died. The Scripture nevertheless teaches that the

---

[28] This concept of marriage, endorsed by biblical law, is largely lost in modern culture. The Apostle Paul in teaching marital love and faithfulness indicates that the disintegration of the Divinely established principles impacts negatively on the capacity of those principles to teach God's relationship to His Covenant people (Eph 5:22-33).

Chapter Thirteen *The new home of the bride, 21:1-4*

citizenship of the saints, even those still living on earth, is in heaven (Phil 3:20), where their names are written in the Lamb's Book of Life (21:27). Perhaps the principal message we should learn from the rich and radiant description of the Holy City as the bride is the wonder of the future glorification of God's Covenant people in the Age to Come.

The New Jerusalem (cont'd)

21:5. **He who was seated on the throne said, "I am making everything new!" Then he said, "Write this down, for these words are trustworthy and true."**

[6]**He said to me, "It is done. I am the Alpha and the Omega, the Beginning and the End. To him who is thirsty I will give to drink without cost from the spring of the water of life.** [7]**He who overcomes will inherit all this, and I will be his God, and he will be my son.** [8]**But the cowardly, the unbelieving, the vile, the murderers, the sexually immoral, those who practice magic arts, the idolaters, and all liars—their place will be in the fiery lake of burning sulfur. This is the second death."**

21:5-8   The Inheritance Covenant Affirmed   Exposition

The One who is the responsible creator of all things guarantees also the recreation of His work according to His original plan. He is "the Alpha and the Omega, the beginning and the end." The bride's inheritance is affirmed by the ancient covenant formula, "I will be his God, and he will be my son." Jesus insures that His bride will be ushered into her new home and that her welfare will be provided eternally. Not only will her habitat again be made perfect but the needs of her psyche, her inner being, will be fully satisfied by the river of life, the provision for her spiritual sustenance. This sustenance derives from her living in intimate relationship with her Creator, her covenant God.

The old sin nature in our immortal life will be forever gone and we will be disposed only and always to honor God with faithful, obedient living. All who have rejected this, God's gracious provision of everlasting life, will suffer everlasting destruction in the lake of fire—the second death.

21:5-8   The Inheritance Covenant Affirmed   Notes

5. This verse implies that the human author is not composing the Book of Revelation as the product of his own reflection upon earlier Scripture or even as the result of his own inspired psyche but, as indicated in 1:11, by a process in which the substance of the revelation was dictated to him by what was revealed in the vision he experienced. The command, **Write this down**, is reiterated here to emphasize the great importance of the words, "I am making everything new!" **Everything** may imply the totality of all that had remained of God's original creation. **New** may be understood, not necessarily in the scientific, materialistic sense, but more probably in the qualitative sense in which we are to understand that the entirety of what was cursed in Adam's fall will be perfected in the new world to become the eternal habitat of God with His people. **6. It is done** suggests that what God had originally set out to accomplish will with the new heavens and the new earth be at last completed! This profound truth is addressed by the Apostle Paul in Rom 8:19-21:

> The creation waits in eager expectation for the sons of God to be revealed. For the creation was subjected to frustration, not by its own choice, but by the will of the one who subjected it, in hope that the creation itself will be liberated from its bondage to decay and brought into the glorious freedom of the children of God.

Alpha and Omega, the Divine name here translated "the Beginning and the End," in context suggests that the perfection of God's original creation will be restored in His new world. **8.** The expression **second death** should be understood as the first, that is, as literal death (cf. 2:11; 20:6, 14).[29]

The New Jerusalem (cont'd)

21:9. **One of the seven angels who had the seven bowls full of the seven last plagues came and said to me, "Come, I will show you the bride, the wife of the Lamb."** [10]**And he carried me away in the Spirit to a mountain great and high, and showed me the Holy City, Jerusalem, coming down out of heaven from God.** [11]**It shone with the glory of God, and its brilliance was like that of a very precious jewel, like a jasper, clear as crystal.** [12]**It had a great, high wall with twelve gates, and with twelve angels at the gates. On the gates were written the names of the twelve tribes of Israel.** [13]**There were three gates on the east, three on the north, three on the south and three on the**

---

[29]See above our exposition of 20:10.

west. ¹⁴The wall of the city had twelve foundations, and on them were the names of the twelve apostles of the Lamb.

¹⁵The angel who talked with me had a measuring rod of gold to measure the city, its gates and its walls. ¹⁶The city was laid out like a square, as long as it was wide. He measured the city with the rod and found it to be 12,000 stadia in length, and as wide and high as it is long. ¹⁷He measured its wall and it was 144 cubits thick, by man's measurement, which the angel was using. ¹⁸The wall was made of jasper, and the city of pure gold, as pure as glass. ¹⁹The foundations of the city walls were decorated with every kind of precious stone. The first foundation was jasper, the second sapphire, the third chalcedony, the fourth emerald, ²⁰the fifth sardonyx, the sixth carnelian, the seventh chrysolite, the eighth beryl, the ninth topaz, the tenth chrysoprase, the eleventh jacinth, and the twelfth amethyst. ²¹The twelve gates were twelve pearls, each gate made of a single pearl. The great street of the city was of pure gold, like transparent glass.

21:9-21   The New Jerusalem, the Bride   Exposition

One cannot escape the conclusion that this description of the New Jerusalem recapitulates with added detail the revelation of verse 2. In verse two the descent of the "city" is indicated; then, the angel of verse 9 takes John to a high vantage point where he can view the city in more detail.

As one reads the description in 21:9-22:5, it should be obvious that we are dealing with highly metaphorical language and not with a physical three-dimensional city. The size alone is a sufficient indication of this, as its 12,000 stadia in length, breadth, and height (v. 16) amounts to approximately 1400 miles in each of the three dimensions! The enormous walls (v. 17), if literal, would serve no purpose in the earth made new where defensive structures implying hostile forces and warfare are entirely uncalled for. Moreover, the existence of the ungodly outside the city as described in 22:15 can hardly be taken literally as in the new earth.

On the contrary the city is identified not as eternal and wonderful real estate supernaturally constructed but as "the bride, the wife of the Lamb" (v. 9). This is sufficient to teach us that we have in this elegant description a glorious revelation of the supernatural, beautiful character of the community of God's redeemed people in the eternal Age to Come. The cubic, three dimensional symmetry, the pure transparent gold, the precious gem stones, the gates of single pearls, etc., reach beyond our capacity to transfer such details in allegorical fashion, even to redeemed humanity, but rather contribute to the reader a sense of awe and wonder at the coming life in the new heavens and the new earth.

21:9-21.   **The New Jerusalem, the Bride**   Notes

9. One of the seven angels associated with the seven last plagues now is instrumental in exhibiting the Holy City, the Lamb's wife. The contrast is no doubt deliberate, intended to lend emphasis to the glory of the redeemed in their future life. **10.** The origin of the city, as seen **coming down from heaven**, teaches the Divine origin of redemption, as well as the glorified state of the redeemed.[30] **11.** The term, **Jasper**, was used in antiquity of any opaque precious stone, including a variety of colors, mostly reddish (cp. 4:3).[31]. Here Jasper is "clear as crystal" probably to suggest the brillance of the shekinah as a manifestation of God's presence in the city. **12.** The **twelve gates** are each named for one of the twelve tribes of Israel, indicating the eternal significance of the elect nation. The **twelve angels** guarding the gates again affirm the impregnability of the chosen people in their eternal home. **14.** The **twelve foundations** named for the **twelve apostles** affirm the unity of the Old and New Covenants in the redemptive economy of God's Word. **15.** The cubic proportions of the New Jerusalem (**12,000 stadia** in length, width, and height) mimic the comparable dimensions of the most holy place in the temple (1 Kgs 6.20) and thereby suggests the holiness of the Bride as she has been prepared for her Husband. **19-20.** The **every kind of precious stone** which decorated the twelve foundations of the city appear to be itemized to

---

[30] A comparable indication is found in Heb 12:23, where it states that the names of the saints of old are written in heaven (cp.Rev 21:27). Cp. Eph 2:19-22.

[31] Bauer, W.; F. W. Gingrich, and F. Danker, *A Greek English Lexicon of the New Testament and Other Early Christian Literature* (2nd ed.; Chicago: University Press, 1979), 368; J. M. Ford, *Revelation*. (Anchor Bible; Garden City, N.Y.: Doubleday, 1975), 335.

enhance the image of the city as a symbol of the immortalized Bride of Christ.[32] The probable array of colors is suggested below:

1. Jasper–opaque red?
2. Sapphire–transparent blue
3. Chalcedony–uncertain?
4. Emerald–transparent green
5. Sardonyx–opaque brown
6. Carnelian–reddish or brown
7. Chrysolite–yellow topaz
8. Beryl–sea green or blue
9. Topaz–yellow or brown
10. Chrysoprase–apple green
11. Jacinth–blue or yellow-red
12. Amethyst–transparent purple

21. In addition to these precious gem stones, **the twelve gates** are carved each from a huge single pearl and **the street of the city** is paved with "pure gold, like transparent glass." The splendor that is ascribed to the New Jerusalem as the Bride of Christ boggles the mind!

The New Jerusalem (cont'd)

21:22. I did not see a temple in the city, because the Lord God Almighty and the Lamb are its temple. [23]The city does not need the sun or the moon to shine on it, for the glory of God gives it light, and the Lamb is its lamp. [24]The nations will walk by its light, and the kings of the earth will bring their splendor into it. [25]On no day will its gates ever be shut, for there will be no night there. [26]The glory and honor of the nations will be brought into it. [27]Nothing impure will ever enter it, nor will anyone who does what is shameful or deceitful, but only those whose names are written in the Lamb's book of life.

---

[32]Beale points out that the twelve stones are the same gems as those on the high priest's breastplate and that these stones symbolized the twelve tribes of Israel (Exod 28:17-21). Several of the gems are listed with names differing from Exodus but those names are semantic equivalents. One should note that the stones which on the breastplate represent the Israelite tribes are identified with the foundations of the walls, representing the Apostles. (G. K. Beale, *The Book of Revelation* [Grand Rapids: Eerdmans, 1999], 1080-1082) This indicates that the Church is numbered with Israel, the faithful Covenant community of the Old Testament. This also appears to be another example of Israelite typology in the Book of Revelation.

21:22-27 **The Lamb, the Light of the City** **Exposition**

The temple, an instrument of the former redemptive economy, will have no place in the new world of Earth made new. The worship of God will be instinctive and normal for its inhabitants, the bride of Christ. That the "city" "does not need the sun or the moon to shine on it" should be understood not as a statement about the astronomical world,[33] but as an allusion to the quality of life as illuminated by the holiness and glory of God (cp. Isa 60:3-5a). That the gates will never be shut indicates that there will never be the need to protect God's people from an enemy. Nothing shameful or deceitful will have a place in the new world. Nations and kings will nevertheless have their place as God's redeemed people (v. 24), but all will be righteous in the Age to Come.

21:22-27 **The Lamb, the Light of the City** **Notes**

22. Here, **the temple** (Gk. ναός, *naós*, "sanctuary"), as context indicates, refers to the temple in the concrete sense of an institution and a building. **23.** The fact that **the Lamb is its lamp** indicates that "light" is not used in the literal sense but as a metaphor for truth and for that which illumines the inner being (cf. BAGD, 872.3). We know from His post-resurrection ministry that Jesus Christ as a Lamp is not a source of light in the literal sense. **24.** The word, **Nations** (Gk. ἐθνοι, *éthnoi*), appears here to have at least a quasi-political sense, as the nations are mentioned in close connection with kings. Politics on the new earth will be cleansed of the evils which we experience as normative in this life. Though some needs for civil structures may still exist, rulers will surely exercise authority with loving beneficence. Moreover, rulers will receive the honor that is their due. **25.** The statement that there will be **no night there** continues the metaphorical use of light and darkness. One need not deduce from this that the earth will no longer rotate or orbit around the sun.

---

[33]George E. Ladd, *Commentary on the Revelation of John* (Grand Rapids: Eerdmans, 1972), 284.

Chapter Thirteen   *The Lamb, the light of the city, 21:22-27*

The River of Life

22:1. **Then the angel showed me the river of the water of life, as clear as crystal, flowing from the throne of God and of the Lamb ²down the middle of the great street of the city. On each side of the river stood the tree of life, bearing twelve crops of fruit, yielding its fruit every month. And the leaves of the tree are for the healing of the nations. ³No longer will there be any curse. The throne of God and of the Lamb will be in the city, and his servants will serve him. ⁴They will see his face, and his name will be on their foreheads. ⁵There will be no more night. They will not need the light of a lamp or the light of the sun, for the Lord God will give them light. And they will reign for ever and ever.**

22:1-5   The River, the Life of the City   Exposition

The details in these verses are clearly intended to teach the reader that that life in the new world will be like God's original plan for His creation, as exhibited before the Fall in the Garden of Eden. The idea of a river flowing down the middle of the main street was not entirely new to the first-century reader. To this day one can see this architectural arrangement in the ruins of ancient Perga, where an open aqueduct at ground level divided the main street, providing an abundance of public water for the city. The stream in the restored Eden is forever pure as it flows from the very throne of God. This river is the corollary to the river in Ezekiel's vision of chapter 47:1-12 in which the water was flowing from under the threshold of the Temple. The water from the throne of God waters the trees on each side of the river to provide whole-some fruit for the nutritional needs as well as the pleasure of life in God's eternal household. Absent from the restored Eden is the tree of the knowledge of good and evil for "no longer will there be any curse" among God's people. They have been made eternally righteous! This inherent righteousness will be their light as they reign with God forever and ever."

22:1-5   The River, the Life of the City   Notes

1. The metaphorical description of the New Jerusalem continues in chapter 22:1-5. The **river of the water of life** which flows from the throne of God is comparable to the "living water" about which Jesus spoke in His conversation with the Samaritan woman (John 4:10). Such living water will be the normal experience of immortal life for all the inhabitants of the new earth, life derived from God and therefore described in symbol as flowing from His throne. 2. As **flowing down the middle of the great street of the city**, it is given a central place in everyday life, as was sometimes the case in an ancient city where an abundance of water was a fundamental necessity.

22:6. **The angel said to me, "These words are trustworthy and true. The Lord, the God of the spirits of the prophets, sent his angel to show his servants the things that must soon take place."**

Jesus is coming

[7]**"Behold, I am coming soon! Blessed is he who keeps the words of the prophecy in this book."**

[8]**I, John, am the one who heard and saw these things. And when I had heard and seen them, I fell down to worship at the feet of the angel who had been showing them to me.** [9]**But he said to me, "Do not do it! I am a fellow servant with you and with your brothers the prophets and of all who keep the words of this book. Worship God!"**

[10]**Then he told me, "Do not seal up the words of the prophecy of this book, because the time is near.** [11]**Let him who does wrong continue to do wrong; let him who is vile continue to be vile; let him who does right continue to do right; and let him who is holy continue to be holy."**

[12]**"Behold, I am coming soon! My reward is with me, and I will give to everyone according to what he has done.** [13]**I am the Alpha and the Omega, the First and the Last, the Beginning and the End.**

[14]**"Blessed are those who wash their robes, that they may have the right to the tree of life and may go through the gates into the city.** [15]**Outside are the dogs, those who practice magic arts, the sexually immoral, the murderers, the idolaters and everyone who loves and practices falsehood.**

[16]**"I, Jesus, have sent my angel to give you this testimony for the churches. I am the Root and the Offspring of David, and the bright Morning Star."**

¹⁷The Spirit and the bride say, "Come!" And let him who hears say, "Come!" Whoever is thirsty, let him come; and whoever wishes, let him take the free gift of the water of life.

¹⁸I warn everyone who hears the words of the prophecy of this book: If anyone adds anything to them, God will add to him the plagues described in this book. ¹⁹And if anyone takes words away from this book of prophecy, God will take away from him his share in the tree of life and in the holy city, which are described in this book.

²⁰He who testifies to these things says, "Yes, I am coming soon." Amen. Come, Lord Jesus.

²¹The grace of the Lord Jesus be with God's people. Amen.

22:6-21 The Sure Return of Jesus Exposition

With verse 6 we enter the conclusion to the Book of Revelation. The message of the angel affirms that the words of the revelation "are trustworthy and true." By affirming that the Lord is "the God of the spirits of the prophets," he implies also that the revelations of this book have authority equivalent to those of the Old Testament prophets, and that the reverse is also true. Verse 6 reiterates the declaration found in the introduction in 1:1 and 4:1 that the things predicted "must soon take place."[34]

An emphatic announcement from the Lord Jesus Himself is found in verse 7, "Behold, I am coming soon!" This is repeated verbatim in verse 12, where it is followed by the Lord's notice of the consequence of this grand event: "My reward is with me, and I will give to everyone according to what he has done." This is a most solemn statement, even for the believer who has received from

---

[34]As the two previous references cited, we understand the verbal action here as ingressive, with the result that the translation should read, "must soon *begin to* take place." The alternate translation, as adopted by those of the futurist school, is that ἐν τάχει means as in some other texts, "suddenly" or "quickly" (Acts 12:7, 22:18; John F. Walvoord, *The Revelation of Jesus Christ* (Chicago: Moody Press, 1966), 333, 35). Some of the texts Walvoord cites to support "quickly" are better translated in the temporal sense, "soon," as e.g., Luke 18:8; Acts 25:4; Rom 16:20. It seems to this writer that "suddenly" or "quickly" is contextually a less appropriate idea for 22:6 and parallels than "soon."

Jesus assurance of his eternal reward through the grace of the Gospel and the atoning work of the Savior. It is a judgment of works for each individual—"according to what he has done" (cf. Matt 25:31-46). This will be a time when the believer's salvation will be based entirely on the Savior's work and not on our own. Nevertheless, our place in the eternal Kingdom on the earth made new will be conditioned on how well we have served our Savior in this life (Matt 25:14-28). The promise of Christ's return is repeated a third time in verse 20, rendering it even more emphatic as our Lord's final message to His waiting church!

Verses 8 and 9 affirm the human author, John, as the one entrusted to communicate the testimony of Jesus Christ. This, he wrote, not as the product of inspired personal reflection and research, but as what in Spirit-inspired vision he heard and saw. As he tried to pay homage to the angel he was reminded that he shared with the angel, other prophets, and all believers the place of a servant. Worship should be directed only to God.

"Soon" here in 22:7, 12, 20 must be understood to mean "suddenly," as nearly 2000 years have passed since our Lord's statements.[35] The ambiguity of ταχύς, *tachus,* may be deliberate as it heightens the mystery of imminence as associated with the time of Christ's coming. He will come as a thief when not expected (Rev 3:3; 16:15; Matt 24:42-44).

Revelation 22:10-11 reflect the prophecy of Dan 12:9-10. What is sealed in Dan 12:9 has been opened in the prophecies of Revelation. Therefore, the forecast of Dan 12:10 is now to be realized: "Many will be purified, made spotless and refined, but the wicked will continue to be wicked. None of the wicked will understand, but those who are wise will understand." Rev 22:11 addresses Dan 12:10, the time of the Second Advent, with "Let him who does wrong continue to do wrong; let him who is vile continue to be vile; let him who does right continue to do right; and let him

---

[35]For an extended discussion of various interpretations of "soon" (ταχύς), see Beale, 1134-1136.

who is holy continue to be holy."[36] The rhetorical form of this admonition is intended to elicit an immediate response to the message of Revelation. This urgency is explained in the words of Jesus, himself, in verses 12-15, where He again affirms His second advent to judge "everyone according to what he has done." Jesus is "the Alpha and the Omega, the First and the Last, the Beginning and the End. Blessed are those who wash their robes, that they may have the right to the tree of life and may go through the gates into the city" (13-14). This urgent invitation is repeated in verse 17:

> The Spirit and the bride say, "Come!" And let him who hears say, "Come!" Whoever is thirsty, let him come; and whoever wishes, let him take the free gift of the water of life."

This evangelistic message is close to the heart of the book. The invitation is continued in our Lord's final words of verse 20, "'Yes, I am coming soon.'" He surely will come both for judgment and for reward. To which, the writer, John, responds, "Amen. Come, Lord Jesus."

We conclude our study of the final prophecy of Jesus with His gracious invitation to receive eternal life, and so realistically to prepare for His return to establish His kingdom on the earth made new.

---

[36]The Greek aorist imperative should not be understood as a command, "He who does wrong *must* continue to do wrong," but as an exhortation, "Let the one who does wrong still do wrong," etc. "The imperatives in Rev. 22:11 are probably hortatory" (A. T. Robertson, *A Grammar of the Greek New Testament in the Light of Historical Research* [Nashville: Broadman, 1934], 947); so read the standard versions.

Appendix One

Observations Regarding the Special Hermeneutics of Apocalyptic

Biblical hermeneutics is often defined as the science and art of biblical interpretation.[1] It is a science because the process of interpretation must be guided by the nature of language and language communication. It is an art not because it is abstract and therefore arbitrary but because it is a discipline that requires skillful application. The nature of language interpretation has been codified into well-known rules that are generally recognized by scholars. Legitimate biblical interpretation must recognize the unique nature of the Bible as the Word of God, as well as its place in ancient literature. It must also reflect a knowledge of the ancient languages in which it was written, as well as the many kinds of literature (genre) which it contains. Bible-believing scholars who write commentaries on the Book of Revelation are aware of these facts.

In this essay this writer intends to address several key principles of hermeneutics which govern his understanding of the Book of Revelation:

1. Perhaps the most fundamental principle is the fact that the Bible is not ordinary ancient literature but it is in fact the Word of God. This is plainly taught by the biblical writers as affirmed by Jesus Christ (John 10:35; 17:17) and reiterated by His apostles (2 Tim 3:16; 2 Pet 1:19-21). This sanctity of Scripture should lead anyone who assumes the responsibility of interpreting Scripture to exercise great commitment to avoid innovation and to take utmost care in applying the principles which must govern correct interpretation. This is emphasized by our Lord Himself in the closing words of His testimony in Rev 22:18-19.

2. The second principle of biblical hermeneutics reflects the fact that both Testaments are the Word of God. They therefore are a unity of truth. What is taught in the Old Testament is not in any way contradicted by what is taught in the New. Both Testaments exist as a harmony.

---

[1]This definition probably should be attributed to Bernard Ramm, *Protestant Biblical Interpretation*, (Grand Rapids: Baker Book House,1970), 1.

Abraham as well as Paul was saved by faith in the atoning work of Jesus Christ (Romans 4; cf. Hebrews 11). If "the Scriptures cannot be broken" (John 10:35), progressive revelation cannot be taken to imply that the New Testament corrects the Old. What was revealed in Old Testament type is fulfilled in New Testament antitype.

3. The third principle of hermeneutics which also grows out of the first is that called the literal principle. This is not the idea that the Bible includes no figures of speech, but rather that the language of the Bible must be taken in its ordinary or plain sense. The reader is not to superimpose any meaning other than that which is given by the natural sense of the text. When interpreting narrative text the natural sense of the language should be easy to recognize, but when seeking the natural sense of an apocalyptic book like the Book of Revelation, this discipline is much more complicated and demanding.

Sometimes theological assumptions may lead the interpreter to wrong conclusions. An example of this is the so-called Replacement Theology, the idea that explicit promises made to Israel in the Old Testament regarding Israel's restoration to their covenant land (see, e.g., Ezekiel 36) are replaced in the New Testament so that they are fulfilled by the church in the Gentile world as the new Israel. To make this replacement one must make the words of the prophets mean something contrary to what they plainly say, and contrary to the manner in which they must have been understood by the original readers in their historical context. If this were true, those promises can no longer be taken literally.

In Revelation, disregard for the literal principle leads many to replace the plain language of chapter 20 for an allegorizing amillennial interpretation advocated by Augustine in the fourth century. It is easier to understand how, when allegorizing was commonplace, Augustine and his followers in the Medieval Church, or even the early Reformers fell into this error, but more difficult to grasp how contemporary scholars in the 20th and 21st centuries have perpetuated this diversion from the literal principle of hermeneutics.

Neglect of the literal principle is also involved with the interpretations of the futurist school. The idea of the church-age parenthesis appears to this writer to be derived from an allegorizing inference suggested by dispensational theology that because the Seventy Weeks prophecy of

Appendix One   *The special hermeneutics of apocalyptic*   473

Daniel 9 is addressed to Israel it has no application to the church age.[2]

---

[2]Many doctrinal aberrations arise on account of inferences drawn from perceived implications of a text. The interpreter needs to be careful to distinguish between inferences which are required by the text and those inferences which may seem to some to be reasonable but are in fact unnecessary. An unnecessary inference should never be used as proof for a biblical doctrine. It seems to this writer that one of the necessary inferences to be drawn from a time prophecy is the duration of the time predicted. This is in fact generally recognized when interpreting such other time prophecies as the 40 days predicted for Israel's sojourn in the wilderness (Num 14:34), Ezekiel's prophecy of the times of the punishment of Judah and Israel (Ezek 4:4-6), Jeremiah's prophecy of 70 years' desolation of Jerusalem (Jer 25:11-12; Dan 9:2), and the 1260 day prophecy of Dan 12:6-7, 11). Why should the rule not apply also to Dan 9:24?

However, the Apostle Paul teaches that Gentile believers are grafted into the olive tree that represents the covenant nation (Rom 11:17-24). A biblical theology addresses the covenant family as one, including both Jewish and Gentile believers (Eph 2:11-22). A literal interpretation of Dan 9:24-27 introduces no church-age parenthesis; it must be introduced as a theological intrusion into the text and as a violation of the very concept of a numerical time prophecy. Moreover, Dan 9:24, which gives a summary of the content of the 70 weeks makes no mention of Antichrist, though Antichrist factors largely into the futurist interpretation of the seventieth week.

In a similar manner, the literal principle is violated when the futurist school inserts a church age-parenthesis into the Book of Revelation. This it does when it infers from Rev 1:10 that the Apostle John was transferred in vision to the beginning of the 70th week after the alleged church-age parenthesis to witness the eschatological Day of the Lord.[3] This unindicated inference distorts almost the entire prophetic message of our Lord with innovative and unnatural interpretion. Moreover, it responds affirmatively to the Jesuit Ribera's attempt to displace the Reformers' Papal Antichrist doctrine.

4. Another hermeneutical principle dictates that an ancient document such as those that constitute our Bible should be understood as the original recipients in their cultural and historical situation should have understood it. One of the charges commonly made against the historicist school of interpretation is that a prophecy which was to have its fulfillment thoughout the course of history would have had little or no meaning for the first-century churches to whom it was originally written. For that reason we have endeavored in our commentary on the prophecies of

---

[3] For the futurist defense of this claim, see John F. Walvoord, *The Revelation of Jesus Christ* (Chicago: Moody Press, 1966), 42. Th1s strange innovation also conflicts with the fact that Christ's letters to the seven churches follow in chapters 2 and 3. For this writer's refutation of Walvoord's theory, see Oral Collins, "Good Question," *Henceforth* 7 (Spring, 1979).103-107.

Revelation to address as primary what it would have meant to those churches in or about A.D. 96, the date the Early Church assigned to the book. As one reflects on this criticism of historicism, one might well conclude that on that premise very nearly all the prophecies of Scripture would have been meaningless to the original recipients. Admittedly, the problem of meaning was exacerbated by apocalyptic symbolism, but most of the symbolism had precedent in their Old Testament Scriptures or in other writings known to Jewish and early Christian believers.

Moreover, it should be recognized that meaning adheres to the text itself and not to the question as to when and how a prediction is fulfilled. For this reason, we have separated our exposition of text from consideration of the fulfillment question.

Further, the meaning for the recipients of an unfulfilled prophecy has two practical aspects: 1. What is predicted? and 2. Given the prediction, how should one respond practically in everyday life? The fact that the second aspect is transtemporal does not eradicate the temporal implications of the first.

5. Finally, there are hermeneutical principles inherent in the genre, that is, the distinctive *kind* of literature we are dealing with in the Book of Revelation. This is appropriately defined by scholars as "dream-vision apocalyptic." The term derives from the fact that such visions are often received by people who are sleeping. This is illustrated primarily by the visions of Nebuchadnezzar and Daniel in the Book of Daniel (Daniel chs. 2, 4, 7, 9, 10-12). In the Book of Revelation, the writer testifies to having been "in the Spirit" when he received the revelation which constitutes the bulk of the book. Our understanding of "dream-vision" in Revelation is largely based on the visions of Daniel. Because several of these visions come to us with with interpretation we do not have the option of concluding that their predictions are primarily transtemporal. They clearly indicate several characteristics of biblical dream-vision apocalyptic: 1. The predictions clearly forecast future temporal events. 2. They commonly forecast such events in symbolic language. 3. They characteristically present these forecast events in a single chronological sequence.

In none of the visions of Daniel is there found cyclic or parallel chronologies such as those scholars find who interpret the Book of Revelation as if the seal, trumpet, and bowl prophecies predict parallel or synchronous chronological events. To base such interpretation on the fact that several of Daniel's visions as compared with each other display parallel chronologies does not indicate a valid precedent for finding parallel chronologies within a single vision such as that of Revelation.

It is this author's conviction that the reader is not justified in creating what amounts to a new genre for understanding the Book of Revelation, especially in light of the fact that the message of the book is dependent on the dream-visions of the Book of Daniel. The above-listed principles should therefore govern our approach to the Revelation. This is especially important on account of the fact that the book presents itself as the witness of our Lord and Savior, Jesus Christ (Rev 1:2, 22:16, 20).

Appendix Two

Observations on the History of Apocalyptic Interpretation

The purpose of this essay is to call the attention of the reader to the principal elements in the historical processes that gave rise to the several divergent approaches to the Book of Revelation. These characterize the interpretations of leading scholars in the Christian church as we begin the twenty-first century. I believe these disparate understandings of our Lord's last message to His church create a very serious problem for several reasons:

1. The Message of the Book of Revelation, as our commentary has pointed out, is not only Apostolic as received and written by the Apostle John, but it purports to be the final testimony of Jesus, the Messiah and the Lord of His Church.

2. The Book of Revelation is introduced with the unique promise of a special blessing to those who read or who hear its message and who take it to heart (1:3). Moreover, this message concludes with a warning of judgment reserved for anyone who adds to or who takes away from its prophecies (22:18-19).

3. The practical result of the several disparate understandings of the Book of Revelation has exacerbated the inherent difficulty of interpretation with the result that much of the message of the book is lost to many who have either given up on the effort to understand it or who have been led to adopt a false interpretation. Of the four primary approaches to interpretation of the prophecies of the book, three must be false, as they are mutually exclusive of one another.

4. Much popular preaching and teaching on the Book of Revelation is done with little or no introduction to the fact that there are alternate ways to interpret the text and to understand our Lord's message. This may even result in the construction of eschatologies that appear to be foreign to what is taught in the rest of Scripture. Some denominations have even

found explicit reference to the members of their sect in the book, as for example, in "the 144,000" (Rev 7:4-8 and 14:1, 3).

The above problems are further enhanced by the tendency of the several schools of interpretation to try to prove that their approach was the one believed and taught by the Apostolic and Early Church, that is, the church of the second and third centuries.

As this writer is convinced of the historicist interpretation, he will in this essay attempt to show that the Apostolic church was essentially historicist and further indicate briefly how the several alternate schools originated.

The Early Church

The primary principles which characterize the historicist school are 1. The prophecies of Revelation not only teach principles for practical application but they predict actual events which were to occur in the context of the future course of history. This is characteristic of biblical predictive prophecy in general, including the apocalyptic prophecies of the Book of Daniel. This characteristic is nevertheless largely rejected for Revelation by those who affirm that the predictions in the book are mostly transtemporal in nature. 2. Historicists also hold that the events forecast in Rev 4:1-22:15 begin to occur soon after the publication of the Book of Revelation near the end of the first Christian century. This principle was commonly assumed in the Early Church with one possible exception, that is, Hippolytus, bishop of Portus (ca. A.D. 170-236). Hippolytus, in his work, "Treatise on Christ and Antichrist," states with reference to the 70th week of Daniel 9 that "by one week . . . he [Daniel] meant the last week which is to be at the end of the whole world."[4] Hippolytus says nothing, however with respect to a church-age parenthesis between the 69th and 70th weeks of Daniel 9, as taught by the futurist school. As he commonly allegorized texts after the custom popular in his day, he may not have assumed a literal chronology for the 70 weeks prophecy.[5] The futurist school also appeals to the fact that the Apostolic church did not adopt the year-day principle when interpreting the numbers in Revelation. Historicists agree that this practice did not become common until after the passage of the first millennium of the church age. Part of the providen-

---

[4] Hippolytus. "Treatise on Christ and Antichrist," *The Ante-Nicene Fathers: Translation of the Writings of the Fathers Down to A.D. 325*, ed. by Alexander Roberts and James Donaldson (Eginburgh: T. &. T. Clark, n.d.; repr. Grand Rapids: Eerdmans, 1986), 5.204-219.

[5] On Hippolytus' practice of allegorizing as comparable to that of Origen, see Philip Schaff, *History of the Christian Church* (Grand Rapids: Eerdmans, 1950), 2.767.

tially mysterious aspect of the prophecies of Revelation is the ambiguity of the numbers. Otherwise, the Early Church would have not retained the principle of imminency in their expectation of the return of Christ. After the first millennium, the year-day principle began to be recognized. Futurists also hold in common with the Early Church the understanding that the war with Antichrist was still future, though Scripture clearly teaches and it was commonly recognized that the Antichrist would rise out of the fourth beast of Daniel 7, the Roman Empire.

With these observations, we can put to rest the claim of the futurist school that the church of the first three centuries held to a futurist eschatology. The facts teach us that the Early Church was historicist, although some tenets later claimed by futurists were characteristic also of early historicism. The facts also indicate that the most fundamental tenet of futurism, the church-age parenthesis theory, cannot be found in the interpretation of the Early Church.

The Byzantine and Medieval Church

For our purposes we date the Byzantine Church from the time that Constantine moved the capital of the Roman Empire to Byzantium, A.D. 330. Constantine's establishment of the state church and the doctrines that accompanied it to enhance the status and political power of the church caused profound changes in its eschatology and the interpretation of Revelation. This can be illustrated by several changes he introduced into the church:

1. He authorized and financed the construction of many cathedrals in the Roman world. A cathedral derives its name and function from the fact that it embraces the chair of the local bishop. These immense and beautifully designed buildings greatly enhanced the office and the prestige of the bishopric.

2. He not only gave to the office of bishop enhanced ecclesiastical powers but he assigned to them civil authority within their districts. He enlarged the bishops' compensation, so that they became wealthy and their office became coveted for its temporal advantage.

3. He elevated the bishop of Rome to archbishop and made him the representative of Christ in the church. He fostered the idea that Christ's millennial reign was fulfilled in the rule of the bishop of Rome over the church. This had the effect of replacing the predominently premillennial

theology of the Early Church with postmillennial and amillennial theories which relied upon allegorical interpretations of Revelation 20. This resulted at length in a declaration of Pope Damasus at the Council at Rome (A.D. 373) banning premillennialism. Premillennial interpretation was soon replaced by allegorical and spiritualizing interpretations, not only of Revelation 20 but of the rest of the Apocalypse as well. This practice continued to dominate the interpretation of the Book of Revelation in the Catholic churches of the East and West through the Middle Ages until the Reformation. There is reason to believe, nevertheless, that historicist interpretation persisted in the "wilderness churches" that resisted submission to Roman Catholicism.

4. The establishment of the state church and the elevation of the bishop of Rome under Constantine also had the effect of countering the Roman Antichrist doctrine. Allegorical interpretation reduced the interpretation of Antichrist to a transtemporal principle instead of a particular person or power which was to arise to wage war against God's covenant people. (See Appendix 4.)

Reformation and Counter-Reformation

The Reformation brought with it the translation of the Bible and its restoration to the laity. It also restored literal interpretation and largely displaced for the Reformation churches the process of allegorizing which had originated in Alexandria and permeated the Catholic churches of both East and West. Reformed commentaries began to appear which returned to historicist exposition. The doctrine of the Roman Papal Antichrist, which had been held by the pre-Reformation Protestant sects such as the Albigenses and the Waldenses was proclaimed and popularized by the Reformers as inherent in the movement.

During the heat of the 16th-century Reformation movement, a priest who came to be known as Ignatius of Loyola founded (A.D. 1540) a new order of Roman Catholics which designed to be totally supportive and submitted to the authority of Jesus, as represented by the reigning Pope. The society came to be called The Society of Jesus or The Jesuits.[6]

During the years following the posting of Luther's theses, Reformed historicist commentaries on Revelation began to appear. Chief among these were the commentaries of Bale (1556-57?), Bullinger (1557), Foxe (1586), and Brightman (ca. 1600), all of which identified the Antichrist with the Roman Papacy.[7] With such publications which

---

[6]Malachi Martin, *The Jesuits: the Society of Jesus and the Betrayal of the Roman Catholic Church* (New York: Simon & Schuster, 1987), 145, 162-163.
[7]Elliott 4.442-474.

together with Reformed preaching undermining the authority of the Papacy, the newly instituted Society of Jesus responded with two major commentaries on Revelation.

The first was written by the Spanish Jesuit priest Francisco Ribera in 1590.[8] He adopted an essentially historicist approach, bridging the church age with the seal prophecies, then interpreting Antichrist of some future Roman Pope. The second Jesuit commentary was written by another Spanish priest, Alcasar. However, Alcasar took an opposite approach, identifying Antichrist with pagan Rome, anticipating the modern preterist school which later was advanced by Hugo Grotius and the German rationalists.[9] Both Jesuits allegorized the millennium as Ribera adopted Augustinian amillennialism and Alcasar took a postmillennial position with the milliennium having begun with the elevation of the Papal state church under Constantine. Ironically, elements of the futurist interpretation of Ribera and of the preterist interpretation of Alcasar have come to dominate Protestant interpretation in the twentieth and twenty-first centuries.

Interpretation in the Modern Period

Historicist interpretation prevailed among Protestant commentators who adhered to the authority of the biblical text through the 18th and early nineteenth centuries. However, about 1830 a prophetic movement in England developed which advocated a pretribulation secret rapture prior to the disclosure of a future individual Antichrist and tribulation.

The origins of these developments are somewhat obscure but several leading personalities are well known including Edward Irving, a Presbyterian pastor in London, John Nelson Darby, an Anglican who became one of the principals in the Plymouth Brethren movement, S. R. Maitland, Anglican curate of Christ's Church, Gloucester, and librarian at the Library of the Archbishop of Canterbury, a public research library of renoun. Strangely another influencial person in the movement was a young Scottish maiden named Margaret Macdonald, whose charismatic revelations fueled the concept of the pretribulation rapture theory. involved two comings of Christ, one to rapture His church before the tribulation and the other coming with His church after the tribulation. The Macdonald family

---

[8] *In Sacrum Beati Ioannis Apostoli, & Evangelistiae Apocalypsin Commentari*j (Lugduni: Ex Officina Iuntarum, 1593).

[9]Elliott, 1.481-485.

lived in Scotland but had connections with Irving, who was of Scottish origin.[10]

The idea of a two-staged coming of Christ appears to have been found also in this pretribulation movement by the influence of another Spanish Jesuit priest whose name was Lacunza, though he published under the pseudonym, "Rabbi Juan Josafat Ben Ezra." A theory inferred from Lacunza's work posits the idea that the 70th week of Daniel 9 falls between the Parousia (Christ's coming for His saints) and the Epiphany (Christ's coming with his saints). On this view, all the predicted events of the seven-sealed scroll are to occur during the 70th week.[11]

In 1833, the Tractarian Movement (also known as the Oxford Movement) arose in the Anglican churches, which further advanced the pretribulation movement, as it advocated a future individual Antichrist instead of the popular posttribulationist Papal Antichrist doctrine, formerly popular among Protestants. This movement was initiated by Anglicans in an effort to promote greater unity between the Anglican and the Roman Catholic Churches. It was promoted with an extensive series of tracts advocating more Romanist practices and doctrines.

One of the byproducts of the Tractarian Movement was the promotion of the Roman Catholic futurist approach in the interpretation of Revelation. Two of the preachers were J. N. Darby and C. I. Scofield. Scofield later with Oxford University Press published his Scofield Reference Bible which had the effect of popularizing the futurist, pretribulationist interpretation among many evangelical Christians. This interpretation was held by D. L. Moody and other founders of Moody Bible Institute, which became a very effective propagator of the futurist school in the twentieth century. Moody graduates founded numerous Bible Institutes which further advanced the popularity of futurism in the U.S. Dallas Theological Seminary with professor and president John F. Walvoord has been one of the principal advocates at the graduate level. On the other hand, many who adopted Ribera's futurist eschatology nevertheless did so while maintaining posttribulationism.[12]

---

[10]Readers who are interested in more detail can consult Dave MacPherson, *The Incredible Cover-up* (Plainfield, N. J.: Logos International, 1975), especially pp. 27-35 (available from http://www.armageddonbooks.com/historicist.html); Duncan McDougall, *The Rapture of the Saints* (Blackwood, N.J.: O.F.P.M. Publishers, 1970), en passim; George Eldon Ladd, *The Blessed Hope* (Grand Rapids: Eerdmans, 1956), 35-41. The full text of McDougall's work is available on line at: http://www.aapi.co.uk/mansbacher/rap-tureOfTheSaints.htm (Feb. 17, 2007).

[11]McDougall, 29-32. Lacunza's book can be purchased from Still Water Revival Books (http://www.swrb.com/).

[12]Ladd, *Blessed Hope*, 41-60.

Appendix Two — On the history of interpretation

One of the foundational innovations of the Protestant futurist school has been the introduction of a "church age parenthesis" into the time prophecy of the Seventy Weeks of Daniel 9. This results in postponing the seventieth week until the very end time. This is understood in terms of a future antichrist and a future tribulation.

Given the Jesuit origin of the principal ideas which characterize the futurist interpretation of the Book of Revelation, one should suspect that the principal objective of the Jesuits was to deflect the Reformation doctrine of the Papal Antichrist.

As indicated above, the preterist school introduced by the Spanish Jesuit, Alcasar, was taken up by the German scholar, Hugo Grotius, and the German rationalists. These scholars practiced a humanizing understanding of biblical prophecy which rejected the supernatural inspiration and integrity of the Bible. They tended to interpret prophecy as history written after the events "predicted." For example, they alleged that the author of Daniel used "Daniel" as a pseudonym and actually lived in the days of the Maccabees after the events predicted in Daniel 11 had actually occurred. The critics alleged that this author was actually ignorant of the true course of history and therefore invented a world empire, the Median empire, in the sequence of the four empires required by Daniel's image of chapter 2 and the four beast kingdoms of chapter 7. On this reconstruction the four world empires that were to precede the kingdom of God were 1. the Babylonian, 2. the Median, 3. the Persian, and 4. the Grecian.

The preterist approach to Revelation follows the Jesuit Alcasar in interpreting the prophecy in terms of the pagan Roman Empire. They usually identify the Antichrist with Nero and the tribulations implicit in the prophecies with Nero's persecution of Christians, all of which they view as having been written not as prophecy but after the events "predicted."

Elements of Preterism have become popular alternatives to historicism and futurism in the 20th and 21st centuries, even among some evangelicals who adhere to the inspiration and authority of the Bible. Such scholars often adopt a pre-A.D. 70 date for the writing of Revelation, contrary to the memory of the Apostolic church.

Other twenty and twenty-first century scholars have apparently invented a new genre of apocalyptic literature by treating the predictions of the Book of Revelation as largely transtemporal, that is by assuming that they do not predict specific events but rather only introduce principles that apply throughout history. Surely, this is contrary to the apocalyptic visions of the Book of Daniel, several of which are given with event-oriented interpretation.

The above cursory review highlighting the divergent directions in which interpretation theories have moved, especially in the 19th-21st centuries indicate the importance of our effort to revive the historicist tradition that characterized pre-Reformation evangelicals and Reformed interpretation in the modern period though much of the 19th century.

Appendix Three

Continuous or Parallel? a Question of Chronology in the Book of Revelation[1]

A few preliminary observations may be appropriate. Twentieth and twenty-first century commentators, if they do not altogether ignore the works of the historical school, almost always dismiss them on the ground of their disagreement with regard to predicted events. Nevertheless, in the effort to compare and classify, one can observe that within all schools there are numerous differences of interpretation which lead to variant conclusions about the Book. We do not have space here to pursue all the implications of this but one could make a case for a larger consensus on the principal points among the historicist interpreters, especially those of the seventeenth through the nineteenth centuries. Moreover, agreement among interpreters is not a hermeneutical principle for determining meaning. But more on that below.

In the historical interpretation of the Apocalypse, the question as to whether the seals, trumpets, and bowls should be viewed as parallel or continuous, a matter of literary structure, both historically and logically precedes the introduction of the several schools of interpretation and the issues of prediction and fulfillment that divide them. With the development of the schools in the post-reformation years, there no longer were only two divergent approaches to understanding Revelation, there emerged at least eight. This illustrates the critical nature of the issue. Not only do the four major schools introduce substantively different approaches to the book but within each school are some who treat the structure as parallel and some who treat it as continuous. This distinction, by itself, is a radical divergence which will determine the reader's conclusions about much of the content. Having pointed up the seriousness of the issue, we proceed to address it.

---

[1]This essay is an edited version of an article previously published as a chapter in the book, *Our Destiny We Know: essays in Honor of Edwin K. Gedney*, published by Venture Books, Charlotte, N. Car. in 1996 (used by permission).

The Case for Parallel Structure

Those who prefer the parallel approach to the structure of Revelation offer one or all of the following arguments for a parallel chronology for the seals, trumpets, and bowls:

1. The several visions of Daniel forecast events which run parallel to each other. This is particularly apparent of the great image vision (ch. 2) and the vision of the four beasts (ch. 7), to a lesser degree also of the vision of the ram and the goat (ch. 8), the seventy sevens (ch. 9), and the Little Apocalypse (chs. 10-12).[2]

2. From an internal standpoint, Andrew Steinmann argues typically from parallel structures within the book that those sections should be viewed as chronologically parallel. The seals, the trumpets, and the bowls are prime candidates for parallel enumeration and partially parallel internal structure and style.[3] Other elements of the book, such as the seven churches (chs. 2-3), viewed as prophecies of seven periods extending through church history, the little book section (chs. 12-14), or the millennium (ch. 20), understood amillennially, may be brought forward with the suggestion that because these may be seen as chronologically parallel, the case is strengthened for the seals, trumpets, and bowls.

3. The language of the sixth seal (Rev 6:12-17) is commonly associated with the Day of the Lord prophecies in the Old Testament. It is so strongly worded as to point to the end time Day of the Lord.[4] This is followed after the sealing scene (7:1-8) with a heavenly celebration which appears to indicate the beginning of the age to Come (7:9-17).

4. Heavenly celebration scenes occur at the end of each of the three series. The aforementioned occurs after the sixth seal (7:9-17). Another occurs after the sounding of the seventh trumpet (11:15-19) with the announcement that "the kingdom of the world has become the kingdom of our Lord and of his Christ, and he will reign forever and ever" (11:15b). After the seventh bowl, again there is a magnificent scene of heavenly celebration (19:1-8) just prior to the final battle of 19:11-21.

5. The detailed chronology that results from the continuous model places too heavy a burden on the reader to know the historical facts of his-

---

[2]G. K. Beale, "The Influenc of Daniel Upon the Structure and Theology of John's Apocalypse," *JETS* 27 (1984), 420-421.

[3]Steinmann, Andrew E. "The Tripartate Structure of the Sixth Seal, the Sixth Trumpet, and the Sixth Bowl of John's Apocalypse" (Rev 6:12,-7:17; 9:13-11:14; 16:12-16," *JETS* 35 (1992), 76.

[4]William Cuninghame, *A Dissertation on the Seals and Trumpets of the Apocalypse* (4th ed.; London: Th. Cadell, Hatchard and Son, and James Nisbet, 1843), 18, 21.

tory in order to interpret the book. One may also assume that most of the prophecies would have been unintelligible and therefore largely irrelevant to the first-century reader.

These are the major arguments which support the parallel interpretation of the seals, trumpets, and bowls.

The Case for Continuous Structure

Those who are convinced of the continuous relationship between the seals, trumpets, and bowls put forward the following observations:

1. The dream-visions in the Book of Daniel were understood to predict a consecutive series of specific conditions or events, represented by a series of symbols. Because the Apocalypse picks up the dominant themes and the style from these visions of Daniel, one should assume it was intended to be read as the same kind of literature. There is clear internal evidence that the Book of Revelation is an expansion on the Book of Daniel, especially on the vision of the four beasts of Daniel 7. Revelation should, therefore, be understood according to the same method of interpretation as those visions. All recognize they are in structure continuous.

2. Hundreds of other apocalyptic visions commonly read by Jews and Christians in the first century constitute a literary tradition of inter-biblical literature which developed after analogy with the dream-visions of Daniel. These visions forecast continuously consecutive events or conditions. So the readers would have been conditioned by their familiarity with the genre to read the structure of Revelation continuously. A good example of such pseudepigraphic literature is the Eagle Vision of 4 Ezra 11.[5] There is no precedent of comparable parallel structure within a "dream-vision" in the several hundred extant apocalyptic works believed to have existed at the end of the first century A.D.

3. The literary character of the three sequences lends itself naturally to a consecutive understanding. Seals were usually used to open, thus to begin the reading of a scroll. A reasonable inference is that the trumpet and bowl sequences forecast events to occur after the opening of the seals. The trumpet, as an instrument of announcement, is appropriate for the judgments which precede the introduction of Antichrist in chapters 12-13. The bowls, indicating the wrath of God poured out on Antichrist, logically follow after chapters 12-13.

---

[5] The primary source by which the reader may access the extra-biblical apocalyptic literature is the work edited by James H. Charlesworth, *Apocalyptic Literature and Testaments, The Old Testament Pseudepigrapha*. Volume 1 (Garden City, N.Y.: Doubleday, 1983). This contains the text of most of the important works, together with introductions and explanatory notes by leading scholars in the field.

4. Internal indicators logically imply that a chronological sequence is intended. An example of this is found with the opening of the fifth seal in the advice given to the martyrs, to wait until the number of their fellow servants to be killed was completed (6:11). No subsequent martyrdom is predicted in this series. Another example is the marking of the covenant people in the first series under the sixth seal (7:1-8), a reference to which is found subsequently in the second series under the fifth trumpet (9:4).

Evaluation of the Parallel Approach

Before we consider several other issues of consequence, we begin with an examination of the case as presented above. Item one defends a parallel approach on the ground that Daniel's visions complement one another and are chronologically parallel. This is an attractive analogy. However, to approach the issue hermeneutically, one should proceed from the standpoint of the dream-vision as genre and compare the one vision of Revelation with any *one* of the visions of Daniel. Typically, scholars use the analogy with Daniel to show how apocalyptic uses symbols but the chronological aspect of such symbols in the genre is ignored.[6] When the chronology of any one of the visions is compared with the vision of Revelation, the argument for parallelism dissolves.

The second item in the case for parallel structure appeals to internal evidence in Revelation. Many popular expositions find evidence for chronological termini in the scenes of heavenly celebration or of judgment. While these may be so understood, the evidence is at best ambiguous, as the differences among those who defend the parallel view indicate. The problem of knowing where to divide the book is far reaching. Space does not permit us to illustrate this fully here but within each school there is considerable divergence of opinion, even among reputable scholars who adopt the parallel interpretation.

William Hendriksen, who is very dogmatic about his own division, nevertheless states that "there is no unanimity with respect to the exact boundaries of each section."[7] Robert H. Mounce cautions the reader and calls attention to "this rather complete lack of consensus about the struc-

---

[6] Graeme Goldsworthy, *The Lamb and the Lion: the Gospel in Revelation* (Nashville: Th. Nelson, 1985), 14-17.

[7] In support of this, Hendricksen lists eight men, including such eminent scholars as Louis Berkhof, William Milligan, and B.B. Warfield. He then notes that all "favor seven-fold division, but the views and systems of division differ." In spite of this Hendriksen states that "the division . . . is very clearly provided by the book, itself . . . ." (William Hendricksen, *More Than Conquerors: an Interpretation of the Book of Revelation* (Grand Rapids: Baker, 1952), 28, 259, n. 2).

ture of Revelation."[8] R. C. H. Lenski is skeptical of any parallel analysis and argues for a "vista" approach without fixed lines.[9] After listing indicators of the end of the world he states,

> Yet we are unable to use any of these features for making divisions in a convincing way, although it has been attempted.... We frankly give up the attempt to divide this book in an ordinary way. At most one could detach 1:9-3:22, and again chapters 21 and 22, but what about all that lies between?

Such hesitancy is rare among commentators but the critical nature of the problem is well illustrated by the differences of division among those who adhere to a parallel chronology. Of those this author classified, 67% of those who decided for parallel structure have been historicist interpreters, whereas 85% of preterists and 78% of futurists opted for the continuous model.[10] This suggests that the decisive reason for a parallel view may not be internal evidence of the text but the desire for a shorter and less detailed chronology of fulfillment.

This raises a very interesting hermeneutical question. Is the fulfillment of a prophecy the meaning of the text? To state it another way, Does the meaning reside in the actual event, in the correlation of an event with the text, or in the text alone? For those who still adhere to grammatico-historical interpretation, the answer should be obvious--meaning resides in the text and the text does not identify the fulfillment. The text of apocalyptic vision prophecy presents only largely symbolic language. The meaning must be correctly exegeted in generic, conceptual terms. Fulfillment, on the other hand, must be decided by analogy, a correspondence between the text and the event, the event as part of a series of predicted events. This being true, to wrongly identify fulfillment, as has often occurred (with too little discernment and too much dogmatism), is not necessarily to adopt a different meaning or to change the interpretation of the text. Those who adopt a parallel model must do so, not because of disaffection for alleged fulfillments by continuous interpreters but on the ground of internal textual evidence.

The question then remains, Does internal evidence suffice to determine parallel structure? Is there any hermeneutical principle established in the apocalyptic genre for such repeated chronological cycles? Or

---

[8]Robert H. Mounce, *The Book of Revelation* (Grand Rapids: Eerdmans, 1977), 46.

[9]R. C. H. Lenski, The Interpretation of John's Revelation (Columbus, Ohio: Wartburg, 1943), 24-25.

[10]The case is even weaker for the parallel view prior to the 20th century. Of 16 preterist, 12 futurist, and 4 philosophy of history works examined, 1 futurist, 1 preterist, and 2 philosophy of history parallel commentaries surfaced.

can the occasional scenes of celebration and/or end-time event be accounted for as proleptic within a continuous structure? Is there any intrinsic textual problem with the majority opinion that the three series seals, trumpets, and bowls flow naturally in a linear series. My survey indicates that a strong majority think not.[11]

For many, the most persuasive argument for a parallel construction is item three, above, the prophecy of the sixth seal (6:12-17), the "great earthquake." Parallel interpreters have always taken the language of this seal to indicate either the end of history or the introduction of its final events. Appeal is usually made to the prophets who use this language to describe "day of the Lord" judgments against various nations. Some take the language at least semi-literally. Even many futurists who hold to an essentially linear interpretation identify the sixth seal with literal signs in the end time and find the trumpets and the bowls following in quick succession thereafter.[12] Others correctly recognize metaphorical language here rather than literal earthquake or celestial phenomena. For accurate interpretation two points require consideration. 1. What is the contextual meaning of such language where it occurs elsewhere in Scripture? 2. What is given in Rev 6:12-17 to aid our interpretation? A few texts will suffice to address these questions.

Rev 6:13-14 reads, "The stars of the sky fell to the earth. . . . The sky receded like a scroll, rolling up." This unusual figure is evidently an allusive reference to Isa 34:4, "All the stars of the heavens will be dissolved and the sky rolled up like a scroll; all the starry hosts will fall."However, the Isaiah text is not a prediction of the end-time day of the Lord but a prophecy of the ancient destruction of Edom, as it says, "For the LORD has a day of vengeance. . . . Edom's streams will be turned into pitch. . . . From generation to generation it [Edom] will lie desolate. . . . The desert owl and screech owl will possess it" (34:8-11). The ancients associated the power of rulers with astronomical signs, so that heavenly bodies were common symbols for the authority of kings and their subordinates. Many illustrations of this have been found, some carved on stone steles with the king's laws. The destruction of a nation or its government is represented by the fall or darkening of celestial bodies.

---

[11]The survey to which I refer was published in the previous chapter of the book from which this essay was adapted: Oral Collins, "Continuous or Parallel? The Question of Chronology in the Book of Revelation: a History of Interpretation." Pages 139-163 in *Our Destiny We Know: Essays in Honor of Edwin K. Gedney*. Edited by Freeman Barton. (Charlotte, N. Car.: Venture Books 1996). For survey results, see below, p. 505.

[12]Ribera and many futurists after him have taken the latter view and thus maintained a continuous structure for the Apocalypse by placing the trumpets and the bowls during an end-time "seventieth week" (Dan 9:27a). Some have held that the seals span the church age and others place all the seals at the end time.

Rev 6:16b, 17 says, "Hide us from him who sits on the throne and from the wrath of the Lamb! For the great day of their wrath has come, and who can stand?" This may be an allusive reference to Zeph 1:14, which reads, "The great day of the lord is near . . . ." Zephaniah during the days of Josiah, in context explicitly referred this demonstration of divine wrath to the destruction of Judah by Babylon, a prophecy fulfilled in the sixth century B.C. The careful exegete will allow context to rule meaning and recognize hyperbolic language when it is used.[13] From the use of such passages in the prophetic books of the Old Testament, one who interprets Revelation is obliged to observe both their temporal application and their use of hyperbole. Though there is no question about the emphatic nature of this collage of textual allusions, they do not prove an end-time reference for Rev 6:12-17.

This conclusion has been recognized in several commentaries of repute. Charles points out that the words cannot be taken literally for after the stars have fallen to the earth, the sky has been rolled up, and the mountains removed from their place, men could not then hide in the caves of the mountains.[14] The language must be hyperbole. Mickelsen states with reference to the hyperbole of the passage that "there is no way to push this language into literal, scientific statements."[15] Beckwith states,"Many interpreters have failed to give their proper value and nothing more to the words, 'the great day has come' (6:17), which are not those of the Seer announcing an actual fact; they are the language of terror-stricken men who misinterpret the portents around them, as signs that the last day is actually breaking upon them." (Beckwith, 528). Walvoord, quoting Ironside, states, "It is therefore not a world-wide, literal earthquake that the sixth seal introduces, but rather the destruction of the present order political, social, and ecclesiastical . . . ."[16] Though other futurists, as well as some preterists, interpret the sixth seal in terms of literal phenomena, though recognizing exaggerated language, the Old Testament prophets generally if not always used such symbols metaphorically to indicate God's imminent, temporal judgment in the collapse of

---

[13]One should not resort from such texts at the risk of a sound hermeneutic to double meaning (or double reference). For a careful and wise treatment of these and other such "Day of the Lord" passages, see J. Barton Payne, *Encyclopedia of Biblical Prophecy* (New York: Harper & Row, 1973), 131-133, 440.

[14]R. H. Charles, *A Critical and Exegetical Commentary on the Revelation of St. John* (ICC; Edinburgh: T. & T. Clark, 1920), 1.179.

[15]A. Berkeley Mickelsen, *Daniel & Revelation* (Nashville, Tenn.: Th. Nelson, 1964), 186.

[16]John F. Walvoord, *The Revelation of Jesus Christ* (Chicago: Moody, 1966), 136.

ruling powers. Parallel-historicist interpreters should not assume that an end-time reference is required.

Another difficulty with the end-time interpretation of the sixth-seal prophecy is its place in the context. It is immediately preceded by the instruction to the martyrs that they are "to wait a little longer" until a further time of martyrdom is completed (6:11). If the sixth seal introduces the end, there is nothing more of martyrdom. Moreover, the sealing of the 144,000 comes immediately *after* the sixth seal as preparation for tribulation as indicated by the blowing of the four winds of 7:1. Then further to assure those facing tribulation a proleptic victory celebration follows in 7:9-17 for those who have experienced this "great tribulation" (7:14). We reach the end of the series before the subsequent tribulation. The celebration must be proleptic whether one chooses the parallel or the continuous model. Logically, if one is to infer a parallel model, then the sealing message o 7:2-8 should fall within or after the trumpet series. The point of such observations is that the three series, if parallel, should each be self-consistent and not logically and chronologically interlaced and interdependent.

This brings us to item 4 in the above list of reasons for the parallel view. The heavenly celebration scenes are taken by many parallel interpreters as indicators of the arrival of the coming age. The three relevant to our study are the celebration of the white-robed multitude after the sealing vision (7:9-17), the celebration of the twenty-four elders after the sounding of the seventh trumpet (11:15-18), and the celebration of the great angelic multitude after the seventh bowl (19:1-8).[17] Each celebration clearly anticipates the time when the saints enter their eternal reward.

However, in no case does the celebration come at the end of the temporal events indicated in the series. The celebration of 7:8-17 comes *before* the tribulation envisioned by 7:1-7 and *before* the 7th seal. The celebration of 11:15-18 comes *after* the seventh trumpet(11:15) but *before* the "third woe" announced in 11:14. Subsequent judgments are also announced in 11:19. Even the last celebration scene in 19:1-8 precedes the final battle and second coming of Christ indicated by 19:11-21. According to either the parallel or the continuous model these scenes must be proleptic and none can be taken to indicate the chronological end of a parallel

---

[17]This heavenly multitude must consist of angels because they refer to the redeemed saints in the third person (v. 7).

series.[18] Moreover, the pattern is different in the seals than in the trumpets and bowls. The celebration *precedes* the seventh seal whereas it *follows* the seventh trumpet and the seventh bowl. If the chronologies were parallel, scenes celebrating *final* victory should occur at the *end* of each sequence.

Now to consider item five in the case for the parallel model. Does the continuous interpretation of the seal, trumpet, and bowl series result in interpretation too detailed and complicated? Surely a parallel understanding of the book makes much fewer demands on the reader who looks for fulfillments. This is especially helpful to those who adhere to the historical school. Analysis which spans the entire book with a seven-fold sequence will focus on more general aspects of history and thus require of the reader who looks for fulfillment a less detailed knowledge of history. On the other hand, to look at the procedure another way, selection of the specific things predicted may be more arbitrary and difficult.

Parallel-historical interpretation often attributes no particular meaning to the details of the symbolism. This generalized approach is another departure from the ancient way of understanding apocalyptic literature. With Daniel and the extrabiblical dream-vision apocalypses, the reader is to assume that the details were given to indicate aspects of prediction which had (or will have) detailed fulfillment. This is evident in the interpretations given in Daniel (2:37-45; 4:24-26; 7:17-27). The same hermeneutic should apply to Revelation.

Whereas most of the older scholars since the Reformation who have preferred the parallel model, such as Pareus, Vitringa, and Cuninghame, took an event-oriented approach to prediction, more recently writers like Hendriksen find, for the most part, only principles that govern history. The latter involves a different hermeneutic than the former. One may question whether interpretation of vision-type apocalyptic prophecy as prediction only of principles has any precedent in Scripture or whether such is true prophecy. Is Revelation a different kind of apocalyptic from Daniel? If so, on what ground? On the other hand, prophecy as prediction does teach principles, both principles of personal conduct and principles of divine providence. Often commentaries concerned with fulfillment

---

[18]Proleptic scenes in apocalyptic are comparable to the prophetic use of the Hebrew perfect tense in the Old Testament prophets to indicate as already accomplished a thing which is certain to happen in the future. See, for example, the literal rendering of the prophet's prediction of the future captivity of Israel in Isa 5:13, "Therefore my people *are gone* into captivity . . . " (KJV, emphasis mine). This idiom is not conveyed to the reader of the modern versions. The NIV translates this, "My people will go into exile." See Isa 9:2-4, 6.

neglect to expound such principles. Nevertheless, true predictive prophecy also anticipates particular event-oriented fulfillment. One need not sacrifice one for the other.

Contemporary evangelical scholarship is often a blend of several of the traditional schools—futurism, preterism, and philosophy of history (Ladd and Beasley-Murray)[19] or preterism and philosophy of history (Hendriksen).[20] Ladd states, "The correct method of interpreting Revelation is a blending of the preterist and the futurist methods. The Beast is both Rome and the eschatological Antichrist and, we might add, any demonic power which the church must face in her entire history" (14). This last assertion is philosophy of history (transtemporal interpretation). When taken purely it eschews a quest for chronological fulfillment and instead looks for types or principles which may have recurrent expression throughout history. However, I suggest that those who defer from prophecy as prediction to philosophy of history simply confuse interpretation with application.

The practical application of a predictive prophecy must address several questions:

1. What principles are implied by the prediction?
2. How may these principles be applied in my situation?
3. What kind of event, circumstance, or condition is predicted?
4. What practical application may be inferred from this prediction?
5. Has the prediction been fulfilled in part or in whole?
6. What practical lessons can I learn from the fulfillment?

Strictly considered, only questions 1 and 3 involve interpretation of the text, although consideration of number 5 may throw new light on 3 and require revision or refinement. The philosophy of history theory appears to eliminate questions 3-6.

Scholars who take a philosophy of history approach ordinarily do not address the fact that they read the Book of Revelation as they read no

---

[19]Ladd, George E. *Commentary on the Revelation of John.* (Grand Rapids: Eerdmans, 1972); G. R. Beasley-Murray, *The Book of Revelation.* (New Century Bible; Revised ed.; Grand Rapids: Eerdmans, 1978).

[20]Such parallel interpretation usually identifies certain specific events, such as the catastrophic language of the sixth seal in 6:12-17 with the end-time, the male-child prophecy of 12:1-5 with the birth and ascension of Christ and the rider on the white horse in Rev 19:1-16 with the second advent of Christ.

other apocalyptic book.[21] In this, they depart from the historical method of interpretation, which assumes that the language of Scripture should be read and understood in so far as possible as other literature of its kind was originally read. The philosophy of history method is comparable to the allegorizing process that developed in Alexandrian Judaism and in the early centuries of the church. The historical method should lead the interpreter to recognize that vision-type apocalyptic such as we find in Daniel and Revelation is event-oriented prediction.

Evaluation of the Continuous Approach

Those who view the relationship of the seal, trumpet, and bowl prophecies as continuous see the seventh seal as introducing the trumpets and the seventh trumpet as introducing the bowls. The six trumpet prophecies will then have their fulfillment in a sequential manner after the events of the sixth seal. The seven bowl prophecies extend the chronology further after the events forecast by the six trumpets and after the interlude message of the little scroll (Rev 10-14). Historically, the continuous interpretation approach began to develop around the end of the first millennium, then more fully and systematically in the Reformation and post-Reformation period, beginning with Joseph Mede. Although Mede is usually credited with starting this trend, even he viewed the bowls as being poured out mostly during the time of the sixth trumpet and after the interlude message of chapters 10-14.[22]

Preterist interpreters have usually seen the seal prophecies as judgments against the Jewish nation, often dating the book from Nero and beginning the judgments with the Jewish-Roman war of A.D. 66-70 and the trumpets and bowls as extending into the near future. Some futurists, after Ribera, see the seals as traversing the church age and the trumpets and bowls as end-time judgments. Other futurists place the fulfillment of all three series in the end-time. Continuous-historical interpreters find the fulfillment of the three series consecutively in history, usually predicated on Domitianic authorship. They begin the sequence immediately thereafter and extend it to the end time.

---

[21]As stated by Marcus Dods, "This system of interpretation has its attractions, but is certainly out of keeping with the general purpose of Apocalyptic[sic] literature" ("The Apocalypse, "*An Introduction to the New Testament* [London: Hodder and Stoughton, 1888], 244). "Apocalyptic," when referring to the genre rather than to the Book of Revelation should be spelled with a lower case "a."

[22]We have classified Mede with continuous-historicist as that is the place given him in the histories on account of his treatment of the seals and trumpets and the influence he has had on subsequent interpretation.

The continuous model like the parallel one recognizes the presence of interludes, as for example, chapter 7 or 19:1-10. These may be viewed as contemporaneous with their immediate context or they may be viewed as proleptic, looking forward to the consummation. The entire little book section (Rev 10-14) is an interlude. Other examples are chapter 7:1-8, where the sealing of the 144,000 is done in preparation for coming tribulation (v. 3), and 7:9-17, the celebration of the great multitude, oriented proleptically after the tribulation (v. 14) in the age to come (vv. 16, 17). Such proleptic scenes are introduced at crisis points in the prophecy to encourage the church as it anticipates suffering.

Mounce, who himself prefers the continuous approach, quotes Farrer who wrote, "There is not a line in the book which promises us . . . a continuous exposition of predicted events."[23] Continuous interpreters, on the other hand, point out that there is no indication that the three series, seals, trumpets, and bowls, are parallel in structure. There is, moreover, a strong and objective precedent in the visions of Daniel, all of which are continuous. So also comparable dream-visions in the extra-biblical apocalyptic literature.[24]

The extra-biblical apocalypses have greater importance than might at first appear because they were widely read and together with the visions of Daniel would have conditioned the way in which the Book of Revelation was understood. Wikenhauser states, "The author of an apocalypse receives the revelations of divine mysteries . . . mainly through visions, whether ecstasies (when awake) or dreams (asleep)." Such writings "begin with an outline of the history of Israel from the time of the alleged author to the end of time, in the form of a prophecy." He states that the Book of Revelation belongs to this literary category, "Both in form and content the Apc. of John shows close kinship with Jewish apocalyptic writings. It presents a continuous series of symbolico-allegorical visions which the author experienced while in a state of ecstasy . . . ."[25] As the

---

[23]Robert H. Mounce, *The Book of Revelation*. (Revised ed.; Grand Rapids: Eerdmans, 1998), 31.

[24]"The apocalyptist very commonly conveys his meaning by portraying contemporary history in symbolic form, and continuing the symbolic narrative so as to include the supernatural events which he believes to be close at hand"(C. K. Barrett, ed., *The New Testament Background: Selected Documents* [1956; Rev. & Expanded ed.; New York: Harper and Row, 1989], 231). The Eagle Vision of 4 Ezra 11 is offered as a good example of such dream vision apocalypses (232-233, James H. Charlesworth, *Old Testament Pseudepigrapha* [Garden City, N.Y: Doubleday, 1983-1985] 1: 548-551). See also Bruce M. Metzger, *The New Testament: Its Background, Growth, and Content* (Enlarged ed.; Nashville: Abingdon, 1983), 231-239.

[25]Alfred Wikenhauser, "The Apocalypse of John," *New Testament Introduction* (New York: Herder and Herder 1958), 542-544.

entire prophetic section of Revelation (chs. 4:1-22:17) is contained within such a single-vision prophecy, the burden of proof rests upon those who would read it differently from other similar apocalyptic writings, as if it were a unique genre.[26]

Other matters of detail support the continuous approach. The seventh seal and the seventh trumpet do not contain significant prediction but serve to introduce the next seven-numbered series. If the parallel reading were intended, one should expect the culminating judgment of the seventh bowl would have strong correlations in the seventh seal and in the seven trumpet, together at those junctures with some explicit indicators that the chronological clock was being turned back.

There is also an important indication of continuous structure in the series of the three woes. These woes are identified with the last three trumpet blasts (Rev 8:13). The endings of the first and second woes are clearly labeled (9:12; 11:14). Only the continuous chronology can account for the isolated location of the notice in 11:14 for the second woe. The third woe, announced by the seventh trumpet, must be either the descent of Satan (12:9, 12) or the seven bowls "the seven last plagues, for in them the wrath of God is completed" (Rev 15:1, NKJV). Either alternative for the parallel model places the third woe within a different parallel series and appears to violate their proposed chronological sequence. Only the bowl series fills the requirement of the third woe, that is, that it is "the last," the final terror leading to the end (see Beckwith, 668-669, 672). "Last" clearly indicates a chronology of events. The difficulty of a construction which places the third woe somewhere in parallel with the first two is obvious.

That a natural or normal reading of the text results in a continuous model is supported by the great majority of scholars of all schools. Statistically, of the 159 scholars whose works I was able to classify, 104 chose the continuous model and 55 the parallel.[27] Mounce, nevertheless, indicates that the continuous approach "is not accepted by the majority of contemporary writers" (31). It appears that Mounce's statement may be true only if limited to modernist and neo-evangelical authors. Of the

---

[26]Continuous-historical" applies to the three principal structural indicators, the seal, trumpet, and bowl series. The content of chs. 11-14 requires a distinctive chronology. However extraordinary from the standpoint of the genre, a two-fold rationale may be found for this exception: (1) it is, as generally recognized, an interlude in the chronological sequence of the big scroll and (2), if I am correct in my understanding, it is introduced as the content of the little scroll.

[27]However, Guthrie, in his *New Testament Introduction* states that "the majority of interpreters" hold to a parallel or recapitulation model (289). My study and the resulting classification is published in *Our Destiny We Know, Essays in Honor of Edwin K. Gedney* (Charlotte, N. Car.: Venture Books, 1996), 139-163.

51 we classified from the twentieth century, 29 were classed as continuous and 22 as parallel.[28] Six of 7 philosophy of history interpreters chose the parallel model. Fourteen of 19 preterists and 7 of 11 futurists chose the continuous model.

This distribution which aligns parallel interpretation strongly with the philosophy of history school suggests that those who adopt the parallel model are motivated at least in part by the desire to simplify questions of fulfillment. The current trend is toward a minimum of event-oriented prediction. Most scholars outside of the conservative-evangelical camp discount any supernatural element in predictive prophecy.

Conclusion

The parallel model lacks textual evidence and tends to rely for support on considerations at best subjective and secondary to exegesis. From the time of Mede in the seventeenth century well into the nineteenth, our study suggests that the continuous model prevailed with nearly a two-thirds majority. Elliott, who offers a thorough review of the history, was able to state in 1862 regarding the continuous model that most historicist expositors adhered to it. Regarding the preterist and futurist schools, he stated that "both Moses Stuart of the German Praeterist school, and Burgh of the modern English futurist school, alike adopt it."[29] My survey indicates that the majority of the commentaries surveyed at any time from the Reformation until the present day have followed it.

The evidence strongly suggests that the seals, the trumpets, and the bowls should be understood to represent event-oriented prediction in a continuous sequence. The opening of the seals is appropriately preliminary to the remainder of the book. The trumpets follow, announcing events leading up to the conflict with Antichrist (Chs.10-14). The bowls complete the sequence by representing historical judgments against Antichrist which pave the way for the Second Advent, the destruction of the evil powers, the resurrection of the dead, and our Lord's eternal reign.

---

[28]Of 22 published since 1950, 8 were classified with parallel and 14 with continuous. This indicates that the trend in the current century has moved toward continuous.

[29]Elliott, 1.106, n. 1; Stuart, 2.150; William Burgh, *The Apocalypse Unfulfilled.* (2nd ed.; Dublin: Richard M. Tims, 1833), 183.

Appendix Four

The Historical Antichrist

There is a vast literature on the subject of Antichrist with many viewpoints and great variety of interpretation. Our objective in this essay is briefly to show the dimensions of the subject in biblical prophecy and how those predictions have been fulfilled in history.

The word "antichrist" occurs in the Bible only in the epistles of John (1 John 2:18, 22; 4:3; 2 John 7). For our consideration the most important of these texts is 1 John. 2:18:

> As you have heard that the antichrist is coming, even now many antichrists have come. This is how we know it is the last hour.

Writing near the end of the first Christian century, John alludes to a common expectation of a future antichrist. On the ground that many had already come who had the spirit of the last-day Antichrist, he points out that the Christians of his time were living in the last days (see 1 John. 4:3).[1]

The spirit of Antichrist to which John refers was not an outright repudiation of the Messiahship of Jesus. It was Gnosticism, a heresy which invaded the New Testament church which degraded both the deity and the humanity of Jesus (see Col 2:8-10). The gnostics denial was their failure to confess the true union of the divine Christ with his human nature (1 John 4:3). To the Apostle, this was tantamount to a total rejection of both the Son and the Father (1 John 2:23). To pervert the essential doctrine of Christ by word or by action is "to deny" him. This is the common usage of the word "deny" (Greek, ἀρνέομαι, *arnéomai*) in the New Testament (cf. 1 Tim 5:8; 2 Tim 2:12, 13; 3:5; 2 Pet 2:1; Jude 4; Rev 2:13; 3:8). We should conclude, therefore, that the idea of antichrist is not connected with atheism, but with heretical Christianity.

The Greek word ἀντιχριστός, *antichristos* does not simply mean

---

[1] It is generally understood among biblical authorities that "the last days" are the days of the Messiah and that they extend from the time of His first advent and His second Advent.

"opposed to Christ," but "vice-Christ" or "substitute Christ." E. B. Elliott explains this in principle as follows: "When αντι is compounded with a noun signifying an agent of any kind, or *functionary*, the compound word either signifies a *vice-functionary*, or a functionary of the *same kind opposing*, or sometimes both."[2]. This principle is illustrated in the Greek word *ἀντιλυτρον, ántilútron*, "ransom," in 1 Tim 2:6, where it is said that Christ gave himself as a ransom, or payment in substitute, representing the believer. *ánti* appears in the Greek titles for official representatives in the provincial Roman government, *ántistrátegos*, "imperator" (Dion Cassius 41.43) and *ánthúpatos*, "proconsul" (Acts 13:7), in the terms "anti-Caesar" and "antipope," used with reference to rival usurpers of an office. Similarly, the word "antitype" denotes a relationship of correspondence between the symbol and the thing symbolized. We should expect, then, that the word "antichrist" denotes not, per se, one who by his conduct rejects the person or teachings of Christ, but one who as a rival usurps the office and prerogatives of Christ in the world.

This is the understanding of Antichrist set forth by the Apostle Paul:

> "[The Day of the Lord] will not come unless the apostasy comes first and the man of lawlessness is revealed, the one destined for destruction who stands in opposition [ἀντικείμενος, *ántikeiménos*] and exalts himself over all things called God or object of worship, so that he sits in the sanctuary [ναός, *naós*] of God, proclaiming himself to be God" (2 Thess 2:3,4; trans. mine).

Note that Antichrist "stands in opposition" that is, he "stands alongside of" in a corresponding, rival position. He appears here not only as a blasphemous Messianic power (cf. Rev 13:6), but also the head of the Great Apostasy (cp. Matt 24:24).

The background for the New Testament doctrine is found in the prophecy of Daniel seven. It is foreshadowed in a general way by Moses, in Deut 28:47-68. In Daniel, the mysterious and terrible Fourth Beast (Rome) has "a little horn" in which were "eyes like the eyes of a man, and a mouth speaking great things" (7:8). In the interpretation of the dream, the prophecy is expanded (7:24-26):

---

[2] E. B. Elliott, *Horae Apocalypticae* (5th ed. London: Seeley, Jackson, and Halliday, 1862). 1.64, 65, n. 6 (italics his). Elliott then lists 22 compounds with ἀντι with their lexical definitions, 11 of which signify a vice-functionary (e.g., ἀντανδρος, "a man's substitute") and 11 (e.g., ἀνταγωνιστής. "the same kind opposing."

The ten horns are ten kings who will come from this kingdom. After them another king will arise, different from the earlier ones; he will subdue three kings. He will speak against the Most High and oppress his saints and try to change the set times and the laws. The saints will be handed over to him for a time, times, and half a time.

But the court will sit, and his power will be taken away and completely destroyed forever.

Is the Antichrist an individual ruler or an antichristian government? The four great beasts of the vision are "four kings [Aramaic, מַלְכִין, *mâlkîn*] who shall arise out of the earth" (17). But the fourth beast is further described as a fourth *kingdom* out of which ten kings shall arise (23f.) These are represented by horns. Since the first three kings are known to stand for three world governments (Babylon, Persia, and Greece), each of which included several monarchs, the word translated *"kings"* in the prophecy (with their symbols, the horns) means "kingdoms" or "monarchies," rather than "individual monarch."[3]

A further study of the passage above-quoted will yield several additional conclusions about the Little Horn or the Antichrist:

1. The Antichrist is a Roman world government in a succession of Roman governments (a part of the fourth beast).

2. The Antichrist government will be essentially different from the earlier Roman governments.

3. It will arise after the ten kingdoms and in so doing will put down three of them.

4. The Antichrist will take a blasphemous stand against God.

5. The Antichrist will persecute the saints.

6. The Antichrist will allege to change the times (the time prophecies? see below) and the laws.

7. The Antichrist will exercise power (as a temporal government) for a specific period, "time, times, and half a time," at the end of which its dominion will be taken away (cp. Dan 12:7).

8. The Antichrist will finally be destroyed at the coming of the Lord (Dan 7:11, 26; 2 Thess 2:8).

Daniel eleven and twelve treat of other details regarding the

---

[3]Francis Brown, S. R. Driver, Charles A. Briggs, A Hebrew and English Lexicon of the Old Testament (Oxford Clarendon Press, 1962), 1100₂

Antichrist which we will not consider now.

We have in the New Testament an elaborate prophetic commentary on Daniel's vision of the terrible Fourth Beast, the Little Horn of that beast, and its war against the saints. This commentary is the book of Revelation. Revelation, as it has been traditionally interpreted by Protestants and even in pre-Reformation times, is a prophecy of the church in the final Fourth Kingdom, Roman era of the Times of the Gentiles from John's day to the final Kingdom of God. It is presented in dramatic apocalyptic symbols and a central symbol is that terrible monster of Daniel seven!

In Revelation twelve, we are introduced to a great red dragon with seven heads and ten horns. The Dragon is at war with a woman and her offspring, and eventually he drives the woman into the wilderness where she is "to be nourished for a time, two times, and half a time" (12:14). Some external circumstance prevents the Dragon from pursuing the Woman (12:16), and it is last seen standing on the shore of the sea. From this sea arises a beast distinguished by ten horns and seven heads (13:1). At the outset, the Beast is identified with the vision of Daniel, not only by its ten horns, but by the fact that it has inherited some of the ferocious qualities of the three previous kingdoms described there: "The beast that I saw was like a leopard, its feet were like a bear's, and its mouth was like a lion's mouth."

It is apparent not only from the above description but from what follows (13:5-8) that the Beast is to be identified with the Little Horn of Daniel and that it is a prophecy of Antichrist. Bible interpreters from the very beginning have seen in the Dragon a description of the ancient Roman Empire. Its seven heads are best understood to represent successive constitutional governments, of which in John's day five had fallen, the sixth was in existence, and the seventh was yet to come (17:10). (The Roman historians Livy and Tacitus, the latter a contemporary of John, name the six then known governments. They are common knowledge to the historians of ancient Rome (Livy 6.1-2; Tacitus, *Annal.* i.1).[4]

With the introduction of the Beast, we are told that "the Dragon gave to it his *power* and his *throne* and *great authority*" (Rev 13:2). We should understand then that the authority of the old Roman Empire is given to the Antichrist. The passage following describes the reign of the

---

[4]For their use of the terms "head" and "fallen" with respect to these, see Livy 26.16, 40; Cicero, *De Off.* ii.13; cited from Elliott, 3. 106-107.

Beast (Rev 13:5-9):

> The Beast was given a mouth to utter proud words and blasphemies, and to exercise his authority for forty-two months. He opened his mouth to blaspheme God, and to slander his name and his dwelling place and those who live in heaven. He was given power to make war against the saints and to conquer them. And he was given authority over every tribe, people, language and nation. All inhabitants of the earth will worship the beast—all whose names have not been written in the book of life belonging to the Lamb that was slain from the creation of the world..

This description is largely a reiteration of Daniel seven. Once again we encounter the prophetic timetable for the reign of Antichrist, "forty-two months" (Rev 13:5; cp. 11:2). From chapter 12 we know that the same period is defined as "one thousand two hundred and sixty days" (12:6; cp. 11:3), as well as "a time, and times, and half a time" (12:14). The forty-two months indicate that a "time" in prophecy is a year of 360 days. Three and one-half years are 1260 days. (The 360-day year is based on a 30-day month, a precedent for which may be found in the account of the flood. Compare Gen 7:11 with Gen 8:3, 4, where 150 days equal 5 mos.) Is this 1260 days to be understood literally or figuratively on the year-day principle? In the prophecy of Ezek 4:1-17, one day in a prophecy of future judgment equals one year in fulfillment (cp. also Num 14:33, 34). Several considerations favor the figurative interpretation:

1. The book of Revelation is composed largely of prophetic symbols which require figurative interpretation. It should not appear as extraordinary if numbers are used as symbols.

2. The Bible indicates that the meaning of time prophecies will be understood only in the end time (cp. Acts 1:7 with Dan 12:4, 8, 9). The year-day principle lends itself to this Providential design.

3. It has been recognized by the great majority of prophetic scholars that the year-day principle was used to veil the prophecy of the first advent of Christ, the prophecy of the Seventy Weeks (Dan 9:24-27). This would seem appropriate also for the prophecies of the second advent.

4. The literal three and one-half year interpretation must assume that Antichrist is still future, whereas it is said of the seventh head that "when he comes he must remain only a little while" (Rev 17:10). Since the seventh head must have reigned before the fall of Rome in 550 A.D., the 1260 days (or years) cannot with propriety still be future.

In view of these considerations we interpret the 1260 days as years and look for the beginning of Antichrist's reign soon after the fall of Rome and the western Roman Empire (A.D. 550).

A further aspect of the Antichrist prophecies to be clarified is the **ten horns** which appear on all of the representations of the Dragon and the Beast. The cumulative information may be tabulated as follows:

1. The ten horns are ten kings (or kingdoms) which shall arise on the Roman Beast prior to the Antichrist Little Horn (Dan 7:24).

2. They are different in character from the Antichrist Horn (Dan 7:24).

3. Three of the ten kingdoms shall be put down by Antichrist when he arises (Dan 7:24c).

4. With the Dragon the diadems are worn upon the seven heads, whereas with the Beast the diadems are worn upon the ten horns (Rev 12:3; 13:1). Royal power is transferred from the heads to the horns.

5. The ten kingdoms had not yet received royal power at the time that Revelation was written (Rev 17:12).

6. The ten kingdoms exist cotemporaneously together with the Beast (Rev 6:12. Translate *mian horan* "at the same time," rather than "for one hour."[5]

7. The ten kings give over their power and authority to the Beast (Rev 17:13).

8. They will make war on the Lamb, but the Lamb will conquer them (Rev 17:14).

9. They and the Beast will come to hate the Harlot (Antichrist, or "Babylon" after her temporal reign) and they will devastate her (Rev 17:16).

Chapter seventeen of Revelation describes Antichrist as a harlot riding on the beast. Antichrist is no longer a ruling head, but it is the "Harlot Babylon." The Beast is no longer ruled by Antichrist but Antichrist rides upon it, and together with the Ten Kings the Beast turns on the Harlot and desolates her, "devouring her flesh and burning her with fire." The Harlot in verse one is described as "seated upon many waters"; verse three states that she is seated on the Beast. The beast, conceived apart from the ruling heads is the empire as governed by the ten horns ("peoples and multitudes and nations and lands," Rev 17:15; cp. 19:6).

---

[5]Greek accus. of time (Elliott, 3. 81, 82, 150).

Chapter eighteen is a prophetic lament over the fall of Antichrist, or Babylon, combined with a warning to the people to come out of her rather than share in her impending doom. In chapter nineteen, the Beast together with the False Prophet (the Beast from the Earth; see Rev 13:11-18) is thrown into the Lake of Fire to suffer final destruction (19:20, 21).

Until the rise of Darby and the Darbyite dispensational futurist school in the nineteenth century, Revelation was understood by pre-Reformation dissidents and Protestants as a prophecy which bridged the span of history from the days of the author, John, to the return of Christ. From the very rise of the Papacy, pious men have been quick to point out the correspondences between the Antichrist prophecies and the politico-religious position of the Roman Catholic Church. The Antichrist prophecies, together with the heresies the Papacy espoused, constituted the framework for the Protestant Reformers' rejection of the authority of the Roman Pope. This traditional Protestant view of prophecy, far from being outdated, bears directly on our own time and is essential for an understanding of prophetic Scripture.

Though this essay is devoted primarily to setting forth the biblical teaching on Antichrist, it is noteworthy to point out that no less an authority than the great Puritan scholar, Jonathan Edwards gave unswerving affirmation of the view presented above. Edwards is esteemed as having been possessed "with one of the finest minds ever to appear in human history."[6] The above quotation is prefaced by the statement that Edwards "expounded [biblical revelation] meticulously (Gerstner, 1.1). Henry Rodgers wrote that "Edwards was probably 'the most perfect specimen of the intellectual athlete the world has ever seen.'"[7]

> According to Edwards, "The Antichrist is the papacy, Satan's masterpiece as indicated in Rev. 17:18, 'the plainest of any one passage in the whole book.' This passage, which it is 'impossible' to mistake, is the key to the whole Apocalypse. Rome's claim to be Christian makes the Papacy all the more the Antichrist . . . . It 'is more antichristian than is possible for heathenish, Jewish or Mohammedan Churches to be.' 'Their whole religion is blasphemy,' Edwards concludes after listing their false claims such as pardoning sins, turning people over to the

---

[6] From the Introduction to the three-volume work by John H. Gerstner, *The Rational Biblical Theology of Jonathan Edwards* (Powhatan, Va.: Berea Publications, 1991), 1.1.

[7] Cited by Gerstner (1.1) from *The Works of Jonathan Edwards, A.M.*, revised and corrected by Edward Hickman, with an Essay on His Genius and Writings by Henry Rogers . . . (2 vv.; London: William Ball, 1837), 1.xii.

wrath of God by excommunication, and even creating their Creator by transubstantiation."[8]

To conclude this essay, we will recapitulate below the principal points of doctrine regarding Antichrist, and show briefly some correspondences with historical fulfillment:

1. **Antichrist is a Gentile Roman power in a succession of Roman governments (Dan 7:7-8).** The accession of Papal Rome to the throne of the Roman Empire is a fact of history generally recognized by Roman Catholic historians. For example, "The Bishop of Rome mounted the throne whence the Emperors fell . . . ." (Duc de Broglie, *Histoire de l'Eglise* VI, quoted by Porcelli, From Cardinal Manning he quotes, "The abandonment of Rome [by Caesar] was the liberation of the Pontiffs . . . . He [the Pope] was elevated to be, in his Divine Master's name, King of Kings and Lord of Lords. The abandonment of Rome . . . left them free to become independent sovereigns, and to take up the sovereignty the Emperor had just laid down."[9]

2. **The Antichrist's government is essentially different from earlier Roman governments (Dan 7:23).** The Papacy is different primarily in that as a Beast or Gentile, pagan, anti-God power it is an apostasy from within the church, rather than opposition from without.

3. **Antichrist will rise after the Ten Kings, putting down three of them. Dan 7:24.** The Ten Kings are the ten Barbarian nations that ruled the western Roman Empire after Roman fell to the Goths. Odoacer the Goth deposed the Emperor and became king of Italy in A.D. 476. The Roman senate dissolved in 550. In the period beginning about 486 and extending through modern times the number of nations governing this territory have numbered about ten, sometimes one or two more or less, but often exactly that number. Elliott catalogs the list for A.D. 532, which he believed to be the primary reference of the prophecy, as follows: Anglo-Saxons, Franks, Alleman-Franks, Burgundic-Franks, Visigoths, Suevi, Vandals, Ostragoths, Bavarians, and Lombards—ten in all. He shows how these kings took over the Imperial diadem as their badge of Roman

---

[8]The quotation is Gerstner's statement of Edwards understanding of Antichrist, as interlaced with excerpts quoted from Edwards own works, "Notes on the Apocalypse," pp. 97-305 in *Apocalyptic Writings*, v. 5 of *The works of Jonathan Edwards*. (Ed. by John E. Smith from unpublished mss; New Haven: Yale University Press, 1977), 119, n.7; 125-126.

[9]Baron Porcelli, *The Antichrist: His Portrait and History* (2nd American ed.; El Paso, Texas: Lamp Trimmers, 2001), 24-25. Porcelli (p. 25) attributes the quotation from Cardinal Manning, to the Cardinal's work *Temporal Power*, 42-46, 50.

succession, which is thoroughly illustrated on their coinage (Elliott, 3.132-147).

The authority of the Roman Papacy was established by the Eastern or Byzantine Roman Emperor Phocas by Imperial decree ca. A.D. 607, when he conferred upon Pope Benedict III the title of Universal Bishop.[10] It is pertinent to point out that the one whose influence resulted in Boniface's rise to the Roman bishopric, Gregory the Great, had earlier stated that the assumption of this title by a Byzantine pontiff was a "blasphemous and diabolical usurpation" and that "whoever calls himself universal priest, or desires to be called so," is "the forerunner of Antichrist."[11] The three kingdoms put down by the Papacy in this transition period were nations which unsuccessfully resisted the Papal power. These were in 533 the Vandals in North Africa, who also ruled the Mediterranean islands of Corsica and Sardinia within the diocese of the Bishop of Rome; the Ostragoths, who ruled Italy; and later, the Lombards, who had taken over most of Italy by 752 (Elliott, 3.167-172).

4. **Antichrist is a usurper of the office and prerogatives of Christ in the world (1 John 2:18).** The Roman Catholic expositor Cardinal Newman in his *Treatise on Antichrist* states that "Antichrist professes to take His place without warrant. It comes forward instead of Christ, and for Him; it speaks for Him, it develops His words, it suspends his appointments; it grants dispensations in matters of positive duty; it professes to minister grace; it absolves from sin, and all on its own authority. Is it not forthwith according to the very force of the word, Antichrist? He who speaks for Christ must be either His true ambassador or Antichrist" (quoted by Porcelli, 26). The organ of the Guild of Our Lady of Ransom (issue of Feb. 1914) edited by Father Philip Fletcher, said, "If the Pope is not the Vicar of Jesus Christ, he must be Antichrist; there is no middle view" (229; Porcelli, 26). Pope Pius IX states, "I am the Vicar of Jesus Christ, and I have the right to employ the very words of Jesus Christ: 'My Father, those whom thou hast given me I will not lose'" (*Discorsi*, 1872-3; Porcelli, 30). Pope Pius X said, "The Pope . . . . is Jesus Christ himself, hidden under the veil of flesh . . . . All must be subject to him" (Porcelli, 29). The doctrine that the Pope is Vicar of Christ is fundamental to Roman orthodoxy.

---

[10]Archibald Bower, *History of the Popes* (Philadelphia: Griffith & Simon, 1844), 1.425-426.

[11]Philip Schaff, *History of the Christian Church* (Grand Rapids: Eerdmans, 1950), 4.220.

5. Antichrist, the Lawless One, sets himself "above all the law, and thinks to change the times and the laws." (2 Thess 2:3; Dan 7:25). Exemption from law was not only claimed by the Roman Caesars, but repeatedly affirmed by the Popes as the dogma of the Roman Church, and the principle is applied freely to temporal circumstances involving both civil and biblical laws. Pope Gregory IX in his *Decretals* said that the Pope "changes even the nature of things, applying the substantials of one thing to another . . . and a judgment which is null he makes to be real; . . . nor is there anyone to say to him: 'Why dost thou this?' for he can dispense with the law; he can also turn injustice into justice by correcting and changing the law, and he has the fulness of power" (Porcelli, 42-43). Pope Nicolas stated, "Wherefore, no marvel if it be in my power to change times and laws, to alter and abrogate laws, to dispense with all things, yea with the precepts of Christ" (Porcelli, 43). The Popes in their reinterpretation of Scripture annul marriages, annul the second commandment regarding the worship of images, withhold the communion cup from the laity when Jesus said, "all of you drink of it," worship saints and angels, etc. With respect to the times, we may point to the invention of the futuristic interpretation of prophecy by the Jesuit Ribera and its intrusion into Protestantism through the work and influence of the Spanish Jesuit priest, Lacunza.[12]

6. Antichrist assumes a pretentious and blasphemous authority "over all things called God," "setting in the temple (Greek, ναός, *naós*, "sanctuary") of God, and proclaiming himself to be God" (2 Thess 2:4). We take the sanctuary of God here to be the visible church, as it is commonly used by Paul in his epistles (see 1 Cor 3:16, 17; here too "temple" is ναός, *naós*). Many illustrations of the Papal position could be brought forward here from Roman doctrine and liturgy. We cite the following from Pope Pius IX in his address to the Apostolic Union in 1912, "The Pope is . . . the head under whom no one can feel himself tyrannized over, because he represents God Himself. He is the Father (par excellence), because he unites within himself all that there is that is lovable, sacred, and Divine" (Porcelli, 27). Pope Pius XI stated from his throne to a kneeling papal audience assembled on April 22, 1922, "You know that I am the Holy Father, the representative of God on the earth, the Vicar of Christ, which means that I am God on the earth" (*The Bulwark*, Oct. 1922, p. 104; Porcelli, 31).

---

[12]See Duncan McDougall, *The Rapture of the Saints* (Backwood N.J.: O.F.P.M., 1970), 29-32.

7. **Antichrist stands in opposition to God as the head of a great apostasy (2 Thess 2:4).** The full extent and implications of this Roman apostasy is extremely difficult to calculate, but the fact is evident that it has changed the course of history. It may even have been largely responsible, through its encouragement of the humanistic enlightenment movement on the one hand and its morally bankrupt authoritarianism on the other, for the spread of rationalism in the Renaissance and modern era. The Three Frogs of Rev 16:13 come from the mouths of the Dragon, the Beast, and the False Prophet, and are usually identified with philosophic movements which have to a large extent given character to the 20th century.

8. **Antichrist in alliance with the Ten Kings persecutes the true church for the period of its reign (Rev 13:7).** The persecution of Jews and "heretics" (dissenting Christians), has been a dogma of the Roman Church. The practice arose simultaneously and in proportion to the political influence of the Papacy. "Heretics" in the words of Pope Pius X, "are the baptized who pertinaciously refuse to believe some truth revealed by God and taught as of faith by the Catholic Church, for example . . . the various sects of Protestantism" and "Protestantism . . . is the sum of all heresies which existed before it, which have since arisen, and which can still arise to destroy souls . . . and represents all the forms of *rebellion against the holy Catholic Church*".[13] "Pius V declared that he would release a culprit guilty of a hundred murders rather than one obstinate heretic" (Porcelli, 43). The failure of the Roman Church of the twentieth and twenty-first centuries to prosecute heretics, even within her own priesthood, is one of the most convincing evidences of the current fall of Babylon. A Roman paper, *The Rambler* (Sept. 1851) stated, "Believe us not Protestants of England and Ireland, when you hear us pouring forth our liberalisms—they mean nothing. Such a person is not talking Catholicism . . . . If he were lord in the land, and you in minority, if not in numbers, yet in power . . . . If expedient he would imprison you, banish you, fine you, possibly he might hang you . . . but he would never tolerate you" (Porcelli, 64-65). During Rome's warfare against "heresy" it is estimated that many millions were tortured and slain, many burned alive at the stake.[14] During the years 1478-1517 alone, it is estimated by the historian

---

[13]Pius X, *The Compendium of Christian Doctrine* (1906), 131, 398; as quoted by Porcelli, 64; italics his.

[14]For a thorough discussion and documentation of this great tribulation as imposed upon evangelical believers through many centuries, see Daniel T. Taylor, *The Great Consummation* (Boston: Advent Christian Publication Society, 1891), 23-132; publication on demand copy available from Venture Bookstore, Box 23152, Charlotte, NC 28227-0272.

Llorente that 13,000 persons were burned alive and 169,000 tortured (Porcelli, 61).[15]

9. Antichrist will exercise temporal power and thereby persecute the church for 1260 years. (Rev 13:5) The Emperor Phocas came to power in A. D. 606 A.D. and conveyed upon Boniface III the title of Universal Bishop. Boniface was consecrated Pope February 19, 607. Calculating from 607 A. D., the projection points to 1867 for the terminus ad quem. Guinness cited fourteen major expositors between the mid-16th century and 1861 who charted the rise and fall of the Papacy from A.D. 606-1866. These based their calculation on the start of the reign of Phocus, as the more exact date of his decree was then obscure. In 1866 there occurred the famous battle of Sadowa, by which was determined for the first time in Europe the ascendancy of Prussia and Protestantism over Austria and Catholicism. There followed thereafter a rapid series of historic events which culminated in 1870 in the total loss of the Papal territories and, as all historians recognize, the end of temporal power of the Papacy.[16] Since then, the political and spiritual influence of the Papacy has declined, until at the present time the authority of the Pope is questioned, even among the Jesuits and other Roman Catholics.[17]

10. Antichrist will ultimately be devastated by the political forces of Europe (Rev 17:16-18) and will be finally destroyed at the

---

[15]Historians today generally are inclined not to believe the statistics of Llorente, though he was Secretary to the Inquisition in Madrid, 1789-91, and had access to the official archives in 1811. Such official records otherwise are generally not available, so that modern scholars tend to be sceptical and radically reduce the numbers. No doubt many reports were based on estimates and may have erred on overstatement rather than otherwise, but nevertheless they indicate many tortures and deaths by burning. H. Grattan H. Grattan Guinness reports having been present in Madrid at the burning place, Quemadero, when the ash field containing the remnants of burned martyrs was uncovered. He stood chest deep in those human remains in a trench cut by bulldozers for highway construction (*History Unveiling Prophecy* (New Yotk: Revell, 1905), 108); see also Guinness' carefully researched account of the Inquisition in the countries of Europe in *Romanism and the Reformation* (Boston: Arnold Publishing Association, 1893), pp. 165-178. The full text of both of the above books is available at www.historicism.com. Cited 20 Feb, 2007. Guinness was a thorough scholar who not only researched the subject carefully but actually visited several of the sites where the inquisition was carried out. For a brief description of his life and ministry, read "H. Grattan Guinness, Flame of Fire," by Eric Peters at the above web site.

[16]See Clarence H. Hewitt, *The Seer of Babylon* (Boston: Advent Christian Publication Society, 1948), 123-126, 407-412; Malachi Martin, *The Decline and Fall of the Roman Church* (New York: G. P. Putnam's Sons, 1981), 247-258.

[17]See Malachi Martin, *The Jesuits: the Society of Jesus and the Betrayal of the Roman Catholic Church* (New York: Simon & Schuster, 1988), which recounts the opposition of the Society of Jesus to Papal authority.

coming of the Lord (2 Thess 2:8). Only these events, if Rev 17:16-18 was not fulfilled by circumstances in the 19th century, remain to be fulfilled.

It is probable that some Roman Catholics enjoy a saving knowledge of Jesus Christ and others are earnestly seeking to be rid of the evils of the Roman system. This is the time to extend a true Christian witness and the call to "come out of her, my people" (Rev 18:4).

Index of Texts

BIBLE
Genesis
1	211
1:7	104n9
2:7	261
2:9	67
2:17	114
3:1-15	16
3:14-19	457
3:15	113n20, 448n18
3:17-18	115
3:22	67
3:24	106n10
4:10	145, 343
7:11	501
8:3, 4	501
9:12-17	102
9:16, 17	113n20, 229
13:3	113n20
13:16	171
19:23-28	211
22:17	447
32:12	171, 447
37:9	156, 273
37:9, 10	274n5
41:49	171, 447
48:12-22	166
49:9, 10	110

Exodus
7-11	182
7:19	357
7:20-21	186, 356
9:9	356
9:23	184
9:23-25	356
13:21, 22	233
15:11	88
16:32-34	76
19:4	284
19:6	53, 115
19:16-19	104
19:16, 19	182
20:4	217
20:14	212n64
23:29	142n38
25:18-22	106n10
25:31-40	60
27:3	179n7
28:17-21	463n32
30:1-10	207
30:1-11	207
32:32f.	87
34:29-30	62
35:34	398
40:20-21	353
40:34, 35	355
40:35	354n2

Leviticus
4:1-7	207
4:7	145
7:18	388
11:9-12	364
16:12, 13	179
18:22	390
18:26, 27	388
19:36	133n21
20:13	390
21:9	398
24:3-4	60
26	172n78, 194
26:14-33	32
26:14-39	140
26:14-43	122
26:22	82
26:26	133n21, 134n24
26:27-30	32
26:27-39	173n78
26:29	82
26:31, 33-35	115
26:33-39	32

Numbers
1:1	208n55
2	187
2:3	166n71
6:27	93
7:12	166n71
10:9	181
10:14	166n71
13:33, 34	245
14:33, 34	501
14:34	240, 259, 473n2
16:3	71
16:5	165
16:46	179
20:4	71
21:1-16	75
22:11	75n27
22:22	75n27
23:22	113
24:17	84, 187
25:1-3	75

25:2, 3	218	32:43	172n78	10:30-37	82		
31:1-16	75	33:17	113	19:15	106n10		
35:30	241	**Joshua**		**1 Chronicles**			
Deuteronomy		5:14	62	2:3-4:23	166n71		
4:28	212	5:14, 15	228	13:6	106n10		
7:25	388	7:19	337n7	24:1-19	103		
8:5	78	11:4	171	28:5, 29:23	280		
12:23	145	**Judges**		29:10-13	1172 2		
17:6	241	5:31	62	**2 Chronicles**			
18:10, 11	390	6:2	158	3:7	106n10		
18:18, 19	173n78	6:5	210	3:10-13	106n10		
18:22	10, 390	7:12	171, 210	3:14	106n10		
19:9	68n19	14:12	419	20:18	107n15		
19:15	241, 247	21:25	220	29-30	207		
20:13	390	**1 Samuel**		32:20-23	207		
22:21	212n64	2:2	88	**Ezra**			
23:4	75n27	13:6	158	1:2-4	27n39		
27:4	68n19	24:3	158	4:6	27n39		
28	172n78, 194	**2 Samuel**		4:7-23	27n39		
28:15-68	122	6:2	106n10	6:3-12	27n39		
28:32	82	7:11-16	90	7:13	27n39		
28:38-42	115	7:11b-16	110	7:18	27n39		
28:41	82	7:12	145n42	7:20, 23	27n39		
28:44	216n75	7:12-17	84	7:21	27n39		
28:47-68	498	22:12	233	7:27	399		
28:49-68	173n78	**1 Kings**		7:36	67n19		
28:52-57	32	1:21	145n42	8:52	67n19		
28:64-68	32	6.20	462	**Nehemiah**			
29:16-21	80	6:23-26	106n10	1:3	27n39		
30:2	68n19	6:29	106n10	2:12	399		
30:16	68n19	6:32, 34m 35	106n10	2:17	27n39		
30:18	68n19	7:13-22	93	7:5	399		
30:22-29	32	7:29, 36	106n10	**Job**			
31:15	233	8:10-13	354n2	1:6-12	441		
31:16	145n42	16:31	80	1:12	198, 318		
32:11	284	17:1	246	3	204		
32:15-43	32	18:41-45	246	3:8	281		
32:17	212, 218	21:21-22	82	3:20	204		
32:22	340			5:17	197		
32:34	25	**2 Kings**		7:12	281		
32:34, 35 LXX	32	1:10, 12	246	7:21	145n42		
32-35	32	6:17	425	9:13	281		

21:19	25	95:5	218	6:5	62, 172
21:20	339	99:1	106n10	7:23	344
31:6	133	102:25, 26	151	8	218
38:22, 33	184	103:4	93n44	8:7	362, 375
Psalms		104	417	8:19	218
1	187n21, 212	104:3	232	9:2-4, 6	491n18
2:8, 9	267	104:10	187n21	9:6	79n28
2:9	77, 83, 280	105:32	182	10:1-11	398
6:5	117n26	106:28	218	10:2, 19, 21	152
7:1-11	197	106:37	212	11:1	110
8:4	345	107:26	441	13:1-32	391
8:5	92n44	115:1-8	212	13:2	404n53
8:6	281	118:22-27	429	13:13	150n48
9	197	119:137	359	13:19-22	403
9:5, NIV	447	141:2	179	13:21	404n53
9:6, LXX	447	148:4	104n9	13:21, LXX	404
13:3	145n42	**Proverbs**		13:21-22a	403
16:10	62, 90	3:11-12	96	14:4-23	391
18:4	62	5:5	62	14:12-15	198n44
18:4-5	62	8:22	95n46	14:12	187
18:12, 13	182	11:1	133	17:5	342
18:13-15	104	13:24	78	19:4	186
18:13	184	16:11	133n21	19:4-5	186
20:5, LXX	447	20:23	133n21	19:6-10	186
21:4, NIV	447	**Song of Songs**		21:1	185n16
30:9	117n26	6:10	281n15	21:1-12	391
47:3	281	**Isaiah**		21:9	337, 403
62:9	133n21	1	186, 187n20	22:22	87n40
69:28	87, 451	1:4-6	357	24:4, 6	185n14
74:13, 14	281	1:21	386n38	24:18b-20	150n48
75:8	339	1:28	446	24:23	329
78:14	233	2:1-5	91	26:17	275
78:47	182	4	213	27:1	131n16, 281
78:47,48	182	4:3	87	27:2	236n9
80:1	106n10	4:4-6	233	27:13	182
84:11	360	4:5	259	28:2, 17	184
88:10-12	117n26	5:1-7	344	28:5	72
89:9a, 10a	295	5:13	491n18	30:30	184
89:17	113	6	106	32:12	344
89:27	52, 53	6:1-5	100	33:14	340
90:4	436n3	6:2	105	34:4	151, 488
94:12	197	6:4	354n2	34:4a	151n49

Index of texts 515

34:5	131n16	60:10	91n42		212
34:5-17	151n51	60:10-14	447	13:16	337n7
34:8-11	488	60:14	90	13:27	388
34:9, 10	416	60:19-20	281n15	15:2	303
34:9-11a	336, 445	61:6	54	15:16-19	237
34:10	418	63:1-6	423	18:17	164, 185n16
34:13-15	404	62:1-12	447	21:7	122
35:9-13	115	63:4	436n3	25:11	23
37:16	106n10	63:9	178	25:11-12	473n2
38:18	117n26	65:4, 11	218	25:15	339
40:25	90	65:6	451	29:10	23
41:4	56	65:11	218	30-33	429
43:6-11	440n8	65:16	95	31:5-14	115
44:6-20	212	65:17	458	31:7-14	440n8
44:6	56	65:17-25	115	31-33	91n42
44:23	101n2	65:19	458	31:34	24
45:14	91	66:3-6, 14b-17, 24	458	31:34b	406
45:22	185n14	66:6	356n4	31:38-40	447
46:10	131n16	66:7	279, 280	33:15	24
47:1-15	391	66:7, 66:8	279	34:12-22	398
47:6	131n16	66:7-8	275, 279n13	43:11	303
47:8a, 9a, 14	405	66:7-9	458	46:7	375
47:9-15	213	66:7-16	278	46:7, 8	362
48:12	56	66:8b-c, 10, 13a	279	46:23	210
49:2	62, 426	66:10-14a	458	47:9	406
49:23	91	66:22	115, 456	49:12	339
51:3	67	66:22-23	458	49:18	151n51
51:17, 22	339, 380	66:24	340	49:35	127
52:10	185n14	**Jeremiah**		49:36	164
52:13-53:12	116	1:13, 14	185n16	50:1-51:64	391
53:1-9	267n51	1:17	172	50:39-40	404
53:2	110	2:20	386n38	51:1, 2	164
53:6	113	2:21	344	51:13	386n39
53:7	113n19	3:1, 9	386n38	51:17	379, 404
53:7, 8	111	3:6-8	273	51:25	186
54:5	273	4:23b	151n49	51:33	342
54:6	421	4:24	149	51:36	185
54:9, 10	102	4:28	152	51:39, 57	145n42
60:1-22	115	5:14	245	51:42-44	185
60:2	185n14	6:9	344	**Lamentations**	
60:3-5a	464	8:3	204	4:21	379
60:6	91n42	10:3-5, 8-9, 11, 14, 15		**Ezekiel**	

1	100	16:8ff.	82	38:16	366
1:1	231, 425	16:15-22	338, 392	38:22-23	379
1:3	226n1	16:15ff.	386n38	39:17-20	427, 428
1:4	61, 233, 263n47	16:22, 36	387	43:2	61
1:5-24	105	16:26, 28, 29	386	45:10	133n21
1:6, 10	107n13	16:45	82	47:1-12	465
1:10, 15-17, 19-21	106	17:5-10	344	47:12	67
1:13	104	17:10	185n16	48	165
1:13, 18	106n11	18:4b, 5, 9b	445	48:1	161
1:15-21	127	19:10-14	344	**Daniel**	236n8
1:26, 27	102	19:12	185n16	1	210n59
1:27	61	20:47-48	185	2, 4, 7, 8, 10-12	124
1:28	62, 102	21:3-5	131n16	2, 4,7, 9, 10-12	474
2:1	57	23	161	2, 7	299
2:9	102	23:1-49	300n36	2:1-11	213
2:9-3:3	230, 237	23:2-21	392	2:1-49	20
2:9-3:4	233n5	23:3ff	386n38	2:28-29	49n2
2:9-3:9	224	23:5-21	338	2:37-45	293n29, 491
2:10	109	23:5ff.	82	2:38	181
2:28	172	23:25	82	2:39, 40	150n47
3:3	226n1, 237	23:25-29	399	2:44	427, 432
3:4	237	27:26	185n16	2:44b	293n29
4:1-17	501	28:12-19	198n44	3:1	234
4:4-6	473n2	32:7	151n49	3:4	114n24
4:5	259	35:1-9	197	3:4, 7, 29, 31	171n77
4:5, 6	241, 245	36	115, 472	3:4, 29	301n35
4:16	133n21, 134n24	36-37	91n42, 429	3:7	107n15
5:2	184	36:8-11	429	4:1	301n35
8:2	61	36:22-23	429	4:1-37	21
8:4-10:22	105	36:24	429	4:19-33	293n29
9:1-11	197	36:24-28	91n42	4:22	181
9:2	353	36:25-28	430	4:24-26	491
10:2, 7	180	37:1-14, 21-22	440n8	4:30	337, 387, 390
10:4	354n2	37:5	261	5:19	114n24, 171n77, 301n35
10:12	106n11	37:15-22	429		
10:20	105	37:22, 24-25	430	5:27	133n21
14:21	122, 140	37:25	91n42	5:30	407n54
15:6	344	37:26-28	439n8	6:25	171n77, 301n35
16	161, 273	38-39	92, 345, 363, 366	7	11, 21, 21n33, 22, 34n47, 35, 124, 225, 230, 232, 233n5, 264, 271, 275, 293,
16, 23	391, 404	38, 39	444, 447		
16:1-43	300n36	38:2-3	444		
16:7	421	38:8, 9	366		

Index of texts

299,
310, 311, 312n52,
380, 449, 363, 377,
477, 485
7:1-8   321
7:1-28   21
7:2, 3   164
7:3   256
7:4   181
7:6, 7   150n47
7:7-8   504
7:7-28   253
7:7   240, 263, 277, 294, 305
7:7, 8, 21   254
7:7, 19-21   275
7:7, 19-25   123
7:7, 24   393, 394
7:8   14, 21, 22, 230n4, 299, 387, 498
7:8, 20   297
7:8, 20, 21   230
7:8, 20, 21, 24b, 25   232
7:8, 11, 24-26   165
7:8, 11, 24-36   166n70
7:8, 20   298, 390
7:8, 21, 24, 25   122
7:8, 21-25   233n5
7:9   61, 451
7:9, 10   22
7:9, 10, 11   450
7:10   116, 451
7:11   11, 22
7:11, 15   397
7:11, 26   296, 314, 427, 432, 499
7:12   22
7:13   22, 54, 57, 60, 229, 233, 263n47, 342, 343, 345, 451
7:13, 14   267
7:13, 27   113
7:13,-17, 26, 27   122
7:14   114, 171n77, 301n35, 345, 399
7:17   277, 311
7:17-18   299n34
7:17-27   293n29, 491
7:18, 27   345
7:20, 25   389
7:20-21   11
7:21   21, 22, 232, 249, 298, 362, 410
7:21, 25   173n78
7:22   232
7:23   299n34, 504
7:24   277, 299, 311, 501, 504
7:24-26   11
7:24b-26   498
7:24c   502
7:25   22, 235, 236n8, 240, 241, 249, 259n43, 283, 298, 313, 314, 506
7:26   34
7:26b   31
7:26, 27   319n58
7:27   22, 53, 83, 301n35
7:27a   31
8   124
8:1-27   21
8:3   113
8:5-8   181
8:5-12   150n47
8:17   62
8:20, 21   299n34
8:26   109
9   9, 21n33, 23, 161, 162, 240, 472
9:2   473n2
9:4-19   23
9:6, 10   236
9:11-14   33
9:11-16   30
9:16   30
9:24   25n36, 25, 26, 30, 32, 32nn43–44, 122n1, 259, 311, 473
9:24-27   24, 122n1, 473
9:24, 27   480
9:25-27   27
9:25a   27
9:25b   28
9:26   29, 172n78
9:26, 27   28, 32
9:26a   28, 30
9:26b   28, 32
9:26c   33
9:27   25n36, 29, 31, 476
9:27a   488n12
9:27b   31, 33
10:1-12:13   21
10:4-11:1   210n59
10:5   61, 102, 353
10:5-6, 16   228
10:6   61, 80
10:13, 20   228
10:13, 21   178
10:15   62
10:16   102, 228
10:21   286
11:2-12:4   277n11
12:1   87, 178, 286
12:2   31n42, 91, 145n42, 436
12:3   322
12:3, 10   321
12:4   21, 109
12:4, 8, 9   501
12:6-7, 11   473n2
12:7   209n58, 235, 236n8, 244, 499

12:7, 11	311n49	8:8	150n48	4:11-14	181
12:9-10	468	8:9	151n49	4:12, & 14	245
12:9	21, 468	9:11-15	91n42, 429	6:1-8	123
12:10	321, 468	**Obadiah**		8:1-23	91n42
12:11	312n52	15a, 16b	446	9:10-10:12	91n42
12:12	312n52, 340n14	**Micah**		11-14	54n9
12:13	145n43, 340, 344n17	4-5	91n42	11:15-17	91
		4:7	329	12	431
Hosea	391, 403	4:9, 10	275	12:3, 10	431
1:2	82, 338, 386n38	5:2, LXX	263	12:7-14:21	429
1:5	127	5:3	279n12	12:10	54, 55n10
2:3	399	6:11	133n21	12:10f.	54
2:16	421	7:8-20	91n42	13:1	431
2:19-20	273	**Nahum**		13:8, 9	184
3:1	82	1:1-8	197	14:1-4	363
3:3-5	386n38	1:6	154	14:1-6	427, 432
10:8	152, 158	**Habakkuk**		14:2	365
11:10	234	3:3	90	14:4	366, 429
13:1	185n16	**Zephaniah**		14:4-11	329
13:12	25	1:2	153n57	14:5	425
13:13	275	1:3	186	14a, 3, 4a	431
Joel		1:14	153, 489	**Malachi**	
1:7, 11	344	1:14a, 16, 18c	153	3:16	451
1:17ff	345	1:15	151n49	3:2	154
2:1, 15	182	3:8	363	3:5	213
2:1-11	200	3:8-20	91n42	4:1, 2a, 3	335
2:3	197	**Haggai**		4:1, 3	156, 446
2:10	150n48	1:15	208n55, 209n55	4:1-3	427, 432
2:11, 31	154	2:6, 7	150n48	**Matthew**	
2:30, 31	151n49	2:6, 21, 22	150	4:8	267
2:31	415	**Zechariah**	363, 364	5:3-10	90n41
2:32	329	1:7	208n55	5:5	115
3	91n42	1:7-11	123	5:17	66
3:2	365, 427, 432, 344	1:17	209n55	5:32	212n64
3:12-16	342, 344	1:18	113	6:20	70
3:13	225	3:1-7	245	7:13	169, 421
3:16	235	3:8-10	246	8:11	421
Amos		4:2, 3	245	8:20	345
1:2	234	4:2-6, 11-14	241	9:24	145n42
3:8	234	4:6, 10	113	10:23	345
6:6	166	4:10	52	10:28	339n12, 446
8:5	133n21	4:11	245	11:15	302

Index of texts

11:19	345	24:13, 14	122	11:9, 10	117
12:8, 32, 40	345	24:14	113, 171	13:6-24	134n25
12:26	295	24:15	236	13:7-20	122
12:39	86	24:15-28	91	13:14-20	91
13:1-23	96	24:21	172, 173n78	13:24	151n49, 155
13:6	345	24:24	316, 498	13:24, 25	151n50
13:13-30	67	24:25	122	13:26	54
13:24-30	73, 165, 293, 395n50	24:25	87n39	14:32	3
		24:27, 30, 44	345	14:62	54
13:30, 42, 50	340	24:29	151nn49–50, 155	15:38	180
13:36-43	73			**Luke**	
13:37, 41	345	24:30	54	1:19, 26	178
13:40-42	425	24:30, 31	365n14	2:1	184
13:43	62	24:30-31	433	2:35	131
16:13	345	24:31	425	4:5	267
16:18	64, 260, 385	24:32	151	4:34	90
16:19	88, 90	24:42-44	468	8:15	92
16:27	425	24:43	86	8:31	441
17:2	62	25:14-28	468	8:52	145n42
17:6	62	25:31	345	9:23	71
17:9, 22	345	25:31-33	425	9:26	425
18:15-18:18	81	25:31-46	82, 449, 455, 468	10:20	87
18:16	241, 247			12:39	87
18:17-18	65	25:41	340	13:35	429
18:18	88	26:24	345	14:28	320
19:9	212n64	26:29	421	15:32	259
19:28	53, 97, 104, 115, 437, 440	26:64	54	18:8	467n34
		27:51	180	21:6	33
20:2	134	28:19-20	310n49	21:8	220
20:22	380	**Mark**		21:8-26	134n25
20:28	114	1:24	89	21:10-24	122
21:9	429	3:11	107n15	21:20	152
23:32, 35, 36, 38	33	4:11	230, 396n51	21:20, 22	33, 30n41
23:37	91	4:34	89	21:20-24	91
23:37, 38	30	5:37	3	21:21, 22	32
24	155	5:39	145n42	21:22	32, 172n78
24:4-6, 11, 23-26	220	7:20-23	213	21:23	152n54
24:4-13	92	8:38	82, 425	21:24	34, 173n78
24:4-28	122	9:32	3	21:25, 26	151n50, 155
24:4, 5	316	9:44	340	21:25a	151n49
24:5-14	134n25	10:45	114	21:26	152
24:10	55n10	11:9	429	21:27	54

22:30	53, 97, 104, 437	14:30	296	26:14	62
23:29, 30	152n54	15:1-8	96	27:1-44	457
23:30	152	15:2	78	**Romans**	
23:43	67, 68n19	16:7, 13	113	1	197
23:44	180	16:11	71, 296	1:4	62
24:50-51	429	16:24, 26	177	1:18	197
John		17:12	437n5	1:18-23	360
1:1	79n28	17:17	471	2:15	81
1:1, 14	345	19:37	55n10	2:28-29	71
1:3	235	20:24	312n51	2:28	71
1:9	90	20:28	79n28	3:21-27	92n44
1:14	117	**Acts**		3:21, 22	145
2:1-11	419	1:9	263n47	4	472
4	173	1:7	501	4:17	216n75
4:10	466	1.9-11	232	4:22-25	171
4:31-34	97	1:9-12	429	5:12-15	114
5:20	90	1:26	437n5	5:18-19	87
5:25	86n38	2:27	90	5:18, 19	145
5:28-29	438	3:14	90	5:19	92n44
6:37	87n38	4:27	90	5:25	86n38
6:39, 44, 54	438	4:30	90	6:3	86n38
6:40	438	5:31	27	6:4-13	442n13
6:46	319	6:5	76	6:23	446
6:47	90n41	8:1	31	6:37	86n38
6:51	90n41 6:54	9:16	71	8:19-21	115, 460
	90n41	12:7, 22:18	467n34	8:28, 29	169
6:69	89	13:7	498	11:11-29	431
8:44	71	13:48	87	11:17	160n65, 162, 163
9:24	337n7	13:50	71		
10:7-9	90n41	14:2-5	71	11:17-24	26n38, 473
10:35	117n26, 445, 471, 472	14:19	71	11:18	59, 162
		14:27	90	11:25	34
11:9	209n57	15	123n3	11:25-36	91n42
11:11-12	145n42	16:14	79	11:26	447
11:43ff.	52	17:5-9	71	11:26-29	429
12:13	171	17:18	212n63, 218	11:29	429
12:31	71, 267, 296	18:1-21	66	11:33-36	235
12:34	342	19:23-20:1	65	12:1	286
14:6	177	20:28-31	65	12:1, 2	49, 54, 165, 331
14:15-19	113	20:28	79n28		
14:15-21	97	20:29	66	12:1-2	144n41
14:16-18	67	25:4	467n34	12:19	145

Index of texts

13:3, 4	250n26	15:18-23	89	5:14	53
13:5	82	15:19-28	52	5:19-21	213
14:2-3	81	15:19, 22-25	169n75	6:11	6
14:20	82	15:20	70	6:12, 13	123n3
14:22	81	15:22-23	433	6:16	160n65, 430
16:20	467n34	15:24-28	267, 456	**Ephesians**	
16:25-26	396	15:25	281	1:11	126
1 Corinthians		15:27	281	1:13	161, 165
1:8	, 60n14	15:51	145n42, 396	1:14	164
1:24	117	15:52	182	1:22	281
2:6-16	96	15:53	445	2:2	296
2:10	82	16:9	90	2:8, 9	170
3:16	58, 269, 300	**2 Corinthians**		2:11-22	238, 473
3:16, 17	238, 506	1:14	60n14	2:12-19	160n65
3:17	78	1:21-22	161, 165	2:14, 19	162
3:27	83	1:22	163	2:15-16a	240
5:1-13	66	2:2	273	2:19-22	462n30
5:2	80f.	2:12	90	4:30	161, 165
5:4-5	80	3:1	66	5	213
5:5	60n14	3:5-11	81	5:2	179
5:54-56	62	3:18	62	5:3-12	213
6:2	53, 84, 97, 104	4:4	96, 296	5:14	86n38
6:2, 3	115, 437	4:5-6	62	5:22-33	458n28
6:2-3	83	4:6	96	5:25-32	426
6:3	440	4:14	52n7, 169n75	6:10	117
8:8	81	5:1-10	169n75	**Philippians**	
8:13	81	5:10	194	1:29	71
9:25	92	6:10	70	2:5-7	57
10:20	212	6:16	238	2:7-8	60
10:20, 21	218	8:23	61	3:9	421
10:28-29	81	11:1-15	123n3	3:11	456n27
10:28	81	11:12-15	66	3:20	89, 93, 459
11:10	61	**Galatians**		4:3	87
11:29-30	82	1:6-9	123n3, 375	**Colossians**	
11:30	145n42	2:9	3, 93	1:15-18	95
12:10	295	3:1-5	123n3	1:16	235
12:12-26	58	3:6,7	145	1:18	52
14:29	66	4:5	160n65	1:19	79n28
14:32	81	4:23	93	2:1-8	123n3
14:37	81	4:26	273, 329	2:8-10	497
15	, 62	5	213	2:9	79n28, 345
15:5	312n51	5:5	92n44	2:16, 17	285n21

4:3	90	3:15	93	**James**	
4:13	95	4:1	219	1:12	72, 92
1 Thessalonians		5:6	86n38	4:4	82
2:2	60n14	5:8	497	5:16b	180
2:16	25	6:16	445, 448	**1 Peter**	
2:19	92, 169n75	**2 Timothy**		2:4-5	53
3:13	169n75, 425, 426n11	2:12	97, 104, 437	2:9-10	54
		2:12, 13	497	2:12	337n7
4:13-18	169n75	2:19	165, 167, 174	3:16	81
4:14	52n7, 145n42	2:20-21	73	3:21	81
4:15	89	3:5	497	5:4	92
4:15-17	365n14, 438	3:16	471	5:13	338, 391
4:16	182, 456n27	4:6-8	169n75	**2 Peter**	
4:16-17	433	4:8	72, 92	1:10	198
4:17	174, 232, 415, 417	**Titus**		1:19-21	471
		2:13	340	2:1	497
5:1-11	365	**Hebrews**		2:9	25
5:2, 4	87n39	1	197	2:12	446
2 Thessalonians		1:8	79n28	2:15	75n27
1:7	425	2:8	281	2:17-19	198
1:9	117	2:9	117	3:7, 10	335, 340
2:3-12	91, 314	2:10	126	3:8	436n3
2:3	230n4, 250, 298, 506	4:9	286n21	3:8-14	169n75
		4:12	62	3:9	82
2:3, 4	14, 498	6:6	255	3:10	87n39, 150, 156
2:4	296, 297, 301, 313, 387, 389, 390, 507	7:26-8:2	177	3:13	115, 455
		7:26-28	269	**1 John**	
		8:12	406	1:18, 22	249n24
2:7	390	9:4	76	2:1, 2	177
2;8	499, 508	9:5	106n10	2:18	91, 230n4, 505
2:9	295	10:19-22	180	2:18, ESV	321n62
2:9, 10	364	10:34	70	2:18, 22	90, 2:20, 497
3:14-15	81	11	169, 472	2:20	89
1 Timothy		11:10	93	2:23	497
1:1, 9	3	11:39	89	4:1-4	123n3
1:11	186n18	11:40	418	4:3	321n62, 497
1:16, 20	199	12:2	28	5:4-5	83
1:19	101	12:5-11	197	**2 John**	
1:20	81	12:6	78	7	249n24, 497
2:5	219	12:7-11	71	**Jude**	
2:6	114, 498	12:22	93, 329, 417	3-16	76
2:12	345	12:23	417, 462n30	4	497

Index of texts

7	336	101, 124n5, 125n6, 235
9	178	
11	75n27	1:20 85, 242
14-15	425	1:46 104
Revelation	350	2 197
1	36, 195, 229n2, 232	2-3 37, 47, 52n6, 62, 123n3
1:1	37n48, 49n1, 467	2, 3 484
1:1-2	166n72	2:1-3:22 63
1:1-3	47, 48	2:1-7 64
1:1-3:22	47	2:1-22:5 36
1:2	1, 421, 474	2:3 6
1:2, 3	195	2:5, 16 197
1:2, 9	421	2:7 68n19
1:3	1, 475	2:7, 11, 17, 29 302
1:4	63, 178	2:8 62, 66, 113
1:4-8	47, 50	2:8-11 68, 69
1:5	2, 56	2:10 66, 93
1:6	2, 437	2:11 460
1:7	2, 55n10, 84, 233	2:12-13 66
1:8	52, 298	2:12-17 73, 74
1:9	7	2:12, 16 131
1:9-3:22	487	2:13 7, 66, 296, 437
1:9-20	47, 56, 57, 59	2:13, 3:8 497
1:10	60n14, 101, 473	2:14-16, 20-24 123n3
1:10-11, 19	424	2:15 67, 75
1:10-20	36	2:18 339n11
1:11	186n18, 460	2:18-29 78
1:11, 19	398	2:19 197
1:11-3:22	62	2:20-23 67
1:12, 13, 20	242	2:24 82
1:12-16	1, 161	2:26 97
1:12-18	62, 63	2:26, 27 437, 440n9
1:13	229, 353	2:27 83, 280
1:13-16	57, 228	3:1 52
1:14	339n11	3:1b 61
1:14-15	77, 80	3:1-6 85
1:16	131	3:3 468
1:16, 20	199, 274n5	3:4 173
1:17	62, 107	3:5 87
1:18	70, 113, 229	3:6, 13, and 22 302
1:18-29	77	3:7-13 88, 89
1:19	7, 36, 63, 100,	3:7 55n10

3:8	7
3:9	71
3:11	7
3:14-22	94
3:16, 18	197
3:18	70, 87, 339n11
3:19	71
3:19-21	86n38
3:21	108, 437
4	210n59
4-19	161
4-22	9
4:1	7, 36, 37n48, 39, 63, 108, 122, 124, 147, 161, 164, 278, 293n29, 312n52, 398, 425, 467
4:1-5:19	210n59
4:1-22:6	62
4:1-22:15	476
4:1-22:17	494
4:2	100, 100n1
4:2-11	352
4:3	462
4:4	87, 172, 272
4:4, 6	418
4:5	39, 52, 113, 178, 180, 339n11
4-5a	279n12
4:6	107, 127
4:6b	172
4:8	52, 145, 199
4:8b	106
4:9-10	62
4:9-11	116
4:9	62
4:10	103n6, 172, 267
5:1	226n1
5:1-22:5	39
5:2	226n1, 227, 232
5:5	234
5:6	52, 178
5:8	172

5:8, 10, 14 107n15	6:12-17 188	7-17 169, 283
5:9 114n24, 171n77	6:13 199	7:25 299
5:9-10 243, 345	7 105, 493	8:1 125, 147
5:9-14 332	7:1 100n1, 147, 177, 490	8:2 353
5:10 53, 83, 103, 171, 246	7:1-7 174, 239, 239n11, 490	8:3,4 206
5:12 56, 116	7:1-8 71, 160, 174, 199, 321	8:3-5 161
5:12-13 56	7:1-17 147	8:4 206
5:13 117n26	7:2 332	8:5 177, 354
5:14 166, 188	7:2-8 346	8:5, 7 339n11
6:1-2 287	225, 301, 322, 486, 493	8:5b 177n3
6:1-9:21 17	7:3 52n6, 93, 197	8:6-9:19 178
6:1-16 92	7:3, 4 199, 319	8:6-9:21 353
6:1-17 188	7:4 171	8:6-21 92
6:1, 3, 5, 6, 7 105	7:4-8 161, 346, 476	8:7 180, 186, 339n11
6:2 422, 425	7:5-8 165	8:8, 9 369
6:2-3 299	7:7-12 266	8:8-9 164, 357
6:4 199, 343n16	7:8-17 490	8:8b, 9 361
6:8 62, 131	7:8, 21-25 233n5	8-9, 16 160
6:9 52n6, 148, 161, 343	165n69, 169, 170, 417n1	8:9b 177n3
6:9-11 284, 286, 437	7:9 418	8:10 199, 361, 371
6:9-17 72	7:9, 10 417	8:12 188
6:10 89, 418	7:9-17 52, 160, 162, 163, 224, 484, 490, 494	8-13 160, 495
6:11 87, 145, 344, 486, 490	7:9-72 163	8:14 42
6:12-7:17 484n3	7:10 170	8-16 174
6:12-13 186, 449n20	7:11-17 177	8:10 199
6:12-14 233, 379	7:11 105, 107n15	9 211n60, 222
6:12-17 147, 178n4, 188, 196, 281, 484, 488, 489, 492n20	7:12 170	9:1 256, 441
6:12 264, 502	7:13-14 87	9:1-2 435
6:13 199, 281n15	7:13-17 301	9:1-3 457
6:13-14 488	7:13 170	9:1-11 265
6:14 380	7-14	9:1-27 21
6:15-17 148	7:14 87, 92, 163, 164, 170, 171, 172n78, 197, 331, 490	9:3-5 203
6:15 158		9:4 204, 486
6:17 489		9:5-6 204
6:10 117		9:7-10 198
6:12-1 196		9:7-11 200
6:12-13 186	7:15b, 16 170	9:9-13 161
		9:12 42, 193, 194, 195, 265, 495
		9:13-11:14 484n3
		9:13-21 247, 265
		9:14 206, 213, 362

Index of texts 525

9:14, 15	216	233n5, 248		11:15b-19	231
9:14-19	206	11:1	161, 247	11:16-19	193
9:15	206, 211	11:1, 19	161	11:17	199
9:16b	211n60	11:2	162, 247, 299,	12	16, 273
9:17-19	206	426, 439, 447, 501		12-13	233n5, 380, 485
9:17b	211	11:2, 3, 11	209n58	12-14	193, 224, 484
9:19	216	11:3 52n6, 236n8, 245,		12, 13, 17	310
9:20-21	206, 211, 217	246, 259n43, 283,		12:1-6	283, 294
9:20	219, 220	299, 310, 501		12:1-13:18	231
9:21	220, 221, 418	11:3-6	242	12:1-17	224, 287
9	102, 203	11:3-10	291	12:1	273, 288, 304,
9:4	204	11:5	317	385, 425, 427	
9:5-6	204	11:6, 14	299	12:1, 4	199
9:12	100	11:7 52n6, 254, 395,		12:2	279n13
9:15	206	410, 441		12:2, 5	279
9:17-19	206	11:7, 8	146	12, 13	233n5, 271
9:19	216	11:7-9	388	12:3 275, 281, 288n22,	
9:20	219	11:7-10	92, 437	294, 297, 303, 310,	
10:1 110, 226n1, 229n2,		11:8	254	313	
263n47, 403		11:9 114n24, 261, 334		12:3b	275, 393
10:1-11:13	264	11:9, 11	171n77	12:4	303
10:1-14:20	223	11:10	184	12:4, 5	260
10:1-3	228	11:11	100	12:4a	278
10:2	263n48	11:12	232, 269, 340	12:4b-5a	278
10:3b	230	11:13	224, 263	12:5	209n58
10:4	230	11:14 193, 195, 224,		12:5 209n58, 279, 304,	
10:4, 8	340	229 248, 265, 352,		440n9	
10:5-6	235	490, 495		12:5a	279
10:5-6, 16	228	11:14, 15	231, 234n5	12:5b	280
10:6	62, 170, 267	11:14, 15	231	12:5c	280
10:7	229	11:15 92, 195, 383, 490		12:6	244, 311, 389,
10:7b	399	11:15-18	224, 490	501	
10:8-11	229	11:15-19	149n45, 484	12:6, 14	209n58, 386
10:9-11	231	11:15b	484	12:7-9	229n2
10-14 226n1, 493, 496		11:15b-18	269	12:7	178, 236n8
10:11	114n24	11:15b-19	231	12:7, 14	236n8
10:13, 20	228	11:16-18	272	12:9 139n34, 304, 363	
11	249	11:16	103n6	12:9, 12	495
11-12	236n9	11:17	52, 199, 267	12:9, 13	295
11:1-2	268	11:19 161, 224, 268n52,		12:10-12	290, 291n27
11:1-6	247	272, 490		12:10	283, 340, 418
11:1-13	224, 232,	11:19b	177n3	12:11	146, 284

12:12 101n2	13:11 315, 364, 375	14:18 161
12:12b 283	13:12 318	14:20 344
12:13-14 283	13:12, 14 281, 321n61	14b, 17, 18 342
12:13, 15 304	13:13 318	15-16 193, 287
12:14 244, 304, 500, 501	13:14-18 352	15-18 225
	13:14 145n43	15:1-4 72
12-16 148	13:14b 317	15:1 194n37, 195, 265, 281, 362, 378, 495
12:16 304, 500	13:14b-17 324	
12:17 304, 331, 391, 391n45, 421	13:15 146, 317, 410, 437	15:2 165, 339n11
		15:3 145, 199
12:17b 293	13:16, 17 165	15:5 100n1
13 147, 249, 394	13:17 318	15:5, 8 161
13-17 287	13 229	15:6 61, 87
13:1-10 21n33, 22, 38, 224, 303, 305, 314, 427	14:1-5 52, 72, 225, 302, 346	15:7 62, 105, 180, 358
		15, 16 195
	14:1-7 231	16 408
13:1-18 224	14:1 93, 161	16:1-17 161
13:1 186, 256, 285, 289, 304, 305, 311, 394, 441, 457, 500, 502	14:1, 3 171, 476	16:1-21 92
	14:2 61, 162	16:1 180, 340, 358
	14:3-5 285	16:2 165, 367
	14:3 103, 105	16:3 357, 361, 370
13:1, 3 321n61, 389	14:4 87, 145, 146, 331, 437	16:4-6 361
13:2 271, 389, 293, 500		16:5 52
13:3 304, 343, 388, 393	14:4, 5 165	16:5-7 359
13:4 458	14:5 331	16:7 161, 199
13:5 22, 259n43, 290, 310, 374, 501, 508	14:6-13 225	16:8b, 9 373
	14:6-20 327	16:9 337n7
	14:6 52n6, 114n24, 171n77	16:12-16 484n3
13:5, 6 389		16:12 375, 427, 432
13:5-8 500	14:8-13 232	16:12a 362
13:5-9 501	14:8 338, 379, 390	16:13 364, 507
13:5-18 91	14:8, NIV 404	16:13-14 377
13:5a, 6 313	14:8, 9, 17 333	16:14-16 345
13:6 298	14:8, 10 358, 380	16:14 281, 363
13:6 498	14:10 379	16:15 87n39, 468
13:7 22, 114n24, 171n77, 224, 334, 388, 437, 507	14:11 418, 444	16:16 378n34, 427, 432
	14:12 187	
	14:13 143, 344n17	16:17-21 38, 379, 429
13:8 87, 184	14:14-16 232	16:17 356n4, 378
13:9 114n24	14:14-20 225, 232, 347	16:18 149n46, 380
13:10b 301	14:14 54, 233, 263n47	16:19 254, 338, 358, 380
13:11-17 224, 427	14:17-20 343	
13:11-18 503		

Index of texts

16:19-20	378	
17	38, 161, 249, 300n36, 402, 403, 412	
17-18	377	
17, 19	195	
17:1-6	383, 400	
17:1-14	397	
17:1-18	400	
17:1-18:20	429	
17:1-19:10	378n34	
17:1	61, 320n63, 398, 418	
17:1, 5, 18	379	
17:1, 15	397	
17:3-14	91	
17:3	400	
17:3, 7	397	
17:3, 12	394	
17:4	402, 405	
17:5	338	
17:6	146, 411, 437	
17:7-13	383, 400	
17:8	87, 186, 296, 338	
17:8, 11	296, 393, 293n47, 297	
17:10	275, 276, 288, 317, 500	
17:10-14	3408	
17:11	294, 296, 304, 343, 362	
17:12	394, 401, 502	
17:13-14	399	
17:13	502	
17:13a	394	
17:14-18	384, 400	
17:14	502	
17:15-18	397	
17:15	61, 114n24, 171n77, 185, 320n6, 334, 398n52, 502	
17:15a	186	
17:16-18	508	
17:16	394, 399, 401, 408, 502	
17:17	398	
17:18	184, 254, 338, 380, 503	
18	38, 358, 384, 412, 414, 503	
18:1	100n1, 406	
18:1-8	401	
18:2	404n53	
18:2, 10, 21	338	
18:3	408, 410	
18:3a	402	
18:4-5	402	
18:4	105, 340, 509	
18:7b, 18:8	405	
18:9-19	412	
18:9-24	401	
18:9, 10, 15	408	
18:10, 16, 18, 19, 21	254	
18:13, 24	437	
18:17, 19	358	
18:21	110, 226n1, 232	
18:22-23	410	
18:23	418	
18:24	410	
19:1-4	428	
19:1-8	72, 210n59, 266, 415, 484, 490	
19:1-9	412	
19:1-10	415, 493	
19:1-16	127n8	
19:1-20	66	
19:1-21	415	
19:1	61, 100n1	
19:2	146	
19:3	444	
19:4-5	186	
19:4	103, 107n15	
19:5	428, 440n9	
19:6	61, 503	
19:6, 7	428	
19:7	273	
19.8	87, 145	
19:9	68n19	
19:10	66, 420	
19:11-13, 19	363	
19:11-16	412, 415	
19:11-18	92, 415	
19:11-19	364	
19:11-21	366, 378n34, 417, 428, 490	
19:11	145	
19:12	93, 339n11	
19:14	87, 210n59	
19:15	62, 280, 380	
19:15, 21	131	
19:17-19	415	
19:17, 18	195	
19:18	87	
19:19-20	410	
19:19-21	363, 439n8	
19:19	407	
19:20-21	415, 427, 436, 503	
19:20	165, 281, 340, 343, 364, 393, 408, 444, 448, 450n21, 503	
19:21	62	
20	306n41, 428, 442n14, 477, 484	
20:1-4	432	
20:1-6	84, 415	
20:2	22, 283, 363	
20:2, 3	435	
20:3	100, 162, 239n11, 256, 426	
20:4	22, 52, 53, 83, 97, 104, 115, 146, 165, 345, 415, 437, 456n27	

20:4-6	53n8	22:6-21	36	2 Apocalypse of Baruch	
20:4-15	415	22:7, 12, 20	468	1.4, 5; 78.5	30n41
20:4, 6	83	22:8	107n15	10:2; 11:1; 33:2; 67:7;	
20:5	22, 222, 438	22:10-11	468	79:1	391n45
20:5, 12	444	22:11	468, 469n36	**2 Esdras/4 Ezra**	
20:6	72, 83, 437	22:12-15	469	2:42, 43	329
20:6, 14	460	22:13-14	469	3:1-2:28:31; 16:44,	
20:7-9	415	22:13	56, 62	46	390n45
20:7	22	22:14	2, 145	5:4, 5	151n49
20:8	171, 444	22:15	461	11:37-46	234
20:10	340, 415, 444,	22:16	84, 110	12:3132	110
446, 447, 460n29		22:16, 20	474	*Apocalypse of Elijah*	
20:10, 14, 15	199	22:17	469	3:4	426n11
20:11-15	415, 450n21,	22:18-19	471, 475	*Apocalypse of Moses*	
455		22:19	1	13:2-5	67n19
20:11	22	22:20	421	40:1-41:3	67n19
20:12, 15	87	**APOCRYPHA**		41:1	67n19
20:12a	415	**2 Maccabees**		43.2-3	68n19
20:12b-13	415	2:4-7	76	*Joseph and Aseneth*	
20:13-14	62	**Judith**		16:17-19	210
20:14	72, 448	2:20, 24	210	*Jubilees*	
20:14, 15	450	**Sirach**		1:28	329
21, 22	487	28:25	133n21	*Psalms of Solomon*	
21:1-22:6	22	37:24b, 38:1-3	246n19	8:14-20	338
21:1	115, 458	42:2-4	133n21	*Sibylene Oracles*	
21:1b	452	**Tobit**		3:663-668	338
21:2, 27	145	8:20	419	5:143, 159	338, 390n45
21:3	340	12:12-15	178	5:162-165	123n4
21:8	72, 340	**PSEUDEPIGRAPHA**		*Testament of Abraham*	
21:9	273	*1 Enoch*		B *7:7, 8*	273
21:9-22:5	461	9:3	178	*Testament of Dan*	
21:9-27	457	46:1	61	*6:2*	178
21:12	165	24:4-25:6	67n19	*Testament of Levi*	
21:14	165	68:2-5	178	*2:7*	104n9
21:18b-19	456	89:76	178	3:3	426n11
21:20	456	90:.29	329	3:5	178
21:22	199	102:3	426n11	15:10-11	67n19
21:27	87, 459, 462n30	*2 Enoch*		*Testament of Moses*	
22:1-5	466	3:2	104n9	2:4	150n48
22:2	67	17	426n11	10:4	152
22:4	93	20:2-8	178	10:5	151n49
22:5	345			**CLASSICAL AND**	

Index of texts

HELLENISTIC LITERATURE

Aristophanes
PHEE 10 — 76

Aulus Hertius
Bellum Alexandrinus
1 — 128n9

Cicero
Epistulai ad Familiares
3.5 — 95

Dion Cassius
41.43 — 498
71.36-72.34 — 132n19

Dionysius of Halicarnassus
Antiquities Romanae
1.3 — 184n13

Herodotus
2.28, 4.53 — 187n21

Homer
Illiad
700.880 — 128n9

Josephus
Antiquities
6.3.3-9 — 30n41
4.6.6 — 75n27

Lactanitius
Institutiones Divinae
1.1 — 157n60

Livy
Historiae ab Urbe Condita
6.1 — 276n8
6.1-2 — 500
26.16,40 — 500n4
37.41, 38.21 — 128n9

Lucian
3.185 — 128n9

Ovid
Fasti
2.683 — 184n13

Metamorphosis
7.187 — 177n3

Petrus Siculus
13 — 140n35

Philo
De Vita Mosis
1.53-55 — 75

Pindar
Pythian Odes
5.54 — 128n9

Pliny
Historia Naturalis
18:10 — 135n26

Plutarch
Aristides
25 — 76
Life of Pyrrhus
6.43 — 128n9

Strabo
Geographus
12.578 — 95

Tacitus
Annals
1.1 — 276n8

Trebellius Pollius
Vita Clsudius
100.16 — 128n9

DEAD SEA SCROLLS

Rule of the Community
6:8-13 — 31n42

Pesher on Habakkuk,
1QpHab, 2:10ff. — 338

RABBINIC LITERATURE

Babylonian Talmud
Soṭa
35a — 72n25

Midrash
Psa 137.1, 8 — 391

Midrash Pesaḥim
30.191b — 67n19

Midrash Rabbah
Deut 1:4 — 274n5
Exod 15:6 — 274n5
Num 2:13 — 274n5
Num 7:10 — 391n45

Targum on Deuteronomy
33:6 — 72n25

Targum on Isaiah
22:14 — 72n25
65:6 — 72n25
65:15 — 72n25

Targum on Jeremiah
51:39 — 72n25
51:57 — 72n25

EARLY CHRISTIAN DOCUMENTS

Chrisostom
Homilies 4 on
2 Thessalonians — 251

Epistle of Barnabas
4:3-6 — 123n4

Eusebius
Book of Martyrs
Bks. 1-8 — 146n44
Ecclesiastical History
8.1 — 146n44
9.6 — 192n35
10.1 — 155
10.4 — 273n2

Gregory
Epistles
1.6, Ep. 30 — 307

Hippolytus
Refutation of all heresies
7.36 — 67

Ignatius
Smyrneans 1.1 — 70

Iranaeus
1.26.3 — 67
3.11.1 — 67

Martyrdom of Polycarp
  12:2   71n22
Origen
  Numeros Homiliae
RHA

  20.1   75, 75n27

ENGLISH LITERATURE

Shakespeare
  Hamlet
    Act 2, Sc. 2:9   177n3

Index of Subjects

20th century commentators 207n53
42 months 241, 247, 248, 260n43
95 theses 262
180 days 262
666, Number of the beast 319
1260 days 236n8, 240, 241, 244, 247, 249, 257, 260n43, 283, 298, 308, 502
1260 years 247, 248, 290, 309, 502
1260 years, Beginning of 308
1260 years, Expiration of 382
1600 stadia 344
144,000 103, 147, 161, 162, 163, 165, 171, 174, 199, 225, 330, 331, 346, 391, 476, 494
Abaddon 200
Abaside Caliph 202
Abasides 202
Abel 143, 145
Abomination of desolation 33n46
Abominations, Prohibited 388
Abrahamic covenant 171
Abubeker, Saracen commander 203
Abyss 197, 198, 199, 256, 321n63, 435, 436n2, 441, 457
Abyss, Locked and sealed 441
Abyss, Shaft of the 199
Accusative of reference 210
Adam, Fall of 457, 460
Adulterous church 392
Adulterous prostitute 420
Adultery 212n64, 389, 408
Aerial warfare 381
Africa, Roman 142
Africa, Vandals from 190

Age to come 143, 169, 232, 346, 422, 447, 449, 453, 459, 462, 464, 490
Ages of the ages 107
Ahaz, King of Israel 207
Air, Poured out into the 378
Alaric the Goth 189
Alaric's campaigns 190n26
Albigenses 259, 368, 372, 478
Albigenses. Churches of 252, 258
Alcasar (Jesuit priest) 8
Alexander the Great 181
Alexander Severus, Emperor 137n31, 138, 139n33
Alexander VI, Pope 368
Alexandria 141
Alexandrian allegorizing 478
Alexandrian Judaism 493
Alexandrian School 5
Alexandrinus (Gk. ms.) 127n7, 302
Ali Pasha 375
Allegorical interpretation 106n12, 123n3, 476, 477, 493
Alleman-Franks 504
Allemani kingdom 311
Allusive reference 182n12, 386n39
Almansor, Caliph 205, 213
Alpha and Omega 55, 56, 459, 460, 469
Altar, Measurement of 237, 239
Altar of incense 161, 206, 207, 208
Altar of sacrifice 144, 146, 176, 179, 180, 207, 238, 247, 359
Ambrose Anspert 248
Amillennialism 306n41, 329n3, 436n2, 437n6, 442nn12, 13, 452n25, 472, 477
Analogical language 185

Ancient of Days 450, 451
Angel, Mighty 110
Angel of the Abyss 198n44, 200
Angelic beings 103, 105, 107, 170, 172
Angelic choir 116
Angelic Messengers, Three 225
Angelic multitude, Celebration of 490
Angels (messengers), As stars 61
Angels, Myriads of 169
Angels of the presence 178
Angels of the seven churches 61
Anglican Church 377, 480
Anglo-Catholic Oxford Movement 9
Anglo-Saxon kingdom 311
Anglo-Saxons 504
Anointed Prince 24
Anointed Ruler, Identity of 29
Anthropomorphic language 102, 318n58, 450
Antichrist 4, 7, 8, 11, 15, 54, 110, 122, 224, 225, 257, 296, 318, 320, 328, 364, 373, 380, 392, 418, 473, 477, 498, 500, 505
   As Babylon 390, 401
   As coming 230n4
   As different 504
   As Nero 481
   Boasting of 387
   Character of 307
   Deception of 338
   Destruction of 379, 423
   Disassociation from 405
   Disclosure of 333
   Fall of 347, 383
   False prophet 321, 503
   Final judgments against 42
   Forces of 266
   Forerunner of 201
   Future Pope 479
   Harlot/prostitute 385, 400
   In God's temple 300
   Merchandizing of 408
   Pagan Roman 479
   Persecution of "heretics" 506
   Powers of 427
   Prophecy of 500
   Reign of 236
   Rider on the beast 383, 400, 502
   Rise of 42
   Roman 124n4
   Roman Papal 8, 14
   Symbolism of 384, 400
   Temporal power of 362
   Transtemporal principle 478
   Victory of Christ over 42, 122
   War with 122, 230, 231, 340, 395, 477, 500
   Worship of 344
Antichrist doctrine, Jewish roots 166n70
Antichrist's power 247, 388
Antichrist's power, Fall of 400, 403, 415
Antichrist (term) 230n4, 249n24
Antichrist theme 230n4
Antichristian philosophy 369
Antiochus IV Epiphanes 244n15
Antipas 6
Antiphonal song 116
Anti-Reformation movement 377
Antitypical altar 179n8, 247
Antitypical ark of the covenant 269
Antitypical court of Israel 268
Antitypical fulfillment 207
Antitypical Israel 274, 274n4, 278
Antitypical Jerusalem 247
Antitypical symbolism 273
Antitypical temple 240, 247, 269
Antonian Constitution 136
Aoocalyptic language 155
Aorist, Ingressive Gk. language) 49n2
Apocalypses, Extra-biblical 494
Apocalyptic 16, 101
Apocalyptic symbolism 15, 16, 196, 474

Index of Subjects 533

Celestial and terrestrial	15
Apocalyptic writings	100, 101, 122
Distinctive features of	15
Dream-vision style	20
Extra-biblical	15, 19, 113, 494
First century A.D.	1
Nature of	9, 15
Structure of	160
Pseudepigraphic literature	19
Apollyon	200
Apostasy of last days	154, 220
Apostate church	147, 240, 248, 256, 385
Apostate harlot	161
Apostle Paul	269
Apostles, False	66
Apostles, Twelve	102
Apostolic Church	
Witness of	6
Apostolic church	481
Apostolic Fathers	69
Apostolic tradition	69
Application, Practical	492
Aquila	65
Arab Muslim nations	375
Arabia	198, 199
Arcadius	159n64
Archangels	178
Archers	128
Arian barbarians	291
Arian Christians	189n24
Arian controversy	291
Arian emperors	304
Arianism, Influx of	291, 304
Arianism purged	291
Ark of the covenant	106n10, 161, 268
Armageddon as figurative	365
Armageddon, Battle of	363, 364, 365, 376, 439n8
Armies allied with beast	427
Armies of heaven	425
Arnaldistae	258
Arnobius	142
Artaxerxes, King of the Persians	
Decree of	27n39
Artemis (goddess)	65
Ascension of Jesus	280n14
Asceticism	123n3
Asher (Israelite tribe)	166
Asia, Churches of	67
Asia Minor	51, 216, 289, 375
Moslem conquest of	202
Asia, Roman province	37, 51, 58, 65, 66, 70, 142, 284n18
Asian churches	58
Assyrian power	375
Astronomical symbolism	151n49, 187, 196, 449, 488
Athanasius (296-372)	248
Atheism	373, 376
Atheistic communism	376
Atheistic humanism	367
Atonement	113, 144, 207
Atonement, Limited	114
Atonement, Ransom concept	114
Atonement, Substitutionary	243
Atonement, True nature of	247
Atoning death	170
Attila, King of Mongol Huns	191
Augustine, Bp. of Hippo	191, 306n42, 472
Augustinian amillennialism	442n12, 452n25, 479
Augustus, Emperor	288
Aurelian, Emperor	288n22
Aurelianus, Emperor	141
Austria	373
Babylon	166n73, 186, 255, 378, 403, 499
As symbol for Rome	186, 338
As Papal empire	380
Call to come out of	405, 502
Destruction of	151n51, 406, 412
Fall of	42, 110, 387, 401, 408, 410

Index of Subjects

King of 198n44
Symbol for Rome 378
Babylon the Great 358, 387, 390
Bagdad 205, 213, 216
Balaam, Teaching of 67
Balance scales 133, 135, 136, 137, 138
Ballistic missiles 379
Baptism, Infant 123n3
Baptismal regeneration 123n3, 167
Bar Cochba 129
Barbarian conquest of Rome 189
Barbarian conquests 188n22
Barbarian invasion of Rome
Barbarian invasions 129, 188, 189, 190, 191, 201, 203
Barbarian nations of Roman Europe 401
Barbarians 132, 141, 152n52, 190n26, 218, 304
Barley 134
Basic human instincts 213
Battle of Armageddon 415, 426, 430, 431, 439, 440n10, 444
Battle of Gog and Magog 444n15
Battle of Jericho 182
Battle of Lepanto 266
Battle of Milvian Bridge 289
Battle of Navarino 375
Battle of Sadowa 309, 507
Bavarian kingdom 311
Bavarians 504
Beast from the abyss 147, 220n63, 224, 256, 296, 364
  Out of the mouth of 363
  Ten horns of 50, 499
  Throne of 374
  With a lion-like mouth 293
  With bear-like feet 293
Beast from the earth 224, 293, 303, 315, 322, 323, 364, 396, 503
  Lamb-like character 315

Beckwith 103n8
Beghards 259
Beginning and the end 459, 469
Believer/s
  Destiny of 51
  Responsibility to witness 51
Beloved City 443
Belt of finest gold 228
Ben Ezra (pseud. of Emanuel Lacunza) 480
Benedict III, Universal Bishop 505
Berengarians 253
Berengaud 249
Berkshire Christian College 12-13
Betrothal period 428
Biblarídion 233
Bible as Word of God 471
Bible, Restoration to laity 478
Bible translation 262
Bible-believing scholars 471
Biblical apocalyptic 181
Biblical doctrine, Essentials of 395n50
Biblical hermeneutics 471
Birth of the male child 304
Bishop/s
  Authority of 291
  Civil authority of 305, 477
  Exaltation of 201
  Office of 305, 477
  Prestege of 477
  Universal 308
Bishop of Rome 305, 306n41, 477
Black (color) 133
Black horse era 138
Blessed hope 340
Blood of Abel 143
Blood of the Lamb 114, 286, 331
Bodies and souls of men 408
Body 145n42
Body like chrysolite 228
Bohemian Brethren 368

Index of Subjects 535

Bohemians	259	Buying or selling with heretics	
Boniface, Bp. of Rome	201	forbidden	258, 321, 325
Boniface III, Pope	308, 507	Byzantine bishop	306
Boniface VIII	249n22	Byzantine Church	477
Book of life	302, 450	Eschatology of	477
Book of Revelation	1	Byzantium	192, 290, 305
Border warfare	132	Calamity	140
Bosrah, Capital of Edom	423	Caliphate	202
Bost (historian)	258	Calixtines	368
Boston Bible School	13, 13n19	Calling and election	198
Bottomless pit	203	Cannon, Enormous	214, 215
Bow	127, 128	Canon law	219
Bower, Archibald	505n10	Captain of the Lord's armies	228
Bowl prophecies	485	Caracalla, Emperor	136, 137n30
Bowl sequence	175	Cardinal Manning	313
Bowls as third woe	495	Cardinal Pallavicini, R. C. historian	259
Bowls, Era of the	401	Carinus, Emperor	132
Bowls filled with wrath of God	354	Carlovingian revolution	249n21
Bowls, Golden incense	114	Carnelian	102
Bowls, Saucer-shaped	354	Carthage, Taken by Vandals	191
Bowls, Seven	194n37, 195	Carthaginian Wars	134n25
Brass censers	179n7	Casting spells	390
Brethren movement	9	Cathari (sect dissident from the Roman	
Bride, Holiness of	463	Church)	253, 258, 324
Bride metaphor	272	Catharine of Aragon	264n49
Bride of Christ	417, 419, 420, 457, 459,	Cathedrals	477
	463, 464	Catholic churches	219, 222, 478
Bride, Psyche of	459	Catholic hierarchical Christianity	289
Bride, Purity of	420	Cavalry	210, 344
Bride, Wife of the Lamb	462	Celebration of victory	170, 224
Britain, Control in Middle East	375	Celebration scenes	488, 491
Britain, Roman	142	Celebration with harps and song	328
Britian	289	Celestial bodies	156
British Empire, Dissolution of	375	Celestial gods	219
British House of Commons	323	Celestial signs	148, 151n50
Bull Unam Sanctam	313	Celestial symbolism	16, 154,189
Burgundian kingdom	311	Censer/s	179, 180
Burgundic-Franks	504	Ceremonial law	285
Burial at sea	451	Chalcocondylas, Laonicus	215
Burial, Christian forbidden	258	Charelmagne	249, 373
Burning mountain	186	Chastity	390n43

Cherubim	105, 106n10, 127	As Christian temple	60
Cherubim, Wings of	107n13	As covenant people	54
Child snatched up to God	280	As God's temple	144, 238
Childbirth, Pains of	275	As witnessing community	243
Choenix	*134, 138*	As local congregation	58
Choir, Angelic	116	As a Catholic state	291
Choir, Heavenly	290	Corruption of	220, 106
Choral interlude	290n27	Destiny of	11
Chosen nation, Israel	169	Excesses of	146n44
Chosen people	194, 428	Suffering	142
Christ as Redeemer	171	True visible	291
Christ, Eternal reign of	415	Church age	220
Christ, God-Man	144	Church age parenthesis	473, 481
Christ our High Priest	177	Church councils	301
Christ, Person of	123n3	Church government, Reorganized	291
Christ, Redeemer	144	Church history	
Christ, Reign as victor!	379	Early Church	4, 19, 235
Christ, Rejection of	140	Testimony of	6
Christ's everlasting reign	422	Church of Jesus Christ	239, 428
Christian and Missionary Alliance	12	Church of Old and New Covenants	102
Christian burial forbidden	324	Church-age Millennium	477
Christian Faith, Genuineness of	62	Church-age parenthesis theory	8, 122n1,
Christian hope	167	472, 473, 476, 477	
Christian Roman Empire	201	Churches of Asia	58
Christian Rome judged	192	Churches, Seven, As having authority	61
Christianity		Church-state union	201, 203
Legalization of	4	Cicero	134n25
Christianity, Elimination of	146	Cilicia, Moslem conquest of	202
Christianity established	304	Circular reasoning	155
Christianity, Nominal	123	Circumcision	71
Christianity, Recognition of	289	*City of God*	*191*
Christians, Professing	292	Civil servants	437
Chronological indicators	101n3, 327	Civil war	132, 137, 141
Chronological structure	175	Claudius, Empror	251n26
Chronologies, Parallel	474	Clement of Alexandria	4
Chronology, Detailed	484	Clergy endowed with riches	291
Church	161	Clerical immorality	220
Apostate	147	Codex Vaticanus	404n53
As antitypical temple	58, 269	Colossae, Church at	66
As a woman	385	Come out of Babylon	406, 502
As bride of Christ	11	Comenius (historian)	258

Index of Subjects

Coming Ruler 30
Commerce, Interstate 411
Commodus, Emperor 131, 132
Composite enumeration 209
Constantine, Emperor 4, 147, 157, 158nn62-63, 167, 192, 201, 203, 218, 257, 289, 290, 291, 303, 304, 305, 306, 315, 323, 452n25, 477
Constantine, Emperor, As bishop 305
Constantine's revolution 155
Constantinian era 188
Constantinople 192, 213, 214, 216, 217
Constantinople, Seige and Fall of 215, 216, 217, 221
Constantinople, Patriarch of 308n44
Constantius, Emperor 291, 304
Consummation of all things 267, 268
Content of the Little Scroll 327
Context, Rule of 153n57
Contextual interpretation 107n13, 488
Continuous interpretation 483, 491, 493
Continuous model 484
Continuous structure 485, 488
Continuous-historicist confirmation 288, 429
Continuous-historicist interpreters 493
Continuous-historicist interpretation 429, 495n26
Conversion of Israel 55
Coptic Church, Head of 308n44
Corinth 66
Council at Rome (A.D. 373) 478
Council of Arles 258
Council of Chalcedon 306
Council of Constance 259
Council of Narbonne 258
Council of Nicea 291
Council of Tarragona 258
Council of Toulouse 258
Council of Tours 258
Countless thousands 116

Courses 103
Court of heaven 105
Court of Israel 238, 268
Court of the Gentiles 238, 268
Covenant 102
Covenant community 162
Covenant curses 122, 140
Covenant imagery 426
    Covenant institutions of Israel, As reflected in Apocalyptic symbols 16
Covenant Israel, As united with Gentile believers 16
Covenant Land redeemed 115
Covenant law 122, 268
Covenant Nation 150n47
    Apostasy of 115
Covenant people 54, 58, 103, 107, 114, 115, 117, 162, 163, 194, 236n9, 244, 245, 255, 267, 285, 303, 349, 383, 397, 426, 428, 447, 458n28, 459
    Destiny of 50
Creation 56, 105
    God's design for 107
    Redemption of 117
    Restored 380
Creation's song of praise to God 106
Creative genre interpretation 474
Cretan coin 128
Cretan dynasty of emperors 287
Cretan mercenaries 128nn9–10
Cretans 128
Crete 129
    Crown/s
    Diadem 103n7
    Laurel wreath 103n7, 128, 287
Crown of life 72
Crowns 105
    In the court of heaven 104
    Of the twenty-four elders 107
Crusades 213, 216
Cryptic style 183

Crystal	352	Day of Atonement	179
Culminating judgments	195	Day of the Lord	42, 153, 249n24, 415, 473, 484, 488
Culture			
Pagan	151n49	Day of the Lord (eschatological)	59,\ 60n14
Pagan secular	388		
Cup of His wrath	380	Days of vengeance	32
Cup of wine	380	Dead	103n8, 145n43, 451
Cynacus, Bp. of Constantinople	307	Veneration of	167
Cyprian	141	Dead Sea Scrolls	31n42, 103n8, 284
Cyril of Jerusalem	248	Death	50, 62
Cyrus	157	As martyrdom	72
Daimonía (Gk. word)	218	O f Jesus	108
Dallas Theological Seminary	480	Of the Witnesses	258n40, 255, 257, 260, 261
Damasus, Pope	478		
Daniel, Book of 15, 18, 23, 33, 110, 124, 150n47, 481		Of the witnesses celebrated	260
		Second	69, 72, 460
Apocalyptic prototype	18	Death and Hades	450
Apocalyptic visions of 15, 20, 210n59, 215n74, 230, 484, 485, 494		Deception	284
		Decius, Emperor	411
Prophecies of	8, 476	Decree of the Emperor Phocus	309
Fourth beast of	255, 477, 500	Defilement with women	332
Little Horn of Daniel 7	35, 283, 500	Demon worship	212, 220
Modern critical reconstruction of	21	Demons	210, 212, 217, 218, 404
Parallels with Revelation	22	Demons, Spirits of	364
Prophecies of	8, 476	Denarius	134
Seventieth week of	28, 30, 31	Descarte	369
Structure and Meaning of	25	Desert/wilderness	386, 389
Vision of the four beasts	21	Desolations, Determined	31
Vision of the seventy weeks	23, 241	Destruction, Everlasting	69, 225
Visions as parallel	486	Destruction of evil	415
Daniel (person)	24, 24n15	Destruction, Severe	184
As a prophet	236	Details without meaning	491
Danube River	190, 191, 372	Devil	139n34
Darby, J. N.	479, 480, 503	Diadem crown	103n7, 277, 280, 281, 287, 288, 312, 504
Darbyite dispensational futurists	503		
Darius the Mede	23	Diadem crowns	277, 281, 303, 394
Darkening of the sun	374	Diadem crowns, Many	422
Darnel	292n28	Diadem crowns on dragon	287
David, Root of	108	Diadem crowns on horns	293
Davidic King Messiah, Reign of	429	Diaspora, Return of Israel from	429
Davidic kingship	111	Diocletian, Emperor	103n7, 132, 142,

Index of Subjects 539

	146, 147, 158n62, 287, 288, 289, 303, 304, 312, 411	Eagle	106
		Eagle as Rome	234n6
Diocletian persecutions	147, 154, 155	Eagle cry	42
Diocletian, Suicide of	290	Eagle flying in midair	195
Dionysius of Alexandria	5	Eagle shrieking loudly	195
Dispensational theology	472	Eagle, Two wings of	287
Dispensations of Divine grace	413	Eagle Vision	485
Dissenting Christians	367n15	Early Church	219
Dividing wall	162	As premillennial	477
Divination	390	As Historicist	477
Divine judgment	155	Heresy in	123
Divine vindication	143	Earth	152
Doctrinal caricature	257	As home of the saints	115
Doctrines, Erroneous	123	As Roman earth	360
Doctrines, False	123n3	Creatures on	100
Doctrines of demons	220	Renewed	115
Domitian, Emperor	4, 6, 7, 122, 124, 129, 130n14, 134n25, 135, 249, 250, 254, 294, 351, 411	Restoration of	115
		As Roman	131n17
		As swallowing the river	304
		Earthquake 150n47, 156, 180, 180n9, 183, 268, 379	
Domitian, Emperor Persecutions of	251 3, 4, 6	Earthquake, Great	148, 224
Domitianic authorship	494	Eastern church	222, 252
Donation of Constantine	367	Eastern Roman Empire	215
Doxology of praise	105	Eat the flesh	427
Dragon 139n34, 225, 231, 281, 283, 364, 502		Eating the little scroll	226n1
		Ebionism	123n3
And the Woman	224	Economic hardship	136
Cast down	283, 286, 290, 304	Economics	134
On shore of the sea	293	Ecumenism, Papal	376
Out of the mouth of	363	Eden, Restored	465
Seventh head of	287	Edict of Toleration	289, 303
Ten horns of	501	Edom	151n51, 404
War in heaven	289	Destruction of	488
Pursuit of the woman	304	Judgment of	336
Tail of	303	Type of Antichrist	424
Dramatic style in Revelation	17, 171	Type of Rome	418
Dream-vision apocalyptic	124, 161, 312n52, 474	Eighth beast, Reincarnation of the seventh	294, 321
Drunk with blood	388	Egypt	255, 289, 376
Drying up of the Euphrates	363, 374, 375	Exodus from	182n11
Dutch Union of Utrecht	264		

Moslem conquest of	202	Eusebius, Bp. of Caesarea	4, 5, 146n44, 155
Egyptian Empire	186		
Egyptian plague	186	Eusebius, Bp. of Verceil	305
Egyptian plague of boils	357	Evangelical church	262
Eighth head of Roman beast	294, 297, 300, 304, 343, 346, 349, 362, 393, 400, 411	Evangelical sects	257
		Event-oriented interpretation	481
		Event-oriented prediction	238, 493
Eighth Roman Imperial government	294	Everlasting destruction	225, 329, 460
Elders, Twenty-four	102, 103, 107, 114, 116, 169, 170, 172, 224	Everlasting life	170, 460
		Evil, Destruction of	11, 445, 449
Elect as multiethnic	171	Evil-Merodach	299
Election, Assurance of	198	Exarchate of Ravenna	249, 249n21
ĕlĕph (Heb. wd.)	171n76	Excommunication for heresy	324
Elijah	317	Excursus	148
Elimination of heretics	369n18	Excursus on the Little scroll	223
Elliott, E. B.	258	Exodus from Egypt	182
Emblematic scenery	206	Exodus typology	60
Emerald	102	Extermination of heretics	325
Emperor worship	23, 70	Extinction of evil	117, 267
End of this age	232, 423	Extortion	221
Enlightenment philosophies	367	Eyes are like blazing fire	425
Epexegetical	140n36	Eyes like blazing fire	228
Ephesian Church	6	Eyes like flaming torches	228
Ephesian Elders	65	Eyes of cherubim	106
Ephesus	3, 4, 65, 70	Ezekiel (book)	231
Ephesus, Church at	64, 65	Ezekiel, The Prophet	100
Ephraim (Israelite tribe)	165, 167	Ezra (book)	245n17
Era of the Martyrs	146	Face like lightning	228
Errancy in biblical interpretation	10	Face like the sun	228, 233
Eschatology of Revelation	434	Faithful obedience	459
Essenes	284n18	Faithful remnant	222
Eternal destruction	69	Fall of Adam	115
Eternal gospel	337	Fall of Babylon	334
Eternal life	168, 318	Fall of Babylon the Great	349
Eternity of God	56	Fall of Byzantium	265
Ethnic Israel	163	Fall of pagan Rome	157
Euphrates	207, 213n68	Falling stars	148
Euphrates River	202, 205, 206, 207, 208, 211n60, 213, 362, 365, 386n39	False Prophet	
		False prophet	318, 321, 322, 364, 427
Euphrates River, Drying up of	374	False prophet, Out of the mouth of	363
European commonwealth	381	False teaching	284

Index of Subjects 541

Family life	390n43
Family of God	197
Famine	133n21, 134n24, 140, 141
Fatal wound of seventh head	296
Feet like glowing bronze	228
Festival of Tabernacles	182
Festivals, Israelite	181
Fifth bowl of wrath	373, 374n29
Fifth Lateran Council	259, 260, 262
Fifth seal	142, 146, 147
Fifth trumpet	196, 201, 213, 214, 265
Figs	151
Figures of speech	148
Filth of her adulteries	390
Final prophecy of Jeus	35
Final testimony of Jesus	475
Fine linen	417, 425
Fire	211
Fire as an instrument of judgment	177
Fire from heaven	443
First and the Last	469
First flying angel's message	333
First love	66
First resurrection	437
First trumpet	175, 183
First Vatican Council	309
First woe	198, 200, 213
Firstfruits to God	165, 301
Fiscus Judaicus	130, 130n13
Five months	200, 204
Flat earth	164
Flight into the desert/wilderness	280, 283
Florence, Seige of	190n26
Flying eagle	193
Forever and ever	107, 444, 447, 448
Forged documents	367
Formula, 4-2-1	182
Fornication	220
Fornication of clergy	221
Forty-two months	240, 298, 501
Four angels	147
Four corners of the earth	164, 447
Four living creatures	105, 114
Four winds	148, 164, 208
Fourth beast of Daniel 7	124n4, 254, 363
Fourth bowl angel	359
Fourth bowl of wrath	362, 372, 374
Fourth Lateran Council	258
Fourth Roman beast	275
Fourth trumpet	184, 191
France	370
France, Control in Middle East	375
France, Southern Moslem conquest of	202
Francis, Emperor	373
Frankish kingdom	311
Franks	504
French National Assembly	323
French Revolution	367, 369, 370, 373
Frog-like unclean spirits	363, 365, 376
Frogs, Loquacious nature	364
Funeral metaphor	408
Funerary motifs	412
Fury of his wrath	380
Future age	103n6
Future antichrist	481
Future events	164
Future kingdom	291
Future tribulation	481
Futurist eschatology	480
Futurist interpretation	377, 473, 480, 481
Futurist interpreters	156, 477, 489
Futurist school	8, 14, 59, 159, 162n66, 222n84, 318, 467n34, 472, 473, 476, 477, 480
Pretribulation rapture	102n5
Futurist-dispensationalists	161
Gabriel, Archangel	178, 232
Gad, Israelite tribe	166
Galerian	167
Galarius	146n44, 158n62, 289
Death of	289, 290

Garden of Eden 67, 106n10, 465
Garments of white 420
Gates of pearls 462
Gathering of the elect 434
Gaul 142, 190, 289
Gehenna 72, 335, 447
Gem stones, Precious 462
Gemetria 319
General Allenby 375
General resurrection 439n7
Geneva Bible *330*
Genre, Apocalyptic 487
Genseric, King of Vandals 191
Gentiles 169, 238, 244, 247, 249, 447
Gentiles, Uncircumcised
Gepidae 191
German rationalists 479, 481
Germany 191
Gibbon 190n26
Gibraltar, Straits of 191
Glass, Sea of 104
Glorification, Future 459
gnomic present tense 296n32
Gnostic philosophy 167
Gnosticism 69
God 17
  Abiding presence of 173
  Almighty, 51, 184, 267
  As creator 107, 171, 235, 459
  As Creator 51, 56, 144
  As King 105
  As Lord God Almighty 199
  Authority of 235
  Beginning and the end 51
  Covenant people of 239, 359, 396, 398, 406, 439
  Creative power of 106
  Discipline of 126
  Eternity of 267
  Glory of 62, 421, 464
  Holiness of 100, 102, 172, 206, 340, 352, 420, 448, 451, 464
  Judgment of Babylon 410
  Judgments of 105, 126, 173, 352, 400
  Just judgments of 359, 416
  Justice of 340, 343, 344, 409, 418, 426, 448
  Kingdom of 108
  Kingship of 107
  Omniscience of 450
  Permissive will of 196
  Promises of 283
  Providence of 127, 284
    See also Providence of God
  Reign of 421
  Saving work completed 116
  Secret council of 235
  Seven spirits of 104
  Sovereignty of 48, 50, 56, 59, 100, 102, 105, 107, 126, 184, 334
  Sustaining power of 106
  Throne of 105, 343
  Triune nature of 48
  Ultimate Victor 443
  Voice of 380
  Worship of 107, 464
  Wrath of 344
God remembered her 405, 406
God's intervention in history 182
God's plan of redemption 347
Godhead, Second person of 457
Godly government 149
Gog 366, 444
Gog and Magog 415, 447
Gold 179
Gold, precious stones and pearls 389
Gold, Pure transparent 462
Golden Age of Islam 205
Golden altar 207
Golden censer 176, 179
Golden cup 387, 389, 402, 405
Golden incense altar 179, 206

Index of Subjects

Gomorah 151n51
Gordon, Adoniram Judson 13n19
Gordon College 12, 13n19
Gordon, S. D. 12
Gospel, Authority of 243
Gospel of grace 243
Gospel of Jesus Christ 221
Gospel of the Kingdom 122, 170
Gothic invasions 141
Goths 152n52, 189n24, 190
Governmental revolution 148
Grace (Apostolic greeting 51
Grace, Means of 221
Grace of God 50, 170, 172, 194
Grafted branches 163
Grammatico-historical interpretation 430, 487
Grape harvest 341, 343
Great and marvelous sign 350
Great chain 435, 441
Great day of God Almighty 364
Great day of the lord 489
Great earthquake 147, 149, 150n48
Great multitude 160, 164, 171, 174, 266, 301, 417, 420
Great prostitute 385
Great river Euphrates 365
Great star 187
Great supper for the birds 427
Great tribulation 35, 160, 163, 170, 171, 172, 173n78, 197, 331
Great white throne judgment 415, 449
Grecian Empire 150n47
Greece 103n7, 189, 499
Greek church 219
Greek language, Extrabiblical 100
Greek insurrection 375
Greek theater 17
Greeks 218
Green grass 185
Gregory I, Pope 307

Gregory IX, Pope 506
Gregory the Great 193n36, 201, 306, 505
Gregory's congratulatory letter 307
Guinness, H. Grattan 508n15
Gunpowder 214
Hades 62, 117n26, 139, 451
Hades as a place of burial 451n23
Haggai 150n47, 245n17
Hail 268
Hail and fire mixed with blood 183, 184
Hair white like wool 228
Halelujah Chorus 301
Half hour of silence 176, 178
Hallel 418
Hallelujah 417
Hallelujah Chorus 384, 412, 416, 428
Hand-made gods 212
Harlot 502
Harlot Babylon 257, 320n63, 402
Harlot metaphor 392
Harlot riding the beast 400
Harlotry, Spiritual 386
Harps as instruments of worship 114, 351
Harvest of the earth 225, 343, 345
Heads 275n7
Heads of the dragon 303
Heads of the beast 294
Heathen 162
Heaven 103n6, 105, 170
Heaven as the sphere of authority 261
Heaven, Creatures in 100
Heaven/heavens 101n2
Heavenly 102
Heavenly beings 102
Heavenly celebration scenes 484, 490
Heavenly court 105, 171
Heavenly sanctuary 177
Hebraic language 445
Hebraism 424
Hebrew grammar 267n51
Hebrew Christians 55n10

Hebrew language	332n6		351
Hebrew language dual number	209	Holiness of God's people	105
Hebrew language idioms	5	Holiness, Personal	198
Hebrew prophetic-perfect tense	388, 403	Holland	370
	491n18	Holy	99
Hebrew prophets	149	Holy city	1, 457, 459, 462
Hellenism	137	Holy ones	425n11
Henry VIII, King of England	264n49	Holy Place	177, 179
Heresy, Early Church	123	Holy Roman Empire	249, 263, 373
Heresy, Elimination of	258, 368	Holy Scriptures	69
Heretical and schismatic sects	289	Holy Spirit	52, 58, 60, 67, 71, 113, 163,
Hermeneutical question	487		173, 198, 241, 245
Hermeneutics	215n74	Holy Spirit, Indwelling	243
Apocalyptic	210n59	Holy Spirit, Inspiration of	101
Correct	150n48	Honorius	159n64
Erroneous	198n44	Hope of God's people	267, 442n14
Key principles of	471	Hope of redemption and glory	301
Unacceptable	437n6	Hope of the coming Kingdom	59
Heruli kingdom	311	Hope to a suffering church	351
Hesiod, Poet	219	*Horae Apocalypticae* (book)	13
Hezekiah, King of Israel	207	Horns as authority symbols	113, 277
Hieropolis, Church at	66	Horn as symbol	113
High priest (Old Covenant)	58	Horns of Hattin	213
Highways, Military	137	Horns of the altar	207
Hilary of Poitiers	248	Horns, Seven	113
Hippolytus	122n1, 476, 476nn4–5	Horse, Black	132
Historicist interpretation	266, 312n52,	Horse, Pale	139
313n52, 356, 376, 377, 387, 394n49,		Horse, Red	130
429, 478, 479		Horse as a Roman symbol	124, 125, 142
Historicist interpreters	192, 209, 226n1,	Horsemen, Four	123
210, 291, 298n33, 322, 382, 401, 436,		Horsemen in Zechariah	123
478, 483		Horsemen, Two hundred million	206
Historicist method of interpretation	473,	Horses and riders	211
483, 493		Horses tails	216, 216n75
Historicist school	107n14, 207n53, 208,	Hosea (book)	391, 404
215n74, 473, 476, 377, 483, 491		House of Severus	132
Historicist tradition	482	Huge mountain	185
History, Knowledge of	491	Hugh hailstones	382
Holiness	180	Human bloodshed	186
Holiness of God		Human depravity	443
Holiness of God	102, 104, 105, 107, 344,	Human warfare	183

Index of Subjects

Humanistic interpretation	481	Inflation	135, 136
Humiliati (sect)	258	Inheritance	164
Humility, Appropriate	172	Injustice	135, 138, 144
Humility of twenty-four elders	107	Inquisition	143, 220, 258, 263, 508, 508n15
Huss, John	258, 259	Interludes	147, 160, 164
Hussites	369	Intermediate state	62, 103n6, 145n43, 344n17
Hymn of praise to the Lamb	112		
Hymn of twenty-four elders	267	Interpretation	
Hymns of praise	169, 267	*See also Revelation, Interpretation*	
Hymns of promise	267	Counter-Reformational	215n74
Hyperbolic language	489	Historicist school of	14
Idolatries	217	Jesuit	215n74
Idolatry	219, 220	Philosophy of history school of	14, 492
Idols of gold, silver, bronze, etc.	217	Preterist school of	14
Ignatius of Antioch	69	Protestant-historicist	122
Ignatius of Loyola	478	Schools of	7
Illumination of the Spirit	321	Spiritual school of	14
Illyricum, Roman province	140n35, 142, 189, 192, 290,	Too detailed	491
		Transtemporal principle of	14n29
Image creation	221	Typological	55n10
Image of the beast	318, 322, 323, 356	Interpretation, Historicist	
Image of the beast to speak	323	School	107n14
Image to be worshipped	323, 324, 356	Iran	375
Image to speak	324	Iranaeus	4, 69, 123n3, 319
Image worship	123n3, 201, 217	Iraq	216, 375
Images	219	Irenaeus	69
Images of Jesus	217	Irene, Empress	217
Imminency, Principle of	477	Iron scepter	426
Immorality	67	Iron scepter	281
Immortal life	459	Irving, Edward	479
Imperial City	191	Islam, Satanic spirit of	376
Imperial coinage	138	Israel	162, 244
Imperial cult priests	321	National conversion off	55
Imperial law	167	National repentance of	55
Imputed righteousness	145, 171	Restoration of	24, 26n38
Incense	179	Israel as symbol	161
Incense altar	179, 180, 354	Israel, Covenant People	54, 60, 160
Incense bowls	161	Israel (ethnic)	58
Indefinite relative pronoun	442	Israel of God	115, 447
Indulgences	221	Israel, Pre-exilic period	122
Inference, Unnecessary	473n2		

Israel, Regeneration of	429	Beginning of the ministry of	31
Israel, Restoration of	429	Birth of	275n6, 278, 285nn19–20
Israel, State of	418	Blood of	53
Israel's Covenant God	344	Crucifixion of	31, 54
Israelite covenant marriage	421	Death as a ransom	53
Israelite covenant symbolism	385	Deity of	57
Israelite imagery	58, 144, 161	Eternal rule of	11
Israelite priesthood	103	Eternity of	62
Israelite symbolism	161, 244	Exaltation of	99
Israelite temple	179	Faithful witness of	48, 49, 52, 233, 271
Israelite tribes	463n32	First advent of	30
Israelite typology	144, 463n32	First-born from the dead	52
Israelite wedding tradition	428	Future reign	42
Issachar, Israelite tribe	166	Glorification of	58, 59
Italy	189, 190, 289	Glorified	42
Italy ravished	190	Head over the churches	58, 61
Italy, Roman	142	High Priestly office of	58
Izmir, Turkey	70	Incarnation of	60
Jacob	163	Juridical office of	62
James' Naval History	371	Kingly office of	53, 58
Jasper	102, 462	Lamb of God	99
Jasper, Clear as crystal	462	Love of	53
Jeremiah	149, 186, 231	Messianic title	54
Jeremiah (book)		Preexistence of	61
Seventy years prophecy, 23		Priestly office of	53
Jerome	140n35, 191, 248	Prophetic office of	53
Jerusalem	23, 255, 344, 443, 447	Resurrection of	52, 62, 70
Destruction of, 30, 34		Riches of	70
Rebuilt, 28		Savior	59
Jerusalem, Destruction of	152n54, 157, 173n78	Second advent	11, 51, 52, 54, 54n9, 55n10
Jesuits	155, 478, 507	Reign of	458
Interpretation of Revelation	8	Return of	122, 382
Introduction of futurism	473, 377, 481	Revelation of	2
Introduction of preterism	377	Savior	422
Jesus Christ	161, 169	Second coming of	364
As Lord	229	Sovereignty of	2, 61
As Word of God	59, 62	Testimony of	1, 49, 59, 169
Ascension of	280n14	Triumph of	108
Atonement	31, 173	Victor	422
Authority of	61	Voice of	235

Index of Subjects 547

Jewish people   54, 70, 71, 103n8, 130
Jewish apocalyptic writings   21, 274, 494
Jewish covenant people   274n4
Jewish diaspora   173n78
Jewish literature   72, 103n8
Jewish messianism   434
Jewish nation, Roman destruction of   122
Jewish-Roman War   3, 33, 129, 152n54, 493
Jews, Restoration to Palestine   418
Johanine books, Literary style   5
John, Apostle   3, 4, 5, 6, 59, 66, 69, 284n18
   Ministry in the Asian province   3
John, Bp. of Constantinople   306
John the Baptist   284
John the Elder   4
Jordan   375
Joseph   165, 167
Joseph's dream   156
Joshua the high priest   181, 241, 243, 246
Josiah   153
Jovinian   190n26
Judah, Israelite tribe   108, 242, 166, 166n71, 166n73
Judaism   103n8, 124n4
Judaism, Ancient   166n70
Judaizers   66
Judas   437n5
Judean wilderness   284n18
Judges, Civil   437
Judges, Period of the   220
Judgment, Disciplinary   184
Judgment, End-time   328, 408
Judgment, Final   144, 292
Judgment hour has come   334
Judgment, Last   444
Judgment of Antichrist   334
Judgment of Christ   439
Judgment of God   146n44, 154, 155, 156, 177, 182, 183, 192, 194, 196, 198, 206, 208, 221, 231, 234, 247, 334, 359, 379, 382, 387, 400, 405, 415, 426, 436
Judgment of works   468
Judgment, Preparation for   455
Judgment, Retributive   184
Judgment, Temporal   151n49
Judgment, The last   55n10
Judgment, Universal   343
Judgments, Disciplinary   123
Judgments, Future   195
Judgments of God   180, 182, 183, 192, 197, 268, 287, 349, 352, 373
Justice   133, 136
Justice of God   447
Justin Martyr   4
Justinian, Emperor   309
Kerithites   128n9
Keys of the Kingdom   251
Kidron Valley   344, 366, 427, 431
Kilns for brick and pottery   199
King James version   103
King of Babylon   187n20
KING OF KINGS   426
Kingdom, Everlasting   231
Kingdom, Future   21
Kingdom, Gospel of the   122
Kingdom of Christ   267
Kingdom of darkness   318
Kingdom of God   48, 51, 108, 114, 143, 170, 267
Kingdom of priests   53
Kingdom of Satan   143
Kingdoms, Ten barbarian   311
Kings as governments   394
Kings from the east   375
Kings of the earth   386, 427
Kings of the east   362, 374, 376
Kingship of Christ   126
Kingship of the Lamb   116
Labashi-Marduk   299
Lake of burning sulfur   427

Lake of fire	448, 449, 451, 460
Lamb	127n8, 144, 148, 149, 165, 169, 170, 171, 172, 177, 225, 301, 316, 330, 395
See also Jesus Christ, Lamb of God	
Antitypical	110
As a "lamp"	464
As sacrificial victim	112, 113
As the shepherd-king	173
As victorious	112
Atonement by	112, 114, 243
Atoning sacrifice of	331
Blood of the	173, 286
Deity of	112
Jesus as the	99, 103
Name of	332
Praise of	114
Seven eyes of the	112, 113
Seven horns of	111
Sovereignty of	112, 1
Triumph of	113
Worship of	112
Lamb and the 144,000	327
Lamb of God Messiah	329
Lamb's Book of Life	459
Lamb's wife	462
Lamps, Seven	60
Lamps, Tabernacle	60
Lampstands, Seven	
As seven churches	60
Lampstands, Seven golden	60
Land, Restoration to the covenant	429
Lands of Roman Empire	199
Language interpretation	471
Language of praise	117
Last Day	164
Last days	220
Last plagues	194, 382
Last trumpet	182
LATEINOS	*319*
Laurel wreath crown	103n7, 128, 281, 345
Law of God	194
Law of the unchaste bride	212n64
Lazarus	52
League of Nations	375
Left foot on the land	228, 234
Legal idiom	212n64
Legs like burnished bronze	228
Legs like fiery pillars	228, 233
Leopard-like beast	293
Letters to the seven churches	37
Outline of	63
Levi, Israelite tribe	166
Leviathan	281
Leviathan, the gliding serpemt	236n9
Levitical priesthood	102
Libertinism	66, 123n3
Licinius, Emperor	158, 289, 303
Licinius, Emperor, Death of	290
Life and immortality	291
Life of devotion	172
Life to come	69
Lightning	104, 180, 180n9, 268
Limited atonement	114
Linen dress	228
Lion/s	106, 108
As the Lamb	111
As the Messiah	234n6
Heads of	211
Lion of tribe of Judah	110
Lion's mouth	211
Literal as the normal sense	472
Literal interpretation	478
As hyperliteralizing	18
As non-figurative	18
As the normal sense	18
Literal principle	472
Literary criticism, Modern	215n74
Literary structure	483
Literary tradition, apocalyptic	485
Little Book	226n1, 247
Chronology of	225

Index of Subjects

Message of 110, 225
Structure of 225
Little horn antichrist 11, 14, 21, 124, 271, 173n78, 225, 230, 230n4, 234n5, 243, 247, 248, 249, 250, 255, 271, 275, 299n33, 362, 387, 390
Little scroll 40, 223, 224, 225, 226n1, 230n3, 232, 234n5, 292
  As written on back of 7-sealed scroll, 41n50
  Chronology of 265
  Conclusion of 333
  Content of 237
  Eating of 230
  Events of 266
  Literary structure of 226n1
  Message of 41, 193, 223, 224, 226n1, 230, 232, 233n5, 265, 271, 287
  Prophecy of 266
  Purpose of 227n1
  Satanic characters in 363
  Size of 233
  To be eaten 229
Living creatures 105, 106, 114, 116, 127, 169
Living water 173, 466
Livy, Roman historian 276, 500
Local officers 437
Locke 369
Locusts 197, 198, 199, 203, 204
Lombards 504, 505
LORD, Day of the 153
Lord Jesus Christ 229
LORD OF LORDS 426
Lord's Day (Sunday) 59, 60
Lordship of the Lamb 116
Loud peals of thunder 417
Lucian 3.185 128n9
Lucifer 187n20
Luther, Martin 262, 263
Luxor temple 281n16

Lying 332
Maccabean "Daniel" 481
Maccabean wars 244n15
MacDonald, Margaret 479
Macedonia 103n7, 189
Maddening wine of her adulteries 411
Magic arts 207, 212, 220, 221
Magog, Land of Gog 444
Maitland, S. R. 479
Male child 291, 304
  Birth of 289
Man 106
Man of lawlessness 14, 230n4, 249n24, 250, 298n33, 300, 314, 362, 387, 390
Manasseh, Israelite tribe 166, 167
Manicheans 252, 253n33
Man-made idols 212
Manson, William 34n47
Many diadem crowns 425
Many, The (term for elect remnant) 31n42
Many waters 186
Marcus Aurelius, Emperor 128, 131, 129
Mariolatry 219
Maritime battles 370
Maritime commerce 358
Mark as figure for ownership 318
Mark of God 197
Mark of the beast 165, 318, 319, 321, 334, 339, 356, 357
Marriage 390n43
Marriage consummation 428
Marriage contracts 109
Marriage covenant, Ancient 212n64, 338, 404, 457, 459
Marriage law, Biblical 458n28
Marriage metaphor 457
Marriage supper of the Lamb 42, 412, 420, 428
Marriage to Yahweh 391
Mars, Roman god of war 125, 128, 191
Martin Luther 260

Martyrdom 3, 52, 70, 142, 146, 147, 184, 222, 255, 290, 442n12, 486, 490
Martyrdom theme as central 437
Martyrs 2, 53, 143, 144, 340, 391n46, 411, 418, 437, 442
   As mediators 219
   Era of the 146
   Souls of 126
   For the true faith 251
   Literal death of 437n6
   Singing hymns of praise 301
   Under Papal Rome 34
   Martyrs' temples 219
Marxist philosophy 376
Massacre of St. Bartholomew 370
Materialism 69
Materialistic science 369
Matthias 437n5
Maurice, Emperor 306, 307
Maxentius, Emperor 158n62, 289
Maxentius, Death at Milvian Bridge 290
Maximian, Emperor 158n62
Maximin, Emperor 158n62, 289, 303
Meaning, As single sense 150n48
Means of grace 221
Measuring of the Temple 243, 327
Measuring reed 237
Medieval Church 472
Medinat al Salem 202
Mediterranean Sea 457
Mediterranean world 216
Megabyzus, Revolt of 27n39
Men gnawed their tongues 362, 365
Mercenaries 128, 137
Merchants of the earth 408
Message of the Revelation 143, 475
Messages, Three angelic 232
Messenger with Divine authority 233
Messiah 52, 108, 124, 173n78
   First advent of, 28, 30

   As a warrior 425
   As King 279
   As the Lamb 99
   As the Prince 28
   Covenant inheritance of 111
   Death of 173
   Jewish 161
Messiah Jesus 112
Messiah-Savior 173
Messianic age 246
Messianic Jews 166n70
Messianic redemption 182
Messianic typology 207
Messianism, Post exilic 246
Messianism, Hebrew-Christian 418
Metaphorical language 151, 461, 488
Meteor 187
Metonymy 140n36
Michael (archangel) 67n19, 178, 229n2, 286, 289
Middle Ages 220, 221
Middle East 128
Middle Eastern world 216
Midrash pesher 55n10
Mighty angel 110, 226n1, 227, 230
Mighty angel's authority 228
Military tyrants 141
Millennial age 53n8, 415, 437, 439, 443, 453, 455
Millennial era
Millennial kingdom 436
Millennial reign 329, 447
Millennium 434, 484
   Allegorized 479
   Conditions during 452
Millstone cast into sea 410
Millstone, Large 411
Mines, Deportation to 71
Miracles 221
Miracles, Counterfeit 296
Miraculous signs 321, 363, 364

Index of Subjects

Missions, World enterprise	264	Myriads of angels	116
Mithraism	173	Mystery	387, 390, 396
Modern military equipment	443	Mystery Babylon the Great	387
Modern war machines	344	Mystery of God	229, 230, 236
Modius	135n26, 138n32	Mystery of God fulfilled	399
Mohammed	201, 202, 203, 205	Nabonidus	299
Mohammed's conquests	203	Name of the beast	318
Monster of the sea	236n9	Name that no one else knows	425
Montanism	123n3	*Naòs theoû* (Greek)	300
Moody Bible Institute	9, 222n84, 480	Naphtali, Israelite tribe	166
Moon	303	Napoleon	309, 310, 371n25, 372, 373
Moon and stars	187	Napoleon's Italian campaign	372
Moon as lesser authority	275	Napoleonic period	374n29
Moors, Spanish	213	Napoleonic wars	372, 373, 401
Moral decadence	192	National calamity	156
Moral law	285	Nationalistic spirit	400
Moral purity	390n43	Nations	464
Mortal wound	304	Nations as heathen	426
Moses	68n19, 122, 173n78, 246	Natural branches	163
Covenant promises of	24	Natural creation	114
Revelation at Sinai	104	Natural depravity of man	360
Moslem "Capitulations"	204	Nature of man	145n42
Moslem conquests	202, 203	Naval warfare	183, 187, 358
Moslem destruction	151n51	Naval warfare, 1793-1815	371
Moslem world	217	Nebuchadnezzar, King	23, 181, 293n29, 337, 387
Moslems, Degrading policies of	204		
Most holy place	180	*Něphěsh* (Hebrew)	145
Mother of abominations	388, 391	Neriglissar	299
Mother of Prostitutes	387, 391	Nero, Emperor	3, 124, 320, 411, 493
Mount of Olives	366, 429	Nerva, Emperor	59n13, 129, 130, 251
Mount Zion	330	New age culture	207
Multiple fulfillments	309	New Covenant	24, 163, 246, 269
Multitude in white	171	New earth	170, 457, 461
Murders	207, 212, 220	New earth, Inhabitants of	466
Musical interlude	286	New heavens and new earth	456, 457, 460, 462
Muslim abuse of women	204	New heavens and new earth	
Muslim anti-Christian forces	349	New Jerusalem	457, 461, 463
Muslim Caliphate	213	New Testament church	70, 236
Muslim conquests	203, 216	New song	114
Muslim faith, Apostasy to the	204	Nice, 7th General Council at	217
Muslim oppression	204		

Nicolaitan heresy	65, 66, 67	Oriental monarch	277
Nicolas, Pope	506	Origen	476n5
Nile River	186	Orthodoxy, Stagnant	65
Ninety-five theses	260	Ostragoths	191, 504, 505
No night there	464	Ostrogoth kingdom	311
Nominalism, Christian	167	Ottoman territories	375
North Africa	191, 289	Ottoman Turkish conquests	265
North Africa, Moslem conquest of	202	Ottoman Turkish Empire	374
Nuclear warfare	381	Ottoman Turks	213, 215, 216, 217
Number of the beast's name	318	Outer court of the temple	238, 239, 244, 247, 248
Numerical time prophecy	473		
Nyack College	12	Ox	106
Obedience of faith	420	Oxford Movement	9, 480
Obedience of God's people	105	Pacification of Nuremberg	263
Obey God's commandments	331	Pagan gods	151n49, 218
Octavian Augustus Caesar	276	Pagan gods, Worship of	143
Odoacer, Chief of the Heruli	192, 304, 311	Pagan Rome, Fall of	155, 502
		Pagan sacrifices	158n64
Oil	135	Pagan worship	159n64
Old & New Covenants, Unity of		Paganism	146, 158n64
Old and New Covenants, Unity of	458, 462	Paganization of the church	192
		Paganized Christianity	158n64
Old Covenant prophets	173n78	Pagans, Nominally converted	291
Old Covenant typology	112	Pale horse	139, 139n34
Old Testament prophecy	154	Palm branches	171
Olive tree	163	Papacy	7, 123n3
Olivet discourse	122	As Antichrist	249, 249, 376, 473, 478, 480, 481
Omar (Saracen conqueror)	202		
Ommiades	202	As the lawless one	314
Omnipotence of God	196	Atrocities of	367
Omnipotence of the Lamb	113	Decadence of	367
Omniscience of the Lamb	113	Immorality of	221
One fourth of the earth	140	Temporal power of	248, 253, 257, 310, 373, 374, 505, 507
One like a son of man	228, 345		
One thousand years	436	Universal authority of	251
One who makes desolate	33	Papal Bull of Innocent IV	258
One who restrains	250	Papal	
One-tenth of the city	261	Bulls of Gregory IX	258
One-third	184, 185	Colonies	371
One-third		Commerce	402
Ophanim	106	Blasphemies	313

Index of Subjects

Corruptions	400
Decadence	367, 368
Empire	381
Fascism	376
France	372
General councils	322
Infallibility, Decree of	310
Inquisitors	263
Loss of temporal power	400
Persecution of dissenters	367
Rome	258
Territories, Loss of	507
Treasuries	221
Wealth	402
World Confederacy	377
Papias	4, 5
Papyrus	109
Paradise	67, 457
Parallel interpretation	178n4, 199n45, 474, 483, 485, 486, 491
Parallel interpreters	490
Parallel structure	155, 160, 484, 485, 486, 487, 490, 496
Internal evidence for	487
Parthian Empire	128n10
Parthian War	129
Parthians	128
Partitive expression	442
Passing of the "Second Woe	327
Passover of A.D. 30	31
Patarines (sect dissident from the Papal Church)	253, 258
Patient endurance	59
Patmos, Island of	3, 4, 51
Patriarchal family	167
Paul, Apostle	115, 160n65, 163, 269
Paulicians (sect dissident from the Papal Church)	253, 257, 368
Pauline Christianity	253n33
Peace	128
Peace of God	50
Peace of Passau	263
Peace (*shalôm*)	51
Penance	221
Pentecost	113
People of God	54, 105, 107, 114, 123, 163, 164, 206, 224, 231, 246n18, 268, 274, 283, 303, 316, 321, 327, 342, 344, 356, 376, 390n43, 420, 443, 457, 458, 462, 464
Peoples, multitudes, nations, and languages	398
Perga, Ancient	465
Pergamum	70, 296, 316
Pergamum, Church at	6, 72, 73
Persecution	70, 71, 146, 291
Deliverance from	280
Of believers	123
Of dissidents	220, 251
Resumed by Maximin	289
Roman	70
Perseverance	66
Persia	499
Persia, Threat to Rome	203
Persian Empire	150n47
Persian monarchs	281
Persian seige of Jerusalem	203n51
Pestilence	141
Peter, Apostle	198
Petrus Siculus	253, 253n32
Phiippi, Church at	69
Philadelphia Church, Letter to	7
Philip, Emperor	141
Philosophy of history interpretation	312n52
Phocas, Decree of	307
Phocas, Emperor	201, 251, 253, 257, 307, 309n45, 505, 508
Phocus, Date of his decree	308
Photius, Patriarch of Constantinople	253, 253n32
Physical persecution	284

Piedmont, Churches of	252	Praise of the angels	172
Piedmont, Valleys of	259	Prayers of God's people	177, 206, 208
Pindar. Pythian Odes 5.54	128n9	Prayers of the saints	114, 179, 180
Plague	140, 141	Praying to the dead	219
Plagues, Last	194n37	Preaching, Spirit inspired	243
Plagues of Egypt	182	Prediction, Event-oriented	476, 493, 496
Plagues, Seven last	195	Predictive prophecy	491
Plato	218, 219	Premillennial historicists	436, 440n10
Platonic philosophy	167	Premillennialism	4
Pliny the Elder	135n26, 139n33	Premillennialism banned	478
Po River	372	Pre-Reformation history	251
Pogroms	70	Presbyterian Church in America	15n30
Political revolution	150n48	Preterist interpretation	377, 481
Political symbolism	150n48	Preterist interpreters	156, 489, 493
Polycarp	69, 71, 72	Preterist school	159, 479, 481
Pontifex Maximus, Cult of	296	Pretribulationism	480
Poor men of Lyons	258, 368	Priesthood, Elevation of the	167
Pope/s	308n44	Priesthood, Israelite	103
As Universal Bishop	201, 257, 505	Priesthood, Levitical	103
Exemption from law	505	Priests in the millennium	437
Head of Roman priesthood	323	Priests, Kingdom of	51, 103
Pope Alexander III	258	Primasius of Carthage	248
Pope Gregory IX	314, 506	Primogeniture	52
Pope Innocent III	258	Priscilla	65
Pope Leo X	259, 260	Prisons, First century	71
Pope Lucius III	258	Progressive interpretation	244n16
Pope Nicolas	314	Progressive revelation	117n26
Porneuō (Greek)	404	Prohibited abominations	388
Portugal	370	Proleptic	174
Postmillennial interpretation	329n3, 437n6, 479	Proleptic interludes	39
Postmillennial theology	477	Proleptic prophecy	99, 116, 160, 224, 6 267, 327, 328, 417, 488, 490
Postmillennialists	442n13	Promised Land	115
Post-modernism	207, 376	Promises of God	283
Post-resurrection celebration	328	Prophecies, Dream-vision	122
Posttribulationism	480	Prophecy	
Poured out into the air	378	Fulfillment of	49n2
Poured out on the sun	372	As preaching	244
Poverty	70	As prediction	491
Praise language	117	Futurist interpretation	122n1
Praise of God	172	Scroll as	110

Index of Subjects

Prophesying of the Two Witnesses 327
Prophetic perfect 267n51, 405, 408
Prostitute 186, 386, 395, 397
   As a metaphor 386
   As apostate church 402
   Devastation of 399
   Professional 404
Prostitutes
   Mother of 391, 402
   Punishment of 399
Prostitution 390n43
   Imagery of 386
   Spiritual 388
   Symbolism of 389
Protestant historicism 377
Protestant interpreters 203
Protestant Reformation 251, 257, 260, 262, 264, 269, 347, 376
Protestant-historical interpreters 277
Providence of God 30, 49, 127, 130, 133, 140, 154, 163, 164, 165, 174, 175n2, 183, 196, 198, 208, 221, 255, 261, 263, 283, 284, 287, 298, 306, 309, 360, 400, 453, 477
Providence, Permissive 302
Providential control 441
Providential design 244n16
Pseudepigrapha 124
Pseudepigraphic authorship 6
Pseudepigraphic literature 485
Publicani 258, 324
Punishment by God 339
Punishment, Everlasting 336
Punishment of gehenna fire 339
Purgatory 221
Purple and scarlet 389
Quadripartite earth 140n35
Quality of life 464
Qumran 103n8
Qumran covenanters 284, 284n18
Rabbi Akiba 425
Rabbinic texts 285
Radagaisus
Radagaisus (Barbarian general) 190, 190n26, 189
Radical revolution 148
Raguel (archangel) 178
Rahab 281, 295
Rainbow 102, 228, 233
Ramses II, Statues of 281n16
Ransom concept 114
Raphael (archangel) 178
Rapture 9, 101, 174, 182, 415
Rapture theory from Rev 4:1 101
Rationalism 369
Reconciliation through the cross 240
Red dragon 275, 303
Red horse 130
Redeemed as priests 115
Redeemed, Glorification of the 462
Redeemed martyrs 172
Redeemed of all ages 169
Redeemed of all races 169
Redemption 102, 107, 115
   Divine origin of 462
   Of creation 114, 115
   Of God's people 332
Redemptive history 114
Reed for measuring 243
Reformation 14, 263
   Churches 478
   Creeds 14
   Movement 269
   Protestant 8, 478
Reformed interpretation 222
Reign, Eternal 449
Reign of Jesus 449
Reign, Temperal 449
Relics 221
Remiel (archangel) 178
Renaissance humanism 369, 400
Replacement Theology 472

Index of Subjects

Rest of the dead 438, 442
Resumption of the witness 261
Resurrection 145n43
   First 169, 182, 415, 434, 436, 438, 442nn13–14
   Future 67n19, 68, 70
   General 444
   Of Jesus Christ 62, 108
   Of the dead 117
   Of the Roman beast 349
   Of the witnesses 261
   Partial 456n27
   Second 415, 444, 450
Return of Jesus Christ 117, 169, 412, 429
Reuben, Israelite tribe 166
Revelation 350, 376
   Allegorical interpretation 5, 37
   Apostolic authorship 3, 4, 5
   Approaches to interpretation 7
   As apocalyptic genre 19
   As commentary on Daniel 109
   As neglected and misused 1
   As the testimony of Jesus 2
   As the Word of God 2
   Canonicity of 6
   Christ-Antichrist theme 110
   Chronology 149n45, 150n47
   Date of authorship 4, 6
   Conclusion of 36
   Dramatic character of 17, 38
   Date of publication 4
   Final message of Jesus 2
   Futurist interpretation 23
   Grammar of 5
   Hebrew language idioms 5
   Historical orientation 11
   Historical origin 3
   Interpretation of
      19th century 13
      20th Century 13
      Current trends 10
      Futurist church-age parenthesis theory 8
      Futurist school 8
      Historical school 7, 10
      Idealist school 14
      Literal 17
      Negative-critical theories 8
      Neofuturism 10
      Philosophy of History School 14
      Postmillennial 11
      Post-Reformation Protestants 11
      Premillennial 11
      Pre-Reformation 11
      Preterist school 7
      Progressive 472
      Reformation 11
      Roman Catholic 8
      Traditional Protestant 14
      Twentieth century 12
   Message of 7, 227n1
      Sweet and bitter 42
      Introduction to 36
   Literary style of 5
   Non-Apostolic authorship of 4
   Occasion of writing 6
   Outline of 42
   Practical application of 1, 49
   Prediction in 2
   Structure and Theme 35
   Structure of 101n3, 147
      Little scroll 40
      Structural symbols of 121
      Unified structure of 42
   Theme of 7
   Title of 15
   Supernatural 182n11
      Introduction to 35
   Revised English Bible 171
Revival, Grass-roots 263
Revival movement 269

Index of Subjects

Revolution, Political	150n48
Revolution, Radical	148
Rhine River	372
Ribera	480
Ribera (Jesuit Priest)	8
Richard the Lion-Hearted	209
Rider, Death	139, 141
Rider on the white horse	412
Right foot on the sea	228, 233
Righteous acts of the saints	420
Righteousness	145
Righteousness, Imputed	420
River flooding as symbol	362
River of life	459, 466
River ways	183
Rivers and springs of water	359, 372
Roar like a lion	234
Roar of rushing waters	417
Robe reaching to feet	228
Robed in a cloud	228, 233
Robes made white	331
Roman	191
Roman Antichrist	250, 356
Roman Antichrist doctrine	478
Roman Antichrist power	427
Roman Antichrist's disclosure	230
Roman armies	128
Roman authority, Sphere of	262
Roman beast	225
Roman bishop, Preeminence of	306
Roman Catholic Church	15, 219, 252, 253, 257, 258, 478, 262, 347, 369, 376, 478, 480, 503
20th & 21st centuries	507
Abuses of	251
Atrocities	368
Commerce of	412
Doctrine of	377
Errors of	257
Persecution of	252
Priesthood of	376
Sacramental system of salvation	14
Slaughter of dissenters	367
Roman Catholic historians	309
Roman Catholic maritime powers	370
Roman Catholics	509
Roman citizenship	136
Roman dragon	278
Roman earth	184, 343
Roman emperor/s	127, 128, 281
Roman emperor abolished	192
Roman Emperors	
Roman Empire	124, 127, 128, 129n11, 132, 136, 139, 140, 141, 146, 152n52, 184, 188, 189, 191, 203, 208, 231, 299, 304, 305
Christian	159n64, 217
Christianized	167
Conversion of	167, 203
Eastern	213, 214, 215, 216, 221
Fall of	192, 251, 294, 401
Government of	4
Old	8
Pagan	122, 125, 126, 139, 143, 146, 149, 167, 217, 287, 303, 363, 481, 500
Reincarnated	305
Resurrection of	306
Tripartite	289
Western	185n14, 188, 190, 192, 214
Western, Fall of	189
Roman Imperial cult	293, 296, 316, 322
Roman Imperial Taxes	137n30
Roman legions	132
Roman military	131
Roman navy burned by Vandals	191
Roman Papacy	249, 269, 305, 505
Authority of	504
Roman Papal Catholicism	373
Roman Papal church	14
Roman Papal corruption	370
Roman senate dissolved	192

Index of Subjects

Roman warfare 181
Roman world 141, 183, 184, 203, 204, 244, 246, 247, 248, 257, 261, 296, 300, 321
Roman world of the 16th century 217
Romanism 137
Romanist practices 480
Roman-Jewish War 173n78
Rome 124, 184, 255, 304
    As "Mediterranean Sea" 186
    As the "sea" 186
    Barbarian conquest of 189
    Besieged 189
    Burning of 190
    Capital of the Empire 411
    City of God 306
    City on seven hills 393
    Pagan's fall 155
    Pillaged by Vandals 191
    Preeminence of 306
    The "great city" 255
Romulus Augustulus, Emperor 304
Romulus Augustus, Emperor 251
Root of David 108, 110
Rousseau 369
Rule of context 153n57
Rule of God 230
Rule with an iron scepter 279
Rulers, Authority of 488
Rules of Interpretation 471
Rivers 187
Saadeddin, Turkish historian 215
Sabbatarian doctrine 285n21
Sabbath 71
Sacramentalism 123n3, 167, 221
Sacrificial altar 161
Sacrifice of Christ 179n8
Sacrificial altar 343, 354
Sacrificial death 170
Saint worship 219
Sainthood 221
Saints 103n6, 420
    As judges 53
    As priests of God 54
    In heaven 103n6
    Intercession of 123n3
    Resurrected and celebrating 351
    To rule 53n8, 437
    To judge the world 437
    Worship of 218
Saladin 209, 213, 216
Sale of indulgences 413
Salvation 169
Salvation by faith alone 247
Samson 419
Sanctifying Holy Spirit 144
Sanctuary, Heavenly 102
Sanctuary of God 353
Sanhedrin, Small 103n8
Saracen conquests 201, 203, 213
Saracen conquests, Duration of 205
Saracen warriors 202
Saracenic empire 202
Saracens 200n46, 213
Saraqa'el (archangel) 178
Sash of gold 228
Satan 187n20, 198n44, 212n63, 240n11, 295, 317, 321n63, 435, 443, 448
    As active during millennium 436n2
    Acts of 261
    Agents of 210n59
    Ancient serpent 290
    Antichristian war of 304
    Binding of 441
    Death of 448n18
    Destruction of 415
    Empire 139n34
    Fall of 198n44, 286
    Home of 320n63
    Incapacitated 435
    Kingdom of 71, 143, 267

Index of Subjects

Mortality of	448n18
Synagogue of	71
Throne of	296
Type of	187n20
Satanic delusion	168
Satanic dragon power	271, 304
Satanic forces	198, 266
Satanic Roman power	283
Satanic triumvirate	327, 383
Satanic underworld	211
Satanic-serpent power	284
Saturday as true Sabbath	285n21
Saturday-sabbath keepers	391n46
Saudi Arabia	375
Saving death	170
Saving faith	144
Savior (Jesus Christ)	
Sovereign	50
Victorious	50
Scales, Balance	133
Scarlet beast	386, 389, 397, 400
Scepter	281, 426
Schofield, C. I.	480
Schofield dispensationalism	155
Schofield Reference Bible	480
Schofield Bible	9
Scorched with fire	373
Scorpion/s	200, 203
Scripture, Allegorization	167
Scripture. Clear teachings of	219
Scripture, Unity of	117n26, 471
Scriptures prohibited to laity	258
Scroll, Great	108
Scroll, Little	223
Scroll, Seven-sealed	109, 120
Scroll, Writing on back	109, 109n16
Scrolls, Manufacture of	109
Scrolls, Sealing of	109
Scythians	191
Sea battles	183
Sea captains, Lament of	410
Sea of glass	104, 351, 352
Sea serpent	281
Seat	186
Sea turned into blood	186, 190, 358
Seal as mark of ownership	165
Seal, Fifth	142, 146, 147
Seal mark on forehead	165
Seal of God	161, 163, 167, 174, 198, 199, 203, 204, 318
Seal prophecies	485
Seal, Seventh	163
Seal up the words	235
Sealing of God's people	239
Seals, As introductory	127
Seals, Seven	110
Seals, trumpets, and bowls	39
Parallel or synchronous interpretation, 40	
Second advent *See also* Return of Jesus	2, 54, 182, 327, 347, 415, 422, 425, 429, 434, 449, 455, 467, 468, 469, 496
Imminency of	50, 244n16
Second bowl of wrath	370, 371n26
Second death	69, 451
Second flying angel's message	334
Second Temple	150
Second trumpet	183, 186, 187, 190
Second woe	207, 213, 214n69, 224, 247, 265
Second woe	213, 248
Second woe, Passing of	232
Sects, Heretical and schismatic	289
Seljuk Turks	213, 216
Semitic idiom	152, 345
Sennacherib	207
Septuagint version of Deut 32:34, 35	32
Seraphim	105, 106
Serpent	284
Serpent, Seven headed	16
Servant, Suffering	116

servanthood 105
Seven, As symbolic number 110
Seven bowls 194n37, 195, 269
Seven bowls of wrath 225, 287, 349
Seven churches 37, 51, 124, 484
Seven churches, Prophetic interpretation 63
Seven churches, Viewed as prophecies 37
Seven crowns 275, 277, 281
Seven Dutch provinces 266
Seven golden bowls 354
Seven golden lampstands 60
Seven heads 275
Seven heads of the beast 312n52, 393
Seven lamps 161
Seven lamps blazing 104
Seven last plagues 225, 265, 350, 352
Seven spirits 52
Seven spirits of God 104, 113
Seven stars 52
Seven thunders 230, 235
Seven trumpets 160, 175, 176
Seven-fold division 486n7
Seven-headed beast 186
Seven-sealed Scroll 266, 327
Seven-sealed scroll 39, 120, 224, 226n1, 233n5, 234n5
Seven-sealed Scroll, Chronology of 287
Seventh Bowl
Seventh bowl 149n45, 389
Seventh bowl of wrath 378, 382
Seventh head 304
Seventh head, Resurrection of 295
Seventh seal 163, 175, 177
Seventh trumpet 193, 194, 224, 225, 226n1, 229, 232, 236, 266, 268, 387
Seventh trumpet era 232
Seventh-day Adventists 188n22, 391n46, 439n8, 444n15
Seventieth week 161, 162
Seventy Weeks of Daniel 9 31, 481

Seventy Weeks prophecy 472
Seventy weeks prophecy 476
Seventy Weeks prophecy of Daniel 9 9
Seventy-week prophecy 241
Severe earthquake 261, 262, 264
Sextus II, Pope 216
Sexual immorality 67, 207, 212, 220, 388, 404
Sexual orientation 332
Shakespeare, William
  Hamlet, Act 2, Sc. 2:9 , 177n3
Sharp sickle 342
Sharp sword 426
Sheep and goats judgment 449
Sheep and Goats judgment 449n19
Shekinah 104
Shekinah brilliance 462
Shekinah glory of God 102
Ships, Destruction of 187
Shout like roar of a lion 228
Sickle, Sharp 345
Sign (*sēmeîon*) 281
Sign of the cross 289
Silence in heaven 176
Simeon, Israelite tribe 166
Simon bar Kokhba 425
Simpson, A. B. 13n19
Sin catalogs 212n64
Sinai 194
Sinaiticus 127n7
Singing Hallelujah Chorus 384
Singing multitude 330
Sits on many waters 385, 386
Sixth bowl of wrath 362, 374
Sixth head of the beast 316
Sixth seal 148, 151n49, 155, 156, 158, 160, 167, 188, 203, 493
Sixth trumpet 205, 207, 213, 214, 216, 217, 218, 220n81, 221
Sixth trumpet era 219, 248
Sixth trumpet forces 214

Index of Subjects

Sixth trumpet prophecy	265
Sky	148
Sky rolled up	151, 488
Slander	70
Slaves, Christian	158n63
Slaves, Pagan	158n63
Smoke	211
Smoke as from a furnace	199
Smoke of the incense	180
Smyrna	69, 70, 71
Smyrna, Church at	68, 69, 72n24
Smyrneans	70, 71
Indulgences, Sale of	368
Society of Jesus	478, 479, 508n17
Sodom	151n51, 255
Destruction of	211
Sodom and Gomorrah, Example of	336
Son, Exaltation of	116
Son of David	279
Son of God	60
Son of Man	51, 54, 57, 228, 229, 345
As a human being	60
As a Messianic title	21, 60, 229
Coming of the	364n14
Enthroned	437
Rule of	342
Song	
By the twenty-four elders	271
Great song of praise	116
Of the twenty-four elders	287, 332
Of the four living creatures	332
Of many angels	332
Of Moses and the Lamb	351
Of redeemed	162
Of the redeemed	331, 332
Of victory	283
Sons of God	460
Sores, Ugly and painful	370
Soul	145n42
Souls of the martyrs	145, 286
Souls under the altar	144
Source streams	183
South America	372
Sovereign and holy justice	335
Sovereign authority	234
Sovereign authority of Christ	229n2
Sovereign Creator	105
Sovereign grace	176
Sovereign judgment	
Sovereign judgment of God	102, 176, 356, 426
Sovereignty of God	1, 54, 56, 102, 126, 144, 145, 149, 151n49, 164, 170, 172, 176, 182, 183, 199, 208, 231, 234n5, 235, 246, 261, 266, 267, 280, 298, 334, 356, 384, 400, 420, 451
Sovereignty of Jesus Christ	343, 422
Spain	190, 202, 289, 370
Devastated by Vandals	191
Moslem conquest of	202
Spanish *Dominie*	*258*
Spanish Moors	213
Spirit of prophecy	421
Spirits of demons	363
Spirits of the dead, Worship of	220
Spiritual refreshment	173
Springs	183
Springs of water	187, 337
Square earth	164
Staples of diet	134
Star, As ruling authority	199
Star blazing	187
Star, Great blazing	191
Stars	303
Stars falling	151, 488
State church	289, 291, 304, 477
State church established	257
Stephen, Death of	31
Stones, Precious	463
Straits of Gibraltar	191
Structural elements, Main	110, 226n1
Structure, Apocalyptic	156

Substitutionary atonement	145, 173	Targumists	128n9
Suevi	311, 504	Targums	72
Suffering	184	Tax collection	138
Suffering for Christ	71	Tax collectors	137
Suffering Servant	116	Tax on Jews	130
Suleiman the Magnificent	263	Taxation, Excessive	136
Sulfur	211	Taxes, Roman	138
Sun	303	Tell Megiddo	427, 431
Sun and sky darkened	199	Temple	144, 179, 238, 268, 314, 464
Sun as symbol	192	Antitypical	240
Sun as temporal authority	274	Architecture of	165
Sun, moon, and stars	184	As sanctuary	148
Sun, Standing in the	427	As the Christian church	60, 300
Sunday (Lord's Day)	59	Destruction of	238
Superficial reading	155	Imagery as the Most Holy Place	99
Superficial reasoning	155	Israelite	
Suru'el (archangel)	178	Jerusalem	238
Sword	140	Second	150n47
Large	130	Threshold of	465
Of justice	427	Typology of	242
Swords, Roman	131	Temple of Artemis	65
Symbolic language	185, 229, 237, 487	Temporal judgment	151n49
Symbolism	107n13	Temporal power of Papacy	249, 253, 258
Covenant	385	Temporal power, Loss of	373, 389
On monuments	151n49	Ten barbarian kingdoms	312
Apocalyptic	1	Ten commandments	353
Symbols from Old Testament	123	Ten horns	275, 300n35, 400, 401
Synagogue of Satan	71	Ten horns as ten kingdoms	408, 501
Synchronous chronology	178n4	Ten horns attack harlot	400
Synchronous structure	155, 160	Ten horns of Daniel 7	310
Syria	289, 375	Ten horns of the beast	264, 293, 310, 394
Moslem conquest of	202	Ten horns of the dragon	293
Tabernacle, Israelite	58, 144, 166n71, 176, 179	Ten kingdoms	300
Sanctuary of	161	Ten kings	397, 404, 427
Typology of	180	Ten Kings as Barbarian nations	504
Taborites	368	Ten Kings, World of the	387
Tacitus, Roman historian	276, 500	Ten plagues of Egypt	356
Tail of the dragon	289	Tent of the testimony	353
Tails like snakes	211	Terrestrial signs	148, 379
Talmud	67n19	Terrestrial symbolism	150, 154
		Tertullian	251

Index of Subjects 563

Testimony 143
Testimony of Jesus 59, 169, 229, 272, 285, 319, 331, 391, 420, 421, 457, 468
Testimony to Jesus 411
Testimony to the Lamb 301
Text of apocalyptic 487
Textus Receptus 193n36
Theft/s 207, 212, 220, 221
Theodora, Empress 252
Theodoret 219
Theodosius, Death of 188
Theodosius I, Emperor 157, 159n64, 291
Thief, Illustration of the 365
Third bowl angel 358
Third bowl of wrath 372
Third flying angel's message 334
Third heaven 233
Third Lateran Council 258
Third of mankind 206, 210
Third of the sea 190
Third of the stars 289, 303
Third of the sun 187
Third trumpet 183, 187, 191
Third woe 193, 194, 226n1, 265, 267, 350, 352
This age 447
Thousand years 435
Three and a half days 257, 261
Three and a half years 259
Three angelic messengers 333
Three evil spirits 363
Three flying angels 327, 347
Three frogs 507
Three woes 42, 193, 194n37, 195, 201
Throne in heaven 101
Throne of God 102, 104, 105, 107, 112, 113, 116, 170, 171, 172, 174, 179, 224, 301, 330, 450, 351, 465, 466
Throne of the beast 373
Throne of the Lamb 330
Thrones 172

Thrones of judgment 437
Thunder 104, 180, 180n9, 268
Tigris River 213n68
Time designation, Extraordinary 208
Time, times, and half a time 23, 236n8, 241, 283, 298, 501
Times of the Gentiles 34
Timothy 220n81
Titus, Emperor 320
Titus, Roman general 30n41
To give breath to the image 324
Tobias' wedding feast 419
Togrul Beg 216
Tongues cut out 258
Tormented day and night 334
Torture 143, 146n44
Tractarian Movement 377, 480
Trajan, Emperor 66, 69n20, 129
Transtemporal interpretation 312n52, 329n3, 338n10, 394, 474, 481, 491
Transtemporal prediction 362
Transtemporal principles 313n52
Tree of knowledge of good & evil 465
Tree of life 1, 67, 469
Trees 185
Trees, Burning of 183, 190
Tribe of Dan 161
Tribes of Israel 102, 161, 165
Tribes, Twelve
Tribulation 59, 160, 169, 172, 301, 490
Tribulation, The Great 33
Tribute tax 137
Trinitarian creed 292
Triumvirate of evil 388
Truce at Horns of Hattin 209
True Israel 144
True visible church 240, 247, 248, 291, 303, 304, 385, 395
True witnessing Church 268
Trumpet 181, 182
  As an instrument of war 182

Fifth	214	Two witnesses	241, 242, 247, 249, 253, 254, 257, 258, 261, 264, 268, 284
First	183		
Fourth	184, 191	Testimony of	257
Last	182	Time to prophesy	298
Prophecies	181, 193, 485	Tyndale, William	263
Second	183	Typological interpretation	55n10, 286n21
Sequence	175		
Series of seven	149n45, 176, 195	Hermeneutics of	187n20
Seventh	224	Tyre, King of	198n44
Sixth	213, 214, 218, 221	Ugly and painful sores	356, 370
Third	183	Ulfilus, Missionary to Goths	189n24
Turkey	51, 375	Unclean food	388
Turkish armies	214, 266	Unfaithful spouse of Yahweh	385
Turkish cavalry	214	Unity of Scripture	117n26
Turkish conquests	216, 217, 221, 222	Universal Bishop 251, 253, 257, 306, 307, 308, 507	
Turkish Empire drying up	375		
Turkish fleet was destroyed	375	Universal company	169
Turkish invasion threat	263	Urban II, Pope	213
Turkish losses-1820-1911	375	Valens, Emperor	291, 304
Turks	213, 214, 216n75	Valenses	253, 368
Turks, Ottoman	213	Valley of Jehoshophat	344, 365, 427, 431
Turks, Seljuk	213	Valleys of the Piedmont	372
Tutankhamen, King	281	Vandal kingdom	311
Twelve apostles	462	Vandal sack of Rome	190
Twelve foundations	462	Vandal/s	152n52, 189, 505
Twelve gates	462, 463	Vatican	
Twelve stars	274	Annual Report of	412
Twelve thrones	437	Possessions of	413
Twelve tribes	462	Wealth of	374
Twelve tribes of Israel	437	Temporal power	309
Twentieth century interpretation	479	Vatican City	
Twenty-four courses of Israelite priesthood	103	Vatican Council I	309, 374
		Vaticanus, Codex	67n19
Twenty-four elders 103n6, 104, 105, 107, 114		Vaudois	368
		Vegetation, Burning of	190
Twenty-four elders, Celebration of	490	Veil of the sanctuary	207
Two-horned beast	249, 310, 321	Veil of the temple	180
Two hundred million	210, 214	Venerable Bede	248
Two lampstands	241, 242	Vengeance, Days of	32n44
Two olive trees	241, 245	Venus, Planet	187n20
Two resurrections implied	438	Vessels, Temple	60

Index of Subjects

Vicar of Jesus Christ 505
Victorinus 102
Victorious consummation 241
Victory celebration 164, 170, 171, 232
Victory of Christ 266, 428
Victory of Christ's Church 72
Victory of God's people 287
Visible church 247, 248, 268, 395n50
Visigothic kingdom 311
Visigoths 504
Visions of Daniel 312n52
Voice from heaven 235, 237
Voice like sound of multitude 228
Voice like sound of rushing water 228
Voltaire 369
Vulgate Bible 140n35
Waldenses 252, 253, 257, 259, 368, 372, 478
Waldo, Peter 253
War against the saints
    146, 171, 230n4, 231, 248, 249, 283, 298, 400
War in heaven 286
War of the dragon 224
War of the Beast 256, 271
War of the little horn 283, 298
War with Antichrist 236
War with Protestant England 370
War with the beast 255, 284
War with the rest of the woman's offspring 304
Warfare 130
Warfare, Human 183
Warfare, Israelite 181, 182
Wedding celebration 428
Wedding covenant 428
Wedding of the Lamb 421
West Indies 372
Western church 222
Western Europe 191
Western Roman Empire, Fall of 192, 502
Westminster Confession 15, 15n30
Wheat 134
Wheat and grape harvest 327
Wheat harvest 341
White horse/s 422, 425
White robe 145, 173
White-horse Rider 422
White-robed multitude 490
Wicked, Destiny of 445
Wild beasts 140, 142
Wilderness churches 478
Wilderness state 284
Wills 109
Wine 135, 338
Wine of God's fury 334
Wine of her adulteries 386
Winepress of God's wrath 344, 346
Wings of the seraphim 106
Witchcraft 390
Witness
    Evangelical 256
    Juridical usage 242
    To Christ 48
    Of Jesus Christ 475
Witnesses, Two 248
    Death of 252, 256, 258, 259
    Persecution of 251
Witnessing church 242
Woe, Passing of the second 224
Woes, Three 495
Woman and the dragon 224
Woman as the church 272, 290
Woman clothed with the sun 224, 273, 291, 303
Woman's flight into the desert 290, 291, 304
Woman in the wilderness 298
Woman on the Beast 399
Word of God 49, 143, 176, 206, 243, 245, 321, 425, 426
Word of God

Unity of	351	Wrath of God	195, 426
World Confederacy, Papal	377	www.historicism.com	12n19, 508n15
World missionary enterprise	264	Wycliffe	258
World of the church	184	Wycliffites	368
World to come	67, 69	Xerxes	27n39
Wormwood	187	Year-day principle	
Worship	105	31, 72n24, 200, 204, 209, 216, 217,	
In heaven	102	240, 261, 298, 436, 476, 477, 501	
Of God	107, 117, 172, 334	Yezed	203
Of demons	212	Yugoslavia	189
Of departed saints	217, 218	Zebulun, Israelite tribe	166
Of idols	212	Zechariah	242, 245, 246n18
Of the beast	334	Zechariah's vision	242
Of the Lamb	117	Zephaniah	153
Worshipers		Zerubbabel	150, 181, 243
Count of	237	Zerubbabel the Prince	241, 245
In Temple	238		

Index of Modern Authors

Adams, J. E. 377n32
Addis, Alfred 202n48
Aharoni, Yigael 27n39
Ainsworth, Wm. F. 75n26
Alcasar, Luis de 479, 481
Alford, H. 61n15
Alford, Henry 442n13
Allen, Leslie C. 278n12
Allix, Peter 11n18, 253, 253n34, 368n17
Andreas 56n12
Aretius, Benedictus 276, 277n10, 288n22
Arnot, A. B. 162n66
Ash, McKinley 156, 163n66, 188n22, 202n48
Ashe, Isaac 188n22, 202n48
Atkinson, Basil F. C. 12n18, 71n23, 121n2, 156, 157n61 163n66, 188n22, 202n48, 233n5, 309n45, 312, 371n26, 374, 382, 448n18
Aune, David E. 321n65, 354n2, 355, 391n45, 394n49, 398n52, 399, 424n7, 425, 450n22, 451
Bacon, Roger 308n45
Bale, John 251, 308n45, 478
Barclay, William 10, 71, 72, 83n31, 89, 91n42, 106n12, 117n26, 134n25, 152n54, 172, 177, 178, 179n8, 180, 182, 243, 377n32
Barker, Wm B. 75n26
Barnes, Albert (Persons) 12n18, 13, 56n12, 83n31, 140n36, 152n52, 163n66, 188n22, 191n31, 200, 202, 209n55, 210, 220, 221, 233n5, 256n37, 260, 263n46, 268n52, 288n22, 322, 360, 371n26, 372
Barnes, Albert 37n49
Barnes, Timothy 159n64
Barrett, C. K. 494n24
Barton, Freeman 488n11
Barton, Harold 12n18, 156, 163n66, 202n48, 210, 276n9, 288n22, 309n45, 371n26, 372, 376, 381
Bauer, Walter 63n17, 462n31
Baumgarten, Joseph M. 103n8
Bayford, John 202n48
Beale, G. K. 14n29, 49n2, 207n53, 208n55, 210, 211nn60–61, 226n1, 229n2, 233, 338n10, 243, 255n36, 263nn46–47, 273, 274n5, 279n13, 281n15, 284, 312n52, 321n64, 337, 339n11, 340n14, 341, 357, 358, 361n11, 379n34, 386n39, 391n45, 394n49, 407, 424n7, 425, 425n10, 442nn12–13, 463n32, 468n35, 484n2
Beasley-Murray, G. R. 103n8, 127n8, 134n25, 162n66, 211n61, 233n5, 492
Becker. C. H. 202n49
Beckwith, Isbon T. 10, 55n10, 56n12, 71n23, 90n41, 101n4, 103n8, 140n36, 162n66, 166n72, 175, 179n8, 195, 208n55, 226n1, 233n5, 268n52, 329, 337n7, 338, 339n11, 341, 377n32, 489, 495
Behm, J. 233n5
Berkhof, Louis 486n7

Beverley, Thomas 202n48
Bichemo, James 188n22, 202n48
Bickersteth, Edward 202n48, 308n45
Birks, T. R. 12n18, 13, 25n37, 173n78, 202n48, 210
Blass, F. 63n17
Bloomfield, S. T. 12n18, 56n12, 120n2, 156, 195n40
Bloomfield, Thomas 202n48
Boak, A. E. R. 129n11, 132, 137
Boring, M. Eugene 162n66, 377n32
Bousset, W. 90n41
Boutflower, Charles 25n37, 29n40
Bower, Archibald 505n10
Briggs, Charles A. 499n3
Bright, John 27n39
Brightman, Thomas 55n10, 56n12, 67, 70, 71n23, 76, 86n38, 156, 162n66, 178n6, 187n19, 193n36, 195n40, 200n46, 202n48, 277, 288n22, 478
Broglie, Duc de 504
Brown, Francis 499n3
Brown, John Aquila 12n18, 202n48, 308n45
Bruce, F. F. 41n50, 84n34, 91n43, 251, 251n26
Bryce, John 308n45
Bullinger, Henry 202n48, 308n45, 478
Burder 308n45
Burgh, William 496
Burke, Emund 323n67
Burns, Thomas S. 189n25, 190
Burr, G. I. 249n21
Burton, Ernest DeWitt 429n13
Bury, J. B. 213n65, 249n21, 306n41
Cachemaille, E. P. (Persons) 12n18, 13, 25n37, 37n49, 142, 142n38, 156, 163n66, 185n14, 188n22, 195n40, 202n48, 210, 214n69, 263n45, 265n50, 268, 288n22, 291,

300n35, 309, 341, 371, 375, 389
Caird, G. B. 84n34, 134n25, 295n31
Calvin, John 197n42, 278n12
Caringola, Robert 156, 210
Carroll, B. H. 162n66
Carson, R. A. G. 288
Charles, R. H. 5, 41n50, 52n4, 53, 56n12, 62, 70, 71n23, 72n25, 75, 90n41, 91n43, 101n4, 102, 104n9, 110, 110n17, 113nn20–21,122, 128n10, 131n16, 134n25, 135n27, 151, 153n55, 162n66, 166n70, n72, 172, 173n79, 177, 179n8, 180n9, 199, 208, 226n1, 232, 233n5, 236, 236n7, 239n10, 246n19, 268n52, 274n4, 303n37, 318, 320n61, 345, 354n2, 358n6, 377n32, 390n44, 489
Charlesworth, James H. 30n41, 106n11, 166n70, 178, 234n6, 485n5
Chilton, D. C. 377n32
Chytraeus, David 308n45
Clarke, Adam 12n18, 71n23, 120n2, 156, 157
Clement of Alexandria 56n12
Collins, Oral 32n44, 60n14, 8029, 172n78, 488
Cooke, Ronald N. 252n30
Cooper, Edward 202n48
Cooper, Samuel 188n22
Cornwall, Rupert 413
Court, John M. 135n25, 182n11
Cowley, A. E. 424n8
Cox, John 202n48
Cox, William E. 33n46
Craven 202n48
Cressener, Drue 202n48
Crinsoz de Boinens, Theodore 188n22,

Index of Modern Authors

202n48
Croly, George 202n48
Cruse, F. C. 273n2
Cummings, John 25n37, 162n66, 188n22, 202n48
Cuninghame, William 150n48, 159, 162n66, 188n22, 202n48, 312, 371n26, 373, 484n4, 491
Danker, Frederick 63n17, 462n31
Darby, John Nelson 489, 502
Daubuz, Charles 11n18, 120n2, 156, 188n22, 202n48, 208n55, 312
Davis, William C. 202n48
DeBrunner, A. 63n17
Delitzsch, Franz 279n12
DeWette, W. M. L. 377n32
Dodd, C. H. 156
Dods, Marcus 493n21
Dollinger, J. H. Ignaz von 369n18
Donaldson, James 476n4
Driver, S. R. 499n3
Drummond, Henry 188n22, 202n48
Durham, James 12n18, 162n66, 202n48, 211n62, 288n22
Edersheim, Alfred 428n12
Edwards, Jonathan xxvii, 12n18, 120n2, 156, 185n15, 188n22, 202n48, 308n45, 503, 503nn6-7, 504n8
Eerdman, Charles 37n49
Ehrlich, Carl S. 128n9
Eicasmi 288n22
Eichhorn, J. G. 377n32
Elliott, E. B. 11n18, 12n18, 14, 14n28, 61, 37n49, 41n50, 62, 109n16,
120nn1–2, 128n9, 129, 130n15, 132, 134n25, 135, 137n31, 138, 139nn33–34, 140, 140n35, 142n38,
156, 157, 162n66, 177n3, 179, 185nn13–14, n16, 188n22, 189, 190, 192, 195n40, 202, 203n50, 204, 205n52, 207, 208, 209nn55, 57, 210, 211n62, 214, 215, 216, 217, 218, 219nn79–80, 221, 226n1, 232, 236n8, 251nn27–28, 252, 253, 255n35, 256, 257, 258, 259nn41–42, 260, 262n44, 263, 265n50, 266, 268n52, 274n4, 275n7, 277n10, 288n22, 289, 304n39, 309, 311, 312, 319n60, 322, 323, 324, 341, 359nn7, 9, 370, 371, 372n27, 373, 374, 394n49, 418n2, 478n7, 479n9, 496, 498, 500n4, 502n5, 504, 505
Ellis, E. Earle 34n47, 55, 56n12, 152n54
Eusebius 4, 5n3
Ewald, G. H. A. 377n32
Faber, George Stanley 12n18, 120n2, 156, 188n22, 202n48, 230n3, 233n5, 308n45, 371n26
Fairbairn, Patrick 197n42
Faldesius 202n48
Farnham, Benjamin 188n22, 202n48
Farrar, F. W. 34
Farrer, A. M. 494
Ferrero, Guglielmo 136, 137, 287
Fisher, George P. 189n24
Fleming, Robert 188n22, 202n48
Fletcher, Philip 505
Ford, Desmond 25n37
Ford, J. M. 52n3, 56n12, 72n25, 195n39, 239n10, 317, 317n57, 341, 377n32, 434n1, 462n31
Foxe, John 188n22, 252, 369n18, 411n55, 478
French, S. H. 121n2, 156
Frend, W. H. C. 143n40, 147n44
Frere, James Hatley 308n45
Frew, Robert 209n55
Froom, Le Roy Edwin 124n4, 188n22, 251n28, 277n10, 308n45

Fry, John 188n22, 202n48
Fudge, Edward William 446n17
Fulco, D. 276, 277n10, 288n22
Fuller, Andrew Gunton 188n22, 202n48
Galloway, Joseph 188n22, 202n48, 308n45
Gallus, Nicholaus 252n29
Garratt 202n48
Gaster, T. H. 218n78202
Gauntlett, Henry 188n22, 202n48, 308n45
Gaussen, Louis 188n22, 202n48
Gebhardt, Hermann 436n3
Gentry, K. L. 377n32
Gerstner, John H. xxvii, 504nn6, 8
Gibbon, Edward 129, 132, 137, 141, 142n39, 157, 159n64, 189n25, 190,
191, 214, 215, 217, 220, 288, 312, 322
Gibson, Scott M. 13n19
Gill, John 56n12, 70, 202n48, 308n45
Gingrich, F. W. 63n17, 462n31
Godet, F. L. 34
Goldsworthy, Graeme 486n6
Goodwin, Thomas 11n18, 120n2, 156, 188n22, 202n48
Gordon, Adoniram Judson 202n48
Goud, Clarkson 439n8, 440n10
Graham, James 323n67
Grant, Robert M. 142n39
Green, E. M. G. 96n47
Gregg, Steve 370n21
Grotius, Hugo 377n32, 479, 481
Guinness, H. Grattan 11n18, 13, 34, 173n78, 188n22, 202n48, 210, 249,
249n22, 288n22, 308n45, 309, 310,
311n50, 368, 369n18, 371n26, 395n49, 508n15
Guinness, Mrs. H. Grattan 13n24
Guthrie, Donald 5, 6, 495n27
Gwatkin, H. M. 290n25
Habershon, Matthew 188n22, 202n48
Hallam, Henry 221
Harnack, Adolph 135n27
Hatch, A. E. 13n19
Haywood, John 202n48
Heinrichs, Johann 208n55
Hendriksen, William 14n29, 37n49, 162n66, 239n10, 341, 360, 360n10, 486, 486n7, 491
Hengstenberg, E. W. 56n12
Henry, Matthew 71n23, 188n22
Herodotus 27n39
Hewitt, Clarence H. 25n37, 508n16
Hickman, Edward 503n7
Hill, H. F. 71n23
Hinton, Isaac T. 202n48
Hippolytus 55n10, 56n12
Hislop, Alexander 75n26
Hitti, Philip K. 203n50
Hoeksema, Herman 37, 37n49
Holland, Hezekiah 308n45
Holmes, W. A. 308n45
Holtzmann, H. J. 377n32
Hopkins, Samuel 308n45
Horch, Heinrich 188n22, 202n48
Hourani, Albert 205n52
Hughes, Philip Edgcumbe 208n55
Hutcheson, William 12n18, 120n2, 156
Illyricus, Flacius 252, 252n29
Infessura, Stefano 221Ir
Ironside, H. A. 489
Irving, Edward 188n22, 202n48
James, William 371n23
Jenkin, George 188n22
Jenks, William 188n22
Jewett, Paul King 123n3
Johnson, B. W. 12n18, 120n2, 156,

Index of Modern Authors

202n48
Johnson, Paul 369n19
Jones, Henry S. 187n21
Jones, William 157n61, 159n64, 201, 202n48, 218n77, 251n27, 252n32, 253, 291, 305, 307, 368n17
Jonge, Marinus de 425n9
Judex, Matthias 252n29
Junkin, George 202n48, 308n45
Jurieu, Pierre 156, 188n22, 202n48
Katz, Solomon 141, 190, 191, 287
Kautzsch, E. 424n8
Kee, H. C. 166n70
Keener, Craig S. 407n54
Keil, C. F. 25n36, 61, 150n47, 279n12, 299n34
Keith, Alexander 188n22, 202n48, 215n73, 371n26
Kelly, William 202n48
Keyworth, Thomas 188n22, 202n48, 308n45
Kiddle, Martin 91n43, 162n66, 233n5, 239n10
Kinne, Aaron 308n45
Kistemaker, Simon 104n9, 233n5, 303, 311n49, 320n61, 329n3, 341, 342, 255, 356n4, 358n6, 361n11, 389, 390n42
Kittle, Martin 242n13
Kline, Meredith 425n10
Kromminga, D. H. 441n11, 452n24
Lacunza, Manuel 480, 506
Ladd, George Eldon (Persons) 10, 37n49, 53, 56n12, 71n23, 91n43, 101n4, 106n12, 115, 127n8, 134n25, 162n66, 208n55, 341, 464n33, 480nn10, 12, 492
Lake, Kirsopp 124n4
Langdon, Edward H. 188n22
Langdon, Samuel 202n48
LaTourette, Kenneth Scott 189n24, 309, 309n48, 369nn19–20, 370n21
Lecky, W. E. H. 221n82
Lee, Francis Nigel 13, 163n66, 202n48, 211n62, 256n37, 288n22, 330n4, 371n26
Leith, John H. 15n30
Lenski, R. C. H. 239n10, 487
Leod, Alexander 288n22
Levitical 102
Liddell, Henry G. 187n21
Lightfoot, J. B. 418n2
Litch, Josiah 188n22
Llorente, Canon Juan Antonio 369n18, 508n15
Lo Bello, Nino 413
Loades, D. M. 369n18
Lohmeyer, E. 233n5
Lohse, E. 233n5
Lord, David N. 202n48, 371n26
Lowman, M. 202n48
Lowth, Robert 423n6
M'Leod, Alexander 12n18, 120n2, 156, 202n48, 205n52, 210, 214n69
MacPherson, Dave 480n10
Manning, Henry Edward 314n54, 504, 505n9
Mansfield, Peter 205n52, 213nn66–67
Marsh, J. 278n12
Marshall, I. Howard 34n47
Martin, Malachi 377n31, 382n35, 478n6, 508nn16–17
Mather, Cotton 188n22
Mauro, Philip 162n66
McDougall, Duncan 480nn10–11, 506n12
McIlvaine, Charles P. 202n48
Mede, Joseph 11n18, 120n2, 156, 159, 162n66, 164, 187, 188n22, 202n48, 210, 211n62, 214n69, 219n79, 277, 288n22, 304n39, 493, 496
Metzger, Bruce M. 193n36, 423n5,

494n24
Meyers, Carol 150n47
Michaels, J. Ramsey 341
Michelsen, A. Berkeley 56n12, 187n20, 489, 489n15
Miller, William F. 202n48
Milligan, William 377n32, 486n7
Milman, Henry Hart 129n11, 189n25, 221n82
Milner, Joseph 123n3
Moffatt, James 62
Moody, D. L. 480
Moore, George Foote 124n4
Moreland, Samuel 369n18
Morris, Leon 37n49, 76, 341
Mosheim, John L. von 189n24, 251n27, 259, 264n49
Mounce, Robert H. 5, 10, 37n49, 56n12, 62, 71, 71n23, 83n31, 91n43, 96n47, 106n12, 140, 162n66, 167n74, 172, 179, 194n37, 199, 208n55, 209n55, 214n71, 339n11, 341, 359, 421, 486, 487n8, 494, 496
Moyer, Elgin S. 189n24, 248n20
Napier, B. D. 113n19
Napier, John 202n48, 276, 277n10, 288n22
Newark, Tim 192n33
Newman, Albert Henry 253n33
Newman, John Henry 505
Newport, John P. 37, 54
Newton, Isaac 156, 188n22, 202n48, 312n51
Newton, Thomas 12n18, 120n2, 156, 162n66, 188n22, 195n40, 202n48, 203
Nichols, James A., Jr. 120n2, 202n48
Omar (Saracen general) 202
Orelli, C. von 278n12

Osborne, Grant R. 320n61, 321, 331, 339, 394n49
Osiander, Andreas 276, 288n22
Pareus, David 202n48, 260, 277, 288n22, 308n45, 491
Park, John R. 202n48, 308n45
Payne, J. Barton 34n47, 153
Pelikan, Jaroslav 192n35, 217, 217n76
Pennington, Arthur Robert 368
Pile, Thomas 202n48
Piper, F. L. 13n19
Pius V, Pope 507
Pius X, Pope 507n13
Ploetz, Carl 276n9 339n13, 361n11, 371n24
Pond, Enoch 198n43, 202n48
Porcelli, Baron 313, 314, 504, 505, 505n9, 508
Prayers of the saints 178
Priestley, Joseph 305n40
Pusey, E. B. 25n37, 29n40, 33, 299n34
Pyle, Thomas 188n22
Pyles, F. A. 13n19
Ramm, Bernard 471n1
Ramsay, William 79, 86, 86n36, 89
Reader, Thomas 308n45
Reid, Robert 202n48
Renaud, B. 278n12
Ribera, Francisco 479, 488n12, 493, 506
Richardson, Donald W. 41n50
Rissi, Matthias 233n5, 239n10
Rist, Martin 166n70
Roberts, Alexander 476n4
Robertson, A. T. 49n1, 469n36
Rodgers, Henry 503, 503n7
Rollin, Charles 75n26
Rowley, H. H. 19n32
Rudwick, M. J. S. 96n47
Russel, D. S. 19n32

Index of Modern Authors 573

Schaff, Philip
  3, 4, 142n39, 159n64, 192n34,
  203n50, 218, 220, 251n27,
  253n34, 288n23, 289, 291, 307,
  368n16, 476n5, 505n11
Schmucker, John George   202n48
Schoedel, Wm. R.   70n21
Scott, John   288n22
Scott, Robert   187n21, 188n22,
  308n45
Scott, Thomas
  12n18, 120n2, 156, 188n22,
  202n48, 203, 210, 211n62
Scott, Walter   9, 9n14, 162n66
Seiss, Joseph A.   162n66
Shaff, Philip   221n82,
Sherwin, William   188n22, 202n48
Silva, Moisés   361n11
Simpson, A. B.   202n48
Simpson, David   12n18, 37n49,
  120n2, 156, 202n48
Sismondi, J. Ch. L.   220
Smiles, Samuel   369n18
Smith, Ethan   202n48
Smith, H. P.   128n9
Smith, Henry   308n45
Smith, J. A.   319n59
Smith, John E.   504n8
Smith, Wilbur M.   13, 395n49
Spurgeon, C. H.   13, 71n23
Stacy, James   12n18
Steele, David
  12n18, 13, 13n23, 202n48,
  308n45, 309n45, 369n18
Steinmann, Andrew   484
Stuart, Moses   12n18, 208n55, 360,
  377n32, 496
Summers, Ray   71n23
Swete, Henry Barclay

  5n3, 10, 55n10, 56, 61, 62, 71n23,
  83n32, 102n4, 153n55,
  166nn70–71, 178n4, 180, 193n36,
  208nn54–55, 233, 239n10, 341,
  346, 377n32
Tasker, R. V. G.   3n1
Taylor, Daniel T.   173n78, 369n18,
  452n24
Taylor, Hudson   202n48
Tenney, Merrill C.   37n49
Thomas, John   202n48
Thompson, J. A.   428n12
Trapp, John   56n12, 156, 202n48
Turner, C. H.   305n41
Unnik, W. C. van   62
Vandervaal   288n22
Victorinus   59
Vitringa, Campegius   208n55, 491
Walvoord, John F.
  9, 55, 60n14, 102, 480, 103n7,
  162n66, 208n55,
  467n34, 489
Warfield, B. B.   486n7
Welcome, I. C.   439n8, 440n10
Wells, H. G.   191
Whiston, William   30n41, 188n22,
  202n48, 312
Whitaker, Edward W.   202n48
Wigandus, Johannes   252n29
Wikenhauser, Alfred   494
Wolfe, H. W.   278n12
Wood, Hans   202n48
Woodward, W. W.   56n12
Wordsworth, John   288n22
Wycliffe, John   258
Wylie, J. A.
  11n18, 252, 253nn33–34, 368n17
Young, Edward J.   404n53
Zimmermann, Frank   419n3

www.ingramcontent.com/pod-product-compliance
Lightning Source LLC
Chambersburg PA
CBHW052041290426
44111CB00011B/1584